D1731629

Classroom Companion: Business

The Classroom Companion series in Business features foundational and introductory books aimed at students to learn the core concepts, fundamental methods, theories and tools of the subject. The books offer a firm foundation for students preparing to move towards advanced learning. Each book follows a clear didactic structure and presents easy adoption opportunities for lecturers.

More information about this series at http://www.springer.com/series/16374

Tawfik Jelassi · Francisco J. Martínez-López

Strategies for e-Business

Concepts and Cases on Value Creation and Digital Business
Transformation

Fourth edition

 Springer

Tawfik Jelassi
IMD
Lausanne, Switzerland

Francisco J. Martínez-López
Department of Business Administration 1
University of Granada
Granada, Spain

This book was previously published by Pearson Education Limited, London, UK, 2005, 2008, 2014.

ISSN 2662-2866   ISSN 2662-2874   (electronic)
Classroom Companion: Business
ISBN 978-3-030-48949-6   ISBN 978-3-030-48950-2   (eBook)
https://doi.org/10.1007/978-3-030-48950-2

This Springer imprint is published by the registered company Springer Nature Switzerland AG
The registered company address is: Gewerbestrasse 11, 6330 Cham, Switzerland

Preface

Context and Positioning of the Book

When we talked to colleagues and friends in the fall of 2003 about the writing of the first edition of our e-business book, many of them asked whether we were arriving too late with the book. They reminded us that the Internet bubble had burst three years ago and that most online companies had since gone bankrupt. Since then, the thinking has changed. Both traditional bricks-and-mortar corporations such as Tesco, Sony BMG or Mercedes-Benz and pure online companies such as Amazon, Google or eBay have continued to develop and implement e-business strategies, albeit initially with less public attention and media coverage than before. Due to the rapid growth of so-called Web 2.0 applications, online companies such as Facebook or Twitter started to dominate the headlines of the business press.

During our research for previous editions of this book, we found very few books published after the collapse of the dotcom bubble that specifically address e-business strategy issues. We also noticed that there were many excellent books on strategy and many books on e-business, yet there were relatively few books that attempted to bring the two fields together in a comprehensive and rigorous manner.

This book, as its title suggests, attempted to close this gap, and this last edition has been updated and includes a collection of new hot topics. It aims at providing readers with a holistic and integrated view of the realms of strategy and e-business by focusing on strategic management concepts and linking them to actual case studies of companies engaged in e-business activities. It also aims at going beyond the hype by closely analysing examples of failure as well as success in order to help readers assess the underlying drivers for a successful e-business strategy.

Target Readers

Strategies for e-Business is a textbook targeted at senior managers, business strategists, entrepreneurs and consultants as well as participants enrolled in MBA, master's and executive education programmes and students in the final year of their undergraduate education. It should be of interest to general management programmes and seminars as well as to those specialising in e-business, electronic commerce, technology management, marketing, entrepreneurship, innovation management and business strategy.

Key Features

The key differentiating features of this book include the following:
- A comprehensive e-business strategy framework. This framework serves as a comprehensive basis for e-business strategy formulation. It is based on rigorous

and time-proven concepts from the field of strategic management, which were adapted to the specific context of e-business.

- An e-business roadmap. The book contains an e-business roadmap that is meant as a guide to help in the formulation and implementation process of an e-business strategy. It provides an overview of the key issues involved in this process. At the same time, extensive cross-references to the more detailed e-business strategy framework allow the reader to obtain more in-depth information when needed.
- A detailed study approach for e-business strategy. Creativity and analytical ability are of fundamental importance in the strategy formulation process. This book discusses how to improve these qualities through the use of concepts and case studies.
- In-depth case studies. The book contains real-world case studies, which provide in-depth accounts of how companies in several industries and different countries have developed and implemented e-business, electronic commerce or mobile e-commerce strategies. All the case studies result from first-hand field-based research, which the case authors have personally conducted in co-operation with executives and top-level managers of the companies involved.
- Geographic focus on Europe. While most of the existing e-business casebooks focus on companies that are based in the USA, this book focuses primarily on companies operating in Europe and Asia. In addition to the technological aspects discussed in the case studies, the wide variety of countries that are involved helps to provide insights into the specific business environment and national culture that characterise the different countries covered.

Structure and Content

Content-wise, Part I (▶ Chap. 1) presents the broader context of the book. It introduces the key terminology and evolution of e-business and provides an historic overview of the distinct phases that technological revolutions typically go through before reaching their full potential.

Part II suggests a strategy framework for the formulation of e-business strategies.

▶ Chapter 2 introduces the e-business strategy framework.

▶ Chapter 3 discusses the external environment of e-business ventures. This includes an analysis of the macro-environment and the industry structure. ▶ Chapter 4 focuses on the internal dimension of e-business strategy formulation. ▶ Chapter 5 is concerned with generic strategy options, which determine the overall strategic direction of an e-business venture. The issue of sustaining a competitive advantage over time and the dangers that threaten to erode such advantage are discussed in ▶ Chap. 6. ▶ Chapter 7 provides a systematic approach for developing innovations that aim to make the competition irrelevant. ▶ Chapter 8 presents the development of value creation and capture through e-business strategies. ▶ Chapters 9 to 11 address three strategic issues that are of special relevance for e-business companies. These include the internal organisation of an e-business venture (▶ Chap. 9), its relations with suppliers (▶ Chap. 10) and its relations with customers/users (▶ Chap. 11). ▶ Chapter 12 presents the improvement of the evolution path from wired e-commerce to u-commerce. ▶ Chapters 13 to 15 discuss mobile e-commerce, social e-commerce and omni-channel commerce. ▶ Chapter 16 applies a theoretical application approach, illustrating e-business strategies adopted by the two e-commerce giants Amazon and Alibaba. ▶ Chapter 17 reveals strategic trends of e-business.

Part III provides a roadmap for the formulation of an e-business strategy. Through the use of cross-references, this roadmap (presented in ▶ Chap. 18) is closely linked to the e-business strategy framework presented in Part II.

Part IV (▶ Chaps. 19 to 31) provides information related to several e-business case studies.

Getting the Most from This Book

In order to benefit most from this book, we recommend that you try to achieve the following when working through the book chapters:
- Thoroughly understand the theoretical concepts presented in the e-business strategy framework.
- Critically assess the strengths and weaknesses of each concept and determine the context for its appropriate use.
- Apply the concepts when analysing the case studies and make action-oriented recommendations backed up by logical reasoning and supporting arguments.
- Expand the usage of the concepts and the frameworks into other business situations that you encounter in your daily work or study.

To make your learning experience more effective and enriching, the book contains the following features:
- Learning outcomes offer a brief description of what you should have achieved after reading the chapter.
- Different types of boxes are contained in the text body of each chapter to provide added information about the concepts that are discussed.
- Articles are taken from the Financial Times and other sources to provide a journalistic perspective (within the timeframe context) of the issue discussed in the section.
- Critical perspectives present a different, if not opposing, view to the position taken in the main text of the chapter. Weighing the merits of each view is a valuable exercise for gaining a more in-depth understanding of the concept that is presented.
- Blog boxes contain excerpts from blog writers who provide their opinions on current developments in the e-business world. These excerpts provide an additional and at times different perspective to the concepts discussed in the chapters.
- Summaries at the end of each chapter allow you to review the most important points that were discussed in the chapter.

- Review questions help you assess your understanding of the material presented in the chapter. In general, the answers to these questions are straightforward since they are based on the material presented in the chapter.
- Discussion questions help you to transfer the concepts from the chapter into different business contexts. They are also meant as a starting point for discussion with your colleagues and peers.
- Recommended key reading provides a select list of additional books and articles that you can read if you wish to find out more about a specific topic.
- Useful third-party weblinks provide additional information on some material contained in the chapter.

Acknowledgements

We appreciate the assistance of Yangchun Li, Ph.D. student at the University of Granada (Spain) during the update of the theoretical part of this edition. Also, we thank all colleagues who have contributed with case studies.

Tawfik Jelassi
Lausanne, Switzerland

Francisco J. Martínez-López
Granada, Spain

Contents

III   A Roadmap for E-business Strategy Implementation

IV   Case Studies

Author Biographies

Tawfik Jelassi

is Professor of Strategy and Technology Management at IMD. He is also Co-Director of the Orchestrating Winning Performance (OWP) programme in Lausanne and Singapore/Dubai, which is the school's largest executive education programme with over 600 participants enrolled per year. His major research, teaching and consulting interests are in the areas of digital business transformation and leadership in turbulent times. He was granted several excellence awards for his teaching and research in Europe and the USA, and has received two national decorations from the President of Tunisia: 'The Order of merit in the fields of education and science' and 'The Order of the Republic'.

Before joining IMD, Dr. Jelassi was Minister of Higher Education, Scientific Research, and Information & Communication Technologies in the transition-to-democracy Government of Tunisia (2014–2015). Prior to that, he was Chairman of the Board of Directors of Ooredoo Tunisia, the leading mobile telecom operator in the country. Between 2000 and 2013, Dr. Jelassi was Professor and Dean of the Business School at Ecole Nationale des Ponts et Chaussées (Paris). Previously he was Coordinator of the Technology Management Department and Associate Professor at INSEAD (Fontainebleau).

At IMD, Professor Jelassi has been teaching in leadership programmes such as High-Performance Boards, Breakthrough Program for Senior Executives, Advanced Management Program, Building on Talent, and in the MBA program. He has also directed or taught several tailored executive education programmes for companies such as Mitsubishi, Bayer, Unilever, Huawei, Telecom Malaysia, Turkcell, Axiata, SOCAR, Metinvest, Banpu, Office Chérifien des Phosphates (OCP), Engie, Essilor, Adecco, Hilti, Electrolux, Conzzeta, Al Marai, Arla Foods, AS Watson, Carlsberg, SeaDrill, Lyreco, Saudi National Water Company, Julius Baer Bank, Central Bank of Indonesia, Agricultural Bank of China, etc.

Dr. Jelassi's research has appeared in leading academic journals such as *Management Information Systems (MIS) Quarterly, Journal of MIS, Journal of Electronic Commerce Research, Journal of Strategic Information Systems, Information and Management, Decision Support Systems, Decision Sciences*, Theory and Decision, and the *European Journal of*

Operational Research as well as practitioner-oriented publications including *Harvard Business Review*, *MIS Quarterly Executive*, *European Management Journal*, and *Information Systems World*. He has also authored numerous case studies on companies such as BP, Tesco, Nestlé, Otis, Ducati, Nordea, Ooredoo, NTT DoCoMo, Safaricom, Turkcell, Dallara, and Accor Hôtels and written six books, the latest of which is a strategy textbook entitled *Strategies for e-Business* (published in 2014 by Financial Times). His research and case writing work has been recognised by international excellence awards from the European Foundation for Management Development (in 1992, 1995, 1998, 1999 and 2011), the US-based Society for Information Management (in 2000, 2002, 2005 and 2008), the Europe-based Case Centre (in 1999, 2001, 2002 and 2013), and the Brandon Hall Group (2019).

Tawfik Jelassi holds a PhD degree in information systems from the Stern School of Business at New York University (USA) as well as graduate and postgraduate degrees from the University of Paris-Dauphine (France).

Francisco J. Martínez-López

MSc in Marketing, and European PhD in Business Administration (2005), with Extraordinary Doctoral Prize, from the University of Granada (Spain), is Professor of Business Administration at the University of Granada. He taught master's in digital marketing and Executive MBA at the Open University of Catalonia, EAE Business School and Online Business School in Spain.

Dr. Martínez-López has been visiting researcher at the Zicklin School of Business (CUNY, USA), Rutgers Business School (Rutgers University, USA), Aston Business School (Aston University, UK), the University of Chicago Booth School of Business (USA), the Michael Smurfit School of Business (University College Dublin, Ireland), LUISS Business School (Rome, Italy), and the Complutense University Business School (Madrid, Spain).

He has been Editor-in-Chief of the *International Journal of Business Environment* (Inderscience Publishers) and is Associate Editor of the *European Journal of Marketing* (Emerald). He was also a member of the Editorial Board of *Industrial Marketing Management* (Elsevier) for more than a decade. Dr. Martínez-López has co-edited several international journals' special issues and research books for leading publishers of business and management research such as Springer and Elsevier. Likewise, he has published in international journals, such as *Journal of Retailing, International Journal of Management Reviews, Industrial Marketing Management, Internet Research, Electronic Commerce and Research Applications, Journal of Business Research, Information Systems, Expert Systems with Applications, Journal of Small Business Management, Journal of Marketing Theory and Practice, European Journal of Marketing, Industrial Management & Data Systems, Computers & Education, International Journal of Market Research, Computers & Human Behaviour, International Journal of Retail & Distribution Management, Journal of Retailing and Consumer Services, Journal of Organizational Computing and Electronic Commerce,* and *Journal of Marketing Management,* among others. He is chair of the Research on National Brand & Private Label Marketing Conference and the Digital Marketing & eCommerce Conference, both based in Barcelona (Spain).

Introduction

This introductory part sets up the overall context for the book. It contains the following elements:
- A definition of the key terminology used throughout the book
- An overview of the evolution of e-business over time
- An introduction of benefits of e-business adoption

The goal of this introductory part is to provide a guide and context for the content of the book. ▶ Chapter 1 starts out with some definitions of the most important terms used in the book, such as e-business, electronic commerce and mobile e-commerce, and the concepts of strategy and value creation. It then provides an overview of the evolution of e-business over the last decade and recognises five distinct phases: (1) the 'grassroots', (2) the 'rise of the Internet', (3) the 'crash' (or the burst of the dotcom bubble), (4) the 'synergy phase' (5) the 'maturity phase'. Lastly, it describes key benefits of e-business adoption.

Contents

Key Terminology and Evolution of e-Business

Contents

© Springer Nature Switzerland AG 2020
T. Jelassi, F. J. Martínez-López, *Strategies for e-Business*, Classroom Companion: Business,
https://doi.org/10.1007/978-3-030-48950-2_1

1

Learning Outcomes

After completing this chapter, you should be able to:

— Understand what the terms of "e-business," "electronic commerce," "mobile e-commerce," "social commerce," and "omni-channel commerce" mean

— Define the concept of strategy and recognize the different levels of strategy development

— Describe the life cycle of technological revolutions and illustrate it through different examples

— Recognize the four main periods of the e-business evolution over the past decade and explain the peculiar characteristics of each period

— Recognize main benefits of e-business adoption

■ Introduction

The purpose of this chapter is to set the stage for the remainder of the book. To create a clear and shared view of what this domain entails, we firstly want to ensure a common understanding of the key terminology used throughout the book. ▶ Section 1.1 includes definitions of e-business-related terms and concepts as well as some strategy-specific perspectives. Following that, ▶ Sect. 1.2 provides a framework that describes the typical stages of technological revolutions and positions the evolution of electronic business within this framework.

1.1 Key Terminology

1.1.1 e-Business

The term *e-business* is defined here as the use of electronic means to conduct business internally and/or externally.[1] Internal e-business activities may include production, development, maintenance of IT infrastructure, and product management. For example, it may include the linking of an organization's employees with each other through an intranet to improve information sharing, facilitate knowledge dissemination, and support management reporting. e-Business activities also include supporting after-sales service activities and collaborating with business partners. For example, virtual teams in two firms in different locations may collaborate via a secure extranet on research or new product development.

Despite the distinct terminology that is used, e-business should not be viewed in isolation from the remaining activities of a business. Instead, a business should integrate its online e-business activities with its offline business into a coherent whole. For example, customers may now shop, order, and pay for groceries online.

---

[1] For definitions and distinctions between e-business and e-commerce, see Bartels (2016). For distinctions between e-commerce and m-commerce, see Surbhi (2015).

They may choose to either pick up the packed groceries from the physical store, or for an additional fee, they may be delivered directly to the home.

1.1.2 Electronic Commerce

Electronic commerce, or *e-commerce*, is more specific than e-business and can be thought of as a subset of the latter. It deals with the facilitation of transactions and selling of products and services online, for example, via the Internet or any other telecommunications network. It involves the electronic trading of physical and digital goods, quite often encompassing all the trading processes such as online marketing, online ordering (e-procurement), e-payment, and, for digital goods, online distribution and after-sales support activities. e-Commerce applications with external orientation are buy-side (e-commerce activities with suppliers) and sell-side (activities with customers).

e-Commerce may occur between business to business (B2B), business to consumer (B2C), and newer forms of e-commerce include consumer to consumer (C2C – e.g., see ▶ Sect. 1.1.4) and consumer to business (C2B). It is sometimes also referred to as v-Commerce, or virtual commerce. For example, customers worldwide can browse, compare, and purchase Dell computers online via the Dell website.

1.1.3 Mobile e-Commerce

Mobile e-commerce, or *m-commerce*, is a subset of electronic commerce. While it refers to online activities that are similar to those mentioned above in the e-commerce section, the underlying technology is different because mobile commerce is limited to mobile telecommunication networks, which are accessed through wireless hand-held devices such as mobile phones, smartphones, hand-held computers, and tablets. For example, eBay customers can download and retain an eBay "app" (application) to their mobile device and then use it whenever they want to search and purchase products. The app stores their login details and payment preferences, which streamlines the purchasing process.

1.1.4 Social Commerce

Social commerce generally refers to the use of the social web to deliver e-commerce activities and transactions, particularly the use of user-generated content and content sharing. From a business perspective, the socialization of e-commerce can strengthen business relationships with customers, increase website traffic, identify potential opportunities, and facilitate product and brand development (Michaelidou et al. 2011).

In comparison to e-commerce, social commerce enables users to interact with others and create value jointly. The integration and utilization of information and content are implemented through multiple actors instead of a two-way

1

collaboration between a customer and business on online platforms (Liang and Turban 2011). Many leading e-commerce sites recognize the importance of social commerce and include social commerce features in their e-commerce sites. For example, Alibaba, one of the biggest e-commerce companies, provides online discussion areas and facilitates online communities for user interaction. These social commerce features facilitate the exchange and integration of information and knowledge and promote selling and buying delivered through e-commerce platforms. Buyers can use the information and knowledge gleaned through social commerce features to assist in their shopping journeys and purchase decisions.

1.1.5 Omni-Channel Commerce

Omni-channel commerce refers to meeting customer requirements across a range of channels, which may entail physical stores, websites, catalogues, call centers, social media, and mobile apps. Omni-channel commerce requires companies to conduct synergetic and systematic management of various channels and touch points in such a way that the customer experience is optimized across channels and throughout the customer journey (Verhoef et al. 2015).

Most companies do not only rely on one channel, for example, a website or physical stores. Rather, to maximize profit, businesses consider the overall coordinated performance of their business across all channels. Stakeholders and investors will not support a "for-profit" business without a thorough consideration of profits. In the past there was much hype about e-business and e-commerce, which drew attention away from traditional offline industries. Nowadays, many e-commerce companies recognize the enormous value of physical stores and their role in the customer experience. For instance, Amazon launched their cashierless retail store Amazon Go. Amazon users can go into a store, pick goods, and leave. The Amazon app will automatically fulfill the checkout process and send bills to users' smartphone. Secondly, Alibaba planned to open 30 physical supermarkets in Beijing in 2018.[2] Thirdly, Florius is a US company that offers mortgages via its website. Customers can choose to apply using self-service or with assisted service help.

> **Florius Delivers an Outstanding, Online, Omni-Channel Customer Experience with Help from Avaya and Dimension Data**
>
> Seventy-year-old mortgage specialist outpaces the competition with full and self-service capabilities from the company's website enabled by Avaya Contact Center solutions.
>
> Avaya Holdings Corp. (AVYA) today announced that Florius, a division of ABN AMRO, now enables customers to quickly complete all aspects of the mortgage process with new, expanded self- and assisted-service capabilities provided

2   For more details see Chou (2018).

through the company's website. Avaya and Dimension Data, an Avaya channel partner and system integrator, worked closely with Florius to create an outstanding, online, omni-channel customer experience that would set the company far ahead of the competition.

See how Florius is transforming the banking experience in the video here.

The 70-year-old company continually seeks to improve its customer experience and the ability for its 185 employees to enhance interactions with customers. With a commitment to speed up the review of mortgage applications, Florius needed to update its contact center operation to increase flexibility, support for multi-channel interactions, and provide a more holistic view of the customer's journey. Going digital was top of mind, but Florius wasn't just looking to simply implement "cool" technologies. Rather, the business goal was a better customer experience that was first and foremost, personalized and omni-channel, supported by digital capabilities.

"The customer journey is very important to us," said Seif Alhamrany, head of the Advisory Team at Florius. "We are committed to a fast turnaround for mortgage applications, so we need to put the customer in the center, have fast access to as much information as possible, and automate processes as much as possible."

The upgrade included integrating Avaya Contact Center solutions with the company's CRM system, a step that broadened the view of the customer's experience and provided new insights. The addition of Avaya Breeze enables Florius to innovate quickly, allowing the company to take advantage of pre-made, ready-to-use Snap-Ins as well as quickly and easily create and integrate its own applications for a differentiated customer experience.

"We've been working with Avaya for a long time. A year ago we started the conversation with Dimension Data about developing a roadmap to enable us to work better with customers and do more with the brilliant Avaya platform we had," said Alhamrany.

With development of the roadmap, the Florius website went live in March with new, WebRTC video and co-browsing capabilities facilitated by Avaya Breeze Snap-Ins. From the customer interaction to the backend magic that brings it all together, Florius has achieved its goal of creating and delivering a personalized, omni-channel customer experience that sets it apart from the competition. Rather than rest on its laurels, Florius is already looking to the future, one that may include artificial intelligence capabilities and other new or emerging technologies.

"We won't be finished after this," said Alhamrany. "We see this as an ongoing project to delight our customers. We're already talking about next steps and what kind of innovation we'll see. As far as I'm concerned, the sky's the limit." […].

Adapted from Lewandowski (2018).

1.1.6 u-Commerce

u-Commerce stands for ubiquitous commerce. It refers to the wireless, continuous communication and exchange of data and information between and among retailers, customers, and systems (e.g., applications) regardless of

1

location, devices used, or time of day. Richard T. Watson (2000) claims it includes four major features:

- Ubiquitous = represents the ability to be connected at any time and in any place as well as the integration of human-computer interaction into most devices and processes, e.g., household objects.
- Uniqueness = stands for the unique identification of each customer or user regarding his identity, current context, needs, and location resulting in an individual service.
- Universal = is related to everyone's devices which can be used multifunctional and as well as universal—you will always be connected no matter of your place.
- Unison = constitutes the data integration across applications and devices to provide users consistent and fully access to required information independent of device and location. The term unison also relates to fully synchronized devices at any time.

For example, a household refrigerator may have inbuilt sensors that record when it empties of specific foods and automatically adds them to a shopping list and sends an order, including delivery, to replenish them. The machine-to-machine process requires little or no human intervention. Ubiquitous commerce creates several new issues including privacy; it redefines how value is created[3] and requires new business models.

1.1.7 e-Market

An e-Market is an electronic marketplace where business to business (B2B) buyers and sellers trade. Electronic markets are more flexible, convenient, and generally less costly than physical markets. Because they can be real-time, they improve business operations.

There are three types of electronic markets: independent, group-based, and private. Independent e-markets are public markets. Group-based electronic markets are typically for a specific industry. Private electronic markets are established by specific companies for their procurement.

1.1.8 The Concept of Strategy

In addition to e-business, *strategy* is the second key theme of this book. More specifically, we analyze and illustrate how firms develop and implement strategies for their e-business activities and draw lessons and guidelines from the studied practices. However, the term "strategy" means different things to different people. To create a clear and shared understanding of "strategy" as it is used in this book, we firstly consider several definitions of "strategy" and then suggest a common foundation of elements that underpin our use of the word "strategy."

---

3   For more details see Zeng (2018).

Strategy is:

Definition

... the direction and scope of an organisation over the long-term, which achieves advantage for the organisation through its configuration of resources within a changing environment to the needs of markets and fulfill stakeholder expectations. –Gerry Johnson and Kevan Scholes[4]

Definition

... the determination of the basic long-term goals and objectives of an enterprise, and the adoption of courses of action and the allocation of resources necessary for carrying out these goals. –Alfred Chandler[5]

Definition

... the deliberate search for a plan of action that will develop a business's competitive advantage and compound it. –Bruce Henderson[6]

Definition

... the strong focus on profitability not just growth, an ability to define a unique value proposition, and a willingness to make tough trade-offs in what not to do. –Michael Porter[7]

Based on the above definitions, we would like to stress the following aspects that are crucial for strategy formulation[8]:

- Strategy is concerned with the long-term direction of the business.
- Strategy deals with the overall plan for deploying the resources that a business possesses.
- Strategy entails the willingness to make trade-offs, to choose between different directions and between different ways of deploying resources.
- Strategy is about achieving unique positioning vis-à-vis competitors.
- The central goal of strategy is to achieve sustainable competitive advantage over rivals and thereby to ensure sustainable profitability.

---

4   Please see Johnson et al. (2005), p. 10.
5   Please see Chandler (1962), p. 13.
6   Please see Henderson (1989), p. 141.
7   Please see Porter (2001), p. 72.
8   Researchers of strategy engage in heated debate about what strategy entails. Most notably, there are two different schools of strategy. The "design view" of strategy considers strategy as characterized by deliberate planning and objective setting. The "experience view" suggests that strategies develop in an adaptive fashion and depend to a large extent on existing strategies. See also Johnson et al. (2005). The frameworks and concepts proposed in this book focus on the design view of strategy.

1

Having defined the concept of strategy, we can now differentiate it from the concept of *tactics*, a term that is often used interchangeably with strategy. Tactics are schemes for individual and specific actions that are not necessarily related to one another. In general, specific actions can be planned intuitively because of their limited complexity. A business can, for instance, have a certain tactic when it launches a marketing campaign.

Strategy, on the other hand, deals with an overarching formulation that affects not just one activity at one point in time but all activities of a firm over an extended time horizon. To achieve consistency and synergy between different activities over time, intuition is generally not sufficient; it also requires logical thinking and systematic planning. Drawing an analogy with warfare, we could say that while tactics are about winning a battle, strategy is concerned primarily with winning the war.

More recent theory suggests strategy can also be concerned with finding a unique strategic position where there are no competitors, or "blue ocean" (*footnote*), or that converging industries and a more dynamic and open environment require businesses to focus more on complementarities than competition. That is, forming ecosystems of mutually supporting entities who collaboratively create value propositions. For example, see the Financial Times article "Ford Open to Working with Foreign Rivals on Driverless Cars."

> ### Ford Open to Working with Foreign Rivals on Driverless Cars
>
> Electric car manufacturers including Tesla, Toyota, and Waymo have captured market share from major manufacturers including Ford and Volkswagen.
>
> Ford is open to working with other carmakers—previously thought of as competitors—to expand self-driving services internationally, the head of the carmaker's autonomous vehicles business said, adding weight to speculation it may partner with Volkswagen on driverless cars.
>
> The US carmaker and its German peer are in "broad" talks over collaboration in a number of areas, both companies have said. Sherif Marakby, CEO of Ford Autonomous Vehicles, said collaborating in other regions "totally makes a lot of sense."
>
> "Joint investment with people who can complement each other makes perfect sense," he told the Financial Times in an interview.
>
> He said: "The autonomous vehicle development and business costs billions and billions of dollars in one region, so when trying to deploy this across multiple regions it totally makes sense to be joining in on the risk and the reward."
>
> The "opportunity to co-invest not just in the technology but the business and go-to-market and share the reward of that, it does make sense," he added.
>
> Herbert Diess, Volkswagen chief executive, said talks could lead to VW sharing its electric car platform with Ford and the pair collaborating over US manufacturing.
>
> Carmakers and technology groups are developing self-driving systems to reduce road accidents as well as to open up new business models, and many are collaborating to reduce the vast investment costs needed.
>
> BMW and Fiat are working alongside Intel, while Honda and SoftBank have both invested in Cruise, the General Motors self-driving car unit.
>
> Volkswagen is working with Aurora, a self-driving development company founded by Waymo founder Chris Urmson, for its technology.
>
> Source: Adapted excerpt from: Campbell and Waldmeier (2018).

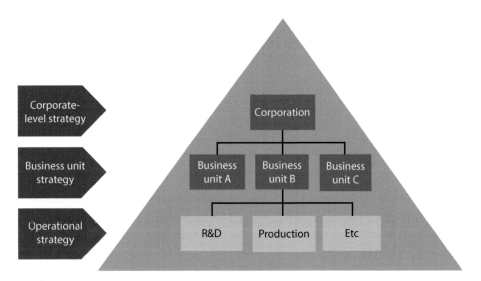

● Fig. 1.1 Three different levels of strategy. (Source: adapted from Jelassi et al. 2014)

It has often been argued that the increasing importance of technology reduces the need for clear strategies. Firms should instead focus on getting their technology to work. This is especially true for the technology that underpins e-business and e-commerce. Yet, technology is not, and cannot be, a substitute for strategy. Overlooking strategy and not considering how a firm can create sustainable competitive advantage is a likely recipe for failure. Just because certain activities are feasible from a technological perspective does not mean that they are sensible from a strategic perspective. Ultimately, information technology (IT) and the Internet should be used not for the sake of using them but instead to create value for customers in a cost-efficient way.

Formulating long-term strategies has become more difficult due to dynamic, rapidly evolving business environments. How long-term can a strategy be when the technological environment is constantly changing? This is obviously a difficult question that has no clear-cut answers. When a disruptive innovation emerges and redefines the basis of competition, previous strategies may become all but worthless. This was the case, for instance, when ► Amazon.com entered the book-retailing market with its online bookstore and when Napster launched its file-sharing platform for online music distribution. Nonetheless, it is important to be aware of the trade-offs that arise when a firm diverts from or ceases a long-term strategy in return for short-term flexibility.

Within organizations, we typically recognize the following three different levels of strategy (see ● Fig. 1.1). They are (1) *corporate-level strategy*, (2) *business unit strategy*, and (3) *operational strategy.*[9]

---

9   For a detailed discussion of different levels of strategy, see Johnson et al. (2005).

1

Amazon Agrees to Buy Whole Foods for $13.7bn

In 2017 Amazon acquired upmarket grocer Whole Foods Market for US$13.7bn, as the ecommerce group seeks to exploit its online scale to challenge the likes of Walmart in food retailing.

Buying Whole Foods, the biggest premium grocer in the United States, radically accelerated Amazon's ambitions in the $800bn US food and grocery sector, specifically for grocery deliveries and payless shopping.

Whole Foods, had been nicknamed "whole paycheck" for its high prices and had same-store sales fall for 2 years prior to the acquisition.

Charlie O'Shea, analyst at Moody's, said the deal was a "transformative transaction, not just for food retail, but for retail in general."

The deal will give Amazon—a company that has built most of its businesses online—a much more significant bricks-and-mortar presence. The online retailer has run its own grocery delivery program, AmazonFresh, since 2007 and has experimented with grocery pick-up kiosks in Seattle.

At the time of the acquisition, German discounters Aldi and Lidl had opened in the United States, risking a price war with incumbents. Walmart looked to discount its prices to retain market share.

Mr O'Shea added: "Implications ripple far beyond the food segment, where dominant players like Walmart, Kroger, Costco, and Target now have to look over their shoulders at the Amazon train coming down the tracks."

Amazon previously unveiled plans to offer a discount for Prime memberships to Americans on government assistance, in an attempt to convince food stamp recipients to do their grocery shopping online. The move was viewed as a direct shot at Walmart, whose core customers come from low-income backgrounds.

Source: Adapted from: Nicolaou et al. (2017).

Amazon Debuts the Store Without a Checkout

In January 2018, Amazon launched "Amazon Go," a futuristic convenience store where shoppers go into a store, pick goods, and leave. The Amazon app automatically fulfills the checkout process and sends bills to users' smartphone. Shoppers are tracked by hundreds of cameras on the ceiling and a computer algorithm that analyzes their every gesture and then tallies up their receipt when they exit. Amazon calls this "just walk out" shopping, because there is no checkout counter and no checkout line, just a few turnstiles.

However, the complexity of the Amazon Go store's design means that it is more of an experimental concept at the moment, rather than a mature technology that can be easily and cheaply replicated.

Dilip Kumar, who oversees the technology behind the Amazon Go store, explains that the store uses computer vision—the ceiling is dotted with hundred of video cameras—to determine what shoppers are picking out. "Five years ago when we started this, we said: can we push the boundaries of computer vision and machine learning to create this effortless experience for customers to come in, take what they want, and leave?" he says. Mr Kumar points to the cameras that nearly blanket the ceiling and explains that the computer algorithm uses these to determine which customer is taking which products. There are also weight sensors on the store shelves, but these are less useful because different items can have the same weight, such as different flavors of yoghurt. "The holy grail is video understanding," he says. "To be able to understand and interpret and know exactly what is happening. Doing this at scale and getting transaction-level accuracy is what makes this challenging."

Source: Adapted from: Hook and Nicolaou (2018).

- **Business Unit Strategy**

Business unit strategy is concerned primarily with how to compete within individual markets. It typically involves middle-level management of a firm who deal with issues such as industry analysis, market positioning, unique competitive advantage, and value creation for customers. When formulating a business unit strategy, the desired scale and scope of operations are considered. Each business unit would typically have a different budget and performance targets that align to the corporate level strategy. Business units typically have a degree of autonomy and agility to respond to changes in customer demand.

For example, e-commerce giant Alibaba in 2019 has nearly 30 separate business units that specifically target market opportunities including in B2B commerce, B2C commerce, C2C commerce, mobile payments, and cloud business. This approach recognizes they are very distinct and dynamic markets with different customer profiles and preferences and different levels of competition. The size of each business unit varies from small teams to large groups of teams and each offers differentiated products and services. It is therefore necessary to formulate a separate business unit strategy with different objectives for each mark.

At a more detailed level, a business unit strategy deals with issues such as industry analysis, market positioning, and value creation for customers. Furthermore, when formulating a business unit strategy, it is also necessary to think about the desired scale and scope of operations.

- **Operational Strategy**

Operational strategy, also known as functional-level strategy, concerns the implementation of the business unit strategy with regard to resources, processes, and people. In the context of e-business, this includes issues such as optimal website design, hardware and software requirements, and the management of the logistics process. It aims to optimize operational effectiveness and minimize costs. Operational strategies use techniques that include business process re-engineering (BPR), value stream mapping (VSM), and total quality management (TQM).

Operational strategies relate to specific functions and are typically more short-term rather than the "whole-of-firm" goals of corporate strategy formulation. Implementation of operational strategies may involve risk management and change management for new processes, tools, and organization structures and customer relationship management. This is discussed further in ▶ Chap. 18.

1

1.1.9 The Concept of Value Creation and Capturing

The ability of a firm to create value for its customers is a critical prerequisite for achieving sustainable profitability. In the context of e-business strategies, the concept of *value creation* deserves special attention because many Internet start-ups that ended in bankruptcy at the end of the Internet boom years did not pay enough attention to this issue. Instead, they were frequently concerned primarily with customer acquisition and revenue growth, which was sustainable only as long as venture capitalists and stock markets were willing to finance these firms.

Nowadays, however, in a more challenging and turbulent business environment, it is critical that strategies focus on what value to create and for whom, as well as how to create and capture value in the form of profits. In economic terms, value created is the difference between the benefit a firm provides to its customers and the costs it incurs for doing so. The concepts of value creation and capturing are discussed in more detail in ► Chap. 8.

1.2 The Evolution of e-Business

Before discussing e-business from a structural perspective through the e-business strategy framework presented in Part II, we firstly want to analyze the evolution of e-business over the past decade and compare it with the life cycle of other *technological revolutions*. Carlota Perez defines a technological revolution as a "powerful and highly visible cluster of new and dynamic technologies, products and industries, capable of bringing about an upheaval in the whole fabric of the economy and of propelling a long-term upsurge of development" (Perez 2002: p. 8).

Technological revolutions are not new. Looking back through history, whether the printing press, steam engine, railway, or car, all such technologies have gone through similar surges. Perez divides the surge of a technological revolution into two consecutive periods: (1) the *installation period*, which consists of an *irruption stage* and a *frenzy* ("gilded age") stage, and (2) the *deployment period*, which consists of a *synergy* ("golden age") stage and a *maturity* stage.

Below, we describe in more detail each stage of a typical surge of a technological revolution[10]:

- Irruption (1). The irruption stage takes place right after a new technology is introduced to the market. Revolutionary new technologies, also called "big bangs," include the mechanized cotton industry in the 1770s, railway construction in the 1830s and, more recently, Intel's first microprocessor in 1971. During the irruption stage, innovative products and services based on the new technology appear and start to slowly penetrate the economy, which is still dominated by the previous technology.
- Frenzy (2). The frenzy stage, also called the "gilded age," is characterized by a sense of exploration and exuberance as entrepreneurs, engineers, and investors

---

10 Ibid. pp. 90–137.

alike try to find the best opportunities created by the technological big bang irruption. Using a trial-and-error approach, investors fund numerous projects, which help to quickly install the new technology in the economy. However, as investors become increasingly confident and excited, they start considering themselves to be infallible. Depending on the technological revolution, they have financed digging canals from any river to any other river, building railway tracks between every city and village imaginable and, more recently, creating online retailing websites for every conceivable product, be it pet food, medicine, or furniture. This process typically continues until it reaches an unsustainable exuberance, also called "bubble" or "mania." At that point, the "paper wealth" of the stock market loses any meaningful relation with the realistic possibilities of the new technology to create wealth.

- Crash (3). The gilded age is followed by a crash, when the leading players in the economy realize that the excessive investments will never be able to fulfill the high expectations. As a result, investors lose confidence and pull their funds out of the new technology. Doing so sets off a vicious cycle, and, as everyone starts to pull out of the stock market, the bubble deflates, and the stock market collapses.

- Synergy (4). Following the crash, the time of quick and easy profits has passed. Now, investors prefer to put their money into the "real" economy, and the successful firms are not the nimble start-ups but instead established incumbents. While, during the frenzy stage, there were many start-ups competing within an industry, the crash led to a shake-out where most of these ventures went out of business. During the synergy stage, a few large companies start to dominate the markets and leverage their financial strength to generate economies of scale and scope. Now, the emphasis is no longer on technological innovation but instead on how to make technology easy to use, reliable, secure, and cost-efficient.

  In order for the synergy stage to take hold, governmental agencies need to introduce regulations to remedy the fallacies that caused the previous frenzy and the ensuing crash and, by doing so, to regain investors' confidence. For instance, following the stock market crash in 1929, the US government set up separate regulatory bodies for banks, securities, savings, and insurances and also established protective agencies including the Federal Deposit Insurance Corporation (FDIC) and the Securities and Exchange Commission (SEC).

- Maturity (5). The maturity stage is characterized by market saturation and mature technologies. Growth opportunities in new and untapped markets are becoming scarcer, and there are fewer innovations resulting from the new technology. During this stage, companies concentrate on increasing efficiency and reducing costs, for instance, through mergers and acquisitions. In today's mature automobile industry, for example, large global manufacturers such as Renault and Nissan or VW and Porsche have merged or established strategic partnerships in order to generate scale effects and expand market reach.[11]

---

11 Note that as one technology reaches maturity, the next technological revolution is about to emerge. As a result, there can be considerable overlap between two technology surges.

1

For a more extensive example of a surge of a technological revolution, consider the evolution of the railway industry in England. Railroads started to become popular in the 1830s. Many entrepreneurs, financed by eager investors, started constructing railway routes throughout the country, which culminated in an investment bubble in 1847. Initially, when building railway tracks, investors sought out those projects that showed a clear need and were easy to build. As the bubble kept growing, investors, searching desperately for investment opportunities, started to fund projects for which there was hardly any demand and that were complicated and costly. Ultimately, railway companies were even building tracks that were running parallel to one another, even though it was obvious that only one track could be operated profitably in the long term.

Inevitably, the railway bubble burst. After the dust settled, the stocks of railway companies had lost 85% of their peak value. After the crash in 1847, when a large number of railroad companies went bankrupt, the industry bounced back, rapidly increasing mileage and passengers and tripling revenues in just 5 years after the bust. After 1850, railways drove much of England's economic growth, and they continued to dominate the transportation market until the automobile became a medium of mass transportation in the middle of the twentieth century (Perez 2002). We can observe similar evolutions with other technological revolutions, such as steel production, steam energy, and, more recently, the automobile.

The above perspective illustrates that the time from the first commercial usage of a new technology to its widespread application can stretch over a period lasting up to 50 years. Within these long periods, the technology's diffusion and growth rates are not continuously smooth. Instead, they are often marked by volatility and a crash, when the initial exuberance and optimism about a new technology fades.

One of the main reasons for these long gestation periods between the irruption and the synergy stages is that it is not sufficient just to have the appropriate technology in place. In addition, managers need to be willing and able to abandon previous ways of doing things and start using the new technology in such a way that it actually creates value. This takes time and requires a lot of experimentation, failure, and fine-tuning.

The development of e-business has been quite similar to that described above. e-Business has changed dramatically since 1993, evolving through the following five periods, which mirror the evolution of the National Association of Securities Dealers Automated Quotations (NASDAQ)[12] in the United States (see ◘ Fig. 1.2) during the same time period:

- Grassroots of e-business (1). Before the widespread commercial use of the Internet, the NASDAQ showed only modest increases. Between 1983 and 1993, it doubled from 350 to 700 points. We refer to this period as the grassroots of e-business which corresponds to the irruption stage in the Perez model.
- Rise of the Internet (2). Even though the beginning of the dotcom boom cannot be determined precisely, we chose 1995, the year when ▶ Amazon.

---

12 The NASDAQ is the main US-based stock exchange for technology companies.

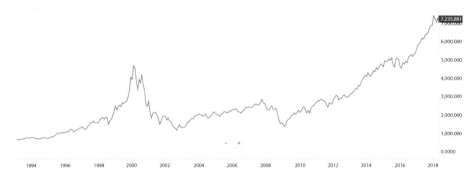

▢ Fig. 1.2 NASDAQ Composite Index 1993–2018. (Source: Yahoo! Finance 2019)

com was launched, as the starting point of the rise of the Internet period.[13] The year 1995 also saw the initial public offering (IPO) of Netscape, the maker of the Netscape Navigator web browser. This was the first IPO of a major Internet company. This period, which corresponds to the "gilded age," is reflected in the strong rise of the NASDAQ index, especially during the late 1990s. At the peak of this frenzy stage, the NASDAQ traded at price/earnings (p/e) ratios of 62, after it had not exceeded p/e ratios of 21 in the years between 1973 and 1995.[14]

— Crash (3). The bubble burst in March and April of 2000, when the NASDAQ index crashed. Between 10 March and 14 April 2000, the NASDAQ dropped 1727 points or 34 percent. By the end of 2000, it had fallen by 45 percent. The subsequent consolidation has been characterized by a more sober approach to e-business and a refocusing on the fundamental drivers of value creation. The NASDAQ continued its decline for another 2 years, albeit at much slower rates, until it bottomed out in early 2003.

— Synergy (4). By winter 2003 there were signs of an e-business revival, as reflected in the rise of the NASDAQ index during the second half of 2003. This trend continued, thus marking the beginning of the synergy stage ("golden age") mentioned in the Perez model.

— Maturity (5). From 2012 we see the emergence of maturity. Digital tools are used more broadly by businesses and consumers. Investor confidence in pure e-business start-ups grows, underpinned by awareness and experience. Start-ups and emergent business opportunities that are not yet cash flow positive are subject to more rigorous assessments of their value creation and financial projections.

---

13 ► Amazon.com was the first firm to add the suffix ".com" to the end of its name, thereby establishing the expression "dotcom," which refers to all types of Internet ventures.

14 The p/e ratio of a company's stock is calculated by dividing its stock price by its earnings per share. For example, if a company made $5 per share in the past year and the share sells for $50, then the p/e ratio for this share is 10. In general, a high p/e suggests that investors are expecting higher earnings growth in the future compared to companies with a lower p/e.

1

In the following sections, the above five time periods are discussed in more detail. The purpose of doing so is to explain with hindsight some of the underlying characteristics of each time period using strategic concepts such as the five forces industry framework, value creation and capture, and economies of scale and scope. These concepts are explained in more detail in Part II of the book.

1.2.1 The Grassroots of e-Business

Before the Internet became a widely used platform for conducting e-business transactions, companies were already using other information and communication technologies (ICT) infrastructures. These included electronic data interchange (EDI), interorganizational information systems (IOS) and public IT platforms such as the Minitel[15] videotext system in France. They enabled companies to connect their business functions internally and also to reach out to their suppliers, customers, and third-party partners.

However, the value creation potential of these technologies was limited due to the high costs involved and the limited benefits that were achieved. System implementation costs were high since most of these ICT infrastructures were more or less proprietary and had to be adapted extensively to the individual needs of each company.

Once implemented and adapted, the ongoing benefits of these systems were further limited due to two factors: the number of market participants and technical incompatibility. Firstly, the number of companies using these IT systems was relatively low compared with today's ubiquitous Internet, thus limiting the number of potential partners to work with. Secondly, even if a company used an ICT infrastructure, its IT systems and applications were not compatible with those of its business partners. This made it difficult at best, if not impossible, to interconnect different "islands of technology." As a result of the above factors, e-business existed only to a limited extent within and across companies or even beyond national boundaries.

1.2.2 The Rise of the Internet

In July 1995, the Internet boom years began with the launch of ▶ Amazon.com, one of today's best-known online retailers. The subsequent 5 years were characterized by great exuberance and the belief in the seemingly unlimited potential of the Internet. During that time period, the profitability and economic viability of companies and business models did not seem to matter much. Instead, metrics such as "click-through rates," or "number of eyeballs" (the number of visitors to a site) were the main determinants for stock market success and media coverage.

---

15 France Telecom closed this service in 2012.

For a more detailed insight into this period, consider the example of ▶ Priceline. com, which allowed people to purchase airline tickets over the Internet. The ▶ Priceline.com IPO on 30 March 1999 issued shares at $16 each, and they soared immediately to $85 each. At the end of the day, ▶ Priceline.com had reached a market valuation of almost $10 billion, which was more than the combined market value of United Airlines, Continental Airlines, and Northwest Airlines.[16] While these airlines had a proven business model, valuable brands, and substantial physical assets, ▶ Priceline.com owned only a few computer servers and an untested business model. In fact, the company even stated in its IPO prospectus that it did not expect to be profitable at any time in the near future, that the business model was new and unproven, and that the brand might not be able to achieve the required brand recognition.

Investors ignored these warnings because they believed that they would always be able to sell the stock to someone else at an even higher price. This investment approach during the Internet boom years became known as the "Greater Fool Theory."[17] In the United States, an estimated 100 million people, about half of the adult population, had invested in stocks at the peak of the bubble. As the stock market kept soaring, more and more people—who had seen their colleagues and friends become wealthy—also started investing in Internet stocks. This meant that the chances of finding a "greater fool" were high—at least during the Internet boom years. The case study on ▶ Covisint.com, which dates back to this time period, illustrates this very same spirit of almost boundless excitement and optimism.

The fundamental driver of the e-business boom was the belief that it would be possible to increase values exponentially because, as explained below, the Internet would lower costs while, at the same time, increase consumer benefits. Costs were expected to decrease significantly because managers and analysts alike believed that Internet ventures would not require heavy investments in expensive bricks-and-mortar infrastructure such as warehouses, retail outlets, and delivery trucks. Instead, they believed that all physical activities could be outsourced to external providers—typically as variable costs based on transaction volumes—while they focused on the technological aspect of the business and on customer interactions.

At the same time, the belief was that, compared with their more traditional bricks-and-mortar competitors, Internet pure play companies would provide far superior consumer benefits, for example, improved customer services and customer experiences. It was thought that combining the two-way connectivity of the Internet with database capabilities and customer relationship management (CRM) systems would create much higher benefits than traditional outlets ever could.

This still leaves us with the question of why so many businesses rushed into this e-market so rapidly during the Internet boom years. Several factors can explain this new "gold rush" (see also ▶ Chap. 7 for a more detailed discussion of early-

---

16 J. Cassidy provides a detailed account of the exuberance and hysteria during the Internet boom years in *Dot.con*, Perennial, New York, 2003, pp. 2–5.

17 Ibid. p. 5.

mover advantages and disadvantages in e-business) including a race to build market share and retain customers and the investment climate. These are discussed below.

By entering the e-market early, businesses tried to capture market share in their respective market segment and to generate scale effects through large sales volumes. They wanted to attract new customers quickly and build up a large customer base. The underlying hope was that once customers had used a website a number of times, then they would be unlikely to switch to a competitor, since they would have to get used to a new website layout and functioning. Furthermore, data-mining techniques would allow online companies to customize their offerings to the specific preferences of the individual customer. By switching to another provider, customers lose this level of customization, at least over the short term.

Internet ventures also aimed to create a customer lock-in through network effects. As more and more customers sign up and provide information about themselves, as is the case at eBay and through ► Amazon.com's book reviews, customers are less likely to switch to competitors unless the latter offer better (or at least similar) network effects. Because of these effects, there was a "winner-takes-all" expectation, whereby a dominant player would outperform competitors through economies of scale and network effects.

Finally, and probably most importantly, the peculiar investment climate pushed companies to spend and expand rapidly instead of taking a more cautious approach. In 1999, Silicon Valley venture capitalist firms such as Sequoia Capital and Benchmark Capital invested an all-time high of US$48.3 billion. This represented a 150 percent increase over 1998, and 90 percent of this money went toward high-tech and Internet companies (Pandya et al. 2002). In order to qualify for venture capital funding, companies had to convince investors that they would be able to grow row rapidly to a large scale and so fuel the hope of a rapid payback on investment.

The investors did not necessarily believe in the future of the start-ups they funded. Yet they knew that as long as stock markets kept going up and people kept buying Internet stocks, regardless of the underlying business model, they could not go wrong. At the same time, investment bankers and venture capitalists who refused to play this "game" also knew that they would fall behind the short-term return on investment performance of their less scrupulous competitors. These perverted incentives contributed significantly to the buildup of the stock market bubble.

1.2.3 The Crash

During 1995–1999, investors and managers had artificially inflated market sizes for dotcom companies and overlooked a number of important issues that led to the subsequent end of the Internet boom years.[18]

---

18 For an excellent discussion of the flawed thinking during the boom years of the Internet, refer to Porter (2001), pp. 63–78.

On the one hand, revenues were artificially inflated through a number of ways. Firstly, in order to gain market share, Internet ventures subsidized customer purchases of their products. For example, Internet retailers such as ► Amazon.com and the pet food supplier ► pets.com provided free shipping and delivery to their customers—even for dog food bags that weighed 20 pounds. Secondly, many customers bought products and services online more out of curiosity than to fulfill an actual need. After the novelty wore off, many customers reverted to their traditional buying behavior. Thirdly, in many instances, revenues for the Internet ventures were generated through stocks from partner companies that enjoyed equally high market valuations.

On the other hand, costs were not represented realistically, which further distorted the true state of the underlying business. In many cases, dotcom companies received subsidized inputs because suppliers were eager to do business with them, which helped them to reduce costs. More importantly, many suppliers and employees accepted equity as payment, expecting that the stock market boom would continue to rise.

The abovementioned factors were reflected in poor operating cash flows that did not reflect the actual Internet ventures' business model in terms of costs and revenues. Furthermore, bank analysts, such as Mary Meeker from Morgan Stanley, who in 1996 wrote the highly publicized *Internet Report*, pointed out that the focus of investors should not be on current earnings but on earnings potential (Meeker and DePuy 1996). Instead, investors were supposed to rely upon indicators including the numbers of online customers, unique website visitors, and repeat online buyers. Consequently, to try to meet investors' expectations, e-managers spent heavily on marketing and advertising to attract site visitors and customers, regardless of costs. As it turned out, however, these metrics might have been a good indicator for spectator traffic on a website, yet they did not represent a reliable indicator of revenue or profitability.

On Monday, 13 March 2000, the dotcom bubble started to burst. Within 3 days, the NASDAQ index slid by almost 500 points. At that time, Jack Willoughby, a journalist for *Barron's*, published an article in which he calculated the "burn rate" of Internet companies. The "burn rate" measured the rate at which these companies were spending money. He concluded that most of the Internet companies would run out of money within a year:

» When will the Internet bubble burst? For scores of Net upstarts, that unpleasant popping sound is likely to be heard before the end of this year. Starved for cash, many of these companies will try to raise fresh funds by issuing more stock or bonds. But a lot of them won't succeed. As a result, they will be forced to sell out to stronger rivals or go out of business altogether. Already, many cash-strapped Internet firms are scrambling for funding.[19]

---

19 Please see Willoughby (2000), p. 29.

1

The article shattered the hope of investors that, regardless of their poor financial viability, Internet firms would always be able to raise more money.

Along with most other Internet firms, the stock of the abovementioned ► Priceline.com started to slide from US$150 at its peak down to less than $2. At this valuation level, the market capitalization of ► Priceline.com could not have bought two Boeing 747 jets. Other Internet companies faced similar fates and either went bankrupt or were acquired by larger competitors, often traditional bricks-and-mortar companies from the so-called old economy. For example, K·B Toys, an 80-year-old, bricks-and-mortar toy retailer, purchased the intellectual property, software, and warehouses of bankrupt ► eToys.com—once one of the most highly praised online start-ups and valued at $10 billion—and relaunched ► eToys.com in October 2001.

Subsequent to the burst of the Internet bubble, which took place in March and April 2000, e-business entrepreneurs, managers, investors, and the media awoke to the new reality and started reflecting on what had really happened. More importantly, they tried to understand the reasons that led to the failure of so many Internet ventures, as well as the flaws in their business models. In addition to the hysteria that had distorted valuations, many of these ventures did not create as much value as was anticipated, and they were also unable to convert their lofty market values into real operating cash flows and profits. Let us look at each of these points in turn.

Overall, the value created by Internet ventures turned out to be lower since costs were higher and benefits were lower than was projected throughout the boom years. The belief that e-business would be comparatively low cost stemmed mainly from the idea that it required only a couple of computer servers and a website to set up an online company. Furthermore, it was thought that doing business over the Internet would be highly scalable since it only required additional computer processing capability to cater for new customers around the globe.

Yet for many online businesses, the costs of developing a website turned out to be only a small fraction of the total costs. For example, during the boom years, ► Amazon.com, on average, paid around $16 for buying and shipping a book. On top of that came $8 for marketing and advertising and $1 for overheads (which included the website development), raising overall costs per book to $25. Average price per book sold, however, was only $20 (Cassidy 2003). The main reason for the high costs was that most costs, including marketing and sales, were not nearly as scale sensitive as the creation of a website. In fact, the acquisition costs of online customers were, in general, much higher than those of traditional bricks-and-mortar companies. Internet "pure player" companies firstly needed to build their brand and then win the trust of online customers.

Furthermore, the notion of the unbundled corporation in which external providers manage the high fixed-cost logistical processes did not work out as expected—at least during those early years when the interfaces between e-business companies and their logistics providers had not yet been clearly defined and stream-

lined. To maintain high levels of quality and reliability, online companies such as
▶ Amazon.com reverted to setting up their own warehouses and distribution centers, thereby adding significantly to overall costs.

It also turned out to be difficult for most Internet companies to establish a sustainable revenue model. As a result, they were unable to achieve a high enough
return on investment to justify their stock market valuation. For example, after
starting operations in April 1998, ▶ Priceline.com managed, by the end of that
year, to sell $35 million worth of airline tickets—at an overall cost of $36.5 million!

The inability of many firms to charge appropriate prices for products and services was due to the following factors. Firstly, the Internet lowered barriers to entry
(see ▶ Sect. 3.2). While in the past it was necessary to operate an extensive physical
network to compete in the retailing sector, many companies from all realms, such
as ▶ Boo.com and ▶ eToys.com, attempted to grow market share by leveraging
the Internet. In the online market for pet food, more than half a dozen web retailers were competing for customers. This led to a price war to attract customers, with
some companies giving away products or services for free.

Secondly, the strategic stakes that were involved further aggravated the competitive scenario. Knowing that only a few online companies per sector would be
able to stay in business, these companies invested heavily and sacrificed profits for
market share. They also hoped that market share would translate into sustained
customer relationships. After all, e-business was supposed to be a winner-takes-all
market. Yet, ultimately the lock-in effect created through high switching costs and
network effects occurred only in a few cases. As websites became more user-friendly,
it also became easier for customers to switch from one provider to another.

With regard to network effects, only companies that relied heavily on consumer
interactions (e.g., eBay) were able to leverage the power of their installed customer
base. However, as long as there was no substantial interaction with other users,
individual customers usually did not care about the size an e-business company's
installed user base.

The final dark side of the boom years was that many companies applied illegal
accounting practices to boost profits. Notable examples include the energy trader
Enron that was once hailed as the model Internet-based company and the telecom
operator WorldCom. Their illegal accounting methods continued undetected,
while the boom persisted and the stock market kept rising. However, when the
market collapsed and investors started to scrutinize accounts more closely the
extent of the criminal activities became obvious, forcing these companies and
numerous others to file for bankruptcy. As with previous crashes, regulatory agencies also reacted to improve investor protection. In July 2002, President George
W. Bush signed the Sarbanes-Oxley Act of 2002, which mandates a number of
reforms to enhance corporate responsibility and financial disclosures and to combat corporate and accounting fraud. In addition, the Act also created the Public
Company Accounting Oversight Board (PCAOB), which has the role of overseeing
the activities of the auditing profession.

1.2.4 **The Synergy Phase**

What messages can we take away from looking at these boom and bust cycles across history? Firstly, in order to enter the synergy phase, it is essential to return to business fundamentals. This includes paying close consideration to issues such as industry structure, value creation, and ways to create profits and a sustainable competitive advantage through the Internet and other technologies.

Secondly, just as the railway, steel, and automobile industries underwent boom and bust phases before realizing their true economic potential, we observed a similar evolution in the e-business sector. The booming "installation" years of the Internet were followed by a bust. Since then, the time has come for the much more profound deployment period of e-business.[20]

At the time of writing the fourth edition of this book, about 20 years have passed since the crash. Companies with established Internet businesses such as Ducati, eBay, Google, ▶ Tesco.com, and Nordea, some who have been documented in this book, confirm that if firms have consistent e-business strategies and implement them successfully, they can create significant value for their customers while at the same time being highly profitable. As a result, the stock valuations of some highly successful Internet ventures, such as eBay and ▶ Amazon.com, have increased beyond the levels of the Internet boom years.

In addition, in recent years, entrepreneurial start-ups have also had substantial success. Ironically, nowadays it seems to be the case that it really does only require a couple of computer servers and a website to set up an online company. Most businesses that had been acquired by large industry incumbents such as Alibaba or Google were founded by young entrepreneurs out of their private homes or college dorm rooms. Businesses such as Flickr, YouTube (within Google), Instagram, and Twitter have built communities around a website offering videos and photos or enabling social networking, all of which do not require heavy investments in marketing (because users mostly took care of this) or infrastructure (because no physical goods were involved).

These businesses, however, had a different starting point than their predecessors of the dotcom period. The actual network infrastructure of the Internet has changed dramatically in the last few years. The spread and penetration of internet means that more people spend more time online. Other tools, for example, video-editing software, have allowed for richer content to be created and viewed, which, in turn, makes it easier for new start-ups to create new service and sites for user-generated content. Furthermore, technology standards such as RSS and AJAX[21] have evolved which makes it easier to keep track of content updates and provide a faster and more convenient web experience.

---

20 See also Mullaney and Green (2003).
21 RSS is a type of web feed which allows users and applications to access updates to online content in a standardized, computer-readable format. AJAX stands for Asynchronous JavaScript and XML. It is a technique for creating better, faster, and more interactive web applications.

Based on these improvements, new web-based services have evolved that focus on fostering communication, sharing, or collaboration. The so-called blogosphere where bloggers create their own content and comment on other bloggers' output is democratizing the web by allowing individuals to engage in their personal journalistic interests ("citizen journalism"), creating articles and media on any possible topic. While web-based folksonomies such as YouTube or Flickr allow their members to upload, label, and categorize content such as videos or photos using tags, other sites allow users to create their own profiles and to connect with other people through a social network. Furthermore, there was a wide variety of services evolving on the web, such as Google's online calendar or word processing and spreadsheet applications, which replicate traditional desktop applications, thus posing a threat to established software industry incumbents such as Microsoft.

By functioning as platforms for its users, these software services allow participants to make various content items available and accessible for others. A common concept for understanding the extent of the growing variety in services and how they create value from a user's point of view is the concept of the "long tail."[22] It relates how the Internet enables niche markets to be accessed easily at negligible cost and in theory therefore by a broader customer base, by allowing the individual to reach and capitalize more on previously inaccessible market niches, described as the "long tail." Search tools, for example, are an integral part of the internet and are needed in order to break down a complex world of choice into reasonable pieces which can be handled and/or are valued by the user.

Still many of the new services are yet to prove that they have revenue models that can achieve sustainable profits. However, highly trafficked sites and high user numbers suggest that the value created by these companies is more significant than the value created by companies during the new economy era. While survivors of the dotcom bust such as eBay and ▶ Amazon.com always had community aspects in their business models and managed to be successful hybrid retailers, companies selling solely digital content have the advantage of completely freeing themselves from the boundaries of a physical world, therefore being even more cost-efficient than others.

Furthermore, investors seem to be more realistic about their protégés' future. Web 2.0 is more about business models and people rather than IPOs. Selling a successful, meaning heavily trafficked, website to one of the established incumbents on the Internet appears to be the modus operandi of exiting entrepreneurs.

1.2.5 The Maturity Phase

In recent years, e-business has become deeply integrated with traditional businesses and our everyday life. The start of the maturity phase refers to a special transitional phase between immaturity and maturity. The immaturity of e-business stems from current emerging new e-businesses and their journey to profitability. For example, the Internet of Things (IoT) is an emerging technology that is far from mature. IoT

---

22 See Anderson (2008).

1

technologies have been applied within many business settings. Retail stores use sensors in clothes hangers to identify customer movement and clothing selections and can display the selected item and its details through an in-store IPS screen, which helps customers to make purchase decisions and/or order their size. The IoT has many potential business applications, but how IoT-based e-business integrates into existing businesses and its potential to generate profits is still undeveloped.

On the other hand, some e-businesses have become mature and developed. Online shopping is a mainstream form of e-commerce. Today's shoppers are accustomed to shopping through a range of websites and apps. e-Commerce giants such as Amazon and Alibaba have created popular online shopping platforms and defined the standard for online shopping businesses, with Amazon hosting more than 300 million customers (2017) and Alibaba hosting a total of more than 600 million customers (2018). As another example, Google popularized the use of search engines in everyday life, particularly search engines on mobile devices, and so search engine optimization is an important activity for businesses to promote their products and services. Businesses pay Google to prominently feature in search results for specific keywords that are relevant to their business.

To summarize, in 2019 e-business is starting its maturity phase, as the Internet and digitization are a necessary part of everyday life and modern business. At the same time, with the evolution of new e-business and e-business technologies, many strategic opportunities remain to be explored by future entrepreneurs.

1.3 The Benefits of e-Business Adoption

Before making a decision to initiate e-business activities, businesses should evaluate the benefits of e-business and also consider their capability, resourcing, demand, and alignment with organization goals. The next section introduces some general potential benefits that e-business may create.[23]

1. *Worldwide connection.* The Internet and other information technologies can connect worldwide information, content, knowledge, and people to a business. E-business provides an approach to access information or contact other people worldwide, often at an extremely low cost.

2. *Organization communication and process.* e-Business communication software allows internal staff to communicate with others and to work with staff in other businesses online. For example, Skype and software for meetings allow "virtual teams" of staff to meet colleagues and discuss projects.

3. *Core business (product/service).* e-Business creates the potential for companies to expand market share through online channels and overcome the physical barriers of face-to-face contact. For example, they may respond to customers anywhere instantly. E-business has also created cross-border competition, for

---

23 This section is based on Pavic, S. (2011). *The creation of competitive advantage in SMEs through e-business*, Unpublished doctoral dissertation, University of Sheffield, Sheffield.

example, domestic retailers can sell goods to customers worldwide through international e-commerce platforms.

4. *Environment.* To some degree, e-businesses can be more transparent than traditional businesses, because anyone can access to an e-business platform that publicly available. A company's marketing-mix can be gleaned through their online profile. Hence, e-business enables companies to be more sensitive to changes within their business environment.

5. *Value creation through differentiation or low cost.* e-Business typically has a lower entry cost in comparison to traditional business. According to neoclassic economics, low entry costs could facilitate the formation of prefect competition since barriers to entry are largely reduced, transaction costs lowered, information asymmetry is reduced, market-dominant pricing is possible, and all with less legislation and regulation than businesses with physical storefronts. e-Business may also help businesses in financial distress. For example, prior to its acquisition by Amazon, sales at Whole Foods' grocery stores were declining. Amazon promoted Whole Foods to its online Prime subscribers and added online ordering of Whole Foods groceries via Prime, and sales rebounded. As e-business matures, more objects can be put online and more customer needs can be fulfilled via e-business platforms. There are endless opportunities to create new value and capture more value for companies knowing how to design suitable e-business strategies.

Summary

This chapter:

— Introduced the definitions of e-business-related terms, including "e-business," "electronic commerce," "mobile e-commerce," "social commerce," "omni-channel commerce," u-commerce, and e-markets and definitions of strategy and value creation.

— Provided a framework to describe the typical periods of technological revolutions. It positioned within this framework the evolution of the Internet and e-business. The five main periods that characterize this evolution are:

  – The *grassroots of e-business* period, which took place before the widespread commercial use of the Internet

  – The *rise of the Internet* period, which started with the launch of ▶ Amazon.com in 1995 and continued until 2000

  – The *crash* (or burst of the dotcom bubble) which took place in March and April 2000 and caused a 45% decline of the NASDAQ by the end of that year

  – The *synergy phase,* which followed the stock market crash and bridges e-business into the next phase

  – The *start of the maturity phase*, which represents a transitional mode of e-business from immaturity to maturity

— Described the main benefits of e-business adoption.

1

② **Review Questions**

1. Define the terms "e-business," "electronic commerce," "mobile electronic commerce," "social commerce," u-commerce, e-markets, and "omni-channel commerce" and describe how they differ from one another.

2. Provide a definition of strategy in the way it is used in this book.

3. What are the three distinctive levels of strategy that can be recognized?

4. Describe the different periods of the life cycle model, as proposed by Carlota Perez.

5. What are the five time periods of the Internet evolution? What are the peculiar characteristics of each period?

6. What are the main lessons that the CEOs of pure player companies (e.g., eBay, ► Amazon.com, Google, and more) might draw from these past years of the Internet?

7. Why do today's traditional businesses introduce digital processes and tools into their business and adopt e business?

8. Omni-channel commerce aims at a synergetic view of all channels. Discuss the potential challenges of managing various channels of an omni-channel business.

9. What do you think are the main elements of strategy formulation? Does the perspective chosen in this chapter correspond to your own experiences and observations? If so, how?

10. Choose two technological revolutions, and discuss their evolution using the Perez framework described in this chapter.

11. Critically reflect upon the benefits of e-business and the potential risks and challenges related to each benefit.

References

Anderson, C. (2008). *The long tail: Why the future of business is selling less of more.* New York: Hyperion.

Bartels, A. (2016). The difference between e-business and e-commerce. *Computerworld.* Available at: http://www.computerworld.com/article/2588708/e-commerce/e-commerce-the-difference-between-e-business-and-e-commerce.html. Accessed 12 Jan 2019.

Campbell, P., & Waldmeier, P. (2018, November 11). Ford open to working with foreign rivals on driverless cars. *Financial Times.*

Cassidy, J. (2003). *Dot.con.* Perennial, New York, p. 148.

Chandler, A. (1962). *Strategy and structure in the history of the American industrial enterprise.* Cambridge, MA: MIT Press.

Chou, C. (2018, January 4). Alibaba to open 30 new Hema stores in Beijing by year-end. *Alizila.* Available at: http://www.alizila.com/hema-to-open-30-new-stores-in-beijing/

Henderson, B. (1989, November–December). The origin of strategy. *Harvard Business Review.*

Hook, L., & Nicolaou, A. (2018, January 22). Amazon debuts the store without a checkout. *Financial Times.*

Jelassi, T., Enders, A., & Martínez-López, F. J. (2014). *Strategies for e-business: Creating value through electronic and mobile commerce: concepts and cases* (p. 8). Pearson Education.

Johnson, G., Whittington, R., & Scholes, K. (2005). *Exploring corporate strategy* (7th ed.). New Jersey: Prentice Hall.

Lewandowski, D. (2018, April 17). Florius delivers an outstanding, online, omni-channel customer experience with help from Avaya and Dimension Data. *Financial Times*.

Liang, T. P., & Turban, E. (2011). Introduction to the special issue, social commerce: A research framework for social commerce. *International Journal of Electronic Commerce, 16*(2), 5–14.

Meeker, M., & DePuy, C. (1996). *The internet report.* Harper Business.

Michaelidou, N., Siamagka, N. T., & Christodoulides, G. (2011). Usage, barriers and measurement of social media marketing: An exploratory investigation of small and medium B2B brands. *Industrial Marketing Management, 40*(7), 1153–1159.

Mullaney, T., & Green, H. (2003, May 12). The e-Biz surprise. *BusinessWeekOnline*

Nicolaou, A., Fontanella-Khan, J., Samson, A., & Hook, L. (2017, June 16). Amazon agrees to buy whole foods for $13.7bn. *Financial Times*.

Pandya, M., Singh, H., Mittelstaedt, R., et al. (2002). *On building corporate value* (p. 8). New Jersey: Wiley.

Perez, C. (2002). *Technological revolutions and financial capital: The dynamics of bubbles and golden ages.* Northampton: Edward Elgar.

Porter, M. (2001, March). Strategy and the Internet. *Harvard Business Review*.

Surbhi, S. (2015). Difference between e-commerce and e-business (with comparison chart) – Key differences. *Key Differences.* Available at: http://keydifferences.com/difference-between-e-commerce-and-e-business.html. Accessed 12 Jan 2019.

Verhoef, P. C., Kannan, P. K., & Inman, J. J. (2015). From multi-channel retailing to omni-channel retailing: Introduction to the special issue on multi-channel retailing. *Journal of Retailing, 91*(2), 174–181.

Watson, R.T. (2000). U-Commerce, the ultimate. *Ubiquity, 2000*(October). Available at: https://ubiquity.acm.org/article.cfm?id=353882

Willoughby, J. (2000, March 20). Burning up: Warning: Internet companies are running out of cash. *Barron's*.

Zeng, M. (2018). *Smart business. What Alibaba's success reveals about the future of strategy.* Boston: Harvard Business Review Press.

Further Reading

A detailed account of different levels of strategy can be found in G. Johnson, K. Scholes and R. Whittington, Exploring corporate strategy. 7th edition, Prentice Hall, 2005.

B. Arthur builds on the insights of C. Perez in the article 'Is the information revolution dead?', *Business 2.0*, 2002, March, pp. 65–73, where he suggests that the Internet economy is undergoing the same evolutionary phases as previous technological revolutions.

B. Henderson uses the metaphor of biological evolution to describe the essence of strategy in 'The origin of strategy', Harvard Business Review, 1989, November–December, pp. 139–143.

C. Perez. developed the five-stage model of technological revolutions presented in this chapter: see *Technological Revolutions and Financial Capital: The Dynamics of Bubbles and Golden Ages*, Edward Elgar, 2002. She draws heavily on the writings of twentieth-century economist J. Schumpeter. Among his important works rank the books *Business Cycles*, Porcupine Press, 1982 and *Capitalism, Socialism and Democracy*, Harper & Rank, 1975.

E. Malmsten (the co-founder of Boo.com), E. Portanger and C. Drazin provide an account of the rise and fall of the Internet fashion retailer Boo.com in their book *Boo Hoo*, Arrow Books, 2002.

For further analysis on social commerce and social layers of the internet, see T. Philbeck, N. Davis and A. M. Engtoft Larsen, 'Values, Ethics and Innovation Rethinking Technological Development in the Fourth Industrial Revolution', *World Economic Forum White Paper,* August, 2018.

For traditional businesses seeking to increase their e-Business, Sunil Gupta describes omni-channel strategy in Gupta, S. (2018). *Driving digital strategy: A guide to reimagining your business.* Boston: Harvard Business Review Press.

H. Mintzberg is one of the most prominent critics of the design or positioning school. For further reading, see *Strategy Safari – A guided tour through the wilds of strategic management.* Prentice Hall, 1998, pp. 114–118, which offers no less than ten different approaches to explaining strategy. His article 'The design school: Reconsidering the basic premises of strategic management'.

Strategic Management Journal, 1990, *11*(3), 171–195, provides a more condensed criticism of the design school.

In 'Profits and the Internet: Seven misconceptions', *Sloan Management Review*, 2001, Summer, pp. 44–53, S. Rangan and R. Adner analyse why the promises of the Internet economy were not fulfilled.

In *The long tail: Why the future of business is selling less of more*. Hyperion, New York, 2006, C. Anderson illustrates how, by using the Internet, companies can capitalise on niche markets better to serve their customers.

J. Cassidy. takes a critical perspective of the development of the Internet economy in *Dot.con*, Perennial, New York, 2003.

Liang, T. P., & Turban, E. (2011). Introduction to the special issue, social commerce: A research framework for social commerce', *International Journal of Electronic Commerce*, *16*(2), p. 5–14.

M. Porter's article 'Strategy and the Internet', *Harvard Business Review*, 2001, March, pp. 63–78, provides an excellent overview of the impact of the Internet on strategy formulation. His recent work updates this. See: Porter, M. and Heppelmann, J. (2014) How Smart, Connected Products Are Transforming Competition. *Harvard Business Review*. November. See also: Porter, M. and Heppelmann, J. (2015, October) How smart, connected products are transforming companies. *Harvard Business Review*.

Pavic, S. (2011). *The creation of competitive advantage in SMEs through e-business*, Unpublished doctoral dissertation, University of Sheffield, Sheffield.

The experience of General Electric provides insight to the challenges and opportunities of e-business transformation. Former CEO Jeffrey Immelt describes the strategy at: J. Immelt, (2017). 'How I Remade GE', *Harvard Business Review*, September. For another perspective, see V. Chemitiganti, 'What we can learn from GE and why digital transformations fail', ITProPortal, 3 October, 2018. Available at: https://www.itproportal.com/features/what-we-can-learn-from-ge-and-why-digital-transformations-fail/

Weblinks

The website www.tutor2u.net provides interesting background information on a number of concepts discussed in this chapter.

www.ecommercetimes.com is an online newspaper specific to e-commerce developments.

The E-business Strategy Framework

This chapter introduces strategic thinking. It encompasses four elements: systematic thinking, creative thinking, vision-driven thinking and market-oriented thinking. It will illustrate the critical success factors of e-business strategy.

We shall propose an e-business strategy framework that consists of the following three phases:
- Strategic analysis
- Strategy formulation
- Strategy implementation

The goal of this part is to provide a comprehensive strategic framework that addresses the crucial elements of e-business strategy formulation. The key elements of the three phases of strategic analysis, strategy formulation and strategy implementation are as follows:
- External analysis of the macro-environment and industry structure
- Internal analysis of key resources and capabilities
- Generic strategic options
- Sustainable competitive advantage
- Exploration of new market spaces
- Creation and capture of value
- Internal organisation
- Interaction with suppliers, customers and users
- Mobile e-commerce and u-commerce strategies
- Implementation of strategy

Contents

Overview of the e-Business Strategy Framework

Contents

© Springer Nature Switzerland AG 2020
T. Jelassi, F. J. Martínez-López, *Strategies for e-Business*, Classroom Companion: Business,
https://doi.org/10.1007/978-3-030-48950-2_2

2

> **Learning Outcomes**
> After completing this chapter, you should be able to understand:
> — Strategic thinking for e-business
> — Critical success factors of e-business strategy
> — The structure and the key elements of the e-business strategy framework

■ **Introduction**

In Part II of this book, we propose an overarching e-business strategy framework that can serve as a comprehensive basis for e-business strategy formulation. This framework should help you address the following:

— Understand the external macro-environment and industry structure of e-business companies.
— Understand internal e-business competencies.
— Choose a specific type of Internet-enabled competitive advantage.
— Sustain the Internet-enabled competitive advantage against imitation and disruptive innovations.
— Create new market spaces through e-business initiatives.
— Link the external and internal perspectives of e-business strategies using the value process framework.
— Make decisions regarding the internal organization of e-business initiatives.
— Interact with e-business customers, suppliers, and users.
— Understand specific issues and applications of mobile e-commerce and ubiquitous commerce (or u-commerce).
— Implement e-business strategies.

To do so, we believe that it is valuable to begin this part of the book by covering rigorous and time-proven concepts from the field of strategic management and then to adapt them to the specific context of e-business. This adaptation takes places in the following three ways:

1. Although the conceptual chapters cover several generic strategy frameworks, they also highlight specific concepts that are important for e-business and help understand recent successes and failures in the field. These include, for example, economies of scale and scope, switching costs, network effects, and transaction cost theory.
2. The strategic framework presents specific e-business concepts such as the virtual value chain (see ▶ Sect. 4.3), the ICDT (information, communication, distribution, and transaction) model (see ▶ Sect. 4.4), and the "long tail" concept (see ▶ Sect. 11.4).
3. All concepts and frameworks that are presented in the conceptual chapters are illustrated through specific e-business examples and case studies. By doing so, we want to link real-world applications with theoretical and conceptual considerations, hoping to make the material more accessible to readers and useful to practicing managers.

2.1 Strategic Thinking in the Field of e-Business

Before explaining strategic thinking in the field of e-business, let us return to ▶ Chap. 1 where we discussed the definition and goals of a strategy. There, we stated that:

> - Strategy is concerned with the *long-term direction* of the business.
> - Strategy deals with the *overall plan for deploying the resources* that a business possesses.
> - Strategy entails the willingness to make *trade-offs*, to choose between different directions and between different ways of deploying resources.
> - Strategy is about achieving *unique positioning* vis-à-vis competitors.
> - The central goal of strategy is to achieve sustainable *competitive advantage* over rivals and thereby to ensure sustainable profitability.

A key theme of the above statements is that a strategy is concerned with overarching decisions that determine the fundamental direction of a company. In this sense, a strategy helps to determine the positioning of a firm in the marketplace and the choice of required resources. The overall goal of developing an e-business strategy is to succeed in using the Internet and other technologies as enablers for achieving a competitive advantage (see ◘ Fig. 2.1). There are several ways of attaining a competitive advantage including, among others, having a strong and unique brand, a large and loyal customer base, innovative products and services, and low-cost production facilities.

Strategic thinking enables senior managers to think systematically, creatively, with vision and a market orientation. It is an important requirement for them to recognize what is most valuable and crucial for their business and to create the optimal strategy.[1] As mentioned in ▶ Chap. 1 of this book, strategic thinking

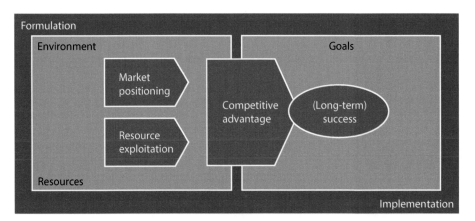

◘ **Fig. 2.1** The goal of e-business strategy is to achieve (long-term) success by building up one or more sources of competitive advantage. (Source: Adapted from Hungenberg (2014))

1　This chapter is adopted from: Moon (2013).

stems from military wars since ancient times, going back to the year 476 BC with Sun Tzu's *The Art of War*. It is an approach that was applied to create a holistic view of war, to fight the enemy, and rationalize the costs of battle. When later applied to business, it's strategic lessons were used to compete with other businesses and secure and defend markets. These days, strategic thinking also concerns itself with identifying new and uncontested markets and/or forming mutually reinforcing ecosystems of complementary businesses who collaboratively create value propositions.

Designing a suitable business strategy in a constantly evolving environment is a complex activity. Strategists need to consider divergent (contrasting) and convergent (unifying) dimensions of an environment. They need to identify and measure the disparities—within and between—the internal and external environment. The analysis then influences the design of a convergent and optimal strategy for the firm. The structure and process of strategic thinking enables strategists to make decisions that encompass and factor in many variables.

Strategic thinking is defined as: "a way of solving strategic problems that combines a rational and convergent approach with a creative and divergent thought process to find alternative ways of competing and providing customer value" (Moon 2013, p. 1699). This definition regards strategic thinking as a way of solving strategic problems, which emphasizes the role of senior managers' strategic thinking ("a subjective matter") in conducting strategic management activities ("objective matters").

Based on this definition and as shown in ◘ Fig. 2.2, strategic thinking includes a creative and divergent thought process. There are four elements of strategic

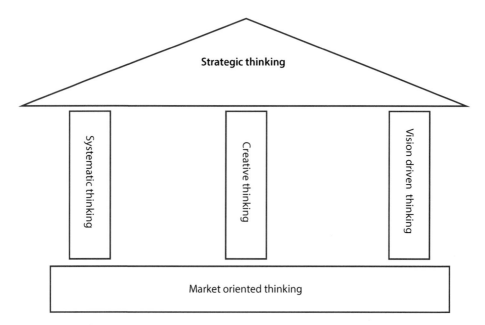

◘ **Fig. 2.2**   Elements of strategic thinking. (Source: Adapted from Moon (2013))

thinking: systematic thinking, creative thinking, vision-driven thinking, and market-oriented thinking. They are described below.

2.1.1 Systematic Thinking

Strategic thinking requires managers to think systematically and holistically. In this case, a business should be viewed as a whole, integrating and articulating organizational activities and components instead of a splintered assemblage of them. This holistic view of a whole e-business or a digital ecosystem is built on the analysis of the internal and external environment of a business.

2.1.2 Creative Thinking

Bonn argues, "strategy is about the development of novel solutions to create competitive advantage. Strategic thinkers must search for new approaches and envision better ways of doing things, in other words, be creative" (Bonn 2005, p. 338). Creative thinking refers to looking at something in a new way, for example, indirectly, laterally, and perceiving new patterns that are not obvious and may be thought of as unusual. The use of creative thinking often achieves unexpected strategic results. e-Business provides many possibilities to combine new and old elements of a product, service, and/or process. The success of the ten most valuable e-businesses in the world[2] may derive from their founders' creative ideas that provide solutions to meet consumer needs.

2.1.3 Vision-Driven Thinking

Creating strategy is a complicated process. There could be various business opportunities available for companies at the same time. Sometimes—especially in dynamic evolving technology industries—a strategic choice is impossible to make solely via analysis. It depends on a sharp sense of vision, an ability to foresee the future and focused determination to achieve desired goals. Central to this is a diligent focus on customers and their needs. In other word, it requires vision-driven thinking.

For example, mass media tends to hype emerging technologies including smart hardware, IoT, blockchain, the cloud, robots and artificial intelligence, and more. There is an ongoing plethora of possibilities and opportunities for e-businesses to assess. The constant churn of new technologies and opportunities may distract managers from their overarching vision and strategic pathway. A visionary does not lose sight of their overarching vision and strategy.

---

2 As of 2018 the ten most valuable e-businesses in the world are Apple, Google/Alphabet, Amazon, Facebook, Tencent, Alibaba, Priceline, Uber, Netflix, and Baidu.

2

2.1.4 **Market-Oriented Thinking**

The importance of markets is self-evident. Markets offer revenues for companies. Market-oriented thinking drives senior managers to regard competitors and customers in a market as strategic design elements. In e-business it requires companies to identify and value aspects of target markets and their incumbents and potential competitors.

For example, a challenge is that e-business markets are no longer impermeable and splintered as distinct segments with barriers to entry. The Internet lowered the entry cost to an e-business market, which made it an almost "perfect competitive market." Amazon, labeled as an online shopping website, now competes in various markets such as fresh food, streaming media, smart speakers, shipment service, e-payment, web service, product advertising, and online shopping.

2.2 **Critical Successful Factors of e-Business Strategy**

Analysis of the Critical Successful Factors (CSFs) of an e-business strategy enables companies to identify key aspects of an e-business strategy that they must support, grow, and/or defend.[3] There are seven types of CSF and they are described below.

2.2.1 **Technology**

The success of e-business depends on applications of technology, for example, an online platform. Companies should provide appropriate infrastructure to deploy technologies into business settings. Security and privacy risks must be mitigated and controlled before launching new IT applications. Strategists should identify the critical technologies within their business and continually optimize them and their use.

For example, technologies require continual updates and upgrades. Almost all popular apps within the iOS and Google Play Store are continually improving their versioning management, e.g., fixing bugs, optimizing user experience, and adding new features or content.

2.2.2 **Customers**

All businesses must identify and monitor their key customer segments and their needs, preferences, and pain points. e-Businesses often fail due to poorly delivered value to customers or poor customer relationship management (CRM). They may create perfect technologies but then pay less attention to who would pay for them, why, and how much they would be prepared to pay.

---

3   This section is adapted from Tsironis et al. (2017).

The Internet enables a firm to reach its customers worldwide, but it can also easily let a firm ignore key customer segments and then gradually lose those customers and consequent market share. Firms should consider communication strategies and CRM strategies when devising e-business strategies.

2.2.3 Suppliers-Partners

Suppliers and partners support the business as it creates and delivers products and/or services to customers. The Internet has revolutionized supply chains of e-Businesses and their business models. Before a firm selects a new e-business strategy, it should assess the potential impact on suppliers and partners and ensure that they too have capability and capacity to work with the new strategy.

For example, to implement "just in time" flexible production schedules and real-time information sharing, a firm should develop a good relationship with suppliers and partners and establish a streamlined direct communication channel with them for infrequent orders of various sizes.

2.2.4 Personnel

Employees are often thought of as the most critical asset of an e-business, because personnel costs typically represent a large part of their fixed costs. e-Businesses tend to require employees with digital literacy skills who can confidently and knowledgeably use the relevant systems or software tools. e-Businesses in specialist or emerging fields may face the challenge of finding, attracting, and retaining the right personnel with the right skills. For this reason, some e-Businesses use global virtual teams—identifying and hiring the best personnel irrespective of where they live and enabling them to work remotely. e-Businesses should invest in continual training of personnel to maintain skills relevancy.

2.2.5 Leadership

The role of leadership is to set the strategy and oversee the delivery of that strategy. They coordinate and motivate teams to act toward achievement of goals. Leaders create a work breakdown structure (WBS) for an e-business strategy and design appropriate roles and responsibilities to achieve the strategy.

There are different types of leaders—informal leaders, authoritative leaders, and more—but for the purpose of this book, we shall typify the leader as a CEO. e-Businesses often require a different type of leadership to "bricks-and-mortar" traditional businesses. Personnel are a significant and critical part of the e-business, so some styles of leadership such as "command and coercion" are suboptimal and may create unhealthy tensions and demotivate personnel. Instead, employees may respond more to collegiate coaching, influencing and pace-setting styles of leadership. Leadership is crucial to e-business.

2

For example, during the initial phase of e-business strategy implementation, investors and shareholders may not see profits because some e-businesses need a long lead time to accumulate scale. This approach requires a strong leadership to motivate the e-business and communicate that the business will definitely eventually profit. This leadership should put a positive tone for e-business projects and provide IT employees with long-term commitments to increase their confidence in the corresponding e-business strategy.

2.2.6 Data, Information, and Knowledge Management

e-Business is usually more knowledge and information-intensive than traditional business. e-Business, particularly those based on data or information services (e.g., the big data companies), will generate a large amount of data, information, and knowledge. This requires the firm to recognize, develop, and use data and transfer it into useful knowledge. Firms can create and capture more value by applying appropriate models of data analysis, for example, identifying consumer behavior patterns by mining consumption data.

2.2.7 Strategic Performance Assessment

Once a strategy has been selected to be implemented, managers must track and evaluate its progress and performance to what was planned. The earlier any negative deviations from the plan are identified the sooner they may be addressed. They do this by setting key performance indicators (KPIs), which is a primary task that senior managers undertake. KPIs are a quantifiable measure used to evaluate the success of an organization, team, and/or employee in meeting objectives for performance.

e-Business companies should not adopt a performance measurement scale directly from traditional companies, because their business models are different and so require different KPIs. For example, the number of downloads and installations of apps is more important KPIs for app publishers than traditional firms because their apps are their key source of revenues. It is important to use the right KPIs, to measure the right performance indicators. In ▶ Chap. 1 of this book, we saw how setting the wrong KPIs can lead to business failure. During the Internet dotcom boom, investors were measuring Internet startups on "eyeballs" and other intangibles rather than cashflow.

2.3 A Systematic Approach to e-Business Strategy Formulation

As stated above, the goal of e-business strategic analysis and formulation lies in identifying and understanding different strategic options and their implications and then iteratively evaluating arguments in favor or against these options. This process does not revolve around finding the *one* right answer, but focuses more on making trade-offs apparent, making decision-makers aware of the implications of different options and helping them make decisions regarding the future based on past and current developments. In this sense, strategic management can be considered to be a "planned evolution"—the alternative to this approach would be an unguided evolution based on pure chance (see Kirsch 1997).

This raises the question of how to go, in a systematic way, about e-business strategy development. As an anchoring point for the remainder of this book, we propose a three part e-business strategy framework consisting of:
1. Strategic analysis
2. Strategy formulation
3. Strategy implementation (see ◘ Fig. 2.3)

The three parts of this framework are dynamically interconnected, that is, they should be regarded as having a feedback loop during the process offering inputs for adjustment and further refinement. Note that in ◘ Fig. 2.3, a given number (inside a circle) corresponds to the specific book chapter in which the listed issue is discussed in detail.

The first part of this framework is the strategic analysis, which consists of two different perspectives: (1) the external analysis and (2) the internal analysis.

The goal of the external analysis, which is covered in ► Chap. 3, is to gain an understanding of developments in the external environment that might have an impact on the e-business strategy of your business. On an aggregate level, the external analysis refers to developments in the broad macro-environment. The acronym PESTEL can frame the external analysis; it stands for changes in political, economic, social, technological, environmental (as in, the natural world), and legal factors that are potentially influential. On a more detailed level, it also entails an

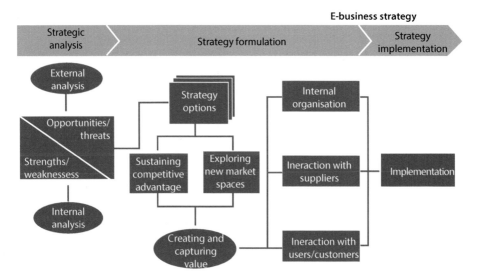

◘ **Fig. 2.3**   The e-business strategy framework consists of three main steps. (Source: Adapted from Jelassi et al. (2005))

analysis of the different players within an industry, including competitors and collaborators, new entrants to the industry, suppliers, and substitutes. This is often referred to as Michael Porter's five forces model (Porter 1979). The outcome of this analysis should help you gain an improved understanding of the opportunities and threats that your business might face in the future.

The goal of the internal analysis, which is discussed in detail in ▶ Chap. 4, is to understand the key resources and capabilities that a business possesses to implement or sustain a specific e-business strategy. Resources might, for instance, refer to a large installed user base (e.g., eBay), large financial capacity for strategic acquisitions (e.g., Google), or a strong brand (e.g., Tesco.com). e-Capabilities refer to a firm's ability through technologies and the Internet to turn resources into valuable products or services.

Based on the insights gained from the internal and external analyses, you should be able to gain an understanding of the strengths and weaknesses that your company possesses vis-à-vis competitors. The overall insights from these two analyses can then be integrated into a SWOT matrix (strengths, weaknesses, opportunities, threats matrix), which raises the four key questions listed in ◘ Fig. 2.4.

Having gained a clear understanding of a company's characteristics and the key environmental and industry developments, we come to the crucial decision of choosing a strategic direction. The choice typically aims to achieve (1) a cost leadership position where a company competes primarily on the basis of low prices and (2) a differentiated position where a company competes on the basis of superior products and services. The strategic options and strategic positioning for e-business are covered in greater detail in ▶ Chap. 5.

Obviously, a competitive advantage that a business possesses today is not necessarily sustainable over time. In the e-business world in particular, there is constant pressure from new Internet startups or incumbent bricks-and-mortar businesses

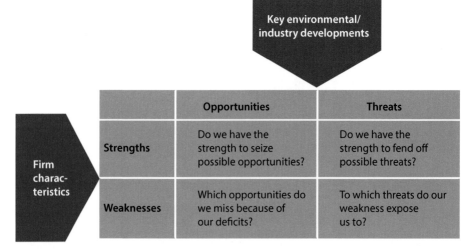

◘ **Fig. 2.4** e-Business strategy formulation entails an internal and an external analysis to identify strengths, weaknesses, opportunities, and threats. (Source: Adapted from Jelassi et al. (2005))

trying to imitate or otherwise outperform existing e-business companies. The issue of sustaining a competitive advantage over time and the dangers that threaten to erode such advantage are covered in ▶ Chap. 6. In particular, ▶ Chap. 6 deals with the threats of imitation and disruptive innovations.

In addition to defending their competitive advantage against imitators, companies can also build up new sources of competitive differentiation by developing new e-business innovations, thereby creating new market spaces that hitherto have been uncontested. The value innovation framework, presented in ▶ Chap. 7, provides a systematic approach for developing these types of innovations that aim at making the competition irrelevant.

▶ Chapter 8 introduces the concept of value creation and value capture. Based on the Good-Dominant logic and the Service-Dominant logic, ▶ Chap. 8 illustrates how a business and customers create value jointly and the causal pathways of value creation and capture.

Following these broad considerations, ▶ Chaps. 9, 10, and 11 address three strategic issues:
1. The internal organization of an e-business venture
2. Its relationships with suppliers
3. Its relationships with customers and users

▶ Chapter 9 deals with a business's internal organization. The concepts of deconstructing the value chain and unbundling the corporation stem from an extensive debate among managers and academics as to how integrated a firm should be in the digital age. During the Internet boom years, popular management thinking suggested that businesses should focus on their core competence (or core business) and outsource all other value-creating activities to external providers. However, this did not turn out to be beneficial for many e-businesses. The main question in this chapter is therefore: "How should we organise internally our e-business activities?" The *Financial Times* article "Connected Devices bring sweeping changes to the factory floor" provides an example of how the Internet of Things (IoT) will change how businesses are internally organized.

Connected Devices Bring Sweeping Changes to the Factory Floor

The Internet of Things is reshaping product design, manufacturing, and distribution.

The interconnection of devices and vast flows of data between machines are transforming factory floors around the world. From robots that work alongside humans to tracking components throughout the logistics system, the Internet of Things (IoT) reshapes the way products are designed and made—and changing the role of humans in manufacturing. Here are the four examples.

▬ Cobots

Cobots work alongside humans and have been spreading across production lines. They are typically smaller, flexible, and mobile, as well as being cheaper than robots. They learn by imitation and are also slower, but cobots are highly adaptable and can be assigned to different tasks. Cobots can perform repetitive tasks that require uncomfortable human movements such as twisting or lifting heavy objects.

— Additive Manufacturing

This is also known as 3D printing, because it involves building objects layer by layer out of substrates such as polymer or metal. Complex patterns based on digital designs that may not be possible with traditional manufacturing techniques can be made with less material and fewer process steps. Additive manufacturing has existed for more than three decades but has been limited by its expense and slowness. However, more real-world applications are emerging—with the potential to remove transportation elements within supply chains. For example, car parts (Porsche), whole cars (Local Motors), and even body parts can be designed and then 3D printed locally.

— Digital Twins

This expression refers to a virtual model of a process, product, or service and is sometimes described as a bridge between the physical and digital world. Data from sensors are streamed from physical equipment to a virtual representation. For example, computer-aided design (CAD) tools can simulate real-world actions.

The concept of a digital twin extends to factory floors, to enable simulation of machinery before anything is built. In the past, production lines had to be switched off to prepare for a new product being made, so downtime can be avoided.

— Supply Chain Tracking

Connected freight and logistics systems used to track at the ship or truck level, but sensors can now be placed on individual pallets of goods.

Separate sensors inside transport vehicles and the final destination factory detect the movement of goods.

Data from these sensors are collated and crunched by computers, revealing the location of a shipment, as well as other factors during transit that affect the goods. Scott Overton, a general manager at Intel explains:

» Maybe it's temperature sensitivity, humidity, vibrations — or maybe [the item] can't be tipped or tilted … All of those kinds of parameters can also be measured, reported and analysed.

He cites a group of drivers of refrigerated trucks on heavily congested roads, who turned off their engines while stuck in traffic. This switched off the cooling systems, but since the refrigeration was back on by the end of the journey, the temperature fluctuations were not always obvious. Connected freight systems on the other hand can make automatic corrections or send out messages to operators, while human intervention is also possible. Furthermore, sensors can indicate when maintenance is required, replacing the need for periodic maintenance with "as needed" maintenance scheduling.

Adapted from: Pooler (2017).

▶ Chapter 10 addresses the upstream issue of supply chain management. The main question here is how to set up B2B relationships with external providers. A special focus is placed on different types of electronic B2B transaction platforms and on third-party e-service providers such as IBX, which is discussed in detail in the case studies section of this book.

▶ Chapter 11 presents some concepts and conceptual frameworks, such the "tipping point," the "long tail," and the "social CRM," which provide insights into how to choose an appropriate e-business strategy for interacting with users.

▶ Chapter 12 presents some conceptual frameworks that are specific to mobile e-commerce and u-commerce applications. ▶ Chapters 13, 14, and 15 specifically discuss mobile commerce, social commerce, and omni-channel strategies.

▶ Chapter 16 presents the strategies employed by the two most biggest e-tailing companies in the world: Amazon and Alibaba. ▶ Chapter 17 looks forward to highlight future trends for e-business.

▶ Chapter 18, which is included in the "Lessons Learned" part of this book, discusses operational issues related to the implementation of an e-business strategy. It also presents an e-business strategy roadmap that covers the main steps (from vision to alignment) of formulating an e-business strategy.

Summary
- This chapter firstly clarified the goal of e-business strategy and introduced strategic thinking in the field of e-business.
- Next, it described the critical success factors of e-business.
- Finally, this chapter provided a brief overview of the e-business strategy framework and its main elements, which are strategic analysis, strategy formulation, and strategy implementation.

? Review Questions
1. What are the four elements of strategic thinking?
2. What are the critical success factors of e-business strategy?
3. What are the key elements of the e-business strategy framework?

References

Bonn, I. (2005). Improving strategic thinking: A multilevel approach. *Leadership & Organization Development Journal, 26*(5), 338.

Hungenberg, H. (2014). *Strategisches Management in Unternehmen* (p. 83). Wiesbaden: Gabler\ Weisbaden GmbH.

Jelassi, T., Enders, A., & Martínez-López, F. J. (2005). *Strategies for e-business: Creating value through electronic and mobile commerce: Concepts and cases* (p. 36). Harlow: Pearson Education.

Kirsch, W. (1997). *Wegweiser zur Konstruktion einer evolutionären Theorie der strategischen Führung.* Herrsching: Kirsch.

2

Moon, B. J. (2013). Antecedents and outcomes of strategic thinking. *Journal of Business Research, 66*(10), 1698–1708.

Pooler, M. (2017, November 1). Connected devices bring sweeping changes to the factory floor. *Financial Times.*

Porter, M. E. (1979). How competitive forces shape strategy. *Harvard Business Review, 57*(2), 137–145.

Tsironis, L. K., Gotzamani, K. D., & Mastos, T. D. (2017). e-Business critical success factors: Toward the development of an integrated success model. *Business Process Management Journal, 23*(5), 874–896.

Further Reading

For a more detailed discussion of the SWOT concept, see Johnson, G., Scholes, K., & Whittington, R. (2005). *Exploring corporate strategy* (7th ed.). Upper Saddle River: Prentice Hall.

For a discussion of strategies in different types of organisations, see Mintzberg, H., Quinn, J., & Ghoshal, S. (Eds.) (1998). *The strategy process: Concepts, context and cases* (4th ed.). Upper Saddle River: Prentice Hall.

External Analysis: The Impact of the Internet on the Macro-environment and on the Industry Structure of e-Business Companies

Contents

© Springer Nature Switzerland AG 2020
T. Jelassi, F. J. Martínez-López, *Strategies for e-Business*, Classroom Companion: Business,
https://doi.org/10.1007/978-3-030-48950-2_3

Learning Outcomes

After completing this chapter, you should be able to:

- Analyze trends in the macro-environment and explain their implications for e-business ventures
- Understand the value of the five forces industry framework for the analysis of industry attractiveness
- Explain the key characteristics of the co-opetition framework and show how it expands the five forces industry framework
- Define industries, segment, and target markets for e-business applications

■ Introduction

» When an industry with a reputation for difficult economics meets a manager with a reputation for excellence, it is usually the industry that keeps its reputation intact. Warren Buffet

e-Business ventures, or any ventures for that matter, do not operate in isolation from their environment. Instead, success depends not only on just what a company does by itself but also on the actions of other actors in the industry, such as competitors or suppliers, and on broader environmental developments such as changes in technology or government regulation. While individual businesses can typically at least partly shape the industry environment through their competitive behavior, the broader developments in the macro-environment can rarely be influenced.

To adjust accordingly to environmental changes, companies need to have a clear understanding of important developments in their external environment. At this stage, for e-business companies, technological changes are of critical importance, since, for instance, an increase in available Internet technologies (such as IoT and smart home tech, AR/VR, machine learning, etc.)[1] open up new possibilities for creating new business models. At the same time, there are also societal changes such as changing demographics and changes in government regulations that potentially have an impact on the sustainability of e-business ventures.

Making sense of this very dynamic environment and deciding how to best do business is a highly complex task; strategists need to filter the multitude of signals to highlight the really important developments. This task becomes even more challenging due to the wealth of public information that is available through media and online sites. As a result, there is just as much danger of information overload as of information unavailability.

One important first step is to organize information about new developments in the macro-environment and cluster them in such a way that they will not be overlooked. As a starting point for such a systematic analysis, this chapter firstly provides a framework for analyzing the macro-environment. Secondly, it discusses Porter's

---

1 For a detailed explanation of these terms, refer to Forbes Technology Council, "Top tech trends in 2019: 11 experts detail what you need to watch," Forbes, 20 December 2018.

3

five forces framework for analyzing the attractiveness of an industry. It also analyzes the impact of the Internet on each force of Porter's framework, i.e., industry rivalry, barriers to entry, threat of substitute products, and the bargaining power of buyers and suppliers. Thirdly, this chapter presents the co-opetition framework, which offers an alternative perspective for industry analysis. Finally, it addresses the question of how to define industries within which to compete and how to segment specific customer groups that a business should target through its e-business offering.

3.1 Examining Trends in the Macro-environment

The macro-environment takes a broad perspective of the factors that influence a business strategy and its performance.[2] Evolving trends in the macro-environment can present significant opportunities and threats to a firm's strategy. Therefore, at the outset of any strategy formulation, it is useful to analyze the trends that characterize the macro-environment in its different dimensions: *political, legal, economic, social,* and *technological* (see ◘ Fig. 3.1).

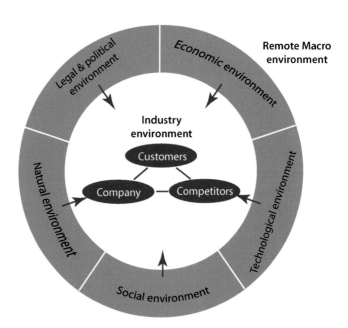

◘ **Fig. 3.1** e-Business companies are impacted by their industry and macro-environment. (Source: Adapted from Hungenberg (2014), p. 90)

---

2   A good discussion of macro-environmental influences can be found in Johnson et al. (2005). A more e-commerce- specific discussion of environmental factors is contained in Chaffey (2002), pp. 143–156.

3.1.1 Political and Legal Environment

The political and legal environment relates to issues on different organizational levels. At country and industry levels, it includes issues such as taxation, company legislation (including monopoly legislation), government subsidies, and other incentives for industries, tariffs, political stability, and interest rates.

Because of the complexity of cross-border regulation, taxation has been a difficult issue in electronic commerce. Yet, because of the boundary-less nature of the Internet, it presents a major issue for governments and a source of opportunity for e-business ventures. For example, multinational companies such as Google, Facebook, and Amazon have been involved in tax avoidance scandals. They reportedly channel online revenue from sales within a country across borders to other countries with a more favorable tax regime. This practice decreases their book profits and subsequent tax payable where their international headquarters are. Upon discovery of this financial strategy, some multinational companies chose to cease rerouting revenues and instead pay tax in the same country where the revenue is generated. For example, Facebook used to reroute its advertising revenues via Ireland and will instead pay tax in every country which has a local office where the revenues are generated[3]. Similarly, the United Kingdom, government plans to create a new taxation approach that taxes revenue rather than profits (see *Financial Times* article titled "Big Tech faces UK tax on revenues, not profits").

> **Big Tech Faces UK Tax on Revenues, Not Profits**
>
> Large technology companies such as Facebook and Google face a tax on their revenues in the United Kingdom after a Treasury Minister said this was the "potentially preferred option" after a government review.
>
> Mel Stride, the Financial Secretary to the Treasury, said in an interview with the BBC that the British government wanted "to move to a situation where we are taxing those activities [of large digital businesses] fairly."
>
> He said: "[Digital platforms with lots of users are] driving a lot of value, so you're looking at social media platforms, online marketplaces, internet search engines — where at the moment the tax regime is not taxing those activities fairly."
>
> His comments come 3 weeks after a government consultation closed on potential changes to taxation of the digital economy.
>
> The aim of the consultation is to tackle long-standing fears that large Internet businesses, such as Amazon, Google, and Facebook, do not pay enough tax following a series of tax-avoidance scandals involving those companies.
>
> Mr Stride said a tax on revenues was the "potentially preferred route to go," although he did not want to do anything that would harm smaller businesses, according to the BBC.

---

3 "Facebook to stop routing ad revenue via Ireland amid pressure over taxes," *The Guardian*, 12 December 2017

3

His comments bring the UK's position on taxing Internet companies much closer to that of its peers in Europe, led by France, which are attempting to introduce a revenue tax that make it harder for US technology giants to cut their tax bills by channeling profits between countries.

Dan Neidle, a partner at Clifford Chance, said that a UK tax on gross revenues would help the government get around "the thorny problem that many internet companies make little profits and [in some cases] huge losses."

However, he also cautioned that some technology companies might respond by restructuring their businesses so that they pay more tax in the United States and less tax overall in the United Kingdom.

"If you want to be kind, this is a proposal intended to discourage the use of tax havens but which won't raise much UK tax. If you want to be less kind, it's a proposal that looks like it's taxing digital businesses, but isn't really," he said.

Sanjay Mehta, a partner at Katten Muchin Rosenman, added: "If this new approach were to be implemented so that revenues were taxed rather than profit, this could dramatically increase the UK's taxing base in the tech sector. However, it would position the UK as an outlier in terms of international taxing standards."

Amazon and Google did not immediately respond to a request for comment. Facebook declined to comment.

In the United Kingdom, Facebook and Amazon have already changed their tax structures to book more of their payments in the country after George Osborne, the former chancellor, first introduced a Google tax on overseas profits. However, their bills are still a fraction of overall revenues.

Facebook in December became the first US tech company to agree to pay more tax outside Ireland by booking more of its ad sales in other European countries.

In 2016, it said it would book big advertising sales generated in the United Kingdom locally, instead of through its European headquarters in Dublin.

Regulators around the world have attempted to develop coherent plans for increasing their share of the tax paid by big US technology companies.

India this month said it could ask companies to pay taxes based on their "economic presence" in a parliamentary bill accompanying the budget.

Source: Marriage and Ram (2018).

Let's now assess how the legislative framework in a country may impact e-businesses. With regard to monopoly legislation, throughout the 1990s, Microsoft was accused of violating its dominant position in the operating systems market by leveraging it to move into other software markets at the expense of competitors.[4] More recently, Google has been criticized for a similar dominance in the online advertising market. When ▶ Amazon.com entered the German market, it was confronted with the price-fixing regulation, which sets a common price for all new books sold in the country. This made it impossible for Amazon.de to compete on the price dimension with rival bookstores.

---

4   "Windows of opportunity," *The Economist*, 15 November 2003, p. 61

Furthermore, in light of peer-to-peer file-sharing networks such as Kazaa or eMule, the dominant incumbents in the music sector (music labels) continue to rigorously criticize "pirates" who download music in violation of copyright laws. Contrary to the interests of the music industry, however (considering the convenience and range of files available) the online file-sharing practice is still highly and widely popular. Filesharers who remix music to create new works provoke further discussion on copyright protection and digital rights management tools. One solution to illegal music downloads is paid file streaming services, for example, another multinational is Spotify, who pay copyright owners a royalty based upon the frequency of plays of a song.

At the individual level, political and legal debates revolve around the extent to which businesses should be allowed to intrude into the private lives of Internet users. This includes topics such as the placement of cookies[5] and aggressive marketing via spam mails and aggregating and onselling user data.[6] The European Union (EU) addressed this to some extent with its complex General Data Protection Regulations (GDPR) in 2018. The GDPR concerns data protection and privacy for individuals within the EU and European Economic Area (EEA) and the export of data outside of the EU and EEA. It aims primarily to give control to individuals over their personal data and to simplify the regulatory environment for international business by unifying the various regulations within the EU. It mandates that businesses that collect personal data must put in place *appropriate technical and organizational measures* to protect that data and users can request companies to delete or change any data the business holds on them. Implementation of the legislation led to many e-businesses changing their operations. Opinion on GDPR is provided in the *Financial Times* article "Europe bets its data law will lead to tech supremacy."

In sum, businesses cannot overlook the role of government and legislation when analyzing the external environment. Through the lens of government, some aspects of e-business create challenges for regulation. Due to the virtual and borderless nature of e-business, it is difficult for governments to regulate, scrutinize, and tax revenues coming from e-business activities fairly. The question of how the "visible hand" of regulators should deal with e-business remains in contention. Some countries or regions, for example, Europe, may introduce stricter regulations to protect taxation and citizens' rights (see the *Financial Times* article "Europe bets its data law will lead to tech supremacy"). Others may view e-business, particularly small and medium-sized e-business startups, as one of the most important boosters of economic performance, for example, the United States and China.

---

5   Cookies are text files stored on a PC that allow the website operator to identify that PC.
6   Spam is unsolicited e-mail messages

3

Europe Bets Its Data Law Will Lead to Tech Supremacy

In several respects, Europe's General Data Protection Regulation is a terrible piece of legislation. Having been so long in the making, it appears outdated even before it comes into effect on May 25. The GDPR is also overly sweeping in scope and largely unenforceable in practice. That is not a great look for what has been billed as a landmark law intended to resound around the world.

Yet, in spite of its manifest flaws, the regulation has already achieved one invaluable goal. It has forced us to focus on how we treat the most valuable assets of our digital age: data. The law's main aim is clear: to compel all organisations to be more transparent and accountable in their use of personal data and to give consumers greater control and choice.

The EU's move seems timely following the outrage surrounding Cambridge Analytica's misuse of Facebook data. The casual way in which 87m users' details were accessed without their consent only reinforced the impression that the big social media companies regard personal data as mulch to be monetized rather than property to be protected.

The very threat of the GDPR has forced every responsible business in Europe to scrutinize how it gathers, stores, and uses data. That is a good thing. The prospect of fines totaling up to 4 percent of global revenues has further concentrated corporate minds.

Yet there are several glaring drawbacks to the regulation. One test of any legislation is how effectively it can be implemented. In that regard, the law is likely to fall woefully short. Such is the complexity of the regulations that it is hard for any company to know whether it is fully compliant. Pretty much any organization could be found in breach.

In Brussels, even the champions of the GDPR privately admit that implementation is likely to be arbitrary and dependent on the effectiveness of national regulators. Ironically, those regulators have been stripped of many of their most expert staff by big companies desperate to hire more data protection officers.

Second, as is often the risk with onerous regulation, the legislation may have the perverse effect of stifling competition and innovation, reinforcing industry incumbents rather than encouraging insurgents. The costs of compliance may also impose barriers to entry.

Third, the GDPR is likely to hobble the short-term development of Europe's artificial intelligence industry, recently identified as a strategic priority. Some trade associations argue that by limiting data flows and raising legal risks, the regulation will chill the sector. If data are the feedstock on which the algorithms gorge, then Europe may be rationing its most precious commodity.

The conclusion of one US tech lobbyist that the GDPR would "kill people" because it would prevent the transfer of medical information may be extreme, but there seems little doubt that Chinese AI companies, almost wholly unfettered by privacy concerns, will have a raw competitive edge when it comes to exploiting data.

Europe's counter-bet is that the GDPR will eventually become the global regulatory norm. Privacy will emerge as a new battleground for tech supremacy. But the early signs are not promising. Outside Europe, the US tech groups seem more intent on evading the law's principles than abiding by them.

Nonetheless, some of Europe's entrepreneurs are surprisingly gung-ho about their chances of competing in what they call the next-generation Internet.

Jason du Preez, Chief Executive of Privitar, a London-based privacy engineering company, argues that users will increasingly gravitate toward businesses that pursue privacy by design. "GDPR is a massive shift and creates an opportunity for businesses to compete on the basis of privacy," he says.

Marc Al-Hames, managing director of Cliqz, a German search engine, compares today's big US tech companies with the automakers of the 1960s. Sentiment swung sharply against the American car industry following the publication of Ralph Nader's crusading book Unsafe At Any Speed, which exposed the manufacturers' disdain for safety. That forced Congress to legislate and provided the opportunity for safety-conscious European carmakers to thrive.

Mr Al-Hames argues that the GDPR should be the first move in a bolder European regulatory campaign to protect the consumer, install digital "safety belts" on the Internet, and tame the big tech groups. "It is then the job of European entrepreneurs to build better, and safer, alternatives," he says.

He is right that only competition can complete what regulation has started. It will be up to consumers to shape the future they want to inhabit.

Source: Thornhill (2018).

3.1.2 Economic Environment

The economic environment refers to broader economic developments within the context of a country, region, or worldwide. Important factors in the economic environment are interest and exchange rates, stock markets, and, more generally, economic growth rates (e.g., gross domestic product, household discretionary income and employment data). The favorable economic environment of the 1990s and the resulting cheap availability of capital contributed strongly to the rapid rise of Internet companies.

This rise came to an abrupt halt with the burst of the "dotcom bubble" and NASDAQ market crash in March 2000 and the subsequent demise of a large number of Internet startups. For example, the launch of some Internet startups such as the online fashion retailer ▶ boo.com was feasible only because capital was accessible so easily at the time. However, during the ensuing consolidation phase, which was characterized by depressed stock markets and cautious venture capitalists, it became much more difficult to gain access to capital, even if the underlying business idea was sound.

Following the NASDAQ crash, the e-business sector has clearly matured over the last few years. For example, global retail e-commerce is projected to become the largest retail channel in the world, with a value of US\$4.5 trillion by 2021[7]. In the

---

7   Orendorff (2017). See also: Grant (2018)

3

more recent past, as e-business companies have shown their ability to operate profitably, investors have once again started to fund young and innovative startups. In contrast to the previous heydays of the Internet; however, investors now seem to be more fiscally responsible and driven by promising business models. In addition to venture capital companies, there are today established Internet companies that are willing to invest in or acquire startups and integrate them into their existing business portfolio. The US$3.1 billion acquisition of DoubleClick by Google or the US$4.1 billion purchase by eBay of the VoIP[8] telephone service provider Skype, which was then sold in 2011 to Microsoft for US$8.5 billion, are prime examples of this newly found confidence.

3.1.3 Social Environment

The social environment considers factors such as population demographics, income distribution between different sectors of society, social mobility of people, and differing attitudes to work and leisure. Social developments were the main driver behind the development of numerous e-commerce applications. For example, if, due to their careers, members of a developed society increasingly become cash rich but time poor, then businesses that address this specific customer segment can create substantial benefits. For example, the online retailer ▶ Tesco.com primarily targets customers who do not have the time or the desire to shop systematically in a physical grocery store.

Other important dimensions of the social environment that impact on the development and use of the Internet are online usage patterns. These can be indicated by the percentage of the population using e-mail or the web for information or transaction purposes. These types of measurements provide good indications of the evolution of the population toward forming an information society and establishing digital habits. For example, the United Kingdom has turned into a "nation of online shoppers" (see the *Financial Times* article "UK turns into nation of online shoppers"). An additional indicator of the social environment is the degree of participation in online communities, such as Second Life[9] or Kitely, where Internet users come together in a virtual world.

The popularity of social networking sites such as Twitter, WeChat, Weibo, and Facebook and professional networking sites such as LinkedIn shows, along with their popularity, reflect that the Internet has become a place for people to interact and share experiences. Unsolicited self-presentation and open communication through social networking sites, apps, or weblogs reinforce the democratization of the web and indicate an important paradigm shift in society, especially among

---

8   VoIP telephony stands for "Voice over Internet Protocol". For acquisition details see Microsoft News Center (2011) and Arrington (2005).
9   For an illustrative example, see, in the second edition of this book, the case study "Second life. Mercedes-Benz enters the metaverse," pp. 525–547.

teenagers and youngsters. Increasingly people aged 50 and above are using social media and the Internet, for example, a study based on a large-scale sample of persons aged over 50 in the United States found 70 percent use social media[10], and a similar pattern is emerging in other countries.

United Kingdom Turns into Nation of Online Shoppers

Britain spends more money online per head than any other developed country, but the love affair with social media may be on the wane, according to research from the UK's communications regulator.

Consumers in the United Kingdom spend almost £2,000 online for goods each year on average—50 percent more than the next-highest valued market of Australia—boosted by widespread broadband access and the experience of home shopping.

"There has been a traditional strong propensity for catalogue shopping among UK consumers and this appears to be translating also to online," said Kester Mann, Analyst at CCS Insight. "There is a good perception and trust in UK postal service to deliver parcels reliably and on time."

The high use of debit and credit cards in the United Kingdom was also cited as an important factor by Ofcom. On the back of the online shopping boom, Ofcom found that two-fifths of advertising spending in the United Kingdom was now online—more than any of the other countries analyzed.

However, the annual report into the Internet economy by Ofcom also found a surprising drop in the proportion of online adults in the United Kingdom accessing social networks each week from 65 percent in September 2013 to 56 percent in October 2014. This was the steepest fall of any of the countries surveyed.

Ofcom suggested that this was because of the rise of less traditional means of keeping in contact with friends that do not use networks such as Facebook and LinkedIn. These include online video sites, games platforms, and instant messaging. Social network use also fell in the United States, Japan, and China.

Ofcom said the popularity of online commerce was boosted by widespread superfast broadband access in the United Kingdom, which is ahead of France, Germany, Italy, and Spain. Nearly eight in ten UK homes have access to broadband services that provide connection speeds of at least 30 megabytes per second.

"The internet has never been more important to the lives of people in this country, and the demand for better connections keeps rising," said Ed Richards, Ofcom Chief Executive. "We are making significant progress in this area. However, we all acknowledge that there is more to do, and this will be the challenge for the coming years."

---

10 Anderson (2017). See also Waldhuter (2017)

More British people also use Internet-connected televisions than in Europe. Almost a quarter of UK consumers have a smart TV and about four-fifths of those have connected it to the Internet. One-third of the online population in the United Kingdom use the Internet to watch TV programs or films at least once a week, the highest proportion of any European country.

Traditional viewing has suffered as a consequence, however, with TV viewing declining more in the United Kingdom last year than in any other country surveyed.

Source: Thomas (2014).

3.1.4 Natural Environment

Minimizing their impact on the natural environment may be challenging for many traditional businesses, particularly polluting businesses such as transportation and logistics and product manufacturing firms. Yet low environmental impact is a selling point of e-business. e-Business can save customer commutes to physical stores, and digital documents minimize use of paper. Furthermore, unlike brick-and-mortar business, e-businesses may require less physical infrastructure and fixed assets and depend less on natural resources, which is very attractive to consumers and regulators. For example, to create and distribute a physical music product (compact disc or vinyl LP) requires time, chemical and plastic inputs, a pressing plant, cardboard or plastic casing, and transportation. To create and distribute a digital music product requires none of these things. As 3D printing gains mass traction, in the near future consumers may purchase codes that they enter into a 3D printer at home and make goods from that.

To leverage off society's increasing environmental awareness, many modern e-business companies use a "green e-commerce" model that aims to minimize their carbon footprint and maximize their sustained contribution to the natural environment. For example:

- Ofo is a stationless bike-sharing company which aims to reduce carbon dioxide emissions by providing stationless bike renting service.
- Ecosia is an online search engine that plants a tree for every search made through it.
- Craigslist and eBay allow individuals to sell used items to others. This "circular economy" concept is an e-commerce model that captures value from used items and reduces expenditure and production on new items that consumes natural resources. Most importantly, individuals' needs can be met at a comparatively low price as they do not need to buy a new one. (See the *Financial Times* article "Luxury Goods Create New Online Market").

Luxury Goods Create New Online Market

Luxury goods companies pride themselves on offering top-quality, exclusive products in sumptuous surroundings. But well-heeled consumers can now save themselves a trip to Bond Street or Fifth Avenue by choosing to buy a "vintage" Patek

Philippe wristwatch or a "pre-owned" Hermes Birkin bag with a simple click of the mouse.

The idea of a secondary market for luxury fashion and accessories is largely anathema to an industry built on the strength of its carefully cultivated brands. Yet as online demand for used luxury goods grows, big brands are divided on how to respond.

Michael Sheldon, Chairman and Chief Executive of Portero, an online trading company that has been called "eBay for the affluent," says some luxury brands are worried about the effects on their primary market. "They seem to have the idea that a luxury brand shouldn't be doing this," he says.

Portero, which trades luxury goods through eBay, says it was founded in 2004 "on the belief that buying luxury online should be effortless and without risk" and it "certifies and guarantees every item" on the site.

Last year the company announced a deal with Tourneau, the watch retailer, to authenticate luxury watches. "We believe [Portero] is legitimising the secondary market of online auctions for luxury goods," says Howard Levitt, Tourneau's President. "We recognise this is the future for buying and selling pre-owned luxury goods online and a way for us to extend our brand to the secondary marketplace."

Others are less sanguine. Lew Frankfort, Chief Executive of Coach, which designs and sells luxury accessories, says: "We prefer our products to be sold in image-enhancing environments only. We don't consider these sites appropriate for the brand."

Yet as some companies speed up their introduction of new product lines, shortening the shelf life of luxury items, more women are looking for ways to empty their closet of last season's fashion and accessories—especially if those items have a resale value.

Daniel Nissanoff, President of Portero and author of *FutureShop: How the New Auction Culture Will Revolutionise the Way We Buy, Sell and Get the Things We Really Want*, says Americans are increasingly trading their possessions in secondary markets—a trend that has important implications for the makers of new goods.

Milton Pedraza, head of the Luxury Institute, agrees. Wealthy baby boomers, he says, "want to forgo the burden of ownership" and "would rather collect experiences," so a secondary market makes sense when they tire of their goods. "They would rather leave their heirs a portfolio of investments than a lot of possessions."

The key issue, says Greg Furman, executive director of the Luxury Marketing Council, a trade group in New York, is that a secondary market has to be "meticulously controlled" because of the proliferation of knockoffs. In 2004 Tiffany's sued eBay for facilitating the trade of counterfeit Tiffany items on the site, claiming the fakes eroded the reputation of its brand. The case is expected to go to trial by the end of this year.

François-Henri Pinault, Chief Executive of PPR, the French luxury and retail group, says that provided the product is legitimate, a secondary market could be good news because it educates consumers about the brand. "It would be better to have used products at a good price than fakes," he says.

Cyrus Jilla, head of European consumer products practice at Bain, the management consultancy, says a secondary market is "neutral to good news" for luxury brands. Many pre-owned items are old lines, he notes. "The truth is today's luxury consumer is very savvy and knows what today's hot item is or not. So it won't impact on today's sales." Moreover, consumers still relish the in-store experience of buying luxury goods, which is hard to replicate online.

Its effect in the long term may be "slightly positive," he says, in that certain consumers may be encouraged to buy a luxury item if they believe it has resale value.

"There are consumers who might find it hard to spend $500-$600 on a luxury item. A site like Portero might encourage them to buy it if they believe it has residual value," he says. "I could see a scenario where it supports luxury goods purchases. I don't think it displaces the typical consumer who goes into the store."

For now, websites offering used luxury items are here to stay. As Mr Pinault says: "You can't stop a customer selling her bag to whomever she wants."

Source: Foster (2006).

3.1.5 Technological Environment

For e-business ventures, the technological environment is of significant importance. Technological innovations (such as the Internet or wireless devices) led to the emergence of new market opportunities and business models. During the early years of the Internet, important drivers of technological developments were standards and languages such as the TCP/IP (Transmission Control Protocol/Internet Protocol), HTTP (Hypertext Transfer Protocol), HTML (Hypertext Mark-up Language), and XML (Extended Mark-up Language).[11] More recently, new web development techniques such as the Internet of Things (IoT) and smart home tech, augmented and virtual reality, machine learning and artificial intelligence, and 3D printing open up new possibilities for e-business entrepreneurship. For example, see the *Financial Times* article "Trying on the future."

Trying on the Future

Just as fashion editors are having to become bloggers and tweeters, retailers should be thinking not just e-commerce but also m-commerce—as in "m" for mobile. With the advent of the 4G world, consumers are about to be able to shop for anything, everywhere, all the time.

Imagine the following scenario, as envisioned by ng Connect, a consortium founded by tech company Alcatel-Lucent to explore the potential of high-bandwidth networks:

---

11 TCP specifies how information should be separated into individual packets and reassembled at the destination. IP specifies how individual packets should be sent over the network. HTTP is a method of jumping back between different files. HTML is a computer language for formatting hypertext files. J. Cassidy provides an informative account of the most important Internet standards and technologies in his book entitled *Dot.con*, Perennial, 2003, pp. 16–24.

» Hanna, a shopper, has her body mapped at an in-store kiosk and uploads a virtual version of herself to the high-speed data cloud. She then goes shopping on her mobile and tries items on virtually. Later, when she goes home, Hanna continues shopping on her smart TV, chatting in real time with an online personal shopper and sending choices to her friends via social networks. Meanwhile she takes in videos offering expert advice on L'Oréal beauty products from the editors of Elle magazine.

This is not far-fetched. Already available in the US, 4G LTE (long-term evolution) offers significantly higher speeds and reduced latency (lag time), which means videos and web pages download instantly. In the United Kingdom, BT and Everything Everywhere are trialing superfast broadband, with a national rollout planned for 2014, and near-4G networks have debuted in the United States, Japan, Sweden, and Norway, with Russia leading the way thanks to Yota, an innovative provider.

"It's not all about speed, but the services we can have when connected to the cloud," says Silvio Fernandez, head of ng Connect Americas. He says the shift to mobile retailing is inevitable, as faster bandwidths make mobile phones our primary connection to the digital world.

"Yes, for over 10 years there was a reluctance to embrace e-commerce, and there'll be a natural reluctance with mobile shopping, but the shift has already started," he says. "I can pay for a coffee with my mobile now in the US."

James Hart, e-commerce Director at the online fashion retailer Asos, says 8 percent of visitors to the sites arrive "via non-traditional sources" such as mobile devices.

"And that number is going to grow exponentially, starting this year, with the proliferation of tablets and cheap smartphones; connected TVs may even gain some momentum this year. In emerging territories there are people accessing the internet for the first time via mobile who may never even use a PC."

However, just as there is no "stop" button on an iPod (only a "pause"), a default "shop" state for consumers will have its pros and cons. According to Holition, which describes itself as an "augmented reality retail specialist," consumers will have access to a wealth of money-saving promotional codes offering more economical shopping.

But Lynne Murray, Brand Director for the London-based company, says there is a less welcome side. "The user will be constantly profiled. The targeting of product based on what you bought most recently may have a negative effect on consumer's attitudes as they switch off to a constant ambush of communication from retailers," she says.

Jonathan Chippindale, Holition Chief Executive, agrees. "Content will need to be presented carefully so as not to appear to interfere or pester the individual with products and services they do not want."

Perhaps the greatest challenge for m-commerce is for mobile phones to be seen as payment devices. So-called mobile wallet technology has yet to be proved secure. Chances are that only when consumers stop leaving their mobiles on café tables while they eat will mobile payments, and thus mobile shopping, come into their own.

Excerpt from: Harkin (2011).

The actual network infrastructure of the Internet has also changed dramatically. The spread of high speed Internet connections and the popularity of mobile devices led to an increasing number of people spending more time online and allowed for richer content to be created and viewed, in turn making it easier for new startups to create new service sites based around user-generated content.

Compliance with common technological standards in wired e-business applications has become more widespread, and so attention has moved to creating and agreeing on new technology standards for wireless devices. Businesses are less likely to invest in technologies where there is no global agreement on standards for use the *Financial Times* article "The Internet risks fracturing into quarters."

The Internet Risks Fracturing into Quarters

Beijing, Brussels, Washington, and Silicon Valley have competing visions for the web.

The Internet, through its most common application, the worldwide web, seems as reliable as electricity or drinking water, and it is recognized as critical infrastructure. But the Internet is not as substantial as it appears—it depends on a precarious balancing act behind the scenes, where technical problems are addressed in the midst of political squalls.

The Internet is a delicate and elaborate arrangement of hardware, software, protocols, standards, organizations, databases, security, telecommunications, and more. The Internet is not just a technical system—it is also social, a massive, tangled interaction involving half the world's population. These people are often erroneously called users; rather, they are participants in this conversation. The Internet influences society, and society influences the Internet.

Why four internets, and not 400 or 4 billion?

Four ideologies are particularly influential, because they have been adopted by state-level actors with the resources to push their visions, fund the science behind them, and, crucially, "sell" them to allies. The four Internets currently coexist in an uneasy peace and even host a parasite. But they are not in equilibrium.

It is possible that one or two could drop out of the picture and one or two become dominant, transforming online public space with repercussions for politics, commerce, and civil society.

Internet technology has two major technical requirements: decentralization (no one in charge, anyone can join) and identification (via a unique Internet protocol address).

The original, what we call the "open Internet" of Silicon Valley, welcomes decentralization and the openness and freedom it allows. But the identification system has led to threats to privacy, and the openness has enabled trolling and fake news.

So critics in Brussels and elsewhere demand a nicely behaved, regulated "bourgeois Internet."

Third, there is a "commercial Internet," whose leaders prize the innovation facilitated by data collection and oligopoly but resist the West Coast vision.

The fourth, the "authoritarian Internet" championed by Beijing, uses the technology to monitor and influence social interaction in order to address security, social cohesion, health and well-being, transport, or climate change.

We must not leave out the parasite: an anarchic hacking ethic allied to paranoid nationalism uses the Internet to spread mistrust. It does not care which Internet it trolls, as long as there is one.

Nevertheless, the authoritarian Internet is the real dilemma. All governments want to engineer good outcomes, and the Internet is a powerful tool for "nudging" citizens to behave in particular ways. But nudging and social cohesion can cross over into control and subjection. Eventually, the Internet's essential openness may be threatened. The Internet is a powerful tool for "nudging" citizens to behave in particular ways technological trends make this a problem now.

I believe passionately that artificial intelligence can be a force for good. AI algorithms are fueled by data created by the web, e-commerce, and social networks. Data are highly regulated in Europe, which is also a fragmented market. They are less so in the United States, where the corresponding advantage accrues to its private sector. In China, data regulation is very different, and its private tech giants conform to the Communist party and government line. Beijing values aspects of the open Internet; social networks often alert the government to problems. However, once alerted, it acts quickly to close conversations down. The government is also seeking to tap the power of social networking with schemes to rank the Chinese people in a social credit system.

China is already using its Belt and Road Initiative to build infrastructure across its hemisphere. We could soon see the addition of an information superhighway initiative where the Internet has room to grow, including Africa—Beijing's influence is strong there—and India. Chinese tech firms have invested billions of dollars in Indian startups over the past few years, and India's Aadhaar ID system is almost purpose-built for authoritarian uses. Even Apple and Google have bowed to Chinese pressure to organize their data and services compliantly. This is not an anti-Chinese argument. Beijing is entitled to regulate as it sees fit, and all governments find the authoritarian Internet attractive to some extent.

A thriving Internet that puts people first should draw on all of these cultures and ideological preferences. We need to recognize this diversity while working hard to ensure that standards remain open and governance conforms to common principles. The technology can promote independence as well as social stability across different societies, if it respects the values inherent in them.

Source: Excerpt from Hall (2018).

See also O'Hara and Hall (2018).

The factors mentioned within the five dimensions above should serve only as a starting point for a careful analysis of the macro-environment. Depending on the industry and country being analyzed, the importance of these dimensions will obviously differ. Needless to say, a comprehensive understanding of the macro-environment is an essential prerequisite for the formulation of a sound e-business strategy.

3

3.2 Examining Industry Structure with the Five Forces Framework

What does the profitability of any given firm depend on? Firstly, a firm needs to be able to create higher value than its rivals. Secondly, it also needs to be able to capture the value that it creates in the form of prices that exceed its costs. If a firm can charge higher prices for its products or services compared with its costs, then it captures large parts of the value it creates. If, on the other hand, prices are driven down by competition, then consumers will capture most of the value.

This highlights the fact that profitability depends not only on the internal competencies and activities of an e-business company, which we shall discuss in detail in ▶ Chap. 4, but also on its environment, that is, the industry in which it competes. In this context, an industry is defined as a group of firms that produce products or provide services that are close substitutes for each other.[12]

As an example, let us consider the personal computer (PC) industry. During the past few decades, this industry has created immense value for consumers, in the form of increased capabilities of desktops, laptops, and tablets. While performance has also increased over the years, prices typically have not risen; instead, they have actually decreased significantly over time, thereby placing heavy constraints on the profitability of most computer manufacturers. In contrast, there are industries such as software development where businesses can capture large parts of the value created. For example, Microsoft became one of the most profitable companies in the world on sales of its computer operating systems. This stark contrast between industries raises the question as to what determines the ability of a company to capture value.

Michael Porter created a five forces framework which outlines the main factors determining a firm's ability to capture the value it creates.[13] In essence, this ability is determined largely by the attractiveness of the industry in which a firm competes. Obviously, the advent of the Internet has profoundly affected the structure of many industries. Yet there are no general conclusions regarding how the Internet affects the structure of different industries; instead, it is necessary to analyze each industry individually.[14]

---

12 For a detailed discussion of industry analysis, see Porter (1998), pp. 3–34.

13 The five forces industry framework is described in Porter (1998), p. 5.

14 R. D'Aveni suggests that levels of competition have risen in the past decade, leading to a phenomenon that he calls "hypercompetition" (see D'Aveni 1995). However, G. McNamara, P. Vaaler and C. Devers have empirically tested this thesis and have not found conclusive evidence for an intensification of competition (see "Same as it ever was: the search for evidence of increasing hypercompetition," *Strategic Management Journal*, 2003, Vol. 24, No. 3, pp. 261–278).

The five forces model provides a guiding framework for understanding the sustainability of profits against competition and bargaining power. The five structural features that determine industry attractiveness are (1) *industry rivalry*, (2) *barriers to entry*, (3) *substitute products*, (4) *bargaining power of buyers*, and (5) *bargaining power of suppliers*. (See the *Financial Times* article "Michael Porter – Academic who shares his values," where Porter reflects on the contemporary suitability of his framework, three decades after its publication.)

Michael Porter: Academic Who Shares His Values

Prof Porter's reputation has put him near the center of discussions with both chief executives and politicians about how to restore US growth and prosperity. Sitting down at his own boardroom table, with a look that brooks no small talk, he blames the depressed state of the economy in part on cyclical factors—retrenchment after the real estate bubble, corporate boards' caution about domestic investment—and in part on "a more fundamental competitiveness problem."

It is predictable that competitiveness is the lens through which Prof Porter sees the problem. At the root of his success was his first article in Harvard Business Review, more than 30 years ago, which outlined the "five basic forces" that determine the state of competition in any industry (customer power, supplier power, the threat of new entrants, substitute products, and rivalry between established competitors). Companies—and subsequently countries—found it a simple and useful way to assess their own strengths and weaknesses and plot forays into new markets.

It still animates Prof Porter, whose steady, high-velocity delivery is punctuated by a mime artist's repertoire of hand gestures (sewing a button, screwing up a jar, chopping a carrot). He points out that globalization has benefited higher-income, higher-skilled people like him. So, having started his career giving speeches on strategy and competitiveness in the United States, he now gets invited all over the world. "The market for me has increased exponentially," he says, "because all these countries are looking for talent." Lower- and middle-income workers, however, have suffered. "We've let all kinds of obstacles fall in the way of the US as an effective and efficient and productive place to do business," he says, citing skill gaps, poor infrastructure, and the burdens of health benefits, regulation, and litigation. At the same time, "other countries have offered a better value proposition."

While Prof Porter retains an underlying optimism, this loss of competitiveness obviously pains him. "This is shocking for the US. If you go back 100 years, you find that the US really was a huge pioneer in public education … The US was a real pioneer in creating a national, very deep university system … The US was a pioneer in the interstate highway system … We stepped to the plate in the past and made very, very bold investments in the fundamental environment for competitiveness. But right now, we can't seem to agree on any of these things."

The financial and economic crisis also sparked a bonfire of many of the widely accepted academic orthodoxies on which the developed world's prosperity was built.

Has it shaken his faith in his theories?

68   **Chapter 3** · External Analysis: The Impact of the Internet on the Macro-environment...

3

Not a bit. Prof Porter says his five forces are, if anything, "more and more and more fundamentally important and visible, because a lot of the barriers and the distortions that would blunt or mitigate these forces and the need for strategy and competitive advantage ... have been swept away" by globalization, the increased velocity and transparency of information, and the decline in trade barriers.

"What I've always tried to do, for better or for worse, is to get at the underlying, fundamental, structural elements of competition and of how firms compete, in a way that's really invariant to whatever best practices happen to exist or whatever trends are," he claims. "So you can do a five forces analysis in 1985 and you can come to one conclusion based on the circumstances of the day, and you can take the same industry in 2010 and it's going to look very different."

In 2008, Prof Porter revisited and revised his five forces article, reviewing the "vast literature" that had emerged around it and concluding that the original theory was robust.

He has also not rested on his prominently displayed laurels. Having outlined the five forces' impact on strategy, he became interested in the competitiveness of locations and nations, as well as in the business clusters that emerge around successful companies. He parlayed this into analyses of inner cities, the compatibility of environmental progress and economic growth, and his latest headline concept: "creating shared value" (CSV)—the idea that corporate activities which advance society will contribute to a positive cycle that allows everyone to grow faster.

Prof Porter insists "CSV" will underpin the creation of "a next and more sophisticated view of what capitalism is all about," but it has stirred up some resentment in the established corporate social responsibility community. Advocates of CSR see Prof Porter's concept as neither new nor different. "It's fundamentally different," he retorts, pointing to the many emails he receives from companies "energised by the idea that they could think about all of these social issues in this different way."

It is also different from his earlier work, which was grounded in data-based research. *The Economist*, for example, criticized "the paucity of evidence." The HBR article Prof Porter co-authored in January cites a series of examples of best practice, such as Nestlé's support for coffee-growers in Latin America and construction company Urbi's "rent-to-own" mortgage-financing plan in Mexico. But as Prof Porter himself says most examples of best practice are "constantly changing, so that means a lot of management literature after a while starts to look a little bit stale."

Could that be the fate of his work on CSV? He admits that finding empirical evidence and support for the concept "is the preoccupation now". But "if companies can start to show the growth in market share [and] profit improvements that they get from pursuing these strategies, I think capital markets will become the biggest cheerleaders."

Eventually, he says, the world will look back and consider the development of CSV alongside China, globalization, and the economic downturn as "one of the big discontinuities of this particular point of economic history."

Few business people would expect to see their strategies outlast them. Prof Porter, by contrast, has no doubt that his ideas will still be fueling corporate, economic, and political strategy long after he has left his institute for the last time.

Source: Adapted from Hill (2010).

3.2.1 Industry Rivalry

Industry rivalry occurs when firms within an industry feel pressure or the opportunity to enhance their existing market position. High intensity of rivalry within an industry results from the following structural factors:

- *Large number of competitors*

If there are numerous competitors in a given industry or business sector, then individual firms may want to make a competitive move, for example, by lowering prices. The Internet has reduced the importance of geographic boundaries, which traditionally limited the number of competitors within a region. Since competitors followed the same strategy, competition became more intense.

- *High fixed costs*

High fixed costs (such as extensive physical infrastructure) create strong pressure to fill capacity, even at the expense of having to cut prices. Consider bricks-and-mortar retail stores, which have specific capacities that must be utilized. To create the necessary turnover, retailers often find themselves in highly competitive price wars. Through the Internet, the ratio between fixed and variable costs shifts more toward fixed costs. Developing software has initially high costs, but rolling it out across different markets has comparatively negligible costs. Thus, industry rivalry tends to increase because e-business ventures want to optimize the use of their capacity.

- *High strategic relevance*

Rivalry increases when firms have a strategic stake to succeed in a given industry. One of the most prominent examples is Microsoft's decision in 1996 to design all its new products for Internet-based computing. This decision led to the browser competition between Netscape's Navigator, the incumbent browser software, and Microsoft's Internet Explorer, a competition that Microsoft was determined to win. In order to beat Netscape, Microsoft offered for free the web server software (which Netscape sold for $1,000) and put 800 people to work on an upgraded version of Explorer. Ultimately, Explorer pushed most competing products out of the market and became the dominant Internet browser worldwide. However, with the rise of Mozilla's Firefox browser and the subsequent launch of Google's Chrome, Microsoft's dominant position was challenged. Fast forward to 2018 and the average usage share of these three desktop browsers is around 12.28 percent for Explorer, 60.64 percent for Chrome, and 11.73 percent for Firefox.

- *Little differentiation between products*

Rivalry also increases when there is little differentiation among products, which then become like commodities. This situation leads to increasing substitution among competing products, thus increasing consumers' bargaining power (see ► Sect. 3.2.4). For example, this is the case in the computer-chip industry where profits are low compared with the value created.

- *Low growth rate of the industry*

Intensity of rivalry also depends on the growth rate of a given industry. Fast-growth industries can accommodate a larger number of providers since, as the overall size of the market expands, each competitor secures a share of the market. In slow-growth industries, rivalry tends to be intense because growth can be achieved only at the expense of competitors.

- *Excess capacity*

When the Internet became an online platform for commercial use, scores of startup companies in different industries embraced it, which resulted in highly intense competition. Venture capitalists and stock markets provided cheap capital, which led to an overinvestment in Internet startups, thereby creating overcapacity.

However, companies need not always be rivals and just that. As explained in ▶ Sect. 3.3, some competitors cooperate with each other, hence the term "co-opetition."

3.2.2 Barriers to Entry

Barriers to entry determine the threat of new competitors entering the market of a specific industry. New entrants, bringing additional capacity and the desire to gain market share, have two negative effects on the attractiveness of an industry. Firstly, new entrants take away market share from existing incumbent companies. Secondly, they bid down prices, which in turn reduces the profitability of incumbents.

Consequently, the profitability of any given industry tends to decrease as barriers to entry are lowered and vice versa. The impact of the Internet on barriers to entry, however, has been less clear-cut than initially assumed, when it was commonly thought that the Internet would wipe out most barriers to entry. In general, high barriers to entry result mainly from the following factors:

- *High fixed costs*

High fixed costs deter many potential entrants because they do not have the required capital and/or the willingness to invest large amounts of money in a risky market entry. While it was necessary in the past to set up an extensive bricks-and-mortar infrastructure to reach out to a large number of customers, the Internet has reduced this requirement. This is especially true for digital goods which can now be distributed online, for example, films, music, news, books, banking, and information services.

The rise of the online peer-to-peer file-sharing systems, such as Napster, illustrates how a single person (Shawn Fanning in this case) with an ingenious idea can threaten a major, long-established industry with a complex and high fixed-cost physical distribution network. Through the Napster platform, individual Internet users were able to exchange music files of their favorite songs, which undermined the traditional business model of the music industry. Subsequently, music businesses attempted to raise barriers to entry again by declaring file-sharing services illegal, yet it is clear that the Internet has profoundly changed the way music gets distributed (for a more detailed account of how the Internet has caused a paradigm shift in the music industry, see the case study in this book on online file-sharing). The pressure on music companies that rely on a physical distribution infrastructure has become so strong that some of them—Bertelsmann's BMG and Sony—merged their music divisions in December 2003.

In contrast, the computer manufacturer Apple recognized that through online distribution, the barriers for entry had been reduced substantially and that the Internet would also be a viable channel to distribute music commercially. It successfully developed the iTunes online music store, which became a highly successful format for selling music online.

In industries that involve the distribution of physical goods or require a high level of personal interaction, the impact of the Internet on barriers to entry is more ambiguous. For example, ▶ Amazon.com initially thought that it could focus solely on the customer interaction aspects of its business and outsource to external providers all activities that would have required substantial investment, including logistics and distribution activities. However, ▶ Amazon.com learned that to guarantee a high level of reliability, it had to operate its own warehouses and distribution centers, which in turn increased the required capital investment. Setup costs for a warehouse averaged $50 million, and operating costs were also significant. In order to finance these infrastructure investments, ▶ Amazon.com was forced to issue more than $2 billion in bonds. In contrast, China's Alibaba does not own any warehouse infrastructure and goods move directly from supplier to customer.

Similarly, in banking, several direct banks initially thought that they could acquire and service customers solely through online channels. The case study of Nordea Bank, however, illustrates that an extensive physical branch network can be crucial for the acquisition of online customers and the selling of more complex financial products. As a result, such physical assets created effective barriers to entry for new online competitors.

Despite these examples of e-businesses using physical storefronts, the use of information and communication technologies (ICT) contributes to reducing the extent of capital that was traditionally required to enter into an industry. As ICT-based outsourcing services become more widely available, the concentration in a given industry decreases. In this context, the strategy of outsourcing non-core elements of a business and paying for services based upon the variable volume of demand is increasingly being used, hence lowering the need for fixed costs. Thus, from a customer's perspective, what used to be in some sectors (such IT services), a fixed cost has now become a variable cost. For example, cloud computing represents a significant change from fixed (server) costs to variable (size in the cloud) costs. This especially benefits small and medium-sized enterprises who are highly uncertain about future information storage needs. (See *Financial Times* article "Cloud computing cuts start-up costs.")

Cloud Computing Cuts Startup Costs

Renting servers by the hour or megabyte removes barriers to entry, making it vastly easier for entrepreneurs to launch, and expand, an online business.

Back in the days of the dotcom boom toward the turn of the century, an Internet entrepreneur had to spend hundreds of thousands of pounds buying computer servers, set them up, launch the service, and then pray that he had guessed correctly on what the uptake would be.

If the site attracted too many visitors, the servers would simply collapse under the weight of traffic. If there were too few visitors, the company was left with a roomful of expensive, underused equipment.

"I remember playing all those guessing games. I spent weeks trying to negotiate different kinds of deals with internet hosting companies: could we have two servers for the first two months, then six for the next two, not really being sure what we would need," says Lachlan Donald, a veteran technologist who is now Chief Technology Officer of 99designs, an Internet marketplace for graphic designers.

If a company got its calculations wrong, it could take days or weeks to get more computer power. "At previous companies it was a nightmare."

The difference is the arrival of cloud computing services, which allow companies to rent computing power by the hour and by the megabyte, making it vastly easier to launch an online business. Startup costs are much lower. "Companies had to borrow a lot of money to buy all those servers. It created a barrier to entry that cloud computing has removed," says Mr Donald. When he helped to launch 99designs, using Amazon Web Services to run the website, the company was set up without any external funding at all.

"Amazon Web Services has been the biggest boon to venture capital-backed companies in recent years. It has meant you can now fund 10 companies for the price of one, and you are seeing new applications being developed that would have been difficult to build cost-effectively in the early days," says Michael Grant, Chief Executive of Cloudscaling, a company that offers cloud infrastructure software.

These services also help to keep down staff costs. "If you are a fashion company, your business is not information technology. Now, you don't have to set up an IT division that is not part of the core business. You can run with minimal IT staff," says Mr Raghavan.

Having computing power on tap like electricity or water has also helped fledgling companies to deal with sudden jumps in popularity. Zynga, a developer of games for social networks, for example, turned to Amazon Web Services in 2009 when users of its FarmVille game jumped from zero to 10m in 6 weeks, and the company had run out of its own data center capacity. "If you are launching an app and you aren't sure how many people will be hitting the site, it makes sense. Even if it is 1m users you will have the flexibility to handle that," Mr Raghavan said.

Mr Grant says that having unlimited amounts of computing power on tap has also helped to spawn new types of companies that would not have been viable before, such as biogenomics businesses offering specialized analysis of gene sequences.

"If you are three guys in a garage and you need 10,000 servers because you are doing some super-fancy algorithmic calculations, the cloud is fantastic for that," he says.

Cloud computing can work for larger companies as well as small ones.

A number of Fortune 500 companies use cloud computing for some of their operations, often where they have want to experiment with new types of services, or create a website around a new product, without huge IT investment.

The cloud might also not work for companies that are too small. It can be complicated designing software to run well on the cloud, warns Mr Donald, and this is something that very small businesses could struggle with. "It is much more technically complex. You need to automate everything and assume everything is going to fail. Although a whole ecosystem of software services companies has sprung up to help with this, it is still has more complications," he said.

Mr Raghavan agrees. "The cloud is not for everyone. If you have a solid business case I would recommend it. But if you just have a concept and don't really know what your audience is, I would not recommend it, because the cloud is not free," he says. "It reduces your capital expenditure costs, but it is not free."

Source: Excerpt from: Palmer (2012).

- *Trust and brand loyalty*

Trust and brand loyalty are essential for customer acquisition and retention. Bricks-and-mortar companies are able to launch online activities more easily than Internet "pure-play" ventures, since they already possessed a respected brand and consumer trust. Pure online businesses, on the other hand, must build their brand which requires investment in marketing. Building trust is even more difficult for a pure online business since, in case of problems, customers do not have a nearby physical branch that they can visit or a customer adviser with whom they can interact face to face. Companies such as Airbnb and Uber address this to some extent by using customer and vendor reviews and ranking systems to enhance the trust of users.

- *A steep learning curve*

A steep learning curve gives a firm an advantage because they have greater experience in the market. A firm may find ways to create more customer benefits or reduce its cost structure ahead of competitors. Any competitor that enters a market needs to accept low returns, while it goes through the same learning experience as incumbents. Alternately, it may find ways to make the incumbents' learning experience obsolete by offering a new way of running the business. For example, Amazon's early start in online book retailing helped the company to stay ahead of its competitors, such as BOL, the online book retailer of Bertelsmann. The latter was never able to catch up with ▶ Amazon.com and ultimately withdrew from the online book retailing business.

- *High switching costs and strong network effects*

High switching costs and strong network effects help an incumbent to keep its customers, even if a new entrant offers a higher value. For example, if retail banking

3

customers want to switch from one bank to another, they need to change their automated bill payments to the new bank account and also inform relevant companies and individuals about the change. The effort associated with doing so could be an effective deterrent for many customers to move to another bank even though the latter offers better value. In the Internet context, the so-called stickiness of a website refers to the switching costs involved with moving from one Internet site to the next. High stickiness makes it unlikely that a user will move from one website to another one. Similarly, strong network effects also tend to increase barriers to entry. The network effects of e-business could be understood by the network externality of Internet platforms. An Internet platform with a large number of users is usually more valuable, and potential users would be more willing to select the platform with a larger network of users, which eventually increases the scale of the user network.

For example, eBay has created strong barriers to entry for potential competitors through the large global customer base it has created over the past few years. For individual customers, it makes sense to switch to a new provider only if they know that all or at least most other current users would make a similar switch as well. Only then would they be able to enjoy the same type of market liquidity as they did before. Similarly, through the creation of strong network effects, social networking sites such as Facebook have established a leading market position. Once users have built up a significant number of contacts and are active in different interest groups on Facebook, it is unlikely that they will switch to another platform unless their contacts migrate with them.

- *Strong intellectual property protection*

Strong intellectual property protection is essential for firms that sell products with high development costs but low reproduction costs. This is the case with digital goods such as music, video, and software. When intellectual property rights are not actively enforced, barriers for new (albeit illegal) entrants are lowered, thus allowing them to push cheap, pirated copies onto the market. Furthermore, without strong intellectual property protection, it will be increasingly difficult in the future to entice creators to create if they will not be compensated adequately.

3.2.3 Substitute Products

About a decade ago, when reflecting on strategy and the Internet, Michael Porter highlighted the role that the Internet could play in creating new substitutes for industries. The intensity of pressure from substitute products depends on the availability of similar products that serve essentially the same or a similar purpose as the products from within the industry. As the availability and quality of substitute products increase, so profits generated within the industry tend to decrease. This is due to the fact that substitutes place a ceiling on prices that firms within the industry can charge for their products. However, the real substitutive power of products must also be assessed taking into account the price of these products and buyers' switching costs as well. The global Internet has helped to increase the pressure from substitute products, especially for goods that are digital by nature or can easily be digitized, as this enhances the variety of products available to customers.

For instance, online music-sharing has evolved quickly and become a formidable substitute for compact discs, thereby threatening the core revenue generator of the traditional music industry in its foundations. In the software arena, Microsoft, the dominant producer of software for computers, faced new substitutes in the form of mobile devices that increasingly provide many of the same functionalities as traditional computers. However, the software for these products is not primarily Microsoft-based.[15] For example, Google developed a free package of online applications, including calendar, email, word processing, and spreadsheet functions that operate as a substitute for Microsoft's high-end Office software package. One response that dominant industry incumbents use to disruptive new startups offering substitute products and/or services is to acquire them, for example, AOL's acquisition of TechCrunch, a web-based publication which offers technology news and analysis; Microsoft acquiring Skype for its VOIP software and LinkedIn for professional social networking; and Facebook's US$1 billion acquisition of Instagram, the mobile photo-sharing application. (See *Financial Times* article "Facebook shows it gets the message with Instagram deal".)

Apps are dominating the fast-growth of mobile-based e-business, with app revenue quadrupling between 2013 and 2018. The best-selling game app, League of Legends (owned by Tencent) received income of US$2.1 billion in 2017, which is greater than many listed companies' whole-year income.[16] iOS and Google Play (two of the most popular app stores worldwide) allow anyone to distribute their app via their platform, reducing the barrier to enter the app market to negligible. However there are also negligible switching costs initially; an app user who dislikes an app can uninstall it immediately and is able to find many other substitutes in app stores. According to neoclassical economics, when a market is still proliferating and profitable, and the entry cost is almost zero, more app developers and companies will enter the market, which could create a "perfect competitive market." Future e-business companies need to consider how to build "an impermeable shield" to protect their interest from other substitute apps in such an intensive competition environment.

Facebook Shows It Gets the Message with Instagram Deal

Remember when it seemed crazy that Google was paying $1.65bn for YouTube? Thanks to the incredible leverage of the web, an online video startup with only 65 employees had already amassed 20m regular users in less than 2 years—though it had nothing in the way of revenue to show for it.

From the vantage point of today's app world, that already looks so 2006.

---

15 "Software's great survivor," *The Economist*, 22 November 2003, p. 70
16 The source of the data involved in this paragraph is Statistica, 2018. Available at ▶ https://www.statista.com

3

Enter Instagram. The photo-sharing app's numbers are more eye-opening than YouTube at the same stage. With only 13 employees, it has garnered more than 30m members in its first 18 months.

The revenue line may still be a big, fat zero—but that didn't stop Facebook from laying out $1bn to secure an icon that enjoys prime positioning on mobile screens everywhere.

If the YouTube deal represented an early flowering of what used to be called user-generated content on the web, the acquisition of Instagram is a harbinger of another new wave: the app that lives beyond the web. It is a place where the influence of the traditional web powers—even one in the ascendant, such as Facebook—is muted, and different rules apply.

Apple ushered in this new world, with the launch of its App Store. The resulting app economy, without much revenue to show for itself, has been floated on a tide of venture capital. But acquisitions like that of Instagram are a harbinger of things to come. In a deal that was, in its way, even more eye-opening, social games company Zynga paid about $200m for the startup behind a simple game called Draw Something: launched only 7 weeks earlier, the game had already attracted more than 35m users.

The platform to support apps like this has come into being remarkably quickly. Apple had sold some 80m iPhones and iPads at the time that Instagram was launched: that number has since grown to 230m, and sales of devices using Google's Android software have exploded. Add in the social network effects that many new services rely on, and this makes fertile ground for app phenomena like Instagram.

The speed with which they emerge and the simplicity of the experience makes it easy to write off such endeavors as small, ephemeral jewels. Yet Instagram packs a punch. As an alternative to importing their Facebook contacts, users can quickly build a new network of people to share pictures with—something that reflects a growing willingness of users to juggle different networks rather than export a single, homogenous Facebook experience to each new online service.

And, thanks to the strong emotional connection that comes from browsing through friends' pictures, Instagram claims to have captured a surprising amount of its users' attention.

How to make money from this will be a big question. Mobile advertising has been notoriously slow to take off. But image-centric services have an obvious appeal to brands that want to create an emotional connection with users. Like the image "curation" site Pinterest, Instagram is an obvious first port of call for brand owners looking to test out future advertising formats that will mix in commercial messages with users' own content.

So what does this $1bn deal say about Facebook? Coming the month before its expected IPO, it should give potential investors pause for thought. Facebook has always displayed a strong sense of paranoia—no bad thing, given the low barriers to entry in its industry—and has used other acquisitions in the past to latch on to new forms of online behavior.

Buying Instagram is an admission that, while its own mobile app is used by hundreds of millions of people, Facebook was not built with mobile in mind. A complex, busy web service can't hope to compete with the simplicity and delight of a purpose-built app like Instagram.

That also explains why many Instagram users are unhappy about a Facebook acquisition, and why Mark Zuckerberg has just picked a big management challenge.

Source: Adapted from Waters (2012).

3.2.4 Bargaining Powers of Buyers and Suppliers

The bargaining power of buyers and suppliers is two sides of the same coin; this is why we discuss them jointly. The bargaining power of buyers tends to be high (and that of suppliers low) if the industry displays the following characteristics:

- *High concentration of buyers*

High concentration of buyers, which allows them to leverage their purchasing power through pooling. One important feature of many B2B e-marketplaces—such as IBX, discussed in the case studies section of the book—is the aggregation of buyers' orders. This helps them to achieve better terms from suppliers than they could obtain individually.

- *Strong fragmentation of suppliers*

Strong fragmentation of suppliers, which makes it difficult to establish a joint approach to pricing. In the personal computer industry, many producers are constantly trying to gain market share at the expense of other competitors by undercutting their prices. This in turn undermines the pricing power of the whole industry.

- *A high degree of market transparency*

A high degree of market transparency, which allows buyers to easily compare the offers of different suppliers. Advanced search tools available on the Internet allow customers to choose from a larger pool of suppliers and to compare prices instantly, thus making it easier for them to find the best deal. This is particularly the case for highly standardized products that can be easily compared using search engines, usually known as "price comparison services," "price engines," or "shopping bots."

Some companies find ways to create their advantage based on the transparency of electronic markets. Two specific actions can be mentioned here: modifying a search engine's outputs in order to increase a company's visibility (e.g., by purchasing a certain position in search results) or practicing what is known as "obfuscation." The latter attempts to obstruct consumers' searches or to at least reduce damage to a company. For example, obfuscation practices increase search friction in online markets. Some forms of obfuscation include complicating a product's description, preventing search engine access to pricing details, or creating several versions of a given product with one of them being very basic and low-price to attract customers but with add-on features with additional costs. These strategies affect digital market transparency and thus may help increase the profit of companies using them.

3

■ *Products are increasingly becoming commodities*
Products are increasingly becoming commodities, resulting in little or no differentiation between different providers. The pricing of commodity products that do not require extensive purchasing advice or after-sales service is especially affected by a higher degree of market transparency and may increase the profit of businesses using them.

■ *Low switching costs and weak network effect*
Low switching costs and weak network effect, which make it easy for buyers to change suppliers.

Conversely, the bargaining power of suppliers is high if the opposite of all or some of the above characteristics holds true. See also the *Financial Times* article "Google buys UK price comparison website for £37.7m."

3.3 Complementing the Five Forces Framework with the Co-opetition Framework

While the five forces framework focuses on the potential negative effects that market participants might have on the industry attractiveness, the co-opetition framework enriches this perspective by highlighting that interactions with other players can also have a positive impact on profitability.[17] These interactions can include (1) joint setting of technology and other industry standards, (2) joint developments, and (3) joint lobbying:

■ *Joint setting of technology and other industry standards*
Joint setting of technology and other industry standards which is often necessary for the growth of an industry. For instance, the Germany-based wireless marketing company YOC joined other wireless marketing providers to set up ethical and data privacy industry standards on how to conduct marketing campaigns over the mobile phone.

■ *Joint developments*
Joint developments between different firms can offer the opportunity for improving quality, increasing demand, streamlining procurement, and sharing costs for non-core activities. Through its Zshops, ► Amazon.com made it possible for other sellers, who are in principal competitors, to sell through the ► Amazon.com website. Similarly, competing car manufacturers (General Motors, Ford, and DaimlerChrysler) collaboratively established an automotive procurement platform to streamline their purchasing processes. It has subsequently been sold

---

17 The concept of 'co-opetition' was developed by A. Brandenburger and B. Nalebuff, *Co-opetition*, Currency Doubleday, 1998. It entails simultaneously cooperating and competing with other companies.

and expanded into e-procurement for other industries. (For more details on Covisint, see the case studies section of this book.)

- *Joint lobbying*

Joint lobbying for favorable legislation is also frequently a prerequisite for growth and market protection.

The value net framework, which is similar to the five forces framework, focuses on the positive aspects of interactions and seeks to identify opportunities for value creation through collaboration. Therefore, it provides a complementary perspective to the one offered by the five forces framework. The "value net" framework looks at four categories of players, which, through their interactions, characterize the market environment. These players are customers, suppliers, competitors, and complementors.

- *Customers*

Customers (who sometimes are the consumers) are the recipients of products or services that a given business offers in the marketplace.

- *Suppliers*

Suppliers are companies that supply the business with resources, including labor and (raw) materials.

- *Competitors*

Competitors are companies whose products or services are considered to be substitutes to the business's own offerings.

- *Complementors*

Complementors are companies whose products are complementary to a business's own offerings. The underlying idea is that customers value a given product more if they can also buy a related complementing product from somebody else. This is the case, for example, with flash storage devices and computers or earphones and smartphones.

The role of competitors and complementors can change depending on the context. For example, with the abovementioned Zshops, ▶ Amazon.com changed competitors into complementors. Instead of looking at them only from a "negative" (or zero-sum game) perspective, ▶ Amazon.com decided that allowing these companies to offer their products on its website would improve its overall value proposition and create a win-win situation for both parties.

Similarly, mobile device manufacturers have complementary relationships with app makers. Mobile devices would not as compelling without apps, see, for example, the *Financial Times* article "Apple and Aetna team up on new healthcare app."

In summary, well-established coalitions in e-commerce are generally more beneficial for the concerned parties than non-coalition scenarios. Likewise, "nonconnex" coalitions, that is, those set up among firms with complementary business activities, are more profitable than "connex" coalitions (those made among close substitutes). One of the main justifications for coalitions lies in the pricing strategies followed by the former coalitions, they are usually more able to attract consumers and even take market share from the competition[18].

3

> ### Google Buys UK Price Comparison Website for £37.7m
>
> Google has snapped up ► BeatThatQuote.com, a price comparison website, for £37.7m as the technology group looks to widen its range of services and strengthen its foothold in the UK financial products market.
>
> BeatThatQuote helps users to compare a range of products including loans, insurance, and utilities. It competes with bigger UK rivals such as ► Moneysupermarket.com and ► Comparethemarket.com as well as providing the underlining technology for price comparison services on other sites.
>
> The BeatThatQuote acquisition, though small, will help Google build on an existing credit card comparison business in the United Kingdom, which will give search engine users faster access to relevant queries. Google has faced criticism from those who claim that its algorithms favor its own products, something the US company denies. Google says its algorithms are impersonal, and it clearly labels its own services. John Paleomylites, managing director of BeatThatQuote, said that by teaming up with Google "we think we can offer more transparency and better pricing information than existing online offerings."
>
> Source: Excerpt from: Watkins (2011).

> ### Apple and Aetna Team Up on New Healthcare App
>
> Latest push by Silicon Valley tech company into healthcare sector.
>
> Apple will gain access to a huge trove of detailed health data as part of a new Apple Watch tie-up with US insurer Aetna.
>
> CVS-owned Aetna and Apple have jointly developed a new app called Attain, set to launch in the coming months. Attain will use the Apple Watch to provide personalized recommendations to users, based on both their health history and live data generated by the wearable device, which offers heart-rate monitoring and workout tracking.
>
> To comply with US data protection regulations, Apple and Aetna have entered into a "business associate agreement" that includes assurances that no personally identifiable information will be shared with the iPhone maker and that it will not be sold, revealed to employers or used for making coverage decisions by Aetna. The health information will be collected on a voluntary basis and only used to support the Attain program, the companies added.

---

18 For a deeper analysis of these coalitions' effects in the e-commerce context, see the chapter by J. Prieger and D. Heil, published in F.J. Martínez-López (Ed.), op. cit.

The deal marks the latest incursion by Silicon Valley into the healthcare sector, while insurance companies look to technology to improve preventive care that can ultimately reduce their payouts.

Tim Cook, Apple's Chief Executive, said on CNBC earlier this month he believed Apple's "greatest contribution to mankind" would come from its work in healthcare.

Using Attain will be voluntary for Aetna members but they will be provided incentives to join, including earning back the cost of the Apple Watch that is required to participate. Spurring sales of wearable devices including Apple Watch and AirPods is becoming more important for Apple at a time when iPhone revenues are slowing.

Users will be able to opt in to sharing Attain data and their broader health history with Apple, providing fuel for analytics and machine learning that the companies need to improve the service. Attempting to head off potential privacy concerns, the companies said that users' health data will be encrypted and will not be used for underwriting or calculating premiums.

"We believe that people should be able to play a more active role in managing wellbeing," said Jeff Williams, Apple's Chief Operating Officer. "As we learn over time, the goal is to make more customised recommendations that will help members accomplish their goals and live healthier lives."

Source: Adapted from Bradshaw and Ralph (2019).

In the personal computer environment, Microsoft's Windows operating system is more valuable (faster and more reliable) when it runs on a computer powered by an Intel microprocessor than on a computer with a lesser quality microprocessor. Yet, Microsoft would typically not be part of Intel's "five forces industry analysis" screen and vice versa. However, whatever Microsoft does is of great importance to Intel. In contrast to the five forces framework where a decrease in the bargaining power on the part of one of the five players leads to an increased attractiveness of the overall industry, this logic for complementors is more different. In the case of Microsoft, Intel benefits if Microsoft's operating system becomes more successful over time, since this also opens up new market opportunities for Intel's microprocessors.

Critical Perspective 3.1
Benefits and Drawbacks of Industry Analysis Tools

Porter's five forces industry framework is one of the most widely used frameworks in the field of strategic management. The framework has numerous positive qualities that have contributed to its far-reaching success. Most importantly, it is a systematic and comprehensive way to analyze industry structure. The five forces that the framework addresses are mutually exclusive and they cover the most important players in a given industry. In addition, the framework claims that there is a monotonic relationship between the power of each individual player and industry attractiveness. This means, for instance, that as the bargaining power of buyers or sellers

3

increases, the industry becomes less attractive. Similarly, as competition increases, the industry attractiveness also declines.

This required monotonic relationship between the power of the actors and industry attractiveness is the main reason why Michael Porter decided not to include government as a sixth force. In an interview,[19] Porter explains why, to his mind, government does not present a sixth force:

> » After much further work using and teaching the framework, I have reaffirmed my original conclusion that government is not a sixth force because there is no monotonic relationship between the strength and influence of government and the profitability of an industry. You can't say that 'government is high, industry profitability is low', or that 'government is low, industry profitability is high'. It all depends on what exactly the government does. [...] And how do you assess the consequences of what government does? Well, you look at how it affects the five forces.

In essence, Porter states that government is a variable that has an impact on the five forces, which in turn impact on the profitability of the industry. Yet, there does not seem to be a direct and, most importantly, no monotonic effect of government on industry profitability. On the one hand, governments in many countries have passed laws to deregulate industries, which has led to a strong increase in competition and reduced profitability for incumbent companies. This was the case, for instance, in the German telecom industry where the entry of numerous new players in recent years is severely threatened the position of market leader Deutsche Telecom. On the other hand, governments might also pass laws that prevent suppliers from colluding and setting overly high prices. This, in turn, reduces the bargaining power of suppliers, thereby making the industry more attractive for incumbents.

The comprehensiveness and clear structure that the five forces industry framework provides is especially valuable during the initial stages of a strategy project when the task is to gain a quick and broad understanding of the relevant players in an industry. Yet, there are also a number of drawbacks associated with the five forces industry framework, which one needs to be aware of. Most importantly, it has been said that the framework is overly static in a rapidly changing business world, where industries are in constant flux. Some academics[20] have questioned Porter's competitive advantage framework in business environments that are volatile, uncertain, dynamic, and ambiguous (V.U.C.A.). It is, indeed, increasingly difficult to define industry boundaries, which are becoming more blurred due to, among other factors, mergers and acquisitions. This does not mean that the five forces industry framework has become irrelevant, since it still helps to pinpoint competitive and industry conditions that are subject to change.

---

19 N. Argyres and A. McGahan published an interview they conducted with Michael Porter in the *Academy of Management Executive*, 2002, Issue 2, pp. 43–53.

20 such as Rita Gunther McGrath of Columbia Business School

> The framework assumes that competitors' behavior and industry structure can be explained by analyzing a single industry. However, frequently there is multi-point competition where firms compete in more than one industry and, more importantly, their behavior in one industry is sometimes determined by competition in other industries. For example, Apple competes in the music distribution industry through its iTunes online store but also in the music player industry, where it sells mobile devices that play music.

3.4 Defining Industries, Segmenting Markets, and Targeting Markets in e-Business

3.4.1 Defining an Industry

As discussed in "Benefits and drawbacks of industry analysis tools," one important challenge that we need to consider when conducting an industry analysis is to define appropriately the industry boundaries. On the one hand, if we define our relevant industry very narrowly, then there will be few competitors, and there is a high probability that the industry will be rather attractive. Yet, there is potential risk that a company from an adjacent industry might enter the industry. On the other hand, if we define the industry too broadly, it becomes overly difficult to reach any clear conclusions.

Consider the example of the networking platform LinkedIn, a narrow definition of the market might limit the industry to online networking platforms, which would focus the competitor analysis on a very small set of companies such as Facebook. A broader definition, including all companies that offer one or more functionalities that LinkedIn offers, would lead to a vast competitive landscape including platforms for job hunting, social networking, business news, and training. This example illustrates that, depending on the industry definition, there could be different customers and competitors that need to be considered.

The key question that always needs to be asked when defining an industry is: Which other products do customers consider are substitutes? Depending on the task at hand, it is possible to use different types of definitions for a given industry. For example, for a more short-term external analysis, it might be sensible to scrutinize closely the main players in the direct environment and thus conduct a rather focused industry analysis. However, if the task is to gain an understanding of longer-term competitive developments and threats, it might be more sensible to adopt a broader industry definition that includes also more remote substitutes and potential disruptive innovations that threaten industry incumbents.

3.4.2 Segmenting Markets in an Industry

Even narrowly defined industries are frequently too broad a category to allow for any meaningful analysis. Consider the car industry, which consists of a broad array of different car manufacturers catering to different customer segments. To conduct

3

an industry analysis that contains both high-end manufacturers (such as Porsche and Jaguar) and mass producers (such as Toyota and Volkswagen) would provide only very limited insights into the attractiveness of the industry. Similarly, lumping together different types of customers, such as private consumers and corporate customers, also does not provide much insight, since their needs are completely different. To remedy this, we need to segment industries and markets within a specific industry into finer units and then decide which ones to target.

Why is it sensible to divide markets into finer segments?[21] We need to do so because different people have different preferences regarding product features and, therefore, appreciate different value propositions. To illustrate, let's look at mobile phones. A busy, young management consultant might value the possibility of checking his/her bank account balance via a mobile phone, while a senior citizen, who may be having some eyesight problems, may not be attracted by mobile e-banking services and prefer to use a bigger computer screen. However, the senior citizen customer group might see value in mobile phones that have enlarged dialing pads, allowing them to key in phone numbers more easily. This example illustrates how differences in customer preferences are the foundation for market segmentation. According to this, a market segment is defined as a group of customers who have similar needs.

Historically, segmenting markets and catering to different needs have not always been as important as they are today. For example, in 1909, Henry Ford started offering car buyers in the United States the Model-T Ford car "in any color they wish, as long as it is black!" By 1926, Ford had sold over 14 million Model-T models. Obviously, with the advent of more sophisticated production technologies and, more recently, the Internet, it has become possible and necessary to segment markets in a much finer way and to tailor different products and services to different customer segments. (See e-Business Concept 3.1.)

3.4.3 e-Business Concept 3.1

- **The e-business market segmentation matrix**

The e-business market segmentation matrix[22] provides an overview of the different participants in electronic business. It differentiates three types of participants— consumers, businesses, and government—who can act as both suppliers/providers and buyers/recipients. This results in the nine quadrants shown in ◘ Fig. 3.2. Below, we shall explain each one of these configurations, taking the perspective of a supplier/provider who is dealing, respectively, with a buyer/recipient, who can be a consumer, a peer or a citizen, as well as a business or a governmental agency. In other words, we shall proceed with the description of the proposed matrix row by row, rather than column by column.

---

21 For an extensive discussion of market segmentation, see Kotler (2005), pp. 251–296.
22 See also Hutzschenreuter (2000), pp. 28–29.

		Buyer/recipient	
	Consumer/peer/citizen	Business	Government
Consumer/ peer/citizen	Consumer-to-consumer (e.g. ebay) Peer-to-peer (e.g. Napster) Citizen-to-citizen (French presidential election 2007)	Consumer-to-consumer (e.g. Amazon.com)	Citizen-to-government (e.g. online tax return forms)
Supplier/ provider Business	Business-to-consumer (e.g. Ducati.com)	Business-to-business (e.g. Covisint.com)	Business-to-government (e.g. online filing of corporate tax returns)
Government	Government-to-citizen (e.g. information about pension statements of citizens)	Government-to-business (e.g. information about most recent legal regulations)	Government-to-government (e.g. exchange of diplomatic information)

◘ **Fig. 3.2** The e-business market segmentation matrix. (Source: Adapted from Jelassi et al. (2005), p. 69)

■ **The consumer/peer/citizen as a supplier/provider**

Through the Internet, consumers can act as suppliers themselves. Consumer-to-consumer (C2C) e-commerce relationships are those where one consumer acts as a supplier and sells goods to other consumers. The most prominent examples for C2C interactions are online auction places, such as eBay, where consumers can sell new and used products to other consumers. When interactions between consumers are not of a commercial nature, we call them peer-to-peer (P2P) interactions. These are voluntary in nature and are free of charge. Examples of P2P sites include YouTube and online music-sharing platforms. Other forms of C2C interactions are social networking sites. Although these interactions are not of a commercial nature, they happen to take place on an online commercial platform that is brokering user-related information.

The second relationship type in this segment is the consumer-to-business (C2B) relationship, where, in general, consumers supply businesses with information about their experiences with products or services. Examples of C2B interactions are the book reviews at ▶ Amazon.com and consumer reviews on Airbnb or Etsy. The information that consumers provide is then shared with other consumers to help them make more informed purchasing decisions. Furthermore, metadata of information on the actual user behavior allows companies to cater to individual needs. For example, collaborative filtering of metadata and algorithms enables ▶ Amazon.com to recommend particular books to a customer by analyzing other users' buying and viewing patterns.

The third category in this segment contains consumer-to-government (C2G) interactions, such as the online submission of tax returns, car registrations online, online collection of census data, and other citizen-to-government interactions. The use of social media by politicians, where they interact with citizens on policy issues, is another example of C2G interactions.

3

- **The business as a supplier/provider**

The most typical form of interaction is one where businesses act as suppliers to other parties. In business-to-consumer (B2C) e-commerce interactions, firms sell products and services online directly to customers.

Business-to-business (B2B) interactions relate to platforms for the online purchase of operational or manufacturing inputs that other businesses need to create their products and services. The e-marketplace platform Covisint which served car manufacturers (as buyers) and component suppliers (as sellers) is an example of a B2B platform.

Business-to-government (B2G) interactions include, for instance, the online submission of corporate tax return forms, submissions to inquiries, and other digital forms of reporting.

- **The government as a supplier/provider**

Compared with the above two categories (consumers and businesses), there have been relatively few examples of government e-commerce activities. However, this is changing, and it can be expected that in the future many governmental agencies' will interact with citizens and businesses online.

The e-business market segmentation matrix shown in ◘ Fig. 3.2 provides a classification of the different interaction types made possible through the Internet. This allows e-businesses to position their own Internet operations within one or more quadrants of the matrix and also to consider the spaces into which they may want to expand.

For example, ► Amazon.com commenced in July 1995 as a pure B2C business, selling books online to customers. It soon added a C2B component by enabling customers to post online reviews to the website. Later, ► Amazon.com expanded into C2C, when it allowed customers to sell used books through its website, using the ► Amazon.com online payment mechanism.

Another example is Nordea, which, like most other banks, was primarily offering retail (B2C) and corporate (B2B) banking services. Through the Internet, Nordea now enables government-to-citizen (G2C) interactions through an online connection with the Finnish government's database that maintains the pension records of Finnish citizens. Through this online link, Nordea customers have instant access to their pension statements, an important feature when deciding, for instance, on a savings plan for retirement. Coincidentally, Nordea bank also offers savings plans for retirement.

There are two main reasons why it is useful to segment markets: (1) gaining insights into customer preferences and (2) getting information about the potential segment size. These two factors are now described briefly:

■ **Insights into customer preferences**

Segmentation enhances the understanding of the target customer group and its preferences. Firstly, this knowledge is helpful in determining how to shape a product and its features (which differ depending on the target customer segment). Secondly, customer preferences help when deciding which distribution channels to select. For example, Nordea Bank identified that older customers were more likely to start using the Internet for online banking services if the option was introduced during a personal face-to-face conversation at a physical bank branch.

■ *Information about the potential segment size*

Segmentation also helps to assess the potential market size. An estimation of the number of customers who might use a product or a service is crucial to forecast potential scale effects, the overall sales turnover, and subsequently the potential return on investment. Webvan in the United States is an interesting case, since it illustrates the disastrous effects of faulty market segmentation and sizing. Assuming an immense potential market segment, Webvan built large, centralized warehouses that could serve a huge customer base. However the number of customers attracted to this service was much smaller than expected. As a result, the picking and packing facilities were underutilized and most of the delivery trucks drove around half-empty. It filed for bankruptcy after 3 years of operation.

Effective market segmentation that actually helps to meet customer preferences is not easy. There are many different ways in which a market can be segmented. Kotler (2005) proposes a number of different requirements that any type of segmentation should fulfil. A market segment should be:

■ *Measurable*

It should be possible to measure the size of a defined segment in order to determine its purchasing power and its unique characteristics.

■ *Substantial*

A segment should be large enough to justify that it be addressed separately. During the Internet boom years, many category specialists entered specific market segments with a very targeted offering. Yet, as it turned out, the targeted segments were not large enough—at least then—to be served profitably.

■ *Differentiable*

The segments must be exclusive and react differently to a variety of marketing approaches.

■ *Actionable*

It should be possible to develop sales and marketing approaches to serve specific segments. For instance, the mobile marketing company YOC designs mobile marketing campaigns specifically to target the segment of 15–25-year-old mobile phone users.

As mentioned above, there are many ways to segment any market. However, depending on the specific product and context, some approaches are obviously bet-

3

Segmentation type	Criteria to be considered
Grographic segmentation	Grographic regions (e.g. continents, countries, states)
Demographic segmentation	Age, gender, income, life style
Psychographic segmentation	Personality type and personal interests (e.g. cash-rich, time-poor)
Behavioural segmentation	Puchasing freqency, usage patterns, etc.

◻ **Fig. 3.3** Segmentation variables are the basis for strategic customer analysis. (Source: Adapted from Jelassi et al. (2005), p. 71)

ter than others. For example, it might be possible to segment the market of Ducati's customers based on hair color and identify blond, brown, black-haired, and bald customers. In all likelihood, doing so will not provide much insight regarding different preferences and also will not be actionable. In this case, a segmentation between male and female groups or between income groups would be much more valuable. The point is that segmentation is not one-size-fits-all; instead, it requires creative thinking to differentiate meaningful market segments.

Below, we outline the main possibilities for segmenting a given market using traditional variables. These possibilities include *geographic*, *demographic*, *psychographic*, and *behavioral* segmentations (◻ Fig. 3.3).

- *Geographic segmentation*

Geographic segmentation entails the selection of specific geographic areas—for example, continents, countries, or specific regions within a country—and tailoring offerings according to the customer preferences within that area or territory. For example, in Europe, certain countries (such as Finland and Sweden) have a very high Internet penetration rate, while others (such as Italy and Greece) do not. Segmenting according to countries or regions can bring out these differences and help to design custom-fit strategies for each region. Websites such as ▶ Google. com recognize whether a user is logged on from Germany or the United States, for example, and displays relevant information in the local language, thus improving the search experience of each individual customer.

- *Demographic segmentation*

Demographic segmentation focuses on different personal attributes of population segments. Demographic segmentation can, for example, identify (1) age, (2) gender, (3) income, and (4) lifestyle. To illustrate the age dimension, YOC has positioned itself clearly to attract young mobile phone users to its mobile marketing services.

Regarding the gender dimension, there are social networks for women's interests, including ▶ *findSisterhood.com* where women discuss motherhood, lifestyles, and relationships and *Women in Technology*[23], an Australian social network for women who work in the technology sector.

---

23 The Women in Technology website is ▶ https://www.wit.org.au/.

■ *Psychographic segmentation*

Psychographic segmentation describes lifestyle characteristics such as describes lifestyle characteristics such as personal interests. For example, the "cash-rich, time-poor" segment of customers has been a primary target for online grocery shopping services such as ▶ Tesco.com. In order to save time for their social activities and hobbies, members of this segment are more inclined to shop online (and pay the delivery fees) than spend hours in a physical supermarket.

■ *Behavioral segmentation*

Behavioral segmentation segments customers based on their use of a product or service. This can be done, for instance, according to usage occasions or usage rates. Dell uses an occasion-based segmentation to group its customers into the following segments: home office, small business, medium to large business, government, education, and healthcare.[24] Segmenting according to usage rates is often useful when different customers show vastly different shopping behaviors. For many firms, 20 percent of customers make up 80 percent of revenues[25]. Placing frequent and less frequent customers into different segments and providing them with different levels of marketing or service may be appropriate. An illustrative example is the low-cost smartphone introduced by Vodafone in association with Facebook that targets heavy users of social networking sites (see *Financial Times* article "Vodafone and Facebook team up on smartphone").

> **Vodafone and Facebook Team Up on Smartphone**
>
> Vodafone and Facebook have teamed up to release a low-cost smartphone dedicated solely to the social networking service, which the operator hopes will sell millions of devices to younger customers and in emerging markets. The Vodafone 555 Blue, manufactured by Alcatel Lucent, comes with a full QWERTY keyboard and a heavily customized operating system that puts Facebook features into the heart of the device, including placing Facebook messages alongside SMS in the same inbox and a dedicated "F" button for sharing to the site.
>
> The phone is expected to retail for around $100—seen as a crucial price point for mass-market adoption—and is billed as the first Facebook-centric device for pre-pay customers.
>
> The two companies hope that it will be popular not only in markets such as India, South Africa, and Turkey where both Facebook and mobile data usage is growing rapidly, but also more established markets such as the United Kingdom, among teenagers and other social networking addicts. Reaching mobile phone users

---

24 This segmentation becomes apparent on the opening page of ▶ www.dell.com, where visitors can choose between different segments.
25 Based upon the Pareto Principle. See also Marshall (2013).

in countries where fixed-line Internet connections are scarce will be vital if Facebook is to reach its target of 1bn users, from 750m today.

Patrick Chomet, Vodafone's group terminals Director, said that its latest device and Vodafone 360 were targeted at "very different segments." "This is part of a movement that we want to accelerate of empowering the mass market on data," he said. "It doesn't do everything ...but it will be better than your Facebook experience on your smartphone because it's not an app, it's the whole phone."

Adapted from Bradshaw and Digital Media Correspondent (2011).

3.4.4 Targeting Specific Markets in an Industry

After dividing markets into individual segments, it is still necessary to determine how to target a specific market segment. There are two main choices associated with market targeting. Firstly, we need to determine which market segment(s) to target. Secondly, we need to determine how many different products and services to offer to the selected market segment(s). As a manager at an online clothing business, for example, you could decide to produce just haute couture for the upper-income class. Another manager might decide that it is more appropriate to produce also sportswear and activewear for other market segments. When deliberating the choices, managers always need to keep two main questions in mind.

Is the market segment or the group of market segments attractive? The attractiveness of market segments can be analysed through the five forces framework (discussed in ▶ Sect. 3.2). To assess the attractiveness of a segment, one could, for example, analyze the overall growth of that segment, its current profitability and current competition within the segment.

Can we compete successfully in this market segment? This depends on a firm's capability and resources to create and capture value through the collaboration and interaction between the firm and customers. For a detailed discussion of value creation and value capture, see ▶ Chap. 8.

Companies can choose from five main possibilities to target market segments (see ◘ Fig. 3.4). These possibilities are (1) *single-segment concentration*, (2) *selective specialization*, (3) *product specialization*, (4) *market specialization*, and (5) *full market coverage*.

■■ Single-segment concentration

Premium providers, such as Net-a-Porter, which specializes in the curation and sale of designer clothing for the higher-income market, frequently concentrate on single segments of a market. This allows them to gain profound knowledge of customers, develop specialized production know-how, and cater exactly to the needs of their specific customer segment. The Net-a-Porter brand is positioned clearly as a premium brand, undiluted by mass market products, which allows them to charge a premium price. Competitors with a broader positioning are likely to over- or underserve this specific customer segment. The downside of single-segment concentration is that if the targeted segment fails to generate the required revenues, then the whole firm is endangered.

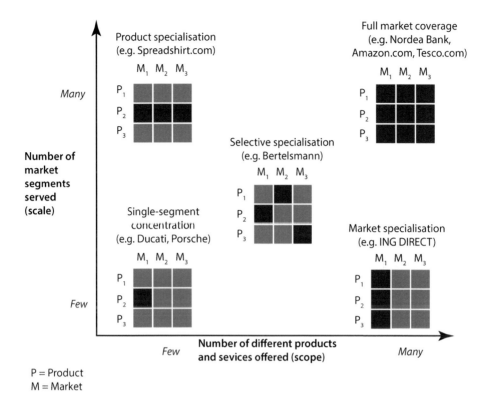

P = Product
M = Market

o Fig. 3.4 Target-market selection depends on the number of markets served and the number of different products and services offered. (Source: Adapted from Abell 1977)

■ ■ **Selective specialization**

A company that pursues selective specialization targets different market segments with different product types. Doing so has the advantage of diversifying business risk. However, it also poses the danger that the firm loses focus and may become vulnerable to attacks by more focused competitors. For example, the German media group Bertelsmann offers a wide variety of media products in the online, print, TV, and radio channels, which target different customer groups.

■ ■ **Product specialization**

A category specialist such as ► RedBubble.com, which focuses on providing printing services, concentrates on one type of service but wants to reach out to as wide a market as possible. The goal of product specialists is to generate either economies of scale or unique insights that differentiate them from competitors. One risk of product specialists is that if their specific product loses favor with customers, they may not be able to cover the fall in revenues with revenues from other products.

■ ■ **Market specialization**

Firms that concentrate on a specific market segment aim to gain a strong reputation and trust with members of the targeted segment and then expand by offering a range of products to the same segment. Cross-selling can be a valuable option to increase revenues, since it minimizes customer acquisition costs.

■■ Full market coverage

Firms that attempt to achieve full market coverage aim to sell a wide variety of product types across the spectrum of target segments. The economic logic behind full market coverage is to create economies of scope by leveraging existing production capacities, technological platforms, and/or a strong brand name. Amazon is an example of a full market provider. Although the company started out selling only new books, it added used books and a wide variety of product categories ranging from baby toys, to pet food, to consumer electronics. Amazon now covers many promising business areas, and some of them are not pure e-business: cloud service, web service, smart speakers, entertainment, groceries, fulfilment, e-payment, and more.

Nevertheless, in conclusion, technological progress increasingly allows businesses to target segments of one and develop a personalized offer in a profitable manner. In this case, companies would practice *micro-segmentation* or the market segmentation taken to the extreme (e.g., see *Financial Times* article "Google searches to become personalised").

Google Searches to Become Personalized

Google has wielded its dominance of web search as a key weapon in its battle with Facebook, with a new approach that draws information from its Google+ social network directly into users' search results.

By including more personal and social information in its results, the new feature also takes Google a big step toward fulfilling a dream long talked about by its top executives: to create a personalized search engine that "knows" its users so well that all the results are tuned directly to their interests.

Known as Search Plus Your World, the new approach marks the most direct attempt yet by Google to use its core service to help it make up lost ground in social networking. However, favoring its own Google+ network at the expense of rivals could heighten regulatory concerns at a time when the company's behavior is already under the microscope in Brussels and Washington.

"They could have done this for Facebook and Twitter and they didn't," said Danny Sullivan, Editor of Search Engine Land. "That will probably make some antitrust people even more anxious over what [Google] is doing."

Alex Macgillivray, Twitter's General Counsel, tweeted that it was "a bad day for the internet. I can imagine the dissension @Google to search being warped this way."

The immediate impact on the rivalry with Facebook is likely to be limited given the newness of the Google+ network and the relative lack of content posted on it, some observers said. "The intent [behind personalisation] is great but I'm not sure today Google+ is of sufficient volume or sophistication," said Martin McNulty, General Manager at Forward3D, a UK search marketing firm.

Google said it would "certainly be open" to including other services, but justified the current exclusion because it "does not have access to crawl all the information on some sites." It also said it only has "persistent access to information from Google+."

With the new feature, content shared privately with contacts on Google+ will be included in search results, though Google said it would ensure that it kept the same levels of privacy as applied on its social network. Google also said it would be able to show profiles of friends when a user enters a name in its search box and that it would suggest interesting people or pages to follow on Google+ in response to some standard search queries.

The changes are part of a shift toward including personal and social information that marks "the most radical transformation ever" for Google's search service, Mr Sullivan said, while also meeting a long-held ambition of the company's leaders.

Eight years ago, Eric Schmidt, then Google Chief Executive, said: "We would like to have a Google that knows you, that understands your preferences."

Making search more personalized, meanwhile, could make it harder for brand owners to use search engine optimization techniques to ensure their pages appear at the top of "organic" or natural results for particular keywords, some experts warned.

As a result, advertisers are likely to switch some their marketing spending away from optimization, said Stefan Bardega, Managing Partner at MediaCom, WPP's media agency. "All of this pours more money into the core business of Google, which is the pay-per-click AdWords model. It will become almost impossible to get the same level of effectiveness in organic results," he said.

Source: Waters and Bradshaw (2012).

Summary
- This chapter addressed the question of where a firm should compete and offered frameworks for analyzing the macro-environment, which includes political, legal, social, and technological factors.
- Secondly, the chapter discussed Porter's five forces as a guiding framework for determining the attractiveness of an industry. It also analyzed the impact of the Internet on industry rivalry, barriers to entry, threat of substitute products, and the bargaining power of buyers and suppliers.
- Thirdly, the chapter introduced the concept of "co-opetition," which refers to businesses that at the same time cooperate and compete with each other. It illustrated how the Internet enables the implementation of such a concept and how it supports the underlying interactions between the businesses involved.
- Finally, the chapter addressed the issues of how to define industries within which to compete and how to segment specific customer groups that a company should target through its e-business offering.

3

❓ Review Questions

1. Explain the impact of the Internet on the macro-environment.
2. Review the impact of the Internet on the five forces industry framework.
3. How can the Internet enable companies to implement the co-opetition concept?
4. Outline the e-business market segmentation matrix based on its two underlying dimensions.
5. Illustrate the five forces industry framework through two e-commerce examples drawn from the same industry: one of an Internet startup and the other of an established bricks-and-mortar company.
6. Choose an e-commerce example and discuss how a company can use the Internet to implement the "co-opetition" concept.
7. Provide a real-world example of your choice for each one of the nine quadrants that make up the e-business market segmentation matrix.
8. Define the industry of ▶ Amazon.com. What are the major players in the industry? What are possible substitutes?

References

Abell, D. (1977). Strategy and structure: public policy implications. In *Proceedings of marketing and the public interest*. Cambridge, MA: Marketing Science Institute.

Anderson, G. O. (2017, December). Technology use and attitudes among mid-life and older Americans. *AARP*. Available at: https://www.aarp.org/content/dam/aarp/research/surveys_statistics/technology/info-2018/atom-nov-2017-tech-module.doi.10.26419%252Fres.00210.001.pdf

Arrington, M. (2005, September 12). Skype sells to eBay for $4.1 Billion. *TechCrunch*.

Bradshaw, T., & Digital Media Correspondent. (2011, July 27). Vodafone and Facebook team up on smartphone. *Financial Times*.

Bradshaw, T., & Ralph, O. (2019, January 30). Apple and Aetna team up on new healthcare app. *Financial Times*.

Chaffey, D. (2002). *e-Business and e-commerce management*. FT Prentice Hall.

D'Aveni, R. (1995). Coping with hypercompetition: utilizing the new 7S's framework. *Academy of Management Review, 9*(3), 45–57.

Foster, L. (2006, February 7). Luxury goods create new online market. *Financial Times*.

Grant, M. (2018, August 14). E-commerce set for global domination – But at different speeds. *Forbes*.

Hall, W. (2018, December 11). The Internet risks fracturing into quarters. *Financial Times*.

Harkin, F. (2011, September 24). Trying on the Future. *Financial Times*.

Hill, A. (2010, September 26). Michael Porter, Management thinker – Academic who shares his values. *Financial Times*.

Hungenberg, H. (2014). *Strategisches management in unternehmen*. Gabler.

Hutzschenreuter, T. (2000). *Electronic competition*. Cologne: Gabler.

Jelassi, T., Enders, A., & Martínez-López, F. J. (2005). *Strategies for e-business: creating value through electronic and mobile commerce: concepts and cases*. Pearson Education.

Johnson, G., Scholes, K., & Whittington, R. (2005). *Exploring corporate strategy*. Harlow: Prentice Hall.

Kotler, P. (2005). *Marketing management* (pp. 251–296). New Jersey: Prentice Hall.

Marriage, M., & Ram, A. (2018, February 22). Big Tech faces UK tax on revenues, not profits. *Financial Times*.

Marshall, P. (2013, October). The 80/20 rule of sales: How to find your best customers. *Entrepreneur*.

Microsoft News Center. (2011, May 10). Microsoft to acquire Skype. *Microsoft*.

O'Hara, K., & Hall, W. (2018, December). *Four internets. The Geopolitics of digital governance*. CIGI Papers no. 206, Centre for International Governance Innovation.

Orendorff, A. (2017, September 1). Global e-commerce: Statistics and international growth trends. *Shopifyplus*. Available at: https://www.shopify.com/enterprise/global-ecommerce-statistics

Palmer, M. (2012, March 1). Cloud computing cuts start-up costs. *Financial Times*.

Porter, M. (1998). *Competitive strategy*. New York: Free Press.

Thomas, D. (2014, December 11). UK turns into nation of online shoppers. *Financial Times*.

Thornhill, J. (2018, April 30). Europe bets its data law will lead to tech supremacy. *Financial Times*.

Waldhuter, L. (2017, February 4). Elderly use of social media and technology on the rise as isolated pensioners get connected. *ABC News*. Available at: https://www.abc.net.au/news/2017-02-04/elderly-use-of-social-media-and-technology-on-the-rise/8240508

Waters, R. (2012, April 12). Facebook shows it gets the message with Instagram deal. *Financial Times*.

Waters, R., & Bradshaw, T. (2012, January 10). Google searches to become personalised. *Financial Times*.

Watkins, M. (2011, March 7). Google buys UK price comparison website for £37.7m. *Financial Times*.

Further Reading

Brandenburger, & Nalebuff B. introduce the concept of co-opetition in their book *Co-opetition*, Currency Doubleday, 1998.

For a detailed analysis of the macroeconomic and competitive implications of e-business, see Prieger, J., & Heil D. (2013). Economic implications of e-business for organizations. In F.J. Martínez-López (Ed.), *e-Business strategic management*. Springer.

For a more detailed coverage of electronic markets' segmentation, see Aljukhadar, M., & Senecal, S. (2011). Segmenting the online consumer market. *Marketing Intelligence & Planning, 29*(4), 421–435.

For a more in-depth analysis of the five forces, see M. Porter, *Competitive strategy*. Free Press, 1998b.

For an extensive discussion of market segmentation and market targeting, see P. Kotler. *Marketing management*. Prentice Hall, 2005, pp. 251–296.

For readers interested in app business, see Roma, P., & Ragaglia, D. (2016). Revenue models, in-app purchase, and the app performance: Evidence from Apple's App Store and Google Play. *Electronic Commerce Research and Applications, 17*, 173–190.

In order to provide practitioners and students a practical yet comprehensive set of templates for applying five forces framework for industry analysis, see: Dobbs, M. E. (2014). Guidelines for applying Porter's five forces framework: A set of industry analysis templates. *Competitiveness Review, 24*(1), 32–45.

Johnson, G., Scholes, K., & Whittington R. discuss the macro-environment of firms in *Exploring corporate strategy*. 7th edition, Prentice Hall, 2005.

Specific examples of segmentation variables in electronic markets are presented in Sen, S., et al. (1998). The identification and satisfaction of consumer analysis-driven information needs of maketers on the WWW. *European Journal of Marketing. 32*(7/8), 688–702.

Weblinks

https://blog.davechaffey.com contains updates about digital marketing and strategy.

https://techcrunch.com/ offers updated and rich information on technology news and experts' analyses.

https://www.ecommercetimes.com provides a sound archive of e-business-related articles and publications.

https://www.emarketer.com/articles/topics/retail-ecommerce provides all kinds of survey reports related to e-commerce.

https://www.icompli.co.uk is a website concentrating on e-commerce laws.

Internal Analysis: e-Business Competencies as Sources of Strengths and Weaknesses

Contents

© Springer Nature Switzerland AG 2020

T. Jelassi, F. J. Martínez-López, *Strategies for e-Business*, Classroom Companion: Business, https://doi.org/10.1007/978-3-030-48950-2_4

4

> **Learning Outcomes**
> After completing this chapter, you should be able to:
> - Understand the meaning of core competence in e-business
> - Assess the impact of the Internet on the value chain
> - Appreciate how a company can leverage the virtual value chain
> - Understand the four virtual spaces of the ICDT (Information, Communication, Distribution, and Transaction) framework
> - Apply the ICDT framework for selecting activities suited for e-business
> - Recognize that companies move from managing an internal value chain to operating along a value network

■ Introduction

This chapter first defines the concept of core competence and discusses it in the context of e-business. It then presents the value chain concept as a way to analyze the individual steps in the value creation process. Thirdly, it introduces the virtual value chain concept and suggests ways for companies to leverage it for value creation. The chapter then describes the four virtual spaces of the ICDT (Information, Communication, Distribution, and Transaction) framework and indicates ways of using it when selecting activities suited for e-business. Finally, the move for businesses from managing an internal value chain to operating along a value network with external partners is highlighted.

4.1 Understanding Core Competencies in e-Business

The goal of strategy formulation is to position an e-business venture so that it can exploit the opportunities that are afforded by its environment and so that it can avoid the risks that it is exposed to. Doing so requires managers of e-business ventures to do two things. First, they need to be able to recognize the opportunities and threats that arise from the external environment. Second, they also need to be able to assess the unique strengths and weaknesses that allow them to exploit opportunities and avoid the threats. A company that is able to align its strengths with the business opportunities and eliminate weaknesses in order to avoid threats creates a "strategic fit" between its internal competencies and the external environment.[1] In addition, competencies are also important from a different perspective, since they can be the source of creating new market opportunities that previously did not exist. That is what Hamel and Prahalad call "strategic stretch" (see Hamel and Prahalad 1993).

---

1   For the concept of strategic fit, see also Venkatraman and Camillus (1984).

4.1.1 Competencies and Core Competencies: A Brief Overview

The terms "competence" and "core competence" have been used widely, meaning different things to different people. Let us therefore establish some basic definitions before proceeding (see ◘ Fig. 4.1).

Most importantly, a *competence* is a combination of resources and capabilities:
- *Resources* are all the tangible and intangible assets of a firm that can be used in the value creation process. Tangible resources include assets such as IT infrastructure, bricks-and-mortar infrastructure, and financial capital. Intangible resources include employee knowledge, licenses, patents, brand name, and corporate reputation.
- *Capabilities* represent the ability of a firm to use resources efficiently and effectively. Skills manifest themselves in the design of processes, systems, and organizational structures. For instance, even before the Internet became a mainstream technology, Dell had already developed significant internal skills in managing the process flow of its direct sales model. Adding the Internet to its value chain was relatively easy, since the necessary skills were already in place.

However, not all competencies of a firm are necessarily *core competencies*. In order for a competence to be considered as core, it needs to be:
- *Valuable.* Customers have to appreciate the value that the competence produces. This can be achieved through either the lowering of costs or the increasing of customer benefit, as perceived by customers.

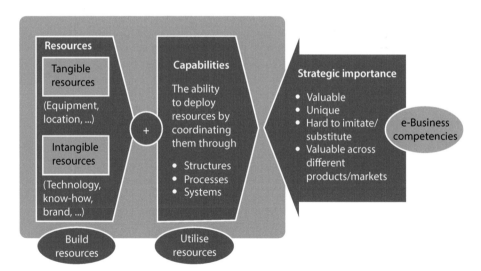

◘ **Fig. 4.1** Distinctive e-business competencies result from the combination of unique resources and capabilities. (Source: Adapted from Hungenberg (2006))

- *Unique*. The competence needs to be unique so that it not only offers a source of value creation but also allows the firm to capture the value it creates in the form of profit. If a competence is not unique, then competition with other firms will drive down profits.
- *Hard to imitate*. The uniqueness of a core competence is sustainable only if other firms find it difficult to imitate that competence. Firstly, competencies are hard to imitate if they require the tightly interlinked participation of many functions or divisions of the firm. Nordea's core competence in the integration of offline and online banking, for instance, is hard to imitate because it requires the alignment of activities across multiple functions and physical and digital channels. Secondly, causal ambiguity also increases the barriers to imitation. Causal ambiguity exists when there is no clear understanding of the sources of a core competence, which makes it hard for an outsider to imitate the competence.
- *Valuable across different products or markets*. A competence is of major value to the firm only if it is not limited to one product or to one market. One of ▶ Amazon.com's core competencies is its ability to manage the flow of merchandise from receipt of a customer's online order to shipping the product to the customer. To create this core competence, it built resources in the form of warehouses and IT infrastructure and created internal skills. As the company moves into different product categories such as toys, home electronics, and clothes, it can reuse these same skills and resources (◨ Fig. 4.1).

Both skills and resources are required in processes that run across the different business functions of a firm. In fact, an important building block of the competence-based approach is that strategy rests less on functional divisions and products (as is the case with the value chain concept described in more detail in ▶ Sect. 4.2) but rather more on processes that cut across different functions (see ◨ Fig. 4.2).

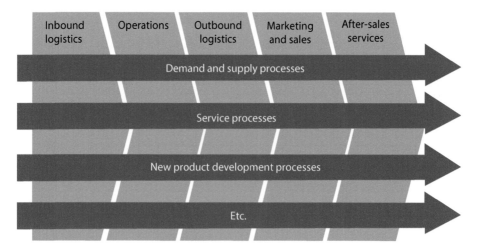

◨ **Fig. 4.2** The core competence approach cuts across different functional areas within a firm. (Source: Adapted from Jelassi et al. (2014))

What Was That About Core Competence Again?

A few years ago, core competence was a popular term. Then the paradigm shift began, unnoticed. More and more often, every IT service provider was able to do it all. It seems impossible for the application user to make distinctions. Direction and credibility are lacking.

It was the automotive industry that kicked off this general chaos in product offerings, in a big way. A company invented a new vehicle class, and, the next moment, competitors copied the concept, fully regardless of firms' core competences. Now every global automotive group offers every conceivable vehicle type, from small car to high-end and from four-wheel drive to the hybrid engine. Of course, the IT sector copied the car makers. Is there any global IT service provider that is not including cloud computing, machine learning, or blockchain in its repertoire?

Core competence is no longer a proof of performance for additional customer-confidence. Evidently today everyone must be able to do it all. Partnerships and cooperations count for little if nobody focuses on their own knowledge and draws upon it. For interested buyers and application users, the market offering thus becomes an unstructured, characterless exercise in randomness. Those no longer able to differentiate based on facts, functions, or performance will take brands and their image as their orientation point. Again, the automotive and consumer goods industries have understood and mastered this challenge well. Car advertising is about lifestyle and image. Sports shoes and sneakers are evaluated on the basis of three stripes or a well-known swoosh.

Evidently the IT sector has not yet come to terms with this paradigm shift. Although almost every market player offers cloud computing, the service providers are still trying to spearhead their market message by using technical terms, instead of highlighting their own company, their own knowledge, and experience.

So is core competence thus irrelevant, behind the times? SAP has set the pace with the paradigm shift, now having its fingers in every IT pie. This includes in-memory-computing databases, blockchain, machine/deep learning, IoT, cloud and mobile computing, etc. People hardly hear anything about the former core competence in FI/CO and HR anymore. So has everything in that activity area already been invented and programmed already? From an SAP customers' perspective, FI/CO and HR still rank among SAP's unmatched core competences. Hardly any other software firm can hold a candle to the global market leader in ERP in these areas. That however does not mean that everything has already been invented with SAP merely needing to rest on its well-deserved laurels. In FI, with continuous accounting, there are highly interesting further developments available already, as SAP Partner BlackLine is impressively demonstrating. In HR the customers are by no means satisfied with "cloud computing" as the direction. SuccessFactors may be enough for some application users, as a minimalist HR/HCM solution in the cloud, but for most users, the simply constructed SuccessFactors is no adequate response to complex HR/HCM processes. Pressured by DSAG, the German-speaking SAP user group, SAP has promised further development of an on-premise HCM solution. Undeniably, SAP does have the core competence for this undertaking at their headquarters in Walldorf.

4

Announcing that it will further develop HCM beyond SuccessFactors, also as an on-premise solution, SAP has revealed an important, necessary decision and roadmap. In this, SAP has remained true to its word. At SAP's Field Kick-off Meeting (FKOM) 2018 in Barcelona, we were told: "We must focus on our customers' strategic priorities to create outcomes."

Simultaneously, however, SAP FKOM 2018 also exhibited the "all IT things to all people" approach: "SAP CoPilot as your digital assistant," which Alexa and Siri are better at "automation through AI & machine learning,"—here too, Amazon, Google, Nvidia, and Microsoft are already far ahead; "IoT is a trigger and enabler for transformation,"—oh really? Outside of any core competence, all SAP is producing with this approach is buzzwords. There are no roadmaps spanning 5–10 years that allow the actual customer to gain any sense of security. Hence, the SAP customers should be cautious and vigilant. This is also because the final message to us in Barcelona lacked any core competence at all: "S/4 Hana growth is strong but start to position yourselves and sell Leonardo now!"

Source: Färbinger (2018).

4.1.1.1 Sources of Value and Core Competencies in e-Business

To understand the sources of value creation and the capabilities to leverage value through e-business technologies, let us first propose a definition: "value is the total value created in e-business transactions regardless of whether it is the firm, the customer or any other participant in the transaction who appropriates that value" (Amit and Zott, 2001: p. 503). The Internet and e-technologies are considered to be strong enablers of value creation because they improve the connections among participants involved in the value creation process. The following four dimensions[2] are regarded as e-business value drivers:

1. *Efficiency.* This relates to efficiency enhancements that may lead to benefits—such as cost savings—in transactions supported by e-business technologies. There are typically higher efficiencies in e-business transactions than in an offline environment. These efficiency gains can be achieved by reducing information asymmetry between buyers and sellers, lowering interconnectivity costs, simplifying transactions, as well as speeding up transaction processing and order fulfillment.
2. *Complementarities.* e-Business technologies foster complementarity by, for example, improving supply chain coordination, functional synergies, and linkages between offline and online channels.
3. *Lock-in.* This dimension is related to customers' (or partners') motivation to engage in a business relationship with businesses that provide benefits supported by e-business technologies. Lock-in effects can be achieved through, for example, loyalty programs of online retailers, offering transactional safety and reliability guaranteed by third-parties, promoting online communities,

---

2   See also ▶ Sect. 5.3.2 for examples of companies that base their business models on one or more of these dimensions.

and allowing customization of products, information, and a website's easy-to-use layout and content.

4. *Novelty.* A source of value creation is the use of e-business for product/service, process, and/or business model innovations.

Taking into account the above framework, how can businesses leverage technologies in order to strengthen their competitive position and possibly achieve a competitive advantage in the marketplace? The key question here concerns not only the suitability of corporate investments in e-business technologies and resources but also the development of e-business capabilities. E-business competencies therefore result from the proper combination of e-business resources and e-business capabilities. The latter is presented in a framework (see Wu and Liu 2010) that explains both the firm's internal value generation (see ▶ Sect. 4.2) through e-business technologies and the external relationships within its value network (see ▶ Sect. 4.5). This framework consists of six sequential stages of interrelated capabilities (or sub-processes) introduced below (see ◙ Fig. 4.3):

1. *Opportunity identification* capability or the firm's ability to identify business opportunities, after both internal and external analyses, and then provide efficient technology-based solutions.

2. *Technology adoption* capability is defined as the firm's ability to properly allocate its e-business-related resources when facing certain business problem.

3. *System development* capability or the ability to obtain suitable e-business systems resources that are necessary to implement the best technology solution.

4. *System acceptance and use* capability or the firm's ability to convince personnel and business partners to routinely use the e-business system(s).

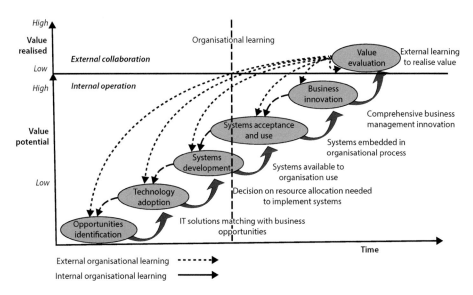

◙ **Fig. 4.3** An extensive e-business capability model. (Source: Wu and Liu (2010))

5. *Business innovation* capability or the firm's ability to introduce organizational changes, innovate, and transform its products' portfolio, resources, partnerships, or the way knowledge is managed.
6. *Value evaluation* capability or the ability of the firm to assess how the value objectives of an e-business are achieved. This capability and the resulting feedback enable organizational learning and a further refinement of the generated e-business value (◘ Fig. 4.3).

4

4.2 Analyzing the Internet-Impacted Value Chain

The value chain framework helps to address the question of how value is created within a company[3] and interrelated activities. In essence, the internal value chain of a company revolves around value creation, where value is created through individual activities of the value chain. It does so by disaggregating a company into strategically relevant units of value.

Ultimately, competitive advantage rests on activities that a firm can perform better or more efficiently than its competitors. There is no general blueprint prescribing which activities should be included in analyzing a company's value chain. However, the following criteria should be used when identifying specific activities for inclusion in a value chain analysis. An activity should:

— *Display different economics.* For example, the development activity of a new software program displays very large economies of scale since the software can be replicated at a negligible cost.
— *Provide high differentiation potential.* These are activities that can greatly increase tangible and intangible consumer benefits, such as product and service quality, convenience, and reputation and are unique and difficult to replicate.
— *Present sizeable costs.* These are activities that add significantly to the overall cost structure of the firm. For instance, in the case study on Ducati, these might be activities related to product development and manufacturing.

On an aggregate level, a company's value chain contains primary and support activities.

To get a better understanding of the ways in which the Internet can change the value chain, we shall take a closer look at how Dell has transformed its value chain of inbound logistics, operations, outbound logistics, marketing and sales, service activities, technology, human resource management, and infrastructure:

▪▪ Inbound Logistics
These consist of receiving, storing, and distributing incoming goods within the company. On a more detailed level, this might include activities such as checking inventory levels and order placement. For example, through close links with its

---

3   For an extensive discussion of the value chain concept, see Porter (1998). A detailed discussion of the impact of IT on the value can be found in Porter and Millar (1985).

suppliers, Dell has radically changed its inbound logistics. When Dell sources monitor from Sony, the boxes are not shipped to a Dell plant from where they are distributed. Instead, Dell has made arrangements with logistics management and courier businesses to pick up the monitors as needed from the Sony manufacturing plant, match them with the corresponding computers, and then deliver them to customers. Doing so reduces the need for warehousing capacity and inventory and removes transportation steps[4] from the value chain.

■■ Operations

Operations are the activities necessary for the making of a product or a service. The Internet has, in many cases, drastically changed a company's production activities. By taking orders online, companies can significantly shrink the time between order placement and production, enabling them to start production in "real time." For instance, through a closely connected website for online orders and production facilities, Dell can build products "just in time" to match orders, thus increasing turnover and reducing inventory costs (Waters, 2003). In other companies such as YouTube, whose value processes are more oriented toward the social web's model (see ► Chap. 11), new technologies enable the user to generate and upload content; therefore the user as content creator and supplier becomes a crucial part of the value chain.

■■ Outbound Logistics

These consist of activities required for delivering the product to the buyer, which can be done either physically or electronically (for digital goods). For example, Dell cut its warehousing costs by ordering products from suppliers only when they were required for production. This approach also reduces Dell's efforts and expenses for outbound logistics because complementary components, such as PC monitors, are shipped directly from the supplier to the final customer. Furthermore, Apple's iTunes proved to be a profitable online distribution channel for digital music, replacing the costly and slow distribution value chain of physical products (compact discs and records).

■■ Marketing and Sales

Marketing and sales activities aim to entice customers to buy a product and to provide the means for doing so. This includes activities such as distribution of online catalogues and online marketing campaigns. For example, the Internet has enabled Amazon to increase sales significantly by acquiring a chain of physical grocery stores in the United States—Whole Foods – to its online subscription service, Prime. In addition, through the integration of Whole Foods into online Amazon channels, the company has added a wide range of supermarket items and Whole Foods-labeled products to its other offerings. While leveraging the online channel for creating incremental sales to its physical Whole Foods stores, Amazon

---

4   Michael Dell describes the PC manufacturer's approach to supply chain management in an interview with J. Magretta (Magretta 1998).

4

also relies on its Whole Foods store network to market the online Amazon channel and Prime subscriptions. Customers who have purchased products online can choose between having the product delivered to their home and picking it up at the closest Whole Foods store.

In other industries, physical sales channels have also turned out to be more valuable than were initially anticipated at the beginning of the Internet boom years. Consider the banking industry, where most industry experts assumed then that virtual banks with no physical presence would be able to outperform their cost-intensive bricks-and-mortar competitors on both the cost and the benefit dimensions. As it turned out, however, bank customers value the presence of bricks-and-mortar branches, where they could meet with an adviser in a face-to-face setting. The example of Nordea Bank in Scandinavia shows how success in the online world depended to a large degree on integrating online activities with sales activities in physical branches.

■■ Service Activities
These deal with the after-sales phase, which includes the installation and maintenance of a product, supplying spare parts and exchanging faulty products. In the case of Tesco, it is possible for customers to return faulty products that they purchased online to a store.

The importance of different activities in the value chain varies from one industry to another. For service firms, operations, marketing, and sales activities are crucial. A retailer of physical goods such as ▶ Amazon.com places a major emphasis on inbound and outbound logistics as well as marketing and sales. To create high levels of consumer benefit, ▶ Amazon.com offers sophisticated sales and marketing tools, such as the personalized recommendation list, which is based on a customer's previous purchases. As part of sales, ▶ Amazon.com has patented the one-click payment mechanism, which allows customers, after having gone through a one-time registration process, to make a purchase simply by clicking on an icon and without having to provide any further information about themselves. Thus, the above-outlined value chain is not a blueprint for analyzing any individual business. Instead, it should be set up based on the individual context of the firm and with the goal of providing a good understanding of how the business operates.

In addition to the primary activities that are related directly to the production and sales process, the value chain also comprises the following support activities:

■■ Procurement
This deals with the primary inputs for different processes within the organization. It includes the purchasing of, for example, machinery, PCs, servers, and office equipment. Procurement is often a crucial element of the overall cost structure of a company.

■■ Technology Development
This includes specific research and development (R&D) for product design. It also refers to development activities that optimize the functioning of other activities of the firm. For example, one of the core assets of ▶ RedBubble.com is its highly

sophisticated website that allows shop owners to easily and quickly create new online shops offering customized designs. Constantly updating and adapting this website to changing customer needs requires a major ongoing investment in technology development.

■■ Human Resource Management

This consists of recruiting, managing, training, developing, and retaining staff. The Internet transformed this activity through online recruiting, web-based training, and intranet-based knowledge management. Human resource issues also influence the choice of an Internet company's geographical location because employees represent the least mobile physical corporate asset. ► Amazon.com, for example, set up its headquarters in Seattle, USA, to be able to attract qualified IT specialists. The growing reliance of companies on globally dispersed remote workforces, enabled by digital communications, is changing the nature of human resource management.

■■ Infrastructure

This refers to a firm's physical premises, including offices, plants, warehouses, and distribution centers. In spite of being an online retailer, ► Amazon.com operates a network of its own warehouses in its key markets to coordinate the logistics of delivery. Digital infrastructure includes computer servers (including cloud computing), data centers, and networking equipment.

In order for a firm to perform certain activities within the value chain, it needs to use certain resources (such as physical, financial, and human resources), as well as technology and practical knowledge. However, the portfolio of these resources and capabilities is not static. As a firm performs certain activities during an extended period of time, it also develops capabilities in-house, as the different departments improve their processes and create assets. In addition, it also develops resources such as improved technology, superior brand reputation, and strong relationships with suppliers and buyers (Porter 1991). For more detailed information on how to organize strategic alignment and value chain, see "Is Anyone in Your Company Paying Attention to Strategic Alignment?."

Is Anyone in Your Company Paying Attention to Strategic Alignment?

One of the best performing corporations is sometimes one of the best aligned. However, who in your organization is listening to how nicely aligned your technique is along with your group's objective and capabilities? In my analysis and consultancy with corporations, I observe that, oftentimes, no particular person or group is functionally liable for overseeing the association of their firm from finish to finish. A number of totally different people and teams are liable for totally different parts of the worth chain that makes up their firm's design, and they're usually not as joined up as they need to be. All too usually, particular person leaders search—certainly are incentivized—to guard and optimize their very own domains and discover themselves locked in energy-sapping inner turf wars, moderately than working with friends to align and enhance throughout your complete enterprise.

4

So, who needs to be liable for guaranteeing your organization is as strategically aligned as it may be? The reply shouldn't be "the CEO" or "the Chairman" or the equal. The job of aligning the trendy company is simply too complicated to be added on to the slate of somebody whose job it's to contemplate a whole lot of different issues, irrespective of how proficient or highly effective they are. Take into account to your personal firm:

Virtually, who on the enterprise stage in your organization is liable for guaranteeing it's as strategically aligned as doable? Is their focus and conduct according to this duty, or is it merely an addition to their overriding day job? Is it the duty of your organization's most senior managers, or ought to or not it's an extra distributed duty? How a lot and the way usually is time devoted in your organization to revisiting its core organizing ideas and discussing how one can construct functionality for tomorrow's buyer, versus specializing in in the present day's enterprise?

How is your organization's management making knowledgeable selections in regard to the association of your organization as a posh system of many shifting and interconnected components—together with organizational capabilities, sources, and administration programs—all aimed toward fulfilling one overarching objective? What frameworks and knowledge do your leaders require to ask good questions, have higher conversations, and make strong strategic and organizational selections?

What capabilities do your enterprise-level leaders require to be efficient at aligning your organization to make sure it's match for its objective? Leaders I've labored with who tackle the problem of strategic alignment describe themselves as needing to be "multi-everything" in outlook and talent. Multi-everything on this sense means multilevel, being able to enterprise stage considering, from 50,000 toes down; multidisciplinary, being "T-shaped," or possessing generalist and specialist data ranging throughout the enterprise; multinational, having no geographical or cultural bias in scope or determination making; multi-stakeholder, understanding the corporate from a number of views and pursuits; and, lastly, multi-phased, selecting to assume within the close to, medium, and long-term regardless of strain for quick outcomes.

If there aren't any apparent solutions to those questions, then there's a good probability that no person is paying sufficient consideration to strategic alignment in your organization. If that's the case, you urgently want to handle this hole in management focus and functionality. Reaching sustainable aggressive benefit by way of superior strategic alignment doesn't occur by chance—it occurs by design, or in no way, and it requires a particular breed of management, which I name enterprise management.

What Do Enterprise Leaders Do?

Not like mainstream concepts about private management, which at their core are involved with mobilizing individuals, enterprise management is worried with mobilizing the sources of a complete firm as a system of many shifting and interconnected components, of which individuals (or "human sources") are only one aspect, and never even essentially an important for growing strategically vital organizational capabilities. Enterprise leaders aren't individual leaders within the conventional sense; they're the system architects of their firm's long-term success.

The aim of enterprise management is to make strategic interventions to make sure an important parts of the corporate's basic design align seamlessly. These parts embrace the corporate's enterprise technique (how the corporate is attempting to win at fulfilling its long-term objective), its organizational capabilities (what it must be good at to win), its sources (what makes it adequate to win, together with its buildings, cultures, individuals, and processes), and its administration programs (what delivers the daily efficiency it must win). These essential parts kind a price chain by way of which corporations carry out their long-term objective, roughly nicely. The worth chain is barely as sturdy as its weakest hyperlink.

Principally, enterprise leaders are liable for:

1. *Envisioning*: Crafting a sturdy imaginative and prescient of what strategic alignment appears to be like at their firm and speaking that imaginative and prescient in a significant technique to others, together with buyers, workers, enterprise companions, and prospects. The imaginative and prescient outlines the important ideas that can inform the corporate's detailed strategic planning, organizational design, operational priorities, and efficiency objectives.

2. *Designing*: Following these ideas, enterprise leaders ought to rigorously design every element of the corporate's worth chain to be extremely complementary of one another and supportive of the agency's long-term objective. Tweaks to the group's design could occur solely episodically; however, the chief's concern with strategic alignment needs to be fixed. The design and administration of the corporate as a posh and adaptive system of many shifting and interdependent parts need to be revisited often, based mostly upon strong prognosis, to make sure it stays match for objective regardless of modifications within the exterior atmosphere.

The problem is there isn't any one-size-fits-all alternative of enterprise technique or associated organizational design that ends in superior strategic alignment. Organizational buildings and cultures, for instance, needs to be as distinctive because the methods they help and make doable, which in flip depend on the group's long-term objective. As an example, to turn out to be extra modern, many corporations try to revamp themselves as agile, extremely related, and open networks of groups and companions by which data is extremely dispersed. The associated fee to that is that network-based organizations are complicated to handle and arduous to manage. For product-centric corporations, the place value administration is the strategic precedence, the comparatively easy, secure, and closed-system hierarchy attribute of "bureaucratic" considering stays in precept one of the best organizational design.[...]

The enterprise management position usually falls to senior executives by default. In some corporations embracing network-based working buildings, the duty can be the area of devoted design groups. No strategy to enterprise manage-

4

ment is better than the opposite. Japanese multinational, Ricoh, for instance, has invested in constructing an extremely networked inner design perform inside its 105,000 sturdy workforce working throughout 200 nations, known as the Future Enterprise Improvement Middle. Its objective is to function on the enterprise-level and lead constructive enterprise transformation throughout all enterprise traces and geographies in keeping with the long-term group technique and future buyer necessities. Constructed to harness rigorous design considering functionality, the various workforce consists of technologists, advisors, analysts, and researchers— not merely profession managers. The considering is that to attain superior strategic alignment within the face of elevated enterprise complexity requires harnessing the collective intelligence and energies of a purposeful workforce of enterprise leaders throughout the group, and their prolonged inner and exterior help networks.

No matter for whom it's a duty, enterprise management is important to design and manage ever extra complicated corporations as extremely successful programs and match to fulfill the calls for of consumers and resist the disruptive maneuvering of rivals. Without it, the chance is that corporations flip-flop between totally different methods and unconnected organizational designs in limitless rounds of reorganization or, conversely, mistakenly preserve the established order and fall behind rivals within the quickly altering market. One of the best corporations is one of the best aligned, however, solely when led by design.

Source: Adapted from: Trevor (2018).

4.3 Leveraging the Virtual Value Chain

In the context of a value chain discussion, it is also of interest to introduce the concept of the virtual value chain (Rayport and Sviokla 1995), which emphasizes the importance of information in the value creation process. Key drivers behind this concept are advances in IT, data availability and analytics capacity, and the evolution of CRM (customer relationship management) systems (see also ▶ Sect. 11.3.1), which have increasingly provided businesses with a vast amount of useful information.

The concept of the virtual value chain suggests that information captured in the physical value chain for activities such as order processing and logistics could be used to offer an enhanced quality of customer service. Based on this concept of recycling information, the virtual value chain illustrates new opportunities to create value by using information captured in the physical value chain. In the past, a lot of information was captured only to support the value-adding processes in the physical value chain, although this information in itself presented potential value for customers.

Opening up new opportunities to make this information available to customers, thereby increasing the value created, is the main goal of the virtual value chain. The latter comprises the following steps: gathering and organizing information, selecting and synthesizing (for privacy) relevant pieces of information that are of value for customers, and finally choosing appropriate formats for distributing the information.

The virtual value chain framework can be used to analyze several of the case studies in this book.

Tesco, for example, has used information that it had access to or already owned to create value for its customers. Through the Tesco Clubcard, Tesco collects detailed customer information about purchasing patterns and preferred products in the bricks-and-mortar environment. When a customer starts buying online, his/her online shopping list is instantly populated with all the products that he/she has purchased during previous visits to the physical store. By leveraging this information, Tesco makes it easier for customers who are new to Internet-based shopping to quickly find the products that they are likely to purchase.

Nordea bank allowed its customers to access their pension statements, which are maintained by a government agency, electronically. The bank also made its online customer authentication process available to other companies that need to use Nordea's e-identification and e-signature services.

▶ Amazon.com has also extensively used information captured throughout its physical value chain to create value. Customers have the possibility of tracking online past purchases and checking the status of delivery. The personalized book recommendation list, where customers receive recommendations based on what other people with a similar profile have bought, is another example of how ▶ Amazon.com has also tapped into the previously unused information stored in its databases. Furthermore, including reviews from other customers and providing sample pages of selected books create value for customers while requiring only marginal investment, since the required information-capturing systems are already in place.

Critical Perspective 4.1

Compatibility Between the Resource-Based View and the Market-Based View of Strategy

Since the beginning of the 1990s, Porter's approach to creating competitive advantage, which is also called the market-based view, has been criticized primarily because of its seemingly one-sided market orientation. The focus of the criticism is that Porter's approach might help to diagnose a specific competitive problem, but it does not provide any means to solve it. Other factors that have an important impact on a firm's competitive positioning, such as internal structure, processes, resources, and capabilities, do not receive adequate attention. To alleviate these shortcomings, a resource-based view was developed, which focuses on the internal perspective of a firm, namely, its core competencies.

For a moment, let us venture out into the theory of strategic management and discuss the relationship between the resource-based view and the market-based view. While many authors assume that the approaches are fundamentally different, there is a growing body of research that suggests that the two approaches are not in competition with one another but rather complement each other.[5]

---

5   For more on this discussion, see also Porter (1991).

4

Although the resource-based view and the market-based view approach strategy formulation from two different angles, they share a common underlying thinking. This reduces the gap between the market-based view (which focuses on the external environment and is activity focused and functionally oriented) and the resource-based view (which is internally oriented and competence focused and takes on a cross-functional perspective). Upon closer scrutiny, the perceived dichotomy between the two views no longer holds, as is shown below:

- Dichotomy between external and internal focus. On the one hand, the market-based view emphasizes the competitive landscape in terms of industry structure (see ▶ Sect. 3.2), which is external to the firm. However, it also emphasizes the creation of competitive advantage through internally executed activities, and the ability to create value through activities is ultimately determined by the quality of internal resources and skills. The resource-based view, on the other hand, starts out with internal considerations of resources and skills. However, any given core competence needs to fulfill the requirements of creating value and being unique and sustainable. This, in turn, requires considerations that are external to the firm and that provide insights into consumer preferences and the competitive landscape.

- Dichotomy between activities and competencies. The market-based view starts out with the definition of activities such as operations or marketing and sales. Yet, to perform these activities in such a way that they create a competitive advantage, a firm ultimately needs to possess superior resources and skills because they are the building blocks of superior activities. The resource-based view, on the other hand, starts out with the core competence as the main building blocks of a competitive advantage. However, competencies that consist of resources and skills create value only as part of activities. A strong brand, for instance, is not valuable in and of itself. Instead, it creates value when a firm is able to spend less money on marketing activities while still achieving the same results in consumer awareness as other firms that need to spend more heavily because they do not possess the same brand reputation. Thus, competencies ultimately also rely on activities as sources of a competitive advantage.

- Dichotomy between functional and cross-functional perspective. Through the analytical framework of the value chain, the market-based view starts out with functional divisions that perform discrete activities. Yet, building on the divisional structure, it also includes a cross-functional perspective when it emphasizes the requirement of fit between different activities that can be achieved via consistency, reinforcement, and optimization. The resource-based view, on the other hand, begins with competencies that are generally cross-functional processes. Yet processes, in the end, also consist of individual activities, which are located in functional units.

4.4 Selecting Activities for Online Interaction with Customers: The ICDT Framework

As e-business has evolved and become more sophisticated, businesses have started to offer increasingly elaborate e-business capabilities. The ICDT model describes the main features that a business can offer to its customers.[6] Essentially, there are four options, which are depicted in ◘ Fig. 4.4.

4.4.1 Information Activities

Information activities include advertising and posting information on the company website. This includes company, products, and service-related information. When the commercial use of the Internet became widespread in the mid-1990s,

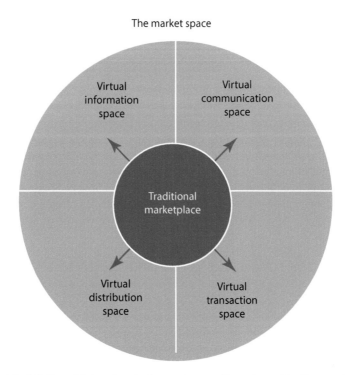

◘ **Fig. 4.4** The ICDT model describes the four main usage dimensions of the Internet in the virtual market space. (Source: Adapted from Angehrn (1997))

---

6 The ICDT model is described in Angehrn (1997).

companies first designed their web presence to provide customers with information about their products and services. At that point, the Internet was not yet tightly integrated with other marketing channels or enterprise resource planning (ERP) systems.

Since then, information provision has rapidly evolved. Today, many companies closely link their Internet advertising with other channels. Information provided over the Internet is no longer of a static nature. Instead, online catalogues are linked closely to warehousing and production planning systems, enabling customers to find out instantaneously whether items are in stock, shipping costs, and when their order will be fulfilled and delivered.

Internet advertising, as one form of information activities, is a common strategy for companies to profit from e-business. Even though it has been criticized due to its intrusiveness and the Internet advertising market has been dominated by digital giants Google and Facebook which represent around 60 percent of the total market, other companies can still find an approach to profitability. For example, Quartz, the business news site, produces first-hand stories, "click-baits," and interesting content to entice online traffic. At the same time, this company sells customized display advertising on the site. For more detailed information, please see the FT article "Quartz Chases Advertising with New Media Initiatives."

Quartz Chases Advertising with New Media Initiatives

Quartz, the Atlantic Media-owned business news site, is increasing its push for advertising, at a time when other publishers are turning to video, paywalls, and e-commerce to counter the pressures of the digital ad market. The company is publishing its first print book, launching new management and lifestyle brands and adding a second daily email newsletter. All of the expansions incorporate new advertising opportunities for Quartz, which derives all of its revenue from ads and event sponsorships.

For its print debut—a book titled *The Objects that Power the Global Economy* that goes on sale on September 6—Quartz included branded content, a form of advertising that drives 60 percent of its revenue. The book, which explores subjects including gene sequencing, blockchain technology, and lithium-ion batteries, is sponsored by Qualcomm, a longtime advertiser, and features a section about the chipmaker's role in mobile communications.

"We're going against the trend, in the sense that we unapologetically believe that there is a healthy and better advertising model to pursue," said Jay Lauf, Quartz publisher and co-president. "It starts with the premise that I don't believe that people hate advertising, they hate bad advertising experiences," he said. "We believe that if you try to create advertising that is an additive, interesting, pleasant experience for the user, you're going to get a better experience for the advertiser."

The privately held company, founded in 2012, does not disclose financial results but is projecting double-digit revenue growth this year. In 2016, it turned a profit for the first time, earning more than $1m on revenue of about $30m, according to a person familiar with the matter. In August, it drew 22m unique visitors to its website.

Quartz's success in building a profitable advertising business comes as many publishers are struggling with the growing dominance of Google and Facebook. The tech giants soaked up 72 cents of every new dollar spent on digital ads in the United States last year, according to eMarketer.

Quartz sells display advertising on its website, mobile app, and newsletters, but the majority of its revenue comes from custom content, such as a chat bot it created for Hewlett Packard Enterprise and the Qualcomm book partnership. As a result, the company's cost per thousand impressions (CPM) is in the $60 range, when the average CPM for display ads in 2016 was $13.88, according to the Internet Advertising Bureau and PwC.

"Their whole philosophy is that they're selling scarcity," said Ken Doctor, media analyst at Newsonomics. "It's why print and traditional broadcast worked. There's a limited space and time." Liya Sharif, Qualcomm senior director of global brand, said the book allowed the chipmaker to advertise "in an unexpected and breakthrough manner." She added: "The audiences for Quartz and Qualcomm align well—these are the people involved in building and shaping our relationships with technology."

For its new management and lifestyle brands, Quartz has signed up new and existing sponsors, including Prudential and Lincoln, which will advertise on the Quartz at Work management site.

Kevin Delaney, Quartz editor and co-president, said the company had identified "untapped appetite" for management and lifestyle coverage. "These are opportunities for readership and, on a business model level, are as big as where ▶ qz.com was when we launched it five years ago," he said.

Source: Bond (2017).

4.4.2 Communication Activities

Communication activities include two-way communication between a company and its online visitors and customers. This can take place via Internet applications such as email and real-time chat. In order to make communication more personal, the online fashion retailer ▶ Landsend.com has included a Lands' End live help icon on its website. By clicking on it, customers can request to be called by a Lands' End employee or to enter an online chat to ask questions and obtain specific product information. In another example, Symphony issued an online communication platform targeting accounting, finance, government, and other sectors. Workers worldwide can use this platform to conduct end-to-end communication which is encrypted and controlled by the user. (For more detailed information, please see the blog box: "Symphony Sets Profit Goal as It Pushes Its Communication Tool as Alternative to Bloomberg.")

In addition to facilitating communication between businesses and their customers, the Internet also facilitates communication between customers who are members of a virtual online community. For some firms, such as eBay and XING, the communication that takes place among members of their online communities is much more important than the communication between the company and its customers.

4

Symphony Sets Profit Goal as It Pushes Its Communication Tool as Alternative to Bloomberg

Symphony Communications Services, a provider of secure communication technology seeking to break the dominance of Bloomberg's communication platform used by investment executives, has set a goal to turn a profit within 18 months. The Silicon Valley, California-based company, has also set a target to more than double its user base to 500,000 by the end of next year and redouble it to one million a year after that, according to its founder and chief executive David Gurle.

"What the market wants is a utility to which they can transform the way they can conduct their business," he said on the sidelines of the Forbes Global CEO conference on Wednesday.

Symphony has 230,000 users and 200 corporate clients, up from 220,000 users and 190 firms last month. Unlike Bloomberg, which sells financial market data, news, and a communications tool to financial sector executives as a bundled offer through its terminals, Symphony focuses on providing a platform for them to communicate and share content.

To better compete with Bloomberg, Gurle said Symphony has joined with its rival Thomson Reuters which provides news and data, as well as data and analytics provider FactSet, to combine their offerings at a lower price than Bloomberg to meet the same customer needs. A Bloomberg spokeswoman in Singapore declined to comment on its sales and pricing strategy.

Information sharing is important to financial asset traders and fund managers allocating clients' funds, since the speed at which they make trading decisions in reaction to market information has huge implications for profits and losses. Gurle said his vision is to "transform" the way people work to make them more efficient through greater collaboration—and sharing information in a secured manner is the key. "Work is becoming more social, electronic, automated and distributed," he said. "You need stronger collaboration with your colleagues whether inside or outside the organisation." He noted that Bloomberg's around 320,000 users represent only 16 percent of the estimated 2 million workers in the global capital markets, with the remaining majority primarily using emails to conduct work-related communication. "So for us, being compared to Bloomberg is really as if our ambition is so small," he said, adding that Symphony's business which he set up 5 years ago and sold to Goldman Sachs and other financial institutions 3 years ago will expand to nonfinancial sectors early next year.

The main industries it will target include accounting, insurance, legal, government, and healthcare. Asked how Symphony is different from other sharing platforms such as Global Relay and ICE Chat for businesses and WhatsApp and WeChat for individuals, Gurle said it lies in its "end-to-end encryption" of content where each customer has control over a unique "key" to decode it. "It is like the key to your house. [The difference is whether] the building [managers] own the key or you own the key," he said. "[In the former case], it is as if your house is secured by them and not by you." Gurle said Symphony expects to sign up another Asia-based client—the Hong Kong operation of a major Chinese investment bank—

before year ends, after it clinched a deal last month to deploy its platform at CLSA which has 1900 employees in the region.

Symphony plans to enter the mainland China market when its platform is approved by regulators, adding that if the Chinese government wants access to certain data for regulatory reasons, it would be the responsibility of its potential clients to meet the request. Gurle rejected concerns the company may have to offer its platform at a low price to compete with Bloomberg, adding that it expects to be profitable by the fourth quarter of next year or the first quarter of 2019. Asked if it plans to go public, he said Symphony will "prepare for" a potential initial public offering but has no concrete plan for one.

The company has raised three rounds of funding totalling US$229 million from 21 shareholders, the latest of which was completed in May this year.

Source: Ng (2017).

4.4.3 Transaction Activities

Transaction activities include the acceptance over the Internet of online orders (commercial transactions) and electronic payments (financial transactions). At the outset of the commercial use of the Internet, there were two main drawbacks associated with online transactions.

Firstly, most Internet users, who were afraid of fraud, considered e-payments were too prone to security breaches so were averse to making personal e-payments, and this perception held back the evolution of e-commerce. However, as payment mechanisms and security matured and trusted e-payment companies evolved—consider, for instance, the case of Nordea—online transaction activities are more commonplace.

Secondly, since payments were limited to credit or debit card transactions, the offering of low-priced products or services (such as newspaper articles) was not economically feasible, since transaction costs would have been prohibitively high. The development of secure online payment systems, such as PayPal and personal Internet banking, addresses this shortcoming.

4.4.4 Distribution Activities

Distribution activities include the online delivery of digital goods, such as software, music, videos, films, and e-books, by enabling customers to download the purchased product(s). The bottleneck that has restricted online distribution to date was the limited bandwidth of online connections. However, as broadband access has become more commonplace worldwide, online distribution is expected to be used increasingly with products and services, especially with those that can be digitized.

Firstly, the online distribution of music, games, television, and movies has become the norm, eventually replacing physical and other traditional modes of

4

distribution. Music streaming subscription services such as Spotify provide a glimpse of the revolution in distribution and new business models. Secondly, professional service providers from different realms, such as consulting and education, will use the Internet increasingly to deliver lectures, presentations, reports, and services to their customers and students.

4.5   Moving Beyond the Value Chain to Value Networks

e-Business ventures do not operate in isolation from other businesses. Instead, their value chains are frequently closely intertwined with the value chains of suppliers and with external partners who provide other support services. The group of partners that a business works with to deliver a product or a service to its customers is called a "value network."

Through the increased use of IT-based communication, value networks have gained importance as businesses outsource numerous noncore activities to outside partners. For more details see the blog box below titled "What i4.0 Means for Supply Chains." As a consequence, the importance of managing external value networks has increased as well. In the context of e-business ventures, this raises a key question of which activities should be maintained in-house, off-shored to different geographic locations, conducted in partnership with competitors or completely outsourced to external providers. See ▶ Chap. 9 for a discussion of this deconstruction of the value chain.

The main partners in a value network are (Deise et al. 2000; Chaffey 2011, p. 330):

- *Upstream value chain partners* which include direct suppliers and business-to-business exchanges.
- *Downstream value chain partners* which include wholesalers, distributors, retailers, and customers. For instance, Tesco delivers groceries to customers within 1–4 hours of ordering, in partnership with external logistics provider Quiqup.[8] Indeed 54 percent of customers now expect to be able to choose which carrier delivers their online purchases,[9] which means e-businesses need to partner with multiple logistics providers.
- *Strategic core value chain partners* are those partners that fulfill core value chain activities. Music streaming service Spotify relies heavily on the major music companies (such as BMG, Warner, and Sony) releasing their content for legal streaming by Spotify customers. Without this content, Spotify would have a very limited repertoire of content and would be unlikely to attract and retain customers.

---

7   Part of the contents of this section is based on Chaffey (2011, pp. 329–331).

8   *Is the Last Mile Solved,* ▶ Veriteer.com [weblog]. Available at: ▶ https://www.veriteer.com/blogs/is-the-last-mile-solved.

9   Metapack, *2018 State of eCommerce Delivery Report – Global Insights*. Metapack Consumer Research Report. Available at ▶ http://www.metapack.com/report/2018-state-of-ecommerce-delivery-report/.

- *Nonstrategic service partners* fulfill functions such as finance, accounting, and travel.
- *Value chain integrators* such as strategic outsourcing partners, application service providers (ASPs), and system integrators provide the electronic infrastructure for a business.

What i4.0 Means for Supply Chains

From boardrooms and shareholder meetings to conferences and collaboration circles, it seems everyone is talking about the Fourth Industrial Revolution (i4.0). Manufacturing executives are increasingly challenged to evolve to remain competitive in this age of rapid technological disruption. Depending on whom you talk to, the disruption for value chains, employees, and business models may be fundamental. In this environment, it is critical for executives at manufacturing companies to separate hype from reality in order to effectively prioritize their business initiatives. They need a clear picture of the current risks and opportunities, and they need to understand what their peers and competitors are doing to drive value and capture competitive advantage.

While most manufacturers are certainly investing into i4.0 capabilities and technologies, few have achieved the scale and integration required to drive enterprise value from i4.0. There are many working toward creating the "factory of the future" or going beyond to evolve to a "digital enterprise," but none have yet to achieve consistent application of those capabilities across all of the corners of their operations. Most are still experimenting with discrete pilots or trialing point solutions. Some have yet to start developing their roadmap for integrating i4.0 into their business and operating models.

We believe that the time for small-scale i4.0 experimentation is coming to a close. Indeed, to win in tomorrow's competitive environment, we believe that manufacturers will need to start being bolder in their vision and faster in their scaling of strategies and actions for i4.0 in a more comprehensive way. Perhaps the best place for all manufacturers to begin with is their supply chain.

Supply Chain: Enhancing i4.0 Value

After years of struggling to improve integration and coordination across the value chain, many manufacturers clearly see i4.0 as a potential solution to some of their more persistent supply chain challenges. Indeed, a fully integrated i4.0 environment could help manufacturers to remove significant friction from their increasingly complex supply chains. It could unlock improved visibility across the network and down into lower tier suppliers to better reduce risk and improve flexibility. It could enhance coordination and innovation through better access to customer and product usage data and deliver scaled yet customized product solutions. And it could deliver improved working capital flexibility by helping to lower inventory levels and sharpen forecasting. The benefits of integration can be significant.

But the real value will come when the value chain becomes a value network— where data is shared fluidly between various nodes in the chain, decisions and

4

demand signals are shared in real-time across the network, and data sources are integrated across systems. That will allow new opportunities to be uncovered and new performance improvements to be achieved.

We recently spoke to some of the world's leading manufacturers, suppliers, and innovators as part of a KPMG-developed framework and benchmarking exercise. What we found is even the leaders of this group demonstrated room for improvement in demand-driven supply chain maturity. However, a few of those investigated are already moving to work (in deep collaboration) with their suppliers and customers to embed value chain considerations into their transformation roadmaps.

What Are the Leaders in i4.0 Supply Chains Doing?

– They are focusing on integration. A few leaders are moving quickly to integrate their suppliers and customers into a demand-driven supply chain. They aim to leverage an interconnected network as the key to future competitive advantage. And they are using the cloud to connect to their suppliers and externally to gain improvements in responsiveness, quality, and cost.

– They are creating the right environment. The leaders are assessing both the opportunities and the risks of greater value chain integration. They are using sensors across all nodes of their operations in order to gather data to help model and predict various supply chain scenarios. And they are improving their controls to reflect the potential for increased cyber security and data privacy risks.

– They are looking for new opportunities to drive performance. Leaders are also rethinking their traditional supply chains and networks to streamline and eliminate unnecessary processes and remove waste by working collaboratively with their suppliers.

Collaboration for Integration

We believe that significant value can be unlocked by driving integration across the extended value chain and creating a platform for the network. This can only be achieved through both technological integration—of systems, platforms, and data—but also closer integration around controls, governance, and cyber security. Further, full cooperation and collaboration between manufacturers, their suppliers, and (possibly) their suppliers' suppliers will drive more value from the platform, not only to improve the success of the partnership but also to identify and monetize the value of the network. Adding the customer into the mix—in a truly interconnected network—will further improve the returns and benefits.

The question then becomes one of control. Leading-edge manufacturers are starting to adopt a "control tower" approach to managing their supply chain, bringing analytics, automation, augmented decision support, modeling, and other capabilities together as a centralized function. Manufacturers can begin by focusing their attention on improving integration with a few select (top tier) suppliers. Once standards have been set, governance and controls have been defined, and protocols have been created, these tools can then be used to drive further integration deeper down into the supply chain.

Source: Heckler and Gates (2017).

Although there are certain similarities between a company's value chain and the value network in so far as both are involved in providing a product or a service to the end customer, value networks and value chains differ in some key dimensions. Most importantly, the value network is characterized by its dynamic nature. Typically, it is much easier to introduce or remove partners from a value network than it is to add or, more importantly, remove functions and employees from a more permanent value chain. Linking external service providers with the internal value chain has become easier through advanced electronic communication. Likewise, depending on the closeness of the interaction, different types of technologies will be used. In the case of strategically relevant and frequently recurring interactions, it might be sensible to install proprietary electronic connections that interlink closely with the systems of each partner. In other cases, email correspondence and video conferencing might suffice.

Here, a company's external e-business capabilities, that is, those abilities which are necessary to successfully create e-business value in value networks, are as important as internal activities, so they should not be overlooked. In Sect. 4.1.2, we introduced an e-business capability model, which emphasizes the importance of managing e-business-related resources and processes with both an inside and outside focus. In the sequel, we provide a summary of what can be called a value network or collaborative core capabilities in e-business:

- *Developing partnerships* or the ability to establish and maintain productive relationships with business partners and customers. Benefits and implications of this capability include facilitating a company's communication with its partners and customers; enhancing the understanding of the industry and the target market(s); and supporting and improving customer relationships through involvement and cooperation.
- *Governing the value network or* the ability of a business, through e-business technologies, to design and coordinate a value network of complementary resources and partnerships.
- *Enabling open innovation.* Companies often have limitations to internally develop all the e-business innovations they need to compete and may choose to use external innovations to support their e-business processes (see also Sect. 9.1.2).
- *Improving co-production and value co-creation.* Involving partners and customers in the value creation process has been a common practice since the 1980s. However, recently, value co-creation has played a central role in what is being referred to as "Service-Dominant logic."[10] The co-creation approach takes even a more important dimension in the prevailing social web context (see also Chap. ▶ 11). Hence, this capability is related to the ability of a business to enhance, through e-business technologies, the participation of its value network's partners and customers in the value creation process.

---

10 The Service-Dominant logic was originally proposed and developed by the US scholars S.L. Vargo and R.F. Lusch. Detailed information about it is available at this website: ▶ http://www.sdlogic.net/.

4

Summary

- Firstly, this chapter defined the concept of a competence as a combination of different resources and skills. It outlined the attributes that a competence must fulfill in order to qualify as a core competence. These are being valuable, unique, hard to imitate, and valuable across different products or markets. It also highlighted the core competence concept in an e-business context.

- Secondly, the chapter discussed the value chain, which disaggregates the firm into strategically relevant activities. It recognized two types of activities within a firm: primary activities (which includes inbound logistics, operations, outbound logistics, marketing and sales, and after-sale service) and support activities (which typically includes firm infrastructure, human resources, technology development, and procurement). It then discussed the impact of the Internet on the value chain.

- Thirdly, the chapter introduced the concept of the virtual value chain, which suggests that information captured in the physical value chain (e.g., for activities such as order processing or logistics) should be used as a new source of value creation to enhance the quality of customer service. It also provided a critical perspective of the resource-based view versus the market-based view of strategy formulation.

- Fourthly, the chapter presented the ICDT (Information, Communication, Distribution, and Transaction) framework and illustrated its four spaces through specific examples.

- Finally, the chapter described how a company can move beyond managing an internal value chain to operating along an IT-enabled value network. It also listed the different types of external partners that are typically members of such a value network and introduced the key e-business capabilities that a firm should develop to successfully manage its value network.

❓ Review Questions

1. What is a competence, and what criteria does it need to fulfill in order to qualify as a core competence? What makes a competence distinctive for e-business?

2. What are the primary and secondary activities of the value chain? How does the Internet impact on these activities?

3. Through what measures can a firm improve the fit between activities in the value chain? Explain how the Internet can influence these measures.

4. Define the concept of the virtual value chain. How does it relate to the traditional value chain concept?

5. Describe the ICDT framework and outline how a company can use it for selecting e-business activities and how a company can profit from these activities.

6. What is a value network and who are its main partners? What specific issues does a company face when it moves beyond a value chain to become part of a value network?

7. From the view of a business leader, what should a leader do to ensure the success of value chain in integrating upstream and downstream partners?

8. Discuss whether competence-based thinking is more suitable for e-business strategy formulation than the activity-based approach outlined in the value chain concept.

9. Analyse the value chain of an e-commerce venture that you are familiar with. Explain how the Internet has impacted the primary and support activities of its value chain.

10. Think critically of possible applications of the virtual value chain concept within specific industries and business sectors. Are there some specific business sectors where this concept fits better than in other sectors?

11. Illustrate the ICDT framework through the example of an Internet venture that you are familiar with.

12. Critically assess the ICDT framework and pinpoint its shortcomings.

13. Based on the specific context of the e-commerce venture that you considered in question 2 above, how could this company move beyond managing an internal value chain to operating along a value network? How could it implement the value net concept and what benefits can it expect to gain from it?

14. Select a real business case, talk with your teacher and classmates about how a company should implement a business project to enhance their core competencies, and reshape their value chain and value network based on their core competencies analysis.

References

Amit, R., & Zott, C. (2001). Value creation in e-business. *Strategic Management Journal, 22*(6), 503.

Angehrn, A. (1997). Designing mature internet strategies: The ICDT model. *European Management Journal, 21*(1), 38–47.

Bond, S. (2017, September 6). Quartz chases advertising with new media initiatives. *Financial Times*.

Chaffey, D. (2011). *E-business and E-commerce management*. Harlow: Pearson/Financial Times, Prentice Hall.

Deise, M., Nowikow, C., King, P., & Wright, A. (2000). *Executive's guide to E-business. From tactics to strategy*. New York: Wiley.

Färbinger, P. M. (2018, May 3). What was that about core competence again? *E-3 Magazine International*.

Hamel, G., & Prahalad, C. K. (1993). Strategy as stretch and leverage. *Harvard Business Review, 71*(2), 75–84.

Heckler, B., & Gates, D. (2017, June 9). What i4.0 means for supply chains. *IndustryWeek*.

Hungenberg, H. (2006). *Strategisches Management in Unternehmen* (p. 143). Wiesbaden: Gabler.

Jelassi, T., Enders, A., & Martínez-López, F. J. (2014). *Strategies for e-business: Creating value through electronic and mobile commerce: Concepts and cases* (p. 82). Harlow: Pearson Education.

Magretta, J. (1998, March–April). The power of virtual integration: An interview with Dell Computer's Michael Dell. *Harvard Business Review*, pp. 72–84.

Ng, E. (2017, September 28). Symphony sets profit goal as it pushes its communication tool as alternative to Bloomberg. *South China Morning Post*.

Porter, M. (1991). Towards a dynamic theory of strategy. *Strategic Management Journal, 12*, 102–105.

Porter, M. (1998). *Competitive advantage* (pp. 33–61). Boston: Free Press.

Porter, M., & Millar, V. (1985, July–August). How information gives you competitive advantage. *Harvard Business Review*, pp. 149–160.

Rayport, J., & Sviokla, J. (1995, November–December). Present the concept of the virtual value chain in "Exploiting the virtual value chain". *Harvard Business Review*, pp. 75–85.

Trevor, J. (2018, January 12). Is anyone in your company paying attention to strategic alignment? *Harvard Business Review*.

Venkatraman, N., & Camillus, J. (1984). Exploring the concept of fit in strategic management. *Academy of Management Review, 9*, 513–525.

Waters, R. (2003, November 13). Dell aims to stretch its way of business. *Financial Times*, p. 8.

Wu, J.-N., & Liu, L. (2010). *E-business capability research: A systematic literature review*. Proceedings of the 3rd international conference on information management, Innovation Management and Industrial Engineering, IEEE, p. 145.

Further Reading

Besanko, D., Dranove, D., Shanley, M., & Schaefer, S. (2003). Provide a detailed discussion of value creation and value capturing. In *Economics of strategy* (pp. 358–402). New York: Wiley.

Porter's, M. book, *Competitive advantage*, Boston: Free Press, 1998, is a seminal work on value creation and the value chain. M. Porter expands on his thinking about competitive advantage in "What is strategy?" *Harvard Business Review*, 1996, November–December, pp. 70–73.

Amit, R., & Zott, C. (2001) specifically discuss this chapter's topic in "Value creation in e-business". *Strategic Management Journal, 22*(6), 493–520.

An up-to-date discussion on collaborative value creation within the e-business framework can be found in: Nelson, M. L., Shaw, M. J., & Strader, T. J., Special Issue on "Collaborative value creation in e-business management". *Information Systems and e-Business Management*, 2012, *10*(1).

Within the field of strategic management, there is a broad literature on the resource-based view. While there was already previous research on the resource-based view of the firm, most notably in 1984 with the article by Wernerfelt, B. (1984). A resource-based view of the firm. *Strategic Management Journal, 5*(2), 171–180, this approach became popular in the mainstream management literature through the work of Prahalad, C. K., & Hamel, G. (1990, May–June). The core competence of the corporation. *Harvard Business Review*, pp. 79–91, and Stalk, G., Evans, P., & Shulman, L. (1992, March–April). Competing on capabilities. *Harvard Business Review*, pp. 57–69. M. Peteraf provides a more recent academic perspective on the resource-based view in "The cornerstones of competitive advantage: A resource-based view", *Strategic Management Journal*, 1993, *14*(3), 179–191.

In the article "Towards a dynamic theory of strategy", *Strategic Management Journal*, 1995, *12*(8), 102–105, M. Porter attempts to reconcile the market-based and the resource-based views of strategy.

Wiengarten, F., Humphreys, P., & Fynes, B. (2013). Article "Creating business value through e-business in the supply chain" offers a timely and detailed theoretical discussion on the use of e-business applications to create value within organisations and their supply chains. In F. J. Martínez-López (Ed.), *e-Business strategic management*. Springer.

For readers who are interested in the concept of core competencies in an organisational setting, see: Hunt, B. (2018, March 14). Getting the most out of your organization's core competencies, *Qualitydigest*. Available at: https://www.qualitydigest.com/inside/management-article/getting-most-out-your-organization-s-core-competencies-031418.html.

For readers who are interested in applying core competencies in real business, see: Rigby, D. K. (2017). *Management tools 2017: An executive's guide*. Bain & Company.

Weblinks

www.ecommercetimes.com provides an archive of e-business-related articles and publications.

http://www.bain.com/publications/industry-insights/technology.aspx provides research reports on how companies implement e-business improvement projects.

Strategy Options in e-Business Markets

Contents

© Springer Nature Switzerland AG 2020
T. Jelassi, F. J. Martínez-López, *Strategies for e-Business*, Classroom Companion: Business,
https://doi.org/10.1007/978-3-030-48950-2_5

Learning Outcomes

After completing this chapter, you should be able to:

- Explain the generic approaches to strategy formulation
- Appreciate the meaning of an "outpacing" strategy
- Assess the risk for companies of being "stuck in the middle"
- Apply business model canvas into business model design
- Understand and learn major e-business models

5

■ **Introduction**

When formulating a business strategy, managers typically choose between two basic options: cost leadership or differentiation. They aim at outperforming competitors either by having lower costs or by offering a superior product or service. A third possibility is an "outpacing" strategy in which they introduce either a cost or differentiation initiative and then quickly follow with the other type of initiative. However, by doing so, they run the risk of failing to achieve leadership in either option and do not stand out from competitors. This is referred to as "getting stuck in the middle." This chapter discusses the above strategy options (lower cost, superior product/service, and outpacing) that are also referred to as or "thresholds." It presents their advantages and drawbacks and illustrates them with examples.

5.1 Examining the Landscape of Strategy Options for e-Business

There are different strategic options that companies can pursue in order to achieve a favorable position in their respective e-business markets. To improve understanding of such options, Michael Porter proposed two generic strategies that build on two distinct types of advantage: (1) a price advantage and (2) a performance advantage.

If a firm wants to be able to compete on low prices, it will adjust its cost structure and aim for a *cost leadership strategy* in its industry. If, on the other hand, it can sustain a higher-quality offering than competitors, then it will aim for a *differentiated strategy* (see ◘ Fig. 5.1).

In addition, there is a third strategy option called *outpacing strategy*, which aims at combining the advantages of a cost leadership and of a differentiation strategy. These different strategy options are discussed in more detail in the sections below.

5.1.1 Cost Leadership Strategies

Consider easyJet, the UK-based low-cost airline. The company's ability to compete on low airfares is primarily determined by keeping costs down throughout its value chain while not compromising its threshold requirements such as the security or

Generic types of competitive advantage

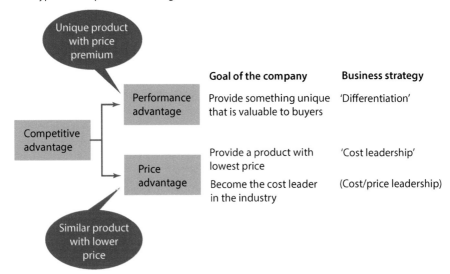

◘ Fig. 5.1 There are two generic approaches to achieve a competitive advantage. (Source: adapted from Hungenberg, 2014, p. 189)

punctuality of its flights. This example illustrates that a firm that wants to attain a cost leadership position in its industry needs to strive to fulfill the following two requirements:

▪▪ Lowest Cost Position

A firm that aims for a cost leadership position has to be able to produce and distribute its product or service at substantially lower costs than its competitors. Lower costs enable the firm to earn profits even in an intensely competitive environment. Note that lower costs do not mean lower prices. It may enable lower prices, or the owner may choose to take higher profits rather than pass the savings on to customers.

▪▪ Benefit Proximity

Having the lowest costs, however, is not sufficient. In addition, a firm also needs to achieve benefit proximity relative to its competitors, which means that it needs to fulfill at least all threshold criteria. If it is unable to do so, then it will eventually have to offer even lower prices, which reduce or eliminate the benefits gained through the low-cost position. For instance, through its unique direct sales model, Dell, until recently, was able to achieve a cost leadership position in the PC industry and pass some of the savings into customers while, at the same time, achieving high levels of consumer benefit through its quality product.

Several levers (including *economies of scale and scope, factor costs,* and *learning effects*) help a firm to achieve a cost leadership position:

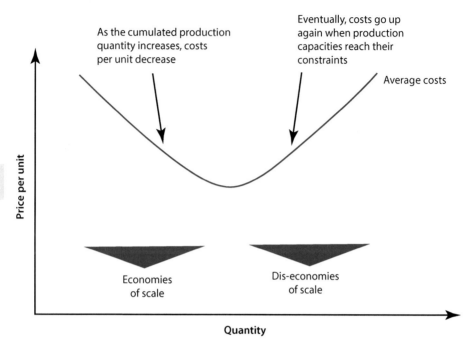

◘ Fig. 5.2   Economies of scale lead to a decrease in per-unit costs as output increases, whereas dis-economies of scale lead to an increase in per-unit costs. (Source: adapted from Jelassi et al., 2014)

▪▪ Economies of Scale

The basic concept of economies of scale is that as a firm increases its product output, it decreases its unit production cost. Why is that so? In general, any production process consists of fixed costs (which do not change as output increases) and variable costs (which go up with an increase in output). Examples of fixed costs are software development, warehouses, and machinery, while examples of variable costs are raw materials and package delivery.

High economies of scale usually exist in production processes that have high fixed costs and low variable costs. As the cumulative production quantity increases, fixed costs are spread out over a larger number of products, thereby reducing the unit production costs (see ◘ Fig. 5.2). Once existing production costs reach their constraints, fixed costs increase again as new facilities are required. Variable costs, on the other hand, increase proportionally with output. For instance, as a mail order company handles more packages, postage costs increase proportionally.

Due to extensive scale effects and efficient IT processes, WalMart in the United States can sell its products at massive discounts in comparison with competitors such as Ahold, Safeway, and Kroger. For example, WalMart sells Colgate toothpaste at 63% of rivals' prices, Tropicana orange juice at 58%, and Kellogg's corn flakes at 56%.[1]

---

1   "Make it cheaper, and cheaper," *The Economist*, 13 December 2003, pp. 6–7

The expectation of high economies of scale was an important reason why Internet ventures were so popular with business managers and entrepreneurs and highly valued in the stock market. In the traditional book-retailing and banking industries, for example, whenever a company wants to expand its offerings to new customer groups, it has to build new branches or sales outlets. Such physical infrastructure requires high capital investments while providing only limited potential for scale economies.

In the early days of ► Amazon.com, founder Jeff Bezos thought that it could limit its investment to IT infrastructure, website management, and call centers and then scale up these facilities depending on customer demand. By doing so, it would not need to make any substantial additional investments while still being able to provide a highly customized service.

The evolution of Internet-based grocery retailing and the different approaches taken by Webvan, now part of the ► Amazon.com family, and ► Tesco.com illustrate further the concept of economies of scale. The strategy of Webvan relied heavily on the realization of economies of scale. It established a centralized and highly automated warehouse chain across the United States at a unit cost of $30 million. This was essentially a fixed cost, because it was incurred separately to the costs of processing orders within the warehouses. The expectation was that variable costs for each shipment would be very low, since the picking and packaging processes were highly automated, thereby reducing the need for expensive labor.

The business rationale was that Webvan would be able to position itself as a low-cost leader while still being able to deliver high levels of consumer benefit through the automated delivery process. It was thought that as customer numbers increased, the warehouses would operate at capacity, which in turn would create substantial economies of scale. The latter were also crucial for the grocery delivery process, whereby delivery trucks were filled at the centralized warehouse and then driven from house to house delivering the items. Costs for the delivery varied only marginally if the truck left half-empty or completely full. Thus, having enough customer orders to fill the truck to capacity was another source of economies of scale in the delivery process. We cannot say whether the above reasoning would have worked out eventually, since Webvan struggled to gain momentum and orders and then filed for bankruptcy only 1 year after going public.

The important insight from this experience is that economies of scale are valuable only if they can be realized, which usually requires a large volume of throughput. ► Tesco.com reached a different conclusion after analyzing the economies of scale potential of warehouse-based delivery. The company decided, contrary to the common wisdom, that it would be sensible to organize the order fulfillment and delivery process out of its existing stores. By doing so, it was able to reduce substantially the need for additional investment in assets which would have created high fixed costs. Furthermore, through this model, ► Tesco.com was able to gradually scale up its operations by adding additional regions on a store-by-store basis.

■■ Economies of Scope

The logic behind economies of scope is similar to that of economies of scale. While economies of scale can be realized by increasing the production of one type of product or service, economies of scope result from expanding the variety of products or services sold using the same research and development, production, and delivery assets.

The main goal here remains the same: it is to spread fixed costs over a wider basis by adding new products or services to the existing offering. Economies of scope can be achieved by extending into different markets and sectors of an industry. ▶ Amazon.com, for instance, has achieved economies of scope through the introduction of additional categories of goods on its website, thereby potentially increasing its share of the wallet of any given customer. It started out by offering only books, and ▶ Amazon.com has since grown its portfolio of product categories such as CDs, videos, electronics, and clothes, using the same technology platform and delivery infrastructure.

Economies of scale and scope should be considered within the context of a specific strategy and not pursued just for the sake of lowering costs. What always needs to be kept in mind is the type of value proposition that a company offers to customers. Adding scale by reaching out to new customer groups, or adding scope by offering new products, might help to reduce the cost position of a firm. In addition to costs, however, it is also important to consider the revenue that can be generated after expanding into different customer segments or adding new product or service categories.

▪▪ Factor Costs

Factor costs represent a crucial cost driver, especially for retailing companies that act as intermediaries. The ability to bargain down input prices, for example, through bulk purchasing, can be an effective lever for lowering costs. Both low factor costs and scale effects are most likely to be realized through high volumes. Thus, a large market share in comparison with that of competitors is generally a prerequisite for being a low-cost provider. The goal of e-marketplaces such as IBX, for instance, is to pool the purchasing power of different business units within an organization, thereby reducing factor costs. IBX was acquired by Tradeshift to aggregate their customer activities in both marketplaces to improve scale effects.

▪▪ Learning Effects

Learning effects can lower costs as a firm improves its efficiency over time, thereby reducing downtime and wasteful activities. For instance, the app business is not static. Companies need to continually update their apps in order to increase user experience. The experience of offering a hot app at app store will help a company to recognize factors or elements that a successful app should have. Hence, for the next generation of certain app, or even a brand new one, experienced companies will better know how to commercialize them.

5.1.2 Differentiation Strategies

A differentiation strategy can be achieved by providing comparatively more consumer benefit than competitors. The main questions for a firm that is striving for a differentiated positioning are: What creates consumer benefit? What is unique? What cannot be imitated? There are tangible sources for differentiation, such as product quality, service quality, speed of delivery, and intangible sources such as brand and reputation.

Similar to the cost leadership approach, firms seeking a differentiated position need to ensure cost proximity to other competitors to guarantee superior value creation. This means that the cost disadvantage has to be small enough so the differentiation advantage can override it.

It is not uncommon for firms to overlook the need for cost proximity when they focus solely on providing the highest-quality product in the market. For example, Apple's development of the iPhone series is a prime example of a differentiation approach to competitors that include Android smartphones.

At this point, it is important to clarify the definition of benefit. While it applies to both corporate customers and individual consumers, let's look at consumer benefit. It is inherently difficult to measure, because consumer benefit cannot be objectively quantified, regardless of place, time, and person. Instead, it varies from individual to individual, depending on:

- Personal preferences. You might derive a high benefit from driving a sports car, whereas your next-door neighbor, who has three children, will get much more benefit from driving a minivan.
- Place. Think of a freezer in the Arctic versus a freezer in the Sahara.
- Time. Think of the benefit of electric light during the day versus at night.

What elements need to be considered when determining the level(s) of consumer benefit?[2] There are a wide range of sources for consumer benefit, which can be divided into *tangible* and *intangible* sources, depending on whether they can or cannot be observed directly (see ◘ Fig. 5.3). Tangible sources of consumer benefit include the following:

Product/service quality. This characteristic refers to the objective traits of a product, such as its functionality, durability (or reliability), and ease of installation. For instance, the quality of Ducati motorcycles can be determined accurately by metrics such as maximum speed, acceleration, fuel consumption, or breakdown rate. In the service dimension, for instance, the quality of ▶ Tesco.com's online grocery business can be measured by the freshness and overall quality of the goods delivered. Furthermore, service quality entails characteristics such as the friendliness and know-how of salespeople or, in the case of a website, the degree of personalization, ease of use, and response time and information quality of online enquiries.

Degree of Product or Service Customization The more a product or service can be adapted to specific customer needs, the more benefit it creates for the individual user.

2 There are numerous approaches available to estimate consumer benefit. They include (1) the reservation price method, (2) the attribute-rating method, (3) hedonic pricing, and (4) conjoint analysis. For a more detailed discussion of these approaches, refer to Besanko et al. (2003).

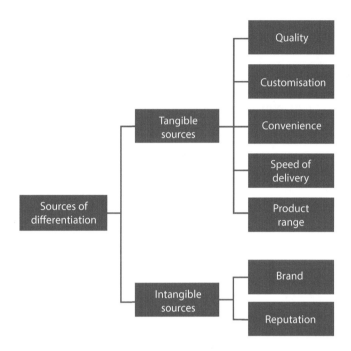

◘ Fig. 5.3   Tangible and intangible sources of differentiation. (Source: adapted from Jelassi et al., 2005)

Dell manufactures its PCs to customer specifications, resulting in two types of benefit. First, all the components that an individual customer values in a PC are included; second, all components that are not valued are left out, thus helping to keep down PC prices.

Convenience   The mental energy, effort, and time that buyers have to spend during the purchasing process need to be taken into account when comparing different providers.[3] This is why people do not drive 10 km to the discount supermarket just to buy one item, but instead go to the local corner store, even though that item might be more expensive there. Through its online grocery service, ► Tesco.com aims at increasing convenience for shoppers and especially for busy people.

Speed of Delivery   The ability to deliver products and services quickly is an important source of consumer benefit. Speed depends on the availability of products, location of the seller, and quality of the logistical process. A firm that has the ability to deliver faster than its competitors because of its management approach, superior process flow, and IT systems and applications can create a significant competitive advantage. ► Amazon.com, for instance, established proprietary warehouses to be able to ensure that products are available and shipped in a timely manner. ► JD.com

---

3   See also Kotler (2002, pp. 60–61).

is an online shopping platform with a 24-hour shipment service, which largely increases the sales volume of products it sells.

Product Range   A broad and deep selection provides an important source of differentiation since it allows convenient and quick one-stop shopping. ▶ Amazon.com is a prime example of a retailer with a deep and broad product range, where customers can find most book titles that are currently in print (and out of print).

Intangible sources of consumer benefit include the following:

Brand   This refers to the perceived traits that consumers associate with the company that is selling a product or a service. A strong brand tends to result from products that meet high-quality standards, yet this may not necessarily be so. It might also come as a result of intensive and innovative marketing activities. Brands need to be built and nurtured in order to use them as a differentiating characteristic in the marketplace.

Most online firms that have not benefitted from "viral growth" (i.e., through word of mouth) typically invest heavily to build their brand. On the other hand, for established physical firms such as Tesco, Nordea, and Ducati, it is easier to acquire online customers because they already have a strong brand from their established "bricks-and-mortar" businesses. Customers recognize them online.

Reputation   The perceived past performance of a company is a major influence on reputation. Customers value reputation because it decreases their purchasing risk. For example, when it comes to making online payments, a company's reputation is especially critical, since many online customers still feel uneasy providing their credit card information to an unknown vendor who they cannot guarantee will deliver their order.

5.1.3 Outpacing Strategies (and the Risk of Getting "Stuck in the Middle")

Porter argues that in order to have a unique and defendable competitive position, it is advisable to seek out one of the above two strategies (Kotler, 2002, pp. 41–44). The underlying assumption is that powerful strategies require trade-offs: a high level of quality usually entails high costs, while a cost leadership strategy usually impairs the ability to provide above-average levels of consumer benefit. As a result, firms that try to be both a quality and a cost leader at the same time tend to end up getting "stuck in the middle," a position that is characterized as neither low-cost nor differentiated.

More recently, Porter's concept of the generic strategies has been challenged by numerous empirically based studies.[4] A main conclusion of these analyses is that, in reality, companies can combine both types of advantage, i.e., a cost and a dif-

---

4   A. Fleck discusses the concept of outpacing strategies in his book *Hybride Wettbewerbsstrategien*, Gabler, 1995.

5

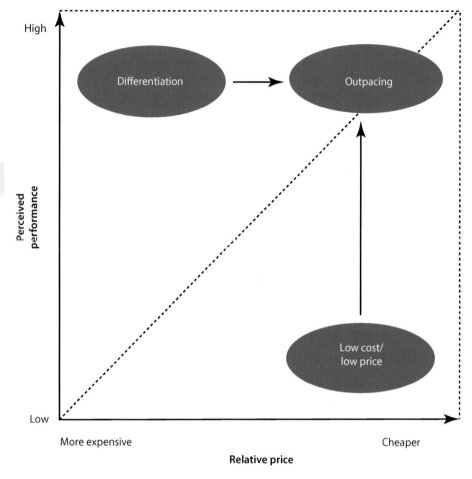

□ **Fig. 5.4**   Perceived performance and relative price position determine a firm's strategy. (Source: adapted from Hungenberg, 2014, p. 194)

ferentiation advantage, following an "outpacing" or "hybrid" strategy (see □ Fig. 5.4).

For example, one possible source for an outpacing advantage is quality management. This can be demonstrated using the example of Toyota. On the one hand, the Toyota Production System increases the perceived use value of Toyota's cars, since, for the past decade, they have proven to be more reliable and functional than the products of most other car manufacturers. On the other hand, the high reliability that guarantees high levels of use value also helps to improve Toyota's cost position by reducing the number of expensive callbacks.

Similarly, during the early 1990s, Tesco competed in the British grocery retailing market primarily by offering low prices. At the time the motto of the company was "pile it high and sell it cheap," in reference to the shelving practice of trying to accommodate as many products in as little space as possible. Over the years, Tesco has refined its value proposition by adding differentiating elements such as the online grocery retailing channel while still remaining highly cost competitive, thereby outperforming competitors on both the price and the quality dimensions. In doing so, Tesco effectively resolved the trade-off dilemma between quality and costs (see the FT article: "A route to profit in the middle market").

A Route to Profit in the Middle Market

Michael Porter was the first economist to become a business guru. He used economic concepts to illustrate issues of corporate strategy. One of his most cited conclusions was the need to avoid being "stuck in the middle." Companies, he said, must either gain a cost advantage or emphasize product differentiation. It was fatal to fall between the two stools of cost leadership and superior quality.

This claim struck me as nonsense. Middle market positions were not only viable but the preferred stance of many successful companies. In debate with Prof Porter, the eponymous chairman of Sainsbury's supermarket defiantly displayed a model truck carrying the slogan "Good food costs less at Sainsbury's"—a celebration of being stuck in the middle. And, when Tesco overtook Sainsbury's in the UK market, it was not by following Prof Porter's advice but by beating Sainsbury's at its own game.

Yet if we look at the UK supermarket sector today, the consensus view is that Prof Porter was right after all. The most successful competitors are Waitrose, firmly at the top of the market, and German discounters Aldi and Lidl, which have placed themselves at the bottom. Tesco, the market leader, along with traditional rivals Asda and Morrisons are under pressure, apparently stuck in the middle. The transformation of fortunes is not confined to the food sector; a remarkable phenomenon in UK high street retailing is the rise of Primark, which sells clothes for less than a hotel charges to launder them. And the most valuable company in the world, Apple, charges premium prices for premium products.

Like many business gurus, Prof Porter wriggled out of the challenge of "good food costs less" by adopting a slippery definition of his proposition. "Don't be stuck in the middle" can be interpreted as meaning that unless you have some cost advantage or product differentiation, you are unlikely to be very successful. That is a proposition so banal as to be almost tautological. A different proposition altogether says that you must emphasize either cost advantage or product differentiation, and if you aim at both, you will not be successful. This may be either true or false. It is disingenuous to use the self-evident truth of the first proposition as support for the empirical validity of the second. And that, I argued back in the 1990s, was exactly what Prof Porter was doing.

Business conferences typically proceed by competitive anecdote. But these debates can never be resolved by repeating slogans and telling stories; you can usually find a narrative to support all but the most outlandish assertions. The only way to find answers is to use more comprehensive data sets, and the combination of market research and company financial statements made such analysis possible here.

My empirical research drew on a database that enabled us to relate perceived market position to return on capital employed. We discovered, to no one's surprise, that high cost with low quality was not often a successful strategy. And low cost with high quality yielded the highest profits. Of course it did. But were you better off with low cost, low quality, or high cost and high quality, or being stuck in the middle with medium quality and medium cost? All produced similar returns.

A product offering is very rarely a sustainable source of competitive advantage because it can readily be imitated. What really matters is enjoying a competitive advantage in the market position you choose—and that typically involves matching your market position to the distinctive underlying resources and capabilities of your business. Waitrose, Aldi, and Lidl are not the beneficiaries, and Tesco and Sainsbury's not the victims, of any verity of business strategy other than the eternal one; the best strategy is to be good at whatever it is you do.

Source: J. Kay, "A route to profit in the middle market," *Financial Times*, 3 March 2015

From a theoretical perspective, the following factors can actually undermine this trade-off: (1) the development of new technologies, (2) wastefulness, and (3) economies of scale and learning effects. They are discussed below.

The development of new technologies. As is the case with the Internet, the development of new technologies offers innovative firms the opportunity, at least initially, to make large leaps in both the cost and the differentiation dimensions. Consider again the example of ► Amazon.com. Compared with other online book retailers and also with most bricks-and-mortar bookstores, it offers the most differentiated product and service, yet at the same time, prices are highly competitive. This is possible because ► Amazon.com has been continuously improving its technology and operations to lower costs as demonstrated by the company's innovative and efficient management of logistics or its introduction of revolutionary products such as the Kindle e-book. This approach is possible as long as the technology is still evolving and serious competition has not yet emerged, though one may at least question its sustainability over time once these technologies become commonplace.

If Internet businesses can persistently have lower costs or offer higher value than their bricks-and-mortar competitors, then there will be two possible scenarios. Firstly, if both types of businesses (i.e., the online and offline businesses) continue to coexist and serve different markets, then competition will take place only between Internet businesses. Secondly, if Internet-based firms turn out to be a substitute for bricks-and-mortar firms, then the latter will increasingly be driven out of business, and the competition will start out all over again among Internet players. Thirdly, industries typically merge online and offline businesses (omni-channel strategies) and maximize profits through a synergetic integration of both. For example, a shopper buys something online and collects it at a nearby physical store. Either way, co-opetition, and with it the need to have a clear strategic position, is likely to increase.[5] Other more mature industries, where new technology developments are of only secondary importance, indicate that it is necessary to seek a more precise positioning.

---

5   For a discussion of economic fundamentals, see Liebowitz (2002).

Many firms and industries are wasteful in their activities. This makes it possible to optimize quality while at the same time reduce costs. When companies are highly inefficient, they can make great strides without having to face the trade-off between quality and costs. However this factor is more concerned with operational effectiveness than strategy. During the Internet boom years, many start-up companies, such as the online fashion retailer ▶ Boo.com, invested lavishly on marketing, public relations events, and travel. Cutting costs in such situations is straightforward because there are no real trade-offs to be made.

Scale economies and learning effects. These might allow a firm to generate significant cost advantages while still pursuing a differentiated strategy. They enable a firm to achieve both low costs (through scale effects) and a superior product offering. Tesco, for example, can offer both its online and offline customers low prices because, due to its sheer size, it can source products at lower purchasing costs than most competitors.

Despite the above factors, the trade-off between differentiation and cost is an important issue to consider in strategy formulation, because, more often than not, a firm cannot excel in everything it does.

5.2 Creating a Fit Between the Chosen Strategy and the Value Chain

Activities in the production and distribution of products or services are not performed in isolation. Rather they operate as a value chain,[6] with each activity considered a link in the process that adds value when complete, and then the next value-adding activity commences. A firm's ability to create a better and unique fit between activities is ultimately responsible for its competitive advantage. Thus, the whole of the value chain is more important than the sum of its individual activities. Sustainability is also created by a unique fit between activities, since it is much more difficult for competitors effectively to imitate a set of interrelated activities than just to replicate one activity.

There are three main levers that determine the fit of activities within a firm: (1) *consistency between activities*, (2) *reinforcement of activities*, and (3) *optimization of efforts*. These are discussed below.

5.2.1 Consistency Between Activities

Consistency ensures that individual activities with their respective advantages build on each other instead of cancelling themselves out. For example, if a company's goal is to differentiate itself from its competitors through a premium product or service, it needs to design activities so that each activity adds to the differentiation

---

6   For different types of strategic fit among activities, see Porter (1996).

advantage. This might be by increasing benefits for customers and creating uniqueness among other benefits. On the other hand, if the goal is to be a low-cost provider, then the costs of each activity should be kept to a minimum while still maintaining the threshold features that are required to stay in the market. A lack of consistency dilutes the positioning of a company.

Why is that so? Porter argues that strategic positions are not sustainable if there are no trade-offs with other positions (Porter, 1996). If a firm wants to provide the highest-quality standards, it usually entails higher costs, while the desire for lower costs usually results in a decrease of quality. This trade-off arises from the following sources:

5

▪▪ Activities

The trade-off results in part directly from the activities involved. Different positions require different processes, resources, skills, and value chain setups. A firm that wants to achieve a differentiated position needs to invest heavily to ensure the highest-quality standards (and, hopefully, to be able to command a price premium). On the other hand, cost leaders need activities that provide the lowest possible cost structure because they want to compete through low prices. Customers of these firms want to receive a basic product or service at the lowest possible price. Thus, a business that wants to be a cost leader and unnecessarily bloats its costs by overengineering its activities is, in fact, destroying value.

▪▪ Image and Reputation

Trying to be both a low-cost and a differentiated provider can easily cause inconsistencies in a firm's image and reputation. It is much easier for a firm to communicate its strategy credibly to its different stakeholders (such as customers and shareholders) when it has a clear position. Think of the car manufacturer Porsche. To develop and maintain its reputation as a premium sports car manufacturer, Porsche needs to position itself clearly with its products and services. Similarly, a low-cost provider such as the US retailer WalMart focuses its efforts on providing its products at the lowest possible costs.

▪▪ Strategy Implementation

It is much easier to implement a strategy within a firm if employees have a clear guiding vision of the strategy and if they do not have to ask themselves with every decision: "Are we competing on low cost, or are we trying to be a differentiated provider?"

The need for consistency emphasizes the requirement that strategy is not just about deciding which activities a company should perform but also, and equally importantly, which activities not to perform. If a company wants to be everything to everyone, it runs the risk of not being able to do anything better than the competition and will end up being "stuck in the middle," where it has neither a cost nor a differentiation advantage vis-à-vis the competition. Porter argues that strategic positions are not sustainable if there are no trade-offs with other positions. If a company wants to provide benefits, this usually entails higher costs, while the desire for lower costs usually results in a decreased value for customers.

5.2 · Creating a Fit Between the Chosen Strategy and the Value...

139

5

5.2.2 **Reinforcement of Activities**

Reinforcement is the second important characteristic of a good fit between the different activities of a company. Its underlying thinking is that competitive advantage comes as a result of how some activities influence the quality of other activities to create higher quality in products or services, thereby increasing the use value for customers. As emphasized above, in terms of the value framework, this implies that the total value created throughout the value chain is larger than the sum of the values created in the individual steps of the value chain.

For instance, if a company has a highly motivated and skilled sales force, it is much more effective if the company also has excellent R&D and production facilities to produce a high-quality product. Similarly, a sophisticated website, such as the one of ▶ Amazon.com, becomes more valuable when it is combined with a warehouse system that allows for fast, reliable, and efficient deliveries. The case of Nordea illustrates the importance of reinforcement. Among other reasons, Nordea is successful because it managed to create a tight fit between all its online and offline banking activities, which allowed the bank to move quickly online a large number of its branch customers. Pure online banks cannot imitate this effective customer acquisition approach, since they do not have a physical branch network. Other bricks-and-mortar banks that tried to follow suit did not realize the importance of closely connecting the online and offline businesses. They opted instead for distinct profit-center structures, thereby creating competition between their online and offline activities. A firm's ability to cross-sell and/or sell through complementary distribution channels is critical, since, especially in the service industry, the cost of acquiring a new customer can be two to three times the cost of selling to an existing customer.

5.2.3 **Optimization of Efforts**

The third characteristic of a good fit is the optimization of efforts. While reinforcement primarily focuses on improving the customer experience by linking up separate activities, optimization emphasizes the importance of cost reduction through the elimination of redundancy and wasted activity. For instance, Alibaba handles around 50 million shipments per day. Dispatching these goods manually would be tremendously inefficient. Thus Alibaba has introduced an automated system for dispatching packages. This system can smartly dispatch shipments to destinations, dramatically reducing the dependence on the labor force and the effort of managing this internal process.

Creating fit between activities through consistency, reinforcement, and optimization of efforts connects the conceptual act of strategy formulation to operational implementation issues, which determine how to choose and structure a company's activities. The value-process framework helps to conceptualize this leap from broad strategy formulation, for example, the low-cost positioning of easyJet, to the actual implementation throughout the different steps of the value chain.

It is necessary to analyze closely the vertical and horizontal boundaries of a firm and to set up the internal organization accordingly, in order to create fit among activities. This requires substantial resources and managerial skills, which also explains why strategy has long-term implications. Changing strategies randomly makes it hard to obtain a competitive advantage, because creating fit takes time and effort. This does not mean that new tools and concepts, such as total quality management (TQM) which might help to increase operational effectiveness, should generally be discarded. Yet it is sensible to implement these tools only as long as they do not alter the fundamental basis of the strategic position and its trade-offs.

5.3 Business Model Canvas

> **Definition**
>
> "The most essential thing for us was to get the business model right, then put the world-class technology under it to support it."
> – John McKinley
> Former US senator

Strategy indicates the general direction of organizational actions, that is, what a firm is going to do and whether it is worth doing so. Tactics represent how a firm fulfills strategy and details specific organizational actions, for example, how a firm does business. There is some space between strategy and tactics. From the view of a corporate president or CEO, strategy is the first issue they should consider, and processes that flow from it is also important for them. Tactics are important but not critical for CEOs because their middle managers are closer to real business contexts and so know more about current situations and so are more equipped to devise specific tactics to fulfill strategy.

Business models are a critical "middleware" delineating how a company conducts value-generating activities at a strategic level (see ◘ Fig. 5.5). These models are what a president or CEO should emphasize because inappropriate business models cannot create, deliver, and capture value. When the firm's generic strategy is settled, corporate leaders can design the corresponding business model to identify how they can achieve the strategy. That is, they think strategically about their value proposition and how the business performs value activities, and key issues related to these activities, to deliver value to customers. Customers pay for that value, which is how a business captures value.[7] Academics George and Bock (2011) describe the differences between strategy and business models:

> ❯ First, strategy is a dynamic *set* of initiatives, activities, and processes; the business model is a static configuration of organizational elements and activity characteristics. A strategy may be reflexive, initiating change within the organization that impacts the emergent strategy; a business model is inherently nonreflexive. Implementing a business model may generate organizational change, but the business model itself is not a description of or recipe for change. Business models are opportunity–centric, while strategy is competitor or environment centric.

---

7   For details on creating, delivering, and capturing value, see Chesbrough (2006).

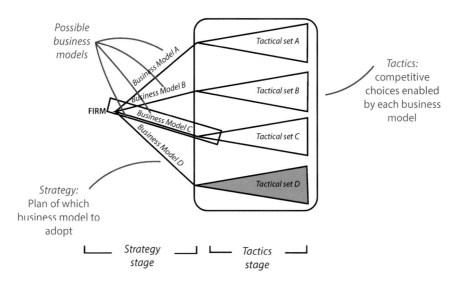

◘ Fig. 5.5 Strategy, business models, and tactics. (Source: adapted from Casadesus-Masanell and Ricart, 2010)

For e-business-oriented companies, business model design is crucial for success. Many e-business-related failures can be attributed to a poor business model, even though many start-ups have advanced technologies and innovative business ideas. These start-ups, particularly small ones founded by technology developers, focus too much on technological aspects of their business and barely think about the commercialization and monetization of their technology at a strategic level.

Today's technology business world is challenging and dominated by multinationals. A leading position of advanced technology is temporary because competitors will find a way to imitate it or use other approaches to outpace the incumbent's leading position. In this case, entrepreneurs should restrain their obsession with technology and invest time in considering the business and strategic aspects of its e-business dimension. The business model canvas is a modern tool to help leaders think strategically about how their firm creates, delivers, and captures value.

5.3.1 A Brief Overview

The business model canvas is a template for documenting new or existing business models. It indicates nine strategic elements of a business separately:
- The value proposition
- Customer segments
- Customer relationships
- Channels
- Key activities
- Key partners

- Key resources
- Cost structure
- Revenue streams

These nine elements reflect different aspects of how a firm creates, delivers, and captures value and make up the business model. Note that large firms with several products and/or services may have several business models that can be distilled into one overarching business model. For example, Amazon has separate business models for its retail e-commerce, web services, home automation, and more, and they may be distilled into one overarching model for Amazon, which will be described later. Other "pure-play" e-businesses with one product or service would have one business model, for example, eBay. By understanding the business model, a leader can then identify how to change that model to respond to changes in the environment that impact on the business. Making changes to the business model can be referred to as business model mechanics.[8]

Value Proposition   The value proposition describes the value a business will offer to customers, either by creating benefits or easing "pain" (solving problems or lessening negative consequences of activities). Because value only makes sense in real contexts, some scholars think that firms can only provide conjectured or imagined value for customers, or offer value propositions. Specifically, value propositions of e-business can be summarized in five categories: price, convenience, efficiency, user experience, and outcome.

Customer Segments   Customers are the determinant factor of business performance. Firms should clearly define their target customers when designing different business models. Detailed information on how customers are segmented can be seen at ▶ Chap. 3.

Customer Relationships   This refers to how a business interacts with customers online and offline. Considering the critical role of customers, businesses need to explicitly identify how they will interact and then develop and maintain their relationship with customers. For example, relationships may be personal, indirect and intermediary, functional, social, or emotional. For example, a customer relationship with ▶ Tesco.com (functional) is different to one with Facebook (social).

Channels   Once the key customers and type of relationships with them are identified, the business then needs to consider how they will reach those customers. Channels refers to different paths through which a business delivers their value to target markets. A firm should think what channels are efficient and cost-effective to reach customers. Channels may include online, through a physical store, and through direct salespeople or resellers. For example, the channels of a film are cinemas, television, digital streaming, and bricks-and-mortar stores (DVDs).

---

8   For more details on business model mechanics, see Osterwalder and Pigneur (2020).

Key Activities   Put simply, a business model is a value activity system, where each activity it undertakes adds value. When creating a business model, ask which activities are most important for creating value as per the value proposition. A business model highlights the activities that if they did not occur, the product or service could not be offered. They are activities which are not easily and quickly replaceable. For example, a key activity of Alibaba is server maintenance (to ensure there is no downtime, especially during peak selling periods such as Singles Day), and a key activity of ▶ Amazon.com is distribution of physical goods.

Key Resources   A business may have plenty of resources, but when creating a business model, identify the key resources that are needed to create value and conduct value activities, as per the value proposition. Resources here can be specialist personnel and intellectual property such as patents, financial assets, and fixed assets (websites, distribution centers, and more). Again, to help identify only key resources, consider whether the product or service could be delivered without them and whether they are easily replaceable. For example, most start-ups have very few physical assets; however, their intellectual property is a key resource.

Partner Network   Partners refers to external agencies that the business relies upon when creating and delivering value. They are not separate to a firm's value activities; they are partners in collaboration. In many cases, the quality of product or service is jointly determined by the focal firm and its partner network. The partner network is a strategic element that firms should take into account. They should identify the partners they depend on to conduct value activities jointly. This aspect is vital within ecosystems. For example, financial services businesses may partner with competitors to merge their "back-office" data processing into one entity that provides services to all businesses within the partnership. Similarly technology businesses partner with hardware manufacturers.

Revenue Streams   This refers to how a firm generates income, for example, via subscriptions, product sales, referrals, advertising and paid placements, and more. Revenue streams are clearly important for company viability because salaries and bills need to be paid. Typically revenues need to be earned before any spending occurs. Revenues are also a critical indicator used by potential investors to evaluate a business. Investor funds are typically not revenues because they must be repaid or take the form of equity, which dilutes earnings.

Cost Structure   This refers to the most important costs for business operations and indicates which resources or activities are "costly" for the company, where most funds are invested. This could include research and development costs, advertising, remuneration of specialists, infrastructure costs, and more. For example, if a key cost was electricity to run servers, a business could minimize that cost by converting to renewable energy, as Google have done.[9] By subtracting costs from revenues, the business

---

9   For more details, see Google, "100% renewable is just the beginning" *Sustainability Google* [website]. Available at ▶ https://sustainability.google/projects/announcement-100/.

can identify whether it captures value in the form of profit. If costs exceed revenues, then it is not capturing value and so needs to reconsider how it creates and delivers value.

In summary, the business model canvas is conceptual, but grounded in evidence. It uses nine components to make explicit the abstract "way of working" within the business. It identifies separate aspects that a leader must consider when designing and improving their business model.

5.3.2 Some Applications to e-Business

The business model canvas is a useful tool to analyze and evaluate a business model. Here we will apply it to two sample companies: Facebook and ► Amazon.com.

5.3.2.1 Facebook

Based on the business model canvas analysis (see ❏ Fig. 5.6), Facebook's value proposition is about helping users to manage their social network. Users are typically individual consumers, but also include companies. Its success lies in its online social platform allowing worldwide users to find, meet, and interact with others, and it offers various forms of content. Content here refers to user-generated content (individuals and also businesses) such as personal updates. Facebook used network effects to build a massive user network that created and gave Facebook content at "zero" cost, and this network gradually became a self-nurturing ecosystem of content: creators (social users and businesses), sharers, distributors, and consumers. Facebook turned this user network into a marketplace and profits from

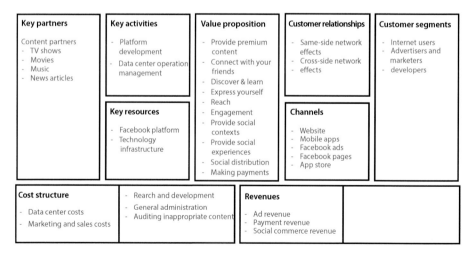

❏ **Fig. 5.6** Facebook's business model canvas. (Source: adapted from Admin, 'Understanding Facebook Business Model', ► Bmimatters.com, 10 April 2012)

targeted advertising on the platform and also sells this aggregated content in the form of user data to marketers and data analytics firms.

The genius of this business model is leveraging the content of social media users, but it is underpinned by a relationship of trust—users trust Facebook to protect their data from misuse. In recent years, as data analytics has evolved and enabled new ways to capture, target, and profit from user data, Facebook has been challenged by breaches of trust, and it has damaged their business:

(a) It's highly targeted advertising model has been criticized by users for an invasion of their privacy. Some do not want to see any commercialization of their social and personal life, particularly advertising based on comments or other content that they have created or shared without knowing that "Facebook was listening in."

(b) Previously Facebook claimed it was not responsible for the content posted by users, but with the dramatic rise of user-generated content, it has become more necessary for Facebook to manage content, which is an additional cost and makes Facebook potentially liable for the content on its platform. For example, the platform has allegedly been misused to spread "fake news."

(c) Facebook sells "aggregated" user data to agencies, some of whom have used it for unethical purposes; see the FT article: "Facebook reveals Russian spending on US election ads." The ethics of this practice have damaged user trust and the reputation of Facebook, leading to a loss of users and regulatory inquiries across several countries.

These malpractices have damaged the business of Facebook, and it is interesting to observe that founder Mark Zuckerberg is pivoting toward another social media platform, Instagram, which Facebook acquired in 2012, and is merging its operations with Facebook.

Please note that in this intermediary business model, users are both customers and partners. Users are also partners because the content they create and provide to Facebook (for free) is then sold to advertisers and data analytics businesses. PayPal is listed as a partner because it is used for sales that are made on Facebook.

Facebook Reveals Russian Spending on US Election Ads

Facebook has found that "inauthentic" Russian actors bought $100,000 worth of advertisements on the social network over the past 2 years, amid investigations into allegations of Russian efforts to influence the US presidential election. Alex Stamos, Facebook's Chief Information Security Officer, said Facebook had shared its findings with US congressional investigators and would continue to work with them. The discovery came after the company probed "serious claims" that there was a connection between Russian efforts to interfere in the election and ads bought on Facebook.

Facebook said in a blog post Wednesday evening that it had found 470 "inauthentic" accounts and pages buying ads from June 2015 until May 2017. These accounts appeared to be operated out of Russia and affiliated with one another, it said. "The ads and accounts appeared to focus on amplifying divisive social and political messages across the ideological spectrum — touching on topics from LGBT matters to race issues to immigration to gun rights," he said.

The platform has become an important hub for political advertising because of its ability to target specific regions—from a whole swing state to an individual county—and to show different messages to various demographic groups, without the ads being shown to other less receptive audiences.

Facebook said the ads bought by the inauthentic accounts did not contain specific messages about the election, voting, or the presidential candidates. About $50,000 was spent on 2200 ads Facebook identified as "potentially politically related" that may have originated in Russia. About a quarter of the ads were geographically targeted, and more of them ran in 2015 than 2016. Facebook has faced criticism since the US election for not doing more to stop misinformation on the platform, where many of the most shared stories were fake, such as a claim that the Pope had endorsed Donald Trump. The company has taken several measures to slow the spread of so-called fake news, from partnering with fact checkers to label stories as disputed to hiring 3000 additional moderators to take down content that breaks its content guidelines.

In April, Mr Stamos' team published a white paper studying how "information operations," such as the campaign thought to have originated in Russia, manipulate public opinion online. Since then, Facebook has taken down several fake accounts in Germany, France, and elsewhere. It is now working on ways to apply the technology it developed to detect fake accounts and inauthentic pages, it said.

Source: H. Kuchler, "Facebook reveals Russian spending on US election ads," *Financial Times*, 6 September 2017

5.3.2.2 ► Amazon.com

"We've had three big ideas at Amazon that we've stuck with for 18 years, and they're the reason we're successful. Put the customer first. Invent. And be patient," Amazon founder Jeff Bezos (Solsman, 2013).

► Amazon.com began as a two-sided market. Initially it empowered sellers to merchandise goods through its online platform and receives revenue from transaction fees. From there it grew to dominate e-business, with New York University Professor Scott Galloway claiming Amazon "is going everywhere and swallowing industries whole (Hough, 2017)." Its business model (see ◨ Fig. 5.7) is a milestone in the evolution of commerce, because Amazon revolutionized how we sell and shop, for example:

- Buyers and sellers no longer need to meet each other face-to-face to purchase goods.
- Shoppers are able to purchase what they want anywhere and anytime.
- Amazon has used economies of scale to push down prices.

But this business model has significant weaknesses too, including:

- Due to the virtual nature of e-commerce, shoppers cannot fully evaluate a product's quality merely by reviewing descriptions and feature points supplied by sellers.

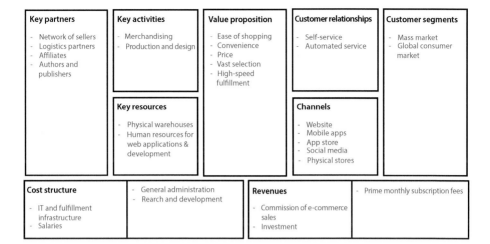

Key partners	Key activities	Value proposition	Customer relationships	Customer segments
- Network of sellers - Logistics partners - Affiliates - Authors and publishers	- Merchandising - Production and design	- Ease of shopping - Convenience - Price - Vast selection - High-speed fulfillment	- Self-service - Automated service	- Mass market - Global consumer market
	Key resources - Physical warehouses - Human resources for web applications & development		**Channels** - Website - Mobile apps - App store - Social media - Physical stores	

Cost structure		Revenues	
- IT and fulfillment infrastructure - Salaries	- General administration - Rearch and development	- Commission of e-commerce sales - Investment	- Prime monthly subscription fees

☐ **Fig. 5.7** ▶ Amazon.com business model canvas. (Source: adapted from E. Noren, 'Amazon Business Model Canvas', *Business Model Innovation Hub*, 9 July 2013)

— Frustration and uncertainty are created when goods are not supplied or when something else goes wrong in a transaction. For example, a buyer may complain about a product that was received with scratches or damage. These scratches or damage may have been caused by either:
  – The seller who sent an inferior product
  – A delivery person who unintentionally damaged the package
  – The shopper who damaged the product and wants to get a new one for free
— It is almost impossible and potentially costly for Amazon to identify responsibility in this "accident."

Over the years, Amazon has iteratively improved its service by honing in on these and other customer frustrations to minimize friction. They now control delivery, provide very rich information to support a shopper's decision process on its site, and offer an excellent return service. Doing so has led to sustained phenomenal growth across geographies and sectors. Amazon has grown from a simple e-commerce company into media streaming (including content creation), web storage, and home automation (Echo), as reflected in its business model below. For more detailed information on Amazon, see ▶ Chap. 16.

To summarize, the business model canvas is a useful tool to clarify, and make explicit, a company's business model. The tool can be applied into various situations. Entrepreneurs in digital start-ups can use the business model canvas to frame their business model and identify their key resources and activities. Established e-businesses can use it to pivot their business model, with business model mechanics. Investors can use it to assess the potential value and prospect of a business.

5.4 Developing Strategy Alternatives: Major e-Business Models

Every day there are new e-business models emerging in the world. Some are tech-based models, such as AI-based business models, IoT-based business models, and 3D print-based business models; some refer to the platform on which e-business performs, such as social media-based business models, app-based business models, and web-based business models. Others follow more traditional criteria to categorize them, such as a revenue model. No two business models are alike, and each organization has a unique business model because different businesses have different resources and competences to create, deliver, and capture value in different markets. This is why a firm should design and develop its own business model based on its current situation and avoid simply copying benchmark business models. That is a path to failure, because the firm may not be able to implement these models in reality due to different contexts.

But no matter how a firm conducts e-business, it is possible to classify the major e-business models. Typical economic agents involved in e-business activities can be divided into three types: consumers, firms, and governments. According to the potential e-business activities between the three economic agents, we get four business model categories: C2C, C2B, B2B, and government-related e-business models. It is noteworthy to mention that some business models can be applied in various settings. For instance, a cloud computing service is used in B2C settings and B2B settings.

A company may have several business models at the same time and have multiple sources of revenue and omni-channels. For example, a shopping mall may entice online consumers to go to its site via social media campaigns. Once in the mall, consumers can receive personalized messages and product recommendations sent to their smartphone using Bluetooth-based technology. When in-store, a consumer could also use their smartphone to scanning codes on items for sale and access product-related information, watch videos, see relevant promotions, and receive e-coupons. When a consumer tries on a new dress in front of a smart mirror, the mirror can virtually accessorize and make other recommendations. When it comes to payments, consumers can use their mobile wallet to pay, so that the mall can automatically calculate the consumer's consumption credit in this mall and send gifts and special promotions to them when their consumption credits reach a specific limit. In this case, the business model of the shopping mall is based on key resources that include multi-technologies (AR, VR, mobile payment tech, image identification tech, etc.) and multi-platforms (social media platforms, a smartphone, a mobile app, a customer relationship management system, etc.). Regarding the diversity of a company's business model, see the article: "The future of retail is happening right now in China." Hence, major e-business models mentioned in this section can inform the creation of other business models.

The Future of Retail Is Happening Right Now in China

If you need evidence of the US retail sector's precarious condition, consider that over 9000 stores closed last year, and another 12,000 are on the chopping block this year, according to commercial property firm Cushman & Wakefield. Despite a 4.2 percent rise in 2017 over the previous year, US retail growth is lumpy and clearly not firing on all cylinders. Every week brings gloomy news of bankruptcies or downsizings. Online sales, meanwhile, have been climbing, underpinning the sector's overall growth. US retail is at a crossroads, with brands and retailers still trying to decide whether e-commerce is friend or foe. On one hand, e-commerce is killing traditional brick-and-mortar business, but on the other, you'll have a hard time finding a company whose future growth strategy doesn't rest on developing its online channels.

New Retail Moves to the Forefront

There's no such quandary 8000 miles away in China, where the "either-or" retail equation is being pushed aside in favor of a model, called "New Retail," melding the best of both the in-shop and online experiences. Leading the way is Alibaba, which operates the country's largest e-commerce platforms and has more than half a billion consumers shopping on its marketplaces. Online sales penetration in China is the highest in the world, but brick-and-mortar retail still accounts for more than 80 percent of total retail sales. Realizing that the future of retail will not be a question of online vs. offline, Alibaba founder Jack Ma unveiled the New Retail concept 2 years ago. Though still young, it's already a game changer for many different types of retail experiences in China. "New Retail is not just super-markets and convenience stores. It's much bigger and more-sweeping than this," wrote Jeffrey Towson, a Peking University professor and private equity investor who closely follows the development of China's retail sector, in his blog earlier this year. "New Retail is a bold extension of Alibaba's strategy of pure digital competi-tion into the physical world. And it hinges on the strange 'economics of participa-tion'…'New Retail' means a massive expansion in their brands and merchants and in the participation and activities of their consumers."

Turning Supermarket Hell into Hema

Who actually enjoys trundling a shopping cart up and down the aisles, searching the shelves, settling for what the store has in stock, standing in line to pay, and schlepping the heavy bags back home? Shoppers have none of those hassles at Alibaba's Hema supermarkets, which the company created to incubate new retail innovations that could be applied to the broader industry. At first glance, Hema looks like most other supermarkets: it sells groceries, fruits and vegetables, and fresh seafood. But this is not your typical grocery store. "I walked into Hema not knowing what to expect–digital extravaganza or shopping made simple. It turned out to be something in-between. I came to see the QR code as the great equalizer," said Steve Stine, whose *Inside Asia* website produced a podcast after a visit to a Hema store in Shanghai. "The entire experience was quick, efficient and painless."

Shopping at Hema is a smartphone-powered experience—you can do it from home or in the store. When you're in the store, you're able to scan a bar code with your phone to get product information. Payment is also cashless, done through the Alipay platform embedded in the Hema app. For some, Hema's "hook" is the ability to choose your own fresh seafood and decide whether you want it to go home with you—raw or cooked—or have it prepared to eat in-store. For those who live within 3 kilometers of the market, Hema's ability to deliver in as fast as 30 minutes is its best asset. Each store serves as its own warehouse and logistics center that collects, fulfills, and delivers customer orders as fast as they come in, online or offline.

Taking the Pain Out of Car Shopping

If you've ever bought a new car, you'll appreciate what New Retail is doing for the experience in China. Instead of visiting one dealer at a time and spending hours perusing mega-lots and facing pressure from a salesman, Alibaba is rolling out "auto vending machines." It recently launched its first with Ford in the bustling southern city of Guangzhou and plans more in the near future. The Ford auto vending machine lets customers browse makes and models inside their app, choose one they want to test drive, pick it up from an unmanned vending machine, and drive it for up to 3 days. After experiencing the car in a no-pressure situation, they can make an appointment to visit a dealer when they're ready to buy. "The technology advancements provided by the Alibaba platform are…giving brands new options to totally rethink how they operate, how they engage with the consumer," said Jason Ding, a Bain & Co. partner in Beijing, who co-authored a recent report on New Retail with AliResearch.

Neighborhood Convenience Stores Get More Convenient

The mom-and-pop convenience store is a sector long in need of a New Retail upgrade. The lifeblood of many communities, some six million of the drinks-smokes-and-snacks shops dot neighborhoods and street corners across China. Most are family-run businesses, with proprietors ordering by gut feel and when products run out. Until Alibaba's Ling Shou Tong program came along, the model hadn't been updated in several decades. Stores are modernized and brightened. They get updated signage. But there's a lot more going on under the hood. Alibaba custom-built an app to digitize the inventory management of each store that lets proprietors know what they need, how much, and when to order. It also tied these businesses into a central warehousing and logistics system. Ling Shou Tong's customer insights can make brands smarter. Snack company Mondelez, for example, filled a need for sweet-toothed customers by producing single-serving Oreo cookie sleeves that stores have strategically placed near the cash register.

Mall Rats of the World, Don't Despair. Here Comes New Retail

And what about malls? While tumbleweeds can be seen blowing through the aisles in the United States, Alibaba has begun pumping up China's malls with a dose of

New Retail. The way to customers' hearts is to have what they want, in the size and color they want and when they want it. The reality of the mall-shopping experience is that you often find the right pants, but not the right size or color in stock. New Retail in the mall means less of a chance that you'll walk away empty-handed. Stores are equipped with "virtual shelves," and if you don't find your size or color in stock, you can still select the product you want on a screen, punch in your size, color and other specs, scan with your app, and have exactly what you want delivered directly to your home. Even the powder room of malls can be a New Retail experience. Step into the ladies' room, and while you're waiting, check out the "magic mirror" on the wall to experiment, virtually, with new makeup colors. Like what you see? You can buy it from the vending machine.

Why Change Happens Faster in China's Retail Sector

To understand why China's retail sector is changing faster than elsewhere, you need to grasp Alibaba's role as a marketplace operator. For nearly 19 years, it has built the backbone of China's giant e-commerce machine, essentially creating a "move-in" environment for brands, as well as an engaging discovery and frictionless purchase process for shoppers. As a marketplace operator, Alibaba offers a panoply of services to brands—advertising and marketing tools, payment systems, logistics and cloud computing, media, and entertainment properties. Brands selling on its B2C platform, Tmall, build storefronts that look just like their own online stores, because the brands own the customer experience and relationship. They also own all of the related analytics. All of that aims to help brands succeed. There's zero competition with Alibaba, unlike in the United States, where online retailers may directly butt heads with the brands selling on their platforms. To Alibaba, success these days also means helping brands go omni-channel. An increasing number of brands are doing just that, tapping Alibaba's New Retail tools, erasing the lines between online and offline. The key to New Retail is the mobile phone, which provides the critical connection between online and offline retail to consumers. Brands in China have an advantage here because they don't need to convince consumers to download and use their apps. That's because they know 500 million consumers already have the Tmall app. The China retail sector is also not torn between propping up legacy business and trying something new. Its brick-and-mortar retail operations are less developed than in the West.

"China is moving much faster than the West in this evolution because the Western retail model is built on legacy systems. China's model is disruptive," said Frank Lavin, CEO of Export Now, a company which helps Western brands sell to China. "China does not have the legacy of malls and big-box stores like the West. China has no traditional retail model to defend."

Source: A. Najberg, "The future of retail is happening right now in china," ▶ Alizila.com, 11 April 2018

5.4.1 **B2C**

B2C e-business models are the most prevalent models for pure e-business.[10] The "B" in question has two meanings. Firstly, it simply means that a company sells products or services directly to consumers, for example, Estee Lauder sells products directly to consumers via its ▶ Esteelauder.com website. Secondly, it means that a company bridges the business activities between business users and individual users, for example, Tmall allows retail companies worldwide to merchandise goods to online buyers. Tmall is a platform for B2C commerce. Depending on the role of e-business companies, B2C e-business models can be further categorized into e-tailers, content providers, portals, transaction brokers, market providers, service providers, and community providers. These are described below.

e-Tailers   The business model of an e-tailer refers to a retailer using Internet-based channels to sell products. These channels not only include shopping websites and apps which have been discussed previously but also include the use of emails and other communications that link to a website. This omni-channel strategy is widely used by bricks-and-mortar companies such as Johnson & Johnson, Walmart, Tesco, and Coca-Cola. The approach of using digital communications to attract consumers into physical stores is informally referred to as "bricks-and-clicks," so that consumers are informed online and can choose to either purchase in-store or online. When purchasing online, the customer may choose to either pick the item up at their local store or have it delivered to their home. A benefit to retailers is that both their physical stores and online stores may use the same point-of-sale system. For example, Office Depot had in place:

- A major logistics network that included 2000 delivery trucks and 30 warehouses that delivered to 1825 stores across the United States
- A real-time inventory database, showing stock available in every store
- A catalog sales operation
- A website

Office Depot was able to exploit these predominantly fixed assets to offer online ordering where customers could order and choose to either pick up in items in-store, or items would be delivered via their existing logistics network.[11]

Content Providers   Content is a digital good in the Internet world. It includes text, video, sound, and data. The scope of the content business is very broad, including online and mobile games, online music, digital animation, e-books, e-learning, and online streaming of films, news and videos, and more. A content owner may use the Internet to provide or distribute their content. For instance, the *Financial Times* uses

---

10   This section is adapted from Laudon and Traver (2017).
11   For more see R. Gulati and J. Garino, "Get the right mix of bricks and clicks," *Harvard Business Review*, 2000, May–June.

▶ ft.com to distribute news, opinions, reviews, and industry analyses and profits from subscription fees.

In the nascent phase of the Internet, there was a culture of freely sharing copyrighted content without appropriate licenses. Some copyright owners would release content so that it could be freely shared, to generate interest, "grow eyeballs," or visits to the site and for the purpose of marketing, branding, and advertising. This created a culture of freely sharing of copyrighted content, which is technically illegal. There were two consequences: the creation of open licenses that allow the legal sharing of content online; but it also led to a wave of takedown notices and other legal action from copyright owners for illegal use of their content online. Content owners suffered a public relations backlash but persisted and launched media campaigns to educate consumers about copyright of online content. Gradually the culture of piracy changed, and consumers began to recognize the need to pay for content online in the same way that they pay offline. The launch and messaging for Apple's iTunes and Music Store was a key enabler of this cultural change, because Apple made it easy to purchase music. At the same time, digital rights management (DRM) tools were created and implemented by copyright owners to manage online access to their content. DRM enabled copyright owners to recognize use of their content, in order to seek payment. Revenues can be incurred from intermediary platforms, for example, as streaming royalties (Spotify, Netflix, and more), or direct sales or rentals (the Apple Store, Amazon Kindle books). For-profit news providers typically require subscriptions to premium content on their websites, which are accessible only after registration. Many content providers use a "freemium" model, in which a portion of content is made available for free, and further, premium content requires some form of payment. They may also receive a portion of advertising revenues from sites that host their content.

Portals   Portals refer to sites that aggregate and curate information from diverse sources like news, weather, search engines, emails, and more. The business model of a portal is based on advertising. A portal can create a large amount of traffic so that it can sell advertising and paid placements. It is very difficult to challenge a the market position of a global portal such as ▶ Google.com, ▶ MSN.com, ▶ Yahoo.com, and ▶ AOL.com because they have captured a dominant position in the market and switching costs may be high for consumers because they use other services of the portal (notably email). But other portals may target one or a few user segments—also known as vertical portals or *vortals*—and can also generate advertising revenue. These *vortals* serve a specialized or niche segment of consumers, for example, ▶ Autohome.com is a *vortal* that specializes in automobile markets and providing curated content related to cars. *Vortals* are attractive to advertisers even though they cannot generate the scale of traffic as generic portals, because advertisers can target a specific segment that directly relates to what they are selling, which improves the potential impact of their advertisements.

Transaction Brokers   When a company is labeled as an e-brokerage company, it means this company leverages the Internet to broker transactions between the supply side and the demand side. For example, Airbnb is an online platform that aggregates lodging service providers and travel fares. A transaction broker adds value by facilitating the completion of transactions and incurs revenues from charging a commission or service fees. As for bricks-and-mortar stockbrokers, they take a percentage of each online transaction activity. For example, TD Ameritrade offers an e-trading platform for individuals and institutions that invest online. Another example is labor platforms, which incur revenue in the same way that they do offline: they typically charge employers for their services. However they may receive additional revenues from advertising placed on their website, and if they are entirely online, their fixed costs are much lower because they may not require physical branches. For example, 51job is an online labor brokerage platform including many talent databases in various industries. This system can help hunters find the most suitable candidates for their recruitment. Revenues are incurred from potential employers through paid placements of job advertisements and direct email marketing campaigns to a targeted group of job seekers. 51job also provides other human resource-related services to potential employers.

Market Providers   Companies can create an online marketplace for transactions between business users and end users. The business model of a market provider is offering, managing, and monetizing the platform. This business model is different from the previous model of transaction broker, because businesses and consumers are empowered by the platform business to conduct commercial activities by themselves. The revenue source of this business model could be diverse and include:

- Businesses which could pay a fee to use the platform.
- The platform which could aggregate and sell user data.
- Advertising and paid placements, among other revenue sources.

For example, Tmall is a platform for B2C transactions founded by Alibaba. It helps many small- and middle-sized enterprises (SMEs) realize their e-commerce strategy at low cost, because Alibaba's business logic is to help SMEs be successful, and then successful SMEs can afford to pay for the placement of their products higher in search results, which compounds their success through greater exposure. Multiply this by many successful sellers on the platform competing for paid placements.

Service Providers   With the emergence of the Internet and other communication technologies, many tasks can be done online. Online shopping is only a small percentage of household expenditure, and businesses that provide face-to-face or in-person services can also use digital strategies. Services such as haircuts, restaurant meals, and home maintenance are provided in person, but service providers use the Internet for promotion. Another type of service provider can aggregate and promote these services. For example, restaurants advertise their menus on their websites. A business may aggregate this information from restaurants across a location and present it in one site, so that consumers can conveniently search across a variety of local restaurants and their menus. They place an order and pay online, and the restaurant delivers the food to their home. Alternately another service provider might deliver it (e.g.,

Uber Eats or Deliveroo). Revenues are typically incurred when the restaurant diverts a percentage of the sale to the platform. Uber Eats charges a delivery fee.

Service providers are trying to bring their offline business and online business together, see the article: "The formula to create a trillion dollar online to offline industry."

Community Providers   Community is an online channel to complete firm-user and user-user interactions. In many cases, firm-hosted online community is a direct channel to allow a company to talk directly with users and also facilitate interactions between users. The business model of a community provider is to use an online community to create and capture value generated from online interactions. For example, an online community is a perfect place for a brand's fans to develop brand loyalty and increase user engagement with the next generation of products. While the online channel may not directly generate revenues, it supports customer retention and can be used for research and development.

The Formula to Create a Trillion Dollar Online to Offline Industry

The unfulfilled promises of online to offline have left us all a bit deflated. It seemed like such a perfect fit; everyone is online and 93% of commerce is still offline; just connect the two worlds, and a massive O2O industry will be born! We've heard this message at every conference since Hootie & the Blowfish were actually popular. So why hasn't this taken off; what's the holdup?

In order to understand what has gone wrong, you have to understand the three core elements that need to be done right in order to create a massive O2O industry. *The offer*—Something that motivates consumers to make a purchase at an offline business

The tracking—How the consumer redeems the offer and how the offline business tracks where it originated from

The monetization—How online companies make money by driving consumers to offline businesses

The Offer

Groupon and LivingSocial almost cracked the code of O2O. They were so close you could taste it, and boy did the copy cats come out in droves. The fact that Google, Facebook, Amazon, Yelp, and thousands of other online companies all started a daily deal website in the same year is unprecedented. The O2O gold rush had begun! You could smell the greed in the air, and it topped out with Groupon's $20B public valuation just 3 years after launch, making Groupon the fastest-growing business in history. But today Groupon is worth less than 10% of that value ($1.75 billion as of 10 January 2016), and there is a graveyard full of failed daily deal sites. So what happened? They screwed up the offer.

Daily deal sites frequently used a 50% off offer. That motivated online consumers by the truckload but wasn't sustainable for the offline businesses. The offer has to walk a fine line of motivational for consumers and sustainable for businesses.

Daily deals were like a "steroid" pumping up businesses fast but then leaving them with a small number of returning customers. What actually works is an "exercise program," like a 10–20% offer that won't drive in as many consumers but will ensure the business has a sustainable marketing source.

The Tracking

Most tracking solutions to connect the online world to the offline world didn't gain traction because they have friction that prevents them from becoming ubiquitous. By friction, I mean anything that requires additional behaviors for either the online consumer (showing a coupon, scanning a QR code, checking in, etc.) or the offline business (installing new hardware, modifying their POS system, or training their staff on a new app).

Daily deals had heavy friction in their tracking because they used the old-fashioned coupon. Even in a digital form, coupons have friction because the consumer has to show the coupon to the staff, which can get awkward on a business lunch or Tinder date. Coupons also require friction on the business owner's part to track the coupons and train staff how to redeem them.

The reason this friction didn't stop daily deals is because the "juice was worth the squeeze." Consumers and businesses alike will put up with friction as long as the reward is worth the pain the friction caused. The higher the reward, the more friction people will put up with. In the case of daily deals, the promise of thousands of new customers was enough for businesses to deal with the hassle of coupons, and for consumers the 50% offer was so compelling that they didn't mind using a coupon. But once you bring the offer into a more sustainable place like 10–20% off, suddenly the friction needs to be less or consumers just won't bite.

Thankfully there are new technologies and data emerging that can remove the friction. Here at Empyr we have formed a direct partnership with Visa, Mastercard, and American Express, so the offline transaction can be tracked using what we all already use to pay, any debit or credit card. This makes it frictionless for both consumers and businesses. Adios friction!

The Monetization

The last piece is pretty simple; you need to create a way for online companies to make money by marketing offline offers. Daily deals monetization strategy paid out about 25% of the purchase price to the online company that marketed the offline offer. This was very compelling and is the reason why just about every consumer-facing Internet company on the planet jumped into daily deals.

Here at Empyr we've created a similar monetization opportunity for O2O except this time the revenue share is more sustainable. The way it works is simple; offline businesses share a portion of the revenue they generate from a sale (usually around 10%) with the online company that drove in that sale. It's a pay-per-sale model for offline businesses, and it's a big revenue generator for the online companies because they make money on every offline purchase. Unlike daily deals, Empyr offers are always on, so the online companies that promote these offers make less than a daily deal in the short term but more in the long term, again like an exercise program rather than a steroid.

So just how big is this monetization opportunity? According to the US Chamber of Commerce, 93% of all commerce is offline, or $4.5 trillion dollars per year.

The Formula

In summary, the formula for a trillion dollar O2O industry is:

1. A compelling offer for consumers that is sustainable for businesses, such as 10–20%
2. A frictionless way to track the offline purchases, such as using credit/debit card tracking
3. A huge monetization opportunity to attract online companies who promote the offers

In a nutshell this is what we do at Empyr and why the time is finally here to build a large, sustainable online to offline industry.

Source: J. Carder, The formula to create a trillion dollar online to offline industry, *Empyr*, 2016

5.4.2 B2B

B2B is not just different from B2C because it is business to business rather than business to consumer. A business that produces goods will typically procure the same inputs from several suppliers using repeat orders and may sell to multiple business customers repeatedly, forming a long-term relationship.

There are several other distinctions. Firstly, B2B business usually involves orders of bulk volumes that may vary within each transaction. Bulk purchases increase the formality of contracts in B2B business. Secondly, because they are larger and so involve greater financial risk, B2B deals can be complex. For example, businesses vying for an order with a new corporate customer will invest a lot of time, resources, and energy on demonstrating their financial viability so that the purchasing business trusts them enough to place an order. During the fulfillment process, the seller must ensure that what is delivered meets contractual obligations. The customer can penalize the supplier, for example, by not paying the final installment. Thirdly, e-business processes can be knowledge-intensive and use specific technologies (e.g., enterprise resource planning or electronic data interchange, to be discussed below), so a company needs specialists to communicate the value of using e-business to another company that it aims to work with. Lastly, business activities between firms are conducted across various departments, which require intra- and interorganizational cooperation and collaboration. Some businesses may have a dedicated procurement unit to handle B2B e-commerce. Below are some modes of B2B e-business.

A Company's e-Business Site   Service providers offer ERP (enterprise resource planning), mobile computing services, cloud computing services, and other services through their websites. These websites are accessible only to authorized business clients because they contain "commercial-in-confidence" data. These clients can securely login in via the web at anytime and from anywhere. The sites may enable different levels of access and have a different system interface and various management authorizations, which depend on client needs and requirements. The ERP service provider gains revenue through selling or licensing the system and also from add-on services or management consulting. For example, IBM once focused on hardware-related businesses, particularly the production and merchandising of PCs. But with the intensification of competition on PCs, it became much more difficult for IBM to sustain its leading position in IT industry. So IBM pivoted its focus from the production of products to provision of IT-related services. This "servitization" strategy (shifting from manufacturing to services) re-created IBM's competitive advantage in the IT industry.

e-Procurement   Some companies may manage a complex variety of suppliers and partners with different procurement processes. E-Procurement companies provide solutions for companies to improve the management of their procurement activities, mitigate procurement risks, and enhance procurement performance. For example, SAP Ariba offers procurement software and cloud storage for its customers to collaborate more effectively on contract management and financial supply chain management. It provides a consistent online platform for suppliers and procurement companies and centrally and securely manages all processes from contracting to payments processing.

Vertical Market Network   A vertical market includes several businesses and customers that are interconnected around a particular niche market. The niche market may be specific to an industry, profession, or trade, or focused on a particular demographic with specialized needs (e.g., working mothers). Businesses in a vertical market share similar interests and may collaborate on joint research and development, or partner to manage their supply chains. A provider within a vertical market can typically charge a higher premium for providing specialized services to a market niche.

For example, ▶ Exostar.com provides information management services to highly regulated industries so that they may securely collaborate and mitigate risk throughout their value chains. The online vertical network platform is similar to a digital ecosystem because Exostar has enabled participants in highly regulated industries to achieve a mutually beneficial purpose. For more on digital ecosystems, see the article: "Creating a digital ecosystem that benefits your business."

Creating a Digital Ecosystem That Benefits Your Business

The digital landscape has changed remarkably in the past decade, and new advances in technology are paving the way for more revolution. Perhaps one way the digital transformation has changed business most is in the way we share information. In essence, the digital revolution has become the digital evolution. New advances in technology mean that businesses need to keep pace faster and faster if they want to survive in the world of big data.

We're no longer silos of enterprises, consumers, and things. Instead, we all share one digital ecosystem. Gartner defines a digital ecosystem as an "interdependent group of actors sharing standardized digital platforms to achieve a mutually beneficial purpose." In other words, it's a blurry line between business and industry. Here are five tips for building a clear and beneficial digital ecosystem with scalable collaborations.

Create an Open Collaborative Environment

Seek an environment that is digital ecosystem-ready, and get your company on board by preparing your organizational attitude and management. A recent survey by Gartner of more than 2500 chief information officers found that spending is on the rise for digitalization, despite only a modest increase in IT funding. Currently, CIOs are spending an average of 18 percent on digitalization; expect that number to increase to 28 percent by 2018. The research also revealed that the major differences between companies classified as top performers were the creation and participation of a digital ecosystem. To get to the top of the pack, enterprises must focus on their organizational capabilities. An IT skills gap will hinder your attempts to create a digital ecosystem; bimodal IT will be essential for companies in making a collaborative environment. This allows for the ready adoption of new technologies and adaptation of things and people into the ecosystem.

Foster Cooperative Relationships

Relationships are at the heart of business. The key to building and maintaining your digital ecosystem is to keep those relationships at the forefront. I think we sometimes fall into the trap of neglecting our customers' best interests in favor of maintaining our status quo. But we no longer have the luxury of standing still, especially when the markets are shifting so quickly because of the digital transformation. A market disruption is good in this case—provided your business is on the right side of the disruption. To remain competitive in an ever-changing marketplace, you need to build your digital ecosystem with a focus on customers. Listen to their concerns and frustrations, and be proactive in addressing their needs. Partner with those who share your vision—start-ups and entrepreneurs are masters at this approach, and it's time we took a page out of their book.

Support a Culture of Innovation

How do you organize your innovation? Do your new ideas follow a top-down processing approach? Truly collaborative environments tear down silos and foster collaboration at every level of business. Don't think about your business in terms of

5

hierarchy. Instead, embrace the idea that every member of your digital ecosystem is a valuable player who can drive the success of your enterprise. Create incentives for innovation, and consider how all partners and suppliers contribute to your business development. Partners will drive innovation and growth as you adopt, consume, scale, and leverage innovation for a lasting impact. We see this in the tech industry all the time with open source software and coding project. It works!

Assemble Agile Management

The need for your business to be agile has never been greater. However, agility is no longer capable of keeping a business ahead; it merely lets you keep up with the pack. Managers must ensure their organizations can pivot with market shifts, even dropping or switching partnerships if the going gets too rough. The ability to adapt to new conditions will be a driving factor in maintaining your digital ecosystem, as partners and suppliers change and customer needs evolve.

Invest in the Right Digital Technology

A holistic ecosystem is a conglomerate of people, things, businesses, and technology. Invest in both core and emerging technologies to build your digital ecosystem DNA. Cloud services, analytics, management, and security are currently the biggest planned investments in technology, according to the Gartner report. A differentiated approach is essential to modernizing your technology core and preparing your enterprise for the future.

Those who invest in creating a digital ecosystem will find themselves better prepared to take on the challenges of modern business. It's an exciting time for business, and I think the collaboration between members in an ecosystem will only benefit consumers in the long run.

D. Newman, "Creating A Digital Ecosystem That Benefits Your Business," *Forbes*, 20 December 2016

Open Online Marketplace   This refers to a marketplace for companies to seek potential business partners and make online purchases. This online marketplace is different from e-procurement service companies, even though it supports e-procurement too. It focuses on promoting platform-intermediated transactions, so that the marketplace provider can take a percentage of each transaction. For example, Alibaba's ▶ 1688. com and Amazon Business are two online B2B marketplaces. They allow suppliers and e-retailers worldwide to use their platform to find new clients and broaden markets.

5.4.3 C2C

When it comes to a realm without an explicit business agent such as C2C and G2G, these e-business models do not have to generate financial value. For example, non-profit companies create online "green" communities for volunteers to communicate the value of environment protection to local citizens. This creates social value rather than financial value. Hence, C2C businesses cannot be evaluated solely from a business perspective; in some cases they should identify the social, emotional, or environmental value of a C2C business. Companies can also seize business opportunities from C2C businesses. For example, establishing an online marketplace for used items, such as Craigslist, not only facilitates the re-purposing of unused items but also allows the marketplace to profit from transactions in a way that is similar to the eBay model.

C2C e-business is not as developed as B2B or B2C e-business because popular C2C business platforms are still emerging, particularly those that use social media and mobile devices. C2C e-business is significantly different from B2B or B2C e-business. Basically, it provides a platform that mobilizes the skills, knowledge, and resources of participants to create socialized value. The productive role of the firm in C2C business is weakened. Contrarily, a firm can play a supportive role in facilitating the consumer value creation and capture process. Firms can provide platforms, resources, incentives, and information security to empower every individual to create value. Below are some types of C2C businesses.

Online Transaction Platform   This refers to an online platform where sellers and buyers all are individual users. The platform may generate revenues by taking a small percentage of each sale. For example, eBay facilitates the sale and purchase of goods between consumers (typically not businesses) of new and used items.

Online Social Platform   Consumers enjoy social interactions with other consumers on online platforms such as Facebook. Basically, there are two approaches for an online social platform to monetize social platform users. They can directly monetize users by charging a subscription fee, or take a percentage of users' commercial activities as in an online marketplace. On the other hand, social platforms can sell advertisements or paid placements. For example, Facebook is an online social platform, and its major business model is based on advertising, which represents more than 90% of total income.

Online Classifieds Platform   This kind of platform provides diverse classifieds for users such as tutoring, lodging, selling pets, delivery services, etc. The classifieds platform usually services local citizens and may sell advertising or paid placements. It differs to transaction platforms in that the transaction may be negotiated offline rather than via the platform. For example, consumers can offer services informally via Craigslist.

Online Crowdfunding Platform   This new e-business model has emerged in recent years and is based on the Long Tail theory of Chris Anderson (see Anderson, 2006), which has been described elsewhere in this book. For example, Kickstarter is one of the most popular online crowdfunding platforms. People who want to develop a new venture or project can create a proposal and ask others to fund them, with incentives and rewards for doing so. For example, an artist may seek funds to record an album in a major studio, and in return funders can receive a copy of the new album. The value of online crowdfunding is more than purely financial rewards, but also offers intangible social rewards to customers who support projects on the site, sometimes to the extent that the projects become real sustainable businesses. It largely promotes individual or small team entrepreneurship. Anyone who cannot fund their dream by themselves can use Kickstarter to potentially reach and leverage a large population that has the willingness to invest. But people would not get funded just by putting an idea on these online crowdfunding platforms; they need a clear strategy and mission, to project their ideas simply and powerfully so that they stand out from other people who are seeking investment funds on Kickstarter (see the FT article: "How to get the most from crowdfunding — and the risks to avoid").

5

How to Get the Most from Crowdfunding—and the Risks to Avoid

For something that is considered a very "now" way of raising money, crowdfunding has its roots in something very old-school: prog rock. It is generally acknowledged that modern crowdfunding was invented by Marillion, a band better known for "Kayleigh" (and a generation of girls bearing the name) than for technological innovation. In 1997, short of cash to make its next album, the band emailed its 6000-strong database of fans asking if they would buy the album in advance. Some 12,000 advance orders later, the album was made, and the idea of offering perks in return for speculatively stumping up cash was born.

Two decades on and crowdfunding is part of the financial landscape for start-ups that want either to raise cash additional to venture capital funding or to get a nifty idea off the ground. The main platforms are Kickstarter and Indiegogo, but there are many others, from GoFundMe, which is used for donations to personal projects, and JustGiving, which raises cash for causes and charities, to MyFreeImplants, which helps women to raise money to pay for cosmetic surgery. Would-be donors are exhorted to "help the women of your dreams achieve the body of their dreams."

Christian Smith, founder of TrackR, which makes Bluetooth tracking tags for items from keys to pets, harnessing what he calls "crowd GPS" to locate lost items, used Indiegogo to raise more than $1.75 m in 2014 to fund the business. However, that was supplementary funding: before taking to Indiegogo, Smith had already done a preliminary funding round and has since added more than $10 m from venture capital. Meanwhile he has another Indiegogo campaign under way for further product development which has raised more than $210,000 so far.

Smith stresses that crowdfunding is not a case of putting a project on Kickstarter or Indiegogo and waiting for the cash to roll in. Indeed, according to a study commissioned by Kickstarter and carried out by Ethan Mollick of the University of Pennsylvania, "careful planning is required both to set these goals [of delivering a product on time] and to prepare for a crowdfunding success." Smith stresses the preparation he put in. "We set up our own crowdfunding site to test the response and conversion for the TrackR wallet and after we had raised a bit of money on our site, then we took it to Indiegogo." Building an audience before launching is important, he says. "You want to be in conversation with hundreds or thousands of people before you launch. If you can understand what they're interested in and get them interested in what's brewing, then people will be more interested when you do launch."

The "conversation" part of this is key. Being well-known can propel your project to undreamed of heights. Exploding Kittens is a card game created by computer game designers Elan Lee and Shane Small, and Matthew Inman, founder of the hugely popular online comic The Oatmeal. The game launched last year looking for a modest $10,000. The immediate buzz on Twitter drove supporters straight to the crowdfunding page. Eight minutes later, Exploding Kittens had exceeded its goal, and when the project closed less than a month later, it had raised $8.8 m. By the time the game shipped in the summer, it had become the most backed Kickstarter of all time, with 219,382 supporters.

However, there are also spectacular failures. Zano, a mini-drone, raised more than £2 m from 12,000 backers, yet failed to get off the ground when its creators could not make it work. To its credit, Kickstarter, which says "active governance is important to our platform; trust is important," commissioned Mark Harris, a freelance journalist, to write a comprehensive postmortem of the Zano project, giving Harris complete editorial freedom. The result revealed, in his view, that there had been hubris and overreaching from the company, as well as poor financial controls.

Kickstarter has resources for founders and would-be founders, such as the on-line Creator Handbook. The problem with crowdfunding, however, is that it leaves due diligence up to backers. A Kickstarter campaign for Shield "signal-proof hats" achieved its funding goal of £13,000 despite allegations that the hats were based on pseudoscience and fear of "electrosmog." Kickstarter received complaints about the project but left it running. Failures inevitably dent confidence in crowdfunding, yet the big successes mean it is nonetheless an attractive way of raising capital. So what is the lesson for entrepreneurs? If you have done your homework and have a clear strategy for engagement, well-defined manufacturing processes in place, and a project that catches the imagination, then you stand a good chance of hitting your target while avoiding the need to give VC funders a stake in your business.

And what of TrackR? Problems with delivery soured the relationship with its backers, though Smith says: "We did our best to be very open with what was happening on the engineering side." He warns: "A lot of problems you'll face are unexpected." But the TrackR devices are in some ways a metaphor for crowdfunding itself. The tags work by checking in with other people's phones running the app, which is great if you leave your phone in a New York restaurant. However, TrackR clearly has yet to catch on in West London, as the app could not locate my cat. And there's the thing: crowdsourcing has to tap into enough of the right people to be really effective. [...]

Adapted from K. Bevan "How to get the most from crowdfunding — and the risks to avoid," *Financial Times*, 22 May 2016

Online Crowdsourcing Platform   This refers to a platform on which individuals can outsource their tasks to others. A crowdsourcing platform can be used by companies or individuals to reach a large population of online users. For example, Amazon's Mechanical Turk is an online crowdsourcing platform. Participants may post a survey on the platform and quickly receive many responses. The cost of doing so is low in comparison to regular face-to-face surveys. 99designs is another crowdsourcing platform, and it focuses on crowdsourced graphic designs. A client may post a design brief on the platform and choose from one of the four packages that the platform offers (with different payment terms). Upon payment, the project is turned into a contest between more than one million professionals on the platform. The client chooses the winner, and they win a prize.

Sharing Economy   The sharing economy business model overlaps with other C2C business models to some extent. This new business model depends on the sharing of resources. Airbnb is a typical case of sharing economy. House owners can offer rooms or an entire home to Airbnb members. This way, house owners are able to use assets that otherwise may lie dormant, and Airbnb charges a booking fee per each successful transaction. Some online platforms—such as social platforms that focus on sharing digital content—can also be viewed as a kind of sharing economy.

The asset structure of businesses based on the sharing economy is usually light because the assets are owned (and shared) by others. For more details on the sharing economy, please read the article "What exactly is the sharing economy?" -asset business model because most firm assets are owned by others.

> ### What Exactly Is the Sharing Economy?
>
> When I first attended Davos in January 2013, I asked everyone I met if they'd heard of the term "sharing economy." Ninety percent of people said no, 5% assumed I was talking about barter exchange, and the remaining 5% acknowledged new technologies, and peer-to-peer networks were enabling emergent business models. It was difficult to find anyone who had used Airbnb or BlaBlaCar. Later that year I co-founded the Forum's Sharing Economy Working Group with other Young Global Leaders, with the goal of building awareness, visibility, and expertise throughout the Forum's communities.
>
> Fast forward to 2017 and the reality is vastly different. Not only is the sharing economy in the news daily, it also has spurred a growing—and at times mind-boggling—list of related terms. To many people, the sharing economy and gig economy are the same thing. But in fact, almost nothing could be further from the truth. […] As the sharing economy has grown, it has become a victim of its own success. Some people have charged that much of today's sharing economy is not really "sharing," an allegation that is partly right. While on the one hand, there are many platforms that espouse the true spirit of sharing—underutilized assets and building community—on the other hand, increasingly there is "sharewashing" going on: companies latching onto the term because it makes them part of a hot trend. Who doesn't want to conjure up notions of community and cooperation?
>
> An example of terminology confusion is Uber. Is it ridesharing when a driver leases out a car that they did not own before, in order to provide rides that they would not have taken otherwise? Hardly. Yet, too much of the public and media, Uber is one of the most touted examples of the sharing economy. That said, newer offerings such as Lyft Line and UberPool are wonderful examples of ridesharing: they enable more efficient use of cars, full stop. But they represent only a fraction of current rides provided. More broadly, when an entrepreneur claims to be the "Uber of X," that is an immediate red flag of questionable sharing-economy status.
>
> So what is the sharing economy? And how should we distinguish among the various "new economy" models in the headlines? Here is a summary list that will

clarify the confusion and provide guidance to companies, policymakers, individuals, and investors alike:

- *Sharing economy*: focus on the sharing of underutilized assets, monetized or not, in ways that improve efficiency, sustainability, and community.
- *Collaborative economy*: focus on collaborative forms of consumption, production, finance, and learning ("collaborative consumption" is closest to the orthodox sharing economy definition).
- *On-demand economy*: focus on "on-demand" (i.e., immediate and access-based) provision of goods and services.
- *Gig economy*: focus on workforce participation and income generation via "gigs," single projects, or tasks for which a worker is hired (limited overlap with skill sharing).
- *Freelance economy*: focus on workforce participation and income generation by freelancers, also known as independent workers and self-employed (limited overlap with skill sharing; freelance engagements are often longer and/or deeper than gigs).
- *Peer economy*: focus on peer-to-peer (P2P) networks in the creation of products, delivery of services, funding, and more.
- *Access economy*: focus on "access over ownership" (overlaps with sharing, though sharing is by no means requisite).
- *Crowd economy*: focus on economic models powered by "the crowd," including but not limited to crowdsourcing and crowdfunding.
- *Digital economy*: focus on anything powered by digital technologies.
- *Platform economy*: focus on anything powered by tech-centric platforms.

It is entirely possible that one platform can fall under multiple definitions. For example, TaskRabbit is arguably part of the on-demand, gig, collaborative, and sharing (assuming the Tasker's skills were previously underutilized) economies. Airbnb's homesharing inventory is clearly part of the sharing economy, while full-time short-term corporate rentals are not necessarily so and more likely are in the access economy.

Moreover, the sharing economy is not defined the same way around the world. Nowhere is this more apparent than in China. Ever since declaring the sharing economy a national priority in 2015, and that sharing would comprise 10% of China's GDP by 2020, the Chinese government has taken an increasingly broad view toward what is included.

Today, what we term the digital economy in the West—for example, Amazon and Netflix—China defines as the sharing economy. The result is a unique set of nuances and challenges, not least for policymakers and economists trying to measure its size and impact and media trying to report accurately on the issue.

The sharing economy is not black and white: it is a spectrum, and it is increasingly crucial to understand its different shades. Ultimately it will become simply part of the economy, without special terminology, but we are not there yet. Entrepreneurs, journalists, governments, and (perhaps most of all) users of and participants in these new economy platforms have a duty to be clear about whether and what we are, and are not, sharing.

Source: A. Rinne, "What exactly is the sharing economy?," *World Economic Forum*, 13 December 2017

5.4.4 Government-Related e-Business Models

The role of government as an important economic agent cannot be overlooked. When reviewing government-related e-business models, note that governments also consider nonfinancial factors before launching IT-based business activities such as social governance, citizens' welfare, social impacts, politics, environment, and more.[12]

Paperwork-Related e-Business Models   Governments use information and communication technologies to replace physical paperwork. Services where e-business has replaced paperwork include the issue, renewal, or legalization of documents including identity cards, passports, licenses, election cards, contracts, and transactions. The replacement of paperwork with e-business also streamlines processes and so is more efficient for citizens. For example, in 2014 the Estonian government created a new virtual residency, or e-residency, that allows non-Estonian residents access to Estonian government services including company formation and taxation. Upon registering online, the Estonian government supplies them with a smart card that includes their digital identity and which can be used to sign documents electronically. The program was successful, despite two separate security incidents. Another example is e-registration: the online registration of contracts. Many contracts or transactions may need to be notarized to have legality and enforceability. E-registration and e-citizenship are designed to significantly reduce the amount of paperwork.

e-Transportation   It refers to government services related to road, rail, water, or air transportation. In detail, it includes various online-enabled activities: (1) ticketing; (2) vehicles status; (3) drivers licensing; and (4) payments of transportation fees or taxes. Citizens in many cities now use smart cards for public transport, and the cards are linked to a customers' bank account to automatically top up when funds run low.

e-Health   e-Health refers to the management and enablement by governments of digital patient medical records and their use within medical providers including hospitals and doctors. e-Health can enable doctors to see all medical records and services that have been provided to a patient, so they can provide a more holistic diagnosis. This approach helps citizens who move frequently (where often medical records remain behind in physical filing cabinets), and the aggregate database of medical records can be analyzed to identify, prevent, and control outbreaks of infectious diseases. However the centralized retention of such records raises privacy and security concerns.

e-Democracy   Democracy needs the participation of citizens. Government "e-democracy" strategies and tools can enable citizens to engage in democratic processes digitally, including voting, voicing opinions and providing feedback, and lobbying. Governments may choose to openly release large-scale data sets on their

---

12 This section is adapted from A. A. Joshi, Scope of E-Governance, *E-Governance in India*, 2008.

services, policies, decisions, and activities to increase transparency for government accountability. When combined with the declining cost, increasing power, and ease of use of data mining and filtering software, citizens and journalists can now identify malpractice in the public service.

For example, in 2009 under a Freedom of Information request, a journalist in the United Kingdom was provided with over a million documents relating to expense claims of Members of Parliament (MPs) in paper format. To analyze them for any mistaken claims, a team of journalists scanned them into cloud-based storage and made them publicly available online with software search tools. They invited citizens to analyze the claims of their local MPs and to highlight any that were questionable for the journalists to investigate. 170,000 documents were reviewed in the first 80 hours, and within a few months about half of the 460,000 claim documents were reviewed by 26,774 registered readers (Daniel and Flew, 2010). In response to errors found and media reportage, the government launched a full investigation into MP expense claims and found, of those that had not been repaid before the investigation, over £1 m were deemed improper and four MPs stood trial for fraud.[13]

In practice there are many challenges in this strategy, and they are explored in the FT article: "The dangers of digital democracy".

e-Administration   Information and communications technologies can underpin the digital administration of government, internally and externally. e-Administration aims to reduce the communication friction between different departments, to streamline operations, and increase the rate of responsiveness to citizens.

e-Police   e-Police refers to the use of information and communication technologies in police activities such as interrogating databases of criminal records to narrow the scope of an investigation, or communicating or sharing files digitally. e-Police is distinct from and broader than cyber police, which is a sub-branch of policing that focuses on reducing cybercrimes.

e-Court   This refers to the use of ICT in judicial processes. For example, modern courts can include remote participants in court hearings via videoconferencing, they may send online summons and warrants, and make available on specialized portals the content of judgments and decrees.

e-Taxation   Taxes are a major income source of government, and in many countries, citizens can fill in and submit their tax returns online, and the processing and payments of taxes and duties can also be made online through e-taxation platforms. Citizens can enter their bank details for the tax office to directly deposit their tax returns. The tax office in some jurisdictions can also connect to banks to scrutinize activities in bank accounts of persons under investigation.

---

13 A. A. Joshi, Scope of E-Governance, *E-Governance in India*, 2008, p. 4.

e-Tendering   This refers to the use of ICT in online tendering and procurement. Some governments use online procurement tools for their tenders. This means that online public tendering is more transparent, applications are received and recorded systematically, and the process can be accessed by all possible tenderers.

Undoubtedly, governments can seize various benefits from e-businesses, and by doing so, they can increase the welfare of citizens, businesses, and society. In many cases, major technology companies collaborate with governments and public institutions because there are benefits to both. Governments may need technology businesses because they can typically innovate faster than governments. Businesses need governments who represent a large customer base and source of work. However, this is a two-sided sword with several challenges. On the one hand, government officials may seek access to the citizen data these companies manage, for example, to avoid crimes or terrorist attacks. On the other hand, the supply of that data may expose individuals to perceived Orwellian-like governmental surveillance and invasions of privacy. This is why major technology companies are still reluctant to enable access by government officials to their customer databases. Brands, reputation, and trust are important key resources in business models.

The Dangers of Digital Democracy

Justin Trudeau, Prime Minister of Canada, had a great line in his Davos speech last week: "The pace of change has never been this fast, and yet it will never be this slow again." For me, that was the key message of the World Economic Forum. The headlines may have talked about President Donald Trump's "America first" speech, but the back story was the fragility of nation states in a time of technological change.

The topic of "the digital economy and society" was the most popular this year at the WEF in terms of the number of sessions and social media buzz—and no wonder. The dirty secret of Davos is that the much-lauded "Fourth Industrial Revolution"—shorthand for the rise of ubiquitous automation, big data, and artificial intelligence—is making most people less, not more, secure, at least in the short term. The ability of a range of companies—in insurance, healthcare, retail, and consumer goods—to personalize almost every kind of product and service based on data streams is not just a business model shift. It is a fundamental challenge to liberal democracy.

Consider the changes being wrought in the insurance business. For 200 years, it has been based on the notion of risk pooling: average the cost of insuring individual homes, cars, and lives, and then divide the cost among the collective. In the age of data, insurance groups will be able to take information from tracking boxes in our cars or sensors embedded in our homes and use it to craft hyper-personalized policies. For example, you might be rewarded for putting a new plumbing system into your own old house (the sensors will measure how well it works), or stopping more quickly at red lights. But you might also be blamed when your 16-year-old puffs weed in his bedroom (smoke detectors will relay the message to your insurer in real time), or if you fail to shovel the snow off the front stoop before it ices up (now insurers could know exactly when and if you did and limit their own risk of liability if a passerby slips). Of course, you'll be able to opt in and out of all this, though probably not very transparently or cheaply (consider that on commercial platforms such as Facebook or Google, you basically have to forfeit your rights to use the product or service easily). But the more disturbing implication is that there may now be an uninsurable underclass who can no longer be floated by averaging. Who will insure them? Most likely subprime lenders or the state.

Another dirty secret of the digital age. Just as the US government has for years subsidized low-cost retailers that do not pay their workers a living wage, the government will probably be asked to underwrite the safety net for a new digital underclass. The problem is that the public sector does not have the capacity to do this. It is coping with trillions of dollars of debt that has been created since the financial crisis, not to mention more partisan politics that make it tough to create consensus on much of anything. As digital bifurcation grows, it is very likely that disenchantment with the state will increase as well, fueling the vicious cycle of political disenchantment and dysfunctional economics.

The other risk is that rather than demanding more, not only of governments but of the companies that are monetizing our data, citizens will remain passive. It's a topic that financier George Soros addressed in his speech at Davos, where he noted that technology groups were "inducing people to give up their autonomy... it takes a real effort to assert and defend what John Stuart Mill called 'the freedom of mind'. There is a possibility that once lost, people who grow up in the digital age will have difficulty in regaining it." Mr Soros noted the risk of "alliances between authoritarian states and these large, data-rich IT monopolies that would bring together nascent systems of corporate surveillance with an already developed system of state-sponsored surveillance." It sounds Orwellian, but it is the state of play in China, where the country's big technology groups and the government are closely aligned. Indeed, some of the digital scientists I spoke to in Davos professed envy for the ease of data gathering even as they expressed their concerns about the political implications.

This is why the most optimistic moment I had in Davos was with Illah Nourbakhsh, a Professor at the Robotics Institute of Carnegie Mellon, who, having become quite worried about the points I have just made, launched a project to educate elementary school children about the power of data, its risks and rewards, and how to use it to advocate for themselves. Under the scheme, children might track, say, the number of cars idling outside their school, calculate the potential pollution generated, and then call a family meeting to discuss how to "challenge the incumbent power structures," as Mr Nourbakhsh says (translation: push their principal for new parking rules).

The idea is to create a new generation of citizen scientists who understand the power of data. I predict that if they truly do, they will start to demand a lot more ownership and control over it themselves.

Source: R. Foroohar, The dangers of digital democracy, *Financial Times*, 28 January 2018

5

Summary

This chapter focused on strategic options in e-business markets. First, it reviewed generic strategy options for value creation in e-business. These options revolved around cost leadership and differentiation strategies.

Secondly, this chapter discussed the concept of being stuck in the middle, which refers to companies that focus on neither a cost leadership nor a differentiation strategy. These companies face the risk of not possessing any competitive advantage vis-à-vis more specialized rivals. However, there are also factors that can allow a firm to outpace its rivals by offering both lower costs and differentiation. These include the development of new technologies, wastefulness of companies, scale economies, and learning effects.

Thirdly, this chapter discussed how to create a better fit between the chosen strategy and value chain activities in order to achieve a sustainable competitive advantage. It described the three main levers that determine the fit of activities within a firm. These are consistency between activities, reinforcement of activities, and optimization of efforts.

Fourthly, this chapter introduced the concept and importance of business models. It illustrates how to use business model canvas to design and analyze a business model synthetically.

Finally, this chapter presented major e-business models. They are B2B, B2C, C2C, and government-related e-business models.

❓ Review Questions

1. What generic strategies can a company use to create value for its customers?
2. What levers can a company use in e-business to create a cost or a differentiation strategy?
3. Why do some companies end up being "stuck in the middle"?
4. What are the factors that allow a company to pursue an outpacing strategy?
5. What are the three main levers that determine the fit of activities within a firm?
6. What is a business model? Why is it important for e-business strategy?
7. What are the nine components of a business model?
8. What are major e-business models? What are the differences between them?
9. Analyze how the Internet can help companies not to get "stuck in the middle." Illustrate your answer through an actual example.
10. Discuss how an Internet venture can outperform its competitors on both the price and quality dimensions. Provide some examples to support your arguments.
11. Consider an Internet venture that you are familiar with, and think of ways in which it could further improve the fit between its activities through consistency, reinforcement, and optimization.
12. Select an e-business company, and use business model canvas to analyze its business model.
13. Imagine you are going to start an e-business, and design a specific e-business model for your business.

References

Anderson, C. (2006). *The long tail. Why the future of business is selling less of more.* New York: Hyperion.

Besanko, D., Dranove, D., Shanley, M., & Schaefer, S. (2003). *Economics of strategy* (pp. 416–419). John Wiley.

Casadesus-Masanell, R., & Ricart, J. E. (2010). From strategy to business models and onto tactics. *Long Range Planning, 43*(2–3), 204.

Chesbrough, H. W. (2006). *Open innovation: The new imperative for creating and profiting from technology* (pp. 63–92). Boston: Harvard Business Press.

Daniel, A., & Flew, T. (2010). The Guardian reportage of the UK MP expenses scandal: a case study of computational journalism. In *Record of the Communications Policy and Research Forum 2010* (pp. 186–194). Sydney: Network Insight Pty. Ltd..

George, G., & Bock, A. J. (2011). The business model in practice and its implications for entrepreneurship research. *Entrepreneurship Theory and Practice, 35*(1), 102.

Hough, J. (2017). Tech giants play the game of thrones. *Barrons.*

Hungenberg, H. (2014). *Strategisches management in unternehmen.* Gabler.

Jelassi, T., Enders, A., & Martínez-López, F. J. (2005). *Strategies for e-business: creating value through electronic and mobile commerce: concepts and cases* (p. 112). Pearson Education.

Jelassi, T., Enders, A., & Martínez-López, F. J. (2014). *Strategies for e-business: creating value through electronic and mobile commerce: concepts and cases* (p. 109). Pearson Education.

Kotler, P. (2002). *Marketing management.* Prentice Hall.

Laudon, K. C., & Traver, C. G. (2017). *E-commerce: Business, technology, society* (10th ed.). Pearson.

Liebowitz, S. (2002). *Rethinking the network economy* (pp. 115–117). Amacom.

Osterwalder, A., & Pigneur, Y. (2020). *The invincible company: Business model strategies from the world's best products, services, and organizations.* New Jersey: Wiley.

Porter, M. (1996). What is strategy?, Harvard Business Review (pp. 70–73).

Solsman, J. E. (2013). Bezos to post: You too can be like Amazon, in 3 simple steps. *CNet.*

Further Reading

M. Porter's book Competitive Strategy, Free Press, 1998, provides detailed accounts of different generic strategy types.

B. Henderson emphasises the importance of differentiation as a key element in strategy formulation when he compares strategy to biological evolution in 'The origins of strategy', Harvard Business Review, 1989, November–December, pp. 139–143.

An updated approach to e-business models can be found in 'Value creation in e-business models' (by A. Rodríguez, F. Sandulli and D. Sánchez), F.J. Martínez-López (Ed.) Research Handbook on e-business Strategic Management, Series PROGRESS in IS, Springer, 2013.

George, G., & Bock, A. J. (2011). The business model in practice and its implications for entrepreneurship research. *Entrepreneurship Theory and Practice, 35*(1), 83–111.

Weblinks

www.ecommercetimes.com is an online newspaper containing articles on a variety of e-commerce topics.

www.strategy-business.com is the online edition of the management magazine strategy+business (s+b).

https://canvanizer.com/new/business-model-canvas is a site for creating business model canvases.

Creating and Sustaining a Competitive Advantage over Time

Contents

© Springer Nature Switzerland AG 2020
T. Jelassi, F. J. Martínez-López, *Strategies for e-Business*, Classroom Companion: Business,
https://doi.org/10.1007/978-3-030-48950-2_6

Learning Outcomes

After completing this chapter, you should be able to:

- Understand the requirements for a successful imitation and the barriers to imitation
- Appreciate how companies can assess the threat of a disruptive innovation
- Identify the ways that companies can follow in order to deal with a disruptive innovation
- Recognize the cognitive frames that companies can adopt when facing a disruptive innovation and understand the reasons underlying their contradicting nature

■ Introduction

This chapter firstly discusses the fundamentals of competitive advantage and how a company can create and sustain it. It then focuses on how to deal with the threats of a disruptive innovation in e-business. More specifically, it stresses the importance of understanding the fundamental process of disruptive innovations and determining the underlying reasons for the incumbent's failure. Next, the chapter suggests some questions that companies need to ask in order to assess the threat of a disruptive innovation. Possible ways for dealing with a disruptive innovation are then suggested. The chapter concludes by providing some ways for selecting the appropriate cognitive frame (mindset) for an efficient response to a disruptive innovation.

6.1 Understanding the Fundamentals of Competitive Advantage in e-Business

The analyses of external opportunities and threats and internal strengths and weaknesses are important steps in the strategy formulation process. Yet, ultimately they provide only the basis for deciding how a company is to compete in the marketplace. The decision about competitive positioning is at the heart of strategy development, which is the focus of this chapter.

Since the concept of competitive advantage is not trivial, it is useful to look at the requirements that need to be fulfilled in order to gain this type of advantage vis-à-vis rival firms. The strategic triangle (see ◘ Fig. 6.1) addresses the main drivers of competitive advantage. In essence, a company needs to take into account customer needs, competitors' offerings, and its own offering. The goal of this framework is to address the following four questions regarding the underlying drivers of competitive advantage:

1. Is the price/benefit ratio (also called value for money) that we offer better than the price/benefit ratio of our best competitor? Having only a low price is usually not enough to entice a customer to purchase a product (or a service). In addition, the product needs to fulfill minimum customer requirements to be considered attractive. Similarly, a product with a superior performance still needs to be priced within the range of the customer's ability to pay.

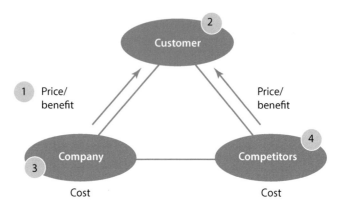

6

◘ Fig. 6.1 The strategic triangle addresses the main drivers of competitive advantage. (Source: Adapted from Hungenberg, 2014, p. 185)

2. *Is the value that we offer to our customers perceivable and important to them?* Customers need to be able to recognize the value of the product that is offered to them, and they also need to consider it to be important and worth paying for.
3. *Are the costs for making the product (or service) lower than the revenue that it generates?* This requirement should be quite obvious; however, during the Internet heyday (until 2000), there were numerous business models that had such a high cost structure that it would have been difficult to offset these costs through revenues. For instance, at that time an online pet food retailer was offering free shipping, which turned out to be an unprofitable business proposition, since the shipping costs (think about a 20 lb dog food bag) destroyed any margins that might have existed in that business.
4. *Is this advantageous position sustainable into the future?* Once actual and would-be competitors find out that a specific way of running a business proves successful, they will typically attempt to imitate this source of competitive advantage. Although companies rarely succeed in building a competitive advantage that is sustainable for an extended period of time, companies such as eBay and XING managed to create a sustainable advantage through strong network effects.

The framework depicted above highlights the fact that the creation of benefits, as perceived by customers, presents one core element of strategic decision-making. In this context, it is useful to differentiate between two kinds of benefits: (1) those that customers consider to be *threshold features* and (2) those that they consider to be *critical success factors*.[1]

- *Threshold features* are the minimum requirements that a firm must fulfill in any product or service. If a firm cannot meet these minimum requirements, then it will get excluded from the market because customers will not even consider that firm's offering. A threshold feature might be, for example, a website with

---

1   For a detailed discussion of threshold features and success, see Johnson et al. (2005).

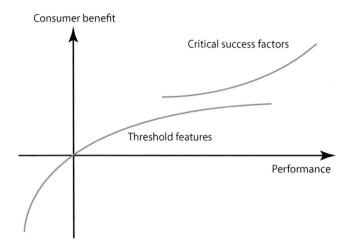

◘ Fig. 6.2 Impact of threshold features and critical success factors on consumer benefit. (Source: Adapted from Hungenberg, 2006, p. 185)

functioning links or a secure payment mechanism for online transactions. Improving threshold features beyond a certain point has only a marginal impact on customer satisfaction (see ◘ Fig. 6.2), which implies that these types of features are not suitable for differentiating a product.

— *Critical success factors*, on the other hand, are those crucial benefits for a customer's decision regarding a given offer. At ▶ Amazon.com, these features include the large selection of books, their reviews, as well as the convenient and fast shopping experience that is made possible through the company's one-click ordering application. At Nordea Bank, critical success factors include the ease of use of the online banking site and the variety of e-business services that are offered through it.

To summarize, both threshold features and critical success factors create consumer benefit, but only the latter help a firm to differentiate itself from its competitors by creating superior consumer benefit.

6.2 Creating Competitive Advantage Through e-Business

Many companies try to profit from e-business, and many have failed. This is because technology does not generate revenue per se, while buyers or payers do. Moreover, from a customer view, competitive advantage is the extent to which a firm distinguishes its product or service from other competitors. Hence, creating competitive advantage is critical for the success of e-business. We will illustrate a traditional company business model to create competitive advantage and then highlight the role of e-business integration in creating competitive advantage.[2]

---

2   This section is adopted from Pavic (2011).

6.2.1 A Traditional Company Business Model to Create Competitive Advantage

Basically, the creation of competitive advantage needs to meet two conditions (Ghemawat and Rivkin, 1998). On the one hand, a firm must be able to provide something unique and valuable, so that someone in the firm's network such as suppliers, consumers, and partners would miss it and no one contemporarily can substitute its position. On the other hand, competitive advantage does not derive from some star employees or core departments, but depends on the full range of a firm's activities from design to post-purchase service. These two prerequisites for creating competitive advantage indicate that competitive advantage is an outcome systematically influenced by internal and external aspects.

In order to create competitive advantage, a traditional company needs to conduct supporting and primary activities to mobilize resources and foster capabilities, wherein IT infrastructure plays a supportive role in this process (see ❏ Fig. 6.3). A firm's competitive advantage is jointly determined by its internal aspects, for example, resources and capabilities, and external factors, for example, its competitive environment, which could be represented by Porter's five forces and other general aspects of its business environment. This advantage leads to profits and organizational growth, which enables the company to spend more resources on this

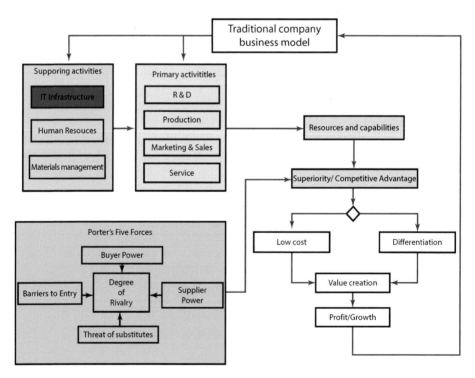

❏ **Fig. 6.3** The process of creating competitive advantage. (Source: Adapted from Pavic, 2011, p. 227)

process. Based on this model, a company plays a key role in creating its competitive advantage. The creation is internal to an organizational action and iterative from a previous outcome generated by the process. This insight also reinforces that competitive advantage cannot be created solely by star employees or core tech departments, as previously mentioned. Leaders need to infuse a strategic mindset or strategic thinking into this business model and organize internal and external aspects strategically and holistically. Regarding the current business environment where new technologies and disruptive innovation emerge every day, leaders need to play three roles in managing the current situation and turning creativity into competitive advantage. For more details see the article: "Leaders can turn creativity into a competitive advantage."

Leaders Can Turn Creativity into a Competitive Advantage

In 1985, Peter Drucker made a hopeful case for an entrepreneurial society in which innovation and the creation of new businesses would more than compensate for job losses stemming from the retreat of manufacturing industries in the United States and other developed economies. Since then, the United States has increasingly come to rely on innovation and entrepreneurship to drive growth—but we haven't achieved the scale of entrepreneurial society we need to offset the effects of globalization and automation.

One reason for this is the increasing speed of change itself. Technological innovations like high-speed trading and digital marketing enable competitors to emerge, thrive, and disrupt companies far faster than ever before. This "VUCA" environment rewards innovation, but it also punishes failure more harshly. The result is that while we may be creating many new businesses, we are destroying existing ones faster than ever before. The average life span of companies in the Fortune 500 has dropped precipitously over recent decades. A second reason is that our assumptions about good management practices are out of date. Since the 1980s, management practices like the Toyota Production System that promote efficiency, quality, and scale have done wonders to lift the quality and profitability of global manufacturing. But in a business environment that is spectacularly unpredictable in almost every way, efficiency is no longer the most sensible—or at least not the only sensible—strategy.

What we need is a shift in emphasis from operational competitiveness toward creative competitiveness—the capacity of organizations and society to create, embrace, and successfully execute on new ideas. How can we foster creative competitiveness, especially in big, established corporate ecosystems? All of our management practices need to be updated: how organizations are structured, how we deploy capital, how we interact and collaborate with broader networks, what tools and technology we embrace and deploy, what we measure, what markets we target, who we hire, and how we lead. Of these, how we lead and the kind of culture we create are the essential starting points.

When our goal is efficiency, our concept of governance includes ensuring standardization, high levels of coordination, careful assessment of risk, and, of course,

6

the elimination of waste. When we want to be creatively fit, governance looks quite different. It should be, and feel, more nurturing. It should focus on speed of learning and rigorous experimentation. It benefits from an attitude of abundance. Nurturing a creatively competitive organization requires curiosity above all else. Asking the right questions is more important (and more difficult) than having the right answers. One of my favorite Victorian entrepreneurs, Isambard Kingdom Brunel, asked the seemingly ridiculous question, "How can I create the experience of floating over the English countryside?", in his quest to building the first large-scale, long-distance railway service in England.

At IDEO, we have identified three roles that leaders of creatively competitive organizations take on at different moments in the continuing cycles of innovation. Essentially, leaders need to be able to lead from every direction: from the front, from behind, and from the side.

The first of these roles is that of the *explorer*. This is the stance that is closest to the governing, decision-making, leading-from-the-front style we're used to seeing in efficiency-led organizations, except for one crucial difference. The explorer leads from the front not by issuing directions, but by asking strategically purposeful questions. These set the organization off on explorative quests that, if they're successful, will bring great value. For example, when Dean Logan, Registrar-Recorder and County Clerk for the County of Los Angeles, was charged with renewing LA's voting system, he could have simply asked for quotes from the standard vendors. Instead he asked the following question: "How can we free ourselves of the constraints of the current state to allow for the possibility of a voting experience that is responsive to voters and adaptable to ongoing changes in human behavior and advances in technology?". This, along with a second question, "How can we design a voting experience, and a system that supports it, that conveys the significance of the act of voting—both on an individual basis and the significance for community?", empowered his team to think differently. He gave them permission to explore ideas that broke with tradition, were more human centered, and even challenged assumptions about what was possible within the regulations. The resulting system promises to be more convenient, more inclusive of a wider range of citizens, and more adaptable to future change.

The second stance is that of the *gardener*, who fosters the conditions in which creativity can thrive. This kind of leading from behind requires forethought and careful investment. By nurturing new capabilities, providing spaces and tools that encourage creativity and collaboration, and protecting the tender shoots of innovation from the efficiency-led behaviors of the organizational core, the gardener releases the creative potential of the organization. Scott Cook, founder and Chairman of Intuit, has spent considerable time helping his organization develop rigorous methods for creative experimentation. He has hired new kinds of talent, including people with more creative experience and who have greater comfort with ambiguity. He worked to develop a playbook to aid teams in practicing innovation experiments, and he has sponsored experiments at the edges of Intuit's markets (in developing countries, for instance) so as to create opportunities for fast learning. These are all things that required the planning and forethought of a good gardener.

The final and most challenging role is that of the *player-coach*. This kind of leading from the side requires a lot of confidence. Leaders must engage in the act of the innovation without dominating it. The job of the player-coach is to anticipate obstacles that the team may not expect, to nudge and guide the cycles of experimentation required to bring ideas to life. Whereas the gardener can prepare the ground in advance, the player-coach must be "on the field" working with teams as they are developing their ideas. To do so requires deep levels of engagement with the ideas and knowledge of the organization. A case in point is Neil Grimmer, founding CEO of Habit. The lessons learned from co-founding his first venture were vital in the successful development of his second. This time, he relied on a talented cross-functional team to develop the new product, instead of being the lead product developer himself. As player-coach, he offered insights and perspectives on the business and how the design needed to meet those requirements. He was in the project room with the team but knew when to step back and let them do their thing.

While leading for creativity is just the first of many new practices required of creatively competitive organizations, it is the one on which all others depend. Nothing is sure to shut down the engine of innovation faster than leaders who behave as if creating and executing on new ideas is just another item on their efficiency-oriented checklists.

Source: T. Brown, "Leaders can turn creativity into a competitive advantage," *Harvard Business Review*, 2 November 2016

6.2.2 The Role of e-Business Integration in Creating Competitive Advantage

e-Business can be a facilitator or an inhibitor in creating competitive advantage. As we discussed in ▶ Chap. 1, e-business adoption can generate many benefits for companies such as efficiency and convenience. At the same time, it is noteworthy that e-business can also inhibit or undermine a company's competitive advantage if it is not integrated properly with physical business. Statistics show that 95 percent of Internet companies fall short of meeting projections, 80 percent fail to see projected return of investment, and 40 percent liquidate and lose most or all investment.[3] Companies need to understand that e-business is more than just purchasing IT and deploying IT systems. They should internalize the external e-business into their processes, structure, and conventions. The organizational culture may also adapt. The process of e-business integration can be divided into four stages (see ❏ Fig. 6.4).

---

3   Source of data: "What do you expect from all the Internet startups for the next following years?" Elektrarna, n.d. Available at ▶ http://www.elektrarna.info/expect-internet-startups-next-following-years/.

6

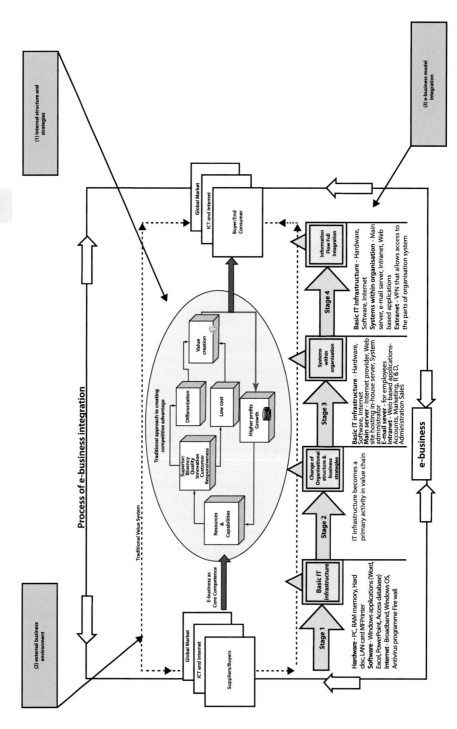

□ **Fig. 6.4**   The role of e-business integration in creating competitive advantage. (Source: Adapted from Pavic, 2011, p. 128)

■ *Stage One: Purchase and Install Basic IT Infrastructure*

Stage one is a primary stage of e-business integration, which is seen as a starting point for an e-business-enabled competitive advantage. A company needs to invest in basic IT infrastructure for the business to grow. After acquiring related software and hardware, a company then needs to install the IT infrastructure.

■ *Stage Two: Change Organizational Structure and Business Strategies*

At this stage, a company needs to acknowledge that e-business is an integral part of their business model. It now has a new way to create and capture value: e-business. To some extent this requires a company to change its organizational structure and business strategies. For example, a company may need to consider creating a CIO (chief information officer) role and including the CIO within the strategy-making group.

■ *Stage Three: Internal Integration of Systems and Organization*

After stage two, a company would typically know what it wants to do with e-business and would be more prepared to devise an initial strategic plan to develop e-business. To support the realization of strategy, a company may need to purchase and install more detailed IT infrastructure and deepen the integration of systems and organization. For instance, a retailing company creating an online selling channel could find that most of its targeted customers shop via mobile apps. This would lead the company to invest more in m-commerce technology and focus on its mobile business.

■ *Stage Four: Thoroughly Integrate e-Business with Internal and External Aspects*

As previously mentioned, internal and external aspects jointly influence the creation of competitive advantage. The previous three stages are used to prepare the company for the thorough integration of e-business with the full range of internal activities and the external network of suppliers, partners, and customers. This stage is determinant because competitive advantage will not actually be created unless internal activities are aligned with e-business and the company can provide competitive products or services to external actors.

❯ In summary, the role of e-business integration is crucial to creating e-business-based competitive advantage.

The integration process mainly goes through two phases. One phase is that a company needs to internalize or absorb e-business into their organizational structure, processes, strategy, conventions, and even culture. Another phase is that the company needs to "sell its e-business" to external actors, particularly customers who should see how the corresponding products or services are distinguished from other options. Moreover, because creating competitive advantage is a dynamic, reflective, and iterative process, and today's e-business-based world is competitive, a company hoping to use e-business to create competitive advantage should transition through these two phases repeatedly, which means that it should embrace new information technologies and promising e-business models. For example, it is hard to place today's Amazon within one e-business category, whereas when Amazon was founded, it was simply an online bookstore. Looking through the trajectory of Amazon's development, it is clear that Amazon integrates new e-business solutions to improve customer value and expand its competitive advantages in various industries. For more information on Amazon's growing competitive advantage, see the article: "Amazon's competitive advantage isn't cost or convenience, it's this."

Amazon's Competitive Advantage Isn't Cost or Convenience, It's This

Competitive advantage, as we know it, has changed. To stay relevant in today's constantly changing competitive landscape requires the capacity to continually learn, evolve, and grow into a better—more valuable—version of what you were yesterday. Competitive advantage today isn't a matter of lowering costs—anybody can slash prices. It's not a matter of hiring "better" people, although the human element is certainly a factor. It's not solely a matter of corporate responsibility either, even though purpose is important. And it's not a matter of a faster time to market despite the fact that failing fast informs sooner. No, competitive advantage is a matter of adaptability. Here's why.

Apple. Originally a computer company, the $800 billion dollar tech giant has adapted its focus to include self-driving cars, augmented reality, and even the payment space historically controlled by banks.

Google. The company that originally started as an online search engine built Android which now owns the majority of market share for mobile operating systems. It also ate the GPS navigation and mapping industries for breakfast and is working on Internet-beaming balloons (what?!) as well as self-driving cars. Hey, why not?

Facebook. No longer "just" a social networking site but a technology powerhouse intent on creating augmented-reality glasses as well as ways to let you type with your brain [...].

Amazon. Amazon's original focus was on selling books, and needless to say, they've adapted quite a bit. You can purchase anything—anything—through Amazon with the blink of an eye and have it delivered to your doorstep the next day. If that's not convenience, then I don't know what is. Quite honestly, I don't even know where to begin with Amazon because there's pretty much nothing they don't do. The point is they've evolved this far because they value change, and they value adaptability.

What do all of these companies have in common? Billions and billions of dollars—because they learned to adapt. They have built and sustained a competitive advantage because they learned to adapt. That's why the merger between Amazon and Whole Foods makes sense. Here you have two completely different companies fusing together to forge not only a new alliance but a new opportunity that, as a result, offers a new competitive advantage: options—a one-stop shop for everything you need, now including organic produce. However, adaptability isn't easy. Here are a couple things to remember when adapting to change:

Adapt Through Teams

Aside from the psychological benefits of mutual support (misery loves company), teams are one of the best ways to effectuate long-lasting organizational change for a number of reasons. First, members learn to work together. Determining how work will get accomplished between Amazon and Whole Foods employees will be a challenge since each company has its own distinct cultural norms. The fastest way for people to learn how to work together is to work together. Things don't get any easier by ignoring them. If you want to move the needle—in anything—you've got to start moving. Period. Teams are no different.

One lesson we learned in the special operations community was the value of cross-pollinated teams. Meaning, we would take a member from one team and rotate him through another team, often to his dismay. What this did was reshape individual identity from one team to a collection of teams so that he had a wider panoramic view of the organization. He was able to bring with him the lessons learned from one team and share them with another which fortified the collective capacity of the organization.

Establish a New Narrative

One of the biggest challenges in any merger is redefining who you are—your organizational identity. The roots of identity run strong—especially in the case of Amazon and Whole Foods—which means there'll be natural resistance to assuming a new one. For Whole Foods the challenge will be preserving its roots under the Goliath-like shadow of Amazon. It'll be incumbent upon leaders to redefine "who we are" and why a new identity is important. This isn't something to be taken lightly. In fact, it's an extremely difficult challenge to reshape one's personal belief system. Just imagine, as an Amazon or Whole Foods employee, everything by which you've defined yourself—the beliefs, values, and how work gets accomplished—is going to change. At the very least, they'll be challenged. This is a difficult concept to grasp let alone accept.

Communicating this new message will require two things: clarity and consistency. The message must be clear as to why things (i.e., culture, work processes) are changing because when people know why, they feel like they're part of the solution. Of course repetition is the mother of all learning, so reinforcing this message consistently is the other piece of the puzzle. And I don't mean hosting an all-hands every once upon a time. A message of change and "newness" must be conveyed every day, in every meeting, and with each directive. Like I said, change isn't easy.

Existing businesses who don't proactively adapt to change will get bulldozed for those that will. It's that simple. In today's competitive environment, it's the companies who willingly adapt to change who stay relevant.

Adapted from J. Boss, "Amazon's competitive advantage isn't cost or convenience, it's this," *Forbes*, 20 June 2017

6.3 **Sustaining Competitive Advantage**

Most firms want to continually profit from their business, so a competitive advantage is not sensible if it cannot be sustained over time. The firm and its competitors determine a sustainable competitive advantage, so in general, there are two ways to sustain a competitive advantage. This section will firstly discuss how a company prevents others from imitating its advantage and then illustrate specific strategies to sustain competitive advantage.

6.3.1 **Building Up Barriers to Imitation**

6

Maintaining a competitive advantage, be it through cost leadership or through a differentiated position, is a difficult challenge for most companies, especially in the realm of e-business where there are few sources of competitive advantage that remain stable over time. Consider, for example, the rise of Netscape Navigator, the most prominent web browser in the mid-1990s. At that time, Netscape Navigator had a global market share of over 80 percent. When Microsoft started to include online capabilities in all of its software products, it also developed Internet Explorer, essentially an imitation of Netscape Navigator, albeit with more advanced functionalities. Ultimately, Netscape lost its dominant position to Microsoft.[4]

However, successful imitation is not trivial, and there are measures that companies can take to reduce the risk of being imitated. Below, we discuss the requirements that need to be fulfilled for a competitor to imitate successfully, and we also discuss the barriers to entry that incumbent companies can build to prevent others from invading their market (see ◘ Fig. 6.5).[5]

Firstly, in order to identify a successful business model, potential imitators *must be able to identify* its competitive superiority. In the case of nonpublic companies, finding out about successful business models is not trivial since there is frequently no hard data available regarding profitability or even sales. During the writing phase of this book, we had an interesting exchange with the leading German auction platform ► www.My-Hammer.de where private homeowners place requests for painting or repair jobs and carpenters and other craft workers offer their services to them. The business model has proven to be highly successful in Germany and would have provided an excellent source for writing a case study. Even though, in principle, the management of MyHammer was interested in collaborating in the development of a case study, they finally decided against it, because they did not want to divulge information about their company to potential would-be competitors. Hence, a company should know how to hide or disguise its competitive superiority from potential competitors because these "business secrets" will lose their

---

4   Later on, after the launch of new desktop browsers, the usage market share changed. This question was covered in more detail in ► Sect. 3.2.1, where recent data on the leading browsers in the market (i.e., Explorer, Google Chrome, and Firefox) is provided.
5   For a detailed description of barriers to imitation, see Ghemawat (2005).

Imitator	Incumbent
Requirments for successful imitation	**Barriers against successful imitation**
1 Must be able to identify competitive superiority	• Withhold information about profitability • Forgo short-term profits for long-term success
2 Must be willing to imitate	• Deterrence: signal promise of retaliation • Make commitments to make threat credible • Pre-emption: exploit all available investment opportunities/secure access to resources
3 Must be able to understand sources of competitive advantage	• Tacit knowledge: rely on skills, processes or culture/resources that are implicit • Causal ambiguity: rely on a complex, multidimensional mix of sources
4 Must be able to build/acquire necessary resources	• Base differentiation on resources that are rare/immobile/contracted • Exploit-time lags

◻ **Fig. 6.5** A company can build up numerous barriers against imitation. (Source: Adapted from Hungenberg, 2006, p. 251)

value once other competitors start to imitate them. This is especially important for start-ups or industries where technologies are similar. Ease of imitation will make a start-up with an excellent business idea lose its key source of value capture. Competitors may have richer resources and better capabilities to quickly realize the source of competitive advantage of others. For industries where most firms' technology use is similar, it is more important to protect information that is unique to the company, for example, by ensuring source codes, the core business idea, or business models are confidential, or enabling the company to capture value before competitors identify the know-how.

Secondly, potential entrants in a market *must be willing to imitate* the successful business model. Incumbents can take measures to prevent them from entering the market. One way to do so is through deterrence. For instance, if a low-cost competitor wants to enter a market, existing companies might signal to the new entrant that they will retaliate by also lowering their own prices, which would render the market entry unattractive. Furthermore, to make threats from potential imitators credible, it is often helpful to increase barriers to entry, for example, to invest substantially in assets that will generate economies of scale. Finally, it is also possible to preempt potential competitors by exploiting all available investment opportunities and by securing access to scarce resources (such as patents or specialist personnel). For instance, preemption might entail acquiring a small competitor with the sole purpose of ensuring that other, potentially more threatening, would-be competitors do not acquire the company and its know-how.

Thirdly, potential entrants *must also be able to understand the sources of competitive advantage*. Most frequently, the competitive advantage does not just result from one resource or capability; it also results from the complex interplay between multiple different factors that might not even be clearly understood by the incumbent company itself. Obviously, acquiring this type of tacit knowledge is even more difficult for outsiders who do not have direct access to the company. Also, the causal linkages between different factors that lead to a competitive advantage are not always clear. For instance, it is not entirely clear whether it is the free time that developers at Google have to work on their pet projects that contributes to the success of the company, or whether it is Google's success that allows management to give this time to developers. Valuing implicit factors such as culture is also a barrier of imitation.

Fourthly, a would-be imitator *must also be able to build or acquire the necessary resources and capabilities* successfully to copy the incumbent's business model. The most promising way to provide protection from this is to base the competitive advantage on resources that are rare, immobile, or contracted. For instance, a core element of Facebook's competitive advantage lies in its broad membership base of more than two billion users. Replicating this membership would be very difficult for a potential imitator. A company should patent their core technologies if possible, to prevent rivals from imitating it.

6.3.2 Specific Strategies to Sustain Competitive Advantage

Building up barriers to imitation is not enough to sustain competitive advantage. A company achieving a temporary advantage may notice that the advantage erodes gradually as competitors provide comparable or even better solutions than the leading company.[6] Here's what businesses should also consider to sustain a competitive advantage:

Foster a Flair for Innovation   Companies should continually push innovative activities—rolling out new improved features or new products to market to satisfy customers. Innovation is a critical enabler allowing companies to acquire new customers and retain loyal customers who have been very satisfied with what the company is offering. To foster a flair for innovation, companies should create an innovative environment within the organization and set incentives for employees to provide creative ideas and support creative talents.

Provide Superior Customer Service   Offering a competitive product does not equate to a competitive advantage. For customers, value-in-use is more crucial than value-in-exchange. Providing a good customer service can help companies sustain their advantage, because customer service adds value to products, increasing the value-in-use of products. Customers' value perception of a product is usually positively associated with their loyalty and willingness to buy. This explains why some small business owners fail, even though they continually provide decent products. For example, a restaurant can offer quality food, which other competitors cannot do.

---

6   This subsection is adopted from Hill (2018).

This would attract many consumers at first. But the restaurant's advantage could start to erode as customer numbers increase and it struggles to provide consistent service quality.

Keep a Low Cost Structure   An advantage is not "sustainable" if it cannot be achieved efficiently. This is a difference between technological advantage and competitive advantage. According to neoclassic economics, a business is still valuable before its marginal cost surpasses its marginal revenue. When its marginal cost surpasses its marginal revenue, it is not worthwhile for a company to invest more in the business because it will not maintain its current revenue level. This explains why some companies can sustain their leading position in their industry. For example, Samsung is a leading company in electronics. The sustainability of its competitive advantage may be due to its low cost structure by efficient mass production and innovations of major products. Keeping a low cost structure can help Samsung to sustain relatively high profit margins. If competitors try to compete with Samsung on price, they need to be able to sustain thin profit margins.

Brand Equity   A company's brand equity can be a powerful weapon to sustain a competitive advantage. Customers loyal to a brand tend to choose the brand's products instead of rivals'. Companies should value the role of brand equity in sustaining competitive advantage and focus on improving brand equity over time.

Cement "Cash Cows"   Some businesses' competitive advantage will erode over time, and the business may face decisions to either cut inputs or shut it down. Sustaining a competitive advantage is an endless game. Companies cannot keep the advantage if they start to "relax," because markets are constantly evolving, and competitive rivals will catch up or even win over the market. The Boston Consulting Group created a growth-share matrix for companies to analyze current businesses. Cash cows are business units within a company or companies with a high market share in a slow-growing industry. These businesses are usually staid in a comparatively mature market, but companies tend to nurture them for as long as they can to maintain marginal profits. For example, Netflix is viewed as a leading corporate in online streaming industry, yet it still cements its advantage in offering up-to-date content and service.

6.4 Dealing with the Threats of Disruptive Innovations in e-Business[7]

Let us look back to the mid-1970s. During those years, Apple introduced the first personal computer (PC) in the private consumer market. The Apple II, developed by Steve Wozniak, was technologically inferior to the then dominant minicomputers that were first developed in the 1960s. They were the size of a large refrig-

---

7   For a detailed and comprehensive description of the theory of disruptive innovations, see Christensen and Raynor (2003).

erator, cost $20,000 or more, and were sold to accounting departments and other corporate users that required advanced computing capabilities. When confronted with PCs, highly successful minicomputer manufacturers such as Digital Equipment Corporation considered them to be "toys" that were of no interest to their demanding corporate customers. As a result, they did not invest in this new technology.

Due to its technological simplicity, however, the Apple was also much cheaper (an Apple II was about $2000, while a minicomputer cost at least $20,000), and it was much smaller (an Apple II had the size of today's PCs, while the minicomputer was as big as a closet) and much easier to use than a minicomputer. As the technological performance of PCs improved over time, they attracted new users who hitherto had not been using computers and also caused customers, who had previously bought minicomputers, to switch over to PCs. Interestingly enough, by then, incumbent manufacturers of minicomputers were unable to integrate PCs into their existing business models, which, ultimately, led to the demise of the minicomputer industry.

6.4.1   Understanding the Fundamental Process of Disruptive Innovations

This failure of once highly successful incumbents and the parallel rise of successful start-up companies is not uncommon. Disruptive innovation theory attempts to explain the reasons for this seemingly inexplicable demise of established incumbents. The fundamental assumption of the theory of disruptive innovation is that there are two distinct types of circumstances that companies can find themselves in: (1) *sustaining circumstances* and (2) *disruptive circumstances.*

In sustaining circumstances, established companies develop innovative products that help them to generate higher margins by selling better products to the most demanding customers. Sustaining innovations can be year-by-year gradual improvements, such as increased processing power and larger storage capacity of PCs or added features on a current operating system. Somewhat counterintuitively, sustaining innovations can also be of a groundbreaking, radical nature that helps companies to leapfrog their competitors. For instance, the transition from electromechanical to electronic cash registers was a radical but sustaining innovation. NCR (National Cash Register) dominated the market for electromechanical cash registers but missed the new technology in the 1970s, which led to a drastic decrease in sales. Yet, NCR decided quickly to introduce its own electronic cash register and, through its extensive sales organization, was able quickly to regain lost market share.

Whether incremental or radical, what all sustaining innovations have in common is that they entail a better product that can be sold for higher profit margins to the best customers. As the example of NCR shows, while incumbents are often not the first to develop a sustaining innovation, they generally succeed in their large-scale commercialization of that innovation. This is due to the fact that, compared with their start-up competitors, incumbents tend to have more financial resources and a large customer base and have the internal resources and processes to push the innovation onto the market.

In contrast to sustaining innovations, disruptive innovations are not focused on bringing better products to existing high-end customers. Instead, they usually tend to be significantly worse in the performance dimensions that traditionally were important in the industry. However, before providing specific examples of companies whose offerings are based on disruptive innovations, let us briefly mention that even the Internet and e-commerce could be used as a type of disruptive innovation for commerce. Attributes which support this claim include the following (see Lee, 2001):

- The economics of exchanging information, which enable the simultaneous achievement of reach and content richness
- Network externality effects and economies of scale
- The speed of exchanging information and content that drive connectivity and interactivity.
- The economics of abundance, as information and digital products can be reproduced and distributed at almost no marginal cost
- Merchandise exchange, when a large selection can be offered without the necessity of having a large physical display
- Prosumption, which means that the active participation of consumers is technically and economically viable if customized exchanges are offered.
- The generated value which transcends industrial sectors

Furthermore, the evolution of e-commerce reveals three main categories of commerce innovations (see ◘ Fig. 6.6): Internet-wired or traditional e-commerce (i-commerce), mobile commerce (m-commerce), and ubiquitous commerce

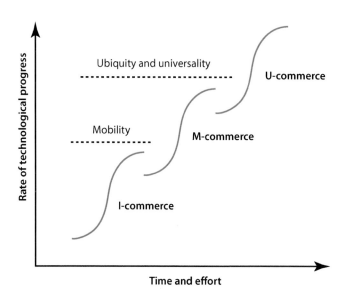

◘ **Fig. 6.6** S Curves of e-commerce innovation: from i-, m-, to u-commerce. (Source: Adapted from Wu and Hisa, 2008, p. 97)

(u-commerce).[8] While the evolution from e-commerce to m-commerce could be considered as radical, the move from m-commerce to u-commerce is more disruptive in terms of both technology and business models (see Wu and Hisa, 2008).

In order to succeed in their e-commerce initiatives, it is important that companies identify the key disruptive attributes for their e-strategies and related business models. The same logic applies when designing new products and services. The origins of Apple are very paradigmatic in this regard. The Apple II computer, for instance, had far less computing power than minicomputers. Yet, this disruptive innovation of Apple offered other benefits such as ease of use, convenience, and, most importantly, a lower price. As a result, initially it primarily appealed to less demanding customers who were willing to pay less for a computer. At the time there was no PC on offer to consumers, they would probably have not purchased a clumsy and expensive minicomputer. Apple essentially created a new category for consumers. This is a typical strategy that has been followed over time by technology-based start-ups.

Over time, customers demand increasingly higher performance from the products they purchase. However, technological progress typically evolves faster than customers' demand for better performance. This implies that technologies in their early development stages may not fulfill customer's performance requirements, but continue to evolve and then outstrip the requirements of customers. Consider the functionalities of Microsoft Office and how they have evolved over time. Early versions were characterized by frequent crashes and incompatibilities with other programs and lacked important functionalities. During that time customers were underserved, i.e., they did not get as much performance as they asked for to do the jobs they wanted to do. Over time, the Office package continued to improve, reliability and compatibility increased, and new functionalities were added. Now Excel and Word have become so powerful and "all encompassing" in their functionalities that most users only use a fraction of what these tools offer. Undoubtedly, the few high-end users who require cutting-edge functionalities for their work are pushing software packages to their limits, but this customer segment is probably fairly small.

As more customers are overserved by the expanding functionalities of Microsoft Office, opportunities open up for disruptive innovations that address this segment with less powerful, yet cheaper and more convenient, offerings. Consider Google's spreadsheet, word processing, and calendar software that can be accessed online free of charge. Although these packages are certainly not as good as the Office software, they are in all likelihood good enough to meet the needs of less demanding users. Incidentally, these users also happen to be the customers who provide the lowest profit margins to established incumbents anyway. As a result, the latter are typically not upset to see them leave. However, the theory would suggest that as Google's software improves over time, it would eventually reach a point where its performance is good enough to meet the demands of mainstream customers. At that point, the mass market switches over to the new technology.

---

8   For an in-depth description of these types of commerce, see ▶ Chap. 12.

6.4.2 Discovering the Underlying Reasons for Incumbents' Failure

The pattern that is described above raises the question of why these types of disruptive innovations take place over and over again in different industries and countries. Frequently it is argued that it is the inability of companies to develop the appropriate innovations that later turn out to be successful. Yet, established companies, for instance, Kodak with digital imaging, do constantly innovate and oftentimes even develop the technologies that later turn out to be the disruptive innovation.

Instead, the driving force behind the inability of incumbent companies to commercialize these innovations successfully is not located in R&D departments, but instead in how companies allocate their resources (i.e., management time and financial resources). Here, the theory of resource dependence provides interesting insights that explain more fully why incumbents fail in the face of disruptive innovations. The theory states that it is actually customers and investors—not managers—who control the allocation of resources in an organization. This is so because companies that invest in projects that do not satisfy the needs of their best customers and do not suit the risk structure of their investors will not receive the necessary funding over the long run. Furthermore, companies generally generate most of their profits from their most demanding customers who are willing to pay premium prices for more sophisticated products. At the same time, profit margins from customers in lower segments are generally much lower, and the business would rely on volume of sales. Consequently, innovation efforts tend to revolve around the improvement of products at the high end. The work of Charles O'Reilly and Michael Tushman identified that some businesses can successfully exploit iterative improvements to their processes and products while at the same time experimenting with and exploring innovations with disruptive potential. The businesses are able to do this by clearly separating both "explore" and "exploit" functions, which O'Reilly and Tushman (2004) refer to as "ambidextrous organizations."

Similarly, when deciding whether to maintain or even increase their stake in a company, investors look for innovations and other growth initiatives that promise a substantial increase in revenue, which then translates into a share price increase. Since the market potential of disruptive innovations is typically small during the early years and cannot be measured precisely, developing a solid business plan is largely guesswork, which makes it hard to sell to investors.

> ❯ The problem for incumbent firms would be less critical if new competitors entering the market with disruptive innovations remained in the low-margin market segments. Yet, once disruptors have entered a market, they are motivated to move upmarket into more demanding customer segments in order to increase their profit margins. For their part, incumbents are motivated to flee upmarket into their most demanding customer segments since that is where their most profitable customers are located. This asymmetric motivation is at the core of the innovator's dilemma.

6.4.3 Asking the Right Questions to Recognize the Threats of Disruptive Innovations

The main contribution of the theory of disruptive innovation is that it challenges conventional management thinking that is perfectly logical and rational in most situations yet leads to failure in the face of a disruptive innovation. Before discussing the key questions that need to be asked to recognize threats of disruptive innovations, we want to take a closer look at the key fallacies of conventional thinking that lead to failure in the face of disruptive innovations.

Firstly, conventional thinking would suggest that most advanced customers who are using cutting-edge, high-quality products will be able to recognize imminent changes in industry structure. In contrast, disruptive innovations have their roots with those customers who are overserved by existing products or with those users who had previously not been using the product.

Secondly, conventional thinking would also suggest that managers need to pay most attention to the largest competitors in their industry. In contrast, companies that disrupt industries frequently are not even on the competitive radar of those companies that are competing in that industry. They may come from another industry.

Thirdly, conventional thinking suggests that those companies with the most resources that can be spent on activities such as R&D or marketing are likely to be successful. In contrast, those companies that succeed with disruptive innovations leverage asymmetric motivation and serve those customers that their competitors are unable to serve, or do not want to.

To counter these traps of conventional thinking and to determine whether there exists a threat of a disruptive innovation in their industry, managers of established incumbents need to ask the following set of questions dealing with (1) non-served customers, (2) overserved customers, and (3) the disruptiveness of the innovation relative to competitors:

Non-served Customers   Is there a large group of people who previously did not have the money or the skills to purchase the product themselves? Did customers have to go to a central, inconvenient location to purchase the product? For instance, families with grown-up children who wanted to sell the clothes and toys they no longer needed belonged to the group of non-served customers because they had the desire to get a job done but did not have the appropriate means to do so, with the exception of a garage sale or the local secondhand store, both of which have a very limited market potential. eBay provided a simple and relatively cheap format to extend this market to a much broader audience, thereby substantially increasing the revenue potential.

Overserved Customers   Are there customers at the bottom end of the market who would buy the same product with fewer features for a lower price? Is it possible to build a profitable business model while keeping down prices? One important factor of overserved customers is that they do not use many of the features that are offered in the most up-to-date version of a product. As we showed above, the market for spreadsheet and word processing software contains numerous customers at the bottom end of the market who would be willing to work with fewer features, as offered by Google's free online version. For overserved customers, price or other performance features that had not been important previously become the primary drivers for purchasing and use decisions. In contrast, underserved customers are eagerly awaiting the next upgrade or new product version.

Disruptiveness to Competitors   Is the innovation disruptive relative to all relevant rival companies that are currently competing in that market? This question emphasizes the crucial point that a technology or business model is never disruptive in absolute terms but only in relation to an existing technology or business model that is already used by established companies. For example, the Internet as a technology is neither disruptive nor sustaining. Instead, it is an infrastructural technology that can be used in either a sustaining or disruptive way. Thinking of the Internet as only a means to disrupt established firms and failing to look at the whole market was actually a critical failure factor for many dotcom start-ups during the early years of the Internet. For instance, the online retailing of PCs was certainly highly disruptive relative to manufacturers who were selling their PCs through physical stores. Consequently, companies such as HP or Compaq were threatened by the rise of Internet-based retailing. Yet, for other companies such as Dell, the Internet was a sustaining innovation. Previously, Dell had used the telephone and fax as primary sales channels, and the Internet was a natural extension to serve better its existing customer base and to attract new customers. As a result, Dell had the incentives and resources to compete in the online world, and it did so very successfully, becoming by the end of the 1990s the world's largest PC retailer. The disruptive innovation theory would have predicted that new start-up companies attempting to sell PCs over the Internet would have been successful if they only had to disrupt competitors such as Compaq.

The banking industry is another example where the Internet had a sustaining impact. Nordea successfully integrated the Internet into its value proposition because it was a way to improve services to existing customers by offering online access to bank account statements, bill payments, and more. In contrast, pure Internet banks that sprung up in droves during the late 1990s have been struggling to make significant inroads into the banking industry or to sustain significant growth.

The questions raised in the above three areas aim to increase your awareness of disruptive threats and provide the basis for appropriate responses, which is discussed in the following section.

6.4.4 Finding Ways to Deal with Disruptive Innovations

A large part of the literature on disruptive innovations discusses the question of how incumbents can react successfully once they realize that a specific innovation has a disruptive potential (see Ghemawat, 2005). In principle, there exists a broad spectrum of possibilities ranging from not responding at all to leapfrogging the disruptor. The different possibilities with their respective advantages and disadvantages are discussed in more detail below.

Not Responding At all   This is what many traditional firms did when e-business ventures started to enter the market on a large scale in the late 1990s. At that time, typical justifications of such no-response strategy were voiced through statements such as:

- "Internet ventures are not my business."
- "e-Commerce will only make up a small niche of the overall market and is therefore not attractive for our company."
- "We don't want to set up an online channel that could cannibalise our physical operations."
- "We don't have the IT skills or the necessary IT systems to compete online."

6

Obviously, managers were (and still are) bombarded with a myriad of new technologies and business threats and opportunities on a daily basis. The challenge for them is determining which of these threats and opportunities could materialize in the future. Yet, in the face of substantial threats, paying too little attention to a changing environment is often more hazardous than paying too much attention.

Migrating/Harvesting   This is a less passive form of response than not responding at all. While the above strategy of not responding is quite often based on ignoring or not properly assessing the underlying facts, the migration strategy is based on a conscious decision to "milk existing resources." This means, for instance, that if the book retailer Barnes & Noble had come to the conclusion that Internet-based book retailing would overtake physical book retailing, it would have stopped investing in its network of physical bookstores.

Defending   This is an active response to the new threatening business model. When defending their existing markets, incumbents need to improve their business model in such a way that they are able either to lower their prices or disproportionately to increase the benefits they provide to their customers. However, this option is usually difficult to implement successfully because the new business model or technology tends to have faster improvement dynamics than those created through a defensive strategy. Other defense tactics include public relations campaigns and lobbying. The music industry used these approaches against Napster; however doing so led to a customer backlash.

Straddling   This means to rely on the old business model while simultaneously introducing a new model. This can either be done as a transitional hedge to determine the potential of the new technology or be set up right from the start as a long-term strategy where both models will coexist. This strategy attempts to combine the best of both worlds, for example, to continue profiting from the old business model while simultaneously gaining traction in the new business model.

While this option might seem to be the more promising at first sight, it also entails major risks in certain scenarios. Firstly, timing is a key risk. Continuing to invest in something that may no longer work might mask a company's unwillingness to make tough choices. As we pointed out previously, the willingness of top management to make tough trade-off decisions is one of the cornerstones of strategy formulation. Secondly, when companies try to integrate the disruptive innovation into their own existing business model, this frequently leads to "cramming." Cramming means that the new technology is primarily used to improve the existing business model. For instance, the newspaper industry provides an interesting example of how publishers initially attempted to cram Internet-based news publishing into their existing business model. In the late 1990s, the *LA Times*, like many other newspapers around the world, recognized the importance of the Internet and decided to enter this market with an online version of its print edition. In essence, it opted for a straddling strategy. Yet, as in most cases, it was primarily the journalists and editors of the traditional print version who became involved with the creation of the online format. This has resulted in an online edition that mirrored largely the print edition with the same content and similar layout. Yet, such newspapers did not leverage the distinct advantages of electronic publishing such as discussion boards, site-searching tools, and breaking news from third-party sources. The following quote by a newspaper executive sums up this inability to operate two distinct businesses simultaneously:

» Where I think we missed the boat is that we saw it [the Internet] as an extension of the newspaper. […] Our Internet operations were really run by people who came out of the newsroom, so they were editors who tended to look at this [online channel] more as a newspaper. (see Gilbert, 2005)

Switching Completely This is a more radical response than straddling, since it entails a complete switch to the new business model. The obvious attraction of this option is that it focuses all managerial and financial resources on the strategy, which helps to avoid distractions (as was the case in the straddling examples mentioned above) and creates a sense of urgency and momentum. Yet, it is also the riskiest of all options since there is always a high degree of uncertainty associated with these types of innovations. Furthermore, it is questionable whether the resources and capabilities that are valuable in a current environment will apply and be valuable in the new business model. For example, physical stores and expertise in their management may not be resources and skills that are needed to manage an online venture.

Leapfrogging the Disruptive Competition This means that a company tries to out-substitute the substitution. From a long-term strategic perspective, this option is highly attractive, yet it requires a very deep understanding of how technology and market demand will evolve. It is not enough to have just a clear understanding of which future technology could be successful. In addition, it is also essential to get the entry timing right, because entering a market too early can be just as detrimental as entering it too late. For example, when ► Amazon.com was selling physical books online, Barnes & Noble may have leapfrogged ► Amazon.com by selling books in a digital format (as e-books); it would have leapfrogged by skipping one technology generation. Obviously, doing so would not have been an easy task, especially considering the fact that ► Amazon.com was in all likelihood better equipped to make the move to digital goods than Barnes & Noble.

6.4.5 Selecting the Appropriate Cognitive Frame for Efficient Responses

In recent years, management researchers have further developed the theory of disruptive innovations, mainly driven by anomalies that the existing theory could not explain. In this section, we want to delve more deeply into these extensions of the theory.

One of the most important claims of the disruptive innovation theory is that incumbent firms do not invest in disruptive innovations because they focus on the needs of their best customers, which leads to resource dependence. This lack of resource, the theory goes, explains why they are unable to commercialize disruptive innovations successfully.

Yet, more recent research has shown that there are, in fact, numerous companies that have invested substantially in disruptive innovations, but still failed. Consider, for instance, Kodak's move into digital photography in 1996.[9] George Fisher, then CEO of Kodak, knew that digital photography would eventually threaten Kodak's core business. He and other senior executives at the company were tempted to ignore it because the profit margins were much lower than on the core business and digital photography also did not address Kodak's traditional customers. Nonetheless, Fisher rallied support from his top management and invested more than $2 billion in R&D for digital imaging. Yet, because Kodak was so worried about the threat, most of the money was spent before it became obvious how the market would develop. Instead of basing the new digital products on home storage and home printing capabilities, which later turned out to be the successful business model, Kodak invested hastily in 10,000 digital kiosks in its partner stores and committed itself to price points and product specifications that were difficult to change later on. Industry outsiders, such as Hewlett Packard, Canon, or Sony, in contrast, invested in the home storage capabilities, thereby driving the development of digital photography.

A similar development can be observed in the newspaper industry. Initially, most newspapers underestimated the potential of the Internet. In the mid-1990s, only a small number of Internet users were getting their news from online sources. At that time, most readers of physical newspapers did not even have access to the Internet.

Thus, managers who tried to secure funding for Internet initiatives in the early 1990s, before the threat of the Internet to the existing business model became obvious, had a hard time convincing management of the potential of the Internet. As a result, newspaper companies did not enthusiastically embrace the opportunities of online publishing. The report of an online publisher of an established newspaper company sums up this sentiment:

» I had trumpeted the new business to everyone and asked for their cooperation with the online group. One day, I asked a staff member of the online business how things

---

9   For a detailed account of Kodak's foray into digital photography, see Gilbert and Bower (2002).

were going and if the newspaper staff was helping out. He told me that he had recently asked for some help and the response was, 'Get the hell out of here; I've got a real newspaper to get out'! (Quoted in Gilbert, 2006)

Only when it became obvious in the late 1990s that Internet portals, such as Yahoo!, or job search sites, such as ▶ Monster.com, were threatening the traditional profit pools of classified advertisements and job posts did the newspaper industry wake up to the potential impact of the Internet on their business. This sentiment is exemplified through this publisher's statement:

» I live in terror that some big thing is going to happen and I don't see it coming (Gilbert and Bower, 2002).

This sense of threat and urgency was then also translated in substantial investments in the new technology. For instance, at one newspaper company that was studied, staff for online operations increased from 15 to 40 people within a matter of months.

Interestingly enough, however, the framing of the threat also had a strong influence on the response patterns of top management. In the face of a threat, the typical reaction pattern of top management is to centralize decision-making at the top and to reduce experimentation. For instance, line managers of the online sites received sample budgets, marketing plans, and checklists that they had to adhere to. One top manager remembers:

» It was very centralized in the beginning, which was very uncharacteristic, because the culture is very much to let each newspaper run its own business. We had a basic business model for every [online] site. We gave them money. We told them they could hire people, but we told them exactly how to run the site (Gilbert and Bower, 2002).

The resulting websites were simply longer versions of the printed newspaper—with more than 75 percent of the content directly imported from the print edition. The features that other Internet start-ups in e-publishing had long integrated, such as customization and community building, were not included. In the advertising realm, the company also did not experiment with new revenue sources such as demographic advertising, email marketing, and classified services.

The important insight of this example about the newspaper industry's reaction to the Internet is that the cognitive frame (mindset) with which top management approach a disruptive innovation strongly influences both how many financial and management resources are allocated and how the innovation is implemented within an organization. In essence, management faces a framing paradox that is difficult to resolve.

If, on the one hand, a mindset is used that focuses primarily on the opportunities that are opened up by the disruptive technology, then, so the theory goes, there will be plenty of freedom for line managers to experiment with novel ways of employing the technology. However it will be difficult to get the required resources approved. If, on the other hand, a mindset focusing on the threat is used, the willingness to invest in the new technology will be much higher. But because of the importance of the new technology and the associated apprehension, centralization of decision-making and a lack of experimentation will result in a lackluster implementation of the new technology within the corporation.

This raises the question of how businesses can possibly manage these two opposing mindsets at the same time. The example of the newspaper industry revealed that newspaper companies that managed the integration of the new Internet-based news publishing more successfully shared two common characteristics.

Firstly, they received advice from people outside of the newspaper industry. In one case, the opinion of a CEO had been shaped by the recommendations of a friend who had been based in Silicon Valley where he was observing the changes created by the Internet. In addition, they also hired industry outsiders who had gained previous online experience in other unrelated industries.

Secondly, they decided to separate the online organization structurally from the print organization. During the early years of e-business, most newspaper companies had decided to integrate the online organization with the print organization motivated by the desire to leverage the assets of the print business. This is summarized by the following CEO quote:

>> Our basic goal is an integrated strategy. [...] In the local information market, the newspaper has an advantage. To separate the online unit from the newspaper is to give away a lot of that advantage.

However, the influence of outsiders also led newspaper companies to reconsider this initial strategy. The structural separation combined with the hiring of industry outsiders allowed the separated online unit to frame the Internet as an opportunity instead of a threat as had been perceived by the parent organization. One online manager of a separated website reported:

>> When we simply changed our name from the newspaper name to 'the ▶ city.com' [...] it changed people's expectations of what would be on the [web]site. This, in turn, changed how people in our online organization viewed who they were and what they were producing. (Quoted in Gilbert, 2005)

Another manager of a separate online division reported:

>> Now that we are separate, we own the opportunity in a way we never did when we were still with the [physical] newspaper.

This thinking in terms of opportunity allowed the online organizations to think creatively about developing new revenue streams without having to worry about cannibalizing the existing print business. A website editor who came from the print business commented about the online director who was brought in from outside:

>> He is constantly seeing digital media in different ways than I am used to or appreciate. At first, this bothered me, but now that I see it working, I increasingly endorse the input.

These new revenue sources, which hitherto had not been used by the online editions of newspapers, included fee-based archival access, email marketing, email list rental, fee-based data analysis, and behavioral and demographic targeting.

Summary
- This chapter first discussed the fundamentals of competitive advantage, which helps companies identify "real" competitive advantage.
- It illustrated how a company creates its competitive advantage and what role e-business plays in the process of creating competitive advantage. Companies need to internalize and externalize e-business to forge it into their business model.
- This chapter discussed how a company sustains its competitive advantage. This section showed how a company builds barriers of imitation and specifically strategies for sustaining competitive advantage.
- The chapter then focused on how to deal with the threats of a disruptive innovation in e-business. More specifically, it stressed the importance of understanding the fundamental process of disruptive innovations and determining the underlying reasons for the incumbent's failure.
- Next, the chapter suggested some questions that companies need to raise in order to assess the threat of a disruptive innovation. These questions deal with (1) non-served customers, (2) overserved customers, and (3) the disruptiveness of the innovation relative to competitors.
- Possible ways for dealing with a disruptive innovation are then suggested. These include (1) not responding, (2) migrating/harvesting, (3) defending, (4) straddling, (5) switching completely, and (6) leapfrogging.
- The chapter then discussed the issues underlying the selection of the appropriate mindset for an efficient response to a disruptive innovation. It concluded by stressing the need for incumbents facing a disruptive innovation to adopt two contradicting cognitive frames: one that primarily focuses on the opportunities that are opened up by the disruptive innovation and one that focuses on the threats that are created by the same disruptive innovation.

? Review Questions
1. How can a company say it has a competitive advantage in a business?
2. What is the process of creating competitive advantage?
3. What role does e-business play in the process of competitive advantage creation?
4. What are the requirements for successful imitation and the barriers to imitation?
5. What strategies can a company employ to sustain its competitive advantage?
6. What questions do companies need to ask in order to assess the threat of a disruptive innovation?

7. What possible responses can companies consider taking to deal effectively with a disruptive innovation?
8. What are the main cognitive frames that companies can adopt when facing a disruptive innovation? Why are these cognitive frames contradictory in nature?
9. Are you loyal to some brands or products? Discuss with your classmates the factors causing these brands or products' competitive advantage.
10. Can you find examples of how companies build up barriers to imitation? Pick out specific examples from different industries and explain what these companies did. Were they successful in their attempts?
11. Consider different industries of your choice (e.g., music, book retailing, or others) and analyze whether they are faced with the threats of disruptive innovations. If so, discuss how the new entrants are attempting to compete. Also, discuss the reactions of the incumbents.
12. Why did Intel develop the Celeron chip? Why have low-cost airline companies (e.g., Ryanair) succeeded over incumbent companies (e.g., British Airways)? or Why has online banking (such as ING Direct) gained such market share to traditional, full bank services? Can you explain this decision using the disruptive innovation logic?

References

Ghemawat, P., & Rivkin, J. W. (1998). *Creating competitive advantage*. Harvard Business Review.
Ghemawat, P. (2005). *Strategy and the business landscape* (p. 106). Prentice Hall.
Gilbert, C. (2006). Change in the presence of residual fit. *Organizational Science, 17*(1), 150–167.
Gilbert, C. (2005). Unbundling the structure of inertia: Resource rigidity versus routine rigidity. *Academy of Management Journal, 48*(5), 741–763.
Gilbert, C., & Bower, J. (2002). Disruptive change: when trying harder is part of the problem. *Harvard Business Review*, 95–101.
Hill, B. (2018). Why are some firms able to sustain competitive advantage over their rivals?. Smallbusiness.chron.com.
Hungenberg, H. (2006). *Strategisches management in Unternehmen*. Gabler.
Hungenberg, H. (2014). *Strategisches management in Unternehmen*. Gabler.
Johnson, G., Scholes, K., & Whittington, R. (2005). *Exploring Corporate Strategy* (seventh ed.). Prentice Hall.
Lee, C. S. (2001). An analytical framework for evaluating e-commerce business models and strategies. *Internet Research, 11*(4), 349–359.
O'Reilly, C., & Tushman, M. (2004). *The ambidextrous organization*. Boston: Harvard Business Review.
Wu, J.-H., & Hisa, T.-L. (2008). Developing e-business dynamic capabilities: An analysis of e-commerce innovation from I-, M-, to U-commerce. *Journal of Organizational Computing and Electronic Commerce, 18*, 95–111.

Further Reading

Christensen, C. (2011). *The innovator's dilemma: The revolutionary book that will change the way you do business*. Harper Business.
Christensen, C., & Raynor, M. (2003). *The innovator's solution*. Harvard Business School Press.
Pavic, S. (2011). *The creation of competitive advantage in SMEs through e-business*. University of Sheffield.

Weblinks

Consult www.innosight.com for up-to-date research findings and practical implications of the disruptive innovation theory.

www.innovationmanagement.se is an online knowledge center for creating value with innovation management. This site offers insights, case studies, solutions and a multitude of useful and cutting-edge content for today's companies.

www.christenseninstitute.org/blog/ is the blog of the Christensen Institute, named after Clayton Christensen.

www.blueoceanstrategy.com/blog/ is the blog of academics focussed on blue ocean strategy.

Exploiting Opportunities of New Market Spaces in e-Business

Contents

© Springer Nature Switzerland AG 2020
T. Jelassi, F. J. Martínez-López, *Strategies for e-Business*, Classroom Companion: Business,
https://doi.org/10.1007/978-3-030-48950-2_7

Learning Outcomes

After completing this chapter, you should be able to:

- Explain how firms can open up new market spaces and thereby create completely new types of value
- Understand how to draw a value curve and gain insights through it
- Explain the six paths framework and be able to use it for value creation in e-business
- Appreciate the importance of finding the right time to enter a market
- Recognize the advantages and disadvantages of being an early mover in e-business

■ Introduction

The strategy options presented in ▶ Chap. 5 mainly focus on the traditional form of competition, which assumes a clearly defined set of competitors within an industry. The key performance measure is relative performance vis-à-vis competitors. As a result of this competitor-focused competition, improvements tend to be incremental through an increase of benefits or a decrease of costs. An alternative way to approach strategy development is to move beyond the sole industry focus and look for new market spaces across different industries.[1]

Doing so allows a firm, at least temporarily, to break out of the cycle of ever-increasing competition within an industry, either by redefining the industry competition or by creating a new industry. The goal of this approach is to drastically increase consumer benefit while at the same time reducing price.

This chapter will first describe what today's business world looks like: sectors without borders. This section will help readers understand this new characteristic of e-business. The next three sections of this chapter deal with the value innovation logic. ▶ Section 7.5 discusses the advantages and disadvantages of being an early mover in a new market.

7.1 Being Ready for Sectors Without Borders

❯ Sector borders or industry borders are viewed as incumbents' "interest protection." They work like a border between countries, allowing a sovereign state to constrict new immigrants and entrants. However, in today's business world, this institutional protection becomes more and more powerless.

Businesses may run into a completely new competitor who they may have never thought of. For example, Ichiba is a Japanese e-commerce and Internet company. Its e-commerce platform Rakuten Ichiba is one of world's largest e-commerce sites.

---

1   See Kim and Mauborgne (1999), and Blue Ocean Strategy, Expanded Edition, Boston, Harvard Business School Publishing, 2015. See also Johnson et al. (2002).

This "e-commerce company" entered the banking industry and became Japan's biggest Internet bank offering financial products and services that range from mortgages to securities brokerage. Ichiba also owns one of Japan's largest online travel portals and a popular instant messaging app Viber. Conventional thinking suggests that it is usually difficult for a company to succeed in an industry that is outside of its core business, but many successful companies such as Amazon, Alibaba, and Google do not seem to prove this thinking. The businesses of these companies cover a wide range of industries and sectors. Most importantly, many of their businesses are quite successful and competitive in the specific industry! This phenomenon is also widely seen in non-digital businesses. For example, Ping An Insurance, a Fortune 500 company (ranked no. 39 in 2017), was highly successful in its core business of insurance and leveraged from that success to expand into banking, asset management, healthcare, automobiles, real estates, and smart technologies.

Among many factors, digitalization may be the most powerful factor to blur the borders between sectors. Digital technologies empower many companies to expand their current offering and exploit new markets. For example, a smartphone is not regarded as a tool to make phone calls or send short messages. People can use it to purchase clothes, order food delivery, organize accommodation, and pay for taxis—basically most transactions can be made with smartphones. Hyperlinks also give rise to the hybridization of two disparate sites. For example, an online social website can lead a user to an online shopping site via a link, so that this social website can profit from the online shopping business, via a referral fee. Apps are different to a physical marketplace. The fact that they can be edited and enriched allows app developers to roll out new features and functions that can be quite independent from previous versions. For example, WeChat was designed to be an instant messaging app and social media and afterward added a popular mobile payment method and a mobile commerce platform.

New digital technology is a catalyst in disrupting the border between online business and physical business. For example, e-commerce websites may offer images and videos, but they are very different to shopping experiences in physical stores where customers can touch and try. However, augmented reality technologies embedded within e-commerce websites can visualize these products and let customers know what they may look like in their home. This is described further in the *Financial Times* article: "BMW to mix real world with virtual car showrooms." On the other hand, the Internet of Things (IoT) digitalizes many physical businesses because IoT-based sensors can identify signals from various devices and conduct programmed actions even in no Internet environment. For example, a home door lock sensor can identify someone from their voice or smartphone app and unlock access (open the door) to him or her. It can also monitor and provide data on visitors to the home.

Most consumers are willing to embrace one-stop services or integrated businesses via their apps. For example, some apps may be used only a few times per year, while too many app installations can affect the speed of a smartphone. Hence some consumers prefer integrated apps. WeChat became one of the world's largest standalone mobile apps by leveraging the network effects of the large Chinese population of young, technology-savvy consumers. It is a one-stop app that covers almost every need within their daily lives. For more information, see ▶ Sect. 8.5. The trend of integration is not just happening in the app or e-business realm. In fact, the emergence of multi-sector integrations, or "new ecosystems," is likely to speed up in place of many industries.

BMW to Mix Real World with Virtual Car Showrooms

BMW is to become the first automaker to use augmented reality technology to sell its cars, with customers using their smartphone screens to view lifelike three-dimensional models superimposed on their view of the real world. Shoppers can open the boot or doors, "step inside," and even turn on the radio. "[In tests of the app] we saw people ducking down when they were getting into the car, as if there really were a roof there for them to bang their heads on," said Andrea Castronovo, BMW Vice President for Sales Strategy and Future Retail.

Augmented reality went mainstream last year with Pokémon Go, in which gamers hunted primitive, two-dimensional characters displayed on top of real-world images from their smartphone cameras. BMW's initiative, announced at the Consumer Electronics Show in Las Vegas, uses Google's visualization technology Tango, limiting it to Tango-capable smartphones, which are only just appearing on the market. Tango uses smartphone cameras, sensors, and infrared for depth perception. The result allows users to walk around a virtual car and see with precision how it would fit in a particular parking space.

Fiat Chrysler Automobiles showed a prototype at Mobile World Congress last February, but BMW will be the first to integrate the technology into its sales process, allowing customers to save their color options and then order the car. The German carmaker is launching the product in select showrooms across 11 countries for its i3 and i8 models. It then plans to release the app on the Google Play store, giving consumers the ability to visualize a broader range of vehicles anytime, anywhere. Eric Johnsen, Head of Business Development for AR at Google, said bricks-and-mortar stores had suffered from Internet shopping, but AR technology could bring them back. "We've gone full circle," he said. "That's why this is exciting—come to the dealership and imagine any BMW car in the actual environment."

But the technology is also likely to be used for online shopping too, potentially creating challenges for retailers. Accenture, which designed and built the app, predicts that AR will revolutionize e-commerce, allowing consumers to visualize within their own homes any product available to buy on the web. "This goes far beyond automotive … This is going to change the way we buy things on the internet," said Matteo Aliberti, Augmented Commerce Lead for Accenture Interactive. "Websites have very nice pictures, but they are flat," he added. "How do you know what furniture will look like in your kitchen? For remodelling your home, this technology will change completely the way we buy things."

Lowe's, the do-it-yourself home improvement retailer, released a Tango-based app in November that gives customers the ability to visualize and measure home furnishings and fixtures. "Instead of choosing between physical or digital shopping, these experiences are now blending in augmented reality, which unlocks entirely new opportunities for retailers and customers," said Kyle Nel, Head of Lowe's Innovation Labs. Apps such as those from BMW and Lowe's provide an important showcase for Google's Tango, which needs to convince both smartphone makers and consumers of its utility. "With other technologies that became fundamental such as GPS and front-facing cameras, it took a few years before every phone was expected to have it," said Johnny Lee, Tango's Technical Lead at Google. "We'll see some of the same adoption curve."

Chinese smartphone maker Lenovo introduced the first Tango-enabled phone, the Phab 2 Pro, in November, while a second, the Asus ZenFone AR, launched this week at the Consumer Electronics Show. Apple has yet to announce its own plans, but it has made a series of moves to position itself, including the 2015 acquisition of German AR start-up Metaio—originally a side project of Volkswagen. Alongside shopping, where Tango was seeing "good traction" among developers, app makers have applied Tango's AR capabilities to gaming and indoor navigation.

"This is allowing us to solve that chicken and egg problem," said Mr Johnsen. He said there would be "several more" Tango phones released this year and predicted that most premium Android devices will be Tango-enabled within 2 years. "Augmented reality has such huge potential for retail, we're just getting started," he said.

P. McGee and T. Bradshaw, "BMW to mix real world with virtual car showrooms," *Financial Times*, 5 January 2017

The borderless aspect can be a facilitator or an inhibitor for businesses to seek out new markets. In the past, businesses established their boundaries on the basis of transaction costs. Then digitalization largely reduced the transaction costs associated with reaching new customers, online merchandising, and customer services. It is now possible for businesses to use digital technologies to explore new opportunities and markets. But can-do does not mean should-do. The exploration of new markets, particularly markets disparate from previous segments, could harm a company's core business because companies have to create additional resources and capacity to explore new markets and shift their focus onto new business. This strategic change could distract and disrupt the current organization structure, strategy, and/or routines and may challenge the dominant business model. Whether the new market strategy succeeds or not, corporate leaders should review the exploration process broadly and strategically and remove barriers to entering new markets with identified potential. Most importantly, extending a business into a new market is an entrepreneurial action that needs leadership and risk management. See the FT article: "Digital option not for faint-hearted leaders."

Digital Option Not for Faint-Hearted Leaders

Digital transformation is not for a faint-hearted leadership team. Indeed, the authors of a recent study by Deloitte, the management consultancy, and *MIT Sloan Management Review*, the business journal, suggest that risk-taking needs to become the cultural norm for companies with digital aspirations. "For every Google,

Amazon or Facebook taking major risks, hundreds of companies are still playing it safe," says Phil Simon, a report contributor and business author. In doing so, they are simply giving digital disrupters further opportunities to outpace them. "Today, the costs of inaction almost always exceed the costs of action," Mr Simon says.

Textbook cases of businesses that paid the ultimate price for failing to anticipate the effects of digitization would include Borders bookstores, Blockbuster video shops, and Kodak, the photographic technology company. In the United Kingdom, WM Morrison supermarkets did not introduce online shopping until 2014, forcing it into a painful game of catch-up with digitally savvy competitors such as Tesco and Waitrose.

The pace of digital disruption is "sweeping, breathtaking and accelerating," said Richard Fairbank, Chief Executive of Capital One, in a July earnings call about the US bank's second-quarter results. "To win in the digital world, we can't simply bolt…channels on to the side of our business or [transfer] analogue banking services to digital channels." Instead, digital must become the centerpiece of the bank's strategy. Some business leaders, however, seem happy to simply add digital channels to existing systems and processes. The danger with this kind of thinking, say experts, is it allows digital disrupters to maintain their technological lead. Businesses such as Uber, Airbnb, and Netflix were built on—and for—the digital age and have mobile and social media technologies at their heart. Such newcomers do not have older systems and processes to worry about and can focus on fine-tuning customers' digital experiences. As a consequence, they will continue to disrupt more established and less agile competitors.

Martin Gill, an analyst with Forrester Research, an advisory firm, says digitally focused companies need to put their organization's purpose and underlying business model first. Too often, he says, established companies find themselves hampered by existing ways of doing things. Philippe Trichet, Digital Expert Director at Boston Consulting Group, the business consultancy, agrees: "Companies need to be prepared to change everything — how they think and how they breathe." In his previous role as Vice President of Customer Experience at Schneider Electric, the industrial equipment company, Mr Trichet was involved in a digital transformation project that involved 30,000 employees in more than 90 countries. "What made a big difference for us was that we had clear goals and the effort was led from the top," he says. From the chief executive down, a common vision of the benefits the management wanted to achieve was communicated to staff. Says Mr Trichet: "It was made clear that digital transformation would affect everyone, so everyone needed to be involved in delivering it."

The project was deemed a success, despite significant challenges, including a large legacy IT estate and the need to join up fragmented sales, marketing, and customer support processes. The program, says Mr Trichet, was not just about rolling out new IT projects, but about rethinking business processes to achieve greater agility, lower costs, and greater customer satisfaction. He adds that it resulted in increased revenues from cross-selling, improved satisfaction from routing customer service online, and increased efficiency by consolidating 145 call centers into 45.

Case studies: Some technological transformations that have gone well—and others that crashed

- **Failure: BBC's Digital Media Initiative**

  Too much focus on technology, not enough on change management—that was what scuppered this initiative, according to an investigation by consultancy PwC. The program, which was cancelled in May 2013 and resulted in an asset write-down of £100 m, lacked an executive steering committee to assess progress against agreed measures of quality, time, and cost. The project "focused on technology risks and issues, rather than [driving] operational change to business practices in the BBC," said PwC.

- **Success: Capital One**

  According to a mid-2014 report from Capgemini Consulting, this US bank "has an unflinching focus on digital," with about 75 percent of its customer interactions now handled digitally. The bank has also been buying talent: in 2014, it acquired Adaptive Path, a San Francisco specialist in high-tech user experience design; in July it bought Monsoon, a Californian digital design company. "With its radical digital approach, Capital One is not just challenging its own wisdom, but that of the entire financial services industry," say the authors of Capgemini's report.

- **Failure: The Co-operative Bank**

  In 2013, Co-op Bank cancelled an IT transformation program resulting in a £300m investment write-off. This became a part of Sir Christopher Kelly's independent review into the bank's crippling capital shortfall. The project's problems, he wrote, included "changes to leadership, a lack of appropriate capability, poor co-ordination, over-complexity, under-developed plans in continual flux and poor budgeting." Co-op Bank has since launched a £60m digital catch-up scheme that has had its own problems, according to consultancy Verdi.

- **Success: John Lewis**

  UK retailer John Lewis has been one of the most successful companies in the fight-back against online retailers, creating a "bricks and clicks" experience. Online sales account for about 33 percent of revenues. While half its customers buy in store, the rest combine experiences through hybrid services that let customers buy online but collect in store. Last Christmas, group sales were up 5.8 percent year on year to £777 m in the 5 weeks to December 27, helped by a 19 percent rise in the value of online sales year on year.

  Source: J. Twentyman, "Digital option not for faint-hearted leaders," *Financial Times*, 30 September 2015

7.2 Gaining Insights into New Market Spaces Through the Value Curve

The concept of the value curve is used to illustrate how to redefine competition along different dimensions of benefit. In the book-retailing example, these dimensions include price, convenience, selection range, speed, and face-to-face interaction. On these dimensions traditional and online bookstores offer varying levels of benefit.

Sketching the value curves of different companies in a specific industry that have diverging value curves is a valuable exercise to gain an understanding of what drives value creation and how companies are positioned along the key dimensions that determine customer benefit. Drawing the value curves in the book-retailing industry (as shown below) requires us, firstly, to identify the key dimensions of customer benefit. During this first step, it is important to ensure that all key dimensions are listed, for example, selection range or price, and that the dimensions listed are mutually exclusive, that is, they do not overlap logically. Secondly, we need to determine how different competitors rank on each dimension. Connecting the different dots then allows us to draw the value curve for each company.

The visualized profile of the value curves provides the basis for thinking about new types of value curves that might break the existing trade-offs of the existing business models.

7.3 Looking Outside One's Own Box

How can this type of value creation be attained? A firm needs to analyze the way it wants to create value by "looking outside the box," that is, outside the standard business practices of its own industry. Doing so can lead to the discovery of uncovered market spaces between separate industries.[2]

The six paths framework developed by Kim and Mauborgne suggests numerous ways of doing so.

Looking Across Substitute Industries   The main question that needs to be asked here is how customers make trade-offs between different products (or services) that serve as substitutes. The goal is to determine why customers choose one product and not the other and what criteria they use in making their decision. In the traditional business environment, the most severe competition does not necessarily come from within the industry. Customers make trade-offs, for example, between using cash or a credit card, traveling by car or train, and using a pen or personal computer. In the online world, customers make trade-offs between shopping online or going to the store and banking online or going to the bank branch. When Nordea Bank considered this trade-off, it found out that customers who go to the branch value the ease of use of over-the-counter banking. Thus, Nordea set out to develop a highly user-friendly online interface to offer a similar experience as that of a branch office with the benefits (and the lower costs) of an online channel.

Looking Across Strategic Groups   A strategic group consists of firms that produce the same type of products for a certain customer segment. Firms usually compare themselves with competitors positioned in the same strategic group as themselves. Doing so usually does not lead to radically new insights since firms in the same strategic group tend to be similar in their product offerings. Looking across strategic groups

---

2   See C. Kim and R. Mauborgne, 1999, op. cit. and 2015, op. cit.

means looking at what companies do that produce the same basic product for different customer segments, thereby finding out potential new ways of creating value. For example, car manufacturer Mercedes, after analyzing lower-ranked strategic groups, developed the Smart car, which is offered at prices that compete with low-cost cars while still containing Mercedes technology. Similarly, car manufacturers from lower-ranked strategic groups, such as Toyota, developed cars that possess many features of higher-ranked competitors while still maintaining a low price position. Another example concerns tablets, where Apple's iPad set the benchmark of quality, while other companies, such as Samsung, have a similar market positioning. However, Amazon's Kindle Fire can be seen as a challenger offering a cheaper and product with less functionality (an e-reader with low-glare screen), a kind of disruptive innovation as discussed in the previous chapter.

Looking Across Chains of Buyers   The underlying logic of this perspective is that the person in charge of purchasing is not necessarily the one using the purchased product or service. For instance, the procurement department and the corporate user usually have different definitions of value. While price and the purchasing procedure are important for the former, the latter focuses on ease of use. If a firm has previously considered only one of the two groups, taking on the other group's perspective might lead to new value creation. For example, consider any product that a parent purchases for their child. The parent may be advised by doctors in the case of a sick child, educators may advise on content and games, and parents in the peer group may influence the purchasing decision for sports equipment and games. However the user or consumer is the child, and the child may exert some influence on the purchasing decision.

Looking Across Complementary Products and Services   Most products and services are not used in isolation, but instead need others to complement them. Computers, for instance, require software in order to operate. ▶ Amazon.com recognized the power of complementary products when it launched its personalized book recommendation service, which suggests to customers a list of books that may be of interest to them based on their previous purchases. Nordea Bank offers a more targeted form of complementary services through the use of a triggered database, which works as follows. When there is a change in a customer account—for instance, a large incoming money transfer, a change of address, or a change in marital status—a trigger in the database is set off to inform the bank about this change, which then raises a number of questions regarding complementary products. What does this change mean for the customer in terms of financing, long-term payments, insurance, and e-services? Products that align to the questions are then offered to the customer.

Looking Across Functional or Emotional Appeal to Buyers   Products or services often focus either on functional or tangible characteristics (such as durability and breadth of choice) or on their emotional appeal, which is captured by the strength of the brand. Looking across boundaries by, for instance, turning functional products into emotionally appealing products can lead to a vast increment in the perceived consumer benefit. Take the example of the coffee house Starbucks, which has turned a functional mass-produced product (coffee) into an emotional experience for its customers, thus being able to charge a premium price for it.

Looking Across Time   By identifying the future impact of changes in the macro- or competitive environment, a business can adapt its value creation strategies based on the predicted changes. If the business acts ahead of competitors, it takes a higher risk but enjoys the benefit of being first to market. For instance, Nordea realized in the 1980s the importance of electronic channels and swiftly introduced PC-banking services. This helped Nordea to create substantial cost savings while at the same time significantly increasing customer benefit, ahead of competitors.

Looking Across Unrelated Industries   It is also possible to venture out and look across completely different industries to see how value is created there. This is one of the key messages that the case studies in this book convey. Looking across different industries requires creative leaps on your side, but it has the potential to create surprising insights. An insurance salesperson might ask, for instance, what lessons can be taken away from Ducati's exclusive Internet sales of new motorcycle models directly to consumers and to what extent the learning can be adapted to the insurance business.

7.4   Pinpointing Possibilities for New Value Creation

After looking across the above dimensions, different questions arise in the four areas listed below. Answering them opens up the opportunity for new value creation potential[3]:

- *Eliminate.* Does what we do really create consumer benefit? If not, which components or features of our product or service should we eliminate? Even if a company has made a proper assessment of these issues at some point in time, it should then raise these questions again since buyers' preferences are dynamic by nature.
- *Reduce.* Where can we reduce our range of offerings? What major costs do not create benefit?
- *Raise.* Where should we raise the standard of products or services? Where can we increase benefit by expanding our existing offering?
- *Create.* What can we do that has not been done so far?

Tapping into hitherto uncovered market spaces provides businesses with the opportunity not only to capture large parts of the market by taking away market share from competitors but also to expand the overall market size. ▶ Amazon.com, for example, did not just take buyers away from traditional bricks-and-mortar bookstores. It also turned people who previously had not purchased many books into

---

3   A detailed discussion of this approach to value creation can be found in Kim and Mauborgne (1997, 1999).

avid buyers through the depth of its offerings and value-adding services such as the book reviews and personalized recommendations.

However, the move into new market spaces is not a one-time affair, since superior profit will last only as long as competitors do not move into this newly discovered market space. Just as it is with generic strategies, competitors will try to enter the market if they believe that the new model promises attractive returns, thereby eroding profitability through diluting market share. The sustainability of a business depends again on the uniqueness of the positioning and on how difficult it is to imitate this positioning.

Summarizing the value innovation thinking, there are five characteristics that differentiate this type of thinking from conventional competitive thinking:

- *Different assumptions.* Conventional thinking tells us that an industry's value curves follow one basic shape. Value innovation logic assumes that new value curves can be shaped by creatively resolving historic trade-offs.
- *Strategic focus.* Conventional thinking tells us that the primary goal is to pursue a competitive advantage and to beat the competition. Value innovation logic pursues a quantum leap in customer value where competition is no benchmark.
- *Customers.* Conventional thinking tells us that the primary goal is to retain and expand the existing customer base through segmentation and customization. Value innovation logic focuses on the mass of buyers. The focus is on finding the key communalities that customers value.
- *Resources.* Conventional thinking tells us to exploit existing assets and capabilities. In contrast, value innovation thinking poses the question: What would we do if we were starting anew?
- *Offerings.* Conventional thinking tells us to offer the products and services of the industry we are competing in. Value innovation thinking refocuses the thinking on offering total customer solutions exceeding industry boundaries.

7.5 Finding the Right Time to Enter a Market

Early- or first-mover advantages were a major driver for the Internet boom during the late 1990s. No potential entrepreneur or investor wanted to miss out on the profit potential that was promised to early movers. Thus, entrepreneurs rushed into creating or financing Internet start-ups, accepting large initial losses upfront but expecting high returns over time due to first-mover advantages.

Undoubtedly for some Internet start-ups, such as eBay, Yahoo!, and ▶ Amazon.com, early-mover advantages helped to establish and secure a dominant market position. In most cases, however, companies that started out early during the Internet boom have either gone out of business or been acquired by other firms that embraced the Internet much later.

Before moving into a more detailed discussion of early-mover advantages, we want to emphasize that a major difference between the ▶ Amazon.com-like ventures and the bankrupt Internet companies is that ▶ Amazon.com was not only early but also best in class in how it was managed. Since its launch in Seattle (USA) in July 1995, ▶ Amazon.com has strived continuously to improve customer experience while simultaneously increasing operational efficiency, thereby reducing costs. In other industries, early movers were unable to compete with late entrants and eventually went out of business.

Similarly, Amazon, eBay, and other successful Internet start-ups managed to get the timing right and also deliver superior value on a continuous basis. Thus, while early-mover advantages have been traditionally seen as important, some studies suggested not giving this time factor a significant importance in explaining a company's competitive advantage in an Internet market context.[4] Basically, the rationale here stems from the fact that in the digital world, the sources of early-mover advantage (including switching costs or network externalities) may have a weaker effect compared to those in the physical market context. When considering the role played by an early-mover company, an important question to bear in mind is whether a firm can maintain its product/service quality or cost leadership over competitors in order to keep its dominant position in the market.[5]

In the following sections, we first analyze the different types of early-mover advantages and discuss how they affect e-businesses. Early-mover advantages can result from (1) *learning effects*, (2) *brand and reputation*, (3) *switching costs*, and (4) *network effects*. We then analyze early-mover disadvantages, which are (1) *market uncertainty*, (2) *technological uncertainty*, and (3) *free-rider effects.*[6]

7.5.1 Early-Mover Advantages

Learning Effects   *The idea of learning effects is that as output increases, a firm gains experience.*[7] *This allows it to conduct its business more efficiently, thereby reducing costs and increasing quality. When* ▶ Amazon.com *entered the German online book market in 1998, it was able to capitalize on its 3 years of experience in the United States where it had learned online and offline marketing, iteratively improved its website and streamlined its logistics and delivery processes.*

Germany's Bertelsmann Online (BOL), on the other hand, entered the online book-retailing business later and still had to go through the learning process, while ▶ Amazon.com kept improving at the same time. Ultimately, BOL was never able

---

4   See Porter (2001).

5   S. Rangan and R. Adner discuss the pitfalls of early-mover advantages in the Internet world in the article "Profits and the Internet: seven misconceptions," *Sloan Management Review*, 2001, Summer, pp. 44–46.

6   For different types of early-mover advantages, see Besanko et al. (2003). W. Boulding and M. Christen point out that there are also important early-mover disadvantages in "First-mover disadvantage," *Harvard Business Review*, 2001, October, pp. 20–21. Likewise, see R. Varadarajan et al.'s paper "First-mover advantage in an Internet-enabled market environment: conceptual framework and propositions," *Journal of the Academy of Marketing Science*, 2008, 36, pp. 293–328; also, see the chapter by R. Varadarajan et al. published in Springer's research handbook on "e-business Strategic Management," edited by F.J. Martínez-López, 2013.

7   The importance of learning and experience first received attention through the development of the experience curve: Henderson (1998).

to provide a shopping experience that could compete with ▶ Amazon.com's, a shortcoming that contributed to the Bertelsmann Group's eventual decision to abandon BOL.

Brand and Reputation *Companies that enter a market first with a new product or way of conducting business catalyze consumer interest, thus improving their reputation and brand awareness. Furthermore, media coverage creates free and strong publicity, which can enhance the brand and reputation. The business press is always interested in new business developments, successful or not. When* ▶ Amazon.com *went public in the mid-1990s, major business newspapers and journals covered it, thereby creating free and credible publicity. In 1996* The Wall Street Journal *published a front-cover story on* ▶ Amazon.com, *and on the following day, book sales on the company's website doubled.[8] Other early movers such as* ▶ Yahoo.com *and eBay have received similar levels of media coverage. If a business is first to market with an inferior or defective product, the media will cover that too.*

Being an early entrant in a market can also help to build up a strong reputation with customers, provided that the company can meet customer expectations during the first few contacts. This may seem obvious, but many Internet start-ups were unable to do so due to their badly designed websites and the lack of timely and reliable product delivery. One poor e-commerce experience would damage the confidence of a consumer broadly beyond the one business. More successful Internet start-ups such as ▶ Amazon.com managed early on to provide customers with a superior shopping experience. Customers who had a good experience with one provider are unlikely to switch to another. Therefore, any new competitor must provide a higher value than that offered by the early entrant in order to offset the uncertainty of being new and to induce the customer to switch over, to leave a business that they are comparatively satisfied with.

However, an established brand and reputation are no guarantee of lasting success. Since the cost of search, trial, and comparison can be very low in the Internet, information asymmetries are usually reduced, and the inclination of customers to switch to another competitor increases in the digital market space. The case of the search engine Google is an excellent example of how a newcomer managed to overcome the brand recognition and reputation of older and more established rivals such as Overture and AltaVista. Google was able to do so because it offered radically higher user benefits through higher speed and better search accuracy than all other companies. Without doing any massive advertising, Google quickly became the preferred search engine for millions of Internet users.

Switching Costs *Switching costs, also called self-compatibility costs, are felt by a customer when from moving from one product to another. Even if a new product is superior to the one the customer already possesses, the customer might still decide to keep the old product because of switching costs, which, in effect, create a weak form of lock-in. The expectation that switching costs on the Internet would be high was one of the main driv-*

---

8   J. Cassidy discusses the story of Amazon in *Dot.con*, Perennial, 2003, pp. 135–150.

ers behind the race for "eyeballs" and "clicks," whose levels determined the stock market valuation of many companies (more traditional metrics such as price/earnings ratios were not considered to be suitable for Internet start-ups).

The common belief was that once customers got used to the setup of a website, and once they had provided their customer information, they would no longer want to change to a new e-business because of the time cost of reentering their information on a new site. A financial penalty, for example, early closure of an account or contract, may also be a switching cost. This belief turned out to be fatal for many companies that spent heavily on marketing and customer acquisition, only to find that their customers were happily switching to other websites when a competitor offered better value. Michael Porter warned against this false belief when pointing out that switching costs could be very low in the digital market space, considering how easy it is to switch with a few clicks. At the same time, it highlights that offering a superior value proposition is a key source of competitive advantage and that a superior value proposition protects against customer's "switching" to competitors. In particular, the Internet underpins markets where first movers can enjoy an advantage by creating what is known as *noncontractual switching costs*[9], that is, those costs related to switching in a situation whereby the customer is not constrained by any contract.

Four sources of noncontractual switching costs can be identified: (1) switching costs from relearning, (2) switching costs because of customized offerings, (3) switching costs because of incompatible complementary products, and (4) switching costs resulting from customer incentive programs. These are defined below.

Switching Costs from Relearning   These are a result of getting used to a new product. Users of software programs who are thinking about switching from one provider to another often stick with the old product for as long as they can to avoid relearning costs. A classic example is Apple and Windows users. Consider too the case of IBX,[10] which developed a proprietary B2B e-purchasing software platform. Once customers get used to this software and train their personnel to use it, switching to a competitor would entail the time cost of considerable relearning. Similarly, Internet users get used to the functionalities of a specific website and might not want to switch to another website. The more website-specific the knowledge is, the less likely it is that a person will switch to another website. It is worth noting in the IBX example that the more idiosyncratic a website is to use, the higher the barrier to initial use because it takes time to learn how to use it. In other cases, such as with search engines where the usage is easy and intuitive, switching costs are minimal. This was another reason that helped Google to become, within a matter of months, the most popular[11] Internet search engine. As the Internet continues to mature and users become more accustomed to using it, relearning-induced switching costs are likely to decrease.

---

9   Ibid., p. 300
10   Acquired by Tradeshift in 2017
11   However, at the same time, this lack of lock-in is also the greatest danger that Google faces today as competitors, such as Yahoo! or Microsoft (Bing), heavily invest in search engine development. Nevertheless, recent search engines' rankings clearly show the dominant of Google.

Switching Costs Because of Customized Offerings   These result from a firm's ability to adapt a website to the specific needs and preferences of individual customers. Investing in personalization tools is one way to generate customized information and advice and, therefore, to seize the "lock-in" opportunity offered to first movers. Since these tools usually perform better with the accumulation over time of customer's transactions, first movers need a longer period to gather customers' information and maintain their superiority over later entrants.[12] For example, as customers make purchases and search for books, ► Amazon.com learns about their preferences and is then able to make customized recommendations based on previous purchase patterns. Another example is Netflix, the provider of on-demand Internet streaming media, which offers movie recommendations. If customers want to switch to a competitor, they first need to "teach the system" through a number of purchases before the latter can provide them with the same level of customized offerings. Similarly, when ► Tesco.com customers first enter the online retailing site, their shopping list is instantly populated with all the items that they had previously purchased in physical Tesco stores with their Tesco Clubcard. This customization eliminates the initial effort for Internet shoppers to set up their shopping list online. Another interesting example is ► Match.com, the biggest dating website in the world. It achieved a leading market position due to a better knowledge of its users than the competition. In a business where giving the right suggestions to meet "compatible" people is a core part of the value proposition, a higher performance of the system used to do the matches can be a source of competitive advantage.

Switching Costs Because of Incompatible Complementary Products   These result from the inability to use the new product in combination with old products. An illustrative example of this was the introduction of the CD player, which rendered the existing vinyl record collections of music lovers worthless if they decided to switch to the new technology. Through the symbiotic relationship between the iPod player and the iTunes music downloading service, Apple also created high switching costs for customers. When iTunes users contemplated the idea of purchasing a digital music player other than an iPod, they would have faced the switching costs of not being able to play the songs that they purchased through the iTunes platform, since their format was only compatible with the iPod product.

Switching Costs Resulting from Customer Incentive Programs   These occur when firms offer customer benefits in return for their loyalty. A prominent example here is the frequent-flyer bonus programs offered by airlines, where passengers earn free upgrades or free tickets after having flown a certain number of miles with the specific airline. Also, Tesco has created switching costs for customers through its Tesco Clubcard. Owners of a Tesco Clubcard, who have been using it for shopping in physical stores, have strong incentives to prefer ► Tesco.com over other online grocery and non-food shopping sites because they can continue collecting incentive points by shopping online.

---

12 See R. Varadarajan et al., 2008, op. cit., p. 300.

For consumers, it is sensible to consider overall costs, including switching costs, when deciding on a new purchase. With hindsight, it is surprising that switching costs received so much attention during the Internet boom years, since the above-mentioned types of switching had been around before then. Therefore, for many online businesses, there was really no need to gain market share as rapidly as possible and to invest heavily in new technology. History has shown that, in most cases, if a new entrant offers a substantially better product and captures sustainable value, then it will most likely drive the weaker product out of the market, even if there are substantial switching costs.[13]

Network Effects   *Network effects are present when a product becomes more useful to consumers in proportion to the number of people using it.*[14] *There are two types of network effects,* direct *and* indirect*:*

- *Direct network effects.* The strength of these effects depends directly on the number of users of a given device or technology that figures a network effect. An example of a product with strong direct network effects is the mobile phone. While a single mobile phone by itself is essentially worthless, it becomes very valuable when large parts of the population own a mobile phone and can use it to communicate with each other. Similarly, the Internet increases in value for the individual user as the number of users increases. Bob Metcalfe found that the value of a network increases proportionally to the square of the number of people using it. This is known as Metcalfe's law. Thus, if you double the number of participants in a given network, the value for each individual participant doubles, which leads to a fourfold increase in the overall value of the network.[15] This coherence becomes especially relevant in the context of social networking sites where the number of users determines directly the value of the overall network due to the likely interaction between community members.
- *Indirect network effects.* Similar effects also apply with products that require complementary goods, such as smartphones and tablets. Their value increases as the size of the installed user base increases, because more companies offer complementary products such as back shells and glass films.

The first mover's offering is expected to be more attractive to current or potential consumers, due to the size of its network which is usually larger than that of the competition. In fact, network externalities constitute a potential source of competitive advantage for first-mover companies. However, there could be some moderating effects for certain dimensions such as product category, market, industry, etc. Consequently, whether a firm can benefit or not from network effects depends

---

13 S. Liebowitz refutes the frequently cited QWERTY keyboard and VHS/Betamax examples in *Re-thinking the Network Economy*, New York, Amacom, 2002, pp. 47–48.

14 A good discussion and critique of the impact of network effects on e-commerce companies can be found in Liebowitz (2002). S. Rangan and R. Adner also discuss network effects in e-commerce in "Profits and the Internet: seven misconceptions," *Sloan Management Review*, 2001, Summer, pp. 44–46.

15 See vcmike (2006). See also Metcalfe (2013).

largely on the nature of the network. For example, if network effects exist in a publicly owned platform that is open to all firms, then network effects benefit the whole community but do not accrue special benefits to any individual party. The mobile phone and the Internet are open networks where the benefits of network effects accrue largely to customers. If, on the other hand, network benefits are specific to a particular website or community, then the operator of this website can reap benefits from these network effects.

The relevant question is whether, when creating a first-mover advantage, network effects in the digital market space are similar, lower, or higher than those in physical, traditional markets. There are several reasons that explain having higher network effects in the digital market space.[16] They include that there are no physical constraints which limit the number of buyers and sellers involved in a market exchange, and electronic transactions can take place irrespective of time and place. These factors significantly contribute to the ability of early movers to create a critical mass of online customers. In e-commerce, a vivid example of network effects is eBay. On a stand-alone basis, this online auction platform is not valuable at all; its value comes from the millions of users who post products for sale and search for products to buy. This results in a highly liquid market, where it is easy to match sellers and buyers.

Furthermore, the strength of network effects is increased through the information that is posted about sellers and buyers, who both get rated by their peers on criteria such as timeliness of delivery, payment, and quality of the products sold. eBay users who have received strong peer ratings are likely to continue using eBay because of their reputation, which makes it easier for them to sell items. eBay, as the operator of the community, can capture parts of the value, for example, through fees for posting on its website and sales commissions.

Through its book reviews, ► Amazon.com has also created network effects. As more customers use its website and post their comments about books and other products, ► Amazon.com becomes more valuable to other customers, who can retrieve information from many different reviewers about any given book. Other companies, such as ► Douban.com, have turned customer reviews into a complete business model, by creating a website that consists primarily of consumer ratings for different kinds of products.

From the individual customer perspective, switching from a network that is built around a large installed user base is sensible only if everybody else switches as well. It is possible, at least in theory, that a company with strong network effects can induce customers to stay in spite of the advent of new competitors with superior products. Users decide not to switch because they do not want to lose their contact with other users. If the majority of users agree to switch to the new product, however, then all users would be better off to do so as well.

The logic of the Internet boom years was that if companies wanted to generate strong network effects, then they needed quickly to generate large market share, even if the costs for doing so were high. Part of this thinking was also that quality

---

16 See R. Varadarajan, 2008, op. cit., p. 298.

in comparison with competitors was not of central importance, because it was assumed that barriers to entry would increase as a result of network effects, making it difficult for newcomers to attract customers away from their current provider. However, network effects, when they existed, often did not turn out to be strong enough to keep customers at one website. MySpace is an example of this. In fact, there were only very few instances, such as online auctioning, where network effects were sufficiently strong to have a substantial impact on user value. Today, however, where online social networking sites are of great importance, the lock-in due to network effects is more relevant than ever.

Additionally, even if network effects are strong, this does not necessarily mean that consumers will not switch to a new, superior product. When choosing between an existing and a new product, customers do not look just at the existing situation; they also anticipate its future evolution—otherwise, CD players and compact discs would never have become popular. Thus, as has always been the case, in order to succeed, new entrants need to demonstrate the superiority of their product and to communicate broadly that their product presents the most attractive features for the future.

7.5.2 Early-Mover Disadvantages

Businesses entering the market early with a new technology do not necessarily achieve a competitive advantage over their rivals.[17] In fact, there are a number of reasons why a late entrant might actually accrue some benefits. These reasons are (1) *market uncertainty*, (2) *technological uncertainty*, and (3) *free-rider effects*.

Market Uncertainty   *During the early stages of an innovation cycle, it is very difficult to clearly establish customer needs. During the 1990s, Internet start-ups were trying out various business models and value propositions, many of which misjudged the actual consumer needs.*

In banking, for instance, there was a much higher desire for security, trust, and face-to-face interaction than was anticipated when many online financial institutions initially entered the market. In the end, banks with established brand names and branch networks were in a better position than their purely online competitors to fulfill customer needs through a multichannel banking approach.

Market uncertainty is aggravated if the market is not ready for a new product or service. Consumers need to get used to a new product or service before it becomes valuable to them. However, they are reluctant to do so unless there are already a sufficient number of providers in the market. On the other hand, providers will not invest unless they believe that there will be enough consumers to make their investment worthwhile. Both sides face a "chicken and egg" situation, which results in uncertainty regarding future developments.

---

17 For a detailed discussion of first-mover disadvantages, see Liebermann and Montgomery (1998).

Furthermore, the market also needs to be ready from a technological perspective. Many of the online services that turn out to be successful today rely on the widespread availability of always-on, broadband Internet connections. For example, on-demand streaming media such as Netflix, social networking sites such as Facebook, the video site YouTube, or the Internet telephony provider Skype depend on users having access to reliable fast broadband to be able to use their services. Had these businesses launched in the earlier days of the Internet when Internet access was limited and unreliable, they would have failed.

Technological Uncertainty Betting on wrong technologies can be as problematic as overestimating market demand. In mobile e-commerce, for instance, early adopters of the Wireless Application Protocol (WAP) found that this highly praised technology did not deliver on its promises to create superior customer value. Instead, it proved to be very cumbersome to use, with a complicated 35-step procedure to configure a mobile phone for WAP access, long connection time (over 60 seconds), and the tiny screen space of a handset. As a result, customer take-up was much lower than predicted.

Another example is Nokia, which was the dominant mobile phone manufacturer. Nokia's swift decline cannot merely be explained by a risk-averse bet on continuing with Symbian systems instead of iOS or Android. Nokia also looked for "a third leg" to shore out its innovation strategy, but their innovations were too ahead of the market, such as the Internet of Things and multimedia health management. Most importantly we cannot just attribute Nokia's failure to technological aspects. Failing to manage technological uncertainty and innovation is, in many cases, also associated with many other non-technological factors such as strategy, leadership, bureaucracy, organization structure, and more. For more information, please see the article: "The strategic decisions that caused Nokia's failure."

> **The Strategic Decisions That Caused Nokia's Failure**
> The moves that led to Nokia's decline paint a cautionary tale for successful firms. In less than a decade, Nokia emerged from Finland to lead the mobile phone revolution. It rapidly grew to have one of the most recognizable and valuable brands in the world. At its height Nokia commanded a global market share in mobile phones of over 40 percent. While its journey to the top was swift, its decline was equally so, culminating in the sale of its mobile phone business to Microsoft in 2013. It is tempting to lay the blame for Nokia's demise at the doors of Apple, Google, and Samsung. But as I argue in my latest book, *Ringtone: Exploring the Rise and Fall of Nokia in Mobile Phones*, this ignores one very important fact: Nokia had begun to collapse from within well before any of these companies entered the mobile communications market. In these times of technological advancement, rapid market change, and growing complexity, analyzing the story of Nokia provides salutary lessons for any company wanting to either forge or maintain a leading position in their industry.

7

Early Success

With a young, united, and energetic leadership team at the helm, Nokia's early success was primarily the result of visionary and courageous management choices that leveraged the firm's innovative technologies as digitalization and deregulation of telecom networks quickly spread across Europe. But in the mid-1990s, the near collapse of its supply chain meant Nokia was on the precipice of being a victim of its success. In response, disciplined systems and processes were put in place, which enabled Nokia to become extremely efficient and further scale up production and sales much faster than its competitors.

Between 1996 and 2000, the headcount at Nokia Mobile Phones (NMP) increased 150 percent to 27,353, while revenues over the period were up 503 percent. This rapid growth came at a cost. And that cost was that managers at Nokia's main development centers found themselves under ever-increasing short-term performance pressure and were unable to dedicate time and resources to innovation. While the core business focused on incremental improvements, Nokia's relatively small data group took up the innovation mantle. In 1996, it launched the world's first smartphone, the Communicator, and was also responsible for Nokia's first camera phone in 2001 and its second-generation smartphone, the innovative 7650.

The Search for an Elusive Third Leg

Nokia's leaders were aware of the importance of finding what they called a "third leg"—a new growth area to complement the hugely successful mobile phone and network businesses. Their efforts began in 1995 with the New Venture Board, but this failed to gain traction as the core businesses ran their own venturing activities and executives were too absorbed with managing growth in existing areas to focus on finding new growth.

A renewed effort to find the third leg was launched with the Nokia Ventures Organisation (NVO) under the leadership of one of Nokia's top management team. This visionary program absorbed all existing ventures and sought out new technologies. It was successful in the sense that it nurtured a number of critical projects which were transferred to the core businesses. In fact, many opportunities NVO identified were too far ahead of their time; for instance, NVO correctly identified "the Internet of Things" and found opportunities in multimedia health management—a current growth area. But it ultimately failed due to an inherent contradiction between the long-term nature of its activities and the short-term performance requirements imposed on it.

Reorganizing for Agility

Although Nokia's results were strong, the share price high and customers around the world satisfied and loyal, Nokia's CEO Jorma Ollila was increasingly concerned that rapid growth had brought about a loss of agility and entrepreneurialism. Between 2001 and 2005, a number of decisions were made to attempt to rekindle Nokia's earlier drive and energy, but, far from reinvigorating Nokia, they actually set up the beginning of the decline. Key among these decisions was the reallocation of important leadership roles and the poorly implemented 2004 reorganization into a matrix structure. This led to the departure of vital members of the executive team, which led to the deterioration of strategic thinking.

Tensions within matrix organizations are common as different groups with different priorities and performance criteria are required to work collaboratively. At Nokia, which had been accustomed to decentralized initiatives, this new way of working proved an anathema. Mid-level executives had neither the experience nor training in the subtle integrative negotiations fundamental in a successful matrix. As I explain in my book, process trumps structure in reorganizations. And so reorganizations will be ineffective without paying attention to resource allocation processes, product policy and product management, and sales priorities and providing the right incentives for well-prepared managers to support these processes. Unfortunately, this did not happen at Nokia.

NMP became locked into an increasingly conflicted product development matrix between product line executives with P&L responsibility and common "horizontal resource platforms" whose managers were struggling to allocate scarce resources. They had to meet the various and growing demands of increasingly numerous and disparate product development programs without sufficient software architecture development and software project management skills. This conflictual way of working slowed decision-making and seriously dented morale, while the wear and tear of extraordinary growth combined with an abrasive CEO personality also began to take their toll. Many managers left.

Beyond 2004, top management was no longer sufficiently technologically savvy or strategically integrative to set priorities and resolve conflicts arising in the new matrix. Increased cost reduction pressures rendered Nokia's strategy of product differentiation through market segmentation ineffective and resulted in a proliferation of poorer quality products.

The Swift Decline

The following years marked a period of infighting and strategic stasis that successive reorganizations did nothing to alleviate. By this stage, Nokia was trapped by a reliance on its unwieldy operating system called Symbian. While Symbian had given Nokia an early advantage, it was a device-centric system in what was becoming a platform- and application-centric world. To make matters worse, Symbian exacerbated delays in new phone launches as whole new sets of code had to be developed and tested for each phone model. By 2009, Nokia was using 57 different and incompatible versions of its operating system.

While Nokia posted some of its best financial results in the late 2000s, the management team was struggling to find a response to a changing environment: software was taking precedence over hardware as the critical competitive feature in the industry. At the same time, the importance of application ecosystems was becoming apparent, but as dominant industry leader, Nokia lacked the skills and inclination to engage with this new way of working. By 2010, the limitations of Symbian had become painfully obvious, and it was clear Nokia had missed the shift toward apps pioneered by Apple. Not only did Nokia's strategic options seem limited, but none were particularly attractive. In the mobile phone market, Nokia had become a sitting duck to growing competitive forces and accelerating market changes. The game was lost, and it was left to a new CEO Stephen Elop and new Chairman Risto Siilasmaa to draw from the lessons and successfully disengage Nokia from mobile phones to refocus the company on its other core business, network infrastructure equipment.

What Can We Learn from Nokia

Nokia's decline in mobile phones cannot be explained by a single, simple answer: management decisions, dysfunctional organizational structures, growing bureaucracy, and deep internal rivalries all played a part in preventing Nokia from recognizing the shift from product-based competition to one based on platforms.

Nokia's mobile phone story exemplifies a common trait we see in mature, successful companies: success breeds conservatism and hubris which, over time, results in a decline of the strategy processes leading to poor strategic decisions. Where once companies embraced new ideas and experimentation to spur growth, with success they become risk averse and less innovative. Such considerations will be crucial for companies that want to grow and avoid one of the biggest disruptive threats to their future—their own success.

Source: Y. Doz, "The Strategic Decisions That Caused Nokia's Failure," ▶ *Knowledge.Insead.edu*, 23 November 2017

Free-Rider Effects   Learning effects can constitute a first-mover advantage. However, if they cannot be kept proprietary, then competitors will benefit from them without having to make the same mistakes as the first mover(s). In general, developing a market as a first mover is more expensive than just imitating it.

Many traditional bricks-and-mortar retailers who were initially hesitant to enter the online business and then later embraced the Internet profited greatly from the failed experiences of the early movers. They leveraged their well-known brand and installed customer bases to rapidly overtake their pure online competitors. In some instances they acquired them. Thus, for example, WalMart in the United States has become one of the largest Internet retailers by leveraging its strong brand name and synergies with its physical store network.

It is not unmanageable to handle these disadvantages. In order to be a winning first mover, companies should be aware that once stepping into a new market, a company needs to manage the tension between exploring new markets and exploiting current markets, such as reallocating and bundling resources, changing strategies, and reorganizing corporate structures, and more. New markets may be promising; at the same time, they may disrupt the current revenue stream and even cannibalize the competitive advantage of a business in current sectors or industries. For example, Tencent launched the WeChat app which competes with Tencent's dominant instant messaging app QQ. However, it is worthwhile to take careful risks and devise strategies to explore new markets because in today's evolving environment, no sectors or industries can permanently generate the same fixed revenue. To achieve sustainable growth, e-businesses need to be dynamic, flexible, and opportunistic. They need to anticipate and adapt to changes in the environment and explore new markets and business opportunities.

Summary

This chapter indicated that digitalization largely disrupts borders between sectors and analyzed how firms can break away from traditional forms of competition and redefine their value proposition by opening up new market spaces. This can be done first by gaining insights into new market spaces through the value curve. It can also be done through the six paths value creation framework by looking across (1) substitutive industries, (2) strategic groups, (3) the chain of buyers, (4) complementary products and service offerings, (5) functional or emotional appeal to buyers, and (6) time and trends.

This chapter also discussed timing issues for market entry in e-business. More specifically, it analyzed the different types of early-mover advantages and disadvantages that an Internet venture can exploit (or should avoid). Early-mover advantages include (1) learning effects, (2) brand and reputation, (3) switching costs, and (4) network effects. Early-mover disadvantages include (1) market uncertainty, (2) technological uncertainty, and (3) free-rider effects.

? Review Questions

1. What do sectors without borders mean?
2. How can a company look for new market spaces outside its own industry?
3. Explain the six paths framework. How can it be used to create value in e-business?
4. Outline the timing issues for market entry in e-business.
5. What are the advantages and disadvantages that early movers in e-business should exploit or avoid?
6. Working in a group, pick out an e-business company of your choice. Write down what you consider to be the key product/service elements. As a group, discuss and reach consensus on these key elements. Using a chart rate the offering's level on each key element against the main competitors. Do you see competitors with radically different value curves?
7. Adopt the perspective of a new industry entrant, and consider the existing value curves. Use one or two of the paths to experiment with the creation of a new value curve.
   - Industry: Which elements of substitute industries are unimportant/important to target buyers?
   - Strategic groups: Which key elements of the offer compel buyers to buy up or buy down?
   - Buyers: Who are the decision-makers, and how would changing buyer focus affect the key elements?

8. Working in group, assess the "lock-in" network effect of Facebook with its users. Also, how plausible is it that Facebook maintains in the future its hegemony in the online social networks sector? Do you see Facebook losing its leading position in about a decade or so?

9. Select a company just reaching out to a new market, and discuss how this company should manage the tension between exploring the new market and exploiting current markets.

References

Besanko, D., Dranove, D., Shanley, M., & Schaefer, S. (2003). *Economics of Strategy* (pp. 438–446). John Wiley.

Henderson, B. (1998). The experience curve reviewed. In C. Stern & G. Stalk (Eds.), (pp. 12–15). *Perspectives on strategy*: John Wiley.

Johnson, G., Scholes, K., & Whittington, R. (2002). *Exploring corporate strategy* (7th ed., pp. 132–133). New Jersey: Prentice Hall.

Kim, W. C., & Mauborgne, R. (1997). Value innovation: The strategic logic of high growth. *Harvard Business Review, 75*, 102–112.

Kim, C., & Mauborgne, R. (1999). Creating new market space. *Harvard Business Review, 77*, 83–93.

Liebowitz, S. (2002). *Re-thinking the network economy* (pp. 13–48). New York: Amacom.

Metcalfe, B. (2013). Metcalfe's law after 40 years of ethernet. *IEEE Xplore, 46*(12).

Porter, M. E. (2001). Strategy and the internet. *Harvard Business Review, 79*, 63–78.

vcmike. Guest blogger Bob Metcalfe: Metcalfe's law recurses down the long tail of social networks. VCMike's Blog, 18 August 2006. Available at https://vcmike.wordpress.com/2006/08/18/metcalfe-social-networks/

Further Reading

V. Atluri, M. Dietz, and N. Henke, 'Competing in a world of sectors without borders', Mckinsey Quarterly, July 2017.

Building on their insights from the value innovation studies, C. Kim and R. Mauborgne published the book *Blue Ocean Strategy: How to Create Uncontested Market Space and Make Competition Irrelevant*, Harvard Business School Press, Expanded edition, 2015.

C. Kim and R. Mauborgne developed the concept of creating new market spaces by looking outside one's own industry in 'Creating new market space', *Harvard Business Review*, 1999, January–February, pp. 83–93. See also: 'Value innovation – the strategic logic of high growth', *Harvard Business Review*, 1997, January–February, pp. 103–112. And: C. Kim and R. Mauborgne, 'Nondisruptive Creation: Rethinking Innovation and Growth', *MIT Sloan Management Review*, 21 February 2019.

R. Varadarajan et al.' analyze the first-mover advantage in the digital market space in 'First-mover advantage in an Internet-enabled market environment: conceptual framework and propositions', *Journal of the Academy of Marketing Science*, 2008, 36, pp. 293–328; also, see the chapter by R. Varadarajan et al. published in F.J. Martínez-López (Ed.) *Research Handbook on e-business Strategic Management*, Series PROGRESS in IS, Springer, 2013.

Weblinks

www.blueoceanstrategy.com revolves completely around value innovations and provides up-to-date examples of successful innovations and their underlying drivers.

www.innovationzen.com provides information on innovation management, business strategy, technology and more.

Creating and Capturing Value Through e-Business Strategies

Contents

© Springer Nature Switzerland AG 2020
T. Jelassi, F. J. Martínez-López, *Strategies for e-Business*, Classroom Companion: Business,
https://doi.org/10.1007/978-3-030-48950-2_8

Learning Outcomes

After completing this chapter, you should be able to:

- Understand the concept of value creation and value capture
- Master the core ideas of the Good-Dominant logic and the Service-Dominant logic
- Know what role a business and customers will play respectively in value creation
- Learn the causal pathways of value creation and capture

8

■ Introduction

In essence, strategy formulation revolves around the concepts of value creation and value capture. During the Internet boom years, online ventures often did not pay enough attention to these fundamental economic concepts. Nowadays, though, economic viability of any e-business venture is of paramount importance to managers and investors alike. This is why we devote a full chapter to talk about value creation and value capture. First, we will discuss some basics on value creation and capture so that readers can generally grasp the gist of value creation and capture. Second, two distinct perspectives on value creation and capture are introduced. We highlighted the importance of the Service-Dominant logic because it is more fit with e-business. Third, based on the Service-Dominant logic, we revealed the different roles of a business and customers in value creation. Fourth, to bring together, we depicted the causal pathways of value creation and value capture so as to point out the key activities that a business should notice in the pathway. Last, we applied theoretical parts into a business case, WeChat.

8.1 Basics on Value Creation and Capture

Value creation is in vogue in the value-driven business world. However, despite the term "value" can be seen in everyday life, it is also an ambiguous and elusive concept in business. By learning this section, we will separately illustrate basics related to value creation and value capture which are necessary for the study of later sections.

8.1.1 Creating Value

We can illustrate "value" from a variety of economics or business views. Marxists think that labor consumed in a product or service is the sole source of value. To the contrary, marginal economists argue that consumers could have different value perceptions toward completely the same products since the product consumed later in a sequence could be less valuable than the one consumed previously. This is due to the decrease of marginal utility, and therefore value also depends on the marginal utility. Marketing researchers suggest that perceived worthiness unmask the concept of value by providing subjective evaluation metrics such as novelty, appropriateness, aesthetics, and so on.[1] The advantage of using the concept of worthiness

---

1   For more details see Pitelis (2009).

to understand value is that this approach considers both the outcomes (e.g., novel features, aesthetic appearance, and functions) of labor, knowledge, and skills applied into product/service as attributes and the subjective perception of individuals toward the target product or service. The subjective evaluation by individuals must have specific object and evaluable attributes. Based on the above discussion, value is "perceived worthiness of a subject matter to a socio-economic agent that is exposed to and/or can make use of the subject matter in question."[2] Referring to the elusiveness and subjectivity of value, see the *Financial Times* article: "Customer value is difficult to understand."

There are two types of value: use value and exchange value (Bowman and Ambrosini 2000). Use value can be defined as the certain quality of the product or service perceived by individuals when being used. Exchange value refers to the amount paid by the buyer to the seller. Use value is obviously a rather subjective construct, while exchange value is largely determined by the supply-demand relationship in the market. On the other hand, for businesses, value can be conjectured or realized.[3] Conjectured value or imagined value refers to the value that a business conjectures; it can generate by conducting specific activities, for example, developing an online platform in order to sell products online. Conjectured value can be realized via sales. Put another way, value creation is just a hypothetical value proposition before businesses realize value by selling to customers. Hence it is customers instead of the business who materialize value. In each sale, conjectured value fulfilled its realization and forms into exchange value. The problem is that prior to the moment of exchange, value is only imaginary for the business, and at the same time consumers could have quite diverse perceptions of use value on the product. This characteristic of value creation requires businesses to better deliver or communicate the value they make to customers to increase the monetary amount paid by customers in the exchange stage, because customers' value perception of a product does not depend on what a business offers but on what is finally delivered. Context-dependency is another characteristic of value creation. The value evaluation process cannot be isolated from a specific context. It is obvious that in desert the value of a bottle of water for a thirsty traveler is significantly higher than that near a lake.

❯ In summary, the definition of value creation encompasses three processes. Firstly, value facilitators provide value vehicles, namely, goods or services, by applying their labor, knowledge, and skills into the production process. Secondly, customers subjectively evaluate and perceive the worthiness of the product or service in specific contexts. Thirdly, customers acquire the product or service by monetary exchange and start to embed value into the product or service further by applying their knowledge and skills with or without other actors.

---

2   Ibid., p.1118
3   The discussion on the conjectured value is based on the literature: C.N. Pitelis, op. cit., 2009, pp. 1115–1139

Customer Value Is Difficult to Understand

Reflecting on Adrian Wickens' sound points about business prosperity requiring an "understanding of what the customer really values and is willing to pay a premium for," I find the need to stress the word "really." That's because the important concept of customer value is often misunderstood and littered with misconceptions that severely hinder its application in practice. Here are a few examples.

First, low price is often confused with value. The so-called "value" ranges of many retailers are just one example. These are two very different animals: price is what someone pays; value is what they get. So, getting a real grip on value means seeing and interpreting things from the customer's perspective, which can present an unexpected level of challenge.

Second is the idea that customers are primarily focused on price. Over many years, and across many sectors, we have found it rare for more than 15% of customers to choose on price alone. What constitutes customer value for the majority is therefore a more complex trade-off among a host of non-price factors.

Third is the notion of added value. For many organizations, this means providing something extra that normally involves extra costs. Unfortunately, customers do not care about costs. So, if that extra isn't valued by the customer more than any additional price premium, not only is there no added value, but the overall customer value is actually diluted.

Finally there is the idea that customer value can be identified by simply asking. If only it were so easy. Most customers can only readily give feedback on product or service characteristics. While this is useful at one level, it is quite shallow in the scheme of understanding customer value. This helps explain, for example, why such a high proportion of new product introductions, usually validated by standard market research, fail. [...]

The concept of customer value may appear self-evident, but I wonder how many of the companies we read about in the FT have a real understanding and apply it to make happier customers and happier shareholders alike.

Source: Adapted from: J. Bray, "Customer value is difficult to understand', *Financial Times*, 21 February 2017.

8.1.2 Capturing Value

Value capture is the realization of exchange value by economic actors (e.g., businesses, customers, resource suppliers, employees).[4] Creating value is not enough for profit-oriented enterprises. A business providing a value proposition has to monetize the outcomes of value creation by sales. Moreover, the earnings generated from limited sales have to cover expenses and share with other stakeholders and society. Value will slip away if the value creator does not keep all the value that is created

---

4   C. Bowman and V. Ambrosini, op. cit., 2000, pp. 1–15

when use value is high while exchange value is comparatively low.[5] Value slippage can significantly discourage value creators to continually create value. Therefore, it is crucial for businesses to capture more value as often as they can.

Two mechanisms can help us analyze what is behind value capture: competition and isolating mechanisms. Sales and revenues derived from value capture can be regarded as another form of "rents" which heavily depend on the market position, competitive advantage, and unique resources or specific assets of a business. However, the market position, competitive advantage, and the available resource level of a business can vary from time to time due to changes in the external environment. For example, the entry of new competitors will dramatically intensify value capture competition. New entrants provide alternative, or even identical, options for customers. Facing more options, customers have more bargaining powers. According to the classic view of economics, with all other things being equal, the increase of supply (a form of competition) will reduce the exchange price (value) to the point where supply equals demand. The emergence of worthier substitutions (another form of competition) will change the shape of the indifference curve, and customers will purchase fewer current goods. In these cases, the value space created by the previous business would inevitably be narrowed due to the competition mechanism. Further, as the competition becomes more intensive, the business would find it more difficult to retain past sales and thus capture less value. For example, Yahoo was one of the most popular websites in the United States. However, when faced with emerging competitors Google and Facebook, Yahoo failed to sustain its leading market position.[6] In 2017, Yahoo sold its core business to Verizon.

On the other hand, the isolating mechanism is a positive way to prevent the value slippage. Technical, social, physical, market, or legal barriers can prevent competitors from replicating or imitating the business, product, or service. This isolating mechanism forges "an impregnable shell" to protect the value created, and thus the business can capture most value. For example, Microsoft isolates its operation system business from competitors by its high penetration of the market. Most PC manufacturers have to preinstall the Windows operating system into their computers. It is the default system that most consumers are familiar with. Therefore, it is almost impossible for new entrants to compete with Microsoft in the market for PC operation systems.

8.2 Two Perspectives on Value Creation and Capture

There are two leading perspectives on value creation and capture: a Good-Dominant (G-D) logic and a Service-Dominant (S-D) logic. These two perspectives have distinct strategic focuses on value creation and capture, and accordingly, managers should devise different value creation and capture strategies under different perspectives.

---

5   The following paragraphs in this section are adapted from this: Lepak et al. (2007)
6   For more details on why Yahoo failed, see McGoogan (2016).

8.2.1 A Good-Dominant Logic

The G-D logic is a product-centric logic.[7] The product here entails both tangible goods and intangible services. The nature of the G-D logic is that value is embedded during the manufacturing (or farming, or extraction) process, and it focuses basically on the input end and the output end (products). By controlling the input, the line of production can continually produce homogenous and standardized goods. Customers could be an input source and provide useful information on preferences (such as flavor, smell, and tactile information) for final products, but they cannot participate in the production process.

The essence of G-D logic externalizes the demand side and highlights the central role of production, inventory, and operation activities. Individuals' competences such as knowledge and skills are supportive or secondary factors rather than determinant factors for the production of goods. The G-D logic also implies that businesses should shift their focus onto the production of new goods once goods are transferred or sold to customers. In combination, the G-D logic has its business advantage in standardizing the production process and forming economies of scale for manufacturers, but it underestimates the role of customers and other external stakeholders and thus unfortunately lets value created by these actors slip away. For example, Apple will not treat itself just as a hardware manufacturer. Its revenue composition is more than the sales of iPhone, iPad, Mac, and other products[8] but also includes a so-called Apple tax, namely, users' in-app payments include a "tax"—a proportion of the price is simply an acknowledgment of the brand of Apple. Customers are prepared to pay a premium above what is charged by competitors for a similar product, because it is Apple. Through the Apple "tax," Apple captures value from the outputs of numerous app developers and service providers and from Apple users.

8.2.2 A Service-Dominant Logic

During the mid-1990s, American Professors Stephen Vargo and Robert Lusch began collaborating on service-centric framework which later becomes the widely known as the Service-Dominant logic. As the label implies, the S-D logic is centered on service. The concept of service under the S-D logic refers to the application of competences (knowledge and skills) to satisfy beneficiaries. This logic reversed the priority of different resources in the G-D logic. It highlights the value of operant resources which are intangible and dynamic resources and are based on the value creator(s) rather than operand resources which are tangible. It recognizes that static resources need actions to become valuable. As was aforementioned, the G-D logic is an input-output mindset and regards services as units of output. In

---

7   The discussion on the G-D logic is based on Vargo and Lusch (2008).
8   Source: "Apple Reports First Quarter Results," *Apple Newsroom,* 1 February 2018. Available at
     ▶ https://www.apple.com/newsroom/2018/02/apple-reports-first-quarter-results/

contrast, the S-D logic treats service from a process perspective. The role of goods involved in this service process is just "vehicles" for the provision of service. Goods materialize all value of their creators' skills and knowledge (e.g., design philosophy), when it is conveyed to end users. Irrespective of whether a service is provided directly or through a good, the providers' knowledge and skills are the essential source of value creation, not the goods themselves. Nevertheless, this does not mean that goods are less important in the S-D logic.

The two core ideas of the S-D logic are basically that economic activities can be understood as a kind of service-for-service exchange instead of goods-for-goods or goods-for-money. The exchange entails two service processes: one is a process to which people are applying their knowledge and skills to do something for themselves and others; another is a process to which they want other(s) to do for them. Secondly, value is co-created. Value is created by the collaboration of multi-actors rather than created solely by one actor and waiting for exchange (Vargo and Lusch 2017).

S-D logic can offer many insights to e-business, particularly in the age of the social web. This logic revolutionized the notion of value-creating creators and value-destroying consumers. e-Business can provide an interactive, sharable, and popularized online value co-creation platform for producers and consumers. These characteristics of online value creation platform have created the concept of "prosumer" (Martínez-López et al. 2015), which implies that consumers also create value for companies. For example, in an online brand community, users can simultaneously and actively create valuable content for the brand by capturing their use experience, user preferences, and expectations on new products. At the same time, companies can use these consumer narratives to improve products or services, recognize "service opportunities," and capture more value.

In reality the Internet does produce any tangible goods (it is machines or humans that make objects) because it is a data exchange channel (uploading and downloading data) or a communication platform based on information technology. The S-D logic highlights how e-businesses are different from manufacturers or factories which focus on production. e-Businesses should concentrate on how they should use the Internet to provide superior Internet-based services for users in order to capture value. For example, consumers can order a cup of coffee on the Starbucks' app and pick it up at the nearest Starbucks store. This does not mean that the app "produced" the coffee, but rather the coffee shop worker did. In retrospect, many magnificent e-business successes start from recognizing a small "service opportunity." Larry Page and Sergey Brin thought that search engines could be more convenient for Internet users, and this idea eventuated as Google; Jeff Bezos found it would be much effortless for consumers to purchase books online, and then this gave birth to ▶ Amazon.com; Mark Zuckerberg and his roommates found the online social interaction platform could cater to Harvard students' social needs, which lead to the birth of Facebook. All of these cases did not produce tangible goods or products but instead demonstrated the triumph of service-centric thinking. This is also the reason why we introduce the S-D logic here, since it has largely revolutionized the position of goods and the concept of service in business studies, and it relates to the essence of e-business.

8.3 Value Creation Spheres

Now we refocus on value creation. Through the lens of S-D logic, we have understood that goods are important for companies, but should not be the only consideration for managers. Managers should also be aware of the importance of the application of knowledge and skills and the value and power of customers. This section will illustrate different roles of producers and customers in value creation by portraying the provider sphere, joint sphere, and customer sphere; see ◘ Fig. 8.1.

◘ Figure 8.1 defines the roles and boundary of each actor (business and customer) by portraying two overlapping spheres.[9] In the provider sphere, a business will undertake activities for creating potential value such as design, manufacturing, assembling, inventory, post-purchase service, and so on. The business also needs to prepare customers with resources, platforms, procedures, or institution arrangements that empower customers to create value. By undertaking these activities and assisting in the value creation process, the business can be defined as a value facilitator (Grönroos 2011). The joint sphere is a field where there is a two-way interaction between businesses and customers. In the joint sphere, customers help

8

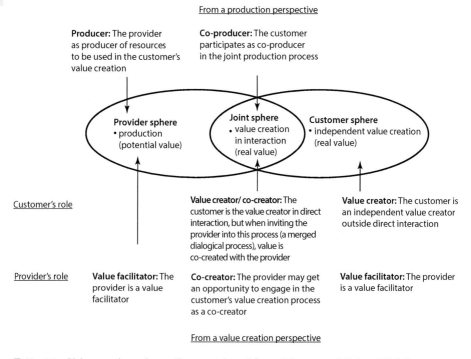

◘ **Fig. 8.1**   Value creation spheres. (Source: Adapted from Grönroos and Voima (2013a))

---

businesses co-create potential or conjectured value through co-design, co-development, and even co-manufacturing of a product. At the same time, businesses could also potentially participate in customer value creation processes and work as a value co-creator. The customer sphere means that customers create value by using the product/service independently of the business. Different customers with differential knowledge or skill levels can create different value. For example, a paper and a pen may just be used for writing for most people, while an outstanding painter could use them to draw a painting worth millions of dollars. In the following subsections, we will describe these spheres in more detail.

8.3.1 Provider Sphere

As it is aforementioned, prior to the moment of exchange, businesses (as providers) can only infer value. After the exchange, customers transform inferred value into real value in their use context. The "real" value here refers to the value of applying the product or service to satisfy customers' need(s) in a certain context, rather than the monetary value occurring in the exchange stage. For example, the real value of a mop is not created by a mop factory, but rather created when someone is mopping in their house. The role of the mop factory in this case is merely providing the person with a mop. Even though businesses do not create any value-in-use or value-in-context, the production processes conducted them result in outputs (products or service and particular features or functions) that customers may choose to use in their value creation process.

8.3.2 Joint Sphere

The joint sphere, as shown in ❏ Fig. 8.1, is a field where value is created by interactions. For example, a restaurant may invite a consumer to taste a dish's flavor before it is put into the market (on the menu). Conversely, a consumer may also complain about the service she or he received and suggests the manager to improve their service. This case would imply that joint value creation processes may occur from provider-customer interactions. In these processes, customers are the most critical force in the joint sphere since only customers can turn potential value into real value, but the provider may affect the customer's value creation process in this sphere.

In the joint sphere, customers might not be able to create the value properly. For example, a customer does not know how to use the product or service. The business, in this case, may be invited by the customer to help him/her acquire enough product knowledge so that she or he can better use it. In that case, value is co-created by the business and the customer. For example, service employees should interact with buyers after purchasing an unfamiliar product online to help them better understand how to use it and increase their perceived worthiness or value of the purchase. Doing so minimizes potential returns—where value did not meet expectations. If the interaction is initiated by the buyer, it is more necessary for employees to interact with buyers; if not, employees should at least be ready and open to customer enquiries. See the Business2Community blog article on value co-creation via social media: "Co-Creating Value Using Social Media Marketing."

On the other hand, the provider could explicitly or implicitly invite customers to participate in the production process. Thus, customers may also co-design, co-develop, and co-produce products or services as "a prosumer." For example, a leading smartphone brand, Xiaomi,[10] creates an online brand community labeled as "Born for Being Fans" for all users to comment on use experience and expectations for possible smartphone features or functions in the future. Xiaomi also recruited thousands of product engineers specifically to collect their feedback to underpin the development of new products.

The approach a business uses to proactively influence customer value creation may be positive or negative or have no effect at all. For example, if a business, uninvited by customers, sends screen pop ups with notifications or short messages, customers may become annoyed and block the business. Similarly the timing of contact with customers is important—for example, many telemarketers call at dinner time. To address this, the business should understand the customer's current context. This may be possible through data analysis, IoT sensors, and other technologies that enable businesses to detect the customer's current context and help them maximize the value-in-use. With reference to ◘ Fig. 8.1, if this happened, it means the business crossed the boundary of the joint sphere and moved into customers' sphere. Doing so would, in theory, allow customers to use the product or service as they wish. Note that GDPR,[11] privacy, and other regulations in most countries legally restrict what businesses can and can't do with customer data.

Likewise, the customer could also cross into the provider sphere actively. This would expand the boundary of the joint sphere toward the provider sphere. In this case, the cross-boundary behavior could be an opportunity for the business to improve their production process and offerings. As for the restaurant case mentioned previously, a customer who complained about the service and asked the manager to change could be an opportunity for the restaurant to realize the importance of service quality and take steps to improve it.

The interactions discussed above indicate that the joint value creation sphere is not fixed. The dynamic of movements within and with the joint sphere depends on the business, the customer, and their interactions. For example, when the business orients itself by S-D logic (it may highlight service in all spheres and enable customer involvement in internal processes), it needs customers who want to engage with the design, development, and production activities. In this instance, the provider sphere and the customer sphere would move toward each other.

---

10 For a global ranking of smartphones, see Yan (2018).
11 The General Data Protection Regulation 2016/679 is a regulation in European Union (EU) law on data protection and privacy for all individuals within the EU and the European Economic Area (EEA).

Co-creating Value Using Social Media Marketing

Co-creating value using social media marketing sounds like a very complex task, but it's a very simple concept. It's the implementation of service-dominant logic that makes co-creating value challenging.

So, now that the first paragraph had totally confused you, let me break this down into common language.

Service-Dominant Logic

Originally, Vargo and Lusch coined the phrase Service-Dominant logic to reflect the notion that all businesses, even ones who made things, rely heavily on service aspects to please customers. An example Bob Lusch uses in his YouTube video is that people buy cars primarily for transportation—a service.

Service-dominant logic is an unfortunate term that also means that service is a major component in all products, even ones manufactured in a factory. Going back to the car example, while you're buying something you can touch and feel, you're also buying a lot of things you can't such as the reputation of the manufacturer, the quality of the service you'll get, etc. And car companies realize these things have a big impact on the brand you choose. That's why you'll hear dealers advertising about their "free service for life" or "free oil changes for life." They know these service elements provide competitive advantage that helps them make the sale.

Co-creating Value

The notion of co-creating value means that firms succeed (gain value) when they provide value to their customers. Although this makes intuitive sense, many firms fail to understand their role in creating value for customers or the notion of customer value gets lost in corporate rhetoric around profits—especially in manufacturing firms where there's a big distance between the firm and customers in both physical distance and time (since customers won't buy products manufactured today for weeks or months).

So, how do firms co-create value with customers and how does using social media fit into this broader notion of co-creating value? I'm glad you asked.

Using Social Media to Co-create Value

Social media is a perfect tool for co-creating value because it increases communication between the company and the customer. In manufacturing, these communications were never there before unless the firm spent a lot of money doing focus groups or collecting survey data. Using social media, firms get unbiased opinions from real customers and prospects at a fraction of the cost.

Collaborative innovation—maybe the most important way using social media contributes to co-creating value is through collaborative new products. If you think about it, firms need new products consumers want to buy, and consumers need new products to solve problems they face. What better way for firms to know what customers need than from the customers themselves. Using social media as a conduit for customer insights is probably the most value aspect for many businesses because they learn customer pain points, discover what customers don't like about their own brands as well as those from competitors, and may even get suggestions from customers on how to improve their brands. For instance, I was working on some software a client purchased. It wasn't working too well, so a colleague and I discussed features we felt were missing by sharing comments as Facebook status updates.

Customer complaints—Twitter has replaced the corporate suggestion box as the preferred vehicle for sharing complaints about failed products. Using social media to hear and respond to these complaints goes a long way toward reducing the damage from these failures.

Share brand messages—firms benefit greatly when customers share favorable brand messages using social media because it amplifies message reach and because consumers believe what they friends tell them much more than messages they get from the firm. But, how does this create value for consumers? Consumers benefit from the micro celebrity, they get from being the go-to person for information. Firms can increase the value received by folks who share your brand messages using social media by recognizing them, thanking them, highlighting their comments, and other tactics that play into their micro celebrity status. Firms can even reward folks who share brand messages with discounts, free product, or other tangible benefits. For example, Red Robin offers discounts through Facebook updates, and users share these updates with friends to claim the discount.

User-generated content—user-generated content creates significant value for both firms and users. When users create a YouTube video or song parody about your brand and it goes viral, you both get a boost. Firms can encourage user-generated content using social media through contests or special offers for folks creating content. Sometimes the simple act of providing space for users to upload content is all it takes to get a lot of content. For instance, NASA maintains a site dedicated to user-generated content where anyone can upload posts, images, etc.

See, that wasn't too hard. And now you have some new tools you can use or new ideas for using these tools more effectively to co-create value for your firm and its customers. If you need help understanding how using social media in co-creating value can benefit your firm, we're happy to help.

Source: A. Hausman, 'Co-creating value using social media marketing', *Business 2 Community*, June 7 2013.

8.3.3 Customer Sphere

In the customer sphere, customers create value independently as this sphere is not open for the outside provider. In this sphere, the customer will use the resources, tools, goods, and rules provided by the business to create real value.

However, the value creation led by the customer is not solely determined by the customer. Apart from the proactive influence brought about by the business, the social, technical, legal environment can play their part in a customer's value creation process. For example, a college student with a basic knowledge on use of Microsoft Office could take some classes to enhance his/her knowledge and skills in using this software, and so could better exploit the possibilities offered by it. The underlying effect of an improvement in his/her expertise with Microsoft Office would be an increased ability to create value when using a computer.

In summary, the value creation spheres built on the S-D logic helps us understand the roles the business and the customer play in the process of value creation by defining and picturing each actor's dominant field. In addition, the spheres also imply that, despite that fact that real value is created by the customer, businesses can improve the "service" as a value facilitator or value co-creator by interacting with customers actively or passively on the business-customer interface.

8.4 The Process and Causal Pathways of Value Creation and Capture

This section will illustrate the process and causal pathways of value creation and capture. Depicting the process and causal pathways helps to understand the elements in the pathways that they should pay attention to and the causality of creating or providing a valuable business for customers.[12]

As is shown in ◘ Fig. 8.2, economic agent(s) would identify a business opportunity – a business idea that might create value for customers. At this moment, the agent can create plans for the realization of this idea and advocate the future business advantage in the target market with his/her business partners, angel investors, potential customers, and many other stakeholders. In order to transform the conjectured value into monetary value, the most direct route is to sell the idea to others, namely, authorizing others to materialize the idea (and pay for it). In this pathway, value finished its duty from creation to realization. This example may apply to franchising or licensing.

The alternative option is more complicated. In reality, it could be very difficult to sell a conjectured value proposition at a satisfactory price. In most cases, this would happen when the agent realizes that the resources and capabilities required to implement the business project are beyond his/her ability. Even if the idea could be easily sold, the agent might ask why she or he cannot capture more value by founding or co-founding an organization. The agent might do this and become an entrepreneur, creating a new business so that she or he can capture more value (Pitelis and Teece 2009) from the idea. The organization's mission in question is to produce goods or service and then market them to customers. Founding an organization is also beneficial for the business to capture value co-created by others, such as suppliers, end consumers, and retailers. In other words, by using an approach of co-creation, the agent may unfortunately lose some value to others in the value chain.

On the other hand, being a founder or co-founder of a new business may sound good, but at the same time they have to take more risks and rely on many other

---

12 This section on the causality of value creation and capture is adapted from C.N. Pitelis, op. cit., 2009, pp. 1115–1139.

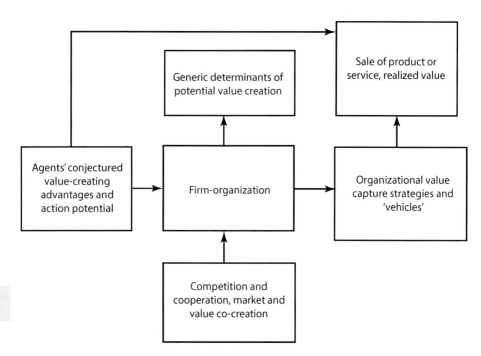

▢ Fig. 8.2 The process and casual pathways of value creation and capture. (Source: Adapted from Pitelis (2009, p. 1128))

determinants (e.g., resources, technology, human resources, organization design, innovation, competence, and so on) to translate the conjectured value proposal into revenue. Furthermore, even if the organization was successfully founded and the value was captured as planned, other competitors could be able to replicate the organization's business model and capture value that would otherwise go to the agent's organization. In summary, the agent should be prudent to choose the pathway to capture the value. However, due to the existence of uncertainty and limited rationality, it is impossible for the agent to confidently predict the potential value and monetary returns generated from the idea since many factors are not predictable and cannot be influenced by the agent. For example, the agent cannot predict with certainty the extent that customers and other stakeholders (whose reciprocal and beneficial value co-creation behaviors are core to the co-creation approach) engage in the production process and contribute to creating value. Therefore, due to the uncertainty of internal and external environments and "guesstimates," organization-based value creation and capture do call for "entrepreneurial spirit" which drives the agent to overcome challenges in the journey from conjectured value to realized value.

As for this book, we are more interested in creating and capturing value via e-business-related strategies. Based on the above discussion, to realize imagined value the e-business creates strategies and "vehicles" to sell products or services and capture value. However, as we mentioned in the value creation spheres, customers, instead of the e-business, are responsible for value creation, and there exists a dynamic joint sphere for the e-business to facilitate customer value creation and to co-create more value, and thus the e-business could capture more value as incremental value is created or added. In this case, according to the S-D logic, value creation and value capture do not grow in a sequence and are not diminished after the financial transaction is complete. When customers have a need for "service," there are opportunities for the e-business to capture more value. To put it in another way, value creation and value capture are intertwined and interact through iterative and evolving e-business-customer interactions. On the one hand, value creation can influence value capture. More value created by customers will widen the value space for the e-business to capture value or set a higher price. On the other hand, value capture can impact value creation. If an e-business squeezes too much customer value, the customer may lose interest in purchasing the add-on services of the business and so will not create more value. For example, even though Blizzard released World of Warcraft (a multi-player online role-playing game) in 2004, the growth of Blizzard's earnings in 2017 can still be attributed to this "aged" game (Hoium 2018). This is primarily because Blizzard keeps updating World of Warcraft and providing new features and expanding the value proposition for players.

The entwined and interactive relationship between value creation and value capture and the existence of uncertainty and limited rationality make it almost impossible for businesses to devise and plan optimal strategies or strategic vehicles to capture more value and adapt to the ever-changing environment. The most difficult problem here is how a business can continually capture value and sustain or even surpass the current value position or what strategies or vehicles it should depend on to do so. Such strategies or vehicles should support companies to enhance and mature its value capture capabilities or model. For example, see the Harvard Business Review article titled "Data-driven Pinterest tactics that drive sales" which shows how to use social media to capture value.

Data-Driven Pinterest Tactics that Drive Sales

People love to talk about the ROI from social media. But ROI doesn't just fall from the sky. If you want your social media efforts to drive actual sales, you need to understand how your customers and potential customers actually use social media in their purchase process. And once you have that understanding, you need to tailor your social media strategy so that it pushes your customers toward a purchase. [Here are some] research findings that can help you tailor your Pinterest strategy […]:

Combat showrooming   Retailers often worry that the Internet has turned brick-and-mortar stores into little more than showrooms: places where customers maul the merchandise and pester salespeople for advice before going online to buy the same products at a lower price. But our study […] showed that social media sends more customers into stores than the Internet pulls out: one in five Pinterest users has bought something in a store after pinning or liking it on Pinterest, and one in three Pinterest users under 35 has done so. If you want more people walking through the door of your store with a purchase in mind, design your Pinterest strategy to send as many people to your stores as to your website.

Drive personal pinning   While 60% of Pinterest purchases were discovered on Pinterest, the vast majority were discovered through the boards or streams of regular human beings: 19% of purchases were discovered through a friend and 24% through a stranger, compared to just 7% being discovered on a retailer's Pinterest board and 10% through Pinterest search. That means you can't rely on your own Pinterest presence to drive significant sales and instead need to think about how to drive repinning (where your viewers and customers share items they find on your pinboards to their own pinboards). To encourage customers to pin items from your site to their Pinterest boards, make sure you include a "share on Pinterest" button on every product page and consider running promotions to encourage pinning (some examples here). To let your customers know that their pinning is appreciated, pay extra attention to the people who share your content the most, by repinning and liking their pins.

Pack images with information   One of the major ways Pinterest influences purchasing is by providing additional information about a product. Any visitor who comes to your site from a Pinterest link should land on a page with relevant information about the product. Better yet, save them the trip by embedding product information directly in the images on your website and Pinterest boards, either with text or (better still) visual cues about product ingredients or usage. For example, compare two images from the Williams Sonoma site, and you'll see that one of them instantly conveys the utility of a new kind of measuring cup, while the other leaves you wondering—but it's the latter image that the company features on its own product page. Featuring the image that contains the most information about a product is the way to succeed on Pinterest.

Pin that deal   Our Pinterest data was drawn from a larger study of nearly 6000 social media users who also told us about the impact of Facebook and Twitter on their purchasing. But where 37% of Facebook users and 32% of Twitter users say that those networks helped drive their purchase by alerting them to a deal, only 19% of Pinterest-driven purchases involved finding a sale or deal through the site. This suggests massive room for growth by incorporating sale notifications into pinnable product images or, conversely, by enhancing the design of online sale announcements, so they are charming or informative enough to get pinned.

Engage with recent pinners   More than 40% of Pinterest-inspired purchases are made within 1 week of pinning, and 80% are made within 3 weeks. That means your best window for nudging customers toward purchase is within 1–3 weeks of the moment when they pin one of your products. This is the time to reach out to customers, ask if they need more information, or simply thank them for sharing. If you're in a business with high-value transactions (like real estate or car sales), it's well worth following up on the indication of interest represented by a pin by using Pinterest's own analytics or a third party tool to see who is pinning items from your site or pinboards. If and when Pinterest finally releases its long-promised API, expect to see the emergence of tools that can automate or facilitate this kind of tracking and response.

> *Talking to Pinterest users about their Pinterest-inspired purchases helped identify specific business tactics that align with the way people actually share and shop online.* Explore the infographic for more insight into how people use Pinterest in their purchasing process, and you may find your own proof of social media ROI.
> *Source*: A. Samuel, 'Data-driven pinterest tactics that drive sales', *Harvard Business Review*, 18 July 2013.

With this overview of the process and causal pathways of value creation and capture in mind, let's now discuss the specifics of how to create and capture value via generic business strategies, business models, and creating barriers to imitation by competitors.

1. *Generic business strategies.* Generic business strategies such as cost leadership, differentiation, and outpacing are proven efficient and effective strategies to capture "the size of the pie" as we discussed in previous chapters (see Chapters 5 and 6). To some degree, market share as the result of these generic strategies represents the extent to which a business has captured value from the market.

2. *Business models.* Business models are defined as a narrative mechanism defining and indicating how value can be created and captured through the business and other actors such as suppliers and customers. The business model here is a strategic vehicle for the company to capture the value framed by the model. According to the nine elements of business model canvas, value propositions in the canvas clarified the conjectured or imagined value proposed by the business. Key activities and key resources make the business distinct from other competitors. The "key" in question indicates what strategic activities the business should focus on and what unique resources they rely on to ensure value creation and capture are processed as the business predicted. Partnership networks, customer segments, channels, and customer relationships delineate the interfaces where the business works as a value facilitator or a value co-creator with actors in the value network and captures value. Cost structure and revenue streams translate realized value into an explicit financial structure, which may indicate the business's future strategic focus. The business will know which business unit has the optimal financial performance and which activities deplete financial resources and can then create specific tactics and solutions in response.

3. *Barriers of imitation.* The Internet dramatically lowers the cost of information transmission and communication and enables the almost "zero marginal cost" of online replication; however this includes unauthorized replication. Governments may put pressure on Internet companies to protect the Intellectual Property (IP) of online content (music, movies, video games, e-articles, and many other digital products). Based on the low cost of cloning, copy-and-paste, and data transmission empowered by the Internet, competitors can price their products or service much more aggressively than the business that owns the copyright of the original product or service and also competes in multiple channels, including traditional bricks and mortar. Some customers would see the lower pricing of "pure-play" Internet-based competitors who do not own copy-

right and revalue the business that operates across channels legally. These businesses become undervalued, and customers move toward lower-priced competitors. Barriers of imitation are a crucial factor for a business to attain sustainable advantage and prevent value slippage. The business could build these barriers by market, social, technical, and legal solutions. For example, digital rights management (DRM) enables some paid applications or software to identify the buyer's computer and only install and enable use on that device. The authorization technology in this case is a typical technical solution to prevent others from installing and using the app illegally. When DRM was first implemented, in response to music piracy, there were many technical issues which created customer frustration. With increasing sophistication, it has become more subtle; users may not know it is there.

8.5 WeChat: S-D Logic Applied into Value Creation and Value Capture

8

WeChat is a mobile social media app developed by China's Internet giant Tencent. WeChat statistics include hosting more than one billion daily active users, and it is known as a "Super App" due to its multiple features and functions such as mobile payments, online shopping, app stores, online ticketing, taxi services, e-learning, and more.[13]

The value creation and value capture activities of WeChat are centered on service and driven by the S-D logic. It is also regarded as one of the newest and most powerful mobile apps since Facebook (last major milestone in the history of Internet business) was launched in 2004.

8.5.1 WeChat and Its S-D Logic

WeChat is a multi-function social media platform. Like Facebook in the United States, WeChat has penetrated the business and life of the majority of the population in China. People are comfortable shopping for fashion-related products on it. Students use it to interact with teachers and submit homework. Industrial workers rely on it to communicate with colleagues and clients. Payers make online or offline payments via WeChat Pay. According to Bloomberg, even bankers and traders use WeChat to make deals (Tu and Hong 2017). The design philosophy of WeChat is to serve users in their everyday life and to build a service ecosystem. The service ecosystem is based on four services:

---

13 For more details on WeChat see Coresight, "Understanding WeChat, China's Super App: Part 1—The Definite Leader in China," *Coresight Research*, 5 September 2018; Coresight, "Understanding WeChat, China's Super App: Part 2— How WeChat Mini Programs Spell Opportunity for Brands and Retailers," *Coresight Research*, 12 January 2019.

1. *Communication*. WeChat can be used to contact others, as per a phone. The interface lists all contacts alphabetically. Users can have one-to-one chats or group chats via text chat, voice call, video call, and video and picture sharing, and most importantly, these are free. This is an example where the value created may exceed value captured from users.
2. *Social Network*. WeChat owns a newsfeed named "Moment" which is similar to Instagram Stories. Moment is a closed online social circle that allows the user to share micro-blogs only with friends. In comparison Facebook recommends content based on an AI algorithm and mixes social content with more ads; however Facebook has also signaled it may adopt a similar strategy (Zuckerberg 2019). A separate section called "Official Accounts" allows business users to advertise.
3. *Finance*. WeChat Pay is an in-built mobile payment system. WeChat Pay is a cashless mobile payment method supporting users to pay for purchases online or at bricks-and-mortar stores. Users can use the WeChat scanner to scan the QR code at the cashier counter or just attach their phone to the near-field communication (NFC)-based register device to make the payment. Users deposit money into their WeChat Pay account and use this account for online ordering (e.g., rail and flight, taxi, food, tickets, hotels, home services, and so on.), payments (such as electricity, gas, and water bills), and public services.
4. *Apps*. WeChat also rivals all app stores in China (including Apple's App Store and Google's Play Store) with its "Mini programs." Through Mini programs, users can use mobile apps on WeChat without downloading or installing these apps. These apps are installed on WeChat's cloud servers. Too many installations can slow the processing speed of a smartphone and eat into its storage capacity. Mini programs address this issue.

WeChat owner Tencent intends to strengthen the WeChat service-centric strategy, expand the service ecosystem, and add more services within the platform (Coresight 2017).

8.5.2 Value Creation and Capture on WeChat

WeChat as a value facilitator WeChat is a comprehensive business platform that includes most features and functions needed for e-commerce. Its system framework is interoperable with almost all websites, including e-commerce sites, and the platform links to third-party commercial websites. WeChat is compatible with many external e-business systems. For example, Chumen Wenwen, founded by former Google engineers, is an information service company based on artificial intelligence that offers a service that is similar to Amazon's Alexa. It's system is compatible with WeChat's Official Accounts, so users can chat with Chumen Wenwen, within WeChat, for example, by asking: "restaurants nearby?" In response Chumen Wenwen receives and identifies the user's location data (encoded by WeChat) and then applies its artificial intelligence-based algorithm to recommend restaurants nearby. The difference between WeChat's Official Accounts and Amazon's Alexa is that the WeChat service was developed by an external company. WeChat is open and compatible with external e-business systems.

Another success factor of WeChat commerce is its convenient payment system. WeChat offers WeChat Pay, a trusted and third-party insured payment system which is compatible with almost all payment settings. When a user purchases a product from another user, she or he can transfer the payment via WeChat with a process that involves simply sending a short message with the amount and the seller's WeChat Pay's number. When funds arrive, a payment notice will inform the seller. The seller has to continue the payment action otherwise the deal will not be confirmed. The integration of WeChat Pay and the seller's e-commerce site adds additional protection for sellers, for example, where a buyer may confirm a purchase but not pay.

In summary, the WeChat e-commerce platform aims to provide all resources, e-business infrastructure, and institutions needed for a wide range of differentiated commercial activities.

Prosumers creating value on WeChat WeChat does not need to actively advertise, brand, and market itself because WeChat users do it for the company. The average time spent by every daily user is 82 minutes.[14] Given WeChat has one billion users, this means an enormous volume of texts, pictures, audio files, and videos are created, shared, and consumed. The chain of value creation and value capture is self-articulated, and WeChat enables this for profit. On the one hand, apart from the holistic service technical infrastructure provided by WeChat, it profits from volume—with the largest number of active daily users (more than one billion) in China[15] creating an online marketplace. On the other hand, WeChat's value creation and capture mechanism allows everyone to create original and interesting content for others, which means that everyone can be a producer and earn money from his/her content. WeChat stresses its protection of the intellectual property of original content creators and offers digital rights management services. Content creators can label their content as "Original" and so prevent other users from directly copying it for use elsewhere. WeChat also values the role of performance. It explicitly presents the "eyeball" rankings of content (clicks, "likes", comments, traffic, daily active users, and others) for advertising sponsors to identify and place advertisements. In summary, WeChat respects the role of users who produce content and has established a mechanism to prevent value created by these users from dispersing to other users. In this way it forms a barrier to imitation.

---

14 For more details on WeChat see Coresight, "Understanding WeChat, China's Super App: Part 1—The Definite Leader in China," *Coresight Research*, 5 September 2018; Coresight, "Understanding WeChat, China's Super App: Part 2— How WeChat Mini Programs Spell Opportunity for Brands and Retailers," *Coresight Research*, 12 January 2019.

15 Ibid.

A road to capture value   Facebook's 2016 advertising revenue accounted for 97% of its total revenue (Facebook Investor Relations 2017). In contrast, the 2016 Tencent advertising revenue equated to 17.75% of total revenue (Tencent Investor Relations 2017). Based on these numbers, we can see that Facebook's profitability is more dependent than Tencent on advertising. WeChat's profitability is built on both advertising and transaction fees, whereas Facebook has no transaction fees. WeChat profits from advertising placements and also takes a percentage from each users who incur advertising revenue on their content. At the same time, users employ e-payment methods for payments or to transfer money. WeChat charges a transaction fee from certain transactions and withdrawals. This makes WeChat's revenue composition very different to the simple advertising model used by Facebook.

Capturing value from mobile payments is not easy. Alibaba, the second biggest e-commerce company in the world, created a mobile payment processing tool called "Alipay" in 2004 and in 2013 overtook PayPal to become the world's largest mobile payment platform. WeChat Pay was introduced in 2014, just after Apple released "Apple Pay" (which is preinstalled on all iPhones). In February 2018, Facebook's WhatsApp reportedly started testing their mobile payment service in Asia with plans to enter the market. As the mobile payments revenue "pie" grows, so too do the number of service providers who wish to take a slice of that pie.

The slice of the pie held by WeChat Pay is growing in a market dominated by Alipay. In 2014, Alipay held 80% of the mobile payments market in China, and WeChat Pay had just launched. In Q1 2017, Alipay's market share had dropped to 54%, while WeChat Pay increased to 40%.[16] Not only does this mean WeChat Pay has taken market share from Alipay, it has also prevented other rivals, Apple Pay and Samsung Pay, for example, from taking market share. The reversal of market shares can be explained by a few reasons. Firstly, the high penetration and high use frequency of WeChat's messaging and social networking service largely increased the exposure of WeChat Pay. Secondly, WeChat Pay dominates in its service and commerce ecosystem. In many cases, WeChat Pay is the only selectable payment method for users to make payments on WeChat, or users are offered a discount if they select WeChat Pay as their payment method. Thirdly, backed by its powerful parent company Tencent, WeChat Pay rivals Alipay (also backed by e-commerce giant Alibaba) at every restaurant, physical store, petrol station, vendor machine, and so on. Consumers in China would be surprised if a shop cannot accept WeChat payments.

In summary, WeChat is a successful example of the adoption of S-D logic. It has built a holistic service-centric ecosystem and respects the role of users in creating value and protects their interests. Put in another way, WeChat has based its value capture strategies and its business model on supporting and protecting the value creation and capture of its users.

---

16 See also Wildau (2017).

8

Summary

In this chapter, we illustrated how value is created and captured via e-business strategies, which can be divided into two parts: theory and practice. The theoretical part can be summarized by following points:

— When creating value, a company needs to focus on the use value as perceived by customers. Only value that is considered as such by customers will eventually translate into value captured in the form of profit.

— Businesses should highlight the role of service in their e-businesses.

— Customers are responsible for value creation. By contrast, a business is a provider, a value co-creator, and a value facilitator.

— Value slippage or bad value capture performance will discourage value creators to continually create value.

— Value creation and value capture are entwined and interact, and they will appear as value creators recognize, develop, and capture one or more service opportunities.

— The business should identify the value capture strategies or vehicles that they depend upon to capture value.

— In order to sustain a competitive advantage over time, a company needs to ensure that its value created is difficult to substitute or imitate, since only value created that can be shielded against current and future competitors will ultimately lead to sustainable profitability.

❓ Review Questions

1. What is meant by "value," "conjectured value," and "realized value"?
2. Why is a service-dominant view important for e-business strategies?
3. How is value created by a business and by customers?
4. What are the causal pathways from conjectured value to realized value?
5. How would you personally define value creation? Does your definition differ from the one suggested in this chapter? If so, how?
6. Discuss strategies for e-businesses to capture value.

Notes and References

Bowman, C., & Ambrosini, V. (2000). Value creation versus value capture: Towards a coherent definition of value in strategy. *British Journal of Management, 11*(1), 1–15.

Coresight. (2017, May 16). Deep dive: WeChat— From messaging app to profitable ecosystem. *Coresight Research.* Available at: https://coresight.com/research/deep-dive-wechat-from-messaging-app-to-profitable-ecosystem/

Facebook Investor Relations. (2017, February 1). Facebook reports fourth quarter and full year 2016 results. *Investor.fb.com.* Available at: https://investor.fb.com/investor-news/press-release-details/2017/facebook-Reports-Fourth-Quarter-and-Full-Year-2016-Results/default.aspx

Grönroos, C. (2011). Value co-creation in service logic: A critical analysis. *Marketing Theory, 11*(3), 279–301.

Grönroos, C., & Voima, P. (2013a). Critical service logic: making sense of value creation and co-creation. *Journal of the Academy of Marketing Science, 41*(2), 141.

Grönroos, C., & Voima, P. (2013b). Critical service logic: making sense of value creation and co-creation. *Journal of the Academy of Marketing Science, 41*(2), 133–150.

Hoium, T. (2018, February 3). What to watch when activision Blizzard reports earnings. *The Motley Fool.* Available at https://www.fool.com/investing/2018/02/03/what-to-watch-when-activision-blizzard-reports-e-3.aspx

Martínez-López, F. J., Anaya, R., Aguilar, R., & Molinillo, S. (2015). *Online brand communities: Using the social web for branding and marketing* (p. 4). Springer.

McGoogan, C. (2016, July 25). Yahoo: 9 reasons for the internet icon's decline. *Telegraph.* Available at https://www.telegraph.co.uk/technology/2016/07/25/yahoo-9-reasons-for-the-internet-icons-decline/

Pitelis, C. N. (2009). The co-evolution of organizational value capture, value creation and sustainable advantage. *Organization Studies, 30*(10).

Pitelis, C. N., & Teece, D. J. (2009). The (new) nature and essence of the firm. *European Management Review, 6*(1), 5–15.

Tencent Investor Relations. (2017, March 22). Tencent announces 2016 fourth quarter and annual results. *WWW.tencent.com.* Available at: https://www.tencent.com/en-us/articles/150006145 9929670.pdf

Tu, L., & Hong, C. (2017, October 16). In China, trading begins on WeChat. *Bloomberg.* Available at: https://www.bloomberg.com/news/articles/2017-10-15/china-s-bankers-cut-bond-deals-where-others-post-dinner-pics

Vargo, S. L., & Lusch, R. F. (2008). From goods to service (s): Divergences and convergences of logics. *Industrial Marketing Management, 37*(3), 254–259.

Vargo, S. L., & Lusch, R. F. (2017). Service-dominant logic 2025. *International Journal of Research in Marketing, 34*(1), 46–67.

Wildau, G. (2017, August 10). China targets mobile payments oligopoly with clearing mandate. *Financial Times.*

Yan, L. (ed.) (2018, February 5). Chinese smartphone firms beat global slump. *Global Times.* Available at http://www.ecns.cn/business/2018/02-05/291509.shtml

Zuckerberg, M. (2019, March 6). A privacy-focused vision for social networking. *Facebook Notes.* Available at: https://www.facebook.com/notes/mark-zuckerberg/a-privacy-focused-vision-for-social-networking/10156700570096634/

Further Reading

Grönroos, C., & Voima, P. (2013). Critical service logic: Making sense of value creation and co-creation. *Journal of the Academy of Marketing Science, 41*(2), 133–150.

Lepak, D. P., Smith, K. G., & Taylor, M. S. (2007). Value creation and value capture: A multilevel perspective. *Academy of Management Review, 32*(1), 180–194.

Pitelis, C. N. (2009). The co-evolution of organizational value capture, value creation and sustainable advantage. *Organization Studies, 30*(10), 1118.

Vargo, S. L., & Lusch, R. F. (2008). From goods to service (s): Divergences and convergences of logics. *Industrial Marketing Management, 37*(3), 254–259.

Choosing the Appropriate Strategy for the Internal Organization of e-Business Activities

Contents

© Springer Nature Switzerland AG 2020

T. Jelassi, F. J. Martínez-López, *Strategies for e-Business*, Classroom Companion: Business, https://doi.org/10.1007/978-3-030-48950-2_9

> **Learning Outcomes**
> After completing this chapter, you should be able to:
> — Describe the spectrum of "make-or-buy" options
> — Identify the main reasons that favor "make" decisions
> — Identify the main reasons that favor "buy" decisions
> — Describe the concept of value chain deconstruction and the role of the Internet within this concept
> — Understand the concept of unbundling the corporation

9

▪ Introduction

Previous chapters discussed the strategic aspects of e-business, and this chapter focuses on internal organizational issues that need to be addressed in order to effectively implement an e-business strategy. We focus on two main questions that are crucial in the context of e-business strategy formulation. The first question is: Which activities within the value chain should we perform in-house and which ones should we outsource to external providers? The second question is: How should we align our e-activities with our physical activities in order to avoid possible conflicts between our online and offline channel offerings? This question, which is addressed in ▶ Sect. 9.4, is only relevant to omni-channel businesses that have both online and offline operations, as is the case, for instance, with Tesco, Ducati, and Nordea (which are featured in the case studies section of this book).

9.1 Reasons Determining "Make-or-Buy" Decisions in e-Business

Consider the joint venture of Sony, Toshiba, and Hitachi that integrated their small and medium-sized LCD[1] screen businesses. The joint venture, named "Japan Display," had several objectives that included strengthening their potential for technological innovation and achieving economies of scale. Another interesting earlier example of a merger is that of AOL and Time Warner. The two firms merged in order to create an integrated value chain in the media industry that spanned from content production to content delivery and leveraged both the physical and online channels. Substantial synergies were expected from this merger. However these synergies proved difficult to achieve, and many critics argued in retrospect that it would have been better to have kept the two firms separate.

From a more historic perspective, let us consider the evolution of the PC industry. In 1985, IBM, which then dominated the industry, conducted in-house all activities in its value chain, from the development of microprocessors to produc-

---

1   Short for liquid-crystal display, a low-power, flat-panel display is used in many digital devices to display numbers or images.

tion, marketing, sales, and distribution. As a result of open standards and the increased use of mass production, this integrated value chain became more fragmented and complex over time. Today companies focus on (and dominate) only some individual activities of the PC industry value chain.

The abovementioned examples illustrate how businesses can choose from a variety of options available to them for making a product or service. They can decide to perform some activities internally ("make" or the so-called *hierarchy* form of governance) or "purchase" them on the open market ("buy"). The different options that companies can choose from are as follows:

1. *Market transactions* involve the purchase from an external provider on an individual contractual basis.
2. *Long-term contracts* involve the purchase from an external provider on a contractual basis, spanning an extended period of time.
3. *Alliances* involve the close cooperation of two separate firms that join up in the production of a certain product or service.
4. *Parent/subsidiary constellations* involve the setting up of a distinct firm that operates separately from, yet under the auspices of, the parent company.
5. *Internal production* involves a process that is managed completely internally, without any outsourcing to external providers.

Businesses that rely heavily on input from external providers include car manufacturers, such as DaimlerChrysler and BMW, and sports goods manufacturers, such as Nike and Adidas. Another example is Dell, which concentrates on tightly integrating different suppliers to deliver components for the PCs that it assembles and sells. At the other end of the spectrum, highly integrated firms, such as Procter & Gamble and Nestlé, perform most functions internally, ranging from production, research, and development to marketing and distribution.

▶ Tesco.com is situated somewhere in the middle of this continuum. On the one hand, Tesco sources many activities that were previously fulfilled by outside providers. Consider, for example, the arrangement that Tesco had reached with the online vendor Grattan. Through this agreement, all the back-end activities of the value chain were outsourced to Grattan, while Tesco only managed the front-end activities. When Tesco recognized the potential business impact of selling non-food products, Tesco Direct was created in-house to provide the services that were previously performed by Grattan. Tesco Direct even decided to set up an internal publishing studio with a staff of 40 employees to produce high-quality photos for the 8000-item print catalogue and the Tesco Direct website. On the other hand, Tesco Direct has outsourced the goods delivery activity to external partners.

Many e-business analysts have argued that the widespread use of the Internet makes it more attractive to increase the reliance on external providers and perform fewer activities internally. In order to assess this claim, we need to analyze the different factors that favor "make" and "buy" decisions and determine how the Internet affects them.

9.1.1   Reasons Favoring "Make" Decisions

There are several reasons and characteristics defining a business context that favor performing activities in-house (i.e., the "make" option).[2] These include:

1. *A strong linkage between activities*
2. *Highly differentiated products and/or services*
3. *Proximity to the company's core business*
4. *Confidentiality of information*
5. *Production cost advantages*
6. *High transaction costs*

Strong Linkage Between Activities   If it is crucial for a company to tightly integrate different activities of its value chain, then these activities should typically be performed internally if that is the only way to achieve such integration. Creating close linkages throughout the value chain can help a firm either to provide superior customer benefit through reinforcement of activities or to lower costs through an optimization of efforts.

Highly Differentiated Products and/or Services   How differentiated a product or service is determines its degree of uniqueness vis-à-vis the competition.[3] In what refers to the "make" versus "buy" decision, a business that aims for differentiation advantage and is considering the potential for outsourcing, should firstly ask if there are qualified businesses, capable of performing the required tasks, to subcontract to. In other words, a potential subcontractor has to satisfactorily contribute to the firm's differentiation strategy, performing the outsourced activity at the value level that matches the business's requirements. On the contrary, if the business cannot find a suitable business to subcontract to, then it would have to consider undertaking itself the particular activity (or activities).

Proximity to the Company's Core Business   Activities or processes that are strongly linked to a company's core business, due to their strategic importance in the value proposition provided, need to be closely controlled and coordinated. Therefore, if a reliable and quality collaboration with a suitable partner cannot be found, the company will have to carry out internally the concerned activity.

Confidentiality of Information   Confidentiality of information is another reason that can lead a business to perform activities internally. The sharing of critical information with external providers, such as research and development methods and outputs, customers, and production methods, may undermine the competitive advantage of a business. Microsoft, for instance, refuses to provide other software development firms with the source code of its software because it fears that doing so would eventually result in a leak into the public domain.

---

2   Contents of this section are partially based on the following articles: Anderson and Coughlan (1987), Anderson and Weitz (1986), Mahoney (1992), and Stuckey and White (1993).
3   For a conceptual discussion of differentiation strategies, see ▶ Sect. 5.1.2.

Production Cost Advantage   In ▶ Sect. 5.1.1, the concepts of economies of scale and economies of scope were presented. If a business can easily obtain, when carrying out certain activities, important cost advantages related to the abovementioned economies, then it should not subcontract but rather integrate these activities internally. In addition, by doing so, the business may be able to create entry barriers or get rid of some competitors.

High Transaction Costs   Costs related to the actual transaction process, also called transaction costs, represent an important factor in the "make" versus "buy" decision.[4] These consist of costs that a business incurs when it relies on the market to make a product or service. Transaction costs arise because of diverse factors, including behavioral aspects related to the economic agents involved in the transaction, the characteristics of the context where the transaction takes place (e.g., its level of uncertainty and complexity), and the inherent characteristics of the transaction being dealt with (such as frequency, asset specificity, level of uncertainty, and more). For instance, in relation to the former factor, buyers and sellers usually have diverging interests, which might make them act with opportunism, or "self-interest seeking with guile," as the Economics Nobel Prize O.E. Williamson put it (see Williamson 1975). The seller wants to maximize profits by charging as high a price as possible, while the buyer wants to keep costs down by paying as little as possible. To avoid opportunistic behavior, a business needs to invest time and effort in searching for an appropriate business partner, negotiating conditions, and monitoring and enforcing the contract.

Which factors or situations cause the possible rise of transaction costs and how does the Internet influence these factors? We now describe some of the most important factors.

Asset Specificity   This relates to the investment needed in order to set up a transaction between two or more parties. A transactional context is said to have high asset specificity, thus creating bilateral dependency between parts, when it is difficult to redeploy an asset to alternative uses outside the original context, without sacrificing the product value (Williamson 1991). For example, before the advent of the Internet, businesses that wanted to engage in electronic transactions with one another had to invest in proprietary electronic data interchange (EDI) systems, which were quite costly to install and rather complex to manage technically, especially if multiple partners spanning different industries were involved. Once such a system was in place, the parties were locked into the agreement because of the high investment made and the limited choice of partners.

Imagine the case of the tire manufacturer Tire Inc., which sources rubber from the rubber producer Rubber Corp. In order to optimize the production flow, Tire Inc. agreed to install a traditional EDI system that connects it to the IT system of Rubber Corp. The two companies drew up a contract and delivery took place as planned. Subsequently, Rubber Corp. informed Tire Inc. that it needed to raise

---

4   Transaction costs are an important concept for explaining firm structures. For a detailed discussion of the impact of the Internet on transaction costs, see Afuah (2003).

prices by 20%, knowing that Tire Inc. needs to keep the business relationship going to recover the investment in the EDI system. Tire Inc. must choose between accepting the price increase, taking Rubber Corp. to court for breach of contract, and terminating the relationship altogether. In any case, Tire Inc. would incur substantial costs. Tire Inc. decided to produce the rubber internally. By doing so, they also avoided transaction costs.

Now, let us think about what this scenario might look like today. Over the Internet, Tire Inc. could connect to the system of Rubber Corp., thereby substantially reducing the need for specific costly IT investments. Rubber Corp. at the same time would not be inclined to try to raise prices because it knows that Tire Inc. could easily switch suppliers. Therefore, transaction costs are now much lower due to lower asset specificity, which makes it more likely that Tire Inc. will outsource activities to external providers.

On the other hand, in this case the Internet dramatically reduced asset specificity. Tire Inc. has more bargaining power with Rubber Corp. because Tire Inc. knows there are other suppliers, which do not have requirements on asset specificity. This also increases Tire's opportunity cost in locking into one supplier. Hence, Rubber Corp has to upgrade or add more value to its supplies otherwise Tire Inc. will reduce the purchase price or look for a better supplier. This case vividly demonstrated how asset specificity influences power structure in a contractual relationship and why the transaction costs lowered by the Internet place more pressure on the supply side.

The Degree of Information Asymmetry Between Involved Parties   Often, a buyer lacks vital information about a seller because it does not know the track record of the seller and vice versa. If a buyer or seller can hide past cases of fraud or other crimes, then it is much more inclined to act opportunistically in the future and try to commit a crime again.

This type of information asymmetry is also easier to remedy over the Internet. Through virtual communities, such as those at eBay, buyers can rate the quality of sellers, and sellers can rate the reliability of buyers. This has a twofold effect. Firstly, any buyer who is considering a purchase can base his/her decision on the track record of the seller. If a seller has hundreds of positive ratings, then it is very likely that he/she will also fulfill his/her promises during the next transaction. Secondly, as the number of positive ratings increases, sellers are more likely to maintain their high standards in order to maintain their reputation. Thus, a self-reinforcing virtuous cycle is set in motion through the rating system, which deters opportunistic behavior, thereby also reducing potential transaction costs (risks).

Because of the lower asset-specific investment and improved information, it follows that the Internet reduces transaction costs. This should, in turn, make it more attractive to outsource parts of the value chain to external providers.

Performance   Businesses aim to create the optimal performance across every part of the value chain. A "buy" decision is in part justified by a low insourced performance compared to that of an external product/service provider. However, some business partners may eventually *perform badly*, requiring either to change the outsourcing provider or to revert to a "make" decision (i.e., to an insourcing approach).

The Level of Uncertainty Within the Business Environment   In uncertain business environments, businesses seek flexibility and agility in their operations. One solution would be to integrate inside the organization the company's main business processes, for greater control. However, a "make" decision may not be the optimal choice for a business since a "buy" approach offers flexibility and choice, two key features that help cope with unexpected market changes. An illustrative example here is the social media strategy of *Yahoo!* In the past, Yahoo! sought to leverage its social connections with users through Yahoo's email, messenger, address book, and more. This represented a clear "make" decision and a corporate integration strategy. However, this approach did not support Yahoo! to achieve its objectives. Finally, the company opted for a social media strategy based on a partnership with Facebook, thus linking its products to Facebook Connect.

On the other hand, if a business foresees an undesirable *dependency* on its partners due to investments in specific core assets, then a "make" decision could be a good choice. Since a partnership cannot always be adequately formalized through a contractual agreement, a hybrid solution between "make" and "buy" could sometimes be more appropriate. At any rate, a more dynamic view[5] of the transaction costs theory suggests coping with uncertainty by avoiding fully integrated business processes, looking for partnerships, and reducing specific transaction assets.

9.1.2 Reasons Favoring "Buy" Decisions

Today, many companies rely heavily on sourcing parts and services from external suppliers. Why should a company buy custom software for their business, instead of building it? See the article "Build vs. buy: how to know when you should build custom software over canned solutions" for more details. There are four main reasons for favoring "buy" decisions:

1. *Difficulty in achieving economies of scale*
2. *High capital requirements*
3. *Specialized know-how*
4. *Higher efficiency of the open market*

These are discussed below.

Difficulty to Achieve Economies of Scale   A business that produces only for its own use usually requires a much smaller quantity than a supplier that produces for many different firms. Therefore, the external supplier has the potential to create larger economies of scale than the individual business that decides to make a part by itself. Dell, for instance, could decide to build its own factories for producing the microchips that it uses in the PCs it sells. However, the investment required for doing so internally is too large relative to the expected output and would make every chip produced pro-

---

5   For example, see Harrigan (1986).

hibitively expensive. Therefore, Dell sources the chips from specialized manufacturers, such as Intel and AMD, who also supply many other computer manufacturers with chips. In fact, Dell has chosen this approach for almost all its inputs. Since it is a large customer for most of its suppliers, it is in a position to capture large parts of the economies of scale in the form of low prices.

High Capital Requirements   If the production of a specific part requires a major investment upfront, such as the construction of a specialized plant, then it may be sensible to find an external supplier that already has the required facilities in place. Doing so might be more expensive on a per-unit basis, yet it reduces the overall risk of a major investment in plant and equipment. For instance, Webvan, the US online grocery retailer, may have fared better if it had relied more on external suppliers when it set up its online grocery business. Instead, Webvan created and organized by itself all parts of the value chain. It invested heavily in a custom-built IT platform, highly automated warehouses and a large fleet of delivery trucks, only to find out that the business model did not work the way it had anticipated. The expensive IT platform, warehouses, and trucks were later sold during the bankruptcy proceedings for a fraction of their original prices.

Specialized Know-How   Specialization effects are likely to be related to economies of scale. A business that produces large quantities of goods also tends to build up substantial knowledge in research and development processes and production methods over time. This specialized know-how should then lead to lower-cost production and higher quality standards, or both. Consider Tesco Direct's delivery system. The company owns large warehouses to organize the logistics of incoming and outgoing shipments. Yet, for the actual shipment process, Tesco Direct relies on specialized logistics businesses that possess strong experience in logistics and delivery and that have over time optimized their processes.

Higher Efficiency of the Open Market   Finally, external suppliers are often more efficient because they are facing continual competitive pressure from other businesses within their specific industry. If performed internally, the production of a subproduct or the provision of a service can become highly inefficient over time due to poorer controls, with commensurate increasing, unnecessary costs. External firms that specialize in producing that same product, on the other hand, do not enjoy the same type of "protection" and are therefore forced constantly to maintain high levels of efficiency, thus keeping down costs.

> **Build vs. Buy: How to Know When You Should Build Custom Software over Canned Solutions**
>
> As a CEO, balancing your company's immediate needs with its long-term growth is both paramount and challenging—especially if your business is a startup. Challenging questions arise, such as whether you should invest aggressively in long-term initiatives or take the less expensive and more conservative approach.

The "build versus buy" decision, for example, is a significant one that many companies face when addressing their software needs.

For my tutoring business, we initially started with off-the-shelf software because it was fast and cheap, but we eventually found that the lack of customization relative to our day-to-day operations ultimately led to inefficient, manual processes. As we grew, these challenges became more and more pronounced, and scalability became harder to reach. Ultimately, we were forced to invest heavily in proprietary software so that we could scale effectively. In retrospect, many of these trade-offs could have been assessed far earlier in our company's lifetime. Building custom software can unlock a host of benefits, but companies should only pursue that strategy if (a) better software can provide a competitive advantage relative to your competitors and (b) you are building a large business that can spread the cost of a proprietary system over a large number of clients. Consider the following questions before making this decision:

Why Should You Consider Investing in Custom Software?

While building custom software is expensive, the return on investment can be well worth it. Remember, however, that significant energy, resources, and time must be dedicated to its development. These tasks associated with custom software may initially make a canned solution seem like the smarter idea, but there are several reasons to reconsider:

- *Off-the-shelf software cannot meet every need.* Canned solutions generally address many of the needs of most companies. If your business has specialized needs, custom software may be better qualified to meet them.
- *Canned solutions are rigid.* The vast majority of off-the-shelf software will not allow you to modify its functionality in a meaningful way. It may be difficult to add or subtract built-in features, leading to either too many or too few functions for your company.
- *Off-the-shelf software may not be compatible with other programs.* Your business might rely on Software A to complete one task and Software B to finish a second related task. If the two programs do not communicate effectively, they may hinder your efficiency. If you build your own software, you can integrate with a wider set of APIs from different software and data partners.

Why Should You Consider Using Canned Solutions and Not Developing Your Own Software?

Under certain circumstances, sticking with canned solutions may be the more sensible option. Smaller business in particular may benefit more by going this route after taking the following factors into account:

- *Limited budget.* The costs that are associated with building custom software may be one of the first and most logical reasons for a business to avoid choosing this option. Canned solutions are cheaper and therefore can make much more financial sense for a company with a smaller budget.
- *Lack of technical proficiency.* If you do not have a strong enough software team with the necessary skills to build out this custom software, it would be wise to

pass on the opportunity until you do have such a team in place. If you cannot hold your software developers accountable for such a project, it will be tough to create great products.

- *Lack of time*. Building proprietary software takes a great deal of time to complete successfully. Businesses that do not have this time available should not immediately pursue it.
- *Great canned software is already available*. If you have a common business, like a restaurant, there are generally canned software solutions available that are already proven to be effective for your organization's purpose.
- *Technology would not be a competitive advantage*. Perhaps your business is a retail furniture store. In this case, building amazing technology would unlikely be a factor that sets you apart from your competition, nor would it likely be something that would help you provide a higher quality service or product at a lower cost and make consumers want to choose your store over others.

How Can Custom Software Help Scale Your Company?

Your business is a dynamic, evolving organization, so it makes senses for your software to adapt and grow with your company as well and not remain static. If you do anticipate your company growing at a fast rate, here are a number of ways custom software can help make your business more scalable:

- *Increased productivity*. Programs that are specifically designed with your needs in mind can enable your team to work faster and smarter. You can create one comprehensive technology platform as opposed to using multiple different programs. An integrated platform can yield major efficiency gains since all the data is one place and users do not have to switch between different websites as part of their workflow.
- *Competitive advantage*. When you rely on the same off-the-shelf software as your rival does, it is that much more difficult to outperform them. By designing your own technology that is ideally suited for your specific business operations, you can garner a competitive advantage relative to your competitors. That advantage grows as you invest more heavily in your proprietary systems.
- *Faster reaction time*. To build great custom software, you must first hire a stellar software development team. Once that team is in place, they can build a variety of products, tools, and systems. As your business needs change and as your industry evolves, being able to quickly shift technology strategies can mean the difference between market dominance and obsolesces.

Despite its initial costs, custom software is well worth the resources it requires if you are hoping to build a business of meaningful scale. Building your own software that is specifically tailored to your company's needs, as well as focused on scalability and efficiency, can help mean the difference between offering a commoditized service and offering a highly differentiated one at a better price.

Source: C. Cohn, Build vs. buy: how to know when you should build custom software over canned solutions, *Forbes*, 15 September 2014.

9.2 Choosing the Organizational Structure for e-Business Activities

In 1998, when Bertelsmann was about to launch its online bookstore BOL, the company faced a difficult question. Should BOL operate as an independent business, or should it be integrated within the company?

Many traditional bricks-and-mortar companies that launched their e-business ventures during the Internet boom years faced the same question and had several organizational options to choose from. The clicks-and-mortar spectrum helps to analyze these different options (Gulati and Garino 2000).

At one end of the spectrum, businesses fully integrate their e-business activities within the firm. At the other end, the e-business operation is completely separated from the company and spun off. Both approaches have distinct advantages and drawbacks and are now described.

9.2.1 Separate e-Business Organization

Let us firstly consider separating the e-business activities from the parent company, an option that was particularly popular during the Internet boom years. Bertelsmann, for instance, decided to launch BOL as a separate business to enter the online market for book retailing. At the time, many other bricks-and-mortar companies chose this separate approach to their online activities because they believed that it gave them the following advantages:[6]

1. *Greater focus.* Due to the fast-moving business environment and the increasing Internet-based competition, businesses wanted to create entities that focused solely on e-business activities and did not have to take into consideration the overall strategy of the firm.
2. *More flexibility and autonomy.* A separate e-business organization structure enabled a more flexible and faster decision-making process. In comparison to an enterprise IT department, parent companies can advantageously allocate more external resources by founding an independent company. Investors, government, and society are typically inclined to support new businesses rather than a restructuring mature business because new companies are agile and usually have more growth potential and a better return of investment.
3. *Entrepreneurial culture.* Established management approaches and business procedures were considered to be inadequate for the Internet world, where "everything" had been turned upside down. To accommodate this change, e-business ventures were often staffed with young individuals who possessed an entrepreneurial drive, strong IT know-how, and analytical capabilities, yet often little knowledge of the industry or experience.
4. *Access to venture capital.* The soaring stock markets of the late 1990s were another reason for separating an online business from its parent company. The

---

6 Ibid.

outrageously high valuations of companies that were focused primarily on pure dotcom businesses (without any physical bricks-and-mortar structures that may hold them back or dilute their business strategy) was in stark contrast to the stable valuations of less riskier traditional bricks-and-mortar companies.

5. *Self-financing.* It is critical for companies to develop e-business, but what is more challenging is to create a well-defined path to monetize e-business by integrating it into existing business operations. In this case, entrepreneurs, particularly in small- to medium-sized enterprises, tend to differentiate their e-business from other business areas. They usually invest in startups for a specific timeframe, during which the startup is expected to become profitable and ideally as soon as possible.

With the burst of the Internet bubble in 2000, many companies that had separated or spun off their e-business activities could not exploit the synergies between their online and offline channels and operations and, therefore, were not able to pursue a clicks-and-mortar strategy. After losing large sums of money on doomed high-valuation dotcom businesses, shareholders wanted to see less rapid decision-making and business pivots and more sustainable strategies and profitable business models.

As a result of lessons learned from the dotcom era, many businesses that initially spun off their e-business operations then reintegrated them into the parent company. A prime example of this development was the case of the Internet bookseller BOL, which started out as a completely separate business with its own management structure and business model. However, as the Internet boom subsided, the online book-retailing operation was reintegrated into the parent Group of Bertelsmann.

9.2.2 Integrated e-Business Organization

Some businesses choose from inception to integrate their e-business activities tightly with their bricks-and-mortar operations. For example, Office Depot seamlessly integrated its website with its physical retailing network. Thus, it was able to leverage from its existing infrastructure of a call center and a vast fleet of delivery trucks. Similarly, when deliberating whether to fulfill orders using its existing store network or warehouses, ▶ Tesco.com opted for an integrated in-store-based fulfillment approach.

Today, it seems that in most cases the benefits of an organizational structure that combines online and offline channels outweigh those of a separated organization. These benefits include:[7]

1. *Established and trusted brand.* Companies moving from the physical world into the online world can leverage the brand, legacy and reputation they have established with their customers in the physical world. Trust is a critical issue in e-business, and it increases when customers can resort to face-to-face interaction when requiring assistance.

---

7   Ibid.

2. *Shared information*. Information about customers can be shared across different channels. For instance, ► Tesco.com uses purchasing information from its online channel to adapt offerings in its physical grocery outlets.

3. *Cross-promotion*. Online and offline channels can benefit from one another through cross-promotion. Nordea uses its bank branch staff to encourage customers to use the online channel. At clothes retailer the Gap, signs throughout its physical stores point to its online presence ► Gap.com.

4. *Purchasing leverage*. Purchasing can be pooled for offline and online channels. This increases a company's bargaining power vis-à-vis its suppliers, thereby reducing purchasing costs.

5. *Distribution efficiencies*. Different channels within a company can use the same infrastructure facilities, thereby increasing utilization and scale effects. Consider Tesco and its store-based picking approach. There, most of the picking is done during the store's off-peak hours when there are fewer customers. At ► barnesandnoble.com, customers can browse and order their books online and pick them up at the physical store. The same option is available, for instance, at Home Depot, the big home furnishings retailer, and at Guitar Center, the world's largest retailer of music instruments, and their related websites: ► homedepot.com and ► guitarcenter.com

6. *Shared customer service*. The offline channel is very useful for providing customer services for the online channel. It is much easier, convenient, and less costly for customers to return defective or unwanted purchases to a physical store than to repackage them and return them by postal mail or courier service. Similarly, employees at physical stores can also help by providing maintenance and inspection work.

As mentioned in several parts of this chapter, there are also some hybrid options spanning the two extreme choices of full separation and full integration. These include setting up joint ventures and strategic partnerships. These approaches seek to combine the technological know-how, nimbleness, and entrepreneurial culture of an online venture with the strong brand name and existing customer base of a bricks-and-mortar business.

Consider, for example, the partnership between ► Amazon.com and the Borders Group, the second largest book retailer in the United States, which filed for bankruptcy in 2011. It illustrates how a major book retailer failed to adapt itself in a timely manner to the new digital business environment, which disrupted the traditional book retailing industry. In 2001, as part of this agreement, ► Amazon.com provided the Borders Group with its e-business solution, technology services, site content, product selection, and customer service for the co-branded "Borders teamed with ► Amazon.com" site. ► Amazon.com recorded all orders that took place through the site and passed on a fixed sales percentage to the Borders Group. Through this agreement, the two companies leveraged ► Amazon.com's strong technological know-how with the Borders group's extensive physical store presence. Depending on availability, customers who ordered through the website had the option to pick up their purchase on the same day at the nearest Borders store. Customers would then receive an e-mail confirmation from Borders, informing them that the purchased item had been picked and reserved under their name for express in-store pickup. Basically, this was the partnership model between the Borders Group and ▶ Amazon.com, whereby Borders got a percentage of the online sales from Amazon. However, although this collaboration agreement was extended after its first years, Borders decided to drop Amazon and in 2008 launched its own e-commerce website ▶ Borders.com. This decision intended to integrate Borders' offline and online channels, thus enabling the company to become a clicks-and-mortar book retailer. However, the worsening financial results of Borders between 2008 and 2011 reflected the company's inability to effectively transform itself in order to meet the new challenges of digital content and online retailing which shifted the book industry's paradigm.

9.3 Value Chain Deconstruction over the Internet

The concept of *deconstruction* builds on the foundations of transaction cost theory.[8] The fundamental idea of this concept is that traditionally integrated value chains within industries get unbundled and reconfigured as a result of two main developments. These are (1) the separation of the *economics of things (physical goods)* and the *economics of information (digital goods)* and (2) the *blow-up of the trade-off between richness and reach*. For example, the value chain of the agriculture industry is fueled and reconfigured by online payment and digital platforms as digital tools enable smallholder farmers to deal with finance-related issues of their business remotely and smoothly. For more, see the article "Financing agriculture value chains in the digital age." The limitations of the concept of deconstruction are discussed in "The limitations of deconstruction and unbundling."

> **Financing Agriculture Value Chains in the Digital Age**
> Agriculture plays a critical role in economic growth, poverty reduction, and food security. The demand for agricultural commodities is increasing, as the world's population surges to an anticipated 9 billion by 2050. It is imperative, therefore, that we find ways to boost agriculture productivity nationally and globally. This cannot be achieved without improving the productivity of smallholder farmers, given that they produce over 70% of global food needs.
>
> Agriculture value chains can provide opportunities for smallholders to access high value markets, advanced technology, and networks of various value chain actors such as processors, traders, and service providers, as well as reduce the cost of doing business. So, what is holding back the participation of smallholders in value chains? Poor access to finance is a critical pain point for smallholders. It makes it hard for them to survive and grow and impedes their participation in a value chain.

---

8   For more detailed discussions of the concept of deconstruction, see Evans and Wurster (1999), and Heuskel (1999).

How Can We Fill the Financing Gap to Integrate Smallholders in Agriculture Value Chains?

In the Philippines, for instance, credit demand in 2014 for priority commodities such as rice, corn, coconut, and sugarcane reached $11.3 billion, while the bank credit disbursed for producing these commodities was only $3.4 billion, leaving a credit gap of $7.9 billion. Smallholder farmers face specific challenges in accessing finance. Lack of formal contracts, credit histories, production records, and their unstable production and income make it difficult for financial institutions to identify risks associated with smallholders. Also, smallholders are spread over rural and remote areas, and their amount of financing they need for inputs and working capital is usually very small. Servicing these needs results in high transaction costs for financial institutions. The question is how to fill the supply-demand gap in financing for smallholders to integrate them into a value chain and vitalize the agriculture sector.

Financing Options

Agriculture value chain finance provides a set of financial instruments that can be applied for agribusinesses at different stages, which helps smallholders access the financing they need to expand. There are several financing options besides bank and nonbank credit. A good example is asset-based finance, or using a firm's valued assets such as accounts receivable, inventory, machinery, and equipment as collateral, or through sale or lease while not depending on real estate securities and third-party guarantees. Asset-based finance offers cash-in-advance with discount, typically faster than traditional bank credit. It provides various forms of financing, such as invoice discounting, purchase order finance, factoring, and warehouse receipt finance; but in reality these instruments are not accessible to smallholders as they are not well involved in value chains.

Digital finance, mainly through Internet banking and mobile banking, will bring more opportunities for smallholders and other value chain actors to access timely and low-cost financing.

Online Payment Is Critical Instrument for Smallholders to Go Digital

A 2017 report by business intelligence firm GSMA estimates that out of over 750 million farmers in 69 countries, 295 million have a mobile phone, and 13 million have a phone and mobile money account in 2016. The report sees as a potential business-to-person (B2P) market a large share of the estimated 350 million farmers who will have mobile phone in 2020. To integrate smallholder farmers into value chains, a balanced development of four key products (payment, credit, savings, and insurance via online and mobile phones) will be needed, together with online trading platforms. Among these products, online payment is a critical instrument to extend digital financial services to smallholders. In general, cash is king in rural areas. Most smallholders do not know what digital payment is and how to use it and are thus hesitant to go digital. Cash payments are often troublesome. Payments can be delayed if there are no bank branches nearby, which may trigger side-selling, selling their commodities to someone outside of a contract, by smallholders.

Smallholders Benefits

But once smallholders experience that digital payment allows them to conduct fast, easy, safe, low-cost transactions in small amounts on their mobile phones, they will start to trust other digital tools. This facilitates shifting from cash to digital. Asset-based finance can benefit from digital technology. For instance, digital production records can fill the information gap between suppliers and financial institutions and can be used for invoice discounting.

Digitizing warehouse receipts is another promising way to help smallholders raise funds, backed by transparent and traceable data on quality and quantity of crops. This system can allow smallholders to access post-harvest loans. Likewise, digital savings can be an important tool for smallholders. Given smallholder farmers' unpredictable cash flow, a digital platform enables them to save ahead for input purchases and prepare for unexpected and urgent expenses, through branchless transactions via mobile networks.

Time to Unlock the Potential of Digital Finance to Support Smallholders

Digital insurance platforms offer reasonably low-cost crop insurance for smallholders. Users can register online and pay their premiums with their mobile phones. Weather-index insurance enables smallholders to effectively manage crop loss risks through automated weather stations and satellites. Finally, online trade platforms can facilitate business connections between smallholder farmers and others on the value chain and further promote trade and supply chain finance. The above are just some of the benefits for smallholders of using digital financial services so they can better participate in value chains. Meanwhile, still many issues remain to further promote digital value chain financing for agriculture.

Developing relevant digital infrastructure and agent networks needs relatively large upfront investment. Comprehensive policy and regulatory frameworks should also be in place to promote healthy digital financial services, and digital finance literacy among smallholders is a must. By addressing these challenges, we can unlock the potential of digital finance to support smallholders on agricultural value chains.

Source: S. Shinozaki, "Financing agriculture value chains in the digital age," *Asian Development Blog*, 30 October 2017.

Let us take a closer look at the first point. How do the economics of things and of information differ? When physical goods, such as a chair or a table, are sold, ownership is transferred from the seller to the buyer. Informational goods, on the other hand, can be used many times, with low (if any) incremental costs. Take a newspaper article that is published online. There is little impact on costs if it is read by ten or ten thousand people. Furthermore, physical goods are location dependent. They cannot be moved easily or quickly, and they often take up substantial space, which is a real cost. Information, on the other hand, can be sent across the globe quickly and only requires disk storage space on a computer server.

In the past, the two different types of economics were combined within a unified business model, which led to compromises. Consider the example of used-car dealerships. What are the reasons for customers to go to a used-car dealership? They want to find out about different choices, go for a test drive, get an attractive financing scheme, and receive a warranty and maintenance services.

In order to provide the customer with as much product information as possible, it makes sense to put many cars on display, so that customers can easily compare between different models and make a more informed purchasing decision. On the other hand, since the information about a car is held in the physical car, maximizing the number of cars in the showroom conflicts with the desire to keep down costs by limiting showroom space and inventory. A further compromise is that, for sales purposes, it is sensible to build large car dealerships in central locations to maximize the number of cars on display. For post-sale servicing purposes, however, it would be much better to have small repair shops located near the car owners' homes.

The online auction company, eBay, has effectively deconstructed the used-car business and has become the largest used-car dealership in the United States. As with a traditional car dealer, eBay offers a wide choice of cars, but unlike physical dealers, it is not constrained by physical space on a car lot. eBay acts as an integrated market maker for sellers, thereby offering unsurpassed choice across the country, or across the world in the case of rare cars. Through the deconstruction and reconfiguration of the value chain with external partners, eBay can offer higher benefits to consumers at reduced costs.

How does it work? Sellers wanting to sell their car on eBay face the problem of not being able to convince potential customers of the quality of their car. To remedy this, eBay works in partnership with the certified vehicle inspection chain PepBoys, which inspects the car and then issues an authorized inspection certificate which the seller can post on the eBay website. The information about the state of the car is even better than in the traditional marketplace, where the buyer, who typically does not know much about cars, has to inspect the car him/herself. eBay also has partnerships with financing companies and with neutral third-party payment operators, which, to prevent fraud, act as proxies to transfer payments from buyer to seller.

Overall, this deconstruction leads to a development called *de-averaging of competitive advantage*. Here, a business picks out individual parts of the value chain and decides to compete on only one dimension through larger-scale, higher degrees of specialization or other factors that contribute to competitive advantage while outsourcing other activities to external providers or even to customers themselves as in the case of online platform *Etsy*, which provides website owners with a shop system allowing for mass customization by sellers of niche products.

Critical Perspective 9.1
The Limitations of Deconstruction and Unbundling

How should we evaluate the applicability of the "unbundling" concept? Its proposition is similar to that outlined in the concept of deconstruction.[9] Both state that different parts of the value chain, here called businesses, should be reconfigured so that the trade-offs, and compromises inherent in integrated firms can be resolved. The examples of eBay and Dell, where deconstruction has worked out very well, thereby rewarding the two companies with high profitability, need to be contrasted with other companies engaged in e-business where this type of deconstruction has been more limited. There are different reasons why deconstruction might not be appropriate for a firm (Porter 2001) including:

- *Lack of linkage between externally and internally performed activities.*
  ▶ Amazon.com, for instance, initially set out with a highly deconstructed business model in which the focus rested on the front end of interactions with customers. Back-end warehousing and logistics were to be left to external suppliers. However, integrating the front end of customer services with the back end with external logistics providers turned out to be more cumbersome than anticipated, and it became impossible to deliver the promised customer benefit in terms of speed of shipment, quality, and reliability. ▶ Amazon.com therefore decided to reintegrate parts of the value chain by setting up a proprietary warehousing system.

- *Increased convergence and ease of imitation.* When key steps of the value chain that previously constituted substantial sources for competitive advantage are outsourced to external providers, this creates the risk that competitors turn to the same vendor, thereby making purchased inputs more homogenous. Doing so decreases the potential for differentiation and increases price competition. Furthermore, it also lowers barriers to entry because new entrants only need to assemble purchased inputs rather than build their own capabilities.

9.4 Unbundling the Corporation over the Internet

The concept of "unbundling the corporation" is very similar to the deconstruction approach.[10] It also argues that companies need to rethink the traditional organization and unbundle their core businesses (or core activities) as a result of falling transaction costs made possible by the Internet and IT advances in general. The

---

9 J. Rayport and J. Sviokla developed a similar concept to the two concepts mentioned here. It proposes an unbundling along the dimensions of content, context, and infrastructure. Since the findings are essentially the same as in the deconstruction and unbundling concepts, we do not elaborate further on this concept. However, for a detailed discussion of this concept, see Rayport and Sviokla (1995).

10 For a detailed discussion of this concept, see Hagel and Singer (1999).

limitations of this concept were discussed in "The limitations of deconstruction and unbundling."

The "unbundling" concept recognizes that a corporation consists of the following three core businesses:

1. *Product innovation*, which focuses on research and development but also includes activities further down the value chain such as market research to identify and understand consumers' preferences. The globally consultancy IDEO, which designs products and services for large corporate customers, is a prominent example of a business that is focused primarily on product innovation.

2. *Infrastructure management*, which focuses on logistics and support functions. This business includes the building and management of physical facilities, such as manufacturing or assembly plants, retail outlets, and truck fleets, for high-volume production and transportation processes. For example, through its extensive physical retail network, ▶ Tesco.com is strongly involved in managing its infrastructure business.

3. *Customer relationship management*, which focuses on the interfaces between the business and its customers. These interfaces include activities such as marketing, sales, and service. Their common goal is to attract and retain customers.

The reason why different businesses conflict with one another is that they have the following differing economic, cultural, and competitive imperatives:

1. *Economics*. In product innovation, speed allows a business to introduce new products to the market sooner than the competition. For this reason speed is a highly valued asset. However, customer relationship and infrastructure management businesses place highest priorities on, respectively, economies of scope (getting a large share of the consumer wallet) and economies of scale.

2. *Culture*. Product innovation focuses on creative employees who are responsible for developing new ideas. This is mirrored in flexible pay schemes and work schedules that are designed to satisfy and motivate employees. A customer relationship business, on the other hand, focuses on external customers, while the focus of an infrastructure business is on costs. To operate large-scale operations efficiently, it is necessary to create a culture of standardization, predictability, and efficiency.

3. *Competition*. For successful product innovation, it is essential to gain access to skillful and talented employees. Developing innovations often does not require large startup costs, as is illustrated by the founders of some e-commerce success stories (such as ▶ Amazon.com, eBay, and Google). Therefore, in product innovation, there are usually many small players, of which few will succeed. In both of the other businesses, however, competition tends to be driven by economies of scope and/or scale, which leads to a consolidation where a few big players dominate the competition.

The problem for integrated businesses is the difficulty of simultaneously optimizing scope, speed, and scale; therefore, businesses need to make trade-offs. For instance, in order to maximize scope, a retailer should provide a vast variety of products, possibly also from external stores.

This is what ▶ Amazon.com has been doing with its Zshop system, which allows other used-book retailers to sell their products through the ▶ Amazon.com website. Doing so makes the site more attractive for customers because they find not only the new ▶ Amazon.com offerings but also used books, which are generally cheaper. From a scope perspective, this makes a lot of sense. However, in the unlikely event that doing so leads to fewer orders originating from ▶ Amazon.com, this would then result in a lower utilization of physical infrastructure, such as warehouses, thereby compromising the company's economies of scale.

Summary

- Firstly, this chapter analyzed the degree of integration of individual activities of the value chain. More specifically, it discussed which activities a business should perform (or "make") by itself and which activities it should source (or "buy") from external providers. Reasons that favor "make" decisions include strong linkage between activities, confidentiality of information, and high transaction costs. Reasons that favor "buy" decisions include high economies of scale, high capital requirements, specialized know-how, and higher efficiency of open markets.
- Secondly, the chapter analyzed how to choose the organizational structure for e-business activities and presented the following four options: (1) in-house integration, (2) joint venture, (3) strategic partnership, and (4) independent business (e.g., a spin-off). It then discussed the benefits and drawbacks of each organizational option.
- Finally, the chapter analyzed the unbundling of the traditional organization as a result of falling transaction costs made possible by the Internet. The unbundling concept distinguishes three core businesses in a corporation: (1) product innovation, (2) infrastructure management, and (3) customer relationship management. These three businesses have different imperatives regarding economics, culture, and competition.

❓ Review Questions

1. Describe the different organizational options along the "make-or-buy" spectrum.
2. In general, which factors determine whether a firm should make or buy a product or a service?
3. Why should a company consider deconstructing its value chain over the Internet?
4. Outline the concept of unbundling the corporation and explain its underlying rationale.
5. What are the different options that a company has when choosing the organizational structure for its Internet venture?
6. What criteria should a company use when deciding whether to integrate its Internet activities in-house or whether to spin them off?

7. Illustrate through different examples how the Internet enables companies to integrate activities across their value chain.
8. Provide examples of Internet ventures that favor (or have favored) either "make" or "buy" decisions.
9. Explain how a company deconstructs its value chain over the Internet and illustrate your answer through an actual example.
10. Provide two examples from two different industries (one related to physical products and one dealing with digital goods) that demonstrate the concept of unbundling the corporation.
11. Critically assess the deconstruction and unbundling concepts and show their limitations using actual e-business examples.
12. Discuss how recent new technologies, such as Blockchain and IoT, impact the structure of organizations and the value chain of industries.

References

Afuah, A. (2003). Redefining firm boundaries in the face of the Internet: are firms really shrinking? *Academy of Management Review, 28*(1), 34–53.

Anderson, E., & Coughlan, A. T. (1987). International market entry and expansion via independent or integrated channels of distribution. *Journal of Marketing, 51*, 71–82.

Anderson, E., & Weitz, B. A. (1986). Make-or-Buy Decisions: Vertical Integration and Marketing Productivity. *Sloan Management Review, 27*(3), 3–19.

Evans, P., & Wurster, T. (1999). *Blown to bits* (pp. 39–67). Harvard Business School Press.

Gulati, R., & Garino, J. (2000). Get the right mix of bricks and clicks. *Harvard Business Review, 78*, 107–114.

Hagel, J., & Singer, M. (1999). Unbundling the corporation. *Harvard Business Review, 77*, 133–141.

Harrigan, K. R. (1986). Matching vertical integration strategies to competitive conditions. *Strategic Management Journal, 7*, 535–555.

Heuskel, D. (1999). W*ettbewerb jenseits von Industriegrenzen*. Campus, 57–72.

Mahoney, J. T. (1992). The choice of organizational form: vertical financial ownership versus other methods of vertical integration. *Strategic Management Journal, 13*, 559–584.

Porter, M. (2001). Strategy and the Internet. *Harvard Business Review, 79*(3), 62–78.

Rayport, J., & Sviokla, J. (1995). Managing in the market space. *Harvard Business Review*, 141–150.

Stuckey, J., & White, D. (1993). When and when not to vertically integrate. *Management Review, 34*(3), 71–83.

Williamson, O. E. (1975). *Markets and hierarchies: Analysis and antitrust implications* (p. 26). New York: The Free Press.

Williamson, O. E. (1991). Comparative economic organization: The analysis of discrete structural alternatives. *Administrative Science Quarterly, 36*, 269–296.

Further Reading

W. Aghina, A. De Smet, G. Lackey, M. Lurie, and M. Murarka, 'The five trademarks of agile organizations', McKinsey.com, January 2018.

R. Coase wrote the first influential article on transaction cost theory in 'The nature of the firm', *Economica*, vol. 4, 1937, pp. 386–405. O. E. Williamson provided an additional foundational perspective on this topic in *Markets and Hierarchies: Analysis and Antitrust Implications*, Free Press, 1975. Also see: O.E. Williamson, 'Comparative economic organization: The analysis of discrete structural alternatives', *Administrative Science Quarterly*, vol. 36 (2), 1991, pp. 269–296.

P. Evans and T. Wurster developed the concept of deconstructing the value chain in *Blown to Bits*, Harvard Business School Press, 1999. For a condensed version of this concept, see, by the same authors, 'Strategy and the new economics of information', *Harvard Business Review*, September–October, 1997, pp. 71–81.

J. Hagel and M. Singer wrote the article 'Unbundling the corporation', *Harvard Business Review*, March–April, 1999, pp. 133–141.

M. Porter criticises the deconstruction and unbundling concepts in 'Strategy and the Internet', *Harvard Business Review*, March, 2001, pp. 72–74.

B. Rosenbloom reflects on several challenges that industrial firms face with their multi-channel marketing strategies. This includes the management of the emergence of eventual conflicts between the different channels, in 'multi-channel strategy in business-to-business markets: Prospects and problems', Industrial Marketing Management, vol. 36, 2007, pp. 4–9.

A.A. Tsay and N. Agrawal, analyse the topic of conflict and e-commerce channels in 'Channel conflict and coordination in the e-commerce age', *Production and Operations Management,* vol. 13 (1), 2004, pp. 93–110.

9

Interaction with Suppliers: e-Procurement

Contents

© Springer Nature Switzerland AG 2020
T. Jelassi, F. J. Martínez-López, *Strategies for e-Business*, Classroom Companion: Business,
https://doi.org/10.1007/978-3-030-48950-2_10

Learning Outcomes
After completing this chapter, you should be able to:
- Understand the basic concepts of e-procurement
- Assess the advantages and drawbacks of e-procurement
- Know the critical success factors of e-procurement
- Master the basic process of e-procurement and the technologies and systems involved in this process

10

■ **Introduction**

In order to produce their own products and services, companies rely on the purchase of raw materials and other manufacturing inputs as well as maintenance, repair, and operating (MRO) goods, from external providers. There are three different types of business-to-business (B2B) electronic marketplaces where companies or other organizations make their purchasing.[1] They are:

- *Industrial markets,* where buyers purchase raw materials to turn them into tangible goods. These markets are primarily used by companies from industries such as agriculture, manufacturing, electricity, or construction.
- *Reseller markets,* where buyers purchase products or services with the sole purpose of reselling them later on. Reseller markets predominate in wholesale and retail industries.
- *Government markets* where government agencies buy goods and services. Transactions in government markets take place, for example, when government agencies make purchases for public administration or to equip the armed forces.

This chapter provides a comprehensive understanding of the basic concepts and issues in e-procurement. Firstly, it presents the advantages and drawbacks of e-procurement. Secondly, it points out the critical success factors of e-procurement. Lastly, it illustrates the steps of e-procurement and diverse relevant technologies and systems involved in it.

10.1 Advantages and Drawbacks of e-Procurement

e-Procurement refers to "the use of integrated information technology systems for procurement functions, including sourcing, negotiation, ordering, receipt and post-purchase review" (Gunasekaran et al. 2009: p. 162). e-Procurement has been evolving since information technologies became widely applied within business communication, specifically business to supplier communication. For more details, see the article: "Technology is transforming procurement operations: here's what you need to know." But e-procurement is not a silver bullet for all businesses and their procurement activities. Businesses need to understand its advantages and drawbacks before adopting it in practice.

---

1   See Chaffey et al. (2006).

Technology Is Transforming Procurement Operations: Here's What You Need to Know

Technology is quickly reshaping just about every aspect of the way business is done. It is a catalyst for change as well as an enabler across industries, and the procurement industry is no exception. New technology provides opportunities for procurement to boost market coordination, introduce new suppliers, enable better compliance, increase capacity and speed, minimize risk, and increase trust by removing human error. These advancements not only enhance the performance of the buyer's organization but also enhance the performance of the suppliers—helping improve the buyer-supplier relationship, collaboration, and innovation. Xchanging recently surveyed 830 procurement professionals across the globe on how technology is transforming procurement. The research aimed to help people understand what technologies are most valuable and significant to procurement and the latest trends in procurement technology.

The United States Leads in Adoption Rates

Procurement functions already adopted a significant amount of technology, witnessed by more than half of respondents who said they already implemented 11 of the 12 technologies listed on the survey. The most widely implemented technologies were savings tracking and spend analytics, with 77 and 76 percent of organizations already having these technologies in place, respectively. This reflects the increased pressure for spending cuts and streamlined processes in today's challenging economic climate. These pressures were also seen in responses regarding the key performance indicators (KPIs) that procurement functions are measured by. The top four KPIs used by companies were cost related with 47 percent citing cost savings realized as the most important, followed by revenue impact at 19 percent, cost savings identified at 16 percent, and cost avoidance at 14 percent.

When looking at current adoption trends, more than two-thirds of companies surveyed already have automation, reporting dashboards and contract management systems in place. Additionally, supplier performance management and market intelligence software are being used by 64 percent and 60 percent of companies, respectively. The highest adoption of these solutions was seen among companies based in the United States (where companies are 8 percent more likely to have all of these technologies in place compared to those in mainland Europe), companies with more than 3000 employees, companies in the retail/consumer goods and manufacturing industries, and companies that outsource parts of their operation.

However, this research revealed an interesting contradiction among procurement professionals: while technology adoption was shown to be relatively high within the industry, a majority of respondents cited more/better technologies as the one change they would make for improved procurement performance. This means that, while technology use is increasing within the procurement industry, procurement professionals are eager to see additional growth and investment in the area.

Capacity Issues Influence Investment Priorities

Procurement decision-makers feel that automation is the future for the function. Process enhancement, automation, and talent development were cited as the biggest investment priorities for procurement professionals at 28, 24, and 22 percent, respectively. These results highlight the capacity issues faced by the industry, as 80 percent of respondents identified procurement team time pressures as a challenge, and 20 percent cited it as a major challenge. Companies with decentralized procurement were 17 percent more likely to consider process enhancement a top priority than those with centralized operations. And, in companies with more than 3000 employees, talent development was considered to be a bigger investment priority than companies with only 500–999 employees.

There is also a discrepancy between C-suite respondents and middle managers on where investment priorities lie. C-suite respondents were more likely to consider analytics an investment priority compared to lower management directors and middle managers. On the other hand, middle managers were nearly twice as likely to consider process enhancement an investment priority compared to C-level executives. Additionally, robotic process automation (RPA) is quickly emerging as a disruptive technology in which companies are looking to invest in the procurement industry. RPA is capable of delivering cost savings, enhanced accuracy, productivity gains, and increased compliance. While RPA left many people feeling threatened by the idea of robots taking their jobs, workers at companies where RPA is already installed are embracing the technology since it frees them up to focus on more innovative and strategic tasks.

Predictive Analytics Will Be King in Procurement

Looking at the procurement industry, it is evident that there are three emerging technology trends that are poised to have an impact on the space: the Internet of Things (IoT), predictive analytics, and social sourcing. Procurement professionals believe that predictive analytics will have the largest overall impact on the industry over the next 5 years, at 80 percent. Additionally, 79 percent believe that IoT will have some impact on the procurement industry in the coming years, and 20 percent believe it will have a major impact.

These results are incredibly positive for the procurement industry, showing that procurement leaders are embracing change, innovation, and technology. But what improvements will these technologies actually bring to the procurement function? Predictive analytics tracks purchasing patterns over time to help forecast a direction of travel and determine where a certain line is headed. This information allows teams to anticipate problems and intervene before it's too late. Procurement teams will benefit from this by staying ahead and responding proactively.

According to Gartner, IoT will "significantly alter how the supply chain operates." This specifically relates to how supply chain leaders access information. IoT will further allow enterprise resource planning and supply chain management to work together by connecting people, processes, data, and things via devices and sensors. IoT in the supply chain and transportation industries is part of today's larger picture digital business landscape by which connected devices enable organizations to work smarter, plan better, and foster more intelligent decision-making processes.

Don't Get Left Behind

While technology is already beginning to reshape procurement, we only just scratched the surface for the impact it will have. Some companies started to recognize the transformation technology is destined to make in the procurement field; procurement leaders who do not recognize and embrace its impact are likely to fall behind. With many processes fit for automation, companies will demand that their procurement efficiency keeps pace with their rivals. This will be critical for long-term success, so be sure your business is ready.

Source: J. Ivancich, "Technology is transforming procurement operations: here's what you need to know," *Supply & Demand Chain Executive*, 11 November 2015.

The most frequently cited advantages of e-procurement are described below.[2]

Transparency   Online procurement ensures access to comparable information for all parties who are involved in the purchasing process, including buyers, decision-makers, and users. In contrast, paper-based purchasing systems can cause confusion in human-based systems, because parties may not have access to the same information. In addition, online systems allow buyers to track and trace the purchase process and to control different aspects such as delivery and internal distribution. Procurement can sometimes be related to corruption, for example, overpayments or preferred vendors who offer less competitive terms or inferior products. It may be easy for small firms to prevent corruption in procurement without digital systems, but for larger companies with hundreds or even thousands of operating units or affiliations across the world, it may be challenging for executives to identify malfeasance in various complicated procurement activities. However, e-procurement can enable authorized staff to access system information (e-procurement and accounts), and this may improve the likelihood of the identification of abnormal transaction activities or corrupt behavior. For example, certain patterns in expenditure or vendors.

Reduced Risk of Maverick Spending   The abovementioned point of higher transparency is closely related to the reduced risk of "maverick" spending that can be achieved through e-procurement systems. "Maverick" purchasing takes place when employees buy items or services that are outside the preferred process or system. Instead of buying from a preferred supplier with which the company has negotiated a contract with discount pricing, an individual might go outside the normal process and purchases that same item at higher prices. Setting up a dedicated system through which purchases are made, and having the means to monitor whether buyers adhere to the rules, lowers the risk of maverick spend.

Price Reduction Through Online Negotiations   Companies typically have various suppliers and a wide range of procurement costs. e-Procurement can help managers

---

2   Ibid., p. 501

manage materials and suppliers to purchase quality raw materials at a reasonable price at the right time. A purchasing business can avoid the unnecessary cost from inefficiencies and frictions of traditional procurement practices that are based on paper or verbal contracts. These practices are suitable for small enterprises with small and regular procurement demands. But for mature, multinational, and market-dominant purchasers that process a large number of contracts, it is very unrealistic to manage them with traditional approaches. e-Procurement can help a business to aggregate long-term and repetitive purchases, so that it can improve its bargaining power with suppliers and reduce costs. For example, Walmart has a very advanced procurement system to predict long-term and repetitive purchases with various suppliers, so that it can reduce its purchasing costs. This approach helps its suppliers to forecast longer-term demand, so improves their stability too. The long-term financial stability of suppliers is beneficial to purchasing businesses. To some extent, e-procurement supports Walmart's cost leadership position in the retailing industry.

In terms of its use in government settings, e-procurement is regarded as a possible measure to reduce procurement waste and costs (see the FT article: Government "wasting billions on procurement").

Government "Wasting Billions on Procurement"

The British government is "wasting billions of pounds on procurement" because it does not know how much it spends on private sector suppliers, according to a leading think-tank.

Although the 17 government departments spend millions of pounds buying services and goods from private companies each year, none could supply "robust data" on how much they spent on contractors, according to research from Reform. When its researchers questioned government departments, it found that "even the most basic questions do not have authoritative answers." As evidence, Reform pointed to vastly differing estimates of government spending on suppliers that ranged from £40bn to £60bn per year from authorities including the former chief commercial officer Bill Crothers, the public accounts committee, and the National Audit Office. Another problem was that civil servants' attention was focused on the procurement process, rather than designing good contracts and monitoring suppliers. This has contributed to a number of expensive botched tenders including the recently ditched deals for the electronic monitoring of offenders.

William Mosseri-Marlio, coauthor of the report, called for greater transparency and accused the government of "wasting billions of pounds because of poor procurement. Straightforward changes could achieve big savings and better services for citizens," he added. The slow progress comes despite pledges in the 2010 coalition agreement by the Prime Minister David Cameron and his former deputy Nick Clegg to "open up government procurement and reduce costs."

The Cabinet Office had pledged to cut procurement times from 220 to 120 working days for all but the most complex goods and services. But although the government has declared this a success, Reform said this had been contradicted by data from the Spend Network, the open data researchers, which suggested that procurement times had increased, and the time it took to win a contract remained the third slowest in

Europe. Pledges to reduce so-called red tape and encourage smaller businesses to bid for work to reduce the number of suppliers judged "too big to fail" also had mixed results, said Reform. One contractor recounted a procurement that involved 137 meetings with the relevant department and a 375-line specification document. Another said they employed 70 administrators to cover the paperwork for just over three contracts.

To improve performance, Reform points to recent successes in moving procurement online, including the introduction of the G-Cloud online market place, which it said made savings of between 20 and 50 percent compared with legacy contracts. It advised the United Kingdom to emulate Estonia and South Korea and use e-procurement everywhere, saving a potential £10bn a year. The Cabinet Office said it had "saved billions of pounds for taxpayers through our commercial reforms, and the Crown Commercial Service and Government Digital Service will continue to work closely together to introduce the latest innovations and ensure we get the best value from every deal." But Alex Hitchcock, coauthor of the report, said the study showed that "commercial skills in the Civil Service are a longstanding concern. Unless the government improves practice, savings from digital procurement are unlikely to materialise."

G. Plimmer, "Government 'wasting billions on procurement," *Financial Times*, 7 March 2016.

Process Optimization   Fully integrated procurement systems eliminate the need to reenter purchasing data, thereby removing potential data entry errors, reducing manual labor, and improving the efficiency of the procurement process. It can also be used to standardize, support, and automate procurement processes, which increase process quality and reduce susceptibility to other errors or flaws. Automated procurement processes can improve the speed and simplicity of order processing. It can reduce the time that is "idle" (e.g., waiting for receipt of contracts via mail or fax) and reduce audit and approval time, shown in ◘ Fig. 10.1. e-Procurement is able to reduce total process times by more than 80 percent. Reduced process times can enhance the ability of a business to change suppliers, which supports agility and sensitivity to external environment. e-Procurement can also enable procurement employees and managers to shift their focus from conventional low-value-adding activities, such as paperwork, to more strategic and crucial activities, such as long-term procurement strategies and strengthening relationships with key suppliers.

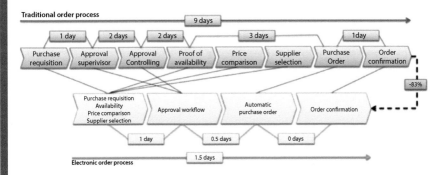

◘ **Fig. 10.1**   Reducing process times through e-procurement. (Source: Adapted from Weigel and Ruecker (2017), 188)

Improved Bargaining Power   With the emergence of web technologies and open e-procurement systems, in theory, any supplier can now trade with any buyer. Access to a wider pool of potential suppliers is an opportunity for procuring companies to bargain with current suppliers: if they do not innovate or lower the raw material price, others may take their position. e-Procurement provides many monopolies with the opportunity to externalize their innovation pressure on suppliers. For example, a monopoly can require a replaceable supplier to decrease its purchase price by 3 percent per annum; otherwise, the monopoly can threaten to replace it with another supplier in their e-procurement database. This mechanism pushes suppliers to innovate and optimize their cost structure.

Yet, there are also a number of disadvantages and risks that are associated with the introduction of e-procurement systems[3]:

Organizational Risk   Depending on the level of integration, which is discussed in more detail below, an organizational restructure may be needed for e-procurement to work. As individual employees are allowed to make e-purchases from their desktop computers, the power and importance of the procurement department in processing transactions decline; however, its oversight of e-procurement practices becomes more complex.

Technology Risk   Implementing an e-procurement system usually involves a substantial commitment to a given technology. This carries a risk of being tied to a marketplace that could decline.

Supplier Resistance   Frequently, suppliers are not eager to enter e-procurement systems since doing so may add to their costs and complexity of operations and may force price cuts (which might conflict with their preference to compete on quality). Suppliers may resist e-procurement practices when it disrupts stocking practices and labor agreements. For example, just in-time' purchasing places the role and costs of warehousing on suppliers rather than purchasers.

10.2 **The Critical Success Factors of e-Procurement**

Introducing e-procurement into a company does not merely involve implementing new software. It creates internal structural and process changes and changes operations with external suppliers.[4] For example, as shown in ❑ Fig. 10.1, many activities in the traditional order process have been removed in the e-ordering process. Estimated improvements that an e-procurement project may deliver can easily turn into disappointment and failure because buy-in from staff or suppliers is not realized or the predicted advantages of e-procurement fail to materialize. For this rea-

---

3   See Chaffey (2006).
4   This section is adapted from: A. Flynn, "Converting to eProcurement: 17 Aspects of Successful Adoption," *Sourcedogg*, 2013.

son, when proposing a new e-procurement project, it is necessary to be realistic when predicting its critical success factors. Otherwise you risk failure by not meeting exaggerated expectations.

10.2.1 The Definition of Deliverables

The clarification of deliverables of an e-procurement project is of paramount importance. Companies need to be upfront and clear about what they want to achieve through e-procurement. Hence, a business can know if, and to what extent, the e-procurement is successful. For example, a company may want to optimize purchase processes and reduce spending through e-procurement. In this case, this company should clarify the processes that are to be changed, the extent to which they change, and the impact on expenditure (cost savings). A clear and understood agreement on the expected deliverables to be generated by e-procurement can help the company to focus on to meeting those deliverables and planning to fulfill broader business goals.

10.2.2 e-Procurement Champions

As mentioned previously, e-procurement requires change in organizational processes and structure. Resistance to change usually arises where e-procurement negatively impacts the power structure and revenue distributions within a business. For example, employees with poor digital literacy may resist or even sabotage new software solutions in contrast to staff with high digital literacy. Therefore an e-procurement champion is needed to lead and manage the change process and to be responsible for the success of e-procurement. They generate momentum to push the introduction of e-procurement and to train affected employees. Of note, e-procurement systems can replace the role of managers' who approve certain expenditures. Inexperienced employees or those with low levels of digital literacy may be concerned about their ongoing roles in the business. An e-procurement champion can not only lead the implementation of e-procurement systems but can also assuage the apprehension of affected staff and through clear, direct communication and training, to improve their confidence in the new business. Finally, e-procurement champions require the executive leadership to provide a powerful project commitment and delegate power and authority to them. This will improve the ability of e-procurement champions to motivate and manage affected staff.

10.2.3 Consultation and Buy-In

e-Procurement includes efforts made by internal staff and external suppliers. Staff use the system to conduct procurement activities. Suppliers should not feel frustrated when using it to bid for contracts. Hence the success of an e-procurement project also depends on these end users. It is recommended that businesses consult with end users and obtain their buy-in prior to implementing an e-procurement project. End users can also evaluate the use ability and the likelihood that they will use the proposed e-procurement system in their daily activities. This and other information from end users can constitute important criteria for selecting an e-procurement system. Moreover, soliciting opinions, help, and support from suppliers or frontline employees can develop a sense of ownership and of being important or considered. Based on consultation with end users, e-procurement champions can develop detailed training programs and action plans.

10.2.4 Ongoing Monitoring

People should not view e-procurement as a success based on immediate outcomes. e-Procurement is not that simple. Short- term implementation outcomes do not include longer-term goals such as reducing maverick purchases and reducing wasteful spending. Furthermore, the adaptability of an e-procurement system within today's rapidly evolving business environment will be revealed over the longer term. For example, see the article below: "Understanding the bullwhip effect in supply chains." Therefore, businesses need to constantly monitor and periodically evaluate their e-procurement performance. Monitoring can help managers to recognize unintended consequences and take corrective measures before they grow into serious problems.

10

> **Understanding the Bullwhip Effect in Supply Chains**
> An efficient supply chain management system is a necessity in order to run a successful business. This results into competitive advantage by providing precise information to suppliers who in turn are able to maintain a continuous flow of products to customers. However, through the several stages of a supply chain, key factors such as time and supply of order decisions, demand for the supply, lack of communication, and disorganization can result in one of the most common problems in supply chain management. This setback is known as the bullwhip effect, also sometimes referred to as the whiplash effect.
>
> Customer demand directly impacts a business' inventory. Very often, companies attempt to forecast demand by gathering a suitable amount of raw materials and resources needed in order to satisfy customer demand in a professional and timely way. However, while going up the supply chain from consumer demand to raw material suppliers, variations can often be amplified, causing issues with time, cost, and inventory in supply chain management. *The Wall Street Journal* describes the bullwhip effect as: "This phenomenon occurs when companies significantly cut or add inventories. Economists call it a bullwhip because even small increases in demand can cause a big snap in the need for parts and materials further down the supply chain." With a thorough understanding of this concept, business owners and managers can avoid costly downfalls and maintain a performing supply chain.
> *So What Causes of the Bullwhip Effect?*

- *Inadequacy.* In a disorganized supply chain management, businesses are likely to face inadequacy between each supply chain link. For instance, by ordering more than required or lesser amounts of a product than is needed due to an over or under reaction to the supply chain beforehand.
- *Lack of communication.* Due to lack of communication between each link in the supply chain, it gets difficult for processes to run efficiently. For example, managers can identify a product demand quite differently within different links of the supply chain and therefore order different quantities.
- *Free return policies.* Sometimes, customers may purposely overstate demands due to shortages and then cancel when the supply becomes adequate again, without return forfeit retailers will continue to exaggerate their needs and cancel orders, resulting in excess material.
- *Order batching.* Companies often accumulate the demand first and may not instantly place an order with their supplier. They usually order weekly or monthly. Therefore, it leads to variability in the demand, for instance, there may be a surge in demand at some stage followed by no demand after.
- *Price variations.* Very often, special discounts and other cost changes can disturb regular buying patterns. What buyers want is to take advantage on discounts offered during a short time period, resulting into irregular production and distorted demand information.
- *Demand information.* It is essential to understand that relying on past demand information to estimate current demand information of a product does not take into account any fluctuations that may occur in demand over a period of time.

The Impact of the Bullwhip Effect on Inventory, Shipping Time, and Overall Cost

The negative impact of the bullwhip effect can prove costly to any company. So as to maintain a manageable and useful inventory, businesses usually work very hard. However, the variables that cause the bullwhip effect can lead companies to have either an excess or lack of inventory which can both be unfavorable for different reasons. Overstated orders based on misguided forecasts lead to incorrect inventory levels.

A surplus of inventory could prove costly to the company, and if consumer demand does not increase, it could result in wasted resources. Moreover, insufficient inventory can lead to poor customer relations due to unfulfilled orders and unavailable products. Such mistakes can seriously affect the goodwill and profitability of an organization.

How to Minimize the Bullwhip Effect?

- *Improved communication and better forecasts.* A good strategy which can be used to minimize the bullwhip effect is through better information, in terms of improved communication along the supply chain or better forecasts. Since managers believe that end user demand is more predictable than the demand experienced by factories, they usually attempt to ignore signals being sent through the supply chain and instead focus on the end user demand. This method ignores daily fluctuations in favor of running level.

— *Eliminate delays*. Another way to reduce the bullwhip effect is by eliminating the delays along the supply chain. Basically, by cutting order-to-delivery time by half in both real supply chains and simulations of supply chains, supply chain fluctuations can be cut by 80%.

— Reduce size of orders and good customer service. Another method to prevent the bullwhip effect consists of reducing the sizes of orders and constantly offering good product prices as a way to prevent surges resulting from promotional discounts. Besides, improving customer service and eliminating causes for customer order cancellations to ensure smooth ordering patterns.

Conclusion: the bullwhip effect can be a serious threat to businesses and should not be taken lightly by supply chain professionals. To prevent the impact of the bullwhip effect, business professionals should be highly aware of this concept and put into practice the ways to prevent it. A good start is to opt for an innovative training and development program to educate employees about the bullwhip effect.

Source: M. Wins, "Understanding the bullwhip effect in supply chains," *Procurement Academy*, 26 January 2018.

10.3 The Steps of e-Procurement

10

E-procurement involves applying information technology into procurement processes. Creating an e-procurement process involves two aspects: firstly, delineating a generic procurement process and secondly, illustrating how and what technologies and systems are applied or involved in the process.[5]

10.3.1 e-Procurement Process

Step 1: Plan the procurement based on an identified need. Companies should firstly identify and confirm a real need to purchase goods or services, particularly for purchases worth a large amount of money. Executive management should consider the strategic effects (resources or capabilities) that their business wants to achieve through its procurement, the advantages it wants to establish or sustain, and an acceptable level of procurement risk. In identification of their procurement needs, they must define target purchases and design specific principles for procurement such as the upper bound and the lower bound of planned purchase spending. At this planning stage, businesses should research their market to identify important information in specific relation to their purchasing needs, for example, who the dominant suppliers are, emerging suppliers, substitute products or services, loca-

---

5   The generic procurement process is adopted from: Australian Government Department of Finance, "Procurement process considerations," 31 March 2019. Available at: ▶ https://www.finance.gov.au/procurement/procurement-policy-and-guidance/buying/procurement-practice/process-considerations/tips.html.

tion of suppliers, standard industry supply terms, and the e-procurement systems that they use. In some cases, company will consult specialists or experts in the specific industry. Obviously, they must also identify and plan for compliance with relevant laws, regulations, and social norms.

Step 2: Scope the procurement. When creating a procurement plan, businesses may look for other buyers who may be interested in purchasing cooperatively. By aggregating demand, cooperative buying improves the ability of a company to bargain with suppliers. On the other hand, businesses that purchase as cooperatives lose some control to negotiate specific terms that relate to their individual business. When planning to participate in cooperative purchasing, a business should also internally estimate the value of the procurement as a stand-alone business, versus the price and terms that are negotiated cooperatively.

Sometimes, it is impossible to value or reliably value the terms of procurement. In this case, buyers must make sure its value is over a basic value threshold. For example, it is difficult to estimate the price of new novel technologies that have never been valued by the market. A company can first analyze its risk-taking capability and estimate possible revenue generated by the new technologies and then set a threshold price based on that analysis. Even though the new technology cannot be valued directly, the company has identified that it is too risky to purchase if its price surpasses that threshold.

Step 3: Determine the procurement method. The selection of a procurement method depends on how each potential method can help a business to achieve its procurement

---

6 Procurement Methods: Obtaining Quality Goods and Services

The procuring department is responsible for acquiring goods and services for a business. This may involve shopping for goods at competitive prices, handling all legal procedures associated with obtaining a contract, budgeting costs for the goods, and studying financial trends to ensure that company money is being spent wisely. [...] Choosing which suppliers a business will use isn't as easy as it sounds. A good sounding product and a good price don't necessarily mean it's a green light for signing on a new supply customer. So what methods does a procurement team member use during the selection process?

Generally speaking, there are six procurement methods used by the procurement team in a company. The actual names of these could vary depending on your company and industry, but the process remains the same. The six times of procurement are open tendering, restricted tendering, request for proposal, two-stage tendering, request for quotations, and single source procurement.

Open Tendering

Open tendering is shorthand for competitive bidding. It allows companies to bid on goods in an open competition or open solicitation manner. Open tendering requirements call for the company to:

- Advertise locally
- Have unbiased and coherent technical specifications
- Have objective evaluation measures
- Be open to all qualified bidders
- Be granted to the least cost provider sans contract negotiations

Arguably, the open tendering method of procurement encourages effective competition to obtain goods with an emphasis on the value for money. However, considering this is a procedures-based method, a lot of procurement experts feel that this method is not very suitable for large or complex acquisitions due to the intense focus on the output process instead of stringent obedience to standards. [...]

Restricted Tendering

Unlike open tendering, restricted tendering only places a limit on the amount of request for tenders that can be sent by a supplier or service provider. Because of this selective process, restricted tendering is also sometimes referred to as selective tendering. Like open tendering, restricted tendering is considered a competitive procurement method; however, the competition is limited to agencies that are invited by the procuring team. The procuring entity should establish a set of guidelines to use when selecting the suppliers and service providers that will be on the invitation list. Randomized selections will not bode well for procuring. This method is selective to find the best suited and most qualified agencies to procure goods and services from. It's also employed as a way for the procuring team to save time and money during the selection process.

Request for Proposals (RFP)

Request for proposal is a term that is used all across the business world. Social media managers receive RFP's from potential clients all the time when a client is seeking a new manager of their venture. This kind of proposal is a compelling and unique document stating why the business is the best fit for the type of project. Similarly, in the procurement world, a RFP is a method used when suppliers or service providers are proposing their good or service to a procurement team for review. [...]

Procurement teams are often on the hunt for the best valued, most marketable items to bring into circulation. A client may feel they have all of the qualifications to fit the needs of fulfilling a specific requirement of a procurement team—but they have to prove it. The agencies writing the RFP's should submit a two-envelope proposal to the procurement manager. The two-envelope process allows the procurers' to review the proposal through and through without knowing the financial component. The financial proposal is sealed in the second envelope and should only be opened after the content of the first-envelope proposal is approved or rejected. This eliminates any persuasion by cost and allows an objective lens to look through when analyzing a good fit. The proposal with the best fit qualifications and best price will be selected. If a lesser qualified (yet still qualified) selection has a lesser price, no contract should be negotiated. The most qualified and appropriate proposal, regardless of price, should be selected. [...]

Two-Stage Tendering

There are two procedures that are used under the two-stage tendering method. Each one of the procedures has a two stage process. This can be disadvantageous for some procurement teams if there is a time limit on securing a contract. In the same vein, this option is more flexible for both parties, allowing more room for discussion to meet mutual needs.

The first procedure is very similar to the RFP method as discussed above. The procurement team receives a proposal with two envelopes—one with the proposal itself and one with the associated financial information. The difference is the bidder is required to submit a technical proposal that highlights their solutions to fulfilling the requirements as specified by the procuring department. This proposal is scored according to the relevance of the solution to the needs of the procurer. The highest scored proposal is invited for further discussion in an attempt to reach an agreement. After the final agreement for the technical proposal is reached, the bidder is invited to submit their financial proposal and then further discussions ensue to negotiate a contract.

The second procedure is much like the above; however, instead of the bidder submitting a fully completed technical proposal, a partial proposal is submitted. The methodology and technical specifications will be included but not to the fullest extent. This allows room for even more customization and discussion. Once the highest qualified bidder is selected, they will be invited to submit a thorough technical proposal along with a financial proposal. The technical proposal will be evaluated, and only then will the financial proposal be opened. The combined score of both the technical proposal and the financial proposal is the grounds on which a bidder is contracted.

Request for Quotations

This procurement method is used for small-valued goods or services. Request for quotation is by far the least complex procurement method available. If you have the option, use this method to ensure a fast procurement process and not a lot of paperwork. There is no formal proposal drafted from either party in this method. Essentially, the procurement entity selects a minimum of three suppliers or service providers that they wish to get quotes from. A comparison of quotes is analyzed, and the best selection determined by requirement compliance is chosen.

Single Source Procurement

Single source procurement is a noncompetitive method that should only be used under specific circumstances. Single source procurement occurs when the procuring entity intends to acquire goods or services from a sole provider. This method should undergo a strict approval process from management before being used. The circumstances which call for this method are:

- *Emergencies*
- *If only one supplier is available and qualified to fulfill the requirements*
- *If the advantages of using a certain supplier are abundantly clear*
- *If the procurer requires a certain product or service that is only available from one supplier*
- *For the continuation of work that cannot be reproduced by another supplier*

In the end, the type of procurement method you choose to use is highly relative to the conditions of the procurement effort and the type of good or service being acquired. All procurement methods follow tight legal frameworks to ensure all standards are being met and quality in the selection process exists. [...]

Adapted from: B. Sponaugle, "6 procurement methods: obtaining quality goods and services," *Udemy*, 29 May 2014.

objectives. For detailed information on six major procurement methods, please see the article: "6 procurement methods: obtaining quality goods and services."

Step 4: Prepare to approach the market. When the method issue is addressed, the procuring business can prepare to approach the market. The procuring entity should check again whether the buying violates relevant legislation or likely will not be agreed to by suppliers. This double check is a way to avoid strategic mistakes involved in the procurement. Moreover, the procuring company should design governance arrangements to avoid potential opportunistic and moral hazard-related behaviors of suppliers.

Step 5: Approach the market. How the market is approached depends on the selected procurement method. Businesses can publish tenders (or RFPs—request for proposals) on public platforms and include essential information (e.g., timing, lodgment mechanism, evaluation criteria, rules, contact officers, and more) to allow suppliers to develop and lodge competitive submissions. At the same time, businesses can use appropriate limitation of liability to design and delimit each entity's responsibility and make clarifications or additional materials available to potential suppliers in a timely and equitable manner.

Step 6: Evaluate submissions and conclude the tender process. Companies should preliminarily evaluate whether submissions are subjected to the explicit principles of the procurement. For example, a critical principle is to see whether the offering from a supplier can help the procuring company achieves procurement goals. The evaluation process must be fair, must be equitable, and must be able to stand up to scrutiny. Businesses should design evaluation dimensions such as BCOR (benefits, costs, opportunities, and risks) and provide sufficient documentation and information for a selection committee to make an informed decision. For example, many Chinese governments now use an online platform for the evaluation process. It contains a database of various experts from different backgrounds and is used to generate an independent list of experts. The experts then evaluate the procurement submissions in a double-blind process—the name of the potential supplier is redacted so cannot be identified by the expert, and the supplier does not know who has evaluated their submission. The experts score each submission based on explicit selection criteria such as BOCR. The highest ranked submission is selected.

Step 7: Manage the contract. A contract is used to ensure a procurement deal operates as agreed. But a contract is not just a white-and-black piece of paper with specifications, requirements, and clauses. It represents a process by which suppliers exchange a specific quantity of operant resources for monetary value. Put simply, a contract indicates that a purchase cannot be defined as a success simply upon signing a contract. There are many instances when suppliers cannot deliver as planned, with knock-on effects to the purchaser including logistics consequences and financial losses. Failure by suppliers to fulfill their contract damage their business reputation and/or lead to potential litigation by purchasers to recover financial losses. Therefore, it is important for procuring companies to manage procurement contracts from a processual prospective. See the article on contract management in procurement contexts: "The procurement process and contract management: the key to managing risk."

The Procurement Process and Contract Management: The Key to Managing Risk

It's no secret. Organizations are losing millions due to cost volatility, supply disruption, and noncompliance fines. An ever-increasing pace of business and rising levels of uncertainty within our global economy have brought about an alarming amount of potential pitfalls for procurement leaders. This means risk management has become a higher priority than ever, and procurement is on the front line of managing that risk. The good news is procurement has a secret weapon: contracts.

While some may consider the contract management process routine or unglamorous, in reality, it's the cornerstone of running a sustainable, successful business and should be considered a key procurement activity. I know nothing more glamorous, actually. Contracts are to procurement practitioners what Q is to James Bond: behind the scenes making every mission possible. For Bond that's stopping Spectre. For procurement that's reducing costs, delivering value, and accelerating growth. Here are three instances when contract management helps procurement teams manage risk and deliver more value.

At the Close of the Deal

Contracts are ground zero for setting expectations for the future and where you assign risk. Each side must assess what level of risk it is comfortable carrying based on the appropriate factors—precedent, probability, impact, mitigation resources, necessity, and so on. During this stage, procurement teams should be collaborating with their legal teams, not circumventing them, to ensure when a contract is drafted, risks are accepted that are fair and manageable. Now is also the time to make sure that any pricing, service-level agreements (SLA), and terms and conditions are carried over from the sourcing phase and written into your contracts.

Advanced features in contract management platforms can simplify this process with capabilities such as approval workflows and templates, guaranteeing an organization's approval policies are respected and all necessary information is included on every contract.

After the Ink Dries

As global regulations proliferate and expectations increase, an audit, or risk assessment, as painful as they can be, is a necessary step in due diligence—helping you hold suppliers accountable and save money in the long run by reducing risk and improving processes and controls. After all, you can't mitigate risk if you don't know it's there. Contract management solutions not only make performing a successful contract audit easier; they make implementing changes and enforcing them easier, too, giving your organization faster processes and the flawless compliance that accelerates growth.

Looking to the Future

Theodore Roosevelt may have said it best when he said, "Risk is like fire: If controlled, it will help you; if uncontrolled, it will rise up and destroy you." If managed well, risk can be opportunity. Procurement needs to create and take advantage of those opportunities. One way to turn the tables in procurement's favor is to embrace technology. Digitizing contract management processes puts every contract online, in one central, searchable repository that is accessible to any internal party with the proper credentials. Procurement teams gain greater visibility into existing contracts and the ability to run reports on a contract portfolio to identify opportunities to fuel negotiation efforts and capture more revenue.

Final Thoughts

If risk management is never operationalized as new suppliers get added, supply shifts, and supply chains change, new and increased risks can go undetected. The best way to circumvent this is by incorporating robust, next-generation contract management into all key procurement activities. Modern contract management platforms drive more visibility, performance, and compliance throughout the procurement process and provide a significant opportunity for procurement to capitalize on its time and resources, as well as outmaneuver volatile market conditions and mitigate or eliminate risk. A contract management platform is quickly deployable, with a rapid time to value. It's not a competitive advantage, it's table stakes. And the stakes have never been higher.

Source: M. Lhoumeau, "The procurement process and contract management: the key to managing risk," *Spend Matters*, 1 August 2017.

10

As shown in ◘ Fig. 10.2, there are seven steps to fulfill a procurement process. But in practice, procurement processes may be more complicated. Businesses may handle many procurement activities simultaneously with multiple suppliers, partners, and other stakeholders. Some suppliers may have supplied the business for years and could be viewed as reliable partners; alternately, some may have little history with the procuring company so may not be as trusted and require closer scrutiny. In terms of purchasing, some purchases may be repetitive and routine, while some may be relatively novel and strategic, with unique risks and benefits for the procuring company. Given the variety in procurement, businesses that to employ digital technologies and systems to help manage procurement processes may reduce spending and risks and improve efficiency and performance.

Various systems and technologies can be used in the different stages of a procurement process. For example, ERP (enterprise resource planning) can be used to identify real purchase needs. E-tendering systems can be used to approach the market and conclude the tender process. ◘ Figure 10.3 displays a generic e-procurement process of purchasing single demands. Procurement is fulfilled through a set of actions from purchase requisition to invoice verification. Of all actions, some are fulfilled physically (see those actions happening in real places), some can be fulfilled solely through electronic methods such as invoice verification, while some may be tackled online as well as offline such as interaction with suppliers. In the next subsection, we will separately introduce major systems and technologies involved in procurement activities.

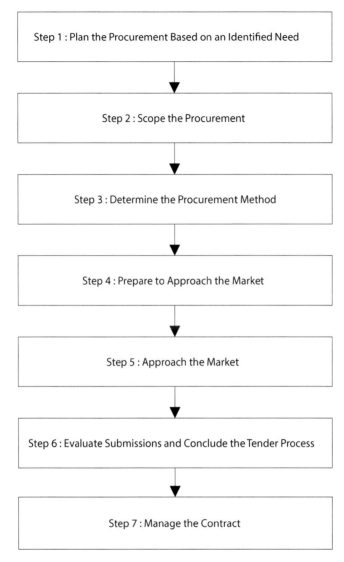

Fig. 10.2 Steps of procurement. (Source: Own elaboration based on the content of this section)

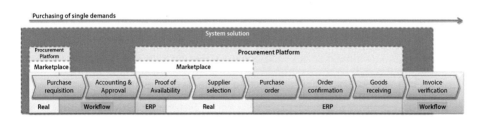

Fig. 10.3 Steps of e-procurement. (Source: Adapted from Weigel and Ruecker (2017), 203)

10.3.2 Technologies and Systems Involved in e-Procurement

10.3.2.1 Systems

Many information systems can play a role in procurement processes. In theory, integrating these systems into one is a way to digitize a procurement process and improve procurement performance[6]:

Stock control systems are designed to facilitate production-related procurement. For example, systems may notify purchasing managers when stock levels have fallen below a certain level and items need to be reordered. They are:

Web-based catalogues present a replacement of paper-based catalogues with search functions to make it easier to locate specific items.

Email or database-based workflow systems integrate the order of the originator, approval by manager, and order placement by buyer. Through the use of one of these systems, orders can be quickly and reliably passed from one person to the next without losing information.

Order entry on website allows users to buy items directly on the seller's website. Yet, since there is no integration with the internal accounting system, purchasing data needs to be rekeyed.

Accounting systems allow the buying department to place orders and simultaneously to pass the information on to be used for internal accounting processes, for example, to make payment upon receipt of the invoice.

Enterprise Resource Planning ERP is widely used for improving business performance and optimizing procurement processes. For example, SAP's Business One is a typical ERP, which is able to automate procurement tasks, highlight trending inventory data, and help procurement managers devise purchase plans. Moreover, Business One can manage supplier and vendor data such as items purchased, prices, transaction dates, and others, which can help companies identify trustable and reliable suppliers and develop good working relationships with them.

Some systems can be directly used for procurement (Corina 2011; Weigel and Ruecker 2017). They include:

e-Ordering e-Ordering has two models, the first is a seller-side model. Many sellers use e-ordering to distribute their goods and supplies to buyers. The second is a buyer-side model. A company displays an e-ordering platform (e.g., an e-ordering catalogue) to its customers. Products or product components in this catalogue are supplied by several suppliers. When a customer places an order, a relevant purchase request is automatically sent to these suppliers.

E-sourcing E-sourcing is a buy-side behavior that enables a business to focus on production of goods and sustaining their core competence. There are three major e-sourcing methods:

---

6   See Chaffey (2011).

> 1. e-Tendering, which refers to the use of IT in sending RFIs (request for information) and RFPs (request for proposal) to suppliers and receiving their replies.
> 2. e-Auction, which enables suppliers to compete on price, so that the procuring company can obtain the lowest possible purchase price.
> 3. e-Informing does not involve transactions, but it is used to gather and disseminate information for internal and external parties.

e-Marketplace This refers to an online marketplace bridging sellers and buyers. An e-marketplace has different degrees of B2B openness (Hoffman et al. 2002). At one end of the spectrum, e-marketplaces with a high degree of openness are those that are publicly accessible to any company. At the other end of the spectrum, e-marketplaces with a low degree of openness are accessible only upon invitation. Based on this distinction, three main types of e-marketplaces are:

(a) *Public e-markets* which are generally owned and operated by a third-party provider. They are open to any business that wants to purchase or sell through the e-marketplace. Because it is easy to enter and leave public e-markets, business processes are primarily standardized and nonproprietary. Products that are most likely to be sold through public e-marketplaces are commodities that need little or no customization. An example of a public e-market is Amazon Business.

(b) *Consortia* are typically jointly owned and operated by businesses that participate in online B2B exchanges. Access is much more limited than in public e-markets, since only equity holders and selected trading partners are admitted. Covisint, founded by General Motors, Ford and DaimlerChrysler, is an example of a B2B consortium.

(c) *Private exchanges* are the most restrictive e-marketplaces in providing access to external parties. They are typically operated by a single company that wants to optimize its sourcing activities by tying its suppliers closely into its business processes. The operator of the private exchange invites selected suppliers to participate in the private exchange and provides them with detailed information about, for instance, sales forecasts or production statistics. In turn, this helps the supplier to optimize its supply chain. In order to achieve this type of close integration, it is generally necessary to build a customized system that tightly integrates the information systems of both buyer and seller. As a result, business relationships in private exchanges tend to last longer than in public e-marketplaces. One of the most prominent examples of a highly successful private exchange is that of Dell with its suppliers.

10.3.2.2 **Technologies**

e-Procurement leverages from many popular technologies. These technologies can be directly or indirectly used to assist in procurement activities.[7] They include:

---

7 This subsection is adapted from: A. Bartolini, "*CPO rising 2017: the procurement event of the year*," SAP Ariba, April 2017.

Cloud Computing   Procurement may need various systems to be integrated. This integration will increase pressure on the IT servers of the focal company, causing slower processing speeds. Cloud-based Software as a service ("SaaS") is hosted, maintained, managed, and upgraded by cloud service providers. By placing operations in the cloud, businesses can relieve the strain on their in-house IT infrastructure that the operation of integrated systems creates. By using the cloud, businesses need less initial investment in IT and require a lower level of internal support to maintain those systems because cloud service providers are responsible for system operations and maintenance.

Social and Collaborative Tools   These tools allow users to digitally communicate with each other and share information, for example, RFPs and bids. Users can co-edit and amend documents online and in real time. This approach has impacted the way that businesses interact with internal and external actors in the supply chain. For more information on the use of a typical social tool; see the article: "Using social media in the supply chain."

10

Using Social Media in the Supply Chain

Global supply chains by definition are very large and include a number of vendors, distribution centers, suppliers, buyers, manufacturing plants, logistics service providers, etc. If social media is embedded in the supply chain, the supply chain can gather information from a broad base of different sources. This collective intelligence can be used to uncover evolving trends or for better-informed decision-making. One such tool to gather and disseminate information throughout the supply chain is social media.

Studies show that 1.5 billion use social media on a global basis with 70 percent of businesses using it. Of Fortune 500 companies, 77 percent use Twitter, 70 percent have an active Facebook page, and 69 percent utilize YouTube. Companies are not using social media to socialize; rather they are using it to grow their business and bring value to their company and their customers. It is estimated that the potential value of social media across the value chain is more than $1 trillion annually.

Social media benefits the supply chain industry in many ways. Companies can enhance communication with customers, generate demand, reduce operating costs, mitigate risk, increase productivity, and enhance marketplace intelligence. If companies aren't participating in social media, they could be at a disadvantage because most of their customers, suppliers, and competitors are.

Social media can help companies generate better ideas for improving supply chain processes and solving existing problems by tapping into the collective insights of supply chain trading partners.

Social media is about building relationships, and it can be used in a supply chain to build and grow relationships among trading partners. Information and knowledge gathered from the use of social media by supply chain partners can provide insight into various issues of the supply chain, industry, competition, etc. It can also be used to build relationships and determine key performance indicators, such as on-time performance of a carrier or slow payments from a shipper. Some companies use social media to solicit information from their customers as a platform for making recommendations for improvement.

The supply chain operations reference (SCOR) is a process reference model developed by PricewaterhouseCoopers LLP (PwC) and endorsed by the Supply-Chain Council (SCC) as the cross-industry de facto standard diagnostic tool for supply chain management. In the SCOR model, there are five key events: plan, make, source, deliver, and return. Social media can be used to capture information associated with various supply chain events.

Social media allows supply chain participants to monitor supply chain events and transactions to keep everyone up to date with current situations, such as a delay in shipping or a carrier failed to pickup a shipment. Twitter messages can indicate the arrival or departure of a shipment from a particular warehouse. Twitter can be used to communicate the need for shipments of a particular type or to alert drivers to accidents and road closures. Social media can provide companies with more timely and insightful information about risks and events, enabling them to make corrective action sooner and thus minimizing the impact of a supply chain disruption.

Examples of Social Media Uses in the Supply Chain:

- Send social media posts to indicate the arrival and departure of a shipment from a particular distribution center or warehouse
- Information about accidents and road closures can be issued that affect delivery times and can be used to reroute deliveries
- Search for the need for shipments of a particular type
- Search for carriers which address a certain territory/area using a certain mode
- Report weather conditions that might affect shipments
- Coordinate supply chain shipments—if you have room on your truck for more shipments, broadcast this info out through the social media to find additional loads.
- Facilitate responses to supply chain disruptions via social media.
- Post-performance information, such as whether a carrier picked up and/or delivered an order on time
- Gain knowledge by discovering influencers and thought leaders.
- Analyze trends, such as number of shipments lost or best day for expediting a shipment.
- Monitor your suppliers and vendors reputation.
- Gain information about different vendors/suppliers, such as the advantages and disadvantages of each.
- Capture and communicate best practices.
- Share supply chain risk identification to uncover vulnerabilities and to mitigate risks in the supply chain.
- Share global regulations and compliance factors to avoid noncompliance
- Collect and prioritize continuous improvement ideas and initiatives.
- Research and find new suppliers, business partners, vendors, carriers, and customers.

> The use of social media is expanding, even in supply chain management, to improve communication and collaboration among supply chain trading partners. Social media brings businesses closer to their customers and provides a platform for communication and building thought leadership, and when executed properly, it can help drive business and provide a significant return on investment. Businesses that ignore social media forgo these opportunities and miss out on potential business development opportunities.
>
> Social media can be an invaluable tool for supply chain professionals looking to identify new innovations, understand commodity and pricing trends, capture best practices, and collaborate with stakeholders, peers, and suppliers. It can improve existing processes, mitigate risk, and increase efficiencies. By tapping the collective insights and knowledge of supply chain participants, businesses can drive innovation within their supply chains, which leads to continuous improvement and business growth.
>
> Adapted from: E. Rusch, 'Using social media in the supply chain', *Manufacturing Business Technology*, 6 August 2014.

Business Networking Platforms   These web-based platforms are a means for companies to communicate with core partners, maintain business relationships, automate procurement activities, and provide actors in the network with the necessary visibility to manage B2B affairs. These platforms are also a convergence point between procurement departments, finance, and other supply chain-related entities. For example, by leveraging the business network Hubwoo, businesses can have peer-to-peer interactions that include advertising their products, listing their business, promoting purchase catalogues, and more.

Mobile technology allows procurement professionals and stakeholders to access systems on the go, reducing the time cost on activities such as invoice approvals. For businesses with mature mobile computing infrastructure, procurement teams can use procurement management "apps" to complete business operations. This may force upstream providers and downstream customers to mobilize their business operations and enhance the overall mobility of the supply chain. For instance, Algarytm's Mobile Inventory management app can optimize inventory management and capture data related to key warehousing activities anytime and anywhere.

Internet of Things (IoT)   IoT devices (e.g., sensors in manufacturing devices or warehouses) can automatically transmit data to a central database, providing stock information for procurement management and automate replenishment decisions. They inform procurement teams about stock levels and streamline purchase decision-making. This approach may minimize risks and, eventually, enhance procurement performance. There are many examples where IoT is applied. Rolls Royce has embedded chips into its aircraft for real-time feedback on the condition of aircraft parts and automatically signal when repair or maintenance is needed, which indicates the timing of procurement or outsourcing.

"Big Data" Analytics IoT-based devices can generate a large amount of data. Businesses and their suppliers can use emerging data analytics tools to analyze business processes, predict future purchases, and find new business opportunities. "Big data" can potentially have significant influence on the supply chain; for more details, see the article: "Leveraging big data as supply chain management changes."

Leveraging Big Data as Supply Chain Management Changes

With the advancement of technology, and the consumer demand for immediate deliveries on the never-ending rise, the importance of Big data in the supply chain will only continue to grow in the next decade. With the amount of data being collected globally, growing at a rate of about 59 percent per year (according to inside big data), we have already seen a major uptick in opportunities for big data application across industries.

The breadth and depth of data generated by the supply chain today are accelerating rapidly, providing industries with metrics that allow them to make smarter decisions. While big data application has been a long journey, the improvements take a vast amount of new data and process and derive impactful insights quickly.

Just like Excel dramatically changed the way supply chain monitoring and reporting was executed, big data platforms are allowing professionals to focus on bigger-picture items instead of monotonous tasks. Supply chain management—as it always has existed—has only risen in profile and importance with the rise of big data. As the world's connectivity increases, companies in retail, manufacturing, and logistics alike need managers who will quickly adapt to new technologies.

With new technology, come new opportunities. We will explore how big data advancements are positively impacting the supply chain, what organizations can do to stay ahead of the curve, and how big data will impact the future of the industry workforce.

How Do Data Advancements Help?

- Big data app integration provides greater contextual intelligence of how supply chain tactics, strategies, and operations are helping achieve financial objectives. The ability to track financial outcomes of supply chain decisions back to financial objectives is important to all organizations. The integration of big data is effective in helping to reduce waste and allows companies to assess where changes can be made.
- Big data is providing improved traceability and cutting down on the potential for lost items while increasing efficiency. Improved tracking allows supply chain managers to more accurately plan timing of essential operations and deliveries.
- Big data provides supply chain departments and organizations with a better understanding of demand and supply, allowing for reduced waste. Along with this demand and supply understanding comes the ability for organizations to react to supply chain issues quickly, reducing the amount of time between the problem and solutions, giving managers the data insights needed for the manager to assess an issue.

- Embedding big data analytics in operations leads to an improvement in order-to-cycle delivery times and improvement in supply chain efficiency. Included in this are analytics that align across a variety of factors, including geo-analytics, transportation logistics, and weather analytics.

While this is just a sampling of how big data has is actively impacting the supply chain, the speed and efficiency in which the supply chain can now run cannot be denied.

What Your Organization Can Do to Stay Ahead of the Curve?

Companies that are achieving significant results using big data analytics know that it's not just enough to have the data available to them—they must be able to take that information and properly analyze it into actionable insights.

It's important for organizations to always stay informed about the new resources that are quickly becoming available. We recommend investing in training programs and ongoing education initiatives. Try working with industry organizations like the Council of Supply Chain Management Professionals (CSCMP) or paying for your employees to attend annual educational events that will expose them to the latest solutions that will help your organization run efficiently.

While the demand for skilled labor remains high, businesses are encouraged to take action to recruit top talent amidst a very competitive landscape. For example, working-based learning partnerships with major universities make it possible for students to work on real-time projects that allow them to become part of a company's supply chain and logistics workforce while still in school. These businesses then have an early opportunity to attract the most talented students graduating from these programs.

Similarly, through apprenticeship programs, businesses can work with community colleges to build out very specific skill-driven programs that give students the training required to receive a job offer after they graduate.

Big Data Will Impact the Future of the Workforce

Big data is turning supply chain managers into "mind readers," allowing them to predict and react to buyer behaviors in new ways. This means, that in the supply chain workforce of the future, the administrative tasks of the past will be reduced greatly, and a higher level of human analysis will be needed.

Supply chain managers don't need to worry about their jobs going away, but statistics show that the need for supply chain professionals will only grow. Their jobs will just shift thanks to big data analytics, where these managers will look at the vast amount of information provided to them and be able to detect actionable items. This higher level of skill will also require advanced education, so supply chain managers of the future should look to join organizations that provide opportunities for ongoing education.

The Future of Analytics

Faster, more accurate forecasting is something that will improve profitability, decrease waste, and lead to satisfaction among customers and clients. The future of analytics is only going to play an increasingly prominent role in supply chain optimization, and machine learning will start to be implemented across the board. Supply chain organizations and managers can take advantage of the new technologies available to the industry and implement changes to become better managers. Adapted from: L. Basel, 'Leveraging big data as supply chain management changes', *Manufacturing Business Technology*, 10 April 2018.

Machine Learning   This refers to technologies that can learn user behavior patterns and can be used to improve user experiences over the process of multiple transactions. For example, the more the number of users who interact with various systems and analytics platforms, the more "smart" and adaptive the systems will become, and the more valuable it will be to businesses. Machine learning can be used to combine spend, supplier, and buyer data with third-party data to provide a holistic view of procurement activities. Systems enabled with machine learning algorithms can be used to predict user needs, and thereby procurement decisions are more subject to data.

Artificial Intelligence (AI)   AI leverages "big data," machine learning, algorithms, and IoT sensors that eventually make integrated systems smarter. AI can process and understand "cause and effect" automatically. AI-enabled tools can proactively serve human by identifying issues and providing in-context notifications and options. Thirdly, AI allows procurement teams to improve management of business operations via data management and analysis and ultimately improve procurement performance. For more information how AI impacts procurement, see the article: "How AI will help procurement advance analytics beyond basic spend analysis."

How AI Will Help Procurement Advance Analytics Beyond Basic Spend Analysis
Leading procurement organizations today don't just measure what they spent. They push their definition of spend analysis to encompass their total value contribution to the business, taking advantage of both conventional and newly accessible data sources to enable true supply analytics. How have they done this? While strong leadership and evolving best practices have played an important role, the simple answer is that analytics technology has finally advanced to the point where it can enable a supply analytics strategy. Key to this evolution is the rise of artificial intelligence within the enterprise, which is now helping procurement organizations gain new insights and shape new strategies not before possible with standard spend analytics approaches. To understand why, here are three examples of how procurement leaders are taking their analytics strategies to the next level with AI.

Strategic Sourcing

The traditional approach to spend analytics helps procurement organizations reduce, avoid or recover costs with their suppliers. Historical analysis of spend data can help somewhat in the supplier selection process, but processing a typical quarterly batch of data is hardly the most actionable information on which to base a strategic sourcing effort. The more intelligent route is to expand the role of spend analysis in strategic sourcing. Using a robust data acquisition, cleansing, and classification process enabled by the latest machine learning methods, procurement can run spend analysis reports before, during and after a sourcing event—a far more complete picture than an out-of-date snapshot.

Before a sourcing event even begins, the standard spend analysis report can now produce demand breakdowns, common cost component analyses, market analyses, and supplier performance analyses, to name just a few. There's no better preparation than heading into a sourcing event with real-time internal and external data. Armed with knowledge about suppliers and current market conditions, procurement should then be able to run real-time reports during event, such as breakdowns by product, service, and carrier; cross-supplier and cross-carrier comparisons; and variance and outlier analyses. These ensure a data-driven strategy carries over into the award decision, and that procurement is getting the absolute best deal from its sourcing process. Finally, procurement should take advantage of real-time classification technology to analyze spend patterns with the selected supplier post-event. This can include spend-to-date reports, invoice analysis, realized savings analysis, and maverick spend analysis, to help keep purchases compliant and tackle pesky tail spend.

Supply Management

Getting a great deal with a supplier is a big win for any procurement team. But after a sourcing event, that supplier becomes just one of many, all of which need to be monitored and evaluated to ensure the relationship is bringing value into the enterprise. The foundational spend analysis program focuses on determining how much the business spent, with whom, in what quantity, where items were shipped, and how they were paid for. The evolutionary approach, however, extends analytics into scenarios beyond the confines of traditional spend analysis such as operations and logistics. This requires an analytics engine that can ingest semi-structured data and other content beyond just transactional data. Machine learning-enhanced analytics services are the only offerings available that can do this quickly and, most important, at human-level accuracy.

For example, instead of just looking at purchase orders and invoices, leading procurement organizations can run reports on inventory turnover and warehouse utilization, helping them determine inventory overhead costs and predict stockouts. They can also analyze a supply base by geography—new geographies and languages often confound prior spend analysis solutions—as well as provide insights into average fulfillment times, underlying commodity and fuel costs, and other overhead costs. While these are just a few examples, the savvy procurement professional understands that spend analysis done right, aided by new capabilities unlocked through artificial intelligence, helps businesses understand the total cost of doing business with a supplier. What's more, this deeper intelligence can be used to compare supplier performance across various benchmarks, presenting procurement with an opportunity to continuously improve the supply services it provides stakeholders.

Risk Management

Beyond value measured in dollars, however, many progressive procurement organizations are expanding their analytics efforts into a critical adjacent territory: risk. The fundamental value of many AI-based analytics offerings is that they offer cleansed and accurately classified data not before available to procurement organizations without significant time costs. But what makes AI even more of a game changer is when procurement enriches this data with external content.

In leading analytics platforms, the data sources that can be added on top of spend data go far beyond integrated market price and commodity data feeds. Users can also integrate financial risk scores, sustainability and corporate social responsibility (CSR) scores, and similar third-party data sources related to risk. With this information, procurement can enrich a spend analysis process to see not just how much it spent with a supplier but also whether that spend is in jeopardy because the supplier is teetering toward bankruptcy, or could balloon because the supplier is based on a politically unstable geography, or is tied to an environmentally harmful production process. AI can uncover trends within these and other key data relationships, leading to broader risk reduction and, in some cases, predictive analytics related to price and margin with suppliers.

Moving Beyond the Foundation

So with all of these potential benefits, why haven't the majority of procurement organizations taken the initiative to evolve their spend analysis efforts beyond merely analyzing what was spent?

In many ways, the historical flaws of spend analysis providers have made realizing such programs unattainable. But with advances in machine learning and artificial intelligence, particularly the power of deep learning, the gaps in analytics offerings are beginning to narrow. Accurate, real-time classification has become the new standard, and prescriptive intelligence based on community-based benchmarks is brining procurement new insights not possible with previous offerings.

Adapted from: N. Heinzmann, 'How AI will help procurement advance analytics beyond basic spend analysis', Spend Matters, 18 September 2017.

10.4 Summary

- Firstly, this chapter introduced the definition of e-procurement and discussed the advantages and drawbacks of e-procurement.
- Secondly, the chapter analyzed critical success factors of adopting e-procurement.
- Thirdly, the chapter first introduced a procurement process and then illustrated a general process of e-procurement and ultimately pointed out technologies and systems involved in e-procurement process.

Review Questions

1. What is the difference between procurement and e-procurement?
2. What are the advantages and drawbacks of e-procurement?
3. Why should companies be concerned about critical success factors of e-procurement? Why are these factors of paramount importance for the success of e-procurement?
4. What is a generic procurement process? What is the difference between a procurement process and an e-procurement process?
5. What technologies and systems are involved in e-procurement processes?
6. Why should (or should not) a company adopt e-procurement practice?
7. How should a company select e-procurement systems and technologies?
8. How do most recent technologies such as IoT, AI, and machine learning influence supply chains and procurement practice?
9. Think of an example business, how should that business use the most recent technologies to improve their procurement practice?

References

Chaffey, D. 2006. *E-business and E-commerce management* (pp. 318–320). FT/Prentice Hall.

Chaffey, D. 2011. *E-business and E-commerce management* (pp. 367–368). FT/Prentice Hall.

Chaffey, D., et al. 2006. *Internet marketing* (p. 494). FT/Prentice Hall.

Corina, P. S. (2011). The role of the e-procurement in the Purchasing Process. *The Annals of the University of Oradea, 1,* 687–691.

Gunasekaran, A., McGaughey, R. E., Ngai, E. W., & Rai, B. K. (2009). E-Procurement adoption in the Southcoast SMEs. *International Journal of Production Economics, 122,* 1–162.

Hoffman, W., Keedy, J., & Roberts, K. (2002). The unexpected return of B2B. *McKinsey Quarterly, 3,* 97–106.

Weigel, U. & Ruecker M. (2017), *The strategic procurement practice guide.* Springer.

Further Reading

An overview on how the Internet changed supply chain management is provided in M. E. Johnson and S. Whang, 'E-business and supply chain management: An overview and framework', *Production and Operations Management*, 2002, *11*(4), 413–423.

Kaplan, S. & Sawhney, M. developed the concept of e-hubs in 'e-Hubs: The new B2B marketplaces', *Harvard Business Review*, 2000, May–June, pp. 97–103.

Hoffman, W., Keedy, J., & Roberts, K. differentiate e-marketplaces according to their degree of openness in 'The unexpected return of B2B', *McKinsey Quarterly*, 2002, No. 3, pp. 97–106.

For an interesting discussion on how the adoption of e-procurement systems and strategies can contribute to a company's value creation and business competitiveness, see W. D. Presutti Jr., 'Supply management and e-procurement: Creating value added in the supply chain', *Industrial Marketing Management*, 2003, *32*(3), 219–226.

10

To understand e-procurement practices in a business-to-business context as well as the success factors and challenges of e-procurement, see R. Angeles, R. and R. Nath, 'Business-to-business e-procurement: Success factors and challenges to implementation', *Supply Chain Management*, 2007, *12*(2), 104–115.

Bartolini, A. (2017). *CPO rising 2017: The procurement event of the year*. April: SAP Ariba.

Weblinks

spendmatters.com is the website of an industry magazine for sourcing and procurement professionals.

www.scmr.com is the website of another magazine, 'Supply Chain Management Review', that provides numerous articles and other resources on managing supplier relationships in e-business.

Choosing the Appropriate e-Business Strategy for Interacting with Users

Contents

We greatly appreciate the assistance of Sebastian Mauch and Matthias Promny (former Masters students at the University of Nuremberg) in preparing this chapter.

© Springer Nature Switzerland AG 2020
T. Jelassi, F. J. Martínez-López, *Strategies for e-Business*, Classroom Companion: Business,
https://doi.org/10.1007/978-3-030-48950-2_11

Learning Outcomes

After completing this chapter, you should be able to:

- Understand the technological developments leading to the advent of Web 2.0
- Recognize how these technological developments made possible the trend of user-generated content and change of behavior.
- Be aware of the evolution of customer relationship management (CRM) to embrace Web 2.0 advances and its potential to address relationships with the new social customers
- Use the insights gained from "mass customization" and "long tail" concepts to increase the richness of interactions with customers
- Use the insights gained from the "tipping point," network externality effects and "viral growth" concepts to increase the reach of interactions with customers

■ Introduction

Since the early days of e-business, which we discussed in ▶ Chap. 1, the Internet has changed dramatically. While years ago it was closer to a "read-only" web with a static and unidirectional information flow, users today have the opportunity to become editors and active content generators on the Internet. In this chapter, we take a closer look at how businesses leverage the new technological capabilities of the Internet to involve their customers and website users more deeply in the information sharing and content creation process.

The chapter starts out by providing an overview of Web 2.0,[1] including the technological advances which led to its advent, the implications for business (including the main guiding principles, services offered through it, users' behavior on the so-called social web[2] and more). In ▶ Sect. 11.2, we analyze the trade-off between richness and reach. Building on this trade-off, we then discuss concepts such as customer relationship management, mass customization, viral growth, the tipping point, and the long tail.

11.1 The Internet and Social Commerce

Compared with its early years, the Internet has become an increasingly interactive platform, thanks to its huge number of users and a large variety of new service sites catering to their users' communication wants and transaction needs. In the following section, we examine the Internet's main technological developments and the applications they have enabled.

---

1   The term Web 2.0 originated from a series of conferences about new web technologies of the same title. These conferences were initiated by Tim O'Reilly, an internationally renowned expert on the Internet and open- source technologies.

2   Although Web 2.0 and social web have been often interchangeably used, the former refers to the new Web 2.0-based applications, while the latter deals with the social aspects of these applications. Furthermore, the social web transcends Web 2.0 and could include future technological advances of the Web.

11.1.1 The Advent of Web 2.0

Web 2.0 has opened up new ways to communicate, share content, and collaborate. It symbolizes a paradigm shift from website provider or supplier-generated content to user-generated content. Tim O'Reilly calls Web 2.0 "the business revolution in the computer industry caused by the move to the Internet as a platform, and an attempt to understand the rules for success on that new platform." Applications should "harness network effects to get better the more people use them."[3] Technological advances in IT have enabled significant changes in the way companies create value and manage relationships with customers and suppliers. More specifically, Web 2.0 can be defined as:

» a collection of open-source, interactive and user-controlled online applications expanding the experiences, knowledge and market power of the users as participants in business and social processes. Web 2.0 applications support the creation of informal users' networks facilitating the flow of ideas and knowledge by allowing the efficient generation, dissemination, sharing and editing/refining of informational content.[4]

Customers and users nowadays have much more information and market power. They are not merely receivers of a company's-generated content as was the case with the previous Web 1.0 capabilities, but they can now produce and share content. This is probably the main technology shift and distinguishing feature of the new Internet and its related business models. Ignoring Web 2.0 capabilities (that activate the role of customers in exchanges, content generation, and value creation) would be a strategic mistake. In other words, organizations must be aware of the new mindset of collaboration and conversation with customers (see ◘ Fig. 11.1) and related Web 2.0 applications (e.g., social networking sites, microblogs, wikis, internal blogging, and more), which among other benefits, support faster decision-making, foster innovation, and enhance effectiveness (Lin et al. 2010).

To conclude this introduction, let us focus on the two key technological advances that underpin Web 2.0: *network infrastructure* and *software capabilities*.

Network infrastructure In recent years, household access to broadband Internet and mobile Internet has increased rapidly. An important driver for this development was the overinvestment during the Internet boom years in fiber-optic cable companies who laid out massive amounts of fiber-optic cable thereby driving down data transmission costs. For Internet users, this increased capacity has resulted in higher connection speeds, which, in turn, translates directly into an improved Internet experience. This attracted more users and made them spend more time online.

---

3   Tim O'Reilly, "Web 2.0 compact definition: trying again,"O'Reilly Radar, Available at: ► http://radar.oreilly.com/archives/2006/12/web_20_compact.html.
4   See Constantinides and Fountain (2008a).

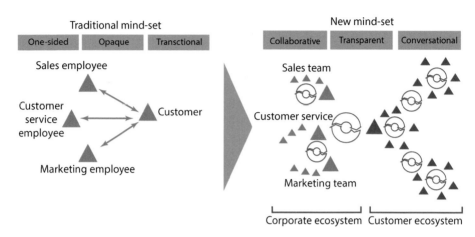

Fig. 11.1 Evolution of the business-customer mindset with the advent of Web 2.0. (Source: adapted from Acker et al. (2011), p. 4)

The rapid decline in *storage costs* in recent years has also had a major impact on companies whose business models rely heavily on storage capacity. Today, it is not unusual to have more than a gigabyte of storage space on an e-mail account such as Gmail or unlimited storage for photos on a social networking site (such as Facebook) free of charge. Depending on the amount of data that needs to be stored, there are different business models in use. For example, online back-up solutions (such as ▶ Dropbox.com, Mozy.ie or ▶ Box.com), that handle a large volume of data, use a subscription model to recover their high storage costs. On the other hand, social networking sites (SNS) try to cover these costs through online advertising revenues.

Software capabilities Capitalizing on technological advances in network infrastructure and the web as a platform, new software standards have emerged that allow for user participation in creating content. The deployment of web application development techniques began to make the Internet experience faster and more convenient for users because it enables websites to reload separately the different parts of a page. As a result, it became possible to surf web pages in the same way as navigating traditional desktop programs. Google Docs, for instance, offers text processing, spreadsheet modeling, and calendar functions that can be accessed directly online from any PC with an Internet connection.

The software has also made it easier for users actually to publish content on the Internet. Initially writing on a website was the privilege of programmers or those having the necessary HTML technical skills. Today, users no longer need to install tools or programs; instead, they log on to their account on the service website that hosts a blog and allows its users to manage their profiles and content for free. Active communities of developers formed around websites and specific programs that either use an "open-source" approach for collaborative software development (as is the case with the Linux operating system) or grant access to an application program interface.

11

The creation and adoption of new syndication formats (such as RSS) enable users easily to track content updates on other websites. By allowing users to subscribe to other people's content, communication, sharing, and collaboration have significantly improved. Blog software installation and administration made it easier for individuals to manage their own web space. WordPress, for instance, is a state-of-the-art blog publishing tool which offers powerful, yet easy to handle customization and administrative features.

11.1.2   Implications of Web 2.0 on the Internet Business Models

◻ Figure 11.2 presents an overview of past, current, and anticipated future web technologies and their applications. Four sequential stages are proposed, with their respective applications. The third step is driven by a significant and expected technological advance: the semantic treatment and integration of the information. This is the milestone of Web 3.0, also called as semantic web, which is the next step for the social web.

❯ In general, Web 2.0 brings about strategic changes in business models. Consumers, who were mainly viewed as a passive adopter/receiver of the value proposal of a business in the era of Web 1.0, are able to be a dominant force in producing and creating value through the power of Web 2.0.

Many companies have aligned themselves to this strategic change and start to leverage the wisdom of the population to produce masses of valuable content. For

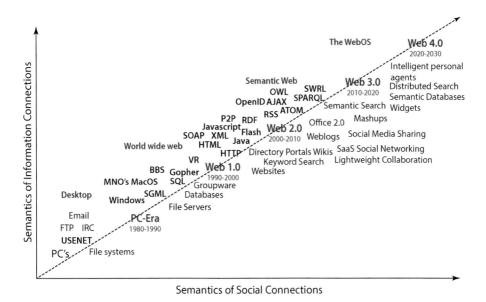

◻ **Fig. 11.2** Evolution of the web and related applications. (Source: adapted from Radar Networks & Nova Spivack, 2007)

example, Facebook barely creates content in platform. Instead, Facebook empowers more than a billion platform users to generate and share content, which underpins Facebook's success in the Internet business world.

The current stage of the web has serious implications for businesses and organizations. The following subsections present important related questions as the main guiding principles of Web 2.0. The most important shifts brought by this web stage are its new functionalities and strategies for businesses to effectively adapt to them.

Main Guiding Principles of Web 2.0 Applications

Advances in web 2.0-based applications have been driven by the following principles[5]:

A focus on service-based, simple, and open-source solutions featuring:

— *A shift toward online services*: from software as a product to software as a service (SaaS). Applications in Web 2.0 are platform independent and usually offered as a free service, easy to access, download, and share.

— *Simplicity*. Web 2.0 services have been designed with an easy-to-use logic offering users numerous customization possibilities.

— *Network effects as a lever to lock-in customers*. Although users can easily shift from one application service to another, they may be deterred from doing that due to network effects and peer usage. An illustrative example here is a Facebook user who would be very reluctant to shift to another social network since (most of) his/her friends are also using Facebook.

Continuous and incremental application development requiring the participation of users not only as passive consumers but also as active contributors.

— *Continuous, real-time improvement*. Web 2.0 applications are characterized by continuously requesting feedback from their users. Such information is used to identify and fix malfunctions, as well as improve the applications' performance.

— *Perpetual "beta version."* Due to the abovementioned continuous feedback loop, Web 2.0 is considered as a "beta version," which is in constant change and evolution.

— *More users: more value is generated through the aggregation of collective intelligence*. An illustrative example here is ▶ Amazon.com or other e-commerce websites that offer recommendations to users based on past behavior. These recommendations (based upon comments, opinions, product or service reviews, and more) can influence a user's purchasing decision.

New Service-Based Business Models and New Opportunities for Reaching Individual Customers with Low-Volume Products

— *Changes in revenue generation and usage models*. Since most Web 2.0 services are offered for free, businesses generate revenues not by charging users but by

---

5   See Constantinides and Fountain (2008b).

selling either online advertising or a premium version of these services. This is the case, for example, of the streaming music provider Spotify which enables users to download for free a basic version containing ads or to pay for an unlimited access to a premium version that has a better audio quality and no ads.

— *From mass markets to individual customers.* This is an important feature of Web 2.0 that will be covered in detail in ▶ Sects. 11.3 and 11.4.

The above principles are complementary with the recent four broad factors (and sub-factors) framework (Wirtz et al. 2010). Note that some of these factors are not completely new, but their impact increased in the Web 2.0 context. ◘ Figure 11.3 lists these factors (and their sub-factors), which include social networking, interaction orientation, user-added value, and customization/personalization. Related actions that companies should make to effectively embrace these four Web 2.0 factors are presented in ◘ Fig. 11.4.

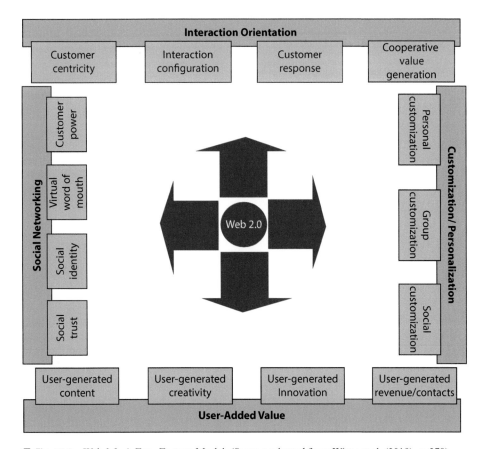

◘ **Fig. 11.3** Web 2.0: A Four Factors Model. (Source: adapted from Wirtz et al. (2010), p. 279)

Factor	Activity
Social networking	• Build your own social networking – e.g. by creating blogs, forums and chats for your website • Check and comment on postings on networks (e.g., review platforms) • Present your company on revalt social networking platforms
Interaction orientation	• Be highly responsive and available 24 hours • Provide users a reward for interaction (social status, prizes, rebates) • Encourage positive *and* negative feedback
User-added value	• Integrate the following tools on your website: user reviews, user-generated information (wikis), media uploads (videos, etc.) • Offer incentives • Use metadata that tracks clicks, recommendations, behaviour, etc.
Customisation/personalisation	• Make good use of available user information as a base for customisation efforts (e.g., build track profiles based on customer history) • Focus on making customisation/personalisation easy to use

◘ **Fig. 11.4** Activities for embracing Web 2.0 in existing Internet businesses. (Source: adapted from Wirtz et al. (2010), p. 284)

Web 2.0 services Different business models for Web 2.0 applications (which are sometimes referred to as Enterprise 2.0) try to seize new business opportunities. Media-sharing portals (such as Flickr and YouTube), free voice-over-IP applications[6] (such as Skype), major online collaborative applications (such as the encyclopedia Wikipedia), and the broad "blogosphere"[7] realm rely on new technologies to promote the collective spirit of the Internet. In general, the plethora of new services and applications can be divided into the following categories:

Blogs and blog aggregators User-generated websites containing continuously updated entries in periodic order. Blogs can be generated through different blog providers such as blogger or WordPress. Several online services such as Technorati provide tools to browse through the sheer number of blogs (often referred to as the "blogosphere").

Wikis or content communities Derived from the Hawaiian word "fast," these websites display content that users can incorporate "as is" or modify at will. In order to assure the quality of its content, Wikipedia, for instance, relies on users' mutual peer content control, article rating, and indexing.

Social networking sites (SNS) These online communities enable users to communicate and connect with each other, build a personal network, as well as share personal content. On these sites, members create a personal profile to present themselves to others, while community providers primarily act as enablers, offering support capabilities as well as search and communication tools. The €482 million acquisition in

---

6   Voice Over Internet Protocol (VoIP) is the routing of voice conversations over the Internet or through any other IP-based network.

7   Blogosphere is a collective term encompassing all blogs as a community or social network. Many weblogs are densely interconnected and have grown their own culture.

2005 of MySpace by Rupert Murdoch's media conglomerate News Corp. made it an early poster child for these new SNS services. Later, in December 2006, the business networking site XING, previously called openBC, staged its initial public offering (IPO), thus becoming the first Web 2.0 company in the world to go public. Nowadays, SNS market leaders include Facebook, which has more than 2.32 billion monthly active users (MAU) as of December 31, 2018,[8] LinkedIn, the world's largest professional social network with about 7% market share, and Twitter with about 12% market share.

Social bookmarking   Users of these services, provided by companies such as Delicious, can collect their favorite websites as bookmarks, using "tags" (short descriptive keywords) instead of the traditional browser-based folder taxonomy. They can also share their favorites with other users who can browse for certain "tags" when looking for interesting weblinks.

Media and information-sharing platforms   The 2008 presidential campaign in the United States has already discovered the huge reach of sites such as YouTube, where users can upload, index, share, and rate a wide variety of videos from around the world, ranging from amateur to professional quality. Another media and information-sharing platform, Flickr, which was acquired by Yahoo! in March 2005 for US$35 million, is similar to YouTube but uses photos instead of videos.

Web-based tools   A variety of services can be accessed directly from the web but offer a degree of customization and functionality that rather resembles conventional programs and desktop applications. There are services providing map and navigation data, such as Google Maps, or websites such as Netvibes that offer a fully customizable desktop surface where users can receive RSS feeds, weather forecasts, e-mail notifications, and other features. Hootsuite users can integrate and customize their social media use into one platform, to both receive and send updates simultaneously across SNSs.

Web-based desktop applications   Even though these applications use the web as a platform, they can be downloaded and installed on a local computer, not just accessed through an Internet browser. Skype was one of the first applications to successfully offer a working service, enabling people to talk to one another over the Internet for free. Telecommunication operators, realizing the disruptive nature of Internet-based telephony, soon jumped on the bandwagon, offering their own VoIP products. Online file-sharing networks such as Napster, Kazaa, Gnutella, or BitTorrent have shown how peer-to-peer (P2P) networks can impact on traditional businesses by eliminating (or decreasing) the friction between producers and consumers, thereby changing users' behavior and causing a paradigm shift in some industries.

---

8   Market data provided by Comscore (an Internet marketing research company), November 2011. Facebook data from Zephoria, "The Top 20 Valuable Facebook Statistics – Updated March 2019," [website], Available at: ▶ https://zephoria.com/top-15-valuable-facebook-statistics/.

Business impact of social networks   Not to be left behind, companies ought to pay attention to the business impact of Internet-based social networks, which are gaining increasing importance worldwide. The rationale for the huge popularity of these networks is manyfold, including[9]:

Social networks are large   Their overall size is continuously growing, with an estimated growth of 20% year on year. There are around 2.77 billion social media users worldwide (2019), up from 2.46 billion in 2017.[10] This is obviously a great audience for businesses to reach, not only as a source of revenue generation but also as a potential pool to capture content generation and value co-creation.

Social networks are active   SNS members are not mere observers but active participants who share personal experiences, personal ideas, and products/service reviews and discuss with and about other people. SNS members can also influence other network users, and businesses should take note, and be careful, of the substantial influential power of certain SNS members.

Social networks are a clearing house of information   Social media users post opinions about their experiences with brands and their likes and dislikes. They also post personal opinions and unedited comments that can have a stronger influence on other people's purchasing decisions than a company's communication and marketing campaigns.

Advertising spending on social networking is strong   Companies are spending more advertising resources on online social networks. Worldwide social media advertising expenditure reached US$31 billion in 2016 and is growing between 20% and 30% year on year (at a time when advertising expenditure is only growing about 4% per annum). It is estimated that total global advertising expenditure on social media will account for 20% of all Internet advertising in 2019 (estimated at US$50 billion).[11] Consequently, irrespective of whether or not it directly leads to sales, if a business ignores or disregards the importance of social media for communication and advertising, then its competitive position may be negatively affected.

Social networks are unique   Some social networks (such as Twitter and LinkedIn) have become part of the daily life of masses of people all over the world.
Social networks are varied and provide access to a potentially large target segments.
    The variety of interest groups that can be found on social networks is very large and constantly growing, for example, academic and research topics, books, music, photography, religions, and many more.[12] It is very useful for a business to

9   See Singh and Cullinane (2010).

10   Source: Statistica, "Number of social media users worldwide from 2010 to 2021 (in billions)," *Statistica. the Statistics Portal,* [website], July 2017. Available at: ▶ https://www.statista.com/ statistics/278414/number-of-worldwide-social-network-users/.

11   Zenith Optimedia, quoted in: Reuters, "Social Media Ad Spending Is Expected to Pass Newspapers by 2020," *Fortune,* 5 December, 2016.

12   For an extensive list of social networking sites, see: ▶ http://www.sociallifenetwork.com/.

easily identify and access particular groups of individuals who match a certain target profile. Also, considering the level of knowledge and engagement these groups have with their topics of interest, businesses can greatly benefit when interacting with groups whose interests are close to their business offers and activities.

Social networks are effective because they consist of consumer-to-consumer content.

As already mentioned, social network users generate content and disseminate it among their peers. In this context, word of mouth and viral marketing can be very effective.

Social networks are easy to use   No proprietary technology or special skills are required to properly use social media networks, thus making them accessible to almost everybody in society. Notwithstanding, unlike traditional media, businesses should manage conversations with target audiences through social networks with dynamicity, continuity, and creativity. Otherwise, their efforts in the social media will be futile.

11.1.3 Understanding User Behavior on the Social Web

Two key developments that led to changing user behavior are (1) the ease with which people can share information through conveniently accessible service sites and (2) improvements in network infrastructure. The Internet has always been about exchanging information; however, we are just starting to tap into the vast potential of the web as a communication platform. ◘ Figure 11.5 highlights the interaction processes that underpin social networking sites. For more information on the impacts of social interactions on business, see the article: "Leveraging C2C: how to influence social interactions about your brand."

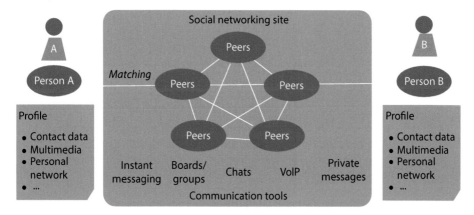

◘ **Fig. 11.5**   Social networking sites help users to pursue their motives of discovery, homogeneity, and sharing by providing various communication tools. (Source: adapted from Jelassi et al. (2014a))

11

Leveraging C2C: How to Influence Social Interactions About Your Brand

The rise of social media has allowed for more customer-to-customer communication opportunities than ever before. Arun Subramanian and Sundar Bhuvaneswaran of Mu Sigma explain how marketers can make the most of C2C channels.

In the wake of digital disruption in the past decade, the marketing landscape has completely metamorphosed, making it more intricate than ever. A quick recap of the past tells us that the digital age of the 1980s and early 1990s had enabled marketers to reap the benefits of cost-effective and one-to-one marketing channels such as emails. With advancements in technology and rapid growth of e-commerce—in the mid-90s and early 2000—marketing channels became more directed and personal. However, the (digital) marketing revolution came with the evolution of social media channels, which enabled people to connect and share, giving rise to a whole new arena of C2C communications. It was just a matter of time for the companies, across B2B and B2C spectrum, to realize the vast potential of capturing and leveraging the "voice of customer" to enable growth and profitability. The transformation, however, is not just limited to the marketplace but also how customers make purchase decisions.

This emerging trend of C2C conversations poses itself both as a challenge and a potential opportunity for marketers to leverage. By committing and channelizing marketing efforts toward collaboration with customers, marketers can infuse a sense of belongingness and ownership in the minds of the best marketing consultants and ambassadors they can bring on board—the customers. These technology-enthusiastic customers of today prefer to interact with fellow customers, across various channels, before zeroing in on a product or a service. To this effect, the role of marketers has become more daunting and challenging, to say the least. There is an obvious "power shift" among manufacturers, marketers, and customers, as customers become critical influencers in the marketing and communication process. Irrespective of the time and mode that a customer chooses to interact with a product or a brand, they expect a seamless and personalized experience in real time. In turn, they influence the purchase decisions of others by sharing experiences—good, bad, or ugly—through channels such as social media, which then becomes accessible to anyone. The outcome, the age-old marketing funnel, which has dictated the marketing scenario for long, has now evolved into a customer hourglass because of customer influence and the opportunity for customers to become brand advocates.

Leveraging C2C Communications to Enhance Brand Equity

In today's time when profit cores can deplete at an astonishingly fast pace, creating brand advocates in the form of existing customers can be highly profitable. These are the individuals who are both buyers and brand marketers. They have a relatively higher lifetime value compared to loyal customers who may purchase more from you but may not necessarily advocate your product or service. To this effect, knowing and understanding your customers better in order to retain them and leveraging the information to attract more customers should always take precedence, especially when they are ready to engage with the brand and share their voice. What does this mean to the brand? Companies must harness the power of customers as they continue to emerge as key contributors to an organization's brand marketing efforts. The below points can help organizations chart a plan to collaborate with customers and be able to drive meaningful results from it.

Facilitate C2C. By creating a seamless multichannel and multi-device ecosystem, organizations should encourage customers to share their experience. They can do so via online forums, social media (fan) pages, reviews, and ratings pages as well as engaging through company promotional videos on video streaming channels such as YouTube.

Create share-worthy content. One important aspect to keep in mind while doing so would be to ensure that the content is helpful and not promotional. The focus should be on driving engagement and not sales. Innovative techniques such as gamification can be leveraged to drive participation while companies can invite customers to co-create meaningful content.

Active participation in C2C. Companies should identify top trends and key influencers that can help them amplify their reach. More so, companies must not hold themselves back while responding to both positive and negative sentiments that play up on the social media radar.

Encourage brand advocates. Having identified the top/key influencers by measuring their impact both on POS purchase and advocacy, companies should encourage them with customized incentives and/or exclusive previews.

The age-old saying, "customer is king," remains true in this new digital setting. In these times when competition is intense and marketing costs are skyrocketing, C2C can offer a compelling arsenal to marketers, provided they drive meaningful engagement with customers. Customers don't just buy a product or service but also share experiences with fellow customers influencing their purchase decisions. Tapping into this potential and using it to their advantage can help organizations at large and marketers in particular to retain not just existing customers but also open channels for new prospects.

Adapted from: M. Read, "Leveraging C2C: how to influence social interactions about your brand," 3 November 2014.

Since the most recent applications usually contain a social component that lets users generate and share content and thereby engage in social interactions, it is important to look at what motivates people to interact with each other on the web. There are essentially three main motives: (1) finding valuable peers (discovery), (2) associating with valuable peers (homogeneity), and (3) imparting information (sharing).

Finding valuable peers (discovery)   One of the basic motives for getting to know people is curiosity and an interest in discovering new things (learning). People like to explore and have an innate interest in communication, either in order to solve problems or for the sake of social conversation. In return, they expect *entertainment* in the form of casual or random conversations or *problem solving* through target-oriented discussions. SNS such as XING (previously called openBC) provide sophisticated search tools that allow users to find other peers who have the information required to solve a specific problem. User satisfaction with a platform is directly linked to (1) the ease with which they can browse through a social network of friends and (2) the accuracy of the search results when they look for individuals with certain characteristics.

Associating with valuable peers (homogeneity)   The motivation to have like-minded people around oneself is as natural as exploring one's personal environment. Just like gregarious animals in nature, people like to surround themselves with their tribe of peers with whom they share personal beliefs, values, or attitudes. Furthermore, *for most* people, conformity increases *security* and *identity*. One fundamental aspect of SNS is therefore the possibility to connect with like-minded individuals, since users provide information about their preferences, tastes, and interests in their personal profile that can be viewed by others. In addition, communication tools such as instant messaging functions, online chats, or private email, provided by some web services, facilitate users' information exchanges according to their individual preferences.

Imparting information (sharing)   People enjoy communicating and sharing what they have learned from their peers. Peers can be relatives, friends, colleagues, mere acquaintances, experts, or social contacts of any other kind. While every individual has a certain personality recognized by others, some like to try to control the impression(s) other people form of them. This *impression management* is closely related to *self-presentation*, where a person tries to influence the perception of his/her image. Self-portrayal and, in more extreme cases, craving for recognition are some of the underlying motives for people to make themselves stand out from the masses and personally express themselves. SNS let people articulate their personality. Depending on the context and focus of the SNS platform, individual profiles contain various data and diverse information and let the individual build and manage an online reputation. Furthermore, this leads to *opportunities* to signal one's competence or interests to others who are in the stage of discovering people. For instance, on media-sharing platforms (such as YouTube), where users can upload and promote their videos, users can present themselves with the content they have created.

11.2 The Trade-Off Between Richness and Reach

As mentioned above, SNS operators can help fuel an individual's communication needs and goals by providing the user with access to diverse information (discovery), like-minded people (homogeneity), and the possibility to provide information themselves (sharing).

Below, we discuss how businesses can address a large number of users and provide them with rich means of communication at the same time, a trade-off that has been considerably weakened by the changes of the Internet leading to Web 2.0. The trade-off between richness and reach focuses on the constraints that businesses traditionally have faced when interacting with existing or prospective customers.[13] In this context, *reach* refers to the number of people exchanging information. *Richness* is defined by the following three dimensions:

Bandwidth   This dimension refers to the amount of information that can be moved from sender to receiver in a given time: email requires only narrow bandwidth, while music and video require broad bandwidth. On a different level, face-to-face interaction (Skype or Facetime) provides a broad bandwidth. This offers an information exchange that goes beyond the content level by also including facial expressions, gestures, and tone of voice. The telephone, on the other hand, is much more limited in its bandwidth since it cuts out the visual aspects of interaction; email is even more limited since it also excludes the voice component of the interaction.

Customization   This dimension refers to the ability to address the needs and preferences of individual customers. For instance, a bank employee at a branch office can provide a much higher degree of customized service than a mass mail advertisement. In a social media context, it refers to the extent to which a user can customize their social media site to reflect their individuality.

Interactivity   This dimension refers to the possibility of having bidirectional communication. Traditional one-way television broadcasting has a very low level of interactivity. The Internet on the other hand is very interactive, since it allows for an almost instantaneous bidirectional exchange of information.

Let us now turn to the historic trade-off between richness and reach. Traditionally, the communication of rich information required proximity to customers and also channels suited for transmitting such information. For instance, rich information exchange takes place in a bank's branch office, where customers talk in person to the bank agent.

However, reaching a large number of customers used to come at the expense of richness, which was due to the limited bandwidth of most mass media devices. This resulted in little customization and a lack of interactivity, as is the case, for example, with a television advertisement. To achieve reach and richness at the same time used to require substantial investments in physical infrastructure and sales force. In other words, scale economies were very limited when a business wanted to expand its customer base—that is expand reach—while still maintaining a high level of richness. Proof of this is the extensive branch network of universal banks through which banks can reach a large number of customers while serving each one of them individually. As the number of customers goes up, so do the costs.

The main argument of the richness and reach framework is that two important drivers of Web 2.0 have also eliminated the trade-off between richness and reach. These drivers are (1) *the increase in connectivity* made possible by the Internet and (2) *the development of common standards* such as TCP/IP, HTML,

---

13   Evans and Wurster (1999).

and XML. Connectivity and open standards have allowed firms to reach a larger number of potential customers while at the same time ensuring a high degree of richness.

Does this concept stand up to reality? In many cases, it does. A global auction place such as eBay would not have been possible in the pre-Internet days. Then, people could sell their used lawnmowers and stamp collections at a local garage sale. There, they had very high levels of richness, where buyers could actually touch and try out the product, yet reach was very limited since, typically, it did not extend beyond the immediate neighborhood of the seller. eBay has created a more liquid by connecting buyers and sellers across cities and countries, enabling them to share rich information about products as well as the reputation of buyers and sellers. For setting up these business models, traditional assets such as a large sales force or an extensive physical branch network, which allowed for richness in the traditional bricks-and-mortar world, would have been more of a liability than an asset. In the case of digital products or services, the concept of reach and richness becomes especially viable.

SNS allow their members to manage more contacts more efficiently than is possible offline; therefore they increase their personal contact reach. In addition, users have more information about their contacts or potential contacts due to their visible online profiles; therefore they also increase personal information richness.

11

Critical Perspective 11.1
The Limitations to Blowing Up the Trade-Off Between Richness and Reach

For several reasons, the elimination of the trade-off between richness and reach has not happened to the expected extent. On the bandwidth dimension, the Internet cannot replicate the richness of face-to-face contacts, which can only be achieved in the physical world.

Dell, the struggling computer maker, recently outlined plans to reverse two decades of reliance on direct sales by broadening its business model to include third-party vendors and retailers. The move to embrace computer resellers, the vendors who design and install computer systems for clients ranging from hedge funds to hospitals, represents a change in strategy for a company that built its business on direct sales of computers to customers over the telephone and through its website.

Dell had previously hinted that it was examining ways to broaden its retail presence, which so far consists of a single experimental store and more than 100 smaller kiosks. Michael Dell, chief executive, said in an interview, published in CRN, a trade magazine focused on resellers: "There are certainly folks out there who don't want to buy direct. So now those customers will have a chance to have Dell product as well." He said the company intended to build on its relationships with resellers and retail partners "not only here in the US, but around the world."

While other computer makers—including IBM and Hewlett-Packard —have long relied on resellers and retailers for a substantial chunk of their annual sales, Dell has shunned such indirect relationships, arguing that direct contact with the customer is the best way to streamline costs and respond to changing demand. Although the company has links with some third-party vendors, it said it had never before viewed the channel as a significant business. Mr Dell indicated that would change. "There is a great interest here," he told CRN. "We're going to ramp it up quickly."

Dell declined to comment on any other retail plans. It has traditionally avoided selling computers through retailers, because it allows the company to avoid carrying costly inventory. Shares of Dell rose 3.3% on Wednesday to $25.49. They had fallen from a high of $41.29 in August 2005, before the company's stumbles began. The rise came in spite of news that Andrew Cuomo, New York's attorney general, had sued the computer maker, alleging that its sales practices had deceived customers. Dell said it intended to fight the suit.

Last year, a series of stumbles led Dell, which was founded by Mr. Dell in his University of Texas dorm room more than 20 years ago, to lose its place at the top of the PC market to HP. This year, Mr. Dell returned to the chief executive role, replacing Kevin Rollins, in an effort to put the company back on track.

Source: K. Allison, "Dell to broaden sales model," Financial Times, 16 May 2007.

11.3 Increasing the Richness of Interactions with Customers

In ▶ Sect. 11.2, we identified bandwidth, customizability and interaction as the main drivers for richness of interaction with users. We now focus on how a business can leverage these drivers in order to foster the richness of interactions with customers. In the following sections, we look at two possible ways of enhancing such richness: (1) customer relationship management supported with IT-based tools. This implies a typical e-CRM but also a CRM based on Web 2.0 applications (or social CRM), and (2) mass customization, which enables the tailoring of products and services to specific customer requirements.

11.3.1 Customer Relationship Management (CRM) ⌃ in a Digital Context

E-Customer Relationship Management (e-CRM) e-CRM refers to the use of the Internet and IT applications to manage customer relationships. As the Internet has permeated all the activities of a company's value chain, e-CRM has also become more important. Specifically, it aims to:
- Create a long-term relationship with customers to offset their acquisition costs
- Reduce the rate of customer defections
- Increase the "share of wallet" through cross-selling and up-selling
- Increase the profitability of low-profit customers
- Focus on high-value customers

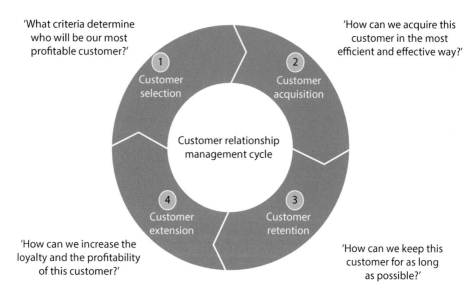

'What criteria determine who will be our most profitable customer?'

'How can we acquire this customer in the most efficient and effective way?'

1 Customer selection

2 Customer acquisition

Customer relationship management cycle

4 Customer extension

3 Customer retention

'How can we increase the loyalty and the profitability of this customer?'

'How can we keep this customer for as long as possible?'

◘ Fig. 11.6   Customer relationship management consists of four elements. (Source: adapted from Jelassi et al. (2014b))

e-CRM comprises the following four main elements: (1) customer selection, (2) customer acquisition, (3) customer retention, and (4) customer extension. They are discussed below ◘ Fig. 11.6.

Customer selection refers to customer segment targeting, which was discussed in detail in ▶ Sect. 3.4.

Customer acquisition includes promotions and other incentives to (1) acquire new customers and (2) entice existing customers to use the company's Internet-based offering. In order to engage a customer in a relationship through the online channel, a firm needs to have at least the customer's email address. More detailed customer profiles include information such as a customer's personal interests, age, financial status, and role in the purchasing process. To acquire this more detailed information, it is usually necessary to offer customers an incentive, e.g., a gift certificate or a free product sample. e-Commerce businesses use a number of different tools to attract the attention of potential customers. Initially, this was done primarily through banner advertising. More recently, marketers have added more sophisticated tools such as "viral marketing," where customers forward a website address or other types of company information to each other via email or SMS. Another effective way of acquiring customers is link building, which ▶ Amazon.com does in partnership with affiliate sites that refer to the ▶ Amazon.com site. For instance, the alumni club of the Leipzig Graduate School of Management in Germany maintains an affiliate relationship with Amazon.de. As part of this agreement, the alumni club's homepage hosts a link to the Amazon.de website and receives a 5% commission on all sales that take place through this link.

11

Customer retention aims to (1) turn one-time customers into repeat-purchase customers and (2) keep customers for as long as possible in the online channel. Customer retention is achieved primarily through two features: personalization and communities. The personalization of a website means it is designed to meet specific customer needs to support creation of "stickiness." For example, if customers want to change their online provider, then they will incur switching costs. Strong online communities with many different users help to create network effects. Both personalization and online communities entice users to stay with a specific website.

Customer extension focuses on maximizing the lifetime value of a customer. Companies achieve this primarily by expanding the scope of an existing customer relationship through cross-selling. Nordea, for instance, is turning toward triggered data mining to cross-sell additional financial products to existing customers. Triggered data mining works as follows: when there is a change in a customer account—for instance, a large incoming money transfer, an address change or a marital status change—a trigger in the database is set off and informs the bank about this change. This, in turn, raises the following question: What does this change mean for financing, for long-term payments, for insurance, and for e-services?

Toward the Social CRM   To effectively manage customer relationships, CRM should be designed by leveraging multiple communication channels, whether they are electronic or not. While the previous section provided a description of traditional e-CRM, this section focuses on the social CRM, which is an extension of the initial concept offering bidirectional exchanges and collaboration with customers as presented in ◘ Fig. 11.1. Through Web 2.0 technology, customers become co-creators of value, and the new emphasis is on developing a customer-supplier relationship through interaction and dialogue (Rodríguez et al. 2010).

To leverage social CRM capabilities for business competitiveness, companies should consider using the following MASTER approach, recently proposed by Acker et al. (2011) and comprising the following six actions:

- *Monitor.* Target audiences that continuously generate data and content and gather useful information about them.
- *Assess and analyze.* Analyze the data collected in the previous stage and identify potential threats and opportunities in social customers, which could be addressed by social CRM.
- *Strategize and structure.* Design and develop specific actions that target customer communities and create value for them. This can be called the platform mix of social or Web 2.0 applications.
- *Test.* Before implementing the social CRM plan, run a small-scale test in order to fine-tune the solution.
- *Embed.* Once social CRM activities are established, it is important to determine their related organizational processes and employee roles, responsibilities, and incentives.
- *Review.* In view of the dynamic business environment surrounding the social web, regularly review the CRM activities and decide on future actions.

SOCIAL CRM	Initial Stage	Mature Stage
Business Functions		
Product Innovation	- Develop products insights from external social networks, leveraging the service as well as marketing insights	- Crowdsource research and development to accelerate product to market and improve the change of product adoption
Social Marketing & Public Relations	- Develop marketing insights from external social networks - Create one main blog, usually by the CEO's office or other upper management	- In near real tme, monitor chatter on social networks, including overall sentiment monitering - Manage the organization's events - Promote corss-deartment blogging and social customer interactions
Social Sales	- Develop sales insights from external social networks - Provide social customers with product information through social media - Develop internal networks to collabrate on sales opportunities and leads	- Develop leads and sales opportunities from social communities - Use peer-to-peer lead generation through social recommendations, referrals, and customer testimonials
Social Service	- Develop service insights from external social networks - Develop internal networks to collaborate on the response to customer issues and service requests	- Develop rapid service response to issues raised on social networksby proactive monitering and establishing in house social support structure - Harness the collective expertise of customers to develop a peer-to-peer social service
Organizational Structures		
People & Skills	- Create isolated social programs typically focused on one department - Leverage select existing emplyees to interest with customers on social networks	- Dedicate a team, decentralized or centralized based on company size, to coordinate social CRM programs all departments - Develop internal speciallized skills to write, develop, and publish social media content such as blogs, podcasts, and multimedia
Culture	- Encourage employees to view social CRM program as a positive new experiment	- Integrate social CRM into the business with a clear mission, ROI, and KPIs - Harness an active and empowered change management program to help customer-centricity, collaboration, and transparency pervade the company's culture
Technology Platforms		
Tools & Systems	- Leverage public and mostly free social media platforms available on the web with no or minimal investment in hardware or software	- Invest in social CRM platforms that are becoming increasingly available in the market with specialization in social sales, social service, or social marketing
Integration	- Do not have to integrate program with in-house platforms such as CRM or business intelligence	- Integrate the social CRM platforms with operational platforms

☐ Fig. 11.7 Embedding social CRM into companies. (Source: adapted from Acker et al. (2011), p. 9)

To effectively embed social CRM in the corporate structure, specific actions should be taken at the following three levels: (1) *Business functions*: product innovation, social marketing and public relations, social sales, and social service; (2) *Organizational structure*: people and skills and culture; and (3) *Technology platforms*: tools and systems and integration. These actions should be considered at the initial stage of rolling out social CRM and at the mature stage (see ☐ Fig. 11.7).

11.3.2 The Concept of Mass Customization

The concept of mass customization acts counterintuitively to the large wave of standardization and exploitation of economies of scale, which originated from industrial economics. The amount of customization in a given product or service is an important determinant driving the richness of interaction between a company and its customers. However, in the past, customization was rather expensive, and customers had to pay a significant price premium, for instance, for the customized

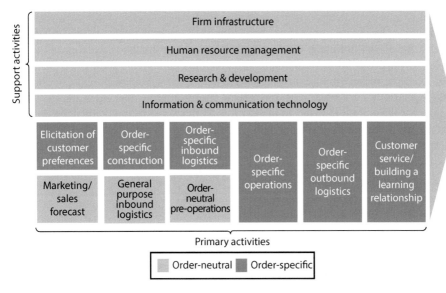

◻ Fig. 11.8 The mass customization value chain puts the user in charge of many steps traditionally performed by the company. (Source: adapted from Piller (2006))

interior of their apartment or car. ◻ Figure 11.8 illustrates how mass customization includes almost all primary activities of the value chain.

If a company wants to pursue a mass customization approach, it firstly needs to elicit the individual customer's preferences, which form the basis for the individual construction of the product. Frequently, the procurement of customization-relevant parts only takes place once the elicitation of preferences has been completed. The most prominent example of a mass customization company is Dell, which lets customers specify exactly which parts should be included in their PC. ▶ Tesco.com also leverages customer data to tailor a shopping list to a customer's needs, for example, by recommending special offers on a one-to-one basis based upon prior purchases.

From a strategic perspective, mass customization opens up the opportunity to pursue an outpacing strategy that combines low prices with superior performance. A mass customization company does not have to opt for one of the two directions of competitive advantage but can simultaneously pursue the two generic strategies using IT and the vast possibilities of user-generated content. On the one hand, mass-customized products are, by definition, highly differentiated, since they are based on each buyer's specifications. For instance, "NikeiD" by Nike allows consumers to design[14] highly differentiated products by letting them choose and combine different materials, textures, and colors for a sneaker or trainer, which is then manufactured and delivered to them. On the other hand, due to efficiency advantages of customer-pulled production, which results in lower business risk and smaller stock levels, mass-customized products are also competitive on the price dimension.

---

14 Source: Nike by you, [website]. Available at: ▶ https://www.nike.com/us/en_us/c/nikeid.

Mass customization options can generally be divided into two different approaches. First, the *soft customization* approach involves only activities that take place after manufacturing. One example of soft customization is to provide customers with the possibility to customize products themselves after their purchase. For example, when users configure the setup of their Microsoft Office software, they essentially customize it to meet their specific needs. The main drawback of this approach is that, in order to allow multiple customization options, the product must have a certain built-in flexibility, which typically results in a relatively high product complexity as well as high development and production costs. Yet, the limited overall variety opens up opportunities for standardization, which in turn leads to economies of scale. From the customer's viewpoint, this mass customization concept is suitable if customization needs change often during product use, which, for instance, is the case with many software applications.

In addition to soft customization, we also recognize the *hard customization* approach, which involves a customized manufacturing process. The starting point of this approach is the splitting of the production process into two parts: a customer-specific part, which is performed in direct interaction with the buyer, and an order-neutral part. For efficiency reasons, the latter should outweigh the former so that economies of scale can be achieved. Nike's NikeiD is an example of a hard customization approach which takes place at the beginning of the manufacturing process. Another example is Mykea,[15] a small Amsterdam-based company whose core business is customizing many Ikea products. Basically, it offers original and creative stickers that are designed to cover the visible part of Ikea furniture. Consumers can select among a wide variety of designs and colors and place the order online. Designs can be easily attached on the surface of the furniture, and customers receive their items in a transport tube with instructions.

As information technologies are increasingly ubiquitous, consumption and production are becoming inseparable (Kozinets et al. 2008), thus making consumers more and more involved in the value creation process. Web 2.0 has therefore enabled collective consumers' creativity and co-production or "crowdsourcing" as it is called.

11.4 Increasing the Reach of Interactions with Customers

SNS can greatly increase the richness of users' interactions. One crucial prerequisite for creating richness is the ability of an Internet service to attract a critical mass of users. SNS can only work if there are enough people registered on them so that users can actually buildup a personal contacts' network of a sufficient scale.

More generally, any e-commerce venture that wants to leverage the power of user-generated content needs to devise a growth strategy that allows it to reach a critical mass of buyers or members, as is the case for SNS. In the following section, we firstly explore how growth can be fostered by tapping into the power of net-

---

15 Source: Mykea [website]. Available at: ▶ http://www.thisismykea.com/.

work effects which may then lead to a "viral growth." We then explain the concept of the "tipping point" and finally investigate the applicability of the "long tail" concept to SNS.

11.4.1 Viral Growth

Any businesses trying to benefit from viral growth need to offer incentives for users to invite others to join the service. Incentives can be intrinsic, such as when users know that inviting other users to the platform will enrich their own experience because they can add them as contacts and interact with them. When these intrinsic motivations fail, a company has to think about providing alternative incentives for users.

Information (in its broadest sense, including everything from a simple fact to new products) sometimes spreads epidemically. Like a virus that spreads by infection, information spreads through word of mouth. (This is actually where the term *viral growth* is derived from.) The mechanism of viral information dissemination is simple and can be compared with the tradition of fairy tales or legends, which spread worldwide only via word of mouth, being retold uncountable times and passed on from generation to generation. Transferred to a broader basis, this means that if only ten people are addressed in the first generation (at the top of the pyramid), 10,000 people can be reached by the fourth generation. This huge potential has attracted the interest of marketing researchers: if viral news dissemination could be systematically implemented as a marketing vehicle, it would have major advantages. Firstly, in comparison with traditional marketing campaigns whose impact is diluted over time, the effect of viral news dissemination is self-reinforced with an increasing degree of distribution, resulting in a sustainable anchoring of information. The reason for this effect is simple: when moving down the pyramid, the absolute number of people further spreading the news gets continuously larger. Secondly, the expected costs of viral news dissemination are low because no additional costs occur after an initial investment to create and initiate the news dissemination (seeding). This is possible because consumers act as a medium to spread the news, once it is seeded. For ways to increase the chances of news about a business going viral on social media, please see the article: "7 ways to up your chances of going viral on social media."

> **7 Ways To Up Your Chances Of Going Viral On Social Media**
> The rapid growth of social media platforms over the past several years has led to significant changes in the way influencers communicate with their respective audiences. Politicians, businesses, athletes, and artists use platforms like Facebook, Twitter, and Instagram to share new ideas, sell new products, and promote their brand. These applications have also made it substantially easier to develop a following by going viral AKA the holy grail for brands the world over. Take, for instance, the app HQ Trivia. HQ is a trivia quiz show that comes on at 3 p.m. and 9 p.m. ET every day and offers contestants a chance to win cash prizes for answer-

ing 12 questions correctly. Over the course of several months, HQ was able to attract hundreds of thousands players every day, with very little traditional marketing. Going viral on social media is a great way to boost your brand presence and attract new customers quickly, but it's not easy.

I spoke to Joseph Ayoub, the founder and CEO of the digital marketing firm Creaze, about the best ways to take your brand viral in 2018. Ayoub has experience scaling brands and working with some of the largest influencers in this space. Here are his 7 tips for going viral on social media.

1. Focus on High-Quality Content Before Investing in Advertising

One mistake many brands make when marketing on social media is focusing on advertising campaigns rather than high-quality content creation. While successful brands certainly have great marketing strategies, they also regularly put out quality content to keep customers engaged. Ayoub tells me that "content is and always will be the key to a brand's success." He added further that "I'd definitely say before investing into advertising, make sure your content is on point otherwise you'll end up wasting money advertising something that doesn't work." So If you're not able to keep customers engaged once they've visited your page with content, advertising is useless.

2. Know Your Audience

NOTE: The following text can easily be classified under blatantly obvious. An important step in going viral is knowing the audience that your content will resonate with. When you produce new content and share it across different social media platforms, it's important to know the type of user that is most likely to share the content with their friends or engage with your brand in the comments. And in the world of never-ending shortage of data we live in, there is no reason NOT to know your audience. Period.

3. Partnering with Influencers

Once you've clearly defined the interests and social media behavior of your target audience, you can use that information to partner with other brands and influencers to increase your chances of virality.

Partnership is a key part of a successful marketing strategy, as it's unlikely you'll be able to reach a large enough audience only using your own social media channels. Reach out to the brands and influencers that are popular with your target audience and arrange a partnership to cross-promote products and new content. This strategy will quickly grow your user base and increase your chances of going viral.

4. Get Your Content Reposted on Popular Accounts

Ayoub worked with Alex from Target, a teenage Target employee that went viral on Twitter after a picture of him was posted online. After the picture was posted, thousands of users retweeted it, and it went viral overnight. He was eventually featured on The Ellen DeGeneres Show after becoming an Internet sensation.

While the post spread relatively quickly organically, Joseph said that it was really "the distribution that these relatable meme accounts that repost popular tweets that made it really stand out and be shown across the world." By cross-posting the content on account pages that already have large audiences, Alex from Target was exposed to a much larger audience extremely quickly.

5. Tell a Relatable Story Through Your Content

One of the things that resonate most with modern social media users is a relatable story. Users are much more likely to share posts with their friends and engage in the comments if they connect to the story you're telling on a personal level. One way to do this is to create a fictional character that is similar to the people in your target audience.

You can create a video series where they use your product or feature your brand throughout their life. If your audience resonates with the character, they'll be more likely to want to associate with your brand.

6. Keep It Short and to the Point

There are more people today than ever before that suffer from attention deficit disorder, better known as ADD. We all have way too many things to distract us in the real world let along the social media one. And then are those devices we cannot live without. Or as one very telling headline in *The Telegraph* put it a few years ago: Humans have shorter attention span than goldfish, thanks to smartphones. Modern social media users have very short attention spans. Make sure the content you produce is easy to read and can be digested by a user in 10 seconds or less. Posts with too much text or videos that are too long will quickly be ignored by users, and your chances of going viral will be much lower.

7. Utilize Interactive Content

One way to get users engaged is to make your content interactive. For instance, post a quiz on Facebook or make a poll on your Instagram story. Users are much more likely to engage with your content if you ask a question that they want to voice their opinion on. Give them the opportunity to comment and share their own ideas. This is a great way to get users involved and increase viewership in as many feeds as possible.

Source: S. Olenski, "7 ways to up your chances of going viral on social media," *Forbes*, 6 February, 2018.

Viral marketing thus aims to find a way of using rapid, widespread news dissemination as a marketing tool, making it measurable and repeatable. The goal is to create a viral marketing campaign as a planned initiative where advertisers develop and spread online marketing messages (viral agents) that motivate the receiver to become a sender. However, there are some barriers to implementing viral news spread as a marketing tool. These barriers include:

Lack of control over people   Viral marketing is consumer driven as opposed to traditional "interruption" unidirectional marketing, which is driven and controlled by the marketer. It is therefore unpredictable and difficult to control the kind of content that people will recommend, when and why. Furthermore, even if people forward the message, what they will add to it or say about it when doing so cannot be controlled.

Lack of control over content   The content of a viral marketing campaign cannot be protected from being tampered with or modified by the people passing it on. Once the news is seeded, there is no way of stopping it from spreading. Thus the danger of a viral marketing campaign backfiring at the advertising company must not be underestimated. *Hotmail*, for example, included an email footer with a Hotmail advertisement in each email that was sent over a Hotmail account. Recipients forwarding such an email could easily modify this footer or add some other content such that the viral campaign would backfire for the initiating company.

11.4.2   The "Tipping Point" Concept

Malcolm Gladwell's (2000) concept of the "tipping point" builds on the idea of viral growth. Based on his observations of different industries and areas of life, Gladwell suggests that news or products sometimes spread at quite moderate rates, and then at some point in time—the tipping point—start to spread rapidly. In one of the original examples used by Gladwell, he analyzed the increase in sales of fax machines in the 1980s. Around 1986, there was a massive surge of sales that can be regarded as the tipping point. Tipping points in new technologies can often be attributed to *network (externality) effects*.[16] These effects also exist in Web 2.0 applications as users benefit from other users joining the platform, for instance, on business networking sites that can provide a vast network of skilled and specialized individuals. Gladwell identified three factors influencing viral spread: (1) the *law of the few*, (2) the *stickiness factor*, and (3) the *power of context*.

The law of the few focuses on the people involved in spreading a message. It suggests that when seeding a message, one has to concentrate on three types of people: connectors, mavens, and salespeople:

- *Connectors* are people with an extraordinary high number of contacts, friends, and acquaintances, who ideally belong to "different worlds," that is, different areas of life. Gladwell argued that almost everyone knows people who seem to be connected across social, geographic, or organizational boundaries and who have a very diverse circle of friends and acquaintances.
- *Mavens* are people who have expertise in various products, prices, or places. Furthermore, they enjoy sharing their knowledge with their friends and acquaintances and other users on Internet platforms. Due to their knowledge and their ability to connect, they also have the ability to start word-of-mouth

---

16 Network effects exist whenever a service has a value to a potential customer who depends on the number of other customers who are already using the same service.

viral news. Numerous online platforms such as ▶ ciao.com, an online product evaluation forum, or ▶ trivago.com, a site where users exchange recommendations about travel destinations, restaurants, etc., leverage mavens to generate content and create traffic on their website.

- *Salespeople* have the skills to persuade others when they are unconvinced. Gladwell provided a typical example for this group of people using an extremely dedicated car dealer. On the Internet, "salespeople" could be a dedicated corporate blogger such as the openBlog, the company weblog of XING (formerly open BC).

The stickiness factor deals with the content of the message that is to be spread. Gladwell postulated that in order to spread epidemically, the content has to be memorable enough to create change and move people to the action stage. Gladwell used the compelling example of the famous television show *Sesame Street*. By testing the single episodes over and over, while monitoring the children's attention, *Sesame Street* managed to increase its stickiness to almost hypnotic levels among its young target group. Viral marketing seems to have a great potential for stickiness, as content spread by peers is more memorable than content distributed by traditional marketing channels.

The power of context focuses on the conditions and circumstances under which viral news can occur. It has two implications:

- *Outer circumstances* have a significant impact on people's inner states. The immediate context of behavior influences people's convictions and thoughts. Even very small changes in certain outer circumstances can cause a situation to tip, for example, a small temperature change may trigger a flu epidemic.
- *Small sub-movements.* In order to create one viral movement, many small movements have to be created first. In order to magnify the viral potential of a message or idea, groups must be close-knit, because in bigger groups, people become strangers to each other and the group loses its "tightness" or cohesion. An analogy could be a fire started by a number of small fires, maybe a bonfire that got out of control or a cigarette that was thrown away carelessly. If the small fires make their way through a wood, they can create a huge forest fire once they come together. This was the case in one of the biggest online viral disseminations to date, the "Coke/Menthos experiments."[17]

11.4.3   The "Long Tail" of Internet-Based Social Networks

To illustrate the concept of the "long tail," Anderson (2006) initially compared online music retailers (such as Rhapsody) with traditional bricks-and-mortar retailers (such as Walmart), just as we compare Internet-based networking (such as ▶ StayFriends.com or XING) to traditional "flesh-and-blood" networking.

---

17 A YouTube video showing an explosion-like reaction when dropping a Menthos, a type of candy, into a bottle of Coke fueled a huge chain reaction of imitators.

Walmart distributes through a large chain of physical stores the variety of physical goods it sells. However, it can only offer a predefined selection of products due to limitations in shelf space as well as the costs of producing (or sourcing), storing, and delivering the goods. Therefore, Walmart and other physical retailers are likely to offer only the "hits" (i.e., in the case of music, the songs and albums which sell best and are most worthwhile providing), just as people in the case of networking will only keep in touch with others whom they consider to be the most "valuable" contacts in one way or another.

In contrast to the above, digital content can be stored, replicated, and distributed at much lower costs. Goods here include media-based products (such as music, photos, and videos) or personal content (such as profiles, online group discussions, and personal networks). At Napster, a (now) legal online music downloading service, 98% of all products sell, and the fact that they sell is the reason enough for carrying them, especially since shelf space is not as restricted as it is in the real world. Since digital products can be offered at virtually no additional cost, it is a viable strategy for online retailers to "sell less of more," that is, to offer a large array of products including those that sell only in small quantities. Due to the fact that digital products bring no additional costs or complexity, they are worthwhile carrying. These niche products make up the "long tail," as opposed to the hits that reflect the "short head" offered by bricks-and-mortar retailers.

Transferring the "long tail" concept to the realm of Internet-based social networks helps us to understand more fully the abovementioned benefits of networking sites. Firstly, via traditional means of networking, individuals almost exclusively contact people they have personally known in the past. For the most part, this is the inner social circle of people that an individual has a strong relationship with, either in business or socially. Via traditional networking, people usually do not have easy access to the contacts of their contacts. Yet, in many situations, such as advice seeking or job searches, we do not benefit so much from the people with whom we have strong social bonds, but we quite often benefit from people we do not know directly or only very superficially—our so-called *weak ties* (Granovetter 1973). By granting access to these weak ties, SNS offer a much larger pool of potentially interesting and useful contacts than the traditional means of physical networking can typically provide.

Secondly, traditional networking allows individuals to stay in touch only with a limited number of people due to time restrictions. It requires simply too much effort to update permanently all contact data in a traditional address book or an Excel sheet, since contacts do not regularly inform the individual about changes in their contact data such as address, telephone number, job position, or email address. Hence, contact data is not always up to date, and the individual might lose track of these people, even if he/she would, in theory, be willing to retain the contact. Relationships thus expire over time due to a lack of interaction. On SNS, however, terminating a relationship requires the user's active intervention; otherwise, a contact will be retained in a user's contact list. Thus, it becomes possible to manage a constantly growing number of contacts without any additional effort. Actively used SNS grant users access to valid contact data at all times, with the profiles acting as a de facto self-actualizing address book.

The combination of the above two factors, that is, the impact of weak ties and the improved contact management, creates a vast potential for online networking. We call this potential the *"long tail" of social networking*.

The X-axis depicts the number of a user's contacts, ranked by networking intensity, while the networking intensity, depicted on the Y-axis, is a function of the contact frequency and the amount and type of information that is exchanged between individuals and their contacts. The "long tail" curve reflects the fact that we tend to have a few people with whom we have very close relationships, whereas there are a lot of people we know only superficially and contact only infrequently.

In addition to facilitating communication between businesses and their customers, the Internet also facilitates communication between customers who are members of a virtual online community. For some firms, such as eBay and XING, the communication that takes place among members of their online communities is much more important than the communication between the business and its customers.

The "short head" on the left contains those contacts that are easily accessible via traditional networking. It consists of a limited number of contacts with which we have frequent contacts. After the "short head," there is a cut-off point beyond which contacts either are inaccessible via traditional networking or have such a low contact intensity that the connection is not worthwhile maintaining and will therefore get diluted over time. Social networking sites offer the possibility to get to know more people and stay in touch with them, even if they are contacted only once a year or even less. SNS grant their users access to these contacts in the "long tail." Therefore, a cut-off point after the "short head" (as with traditional networking) does not exist.

The "long tail" concept has three main implications for businesses that want to access and leverage the "long tail" for their customers:

- *Lengthen the tail.* By giving people access to a large pool of individuals, SNS lengthen the tail of potential social contacts. In the same way, other services revolving around user-generated content provide their users with access to unique and individual content. For example, through Second Life technology users even generate virtual content that is actually traded and sold—for real money.
- *Fatten the tail.* SNS uses a variety of mechanisms to enrich communication between users and thereby fatten the tail by increasing the frequency of interaction. Personal messages, guest books, "poking" people virtually on Facebook, or "Tweeting"[18] about the latest news are ways that increase the overall level of communication between users.
- *Drive demand down the tail.* This can be achieved by shifting users' attention to content that normally is not as easy to find. ► Amazon.com has done this for quite a while with its unique recommendation mechanism, but, today, services like YouTube do the same thing by constantly recommending to a given user similar videos to others that have been viewed, that potentially match his/her interest.

---

18 See: Twitter at ► http://www.twitter.com. The service provides users with the potential of reaching a large number of people. Users post frequent updates about themselves free of charge. The hype around Twitter has resulted in a variety of mash-ups and applications for the service.

Critical Perspective 11.2

Is there unlimited choice and does it create unlimited demand?

While Chris Anderson finds good examples in electronic retailing, empirical evidence has yet to be produced to support his Long Tail theory. Even before publishing his book, Anderson was criticized for his blunt and straightforward statements in several articles in *WIRED* magazine that seemed to turn retailing upside down. However, this is maybe not the case.

The Wall Street Journal's Steve Gomes contradicts Anderson's findings: he claims figures published by Rhapsody contradict the statement that "98% of all products sell"; the no-play rate, meaning songs offered on the website that are not downloaded at all, is more like 22%. Closely related to that is Anderson's statement of "misses outselling hits," meaning the traditional 80/20 rule of making 80% of revenues from 20% of the products offered (the "hits"). Gomes again contradicts using Rhapsody data showing that the top 10% of all songs roughly get more than 80% of all streams.

Shortly after the first wave of comments on his findings, Anderson had to step back from his initial claims and rephrased some of them for the book published in 2006. And still a lively discussion continues throughout the blogosphere about the validity of his claims.

While the potential of the web, especially new developments toward "Web 2.0," to offer more choice certainly exists, the actual question is how this potential can be monetized. It seems that hits still do account for the largest amount of retail revenues, and it is doubtful whether that will change any time soon.

11

11.4.4   Using Machine Learning to Offer Personalization

Today's customers are overwhelmed by a wide variety of information and content. Information overload is a major challenge that businesses need to consider. In many cases, commercial content or messages have been sent to customers but barely arouse their attention. Businesses want to reach and find valuable customers and convert this into sales; see Sect. 13.6.3 about the low conversion rate of PCs and mobiles. In this case, businesses should learn what a customer likes and offer personalized content or messages. This could be difficult and costly for many businesses to access and master customer preferences by traditional approaches because every customer has distinct preferences and typically do not want their preferences and behavioral patterns accessed by businesses. These details are related to an individual's information privacy and security.

Machine learning (ML) may help firms tackle this issue.[19] ML enables computers to learn without explicit programming. Firstly, it allows a computer to use data

---

19 This section is adapted from: B. Ho, "Machine Learning for Personalization and Beyond: 6 Ways Marketers Can Benefit from ML," *Criteo*, 7 December 2017.

to observe, learn, and analyze patterns for inferences without typing in any commands. Secondly, it can grow itself by accessing more data. The more data it accesses, the smarter it becomes, gradually improving its analytics and task completion ability. Eventually, it is able to handle large volumes of data at a rapid velocity and take actions with a high precision. Considering ML's characteristics, it is suitable for businesses aiming to meaningfully and effectively reach customers. Here, we provide a few ways that firms can benefit from interactions with customers through ML.

Usable real-time data   An object's value depends on its context where human-object interactions happen. For example, it is easier to sell umbrellas in a rainy day than a sunny day. Real-time data can help firms understand what a customer is doing and which types of content or messaging they should offer. ML can identify a customer's current context by gathering real-time data (e.g., location, events in that location, possible activities the person is undertaking, whether they are there regularly, and more). In this case, customers will see content or messages tailored to their context from time to time.

Deeper customer insights   ML can collect data related to customer preferences and distinguish what type or style of a message or content will be "liked" by customers. When combined with real-data analysis, ML can analyze content across channels and memorize search records and past activities and purchases. Businesses can then create a fuller profile of customers and offer personalized experiences or recommend content.

Chatbots   ML generates the use of chatbots. Labor-powered customer services are costly and usually cannot produce an excellent customer experience. For example, today's online shoppers are more impatient, and it is difficult to retain shoppers who have been waiting in a queue for minutes before speaking with a customer service representative. In the past, service bots could only competently respond to very limited questions and usually worked as a service portal. However, natural language processing (NLP) techniques enable ML-based chatbots to understand human language and respond more appropriately. For more information on chatbots, see the article: "The value of chatbots for today's consumers".

Personalized recommendations   ML is a powerful weapon to customize recommendations. Recommendation systems are crucial for some content platforms and e-commerce platforms. For example, many people use apps to catch up with current news. But there are a huge number of stories covering various aspects such as politics, sports, entertainment, and more. How could a news platform recommend stories that users are interested in? ML can learn from a user's browsing history, record a user's preferences, and then recommend content which should be most interesting for him or her. For example, Amazon uses this technique to smartly recommend products for shoppers, and doing so increases shoppers' interest in recommendations and raises their purchasing intentions. There are many other applications that offer personalized recommendations.

Smart advertising   Advertisements are an important way for businesses to reach consumers. But they are annoying for many users. Even though some platforms are useful or valuable for users, some may uninstall them purely based on too many annoying intrusive advertisements. Some premium users are even willing to pay a fee just getting rid of in-app advertisements or use software that blocks them. But for most free users, apps monetize them with advertising and also try to decrease the customer loss caused by advertisement displays. To mitigate this tension, ML can take contingent actions, by learning from a user's response to advertisements and search histories. For instance, if a user tends to ignore certain advertisements, they will be replaced by others relevant to the user's recent browsing or shopping histories.

11

The Value of Chatbots for Today's Consumers

The global chatbot market was valued at over $190 million in 2016 and is only expected to grow in the coming years. Chatbots are here to stay, and it isn't hard to see why. According to a study by Aspect Software Research, 44% of consumers said they would prefer to interact with a chatbot over a human customer service representative. What may surprise you, though, is that baby boomers are playing a large role in the future of chatbot use. Despite the stereotypes regarding age and technology, a joint research project between my company, MyClever, and Drift and SurveyMonkey Audience that surveyed over 1000 adults in the United States found that baby boomers were 24% more likely than millennials to see greater benefit from chatbots in five of the nine uses cases studied. Let's take a closer look at how this modern technology is affecting all generations.

Chatbots Can Provide Instant Responses

According to 61% of baby boomers and 51% of millennials, one of the main benefits of chatbots is their ability to provide instant responses to questions. This is great news for brands, suggesting that chatbots could have a serious impact on all customer service needs and open the doors to proactive new ways to service customers. An easy deployment method for service chatbots is to deploy them automatically when a customer is showing signs of rage clicking, which is characterized by erratic clicking of the mouse on a screen when something isn't happening as the consumer wishes. Modern chatbots can be triggered by this action and deployed in real time to propose a solution. Providing proactive, 24/7 service increases the value of the customer experience.

Chatbots Can Answer complex Questions

In addition to simply servicing customers, baby boomers also see chatbot benefits when it comes to getting answers to complex questions: 38% of baby boomers and 33% of millennials feel that chatbots are good at answering complex questions. Complex questions are a part of many customer experiences. In sales, for example, many questions must be asked to evaluate the buyer's situation before the correct solution can be provided: What other tools are you using? What versions of those tools? For what?

I spoke to Guillaume Cabane, former VP of growth at Segment, to learn more about how he used a chatbot to enable greater lead qualification and lead generation.

The bot was combined with other technologies, allowing it to be deployed to specific customer segments with specific talk tracks. This automated complex lines of questions instantly. After 3 weeks of deployment, the chatbots became the number one source of leads for Segment, and year to date, it is the largest single factor of Segment growth. Specifically, engagements have increased fivefold and conversions doubled. The best result, as Guillaume would say, is "100% of my sales reps now love me."

All Buyers and Customers Are Using Chatbots

Baby boomers see significant value from chatbots, and this may be because they have used one recently. Our study found that 15% of all consumers have engaged with a company via a chatbot in the past 12 months. To put that into perspective, 28% of consumers engaged with a brand via social media in the past 12 months, 30% via a mobile app, and 60% via email. While 15% engagement may seem low, yet as a channel, it is beginning to hold its own against these more traditional channels.

Chatbots are only the tip of the iceberg for how consumers and businesses will engage in the future. As more consumers engage via chatbot, it will only be a matter of time before they expect voice assistance like Alexa. Capgemini predicts that in 3 years, 40% of consumers will use voice assistants instead of a company's website or mobile app. Consumers are demanding faster and better experiences, and chatbots fit that bill.

Chatbots Are for More Than Just Service

Chatbots are delivering results far beyond better service. In a recent conversation with customer service expert Jay Baer, he mentioned that he has begun utilizing chatbots as a way of engaging with his audience and distributing content. His initial findings were that chatbot usage leads to ten times the open rate with content and five times the engagement with that content, over email. Chatbots aren't just for responding; they can be used for proactive content distribution as well.

As we continue to move into an increasingly technology-driven society, we must not let our old ideas of consumer behavior stand in our way. All demographics are finding value with chatbots in many different ways. Moving forward, all brands, regardless of their target market, should look to identify places where chatbots can be deployed to drive their businesses forward.

Source: M. Sweezey, "The value of chatbots for today's consumers," *Forbes*, 13 February 2018.

Summary

- This chapter provided an overview of Web 2.0. It discussed why Web 2.0 brings about strategic changes in Internet business models. It explained how advances in network infrastructure and software development led to an increased number of web users and a richer user experience. Furthermore, the chapter depicted the Web 2.0 service variety and showed how it enables better networking and sharing of information and content among peers.

- Social networking sites (SNS) allow their members to manage more contacts more efficiently than is possible offline; therefore, they increase personal contact reach. In addition, users have more information about their contacts or potential contacts due to visible virtual profiles; therefore, SNS increase personal information richness.
- Through the mass customization approach, manufacturers or service providers try to elicit customer preferences and then tailor a product or service to meet their client's preferences.
- Businesses that want to benefit from "viral growth" need to provide incentives for users to invite others to join the service. These incentives can be intrinsic when users know that inviting others to join the platform will ultimately enrich their own experience.
- Viral marketing is a tool that has a strong potential for building brand awareness. Therefore, finding a way (e.g., Gladwell's "tipping point") of controlling viral growth is essential for businesses.
- By giving members access to a large pool of other individuals, SNS lengthen the "long tail" of potential social contacts. They further use a variety of mechanisms to enrich users' communication, thereby fattening the tail by increasing the frequency of interactions. Driving demand down the tail can be achieved by shifting users' attention to content that normally is not as easy to find.
- Machine learning refers to computers that learn without explicit programming. It can be used to improve the reach and interaction with consumers.

11

? Review Questions

1. Review users' motivations for joining Internet-based social networks, and for each one of these motivations, provide an example of real-world social interactions.
2. Explain how Anderson's "long tail" concept can be applied to Internet-based social networks. What are the main similarities and differences between the application of this concept to SNS and to traditional networking?
3. Suggest at least two examples of people you know for each one of the categories proposed in the law of the few by Gladwell's "tipping point."
4. What is machine learning? What benefits can a business reap from it?
5. Assess the following statement: "Unlimited choice creates unlimited demand."
6. Chart the value chain of an Internet-based mass customization service. (To answer this question, you may want to refer to the value chain model shown in ▢ Fig. 11.8.)
7. Considering the evolution of CRM and the advent of Web 2.0, do you think new e-CRM capabilities can impact a company's competitiveness?
8. Can you think of products that do not have the potential of spreading virally through the Internet? For services that have such a potential, is it worth giving up control of the spread of the message about them?

9. Make a critical assessment of the following statement: "The application of Anderson's 'long tail' concept leads to an unlimited choice and creates an unlimited demand." Try to illustrate your answer with some actual examples.
10. Design a viral marketing project with your classmates.

References

Acker, O., et al. (2011). Social CRM: How companies can link into the social web of consumers. *Journal of Direct Data and Digital Marketing Practice, 13*, 3–10.

Anderson, C. (2006). *The long tail: How endless choice is creating unlimited demand.* London: Random House Business Books.

Constantinides, E., & Fountain, S. J. (2008a). Web 2.0: Conceptual foundations and marketing issues. *Journal of Direct, Data and Digital Marketing Practice, 9*(3), 232–233.

Constantinides, E., & Fountain, S. J. (2008b). Web 2.0: Conceptual foundations and marketing issues. *Journal of Direct, Data and Digital Marketing Practice, 9*(3), 234–237.

Evans, P., & Wurster, T. (1999). Richness and reach concept. In *Blown to bits* (pp. 23–38). Boston: Harvard Business School Press.

Gladwell, M. (2000). *The tipping point.* London: Abacus.

Granovetter, M. (1973). The strength of weak ties. *American Journal of Sociology, 6*, 1360–1380.

Jelassi, T., Enders, A., & Martínez-López, F. J. (2014a). *Strategies for e-business: Creating value through electronic and mobile commerce: Concepts and cases* (p. 242). Edinburgh: Pearson Education.

Jelassi, T., Enders, A., & Martínez-López, F. J. (2014b). *Strategies for e-business: Creating value through electronic and mobile commerce: Concepts and cases* (p. 246). Edinburgh: Pearson Education.

Kozinets, R., et al. (2008). The wisdom of consumer crowds: Collective innovation in the age of networked marketing. *Journal of Macromarketing, 28*(4), 339–354.

Lin, S., et al. (2010). Web 2.0 service adoption and entrepreneurial orientation'. *Service Business, 4*, 198.

Piller, F. (2006). *Mass-customization* (p. 175). Wiesbaden: Gabler.

Radar Networks & Nova Spivack (2007). Evolution of the Web. Available at: http://www.radarnetworks.com

Rodríguez, I., Martínez-López, F. J., & Luna, P. (2010). Going with the consumer towards the social web environment: A review of extant knowledge. *International Journal of Electronic Marketing and Retailing, 3*(4), 415–440.

Singh, T., & Cullinane, J. (2010). Social networks and marketing: potentials and pitfalls. *International Journal of Electronic Marketing ad Retailing, 3*(3), 211–214.

Wirtz, B., et al. (2010). Strategic development of business models: Implications of the web 2.0 for creating value on the internet. *Long Range Planning, 43*, 272–290.

Further Reading

Gladwell, M. 2001. *Tipping point.* Abacus, provides further vivid examples of how information can spread virally.

Ho, B. 'Machine learning for personalization and beyond: 6 ways marketers can benefit from ML', *Criteo*, 7 December 2017.

Meerman Scott, D., 2007. *The new rules of marketing and PR. How to use news releases, blogs, podcasting, viral marketing and online media to reach buyers directly.* Wiley, offers an exhaustive guide for businesses to learn to use Web 2.0 communication tools with target audiences.

More practical examples of the 'long tail' concept can be found in Anderson, C. 2006. *The long tail – how endless choice is creating unlimited demand.* Random House Business Books.

See Tseng, M. M., & Piller, F. T. (2005) *The customer-centric enterprise: Advances in mass-customization and personalization.* Springer, for an in-depth look at mass customisation.

See Weber, L. 2007. *Marketing to the social web. How digital customer communities build your business*. Wiley, for a detailed review of the impact of Web 2.0 on marketing activities.

Weblinks

http://mashable.com is a blog dedicated to social networking sites.

http://www.novaspivack.com/ provides interesting information on current and future issues related to information technologies, evolution of the Web, social web applications, and more.

https://www.oreilly.com/ is a widely recognised blog from the US media company O'Reilly Media who started the first conferences under the label Web 2.0.

11

Moving from Wired e-Commerce to Mobile e-Commerce and U-Commerce

Contents

© Springer Nature Switzerland AG 2020
T. Jelassi, F. J. Martínez-López, *Strategies for e-Business*, Classroom Companion: Business,
https://doi.org/10.1007/978-3-030-48950-2_12

Learning Outcomes

After completing the chapter, you should be able to:

- Define mobile e-commerce and outline the key components of the mobile value network
- Recognize mobile e-commerce applications and be able to categorize them
- Depict the advantages of mobile e-commerce over wired e-commerce
- Understand how wireless technologies affect the value chain and influence the industry's five forces
- Understand ubiquitous commerce and its related market strategies

Introduction

The first part of this chapter provides an overview of mobile e-commerce. It highlights (1) wireless technology providers, (2) mobile e-commerce applications and services, and (3) their most salient benefits compared with wired e-commerce.

The second part of the chapter discusses how wireless technologies influence Michael Porter's value chain and the industry's five forces. It also provides some illustrative examples drawn from different industries. The third and final part of this chapter presents ubiquitous commerce, which is the new frontier in the field going beyond wired and mobile e-commerce.

12.1 Mobility and Unwired e-Commerce

Mobile e-commerce, or m-commerce, is a subset of electronic commerce. While traditional e-commerce refers to transactions conducted via fixed or wired Internet terminals, m-commerce refers to e-commerce transactions via mobile devices or wireless terminals (Dholakia and Dholakia 2004). For example, in the earliest days of the Internet, it was accessed through a cable that was fixed to a wired location. Mobile access to the Internet now allows users to be time and location independent and, therefore, broadens traditional e-commerce characteristics. Furthermore, Internet-enabled mobile devices (watches, tablets, and phones) enable users not only to make voice and video calls and use messaging functions but also to make it possible to access databases, retrieve information, download content, and carry out transactions.

There is a consensus regarding the use of mobile devices to establish commerce-related communication processes with the support of mobile telecommunication networks; however, one main distinction concerns the purpose of such communication. In this context, a "restrictive" view of mobile e-commerce links its related communications with the development of monetary transactions (e.g., buying a concert ticket with a mobile device). A broader view extends m-commerce to all mobile services in a variety of sectors including information, communication, transaction, and entertainment.

Obviously, there is a need to distinguish the mobile e-commerce concept and its underlying technologies since the latter are dynamic and evolve over time. The former, mobile e-commerce, offers the following distinguishing features:[1]

- It implies communication, either unidirectional or interactive, between two or more persons or objects (e.g., devices).
- At least one of the parties involved in the communication has to be mobile, i.e., not based on any kind of wired connection.
- The communication process should be maintained in an uninterrupted manner from one place to another.
- At least one of the parties involved should look for an economic profit in the communication process, either in the short or long term.

12.1.1   Understanding the Value Network of Mobile e-Commerce

The mobile e-commerce value network (Müller-Veerse et al. 2001) comprises different players that interact and collaborate within the industry. These players include mobile technology providers such as mobile vendors for infrastructure and devices, wireless network operators, IT enablers, application and content providers, as well as portal providers. The m-commerce value network (see ☐ Fig. 12.1) outlines the multifaceted role of these players. Based on their business focus, the latter offer different kinds of mobile e-commerce services and can be assigned to the application, technology, or service area.

12

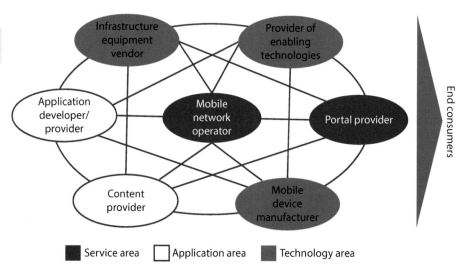

☐ **Fig. 12.1**   The mobile e-commerce value network outlines the key players. (Source: adapted from Müller-Veerse et al. 2001)

---

1   See Balasubramanian et al. (2002).

Mobile network operators (MNOs) are the industries' linchpin. Their close contact with customers positions them at the center of the network and gives them a dominant service role. Since MNOs carry out payment and billing activities, they enjoy a loyal and trustworthy relationship with their customers. Furthermore, since MNOs have access to client data (such as geographical location or Internet behavior), they enjoy a unique and privileged position within the network.

MNOs Differ in Their Service Offerings While offering a wireless network with an Internet gateway implies a low degree of involvement in the mobile value network, providing an additional mobile portal or further access to applications and services increases an operator's involvement. T-Mobile, for instance, not only offers customers voice calls but also promotes its mobile portal "T-Zones" through which it sells content ranging from ringtones and videos to games.

Mobile virtual network operators (MVNOs), such as Virgin Mobile, are a variation of traditional MNOs. They become part of the value network by buying bandwidth from traditional operators for resale to their own customers. MVNOs have their own market presence and a billing relationship with end users and, therefore, share similar characteristics with traditional MNOs. Furthermore, MVNOs sometimes bundle their services with other offerings, such as mobile music, in order to establish a deeper relationship and increase switching costs with their end customers.

Mobile device manufacturers play another crucial role within the industry. They not only determine the design and functionality of mobile devices (including phones, tablets, watches, and more) but also set the communication standards and take care of the pre-installation of browser, operating system, and other applications. Furthermore, device manufacturers have a close relationship with end consumers and therefore play a key role in influencing m-commerce developments.

The competition in the hand-held industry is dominated by companies including Apple, Samsung, and other hardware manufacturers including Huawei, Hewlett Packard, Lenovo, Xiaomi, HTC, and more. Product cycles have become shorter and profitability margins thinner. Mobile device manufacturers have seen their market share erode, thus having to extend their business by developing additional activities. Apple, for instance, creates mobile hardware, software, and services. Data-ready mobile phones, personal digital assistants (PDAs), watches, and similar wireless handsets are converging, thus increasing the functionality of the hand-held device and therefore affecting consumer electronic providers and other industries.

IT enablers provide operating systems, micro-browsers, databases, and other middleware technologies. These enabling technologies determine a user's mobile experience in terms of usability. Companies such as Microsoft, Google (Android), or Apple (iOS) generate revenues from licensing software, leasing, consulting, and/ or maintenance fees. YOC, a mobile marketing service provider from Berlin (Germany), covers activities ranging from the design of mobile marketing campaigns to the provision of content and applications and also acts as an enabler in the mobile marketing space. YOC can thus guarantee a fit between single activities and make users' mobile experience as seamless as possible.

Infrastructure equipment vendors provide the technical backbone of mobile communication networks comprising access points and broadcasting towers. The design and implementation of mobile networks is simpler and more cost-efficient than that of fixed-line networks. Developing countries rely heavily on wireless technology, especially in regions with poor fixed-line telecommunication infrastructure. Furthermore, since mobile networks can reach out to users with limited resources, they cover a broader consumer base than fixed mobile networks.

Portal providers provide the starting page for customer's and bundle their preferred services and applications. Horizontal portal providers cover a broad spectrum of topics, while vertical portals focus on a single subject area and provide in-depth information. Portal providers generate revenues through monthly subscription fees, traffic-based revenue-sharing arrangements with mobile telecom operators, commissions on transactions, advertising, and so forth (Sadeh 2002).

Application and content providers often cooperate with portal providers in order to gain access to customers and make their products (such as news, shopping, and games) available to their target audience. For example, Google Play and the Apple Store are two predominant stores offering a wide variety of apps.

Among the different parties involved in the mobile e-commerce value chain, it *is the end consumers* who represent the most important element, followed by mobile network operators (MNOs). The former represent the demand for mobile e-commerce content and services, while the latter ensure the connectivity and the direct contact with consumers. Other important parties involved in the mobile e-commerce value chain include mobile device manufacturers, application developers, software providers, system integrators, and more.

If the provision of an optimal value to consumers is wanted, critical success factors for mobile e-commerce providers include the following:[2]

Time-Critical Needs and Arrangements   One of the distinguishing features of mobile e-commerce, compared to traditional wired e-commerce, is extending the time and place where users can access the Web. This allows attending to users' use preferences anytime and anywhere and thus represents an opportunity to develop new value-added services.

Spontaneous Needs and Decisions   It is well-known that not all consumers' purchases come from a planned process; many purchases are the result of spontaneous decisions motivated by internal and/or external stimuli. Diverse questions such as, for example, downloading a song, looking up financial information, searching for a book or an electronic product, and more, can be associated with spontaneous needs of consumers that might be satisfactorily fulfilled by suitable mobile e-commerce-based services.

Entertainment Needs   Mobile e-commerce offers clear opportunities to combine mobility and entertainment. It is not unusual that entertainment needs arise at an

---

2   See Anckar and D'Incau (2002).

unexpected time, for example, free time between two consecutive activities. In these situations, without having the possibility of using a wired connection, people could rely on their mobile device to access mobile services and applications (e.g., music, newspaper, ticket reservations, and more). In fact, it could be argued that there is a relationship between these needs and the abovementioned spontaneous needs.

Efficient Needs   Nowadays, time is one of the most valuable assets, so individuals have an increasingly strong need to improve the efficiency of the time used to manage their daily activities. Mobile devices have been conceived to enhance time productivity while being mobile. They enable the management of a broad variety of tasks with unprecedented flexibility of time and space.

Mobility-Related Needs   These represent the main source of value of mobile e-commerce, because fulfilling these needs is at the core of the value proposition that is offered. Actually, this benefit is subjacent to the variety of needs mentioned above. Notwithstanding, there are specific situations where needs are more intrinsically related to the individual's mobility. Examples of location-based services include traffic coordination and management, location-aware advertising and general content delivery, integrated tourist services, safety-related services, and location-based games and entertainment (Jensen et al. 2001).

12.1.2   Segmenting Mobile e-Commerce Consumers and Business Services

Hand-held devices allow for a wide range of wireless applications and services to be deployed in either consumer or business markets. Depending on the context, these applications and services can help to improve lifestyle on a personal level or productivity on a business level. Basic uses of the mobile phone include the following voice, Internet, and messaging functions.

Voice   In addition to basic telephony functions, data-ready mobile phones allow for richer voice applications. Rich voice services use the data connection of a device to offer advanced call capabilities. Compared with traditional mobile voice calls, VoIP (Voice over Internet Protocol) calls are cheaper and can enrich a user's call experience through video support. In a business context, VoIP allows for substantial cost savings and enables a business to maintain voice, image, video, and text contact with its field staff, thus boosting productivity.

Internet   Connectivity to the Internet allows users to access e-mail accounts and has become a major driver of the "fixed-mobile convergence." Voice as well as Internet traffic has shifted from wired to mobile networks and will not only provide wireless Internet access to users in consumer markets but also offer Internet, intranet, and extranet access to business clients. In communication-intensive industries (such as finance, transportation, insurance, public safety, or healthcare), mobile access to desktop applications such as e-mail, contact lists, or spreadsheets is the norm.

Messaging   Mobile messaging services are dominated by SMS and MMS and are widely used for asynchronous conversation through text or multimedia messages. Since blogging has gained importance on the Internet, the interest in other people's lives and the wish to share one's own life are addressed by services like Facebook and Instagram. Twitter takes this phenomenon mobile and implements it through the microblogging concept. Twitter users define their friends online (through the twitter app) and provide their accounts in Twitter and/or their mobile phone number. Then users post a message, or *tweet*, to Twitter, which then becomes available in the Twitter feeds of all defined friends and becomes available on the user's Twitter profile page. This service is free, if accessed through the company's website, which is the typical access method especially as the worldwide penetration rate of smartphones increases. However, messages can also be sent as SMS but at a cost, which varies depending on the mobile phone service provider that is used.

Similar to the idea behind Twitter, mobile messaging can also be used for *notification-based solutions.* That way, real-time sports results or real-time information for decision-making can be delivered to users independent of time and location. Location-based services (LBS) include location-sensitive information in their service. In the business context, this can be of tremendous importance for emergency services. It has also implications for fleet management and the tracking of vehicles or remote mobile workforce management. In consumer markets, localized content such as weather, news, hotels, restaurants, traffic and travel information, and navigation prevails.

▪▪ m-Commerce Consumer Services

The following segmentation focuses on m-commerce consumer services. Consumer services can be classified into four major categories: (1) information, (2) communication, (3) transaction, and (4) entertainment services (see ◘ Fig. 12.2).

Mobile information comprises news, weather, or other information. Many news organizations have developed applications that make content available through mobile phones. Furthermore, users may receive weather and traffic warnings and other location-based information notifications.

Mobile communication includes services that allow users to communicate with each other or with remote systems. Mobile marketing, for instance, is still highly dominated by SMS and used as a means of prompting consumers to a point of sale or to some desired action. In push campaigns, marketing services are delivered directly to the user on the mobile device through a text message. In response-oriented mobile marketing campaigns or pull campaigns, it is the user who initiates the communication by sending in a promotional code that is, for example, found on a bottle or seen on TV.

Mobile entertainment refers to downloading ringtones, games, music, or videos and trivia through wireless technologies. Companies such as Tencent provide a variety of video games to mostly younger users, generating massive revenues. In Japan, mobile entertainment has even become a cultural phenomenon for the millions of commuters who daily spend a lot of time on trains.

Mobile transactions allow users to conduct various transactions over the mobile phone. Mobile e-banking applications give users access to their bank statements or account balance and allow them to pay bills or transfer funds. Users also receive

◘ **Fig. 12.2** m-Commerce consumer services and applications. (Source: adapted from Müller-Veerse et al. 2001)

alerts, for example, in case a payment is due or the account balance has fallen below a specified amount. There are also mobile e-shopping and mobile e-payment services such as M-PESA, which allow users to make ticket reservations, for instance, or take part in auctions (as in the case of eBay). NTT DoCoMo even developed specific mobile phones that let users store credit card information for mobile payments at convenience stores. Nowadays, the world's leading company in mobile payment transactions is Starbucks. Its former CEO Howard Schultz highlighted the importance of its mobile payment system in strengthening its competitive position and increasing its sales turnover. In 2017, mobile payments accounted for 30 percent of Starbuck transactions (Soper 2017). For more information on mobile payments and transactions, please see ▶ Chap. 13.

■■ **m-Commerce Business Services**
Business services can be broadly categorized into mobile supply chain management (M-SCM), mobile customer relationship management (M-CRM), and mobile workforce services and applications (see ◘ Fig. 12.3).

Mobile supply chain management services and applications aim at enhancing the performance of activities along the supply chain and facilitate collaboration with partners, because information sharing can be conducted in real time. Mobile inventory applications alert suppliers, for example, if the stock level of a product has fallen below a predetermined level (push approach) but also allow for remotely checking the availability of items in warehouses and reordering in case of unavailability (pull approach).

Mobile customer relationship management services and applications enhance interactions with customers before, during, or after sale by gathering data about

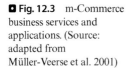

◘ **Fig. 12.3**   m-Commerce business services and applications. (Source: adapted from Müller-Veerse et al. 2001)

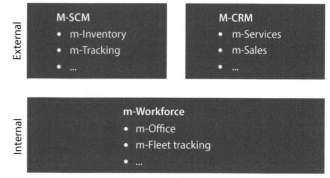

customer preferences, purchased products, and required maintenance. Access to this data enhances a sales agent's productivity and allows for an effective response to customer demands. Therefore, these services help to increase customer satisfaction and company's revenues.

Mobile workforce services and applications support field staff and other employees working on client sites. Hand-held devices give sales teams or managers on the move secure wireless access to corporate LANs and VPNs and to their offices or help track vehicles and dispatch them to new locations.

A classification of mobile e-commerce services and applications for consumer (B2C) and business (B2B) is presented in ◘ Table 12.1.

12.1.3   Comparison of Mobile e-Commerce and Wired e-Commerce

Business opportunities in mobile e-commerce and critical success factors for companies in this field greatly depend on the value proposition that is offered to customers, whether they are end-consumers or business clients. In this context, it is critical to have a good understanding of what can be referred to as the "mobile experience," that is, the relevance and significance of the mobile-e-commerce value provided to customers.

❯ Compared with wired e-commerce, mobile e-commerce has unique value-adding attributes. When formulating a new business strategy, managers need to be aware of these attributes and leverage them service-wise. These unique value-adding attributes are (1) ubiquity, (2) convenience, (3) localization, and (4) personalization. They are now discussed in more detail.

Ubiquity is the most decisive characteristic of mobile e-commerce applications. It means that users are able to use their device at any time and in any location whether to obtain information or perform a transaction. Ubiquity increases the immediacy of communication and is equally valued in consumer and business markets. This is the core attribute and essence of a new form of electronic commerce referred to as u-commerce, which will be covered in detail in ▶ Sect. 12.3.

◘ Table 12.1 Mobile e-commerce applications for consumers and businesses

Category of applications	Details	Illustrative examples
Mobile financial applications (B2C, B2B)	Applications allowing to manage and follow-up financial transactions through mobile devices	Banking, brokerage and payments for mobile users
Mobile advertising (B2C)	Applications turning the wireless infrastructure and devices into a powerful marketing medium	User-specific and location-sensitive advertisements
Mobile inventory managment (B2C, B2B)	Applications aiming at reducing the amount of inventory needed by managing in-house and inventory-on-the-move	Location tracking of goods, boxes, troops and people
Product locating and shopping (B2C, B2B)	Applications helping to find the location of products and services that are needed	Finding the location of a new/used car of a certain model, colour and features
Proactive service management (B2C, B2B)	Applications aiming at providing users with information on services they will need in the very-near-future	Transmission of information related to ageing (automobile) components to vendors
Wireless re-engineering (B2C, B2B)	Applications that focus on improving the quality of business services using mobile devices and wireless infrastructure	Instant claim-payments by insurance companies
Mobile auction or reverse auction (B2C, B2B)	Applications allowing users to buy or sell certain items using multicast support of wireless infrastructure	Airlines competing to buy a landing time slot during runway congestion
Mobile entertainment services and games (B2C)	Applications providing entertainment services to users on per-event or subscription basis	Video-on-demand, audio-on-demand and interactive games
Mobile office (B2C)	Applications providing the complete office environment to mobile users anywhere, anytime	Working from traffic jams, airports and conferences
Mobile distance education (B2C)	Applications extending distance/virtual education support for mobile users everywhere	Taking a class using streamed audio and video
Wireless data centre (B2C)	Applications supporting large amount of stored data to be made available to mobile users for making 'intelligent' decisions	Detailed iformation on one or more products being downloaded by vendors

Source: adapted from Varshney and Vetter (2002)

Convenience is high, since the functionality and usability of wireless devices have increased. Mobile content is inferior to other media in terms of screen size and downloading speed. However, it is superior to other media in terms of convenience and ease of use. Mobile e-commerce is comparable to a convenience store where customers buy daily but in small quantity, whereas wired e-commerce can be compared with a hypermarket where customers spend a lot of money but only occasionally (Steinbock 2005).

Localization of devices and their users is based on the portability of wireless devices and knowledge about a person's location. It enables location-based services that provide their users with location-specific information. This inherent feature to mobility considerably extends the contextualization possibilities of the value proposition. For instance, a store could detect a nearby digital device of a customer and then send commercial information to attract him/her to the store. However, to increase the relevance and impact of the information to send out, the store should also know the individual's interests and any past interactions with the store. This obviously depends on whether the individual at hand has previously introduced his/her main interests and likes in their mobile device(s), enabling connections with external communications that provide physical-sensitive commercial information. Recently, Facebook has launched a service called "Places," which reveals their users' current location. This enables retailers to access this information and then make personalized offers, which could be subsequently commented by users to their friends through this social network. In 2019, however, Facebook is receiving negative publicity for the aggregation and on selling of user data.

The degree of *personalization* in mobile e-commerce is higher than in wired e-commerce. When calling a mobile phone, users call the number of a person and not the number of a location as in the case of a fixed-line phone. Furthermore, as initially demonstrated by Apple's iPhone, and subsequently by other smartphone manufacturers such as Samsung, HTC, and Sony Ericsson, the mobile phone is increasingly integrating different multimedia functions and reflecting the user's lifestyle dimension. However, although it is more challenging to optimize content for the handset's small screen size than for the wired PC, recent technological advances in smartphones and tablets illustrate the move toward a fully-fledged digital convergence.

Mobility in general allows for more flexible and efficient communication; it also enables users to socialize with their peers and friends. Informative and/or entertaining content can be targeted more closely to the user's needs and made more personal by tracking the user's wireless transactions and by drawing implications from these. User-related information can be used to tailor specific products for consumers in ways that were not feasible with traditional e-commerce. However, there are also disadvantages, including (1) privacy and security and (2) device and network limitations, such as screen and keyboard size as well as connectivity and transmission speed.

Privacy and security are decisive prerequisites for all wireless transactions. Users are likely to insist on having privacy and security safeguards. They also need to be in control of their data, especially if it contains information about their geographical location.

Device and Network Limitations   Due to slow transfer rates and limited connectivity, a user's wireless Internet experience can be very restricted. When this is added to the small screen and tiny keyboard of the handset, users are still often reluctant to trial emerging wireless services. However, as mentioned above, current technological capabilities enable companies and organizations to overcome these limitations.

12.2 Strategy and Mobility

Although the wired Internet enables users to access information from any computer around the globe, it is tied to a physical location. Wireless technologies, however, make users independent of place and time. They may be used strategically in most industries, especially those that are information and communication intensive. Being able to incorporate wireless technologies into business operations could result in a first-mover advantage. What makes companies successful, however, is the translation of a first-mover advantage into a sustainable competitive edge. It is important not only to align IT with strategy but also to align mobility with strategy in order to make a company more efficient, attract new customers with a differentiated product or service, and ultimately outperform competitors. In the next sections, we shall:

1. Discuss how to achieve a competitive advantage through wireless technologies
2. Examine how these technologies affect a company's value chain
3. Analyze how they influence the five forces of the industry

12.2.1 Leveraging Wireless Technologies to Create a Competitive Advantage

Mobility benefits mainly those organizations that manage to integrate wireless technologies seamlessly into their business processes. By improving the linkages between their human resources and business processes, companies can substantially improve their overall performance. Wireless technologies strengthen these linkages by making information available where and when users need it.

As seen in ▶ Chap. 8, the creation of economic value depends on the gap between perceived use value and costs. Wireless technologies can increase use value and decrease costs and, therefore, increase a firm's operational effectiveness. Each (primary) activity of the value chain contributes to the aggregate use value as perceived by customers. A more effective mobile workforce, for instance, increases productivity and allows a company to decrease its overhead costs or increase the perceived use value. In the next section, the concept of the value chain will be analyzed in the context of mobility.

The goal of every firm is to outperform its competitors and eventually achieve above-average returns. Long-term strategic positioning means that a company is able to outperform competitors by offering customers a better price/performance ratio than competitors. While economic value depends on a customer's willingness to pay a price for a product that is higher than its production costs, strategic positioning depends on industry forces and the profitability of the average competitor within the industry. The five forces model presented in ▶ Sect. 12.2.3 shows how mobility can affect industries.

12.2.2 Impact of Wireless Technologies on a Company's Value Chain

Companies perform value-creating activities, which are interdependent with activities of suppliers or customers. Michael Porter's *value chain analysis* provides a framework for identifying all of these activities and analyzing how they affect a company's relative cost position and the value delivered to customers. Information technology is relevant to all the primary and support activities of the value chain, since every activity involves the creation, processing, and communication of information. For a detailed discussion of how the wired Internet impacts on a company's value chain, see ▶ Chap. 4.

Wireless technologies help to create new kinds of activities or enable streamlining of existing activities. They influence the design, production, marketing, sales, and support of products, services, and processes.

Support activities can be generically categorized into a firm's infrastructure, human resources management, technology development, and procurement.

The firm's infrastructure supports all the company's activities. Moving from physical (paper-based) activities to digital applications that can be remotely accessed through wireless devices allows a company to reduce its data collection time and operational costs while improving its responsiveness to customers and its overall service level. Salespeople in the field, for instance, can access through handheld devices corporate databases (such as phone directories), and marketers can receive customer feedback in real time or supervise a delivery status.

Mobile technologies can also affect management activities of the *Human Resources* Department, such as recruiting, training, developing, and rewarding staff members. Wireless access in the field to a company's knowledge base, for instance, enables employees to keep in touch with their colleagues (whether in the office or on the move) and also to foster their productivity.

Through wireless devices, a company's *technology development* can improve products, services and processes. It is important to note here that mobile business professionals often seek better on-the-move work tools and practices, while IT managers want to have reliable and secure IT systems and applications. In order to reconcile both dimensions, issues of interoperability, usability, security and privacy need to be addressed early enough in the technology development process.

The procurement of raw materials and other inputs can be improved through wireless technologies. For example, the use of radio-frequency identification (RFID) and Internet of Things (IoT) sensors enables better real-time tracking of goods and inventory items. RFID tags can be automatically read from remote locations and therefore do not need to be held near a reader (or a scanner) as is the case with barcode-based tags.

Wireless technologies can also affect a company's primary value chain activities such as inbound logistics, operations, marketing, and sales, as well as after-sales service.

Through wireless technologies, a company can foster its *inbound logistics* by receiving, storing, and disseminating inputs to products and services. For example, in the context of user-generated content whereby users are an active part of the value chain, mobile technologies can become a valuable input medium. The German tabloid newspaper Bild encourages readers to send in pictures of events or celebrities through MMS. Thus the reader is turned into a newspaper affiliate, encouraged to contribute content to the latest edition.

Operations   In industries where information is a crucial part of the product, wireless technologies can especially add to a customer's perceived use value. For example, phone directory services provide callers with phone numbers and address information. In addition to announcing over the phone the result of the customer query, some service providers offer callers the option of receiving an SMS containing the requested information, from which they may auto-dial the number. By doing so, they better support the caller (who may or may not have readily available writing materials) and improves its overall customer service.

Outbound logistics refer to wireless activities that are associated with collecting, storing, and distributing products or services to customers. Mobile music providers (such as Spotify) enable users to access content instantly while on the move. Also wireless portals (such as Google) deliver to consumers, through mobile applications, various types of information including news, weather, and more.

Marketing and Sales   Mobile marketing approaches enable companies to enhance brand or product awareness; lead consumers to the point of sale; generate dialogue with marketing contacts; increase sales; or support customer loyalty programs. Coca-Cola, for instance, used on-pack promotions in order to entice consumers at the point of sale to buy a Coke. Hand-held devices also allow companies to offer a high level of personalization and the possibility of treating each customer as a segment of one. Renault, during a Motor Show, provided visitors with an RFID-enabled card which allowed them to access Facebook not through a mobile phone or tablet but through pillars located near every car model on display. Once on Facebook, they could click the "like button" with the car model(s) they preferred. Similarly, the clothing company Diesel designed a mobile campaign using Quick Response (QR) codes related with denim attire in its stores. It allowed consumers to obtain price discounts if they scanned the QR code that took to a product page where a "like button" could be clicked, and a post would then appear on the Facebook wall of every person who did this. This campaign actively involved consumers and spread the message through their social network.

Service   As customers become increasingly mobile, businesses need to extend their reach to these customers by offering support services through wireless channels. By doing so, they can respond to customer needs faster than ever before. For example, airlines (such as Lufthansa) allow passengers to make or confirm a seat reservation through an SMS, thus helping customers to save time.

12.2.3 Influence of Wireless Technologies on the Industry's Five Forces

The position of a business within an industry determines its ability to create value for the marketplace. Industries with a high information intensity, a large mobile workforce, and activities can leverage wireless technologies in a significant way.

As stated in ▶ Chap. 3, the five forces model helps determine the attractiveness of an industry in general. In particular, the wired Internet influences each one of the industry's five forces, as do wireless technologies.

Industry Rivalry Since wireless technologies widen the physical marketplace by reducing the importance of geographical boundaries, it increases the number of competitors within an industry and, therefore, tends to lower the attractiveness of an industry. However, for wireless technologies and mobile applications, charges for international roaming continue to be very high and represent an important uptake factor for consumers.

Bargaining Power of Suppliers Companies that embrace wireless technologies can capitalize on a quite unique online channel to reach out to customers and, thus, to reduce the leverage that other suppliers may have in the market. However, these technologies also offer a direct channel for dis-intermediating traditional players in an industry. For instance, Sony BMG considered creating its own MVNO[3] in order to position itself in the growing mobile music market but refrained from doing so due to the high-cost structure and high risk of such a venture.

Bargaining Power of Buyers Wireless technologies can shift the bargaining power to end consumers; they can also complement existing channels and improve the bargaining power over traditional channels. For example, most newspapers are now accessible not only through computers, hand-held devices such as tablets, and smartphones. These devices allow readers to circumvent traditional newspaper stands and at the same time increase access to a greater number of newspapers.

Barriers to Entry On the one hand, wireless technologies can increase barriers to entry by helping companies to streamline some of their business processes and thus contribute to efficient operations. On the other hand, since mobile applications are difficult to keep proprietary, barriers to entry could therefore be rather low, and consolidation in the industry favors incumbents. For example, mobile advertising technology business YOC is facing increasing competition from multimedia agencies that are trying to transfer their competence in digital marketing to mobile marketing. However, the technical complexity involved in creating and managing mobile marketing campaigns favors specialized companies (such as YOC) over multimedia agencies. Furthermore, technical competence in wireless technologies and mobile applications is viewed as a key factor for the sustainability of specialized companies such as YOC.

---

3   Mobile virtual network operator

Threat of Substitutes Companies should view wireless technologies as an enabler for creating complementary opportunities and not just a threat of substitute products or services. Mobile phones and wireless communication networks are substitutes for fixed-line phones and wired networks and, therefore, are becoming a threat to some industries. For instance, O2, the UK-based mobile communication network, is offering customers a "home zone" option, which allows subscribers to make local calls from their handset for cheaper rates.

Businesses should aim to overcome or mitigate these forces to ensure the success of their mobile solutions. For more details, see the article: "Porter's five forces for enterprise mobile solutions."

Porter's Five Forces for Enterprise Mobile Solutions

The Lean Enterprise approach to mobile solutions can take competitive strategy to the next level. At the core of any firm, however large, a very small number of key processes are the "heart" of the value created. Knowing and nurturing these core processes drive the competitive advantage of the firm—the output may be similar, but the throughput must become unique in the industry and difficult for competitors to copy. To effectively compete in today's economy, the core value creation processes must be proprietary and continuously improved. Applying Lean Enterprise Kaizen—continuous improvement—through mobile solutions will raise barriers to entry, increase operational effectiveness, and shift bargaining power in your favor. Pressure from each of the five forces can be reduced.

Minimizing the Threat of New Entrants Investment in a mobile-first approach to Lean Enterprise Kaizen will not only raise barriers to entry against new competitors, it will also create learning curve disadvantages against existing rivals that are no longer as efficient or effective. [...]

- Economies of Scale – As your mobile portfolio begins standardizing work, level-loading process blocks, and driving just-in-time operations, the cost of operations will drive down. The goal will be to reach minimum viable production—doing more of the high-margin activities that differentiate your organization while standardizing the work, focusing the worker, and reducing takt time.
- Technology Protection – The core processes at the heart of your competitive strategy will only provide competitive advantage so long as they remain proprietary, consistent, and scalable. Any business has non-core processes that will benefit from off-the-shelf solutions (i.e., don't reinvent payroll, several providers specialize in that). By identifying a key process that can be transformed, protected, and optimized, higher revenue and margins, better leadership proprioception, and instant data access will disrupt the industry in your favor.
- Learning Curve Disadvantage – Although adoption rates for mobile devices has never been higher and companies everywhere are investing heavily in mobile, whether responsive or optimized web, native apps, or hybrid, very few companies are focusing on process transformation and even fewer on proprietary enterprise solutions. This gives a multiplicative affect to the competitive advantage driven

by an enterprise app portfolio: competitors will need to learn what you do differently and how you built an enterprise app portfolio and adopt a prioritization of disruption and transformation just to keep up.

Minimizing the Threat of Substitution   Threat of substitution is minimized through differentiation and quality assurance. To the extent a product or service is perceived as unique and consistently valuable, the price elasticity of demand can be manipulated in your favor. Mobile apps can facilitate the role of your core processes to this end:

- Differentiation – Streamlining processes that impact consumers will set you apart as an early adopter. Maintain direct communication; make data instantaneous. The consumer is becoming more sensitive to time-to-gratification. Mobile solutions can remove every time a consumer-facing employee turns their back, puts a user on hold, or walks to a back office. This turns sales reps into consultants, fully empowered to get the right product in the consumer's hands with minimal time, confusion, or hassle.

- Quality Assurance – For both internal operations and consumer interaction, mobile solutions establish an intuitive guided workflow that standardizes the work to be done, focusing interaction on small batches of the overarching process. Through business intelligence analytics driven by the application itself, key insights into bottlenecks are simple to find. Furthermore, when kaizen and "standard work" are facilitated by the tools built to make the employee's work faster and more enjoyable (rather than a process document and managerial oversight), updates to the core process are implemented as part of updates to the app portfolio. This is more than MDM version control; it is version control for process transformation.

Minimizing the Threat of Supplier Power   The threat of supplier power is high when there is resource or information asymmetry. Real-time data, and becoming a firm that demands it, shifts this balance. You will have the freedom to determine whether you "put all the cards on the table" or maintain an information asymmetry of your own. Knowing yourself and your suppliers with real-time data as it impacts your core processes will keep supplier power over resource prices at bay.

Minimizing the Threat of Buyer Power   Unless you have exclusive access to a resource or protected rights to intellectual property, the only way to reduce the threat of buyer power is to diversify your revenue stream across a larger portfolio of consumers, whether product or service, B2B or B2C. If your current buyer portfolio is skewed to a small number of large purchasers, streamlining your core processes, standardizing the work, and maximizing (operationally efficient) differentiation will provide a repeatable, scalable business model. If you're contractually obligated not to serve additional buyers, process improvement efforts should focus on heijunka (level loading) and delayed differentiation. The ability to maintain operational efficiency despite the ebb and flow of suppliers and buyers will insulate against the threat they pose.

12.3 · Ubiquity and U-Commerce: Strategy for the Ultimate...

361

12

Minimizing the Threat of Competitive Rivalry Direct competition through pricing wars kills margins industry-wide. To any extent "coopetition" can occur, margins can remain healthier for everyone. Each player positions themselves in the industry such that they compete for a specific market—Player A competes for the price-sensitive, Player B for the luxury experience, and Player C for a reputation for the highest quality. Across a large geographic region, these three strategic positions can be focused territorially. Every mobile app in your portfolio is a tool with a specific purpose. Every tool has one number that defines it: gross revenue, conversion, items per ticket, and EBITDA. Mobile app solutions need to maintain laser focus on the strategic position you intend to maintain and the one number that indicates if your solution is succeeding:

- Competing on Price – Whatever your industry sells, part of the market skews more price-sensitive. If your position in your strategic landscape is focused on low costs, your focus for mobile enterprise solutions should focus increasing operational effectiveness. The goal is to maintain current price and revenue increasing gross margin. This is especially true if your industry is already in a state of no-growth, zero-sum competition.

- Competing on Quality – Every product or service has quality as a perception of value created. For a car, this may mean low maintenance or high safety ratings. Competing on quality is one form of differentiation, and pricing should be higher than price-based competitors. Mobile solutions for these enterprises should focus on real-time analytics, providing transparency to management and the market into actual quality scoring. This "dashboard" is really a marketing tool, whether it is aimed at your executives, investors, or consumers. The other side of these solutions should be process analysis and notification, making any part of the workflow capable of automatically alerting someone that quality is at risk. For more on the fundamental principles of "autonomation," the Toyota Production System is the best introduction.

- Competing on Luxury – Every industry has conspicuous consumption. For products, these are the premium buyers and early adopters. For services, this is the "concierge treatment." Typically, you're combining both tactics when competing on luxury—creating the most pampered experience for the luxury consumer. Mobile solutions in this enterprise space should focus on enabling maximum attention to the consumer and assist in consistency of the consultative nature of the employee workflow.

Adapted from: Keener Strategy (2015)

12.3 Ubiquity and U-Commerce: Strategy for the Ultimate Evolution of Commerce

U-commerce is commerce which is based on today's ubiquitous communication networks. The vowel "u" can be related to terms such as "über," "ubiquitous," "universal," and "ultimate." Each one of these terms represents a particular nuance of the u-commerce phenomenon. This section discusses the evolution from the wired e-commerce to u-commerce and the main distinguishing features of the latter. It also presents a typology of commerce within the u-commerce framework, along with related new forms of marketing.

12.3.1 What Is U-Commerce?

One of the first and widely accepted definitions of u-commerce[4] is "the use of ubiquitous networks to support personalised and uninterrupted communications and transactions between a firm and its various stakeholders to provide a level of value above and beyond traditional commerce."

More specifically, u-commerce goes beyond traditional e-commerce as it integrates unwired electronic communication channels, TV, VoIP, and other technologies to identify and interact with users.[5] It represents a new step in the evolution of markets to which the wired and mobile e-commerce have contributed. However, in view of its unique features, u-commerce could be considered as a definite evolution of commerce. The application of IT advances to commerce has led to the increasing blurring of the physical market constraints. The implicit "space-time" paradigm, on which transactional marketing is based, has now evolved toward the "virtual-now" of the e-commerce era.[6] We are seeing a real materialization of u-commerce, within a ubiquitous space (or u-space) that enables the integration of physical and electronic markets. For example, Amazon Dash Buttons provide ubiquitous commerce. Consumers just press a small button fixed to a product somewhere in their homes, for instance, and Amazon will automatically order, pay, and deliver its replenishment. For more information on Amazon's strategic vision on u-commerce, please see the article: "The dash button was just the beginning: expanding commerce everywhere."

◻ **Table 12.2** The evolution of markets: from traditional to ubiquitous markets

Market	Definition	Theme	Market-driving technologies
Marketplace	Traditional physical marketplace	Exchange of goods and services via face-to-face human interaction, where value is extracted from a physical location	Constructions and mechanical devices: vehicles, trains, airplanes, ships, etc.
Marketspace	Informational marketplace	Exchange of goods and services via computer interaction, where value is extracted from information	Computers
U-space	Transcension and integration of market place and marketspace	Physical and informational are globally integrated to provide value through amplification, attenuation, context and transcension; value is extracted from networks	Ubiquitous networks

Source: adapted from Watson et al. (2004)

4　See Watson et al. (2002).
5　See Galanxhi-Janaqi and Fui-Hoon Ha (2004).
6　See Berthon et al. (2000).

To conclude this section, a synthetic view on the evolution of markets is presented (see ◘ Table 12.2). It is organized along three market types: (1) traditional (physical) market or marketplace; (2) electronic market or market space; and (3) ubiquitous market or u-space.

The Dash Button Was Just the Beginning: Expanding Commerce Everywhere
Brands and retailers are changing the way they engage with consumers who today have access to more choices than ever before. Increasing investments in "customer experience" enhancements, often incorporating technology, highlight the necessity of adapting old business practices to the speed and reality of omni-channel commerce. As brands and retailers consider the role of the Internet of Things (IoT) in their operations and customer experience, they are quickly realizing the potential of simple IoT nodes or "touch points" to facilitate and encourage ubiquitous and immediate omni-channel commerce—the ability to quickly and easily initiate a targeted purchase just about anywhere and at any time.

As retail IoT buzz began to grow in 2015, e-commerce giant Amazon launched the Dash Button—a small battery-powered, Wi-Fi-connected device that promised to streamline ordering of a specific product from a specific brand with the simple push of a button. While some initially saw it as an April Fool's joke, the value became clear as initial curiosity led to satisfied users and significant sales for brands.

In practice, an Amazon user can purchase a $5 Dash Button featuring the Tide logo, for example, pair it to their home network, configure it to reorder Tide laundry detergent via Amazon, and place the button near their clothes washer. When the user needs more Tide, they push the button and Amazon completes the order, shipping Tide to the user without any additional hassle. Many users were thrilled with the consumer experience, as evidenced by the reported acceleration of Dash-initiated transactions to four orders per minute by early 2017—quadruple the previous year's rate, according to TechCrunch. But this is only the start of retail's journey toward ubiquitous omni-channel commerce. While Amazon's Dash program has validated the value of simplicity in the omni-channel consumer journey, it's only an initial, limited step toward solutions that provide an always-available, consumer-optimized communication channel between a brand and an individual consumer.

The First Step: Changing User Behavior
To better serve customers and accelerate sales, brands and retailers are focused on maximizing convenience and minimizing friction throughout the consumer journey. As connectivity becomes more universal and consumer expectations of retail extend beyond physical shops and e-commerce websites, it's reasonable for a consumer to expect that they can buy most products whenever and wherever it's convenient. As a tool to get users to think differently about commerce, the Dash Button has been a successful first step. We now know that shoppers can and will rely on the IoT to simplify their shopping experience, and this means that brands and retailers can invest in technology that creates a direct communication channel and commercial link to consumers.

This "commerce anywhere" approach benefits both consumers and brands, as consumer convenience leads to brand loyalty and a greater likelihood to repurchase. There's room to grow beyond the Dash Button, which payment industry analyst Richard Crone calls "placeholder interim technology." Meaning the Dash Button is a step toward figuring out a more permanent, actionable solution. As it exists today, users face the burden of setup, as well as an upfront fee before a Dash Button can be successfully activated and made functional. On the surface, it appears simple enough, but the concept of a simple one-touch trigger hides a substantial amount of upfront friction, with a setup process that's actually closer to 15 steps.

First, a shopper has to make a conscious choice to order the button in advance of when they might need it. After paying for and receiving the button, the user then needs to install an associated app on their smartphone, which must be connected to the device via Bluetooth and Wi-Fi. And because each Dash Button aligns with one specific product and brand, the consumer has to repeat this process for each device they want to set up. Pushing a physical button also presents its own limitations and issues. As anyone with small children knows, buttons can be irresistible and don't differentiate between users, which could easily lead to unwanted deliveries or the hassle of having to quickly cancel unintended or redundant orders. If the consumer runs out of a particular product but is not near the appropriate Dash Button, the device essentially becomes useless in their moment of need.

In this sense, the idea of commerce everywhere only works if the device is where the customer is, at the precise moment they want to buy. And if you consider the range of products a consumer might want to reorder in this fashion—e.g., cosmetics, toothpaste, laundry detergent, batteries, vitamins, baby diapers, water filters, and light bulbs—it's not unrealistic to think an individual may end up having to manage a collection of several dozen Dash Buttons. That's not an ideal experience and adds yet another layer of complexity most consumers would rather not deal with.

Going Integrated: A Streamlined Solution for Smart Appliances

With higher-end electronic devices constantly getting smarter, the Dash Button has recently begun to appear in home appliances via Amazon's software development kit (SDK) for third parties. Instead of a separate physical button that reorders a commonly used consumable product (from refrigerator filters to dishwasher detergent), the functionality can now be built into smart appliances that are already connected to a smart home network. While the convenience is undeniable, market reach may be limited for some time. Analysts at IHS Technology estimate that fewer than a third of appliances sold in 2020 (31 percent, as compared to 0.2 percent in 2014) will have built-in connectivity, which means that a substantial opportunity exists to add simple "commerce everywhere" capabilities to consumable products and packages themselves.

In addition, "virtual" Dash Buttons can now be placed on websites to enable one-click Amazon ordering from within a brand's own website. While this increases a brand's dependency on a single retail channel, this approach may make sense to

12.3 · Ubiquity and U-Commerce: Strategy for the Ultimate...

365

12

small brands that rely on the e-commerce giant for turnkey fulfillment services. However, this approach acts purely as a digital extension of the Dash concept and does not streamline the customer experience in the real world. These extensions to the "commerce everywhere" concept gradually incorporate new use cases that build channel loyalty to Amazon. As we have previously discussed, adhering so closely to a single sales channel has the effect of creating an intermediary between brands and consumers.

For brands who want to enable the convenience of purchasing anywhere and anytime but need more flexibility in the user experience and distribution channel, solutions are emerging to connect brands with consumers in ways that can leverage one or more preferred distribution partners, depending on the brand's requirements.

So What's Next in "Commerce Everywhere?"

Innovators are introducing consumer-facing solutions that reach a wider range of shoppers, support more diverse products, and eliminate setup friction while preserving the simplicity of placing an order. A recent example of this next wave of commerce-enabled connected objects is a series of NFC-enabled refrigerator magnets [...] launched by liquor company Campari America in support of six popular brands, including Wild Turkey Bourbon, Espolòn Tequila, and SKYY Vodka. When simply tapped with a smartphone, each magnet launches a streamlined e-commerce experience powered by the Drizly delivery platform, allowing consumers to instantly order the product for same-day delivery from a local, in-stock retailer. Hello, Dash Button 2.0! Always available reordering with no Wi-Fi pairing, no initial setup, and no batteries to replace.

The smartphone also adds to the user experience beyond what a simple button can deliver: With a single tap, users can adjust order quantity, try a different vodka flavor, apply a discount offer, or receive a personalized recommendation that increases order size and satisfaction. While maintaining a streamlined ease of use, the smartphone interface to the physical touch point addresses several consumer concerns uncovered in a survey by retail solutions provider Field Agent: setup issues, blind ordering, limited products/brands, and accidental/duplicate orders. By allowing for superior consumer choice and a better experience, brands build customer loyalty, strengthen a direct communication channel, and increase revenues.

Speculating on what could come next, journalist Jared Newman imagined "buttons [built] into the product packaging itself. Each button would work once and would be discarded along with the package." When billions of everyday items can be made interactive with easy-to-use, highly scalable, battery-free technology, brands and retailers can engage with consumers in meaningful new ways. While a single smartphone tap on a product or package could simply trigger the next order with the security of biometric authentication that controls access to our personal device, that same tap could also present timely, contextual, item-specific information to increase consumer satisfaction and loyalty. This experience leverages the flexibility of the cloud: from updated usage tips and loyalty integration to streamlined access to warranty registration, location-aware support, and personalized upsell/cross-sell opportunities.

> The journey to connected consumer engagement will involve multiple solutions, and these approaches will improve in their simplicity, scale, and effectiveness. Amazon's Dash program validated the importance of simplicity in the modern consumer journey and opens the door to approaches that can accelerate the push toward platforms that can deliver "commerce everywhere." Think of the Amazon Dash Button like the Wright Flyer: It's the bold first flight into new frontiers, and the next generation—which has already begun to arrive—is even more comfortable, more cost-effective, and scalable to the billions.
>
> Adapted from: Sutija (2018)

12.3.2   Main Features of U-Commerce

U-commerce is considered as a major new paradigm for the development of electronic transactions, transcending the Internet era by providing ubiquity, universality, personalization, and unison. These are the four main features of u-commerce that are frequently cited:[7] They are now defined.

Ubiquity   This characteristic was previously introduced for m-commerce in ▶ Sect. 12.1.3. In a generic sense, ubiquity refers to all that can be everywhere at the same time. In the context of markets, u-commerce implies the possibility of undertaking transactions everywhere, at any time, and, most importantly, without human intervention in the process (e.g., exchanges that can be automatically processed). As previously mentioned, it is obvious that the Internet and mobile devices enable reach beyond the constraints of the spatial dimension, which has traditionally limited the development of commercial exchanges and transactions. IT and communication technologies continue to evolve from mobility that is linked to devices to another state whereby mobility will become an intrinsic characteristic of the context where individuals, users and consumers will be. Therefore, through u-commerce, there will be a subjacent complex network of interconnected electronic objects helping individuals to go about their daily tasks almost effortlessly. Individuals will become accustomed to moving in this context that, even though they will be surrounded by electronic objects and devices, these omnipresent communication networks will be invisible for them. Their three distinguishing characteristics are now described.

- *Universality.* Although the mobility enabled by electronic communication devices has contributed to the emergence of ubiquitous commerce, compatibility problems among communication standards present challenges for u-commerce. However, it is expected that true convergence of communication standards through universal protocols will allow electronic devices to connect to ubiquitous networks, thus making the universality and ubiquity of e-commerce become a reality for users regardless of their location and context.

---

7   Some of these ideas have been extracted from Watson et al. (2002).

— *Uniqueness.* Mass personalization has been an important feature of some e-commerce value propositions such as that of ▶ Dell.com (for customized PCs) or ▶ Levis.com (for personalized jeans). It allowed the adaptation of a supplier's offer to each shopper's preferences, thus treating each customer as a segment of one. Although mass-customization can be implemented in a variety of ways and to different degrees, u-commerce allows it to reach its fullest meaning. Indeed, through it, exchanges can be unique, taking into account that all contextual factors at hand surrounding a particular consumption experience could be known and addressed. Contextual factors may include:
   - The time of the interaction
   - User's location
   - His/her personal preferences (whether they were explicitly stated or automatically derived from past experiences)
   - His/her possible role (e.g., as a worker, a tourist, a father, and more)
   - And more
— *Unison.* This feature refers to the integration of a person's electronic devices, be it a PC, laptop, tablet, or mobile phone. All these devices will be interconnected and coordinated in real time, so any action realized by the user through any one of his/her devices is automatically updated on the other devices, thus enabling the user's devices to work in unison. This synchronization among electronic devices could be extended to include digital household products and appliances (e.g., a refrigerator), thus achieving the total unison of a person's electronic devices.

12.3.3 From Wired e-Commerce to U-Commerce: The Definite Evolution

U-commerce is thought of as the last and definite stage in IT-based commerce through the integration of all the types of commerce. The latter have served as intermediate steps to this integration and have thus individually contributed to the advent of u-commerce.

12.3.4 Types of U-Commerce and New Forms of Marketing

New forms of marketing approaches and strategies have been suggested in the literature for the u-space.[8] As shown in ◘ Fig. 12.4, the u-space is structured along two dimensions: on the horizontal axis, the time and space of the interaction can be either specified or ubiquitous, and on the vertical axis, the customer's degree of consciousness can range from unconscious to ultra-conscious.

---

8   Contents of this section are an adaptation of the original framework proposed by Watson et al. (2002).

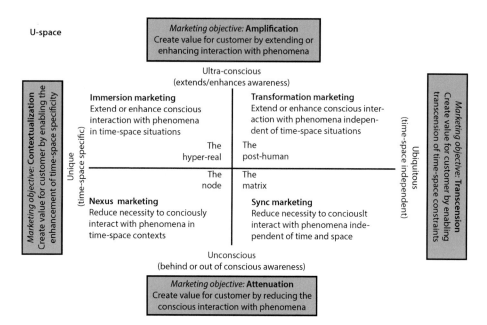

● **Fig. 12.4** U-space: types of commerce and marketing forms associated. (Source: adapted from Watson et al. 2004)

Each one of the four quadrants in ● Fig. 12.4 refers to a particular form or orientation of marketing in the u-space. Thus, in scenarios where time and space are specified, a *contextual marketing* is applied. In a contrasting scenario, businesses need to implement marketing programs that transcend users' temporal and spatial restrictions. This approach is known as *transcension marketing*. Regarding the consciousness dimension, if customers are ultra-conscious, then *amplification marketing* is recommended in order to improve the conscious interaction with objects related to the consumption experience. On the contrary, in the unconscious scenario, *attenuation marketing* is recommended in order to create value by reducing customer's conscious need of interaction with the consumption phenomenon.

The abovementioned u-space dimensions along with their corresponding marketing approaches are used to define four types of ubiquitous commerce: the hyperreal; the post-human; the matrix; and the node. As it can be observed in ● Fig. 12.4, each quadrant represents an area that is a combination of the two u-space dimensions. Consequently, it would not make sense to apply to every dimension one of the marketing approaches related to the four scenarios described above, because these are specific to different situations in the u-space. However, the abovementioned four types of commerce correspond to mixed areas, whereby the applied marketing approach "hybridizes" the four basic forms of commerce. Hence, the four types of mixed marketing forms in the u-space are immersion marketing, transformation marketing, sync marketing, and nexus marketing. We will now present briefly each type of commerce in the u-space with its associated marketing form.

The Hyperreal   This type of commerce is identified through consumption experiences characterized by ultra-consciousness within unique locations. Exchanges between companies and customers have specific time and space dimensions, though technology is used to enhance customer's conscious sensation in such a manner that a normal experience becomes rather unique. For instance, a Formula 1 fan might pay to watch a Grand Prix seated in a physical cockpit with a video feed (through an onboard camera) of his/her favorite driver's experience during the race.

The Post-human   This type of commerce is characterized by an improvement of the consumer's consciousness of a certain phenomenon in a ubiquitous manner (i.e., with no time-space restrictions, wherever the place, whenever the moment). It is in this context that *transformation marketing* takes a leading role. For example, today's virtual learning environments have transformed the way knowledge is transferred and developed, especially when compared with traditional, location-based learning. Through e-learning, the original time and space constraints disappear, and users can access academic services wherever and whenever they need them. Furthermore, as new learning tools are introduced, users' consciousness of their e-learning experience is enhanced.

The Matrix   Here too, time and space restrictions are relaxed; however, customer exchanges usually take place in a conscious way. The idea is that communication infrastructures enable the automatic and de-contextualized execution of customer tasks. This execution is not conditioned by a specific time or place and is not triggered by an explicit customer's action. Therefore, actions here do not result from the conscious will of the customer but from the automatic responses of some IT applications. This quadrant of the u-space uses *sync marketing*, which consists of automatically updating and integrating processes across time and space.

The Nexus   In this type of commerce, operations are also automatically and unconsciously triggered (as in the above matrix case), but these operations are related to a specific time-space context. For example, automatic processes start when customers are in a specific context. It is here where *nexus marketing* takes place, with processes designed to reduce customers' need to consciously interact with a phenomenon in a particular context. For instance, let us think of the following scenario: a person enters a hypermarket; his mobile device detects his location and subsequently accesses his integrated database to check his possible product needs. The latter are defined based on automatic database updates through data feeds received from his refrigerator, kitchen cupboard, laundry, and bathroom. Next, the customer receives a notification, through his/her mobile device, suggesting certain products he/she may need to purchase. All the steps of the above process are automatically performed, without any consumer intervention.

Summary

This chapter started out by giving a definition of mobile e-commerce and depicting the players of the mobile value network. These include mobile equipment vendors for wireless infrastructure and hand-held devices, mobile network operators, IT enablers, application and content providers, as well as portal providers.

By segmenting mobile e-commerce consumer and business services, this chapter illustrated the many uses of wireless applications. While consumer services can be categorized into information, communication, transaction, and entertainment services, business services can be categorized into mobile supply chain management, mobile customer relationship management, and mobile workforce services. A detailed classification of mobile commerce services and applications, both for corporate and individual consumers, was also presented.

Next, this chapter explained the main advantages of mobile e-commerce over wired e-commerce. Ubiquity, convenience, localization, and personalization represent some of the key capabilities of wireless technologies that can be leveraged for value creation.

While the value chain framework exemplified how wireless technologies impact on the primary and support activities of the firm, the five forces framework illustrated how these technologies can affect the strategic positioning of a firm within its industry.

Finally, a brief presentation of the ubiquitous commerce framework, which is considered to be the next stage in e-commerce evolution, highlights the new strategies and applications in the field.

❓ Review Questions

1. Outline the value network of mobile e-commerce and briefly explain its players.
2. Which categories can be used to segment mobile e-commerce applications?
3. What are the advantages of mobile e-commerce over wired e-commerce?
4. Pick two support and two primary activities of the value chain and describe how wireless technologies can affect them.
5. Explain to what extent wireless technologies increase or decrease an industry's rivalry.
6. Illustrate how a firm should strategize its mobile business to overcome the obstacles caused by 'five forces'.
7. Describe the u-commerce framework and its related market approaches.
8. Critically assess to what extent mobile network operators play a key role in mobile e-commerce.
9. Illustrate the advantages of mobile e-commerce through a real-world example.
10. Provide an example of a company that uses wireless technologies for customer relationship management and discuss how it adds value.
11. Pick an industry of your choice and show how wireless technologies affect its incumbents.
12. Reflect on how companies are currently managing the challenges of mobile e-commerce.
13. U-commerce is a strategic trend. Brainstorm a profitable business idea and plan related to u-commerce and defend its suitability before your classmates.

References

Anckar, B., & D'Incau, D. (2002). Value creation in mobile commerce: findings from a consumer survey. *Journal of Information Technology Theory and Application, 4*(1), 43–64.

Balasubramanian, S., Peterson, R. A., & Jarvenpaa, S. L. (2002). Exploring the implications of m-commerce for markets and marketing. *Journal of the Academy of Marketing Science, 30*(4), 348–361.

Berthon, L., et al. (2000). Postmodernism and the Web: Metha themes and discourse. *Technological Forecasting and Social Change, 65*(3), 265–279.

Dholakia, R., & Dholakia, N. (2004). Mobility and markets: Emerging outlines of m-commerce. *Journal of Business Research, 57*, 1391–1396.

Galanxhi-Janaqi, H., & Fui-Hoon Ha, F. (2004). U-commerce: Emerging trends and research issues. *Industrial Management + Data Systems, 104*(8/9), 744–755.

Jensen, C. S., et al. (2001). Location-based services – A database perspective. In *Proceedings of the 8th Scandinavian Research Conference on Geographical Information Science (ScanGIS 2001)* (pp. 59–68). As.

Müller-Veerse, F., et al. (2001). UMTS report – An investment perspective. *Durlacher Research*, 23.

Sadeh, N. (2002). *M-Commerce: technologies, services and business models* (p. 52). Wiley.

Soper, T. (2017, July 27). Mobile payments now account for 30% of Starbucks transactions as company posts $5.7B in revenue. *Geekwire*.

Steinbock, D. (2005). *The mobile revolution: The making of mobile services worldwide*. Kogan Page.

Sutija, D. (2018, February 16). The dash button was just the beginning: Expanding commerce everywhere. *Martechtoday.com*.

Varshney, U., & Vetter, R. (2002). Mobile commerce: Framework, applications and networking support. *Mobile Networks and Applications, 7*, 185–198.

Watson, R. T., et al. (2004). Marketing in the age of the network: From marketplace to u-space. *Business Horizons, 47*(6), 37.

Further Reading

For a detailed presentation of the u-commerce framework, see Watson, R. T., Pitt, L. F., Berthon, P., & Zinkhan, G. M. (2002). U-commerce: Expanding the universe of marketing. *Journal of the Academy of Marketing Science, 30*(4), 333–347.

For an in-depth portrayal of mobile services, see Steinbock, D. (2005). *The mobile revolution: The making of mobile services worldwide*. Kogan Page.

For more information on the categorisation of mobile content, also see Müller-Veerse, F., et al. (2001). UMTS report – An investment perspective. *Durlacher Research*.

Keener Strategy. Porter's five forces for enterprise mobile solutions. *Keenerstrategy.com*, 24 July 2015.

Useful Third-Party Weblinks

www.ecommercetimes.com is an online magazine, which also provides in-depth coverage of mobile commerce topics. n.d.

www.mmaglobal.com is the website of the Mobile Marketing Association, which strives to stimulate the growth of mobile marketing and its associated technologies. n.d.

Strategies for Mobile Commerce

Contents

© Springer Nature Switzerland AG 2020
T. Jelassi, F. J. Martínez-López, *Strategies for e-Business*, Classroom Companion: Business,
https://doi.org/10.1007/978-3-030-48950-2_13

> **Learning Outcomes**
> After completing this chapter, you should be able to:
> - Understand the definition and elements of a mobile commerce strategy
> - Describe factors influencing mobile commerce adoption
> - Describe the value of mobile commerce for businesses and consumers
> - Understand the strategic aspects of mobile payment
> - Describe the variety of mobile commerce apps and tools
> - Realize key challenges that mobile commerce are facing

■ Introduction

Mobile dominates the digital world. With the widespread and increasing number of smartphones, mobile commerce should be the first priority of e-businesses. In 2016, smartphones surpassed computers as the top e-commerce traffic source.[1] According to Comscore, in 2017 the mobile share of total digital minutes in nine main Eastern and Western countries surpassed 60%. Mobile devices can meet our "hierarchy of needs" through a series of key uses, such as a support when traveling, healthcare, banking, and shopping.[2]

This chapter introduces strategic aspects of m-commerce. First, we conceptualize the m-commerce strategy and illustrate its elements to help readers understand its key tenets. Second, as mobile and commerce adoption is a prerequisite for its success, we discuss its potentially influential factors. Third, in order to let readers realize the tremendous value of m-commerce, its value for consumers and businesses is described. Fourth, since mobile payments are a strategic, novel, and profitable business, it is valuable for m-commerce adopters to delve into how they may capture more value. Fifth, practical m-commerce tools and apps are included in this chapter. In many cases, businesses do not need to work with their own apps and can use existing apps and tools to boost their m-commerce. Last but not least, m-commerce has its advantages over traditional commerce but also has diverse challenges that are discussed in the last section of this chapter.

13.1 Mobile Commerce Strategy: Conceptual Foundations

13.1.1 What Is a Mobile Commerce Strategy?

Even though m-commerce strategies are widely used in practice, they are ill-defined. To our best knowledge, we have not seen a well-established concept of mobile commerce strategies. This can be explained by a variety of reasons. On the one hand, due to the increase in mobile sales in recent years, the scale of m-commerce is just "big enough" to be discussed at the strategic level, while researchers need time to

---

1   For more details see Harty (2016).
2   Referring to the mobile's status quo, please see Martin (2017).

develop, refine, and publish their work on the conceptualization of m-commerce strategies. On the other hand, mobile is fundamentally a technical term which creates a challenge for researchers who wish to upgrade it to a strategic level. Here, an m-commerce strategy is defined as:

> ❯ a long-term plan to conduct mobile device-based activities to fulfill commerce-related strategic purpose(s).

This definition is built on the concept of m-commerce (conducting commercial activities through mobile devices), and specifically stresses its strategic aspects, "a long-term plan" and "strategic purpose(s)." Based on above discussion, an m-commerce strategy is not just treating mobile as a complementary channel or an alternative touch point to interact with customers but also a strategic source for businesses to capture tremendous value and realize strategic goals.

13.1.2 Elements of a Mobile Commerce Strategy

Before devising and specifying an m-commerce strategy, businesses should know its elements.[3]

Strategic Purposes   Strategic purposes clearly highlights the business aim, what it intends to achieve through the m-commerce strategy. Different strategic purposes focus on different aspects of m-commerce. For example, a market share-oriented strategy concentrates on capturing the market and places less emphasis on profitability. By contrast, a profit-oriented strategy can focus on users willing to pay a fee, and it thus may cause the loss of market share.

Mobile Devices and Online Platforms   The operation of m-commerce relies on one or more mobile devices and online platforms. Mobile devices include smartphones, tablet computers, smart watches, wearables (headset, goggles, and glasses), smart earphones, and so on. Online platforms can be divided into business-established platforms and user-established platforms. The business-established platforms can be further categorized into the platforms established by the business and platforms established by other companies. Undoubtedly, the characteristics of devices and platforms can significantly influence what the business eventually intends to offer. For instance, smartphones can carry audio and video, while smart earphones can only carry audio. Compared to an online platform established by a third-party company, a business can exert more control over its own platform.

Mobile Architecture   Mobile architecture provides the technical base for m-commerce. There are many types of client architecture (e.g., native, web, hybrid) for the business to select to get the optimal performance. The business also needs to consider

---

3   The discussion on elements of a mobile commerce strategy is adapted from Gopikanth (2015).

the carriage of its service, such as the quality of customer internet connections, their operating systems, and compatibility issues.

User Experience   The user experience is a critical factor that businesses should focus on. Bad user experiences may generate a negative perception of the app by users, who may even uninstall it, which leads to the failure of the m-commerce strategy. Research stated that user experience influences users' in-app shop decisions.[4] At Google's Play Store, if there were many negative comments on an app's use experience (such as too many ads, poor usability, and too many notifications) and many positive comments on a competitor's app (such as an "addictive," works excellently, and easy to use), users would probably download the competitor's app, because user experience is a crucial factor in app choice. As we discussed in ▶ Chap. 8, Internet companies should stress the key role of service. Service-oriented thinking requires businesses to highlight user experience and even build an experience-centric competitive strategy. A decent user experience design could attract more users to download and install the app, enlarge the scale of commerce, and therefore generate more opportunities for monetization.

Lean Development   Lean development refers to the continual improvement of apps with maximum flexibility and minimum waste in the process. Lean development requires businesses to periodically create the Minimum Viable Product (MVP) because MVPs can meet users' demand and at the same time cost minimum resources. Internet users' preference and needs may vary from time to time, and the developer cannot precisely predict the features and functions offered by competitors and when they will hit the market. For example, Facebook made at least 13 attempts to clone Snapchat.[5] Facebook rolled out many Snapchat-style features such as ephemeral pictures, video messaging, and augmented reality lenses. Therefore, it makes sense for businesses to adopt the lean development approach to create their m-commerce strategy.

Partner Strategy   In many cases, e-businesses have to rely on other partners to build their operating processes. Even Amazon, which is capable of building its own massive e-business ecosystem, partners with many software and hardware providers and numerous e-retailers. For instance, payment is a core activity in the commerce process. If a business created their own payment system, users would be cautious to use the payment system due to a perception of risk in the unknown. In this case, the business may consider partnerships with reputable payment companies and focus on its niche segment.

To summarize, strategists should consider internal, external, technical, and strategic elements to develop an optimal m-commerce strategy. For more specific strategies to achieve mobile success, see the article "Six Strategies for Mobile App Success."

---

4   Source: Adhami (2013).
5   For more detailed information, see HAL90210 (2016).

Six Strategies for Mobile App Success

Mobility has changed business forever. It has increased the types of devices (phones, tablets, wearables) and the volume of devices that connect to a company's enterprise resources. There are over 6 billion mobile phone subscribers globally and the rapidly expanding Internet of Things (IoT) market promises to connect tens of billions of devices to the Internet within several years. These mobile and IoT devices have new operating systems that change how we build software and services. These technology shifts also provide a tremendous opportunity to change how every company will engage and transact business with its customers, employees, and partners.

To benefit from these new technologies, corporate data and services must be accessible across smartphones to wearables. Businesses are taking action. More than half of the companies, Lopez Research surveyed plan to build 20 or more enterprise mobile apps this year. Many are also using cloud infrastructure and platform as service solutions to support mobile initiatives. Leading companies in the mobile cloud era will create business and technical strategies where:

— *Flexible platforms enable scalable mobile application development.*
   Once a company moves beyond building five to ten apps, it looks for software tools to scale its development efforts. Platforms provide modules to support critical management elements such as testing, app version control, application catalogs, performance analytics, and security and lifecycle management. Unlike the rigid platforms of yesteryear, today's mobile development platforms are modular, offer standards-based interfaces, and work with multiple front-end design methods.

— *Data should be secured across devices, networks, and clouds.*
   Mobile and cloud computing have changed how data is accessed and where it lives. In a mobile world, the concept of a data perimeter where data can be secured has vanished. Data must flow seamlessly and securely between a corporation's data center, the cloud, and mobile devices. With over 67% of companies supporting BYOD, companies must be able to separate and control business data across personal and corporate-owned devices.

— *Mobile applications move from pretty to transactional.*
   Applications need must connect to data from numerous back-end systems. An application is useless if it can't access the data a person needs. IT should create mobile optimized access to a variety of enterprise systems such as SAP, Oracle, legacy databases, and custom applications. Companies can look to mobile platforms for middleware services to securely connect this data into applications and cloud services.

— *Mobile apps become a collection of data that represents an entire workflow.*
   In the PC world, a person used multiple apps to complete a workflow such as ordering supplies. In the mobile world, data must be collected from multiple systems and presented in a format where a person can take action. This action could be as simple as an approval or as complex as finding and purchasing a product. To do this, companies will use enterprise integration and sync software (mobile middleware) to link data from systems such as enterprise resource planning, databases, and financial systems into mobile applications.

- *The focus shifts from app downloads to continuous improvement and engagement.* The first step in mobility requires designing an application and achieving downloads, but an app isn't successful unless it drives engagement. IT must work with the end customers at the design phase to understand what tasks and features are most beneficial. App developers must build analytics into the app that will help the company understand the mobile app user experience across the entire application lifecycle. For example, IT should test software to improve performance and use analytics tools to measure adoption and engagement. Analytics and testing at both the design phase and initial deployment phase will help companies identify data related problems and usability issues before they result in poor reviews and impact a company's reputation. Common measurements for application analytics include crash reporting, flow visualization, session length, frequency of use, device type, location, and retention.
- *IT leverages the cloud for rich functionality and scale.* In the past, IT had to purchase and deploy all of the technology to maintain mobile devices and to deliver applications. Today, a company can use cloud solutions for application testing, mobile application development platforms, and enterprise app integration. The latest enterprise mobile management solutions allow a company to secure, deploy, and update applications for its employees. IT also has access to highly available infrastructure and distributed data stores to scale the collection and processing of mobile and IoT data. These modular platforms allow IT to purchase exactly what is needed and scale deployments as needed. Mobility has the opportunity to transform our businesses but only if a company evolves to mobile business processes.

The good news is that all of the technologies a company needs to mobile-enable a business are available as a set of modular platform capabilities that can be deployed on premises or in the cloud. In fact, a company can use a combination of cloud and on-premise software to mobile-enable apps and services. With technology solutions readily available, companies can focus on the critical process of defining the workflows that need to be mobile-enabled.

Source: Lopez (2015)

13.2 Factors Influencing Mobile Commerce Adoption

Adoption is a prerequisite of m-commerce success. If end users reject the mobile app or service which a business intends to offer, it is extremely difficult for the business to let users engage in the business and, needless to say, pay for any services or products.[6]

---

6   This section is adapted from Nikou and Mezei (2013).

13.2.1 Fee or Free

A fee or free business model can influence user acceptance of m-commerce. A free app could attract many users, but once it starts levying an access fee, it may very probably drive away most free users. But this does not mean an app has to be totally free, since a profit-oriented company needs to extract revenue from m-commerce and find a way to monetize users. In this section, we illustrate five charging methods. Businesses should consider which method fits their business and consumers/users most.

No Charge   Offering all mobile services for free. A free strategy is a common market strategy of internet companies because they obtain alternate earnings from companies or individuals, for example, sponsors. Advertising is a main revenue source for many internet businesses. For example, advertising earnings represented more than 95% of Facebook's total revenue in 2016.[7]

Usage-Based Charging   Users are charged based on their usage. For example, an Uber user uses the app to call for a ride service. When the ride is done, the app will charge the user based on his/her journey distance.

Bundle Pricing   Providing a few of alternative services (as a bundle) with different price options. In order to decrease the vacancy rate, some flight companies provide travelers with their brand app allowing users to order air tickets in advance. In the app, users will find a number of services (such as package delivery, premium food and drink, insurance, and so on) and selectively customize the services bundle and thus get the final price of the ticket.

Fixed Price   Charging users at a fixed fee periodically (e.g., monthly, yearly). This charging method is widely used by digital entertainment companies. For instance, iQiyi, a movie and drama app, charges premium users a fixed monthly fee to access the newest movies and dramas. Similarly, magazine apps charge subscribers a subscription fee monthly or yearly.

Packet Charging   Charging services in a packet-based method. For example, mobile operators charge smartphone users a packet fee covering certain minutes of active phone calls and gigabytes of data transferred.

13.2.2 Functionality

The functionality of a mobile app refers to the ability of a user to conduct certain tasks. From a value perspective, an app should bring about value (hedonic value, utilitarian value, social value) for the user. Functionality is the value enabler of an

---

7   Facebook's 2016 financial results can be accessed at Facebook (2017).

app. It enables users to do certain tasks that create value for the app owner. Moreover, functionality can be broken down into four aspects:

Simplicity The minimum knowledge required to use an app or mobile service. Businesses should increase the ease of learning for use because a simple, easy-to-use app or service will typically attract more users regardless of the differences in their learning capabilities.

Usability The quality of use positively correlates with user experience. If a user perceives an app has a poor quality of use (e.g., it is a frustrating experience), their perception and use of the app will similarly decline.

Accessibility The extent to which an app or mobile service can be accessed anytime/anywhere and on any device. The use of an app or mobile service depends on many factors, for example, internet quality, the density of mobile requests, and the internet protocol address. Poor accessibility may discourage users to continue to use the app or service because their needs cannot be gratified anytime/anywhere as they wish.

Personalization Offering services that align to personal profiles or behavioral patterns. There is great variation in the preferences of digital customers. It is difficult for businesses to use a "one-size-fits-all" standardized service solution for all customers. For example, products recommended through an app's push notifications may be targeted based on users' browsing history or other existing data that signals their purchasing preferences.

13.2.3 Value Added

To add value is to increase users' perceived worth of an app or mobile service. An individual's perception of worthiness largely influences their uptake. It does not make sense for an individual to adopt a worthless app or service. The value added by an app or mobile service is comprised of the following points:

Mobility Offering real-time information and communication anytime/anywhere. Mobility is a salient advantage of mobile business in comparison to traditional business. Mobility is different from accessibility since it requires more than just connecting to the Internet. Mobility of an app or mobile service relies on the application of the mobile computing capability. For instance, a map app offers location-based information service, which should be able to identify the user's current geo-location.

Content Quality Offering updated, correct, and timely content. Content includes posts, blogs, audios, videos, and more. Improving the quality of content is clearly a value adding strategy and increases user satisfaction.

Features of Certain Occasion Offering mobile services for certain occasions. Mobile services and apps can provide unique services that are tailored to specific activities.

For example, smartphones can act as a "mobile wallet." Consumers who are unwilling to use cash can use a mobile payment app to pay a restaurant bill. A PC cannot do this.

Enjoyment/Entertainment   Gratifying user entertainment needs. The desire for hedonic value is part of human nature. Therefore, a successful app should not only just meet the utilitarian needs of users but also gratify their hedonic needs.

13.2.4 Perceived Worthiness

The three factors discussed above align with a business perspective. The last factor is less controllable for businesses but significantly determines user adoption. Today's e-businesses should not only consider what they will offer but also what their customers will get. Bored, dissatisfied, impatient users of an app can uninstall it without any hesitation because the cost of entry (installation) and exit (uninstallation) is almost zero. Perceived worthiness is defined as the extent to which users think it is worth using, and paying for, the app or mobile service. It is a trade-off between sacrifices and benefits. According to economic rationality theory, the perceived worthiness of an object is a precondition for purchasing or using the object by a rational agent. There are three key aspects related to this construct.

Perceived Service Quality   How well a user perceives the quality of service. Service quality is a critical dimension of an assessment of the benefits generated from an app or mobile service. This construct is a user-centered metric that measures how a user evaluates the functionality and value added by the business.

Perceived Cost   A user's satisfaction with the cost of using the mobile app or service. Perceived cost is a construct measuring the extent to which a user is satisfied with the app or service compared to their monetary, time, and energy consumption. Users will adopt a mobile service or app only if they feel that what they gain exceeds what they give.

Perceived Performance   How well a mobile service of app fulfills a user's needs or goals. In many cases users use mobile services or apps to satisfy their particular needs or conduct certain tasks that otherwise may be undertaken on PCs which have a wider screen. There is nearly always a mismatch between ideal performance and perceived performance. Businesses should minimize the gap by offering a simple, easy, and friendly interface to users.

13.3 Value of Mobile Commerce for Consumers and Businesses

Any good revenue model centers on the value proposition. A profit-oriented business does not adopt m-commerce simply for its prevalence and popularity. It must directly or indirectly generate revenue. At the same time, a successful business, no matter what it is, relies on the value it creates for customers. Hence, managers should identify the value of m-commerce for their own businesses and consumers.[8]

13.3.1 Consumers

"Consumers" is a broad term including consumers of a business as well as consumers of rivals and potential consumers. The value of m-commerce offered by the business can benefit these three groups. For instance, business customers can visit its site using their mobile devices and make purchases; customers of rivals can do the same and compare the price and quality of items; and potential customers can also browse the mobile platform to become informed. Inevitably, the latter two groups are taking advantage of the business with "free-riding" behaviors which mean they captured value from the site, but they purchased from an opponent. Nevertheless, businesses should be aware that the latter two groups can also create value for them. For example, many owners of gasoline-powered cars advocated for the Tesla Model X (an electricity-powered car) via online social networks, even though they did not intend to change their car.

Informational Value m-Commerce allows consumers to access information online. Information is valuable for consumers and empowers them to be informed and make better decisions. For example, it is difficult for a consumer to detect the real value of an unfamiliar product while s/he can Google the product via their smartphone to review online comments and thus make a more informed purchase decision.

Social Value Most online social networking sites such as Facebook, Twitter, and Instagram are widely used via mobile devices. Mobility can also provide social value through mobile social apps or websites. For instance, a person can display a picture of newly purchased clothing via Facebook to enhance their online image, social impact, social identity, and express a sense of belonging to that brand.

Entertainment and Emotional Value As we discussed in the previous section, entertainment is a factor that influences user adoption. Pokémon Go is a viral game app that attracted players worldwide and who enjoy capturing virtual pets. More interestingly for business, the Pokémon company also devised a system by which stores can pay for lures that bring these virtual pets near the store so as to entice Pokémon hunters to visit the store.[9] For those who want to improve their experience of the game, virtual items may be purchase in-app, which incurs revenue for the business. Emotional value is a psychological value that relies on a product's ability to arouse feelings or affective responses. Emotional responses are usually a by-product of watching videos or playing games because they entertain consumers by letting them feel emotional, excited, thrilled, or other affective reactions.

---

8   This section is based on Larivière et al. (2013).
9   The source of the statement can be seen at: Auger (2016).

Convenience Value   Compared to wired e-commerce, m-commerce brings about three kinds of convenience: convenience of accessing the internet, convenience of collecting and spreading information, and transaction convenience. Smartphones can access the internet anywhere within wireless range. Search engines in smartphones increase the ease of searching for information. Consumers can take photographs and send graphical and text messages to friends via smartphones. Last, consumers no longer need to carry their wallet with them when they have a mobile wallet on their mobile device and can make payments using it.

13.3.2 Businesses

We define "businesses" broadly, encompassing the focal business, rival businesses, as well as other related and unrelated businesses. For example, brands sell products to consumers through the Amazon shopping app. The brands receive revenue from sales. Amazon can ask for a commission based upon each sale. Rival apps may receive value from the app too. For example, they can design Amazon-like features (color, layout, buttons, and so on) for their app.

Reducing Costs   Mobile is a cost-efficient communication channel. In comparison to face-to-face contact, short messages, emails, and push notifications are very economic channels for customer contact. Hence by increasingly relying upon mobile channels rather than face-to-face, businesses are able to reduce communication costs.

Consumer Co-creation   As consumers us mobile services or apps on their mobile devices, they also may play a role in the business's service or app improvement process. For example, station-free bike-renting companies like oBike or Ofo offer an app that unlocks bikes nearby. It could be costly for these companies to physically unlock the bikes in person. Their app also requires users to report their ride experience when they finish the ride. This data informs businesses about bike that may be unavailable or broken in a timely manner so that they can fix the broken bikes as soon as possible, to minimize bike downtime and consequent loss of business.

Market Insight and Customer Knowledge   Commercial activities that are undertaken via mobile devices can generate a large amount of data and information for businesses. Businesses should be able to identify useful market insights and learn more about their customers by digging into key datasets and other information. This might include the brands that a consumer purchases and which products achieved the highest sales at the current season.

Real-Time Tracking/Control   In today's digitalized world, most people are very attached to their smartphones, both physically and emotionally. Being connected is a fundamental need in human nature. This habit enables businesses to conduct real-time tracking, to access a users' current location or identify the name and quality of Wi-Fi. Real-time tracking is beneficial for the business and consumers to provide localized, in-time service or information, for example, navigating a driving route through a map app. This approach raises many ethical questions around personal privacy and data management. Some wireless Internet users report feeling "watched" by businesses, namely, a variety of ongoing surveillance activities built by the wireless internet and mobile technology (Su et al. 2018).

Consumer Influence Smartphones are an ideal tool for sharing information. Consumers can easily share their purchases and express their likes or dislikes of a brand through social apps, short messages, email apps, and phone calls. For example, the person who uploaded photos to social media of themselves in newly purchased clothing may quickly find the picture has received many likes and comments from friends. The person's influence is temporarily amplified by a mobile device in this example.

To summarize, m-commerce can provide value for consumers as well as businesses. For e-business companies that intend to devise an m-commerce strategy, it is vital to find a balance point where m-commerce can provide value for consumers and also create value for the business.

13.4 Mobile Payments

13.4.1 Introduction

Mobile payments are defined as making payments through mobile devices. m-Payment does not completely belong to the realm of m-commerce. For example, transferring money to family members or friends does not include commercial activities or exchanges for goods or services. But no matter whether a payment is made for commercial or noncommercial purposes, what really matters is that businesses can receive revenues in this way. Furthermore, m-payment operations do not have to rely on payment apps like PayPal. m-Commerce businesses can require users to add their bank card as a payment method or deposit funds into their online account as a cash reserve. In many cases, users need to create a PIN and enter a number to make a payment. The money will be automatically deducted from their bank account.

m-Payments can be divided into two types: proximity m-payment and remote m-payment. Proximity m-payment is payments made at the point of sale based on proximity payment technologies such as Near Field Communication (NFC) or Quick Response (QR) technology. Remote m-payment is similar to the operation of traditional online payments where funds are transferred from one party to another but via mobile devices. m-Payment is built on multi-sector cooperation:

(a) Mobile network operators and mobile device manufacturers equip smartphones with a Secure Element and a NFC chip for safe memory and operations.
(b) Financial institutions (e.g., banks) control payment terminals and issue credit, debit, or prepaid cards as a payment account.
(c) Vendors purchase new NFC-enabled point-of-sale terminals, handhold readers able to scan QR codes of consumers, or display their QR code as a receipt account to consumers.

(d) Payment service providers transmit, execute, and secure payments for vendors and consumers.

(e) Third-party insurance companies insure the financial safety of payments (Liu et al. 2015).

Despite the fact that m-payment is emerging in business, companies cannot underestimate its enormous potential economic value and strategic position. Uptake of m-payments has grown rapidly, from online stores to brick-and-mortar stores, groceries to restaurants, taxies to trains, and even auto-vending machines, being applied everywhere.[10] Growth is aligned with rising consumer confidence in e-commerce, and it is estimated that 938.2 million individuals—or 36.0% of smartphone users—will use a mobile phone proximity payment app in 2019. Payment app usage is highest in China, where an estimated 81.4% of smartphone users will access such apps in 2019, and markets are rapidly growing in India, Indonesia, Mexico, and Germany.[11] It is estimated that by 2021, 17.2% of the global population will be proximity m-payment users.[12]

To embrace m-payment business opportunities, strategic partnerships among payment companies are common in recent years: PayPal partnered with Synchrony Financial (Feb 2018), Alipay with Verifone (Oct 2017), Apple Pay with DiDi (Sep 2017), Samsung Pay with PayPal (Jul 2017), and more. In 2018, Alipay obtained payment licenses in more than 35 countries or regions. Wechat Pay launched a European trial.[13] Google rolled out Google Pay which brings Google Wallet and Android Pay into one service to rival their competitor Apple Pay.[14] Amazon opened Amazon Go, an unmanned supermarket, that allows shoppers to use the money in their Amazon app to pay for purchases. For more detailed information please see the FT article "Amazon Debuts the Store Without a Checkout."

13

Amazon Debuts the Store Without a Checkout

Five years ago Amazon started working on a secret project: how to eliminate the checkout line in stores. Amazon executives reasoned that most other aspects of physical shopping had been pretty much perfected, except for one thing—nobody likes waiting in line.

The result of that project is Amazon Go, a futuristic convenience store in which shoppers are tracked by hundreds of cameras on the ceiling and a computer algorithm that analyzes their every gesture and then tallies up their receipt when they

---

10 Unless specifically noted, the data source of the discussion below is taken from: *Global and China Mobile Payment Industry Report, 2017-2021*, Reportlinker, January 2018. Retrieved from ► https://www.reportlinker.com/p04627129/Global-and-China-Mobile-Payment-Industry-Report.html/.

11 Source: McNair (2018).

12 The data source of this discussion is Tang (2018).

13 More detailed information can be seen at PYMNTS (2018).

14 More detailed information can be seen at Molina (2018).

exit. Amazon calls this "just walk out" shopping, because there is no checkout counter and no checkout line, just a few turnstiles like those on the underground.

The store, which has been in testing since December 2016 and opens to the public on Monday, represents Amazon's most provocative effort yet to reshape the future of brick-and-mortar retail.

Located in a ground-floor retail spot at the center of Amazon's campus in Seattle, the shop has posters in its windows advertising the "just walk out" shopping experience. To underscore the point, each receipt comes with a "trip timer" so shoppers see exactly how many seconds it took to grab their goods. The items for sale are similar to what might be found in a deli or a corner store, with an in-store kitchen that prepares fresh sandwiches and salads.

Although it was founded as an online-only bookstore, Amazon's aggressive push into physical retail has surprised—and alarmed—many of its retail competitors. The company now operates 13 brick-and-mortar bookstores, several grocery pickup points, and, since its \$13.7 billion acquisition last year, hundreds of Whole Foods stores across the United States.

However, the complexity of the Amazon Go store's design means that it is more of an experimental concept at the moment, rather than a mature technology that can be easily and cheaply replicated. The store was initially supposed to open to the public in the spring of 2017 but was delayed until this month amid reports it was not quite working as expected.

Dilip Kumar, who oversees the technology behind the Amazon Go store, explains that the store uses computer vision—the ceiling is dotted with hundreds of video cameras—to determine what shoppers are picking out.

"Five years ago when we started this, we said: can we push the boundaries of computer vision and machine learning to create this effortless experience for customers to come in, take what they want, and leave?" he says.

Mr. Kumar points to the cameras that nearly blanket the ceiling and explains that the computer algorithm uses these to determine which customer is taking which products. There are also weight sensors on the store shelves, but these are less useful because different items can have the same weight, such as different flavors of yoghurt.

"The holy grail is video understanding," he says. "To be able to understand and interpret and know exactly what is happening. Doing this at scale and getting transaction-level accuracy is what makes this challenging."

He explains that one of the most difficult things for the algorithm to master is when the store gets crowded. "It is much more convoluted when you have 50 people picking up multiple items or browsing," he says. "They are occluded, they occlude each other, items are getting occluded, and the items are small."

Over the past year, the tech team has been improving the algorithm so that it is trained to handle these scenarios, including when customers might partially cover an item with their hand when they take it from the shelf.

To help facilitate identification, certain items in the store such as sandwiches also have a special dot code on top, similar to a bar code but designed with circles and diamonds that make it easier for a camera to read from a distance.

> While Mr. Kumar vowed that the technology was "very, very accurate," he declined to specify when the company might open other Amazon Go stores. "We'd love to build more," he said, without elaborating.
>
> Mr. Kumar also said the company has "no plans" to introduce its checkout-free shopping in any Whole Foods stores, nor in the Amazon bookstores.
>
> Nevertheless, in the year since Amazon first unveiled plans to reinvent the grocery store with Amazon Go, rivals have raced to invest in similar technologies as they battle for market share of the $800bn US grocery business.
>
> Plans have ratcheted up since Amazon acquired Whole Foods last summer. In the ensuing months, bankers have worked closely with their brick-and-mortar clients to help them come up with a tech-centric defense to the threat. [...]
>
> Source: Adapted from: Hook and Nicolaou (2018)

13.4.2 History

The history of m-payments can help us to understand its evolution and changes over the years. Below, a chronological sequence of main events is presented:

- 1994: The QR code is invented.
- 1997: m-Payment starts to emerge.
- 1998: PayPal is founded.
- 1999: Mobile phones can be used for buying movie tickets.
- 2001: The third generation (3G) of wireless mobile telecommunications technology is invented.
- 2004: NFC and NFC-based services are under development.
- 2006: Cloud computing tech emerges.
- 2007: The age of smartphone comes: iPhone and the Droid operating system are released.
- 2009: 4G is released.
- 2011: Google Wallet is released.
- 2013: Alipay launched a financial product platform called Yuebao.
- 2014: Apple Pay and Wechat Pay are launched.
- 2018: Google Pay combined Google Wallet and Android Pay. At the same year, the first Amazon Go store is open at Seattle.

From this evolution, note that the maturity of m-payment technologies is dependent on many technologies from different levels. Cloud computing, NFC technologies, and QR code technologies are developed for the use of m-payment in physical settings. 3G, 4G, and smartphone operating systems are the technical infrastructure that enables m-payments. Various payment apps provide m-payment services for a mass market of users. The invention of Amazon Go represents the perfect combination of m-payments and smart retail, by which payments are smartly and automatically made by algorithm and identification technologies.

13.4.3 Benefits and Risks

e-Business companies must thoroughly reflect on the benefits and risks of m-payments when devising their m-payment strategy, because modifying an m-payment strategy during its implementation could be difficult and costly.

13.4.3.1 Benefits

Increasing the Convenience of Purchases and Payments m-Payment users can make payments anytime and anywhere due to the mobility of smartphones and other mobile devices. Businesses can take advantage of this point to capture more value from impulsive shoppers. For example, many m-commerce businesses focus on simplifying the consumer journey to making a purchase and provide "one-click order" and "one-click purchase" functions which can complete a purchase in a few seconds and thus leave almost no time for those impulsive shoppers to reconsider their purchase decision.

Enhancing Consumer Experience at Brick-and-Mortar Stores What m-payment provides for brick-and-mortar stores is not just a quick checkout.[15] When compared with traditional payment methods such as cash, credit card, or membership card, m-payment is more interactive. For example, when a shopper completes a payment by Alipay, he sees more detailed information on the merchant, and if he likes, she/he can friend the merchant on Alipay. The merchant could offer the shopper an e-coupon via Alipay to implement a loyalty program. Alipay, as the online payment platform, can provide a small random discount for this payment, which is also good for enhancing consumer experience, as the shopper would wonder and expect how much money could be saved in the transaction: "is it a 0.1% discount or a 5% discount?"

Reducing the Work of Cashiers It is estimated that it costs $1 to check out a $100 purchase (Taylor 2016, pp. 159–177). Proximity m-payment saves the time cost. Moreover, fueled by remote m-payment, consumers can pay for their bill anywhere and anytime. For example, when a family finishes a meal at a restaurant, they just get up and leave. It is because a family member, for instance, the father, has paid the bill through a remote m-payment method and an e-receipt has been sent to him through the m-payment app. Businesses do not have to build their own m-payment system, as Starbucks did with its app, because there are a plenty of online third-party m-payment platforms to provide payment services for them, for example, Groupon, Meituan, and Airbnb.

Increasing the Precision of Marketing The routinization of m-payment use in everyday life will provide businesses with more data about consumer preferences and behavioral patterns. Therefore payment companies are able to increase the precision of their marketing strategies, for example, predicting what a consumer would be

---

15 This subsection is adapted from Taylor (2016).

interested in and when and where the consumer will do his/her routine shopping. Merchants who obtain their sales data (payment companies may charge a fee for the information service) could maintain a more accurate inventory level and offer more refine their product offerings in response to identified patterns in demand.

13.4.3.2 Risks

Financial Risk[16]   Financial risk refers to a potential loss of money caused by the use of m-payment. Consumers using m-payment methods may be worried about the safety of their money, for example, hackers access their account and PIN and steal their money. There are two main risk sources. First is free public Wi-Fi. Free public Wi-Fi sounds good but also lets Wi-Fi owners to access connected mobile devices, and as such it is possible for Wi-Fi owners to attain the financial information without authorization. Second are malicious QR codes. QR codes can be doctored and used to implant malicious viruses into smartphones which scanned the code to make a payment. The viruses might steal the smartphone owners' bank accounts and PINs.

Privacy Risk   It is defined as the expected potential loss related to the disclosure of individual private information, like phone numbers, shopping preference, behavioral pattern, and other information generated by the use of m-payment. With the penetration and popularization of m-payment, this problem is even worse. If a consumer frequently uses an m-payment method in his daily life, the payment company could detect his everyday route and behavior pattern (when, where, and what he will do) by his payment records and geo-locations and then make use of such information to practice precision marketing, make personalized recommendation, or even sell that information to other companies. The problem is how m-payment companies convince consumers to trust they will neither use opportunistically their information nor invade their privacy.

Performance Risk   It refers to the possible malfunctioning of m-payment system. Specifically, m-payment apps might not work as expected, and so they could not provide a normal payment; performance of m-payments are affected by many factors, such as data transmission speed, internal storage, responsiveness, processing capability, and Internet quality. For instance, due to a poor internet quality, a frozen payment operation can wear out consumers' patience, and, therefore, they could eventually uninstall such a payment app.

In summary, m-payment can provide benefits as well as involve risks. Managers need to consider both technical and managerial viability of m-payments actually. Technical viability means the payment system can smoothly and perfectly handle enormous payments at the same time. Managerial viability implies the adopting organization can properly integrate and interact with the m-payment system, being able to manage all kinds of contingent payment problems. Retaking the example of using certain remote m-payment method in a restaurant, if many consumers simul-

---

16   This subsection is adapted from Yang et al. (2015).

taneously decided to use it and directly leave without a word to the waiter, how would the staff waiting on customers figure out which table is leaving with a paid check and which could be leaving without having paid? Obviously, this is not a mere technical issue but also a managerial issue. For instance, cashiers and/or employees supervising the tables should be timely updated on the current status of tables, either by an employee in charge of managing the m-payments or, more easily and immediate, configuring the software used to manage tables to automatically update mobile-based payments.

13.4.4 Classification and Variety

There are three main technical solutions of m-payment: reader-based m-payment, cloud-based m-payment, and third-party-based m-payment (Liu et al. 2015, pp. 372–391). *Reader-based m-payment* is to make consumers' payment smartphones communicate with the merchant's checkout terminal or QR code. For example, Santander has reached a strategic partnership with Apple Pay. iPhone users can add their Santander bank card into their Apple Pay and put their iPhone on in-store NFC terminals to make payments. Another type of reader is the smartphone camera. Consumers can open their smartphone camera in the m-payment app and use the camera to scan the merchant's QR code to pay. Merchants can also use a code reader to read consumers' payment code to receive payment. For instance, Alipay and Wechat Pay are two representative m-payment apps based on the QR code tech. Some companies also offer a pluggable device which can connect the smartphone to read the bank card information inside and complete the payment. *Cloud-based m-payment* allows payment credentials stored on cloud servers, and as such m-payment apps can be a mobile wallet for proximity or remote payments. PayPal and Alipay are typical payment apps employing this tech to secure payments by the cloud computing tech. *Third-party-based m-payment* refers to making m-payment through a third-party app. In this case, the merchant authorizes the third-party app to collect money on behalf of him, which means that consumers can just make payments on the app.

Next, we can classify the use of m-payment by four main settings to illustrate the various applications of m-payment in life and work:[17]

Money Transfer in Everyday Life   The most regular remote m-payment occurs in everyday life, like transferring money to friends, merchants, or family members. Cloud-based payment apps work like a "mobile wallet" in this case. Users can use their mobile wallet to conduct any commercial or noncommercial activities. Money is automatically deducted from the user's bank account and go to the receipt's account.

---

17 The classification of m-payments by different settings is based on Pinola (2017).

Point of Sale Payments   Payments taking place at the point-of-sale (POS) in physical stores. In order to cater to those m-payment consumers, many stores have purchased NFC-based POS terminals to allow consumers to use m-payment methods.

m-Payment via a Brand App   m-Payments specific to a brand. For example, consumers who order and pay for a cup of coffee via the Starbucks app can skip the regular queue line in the shop and go directly to a specific mobile-order line to pick up their coffee. It is worth mentioning that in reality this kind of brand apps also allows consumers to order products online and pay in cash.

Carrier Payments   Payments and money transfer do not happen simultaneously. Some services allow users to pay via smartphone, but money is not withdrawn from their bank accounts till they get their monthly smartphone bill. For example, smartphone users buy a ringtone service for their phone; the service fee is automatically added to their monthly phone bill.

13.4.5 Main Mobile Payment Apps

Here we introduce mass market m-payment apps and illustrate their characteristics to help understand how m-payment works in the real business world.[18]

Apple Pay and Samsung Pay   We put Apple Pay and Samsung Pay together because they are two world-leading m-payment applications labeled with each smartphone brand. Apple Pay works with iPhone, iPad, Mac, and iWatch; Samsung Pay works with Samsung Galaxy and Samsung Gear. There is increasing recognition among smartphone manufacturers that smartphone-labeled m-payment services are a valuable business. This is because users can pre-install the m-payment app into their smartphones, and thus their smartphone users can directly use an official m-payment app issued by the smartphone brand. The smartphone-labeled m-payment strategy is reasonable since an individual who buys a smartphone from one of these brands leverages off the comfort that a use has with that brand. Smartphone companies can capture more value by leveraging that trust by providing m-payment service. For example, Huawei, the global top 3 smartphone brand, worked with UnionPay International to roll out "Huawei Pay" in 2016.[19] For a more detailed information on Apple Pay, see the FT article: "Apple Pay: What It Is and How It Works."

Google Pay and Alipay   Google and Alibaba are two of the biggest Internet companies in the world and built their own business ecosystem. Google developed its search engine, Chrome, or its operating system for mobile devices Android, among other

---

18 This section is adapted from Pinola (2017).

19 More information can be seen at: "Huawei Teams with UnionPay International to oll out Huawei Pay Worldwide", *Huawei*, 27 January 2018. Retrieved from ▶ https://www.huawei.com/en/press-events/news/2018/1/UnionPay-Huawei-Pay-Roll-Out-Worldwide/.

things. Alibaba created Tmall, Taobao, Alimama, AliExpress, and so on. Their purpose of developing their own m-payment app was to better serve their users since users of these products need to make payments somewhere. For instance, Android users need to buy paid apps in Play Store; mobile shoppers in Tmall stores—e-retail stores—have to pay for their online purchases.

Snapcash, Messenger Payment, and Wechat Pay To take a piece of the pie, online social networking service companies also joined the game. Money transfer in everyday life is very common and prevalent. At the same time, these online social platforms, Snapchat, Facebook Messenger, and Wechat, have accumulated enough users. Snapchat has 187 million daily active users,[20] Messenger has 1.2 billion, and Wechat has 963 million, where users can transfer money to friends like sending a text message.

Bank of America, Wells Fargo, and JPMorgan Chase Banks are expected to dominate m-payment-related business because m-payment, digital cash, and m-wallet are, at their core, financial services. Bank of America, Wells Fargo and JPMorgan Chase are the three biggest banks in United States and their bank apps can connect to a users' bank account and so more easily provide them with m-payment services. Technology and Internet companies that offer m-payments, such as Apple Pay, Samsung Pay, Alipay, and Wechat Pay, do not have the same level of long-held consumer trust that banks have to protect financial accounts and transactions.

Walmart Pay and Starbucks Walmart and Starbucks are two of the most popular brands worldwide. Walmart supermarkets and Starbucks coffee shops use their own m-payment methods, Walmart Pay and Starbucks respectively, to streamline the checkout process, minimize the requirement for cashiers, and enhance the consumer experience. Their apps can be bundled with other branding or marketing functions such as sending e-coupons, pushing notifications, and communicating brand value.

Groupon and Meituan Groupon and Meituan are two popular e-commerce marketplaces that connect app users with local merchants. Groupon and Meituan offer online group buying and provide online consumers with low prices, localized and quality products or services from nearby service providers, and more. Users can find promotion codes offered by local businesses on the app and make payments via the app. Once the online payment is made, consumers show the code to staff in a physical store and then enjoy a free dinner or movie. Group buying apps help small local business owners who are unable to develop their own m-payment apps. The inclusion of their business within these apps promotes their business and special offers.

---

20 The number of daily active users of these social platforms can be found at: "Daily time spent on social networking by internet users worldwide from 2012 to 2017 (in minutes)", *Statista*, 2019. Retrieved from ▶ https://www.statista.com/.

Apple Pay: What it Is and How it Works

Millions of Britons are now able to pay for everyday transactions using their mobile phones, iPads, and watches following the launch of Apple Pay this week.

The new payments system allows anyone with Apple's latest phone or watch to buy goods worth to £20 at more than 250,000 shops and restaurants across Britain. It is the first time the "tap-and-pay" system has become available outside the United States, allowing users to pay for things by touching their smartphones on contactless payment points. Here we look at how it works.

— *How Do I Activate Apple Pay?*

Opening the Wallet app on the iPhone will ask you to add a bank card to the app. Apple will ask whether you want to add the card that's already associated with your Apple account, and if you do then all you have to do is enter the three-digit security code on the back of your card. Alternatively you can scan a card using the iPhone's camera or type in card details manually.

Your bank will then do a security check. It may send a text with a code you need to enter, ask you to ring its call center or log into online banking. Once your identity has been checked, an image of your card appears in the app, and you can start spending using your mobile. There is no limit to the number of cards you can add.

— *How Do I Use It?*

When it's time to pay, hold the device linked to the account near the contactless reader with your finger on the home button. Your phone will register when it is near a payment terminal, and the card you choose to use most often will pop up on the screen.

You will then need to give a thumbprint on the circular "home" button to confirm your identify. Finally, to pay, tap the device against the card reader. The smartphone or watch will vibrate to let you know the payment has been approved.

— *Will My Bank Let Me Use Apple Pay?*

Banks that launched the service on Tuesday included Santander, Nationwide and Royal Bank of Scotland with its NatWest and Ulster Bank subsidiaries. Other banks plan to launch the service later this year, including Bank of Scotland, Lloyds, M&S Bank, TSB, Coutts, and Halifax.

Barclays said that despite not participating in Tuesday's launch, its debit cards and Barclaycard credit cards will be joining the scheme soon.

— *How Does It Link to My Bank Account?*

Apple Pay will automatically use the customers' default card, although you can switch through the available credit and debit cards at checkout on the smartphone or Watch display.

Once added, all credit, debit, and loyalty cards are kept within the iPhone's pre-installed Passbook app. New cards can be added by taking a photograph. Before you can use the card to pay, Apple requires you to verify with your bank, either using a text message code or a phone call.

Apple has put strict security measures in place so Apple Watch owners will have to enter their card details separately within the Apple Watch app.

- *Where Can I Shop with Apple Pay?*
  Some 250,000 stores—as well as the entire Transport for London underground, bus and rail network—will accept Apple Pay. Individual retailers already signed up to support the system include Starbucks, Costa, M&S, McDonald's, KFC, Pret A Manger, Boots, JD Sports, Co-Op, Nando's, Lidl, and Waitrose [...]
- *How Safe Is Apple Pay?*
  Apple Pay is being touted as safer than "chip and pin" by some experts as it is harder to fake a fingerprint than guess a pin code. Card details are not stored on your phone or iPad. So if your phone is stolen, a thief cannot access your account. Instead, a unique and encrypted code is linked to your phone. It cannot be used by any other device [...]

Source: Adapted from: Warwick-Ching (2015)

13.5 Mobile Commerce Apps and Tools

Commercial transactions are various and dynamic. On the one hand, they include various activities such as shopping, traveling, watch paid movies, and paying for mobile video games. On the other hand, the processing of commercial transactions involves many dynamic tasks: search, target, evaluate, purchase, and post-purchase. Any applications that can help consumers to fulfill these tasks can be seen useful tools for m-commerce. Due to the variety of m-commerce apps and their distinct characteristics, this section structures m-commerce apps into five subgroups and nominates popular m-commerce tools/apps within each group. The classification benefits businesses because it is a way to frame the available options and tools for their m-commerce strategies by asking two questions:

1. What kind of app should we develop for users?
2. What apps or tools should we use to improve our m-commerce?

13.5.1 Classifications of Mobile Commerce Apps

A key strategic factor that businesses should consider is the type of app.[21] m-Commerce apps could be grouped in four categories: commerce-, tool-, entertainment-, or social-centric.

Commerce-Centric Apps Commerce-centric apps allow consumers to shop through the app. Put it simply, these apps are for m-shopping. For example, the Amazon shop-

---

21 This section is adapted from: Zhao and Balagué (2015).

ping app is the mobile version of ▶ Amazon.com. Shoppers can browse millions of products and manage their Amazon orders anywhere and anytime. This app supports price comparisons by typing in keywords or scanning a barcode or an image with smartphone camera. Shoppers can also sign up for shipment notifications so they are informed about when their order is shipped and arrives. Similarly, AliExpress shopping is another popular shopping app issued by Alibaba Mobile. It provides thousands of brands and millions of products, and most importantly, at competitive prices. Shoppers can easily find what they want with the in-built search engine. In addition, there are numerous coupon giveaways, discounts, and promotion codes. AliExpress shopping can also push personalized notifications and recommendations to the shopper.

It is intuitive for businesses to design a commerce-centric app for their m-commerce strategy. Through this app strategy, businesses are able to sell products directly to customers or create an online C2C or B2C marketplace. But there are other app strategies that can capture consumer shopping activities.

Tool-Centric Apps   Apps as tools are designed to provide users with utility. The main goals of tool-centric apps are to recognize the motivations and needs of consumers when using mobile services or tools for personal or business use. For instance, Dropbox is a cloud storage app designed to provide a creative collaboration space for storing, sharing, and editing personal or business files anytime/anywhere. Dropbox gives the basic version of its product away—2GB storage and basic features such as file synching, encryption, and integration with Microsoft Office software. Users, who need more storage capacity and other premium functions, pay a subscription fee for either a Pro or Business edition.

There are tool-centric apps that implicitly market or brand products or services. For example, cosmetic products are typical experience products. Consumers cannot know the actual effect of a cosmetic product until they trial it. At the same time, consumers are not that "brave" and are too time-poor, to try all products at no cost and then select the optimal one. To resolve this problem, L'Oréal issued a cosmetics app called "Makeup Genius." It is a tool to implicitly recommend L'Oréal's cosmetic products. Users firstly create a selfie through the app and then they can try different virtual makeup looks and cosmetic products on their image. When users feel that they are "beautiful enough" through several virtual makeup try-ons, the app will display the L'Oréal's products included in the last virtual makeup.

BMW Driver's Guide App Is Another Type of Tool-Centric App provided by BMW. As the name implies, the app is an owner's handbook for selected BMW models. Users enter a vehicle identification number, and then the app will automatically match the user's vehicle and download the specific model's guidance book. The app helps drivers to resolve problems that are related to the car.

Thus, businesses with tool-centric apps have many options to create value. They can directly charge for their premium mobile service like Dropbox, recommend brands and products in an implicit way like L'Oréal, or just improve the user experience of their products like BMW.

Entertainment-Centric Apps   With the boom of smartphone and other mobile device use, businesses can create revenue through game apps, music apps, drama apps, and so on. For example, Netflix is a leading app for watching TV episodes and movies. Once users have the Netflix membership, they can watch thousands of TV episodes and films via smartphone. Netflix charge a monthly subscription fee through automatic deductions. Spotify is a music app that allows users to access a world of digital music. Users can stream the music by artist or album or create their own playlist. Spotify's freemium business model means that users can use the app for free, but if they want to get better service (with no advertising, no download limit, and a higher song bitrate), they pay a subscription fee.

Designing an entertainment-centric app does not mean providing a mobile game app just for fun. Most entertainment-centric apps are dedicated to cultivate and develop user value in a casual and immersive environment. Irrespective of whether it is selling entertainment products or advertising for other companies or brands, the ultimate goal of an entertainment-centric app is to monetize user attention.

Social-Centric Apps   Social media and e-commerce are the two biggest inventions of the Internet, which may explain why investors become excited when businesses try to fuse the two together. For example, the Facebook app is its most frequently used channel. Facebook launched a variety of commercial features and functions to embrace the "Facebook commerce," such as Pinterest-style buyable product pictures, "Buy" buttons, and Messenger Payments. WeChat is an online social networking service app. It launched its own payment system WeChat Pay to prompt its commercial business, "WeChat commerce." WeChat users can use WeChat Pay to purchase items in posts and tip content creators. Clearly the core function of any social-centric app is social networking services. m-Commerce features or functions play a complementary or secondary role to support shopping via social apps. Meanwhile, for social-centric app businesses, m-commerce acts as an additional revenue source. A key consideration for any social-centric app that offers commerce is to carefully mitigate against users becoming disenfranchised, dissatisfied, and uncomfortable about the commercialization of their social activities and friendships. For example, frequent pop-up advertisements on a social app may lead users to uninstall the app because they disrupt conversations with friends in the app.

In summary, this section has offered a broader view on the variety of apps for m-commerce. We provided four varieties; each of them connects to or facilitates m-commerce from a particular aspect. Businesses should carefully consider options and then select and develop an app that is most suitable for their business. For example, commerce-centric apps focus on e-marketplace or e-tailing. Tool-centric apps can create value for users and companies by offering a form of utility. Entertainment-centric apps focus on the commerce of products or services related to entertainment. Social-centric apps add m-commerce features or functions into online social networking services.

13.5.2 Useful Tools for Mobile Commerce

Next, seven useful m-commerce tools are introduced. These tools are beneficial for mobile commerce from different aspects, and so their benefits are illustrated separately.[22]

Yelp   It is estimated that Yelp has an average of 92 million mobile users per month, with over 100 million reviews in total. Yelp owns both a desktop version and a mobile version, and 72% of total page views and 60% of all content (reviews and photos) come from mobile. Yelp is an ideal place for tourism and new businesses. People initially may search Yelp for an unfamiliar destination, to gauge the online reviews to support a decision about whether or not to visit there. Users rely on the prior experiences of peer Yelp users via their reviews and pictures. Hence, this app is useful for businesses, who should consider creating a presence on Yelp and monitor and respond there to reviews of their business.

Facebook   As at 2019, Facebook has over 1.5 billion mobile monthly active users, and more than 50% of those solely use its mobile version. Facebook has long been regarded as a key place to advertise brands and products to a mass market. Businesses can filter users by specific demographics and then can directly advertise to them. In addition, the business knows which users have visited or referred to the business Facebook page or registered their email address or phone number. However, due to a breach of user trust through mismanagement of user data in 2018, users are leaving Facebook and spending less time on the platform or in app. In response, Facebook has released an algorithm that gives priority to posts related to users' friends and family over brands in their news feed. This decision aimed to strengthen user engagement with Facebook. But it may lessen the attractiveness of Facebook for business investments in advertising on Facebook because their advertisements will decline in prominence.[23]

13

Instagram   Instagram is owned by Facebook, and, as of 2019, it reaches more than 300 million daily users who post more than 95 million photos and videos per day. It is primarily used in-app, and the Instagram website has less capability than the app. Unlike Facebook, Instagram's user demographics lean toward a more youthful audience: 55% users are 18–29 years-old, and 28% are 30–49 years-old.[24] Users in these age ranges are more willing to adopt digital, novel, and new products and services in comparison to older age ranges. Instagram also provides image filters, special effects, and editing tools and is more focused on images and short videos than other information; however, like Facebook it is a rich platform for reaching specific demographic and geographic market segments.

---

22 This section is adapted from Lister (2018).
23 Source: Cao and Sweeney (2018).
24 Regarding the demographics of Instagram, see da Cunha (2019).

WordPress/Medium WordPress and Medium are blogging and website tools that improve the load time of webpages on mobile devices. Reducing the load time is helpful for businesses to retain impatient consumers. They allow website operators to read and edit existing posts or create new content and respond to existing posts from their mobile devices.

SlideShare SlideShare, as the name implied, is an online slide sharing platform, with over 70 million users as at 2019. It is a good place to post and share presentations. SlideShare content will not just be buried somewhere on the site, because 80% visitors come to the site via specific searches which lead them to the target content they want. Moreover, SlideShare has shareable social buttons connecting to social media and a comment section to interact with others.

Google's Mobile-Friendly Testing Tool and Mobile Usability Report Google's Mobile-Friendly Testing Tool is a tool that tests the usability of a website on mobile devices. This tool is very simple—just enter the webpage URL into it, and it will report the friendliness of the site and display a screenshot of how it looks on a mobile device. The Mobile Usability Report works in a similar way but provides a more in-depth examination of a site's potential problems.

Google Analytics Google Analytics is a core tool for tracking and analyzing the performance of any online presence, including mobile devices. It can monitor real-time data, provide a customized report, and represent the report in a dashboard with metrics as selected by the user. Google Analytics is used to monitor website performance, and the data it provides can be used to inform specific actions to improve the online performance of a business. In addition, the user can login in and check the dashboard through a mobile device.

13.6 Challenges for Mobile e-Commerce Businesses

The main barriers to large-scale, worldwide adoption of mobile e-commerce have been the lack of user trust in m-commerce information security, the usability of mobile devices, and the low conversion rate of m-commerce. These are now described.

13.6.1 Trust

As it was the case in the earlier phases of traditional, wired e-commerce, user trust in m-commerce is critical to increase take-up. As was discussed previously, m-commerce creates a wireless Internet environment with benefits and value for customers, but that does not mean customers will readily accept it. m-Commerce provides customers with convenience and improves the user experience, but on the other hand, it also has perceived potential risks related to privacy and security.[25] Customers do not embrace mobile transactions unless they are sufficiently confident that they can rely upon both the m-commerce approach in general and the m-commerce channel.

Trust can be divided into three types:

1. *Trusting beliefs* which means a consumer associates "positively" with m-commerce providers that offer reliability, capability, and a good reputation.
2. *Trusting intention* implies a consumer's intention to believe in m-commerce providers.
3. *Trusting behavior* that a consumer demonstrates to fulfill a commercial activity with m-commerce providers.

Ultimately consumer trust is what businesses want, but beliefs and intentions of trust are the precursor for trusting behaviors, so businesses should consider ways to make consumers identify positive traits with their brand, product, staff, service, and mobile infrastructure.

Desirable goals that businesses should pursue with their m-commerce strategies include the following two groups:[26]

Group 1: Goals that aim to generate initial trust

- Increase the familiarity of customers with mobile technologies and mobile services.
- Build brand reputation as a mobile service provider.
- Provide high-quality information through the mobile channel.
- Work with independent (third-party) certifiers of quality and security for m-commerce, to obtain quality and security certification.

Group 2: Goals that aim to generate lasting trust

- Continuously improve the mobile channel to develop good-quality communication.
- Improve staff competencies with mobile-based services and activities
- Maintain business integrity in the mobile channel.
- Publicly announce the company's privacy policy, notably with e-commerce transactions and in the mobile channel.
- Foster two-way B2C dialogue through the mobile channel.
- Arrange regular external audits to monitor online operations, and actively and transparently respond to irregularities or bad practices.

13.6.2 Usability

Usability of m-commerce depends on the ease of use of mobile devices and applications and, as such, is strongly linked to the quality of interactions in mobile

---

25 Source: Chong et al. (2012).
26 Source: Siau and Shen (2003).

environments. Usability is a measure of the interactive user experience associated with the m-commerce system. As was discussed previously, usability is a crucial factor that influences the rate of m-commerce adoption. In spite of the major advances in usability during the last decade, this dimension remains a challenge for many businesses, especially for those that need to better understand the mobile user experience context and value proposition.

The above-mentioned link requires businesses to consider the following principles:[27, 28]

- Make careful use of graphics and images. This is due to the limited visual capability of a mobile device (as compared to that of a PC, a laptop, or a tablet) and to the fact that rich graphic resources require larger files to download and therefore slow down interactions with users.
- Account for the differences between Android and iOS. Android and iOS are two very distinct operating systems, so it is problematic to simply clone the app from one to another. For example, iOS does not have a "back" button like Android. An app must be tailored specifically to both systems and allow users to operate it intuitively.
- Avoid long lists and give users immediate information on the number of options available, in case they cannot be fully visualized at once.
- Make important options visible to customers. For example, a business website with a clear transactional capability would facilitate the identification of purchase options, shopping cart, and more.
- Provide users with helpful and meaningful error messages, avoiding the use of coded messages without an easily understandable error description.
- Avoid dead ends. Actively test and ensure that all website and app links are active and working properly.
- Format and present content appropriately. Designers should be aware of the specificities (including the limitations) of the mobile context in order to propose appropriate designs.
- Offer consistency in navigation and menu options. Development teams may create many interesting features or content for users but should never ignore how they fit together in a well-organized simple way.
- Provide users with sufficient prompting. Users should be given useful information, which helps them to efficiently navigate through the mobile service or app.
- Minimize user input. In spite of the significant technical advances in mobile devices, users still have some limitations to comfortably and quickly interacting with m-commerce sites or apps, for example, typing in sentences. This shortcoming calls for reducing the users' need to both click on links and introduce more information.

---

27 Source: Condos et al. (2002).
28 Source: Gerber (2016).

- Structure tasks to help users interact with the mobile environment. Mobile services should be designed in such a way that they are presented to users in a logical, well-structured and easily accessible form.
- Simplify the checkout process. Checking out via smartphone may be complicated by the device's limitations. Consumers may have to enter their address and phone number and select a secure payment method—all on a tiny screen. Think of simple approaches to allow a safe and quick checkout. For example, auto-save consumer information related to their address and phone number after they made a purchase, and so consumers just need to confirm the information at the checkout process. Alternately, use an Address Finder plugin to autofill address details after a consumer has typed in their street number and name.
- Stress user testing and feedback. User testing is an obvious strategy to learn about user needs, feelings, and perceptions. Businesses need user testing and continuous feedback to identify potential usability problems; this enables a faster awareness of usability issues that require attention and address them as soon as practical. This dynamic approach is more responsive than static regular app updates. Many businesses still withhold iterative improvements until regularly scheduled updates.

13.6.3 Conversion Rate: The Ultimate Challenge

A conversion rate compares the total number of visitors to a site to the number of visitors who become paying customers/users. This is a vital e-commerce metric because it represents the extent to which the site has captured customer value.[29] First, a conversion rate is a common metric that is typically used by all sites and apps, and so businesses can compare their conversion rate with industry benchmarks. Second, conversion rate analysis can reveal which channels are most efficient and effective in transforming visitors into buyers. Based on the data analysis and other metrics, businesses can devise future strategies and tactics. Third, the rate can be calculated by different demographics. A demographic-based conversion rate analysis is helpful for businesses to identify the most valuable customer segments and the most likely segments that buy.

As for m-commerce, a conversion rate is often employed as a key performance indicator (KPI) to monitor the effectiveness of m-commerce sites and apps. As shown in ◘ Table 13.1, the conversion rate by mobile devices (smartphone and tablet) is always lower than desktop computers. Even for the United States where m-commerce is highly developed, the desktop conversion rate is nearly three times higher than smartphone.

Businesses with omni-channel strategies may acknowledge that consumers use some channels for information and others for purchasing. However, with more people using mobile devices for shopping, it is critical for businesses offering m-commerce maintain their conversion rate to the benchmark level or above; oth-

---

29 The discussion on the importance of conversion rate is adapted from Chaffey (2019).

erwise businesses may be losing potential customers who should have bought products and created sales for them. For example, as shown in ◘ Table 13.1, in the first quarter of 2017, the 1.25% global conversion rate means that more than 98% of smartphone visitors do not buy anything. It should also be considered that, among that 1.25% of buyers, a proportion of those may return goods. As a consequence, how much revenue can a business attract from m-commerce transactions? The low conversion performance, to some extent, raises questions about the real current value of m-commerce.

Mobile dominates 69% of people's digital time but only accounts for 20% of online expenditure. When the five reasons for non-conversion are reviewed, we find wired e-commerce also had similar in its early phases, such as security, transparency, usability, and so on. Similarly, it is acceptable that, as an immature business, m-commerce has weaknesses and shortcomings.

On the other hand, today's consumer behavior is more complicated. No matter what channels are used for e-commerce, it cannot directly offer users tactile information related to a product or service. The tactile information is often important to buyers who may want to judge the quality of products in this way, for example, clothes, shoes, and furniture. This explains why some consumers browse products online but purchase offline, namely, *webrooming* behavior. Imagine a woman is shopping at a physical store and shows her interest in an expensive dress, but she did not have enough knowledge to tell whether the dress is worth the price or not, so she would search the price through her shopping app and would get the same product at the same price and then would finally buy it at the store. From this example, we can see that people sometimes just use shopping apps to collect online information to assist in decision-making. The informative advantage, mobility, and convenience of m-commerce apps indeed provide a lot of value for consumers and businesses, but in this case m-commerce apps unfortunately foster a free-riding behavior. It is a paradox of m-commerce apps and reinforces why businesses use holistic omni-channel strategies.

◘ **Table 13.1** Conversion rates by device by country

	Conversion rates by device	Q1 2016 (%)	Q2 2016 (%)	Q3 2016 (%)	Q4 2016 (%)	Q1 2017 (%)
Global	Desktop	4.23	3.88	3.66	4.25	3.63
	Smartphone	1.42	1.31	1.17	1.49	1.25
	Tablet	3.59	3.44	3.21	3.79	3.14
US	Desktop	4.28	3.94	3.75	4.41	3.73
	Smartphone	1.27	1.16	1.03	1.40	1.14
	Tablet	3.46	3.33	3.08	3.80	3.06

Source: Adapted from Chaffey (2018)

In summary, m-commerce is still undeveloped. For long-term profits and sustainable advantage, businesses using m-commerce need to consider thoroughly and carefully how to address these challenges before formally launching their m-commerce strategy.

Summary

In this chapter, we discussed the strategic aspects of a mobile commerce strategy, mobile payment, and mobile commerce apps and tools.

1. A mobile commerce strategy is a long-term plan to conduct mobile device-based activities to fulfill commerce-related strategic purpose(s).
2. Adoption is a prerequisite of m-commerce success.
3. Businesses need to find a balance point where m-commerce can provide value for consumers and also create value for them.
4. m-Payment refers to making payments through mobile devices.
5. m-Payments can be divided into two types: proximity m-payment and remote m-payment.
6. m-Commerce apps can be grouped in four categories: commerce-, tool-, entertainment-, or social-centric.
7. Trust, usability, and conversion rates are three key challenges that m-commerce is facing.

❓ Review Questions

1. What is a mobile commerce strategy?
2. Why is adoption important for the success of m-commerce strategy?
3. How many kinds of m-payment are there?
4. How many types of m-commerce apps are there? Can you figure out the difference among them?
5. What is a conversion rate of m-commerce?
6. Which aspects should be assessed when designing an m-commerce strategy?
7. How should a business find a balance point where m-commerce can provide value for consumers and also create value for them?
8. Balancing the benefits and risks of m-payments, should a company launch an m-payment plan?
9. How should an m-payments business properly handle user data?
10. How should a business use m-commerce apps/tools to create and capture value?
11. Why are trust, usability, and a conversion rate important for the maturity of m-commerce?

References

Adhami, M. (2013). Using neuromarketing to discover how we really feel about apps. *International Journal of Mobile Marketing, 8*(1), 95–103.

Auger, A. (2016, August). Pokemon Go: Mobile gaming a boon for local retail? *BNP Paribas.* Retrieved from https://atelier.bnpparibas/en/retail/article/pokemon-go-mobile-gaming-boon-local-retail/.

Cao, J., & Sweeney, S. (2018, January 12). Facebook's ad business may power through news feed change. *Bloomberg*.

Chaffey, D. (2018, January 30). Ecommerce conversion rates. *Smart Insights*.

Chaffey, D. (2019, February 19). E-commerce conversion rates—how do yours compare? *Smart Insights*. Available at https://www.smartinsights.com/ecommerce/ecommerce-analytics/ecommerce-conversion-rates/.

Chong, A. Y. L., Chan, F. T., & Ooi, K. B. (2012). Predicting consumer decisions to adopt mobile commerce: Cross country empirical examination between China and Malaysia. *Decision Support Systems, 53*(1), 34–43.

Condos, C., et al. (2002). Ten usability principles for the development of effective WAP and m-commerce services. *ASLIB Proceedings, 54*(6), 345–355.

da Cunha, M. (2019, March 22). 11 Instagram marketing tips for brands in 2019. *Wordstream*. Retrieved from https://www.wordstream.com/blog/ws/2015/01/06/instagram-marketing/.

Facebook. (2017, February 1). Facebook reports fourth quarter and full year 2016 results. *Facebook*. Retrieved from https://investor.fb.com/investor-news/press-release-details/2017/facebook-Reports-Fourth-Quarter-and-Full-Year-2016-Results/default.aspx/.

Gerber, S. (2016, May 26). The eight most overlooked mobile app usability issues (and how to fix them). *Mashable*.

Gopikanth, V. (2015, January 14). Elements of a successful mobile strategy. *Digital Reimagination*.

HAL90210. (2016, November 10). Facebook makes 13 attempts to clone Snapchat. Lucky for some? *The Guardian*. Retrieved from https://www.theguardian.com/technology/2016/nov/10/facebook-clone-snapchat-whatsapp/.

Harty, D. (2016, July 25). Smartphones overtake computers as top e-commerce traffic source. *Bloomberg*. Retrieved from https://www.bloomberg.com/news/articles/2016-07-25/smartphones-overtake-computers-as-top-e-commerce-traffic-source.

Hook, L., & Nicolaou, A. (2018, January 21). Amazon debuts the store without a checkout. *Financial Times*.

Larivière, B., Joosten, H., Malthouse, E. C., Van Birgelen, M., Aksoy, P., Kunz, W. H., & Huang, M. H. (2013). Value fusion: The blending of consumer and firm value in the distinct context of mobile technologies and social media. *Journal of Service Management, 24*(3), 268–293.

Lister, M. (2018, November 28). 13 great mobile marketing tools you need. *Wordstream*. Retrieved from https://www.wordstream.com/blog/ws/2016/10/14/mobile-marketing-tools/.

Liu, J., Kauffman, R. J., & Ma, D. (2015). Competition, cooperation, and regulation: Understanding the evolution of the mobile payments technology ecosystem. *Electronic Commerce Research and Applications, 14*(5), 372–391.

Lopez, M. (2015, July 21). Six strategies for mobile app success. *Forbes*.

McNair, C. (2018, December 17). Global proximity mobile payment users. *eMarketer*.

Molina, B. (2018, February 20). Google rolls out another rival to Apple Pay. *USA Today*. Retrieved from https://www.usatoday.com/story/tech/news/2018/02/20/google-pay-rival-apple-pay/355174002/.

Nikou, S., & Mezei, J. (2013). Evaluation of mobile services and substantial adoption factors with analytic hierarchy process (AHP). *Telecommunications Policy, 37*(10), 915–929.

Pinola, M. (2017, September 22). How to pay with your phone or tablet. *Lifewire*.

PYMNTS. (2018, January 23). WeChat Pay enters Italy. *PYMNTS.com*. Retrieved from https://www.pymnts.com/news/payment-methods/2018/wechat-pay-european-payments/.

Siau, K., & Shen, Z. (2003). Building customer trust in e-commerce. *Communications of the ACM, 46*(4), 91–94.

Su, W., Xu, X., Li, Y., Martínez-López, F. J., & Li, L. (2018). Technological innovation: A case study of mobile internet information technology applications in community management. *Journal of Global Information Management, 26*(2), 193–203.

Tang, A. (2018, February 15). Mobile payment expects to grow 13% globally. *Marketing*. Retrieved from http://www.marketing-interactive.com/growing-no-of-smartphone-users-purchase-on-phone-at-physical-pos-in-2018/.

Taylor, E. (2016). Mobile payment technologies in retail: A review of potential benefits and risks. *International Journal of Retail & Distribution Management, 44*(2), 159–177.

Warwick-Ching, L. (2015, July 17). Apple Pay: What it is and how it works. *Financial Times.*

Yang, Y., Liu, Y., Li, H., & Yu, B. (2015). Understanding perceived risks in mobile payment acceptance. *Industrial Management & Data Systems, 115*(2), 253–269.

Zhao, Z., & Balagué, C. (2015). Designing branded mobile apps: Fundamentals and recommendations. *Business Horizons, 58*(3), 305–315.

Further Reading

Martin, B. (2017, January). Mobile's hierarchy of needs. *comScore MMX Multi-Platform.*

13

Strategies for Social Commerce

Contents

© Springer Nature Switzerland AG 2020
T. Jelassi, F. J. Martínez-López, *Strategies for e-Business*, Classroom Companion: Business,
https://doi.org/10.1007/978-3-030-48950-2_14

Learning Outcomes

After completing this chapter, you should be able to:

- Understand why firms should consider adopting social commerce strategies
- Understand the wide variety of social commerce activities
- Discern social commerce's structure and characteristics
- Understand how marketing mindsets are evolving along with advances in technologies
- Understand value creation on the social web
- Know how firms can monetize social platforms and how advertising and commerce strategies work on social platforms.
- Take social commerce into today's mobile business and understand how to design and configure a mobile social commerce

■ Introduction

Online social platforms are dominating the digital time of Internet users. According to research, most people spend at least 2 hours on social networking and messaging every day (Galer 2018), and businesses should not miss opportunities within this phenomenon to reap more benefits and fulfill strategic purposes.

In this chapter, we will:

1. Discuss why firms should adopt social commerce strategies.
2. Social commerce is more than social advertising and social shopping; we introduce a wide range of social commerce activities from different aspects.
3. Provide the layers that constitute social commerce and illustrates social commerce's characteristics.
4. Introduce marketers' mindset change along with advances in web technologies and then delineate the concept of value creation on the social web. This will highlight that the value creation logic is special on the social web.
5. From a lens of a social platform provider, there are two major strategies to monetize social platforms: advertising strategies and commerce strategies. Eventually, as mobile technology use is influencing all Internet businesses, social commerce strategists need to configure their social commerce into a mobile context.

This chapter also offers a three-layer design for mobile social commerce and a real case to explain how firms apply this design framework into practice.

14.1 Why Should Companies Adopt Social Commerce Strategies?

Businesses should be careful when implementing new e-business strategies. Not only might new strategies deplete firm resources, but they may also lead to fundamental changes in the organizational structure and processes. Moreover, firms should identify and manage conflicts and misalignments between new strategies and previous strategies. S(ocial) commerce strategies may generate new value and business opportunities for firms, but not all firms can capture them effectively and efficiently. There are at least five reasons for firms to adopt s-commerce strategies.[1] Firms need consider them in their real business contexts and decide if adopting s-commerce is strategically worthy.

It makes online shopping more social Shopping should be fun. For commodities with social elements such as fashion and apparel, consumers typically do not want a solitary shopping experience. It may be fun for consumers to shop for social commodities with their friends and family, because they can seek their opinions, which may develop psychological benefits such as happiness and a sense of belonging. s-Commerce realizes this social feature of online shopping, and shoppers can interact with others by sharing pictures or website links. Many e-commerce platforms add social features. For example, Pinduoduo, an e-commerce site founded by an ex-Google engineer, allows online shoppers to send friends shopping links and do online group buying through WeChat. For more detailed information, see the article: "Ex-Google engineer builds $1.5 billion startup in 21 months."

Ex-Google Engineer Builds $1.5 Billion Startup in 21 Months

Colin Huang belongs to a rarefied cohort of Chinese entrepreneurs who launched their careers in Silicon Valley and then returned home to start successful tech companies. Huang, an ex-Google engineer who worked on early search algorithms for e-commerce, is already on his fourth and most ambitious startup. Pinduoduo, or PDD, is a kind of Facebook-Group on mashup that Huang believes could revolutionize e-commerce. PDD just raised more than $100 million, according to people familiar with the matter, valuing the company at more than 10 billion yuan ($1.5 billion) less than 2 years after its founding. Huang, featured in the latest episode of the Decrypted podcast, is one reason China has created as many $1 billion startups this year as the United States.

The idea behind PDD is simple enough. Typically shoppers know what they want before they get online. A person goes to, say, Amazon or Alibaba, plugs in a keyword and then picks out what they want after sorting through a few options or reviews. Huang's idea is to give shoppers an experience more like spending a day at the mall with friends. You share ideas about what you like, get feedback from people you trust, maybe gossip a bit. Then, if you make purchases together, you get a discount. It's a twist on the so-called social commerce, an idea that has been tried with little success in the United States. For a time, both Twitter Inc. and Facebook Inc. put buy buttons on the ads featured in a person's newsfeed. The latter even offered a kind of currency called Facebook Credits. The tests were discontinued because most users don't want to be solicited while hanging out with friends online.

Companies like PDD that start as shopping sites with a social component sometimes work better. Huang has wisely embedded his app in China's ubiquitous messaging service WeChat, used for everything from social networking to mobile

---

1   These five reasons are adapted from: Parker (2017).

payments. To further entice users, he drew on his previous experience with successful gaming apps and made sure PDD was fun to use. "A few companies have tried this before, but no one has really been able to do it," says Huang, who sports a buzz cut and has an unrestrained laugh. "We felt we had a competitive advantage." So far, he looks to be right. Demand has exploded, prompting PDD to move into airy Shanghai offices where Huang expects to double his headcount to 1000. PDD is now the largest private e-commerce company in China by sales volume and is closing in on Vipshop Holdings Ltd., the third largest e-commerce player behind Alibaba Group Holding Ltd. and ▶ JD.com Inc.

PDD's rapid growth has led to some cases of botched deliveries and damaged merchandise, prompting complaints from unhappy customers. The bulk-buying business model has flopped elsewhere too, most famously with Groupon Inc. But Huang has had no trouble finding backers, raising his first round of venture money in 2015 and closing the latest in February. Zhen Zhang, whose Banyan Capital led the first round, was attracted by the simplicity of Huang's concept. "He is taking advantage of people's willingness to save money and tell their friends," he says. [...]

Huang came up with the idea for PDD in part by watching China's two top internet companies—e-commerce giant Alibaba and Tencent Holdings Ltd., the dominant games company and owner of WeChat. Both are big, fast-growing, and successful, but neither could penetrate the other's business. "These two companies don't really understand each other," Huang says. "They don't really understand how the other makes money."

Huang and his team did. They had experience in both e-commerce and games and were convinced there was an enormous opportunity in bringing the two worlds together. Huang raised $8 million from a group of investors led by Banyan in May 2015 and launched the app a few months later. Most people use the PDD app within WeChat. You open up the messaging service on your phone and then click on PDD. The home screen has tabs for categories like food, clothes, and bedding. Once you choose a category, you get a vertical list of products you can scroll through, say lychee or apples in fruits. The app has the feel of a game, with colorful photos and hidden bargains. Deals change every day, and, as you scroll through a category, the discounted price is shown below the image. You click on an image of mangos at 34.8 yuan for eight and find the price is 39.9 yuan if you buy alone. To get the discount, you have to find a friend to join in the purchase. Because you're already on WeChat, you can instantly pitch others.

The motivation can be compelling. Recently, a track suit in red, white, or black was on sale at 48 yuan for a single purchase. You can click a button and pay 29.8 yuan if you say a friend will join. That sends shoppers off in search of friends willing to participate. If you can't find another buyer, you get a refund. Ren Shuying, a Beijing accountant, is a dedicated user. "I check it out every day and chat about products with friends," Ren says. "I've bought all sorts of products-things to eat or wear."

With usage increasing, PDD raised about $100 million in 2016, giving the company the resources to attract more merchants and customers. The total amount of goods sold on the platform, or gross merchandise value, went from 100 million yuan a month in early 2016 to 4 billion yuan a month now, Huang says. That puts PDD just behind Vipshop, a flash sale website that trades on the New York Stock Exchange with a market value of more than $8 billion. "We think we will pass them in the next 12 to 18 months," Huang says, his PR handler shifting nervously nearby. Huang sees PDD as a way to create a richer retail experience for both shoppers and merchants. Customers learn from friends about products or services they love. Producers have the opportunity to customize for small groups of buyers online and innovate in ways that were impossible before. Merchants can also cut out retailers and get more direct feedback from customers. [...]

Adapted from: P. Elstrom, D. Ramli, "Ex-Google Engineer Builds $1.5 Billion Startup in 21 Months," *Bloomberg*, 27 April 2017.

Beauty Content Marketing: Tips from the Estée Lauder Companies' Alicianne Rand

When it comes to social media engagement, beauty brands are, in many ways, leading the content marketing space. From connecting content to commerce, celebrating fans, leveraging influencers, and becoming early adopters on new platforms, they often set the bar for what other industries can achieve through content marketing. We connected with one of the best in the business, Alicianne Rand, Executive Director, Global Content Marketing, for The Estée Lauder Companies, who recently shared her insights as a speaker at ThinkContent London and Content Marketing World. Here, she delves into some tactics that The Estée Lauder Companies' brands—which includes Clinique, M•A•C, Bobbi Brown, Smashbox, and many others—are using to connect with consumers and drive engagement and commerce.

Harness the Power of Social

"People are looking for beauty inspiration on social, sharing on social, and shopping on social," says Rand. It's no wonder that savvy brands are creating and scaling content to meet consumers where they are, she adds, noting that consumers watch 1 billion hours of YouTube a day. "When you consider that Kylie Jenner built a $420 million beauty business in just 18 months primarily by harnessing content marketing on social media, you can see just how powerful those platforms are for the beauty industry," says Rand.

Plus, makeup and skincare are emotional topics that speak to women's inner confidence and are very visual—making them a natural fit for social media. To make sure that content will resonate, brands in The Estée Lauder Companies' portfolio ask these four questions before publishing content: "Does it stop me? Does it reward me? Does it make it easy for me? Does it stay with me?"

Leverage Influencers for Storytelling

"You don't need celebrity star power to be an influencer. Local makeup artists and consumers can be influencers to brands," says Rand. "Social media has created an even playing field where anybody can become an influencer, and some influencers have become their own brands. We see this across YouTube, Facebook, and Instagram. "Influencers have strong relationships with their fans and tell authentic stories, making them great content creators. This is why brands within The Estée Lauder Companies have teams dedicated to influencer engagement – who do everything from identifying influencers who align with the brands' values to partnering with them to tell authentic stories," says Rand.

Use a Full-Funnel Strategy and Measure Success at Each Stage

"When we think about content, we think about every asset that is going to live on our platforms. Some are more advertising- and campaign-focused, and they are all about sales and conversions," Rand says. For each piece of content, the team identifies the narratives, distribution channels, and an amplification plan that will help them achieve their goals. "Some will be need-based, like how-tos, stories around customer pain points, and interests like cooking and travel," she explains. "The result is a content strategy that is seamlessly woven across different channels and platforms from social to online to in-store," says Rand. "We focus on storytelling narratives that help drive the brand forward and hit the right business KPIs every step of the way. Our content strategy needs to drive those goals, and our distribution and paid amplification strategies align with that."

Here are some of the content stops along the funnel:

- Awareness: "Here, we're focused on driving reach and frequency," says Rand. Her team measures share of conversation, unique reach, veiwability, video completion rates, and more.
- Purchase and conversion: This is the information that helps guide purchase decisions. Rand says some of the important metrics here include web traffic, branded and unbranded search, sentiment, and product reviews. "We are also looking at purchase metrics, online and in-store," she says.
- Retention: This type of content is all about keeping your brand top of mind, including metrics like product reviews, an increase in average order value, and repeat purchases.

Put Customers in the Spotlight

More than 40 percent of content related to The Estée Lauder Companies' brands comes from consumers who share their stories. "Consumers are naturally sharing their beauty tricks, tips, comments, and pain points on social. It's happening every single day. We're trying to inspire them to do that even further," says Rand. Some of the ways that The Estée Lauder Companies' brands encourage consumers to contribute to the conversation include asking questions around specific pain points, engaging in dialogue around cultural moments like Coachella or International Women's Day, or posing a challenge, such as "create your best Halloween look and share it with us."

> **Create New Paths to Conversion**
>
> The Estée Lauder Companies is no stranger to experimenting with new technologies to connect with fans. For instance, the Estée Lauder brand recently used augmented reality to help drive conversions in store. The lipstick chatbot, which works on Facebook Messenger and was created in partnership with Modiface, enables Estée Lauder customers to search for and virtually try on Estée Lauder's full assortment of lip shades, each individually shade matched to represent the actual product.
>
> Rand says listening closely to consumers and being willing to innovate are what helps keep the content machine rolling. At the Company, that's no easy task, but it is working. "Every single day, we reach over 100 million people globally through our social channels," Rand says. "And we will continue to innovate the way we communicate through content to build meaningful, long-lasting relationships with our consumers."
>
> D. Papandrea, "Beauty content marketing: tips from The Estée Lauder companies' alicianne rand," *Newscred Insights*, 28 March 2018.

It reduces friction in buying processes   The completion of an online purchase typically occurs on an e-commerce site instead of a social media platform. s-Commerce reduces friction in the customer journey from interest to purchase, which may explain why the use of s-commerce is increasing. It offers the potential for shoppers to complete an online purchase within one platform; it reduces the effort of using both a social media platform and an e-commerce site simultaneously. However, approaches to minimize friction on a shopper's path to purchase are diverse between various platforms. For example, Facebook mainly offers "call-to-action" features for advertisements. Facebook users can tap on an advertisement, and it will lead them to an external site. In contrast, Pinterest is more direct. Pinterest shoppers can find buyable "Pins" allowing them to directly purchase items in relevant pictures. This approach has less friction than the Facebook example.

S-commerce revenue is real   Profitability could be a priority when businesses consider new strategies or business opportunities. For example, advertising is a representative business for most social platforms; Facebook's advertising revenue was US$39.9 billion in 2017, which is an astonishing 49 percent per annum growth (from US$26.9 billion in 2016). As for social shopping, it is estimated that 73 percent of people who have tried social "buy buttons" would do so again (Hutchinson 2016).

It allows firms to access a focus group of millions   Brands can directly or indirectly interact with a mass market of users through social media. For example, Estée Lauder owns a Facebook homepage having 2.2 million followers. It is able to directly convey brand value those followers simultaneously. In theory, this approach is more precise than traditional mass advertising because people who follow a brand on social media usually do so out of interest or loyalty: they are target customers. Moreover, Estée Lauder uses celebrity influencers to reach much more consumers; see the article: "Beauty content marketing: tips from The Estée Lauder companies' Alicianne Rand."

14.2 Classification of Social Commerce

Social platforms can be used to conduct a wide range of commercial activities (see
◘ Fig. 14.1). A social platform can be used for at least three business activities:
social media marketing, enterprise management, and technology support.

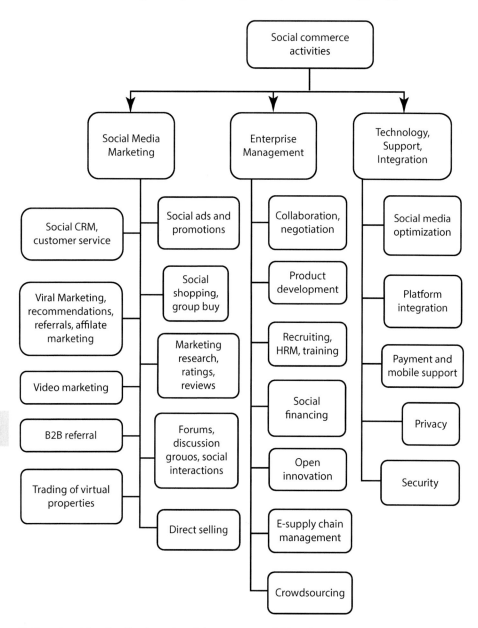

◘ **Fig. 14.1** The classification of social commerce activities. (Source: adapted from Liang and
Turban (2011))

Social Media Marketing Businesses use social media platforms to conduct marketing-related activities. Social media platforms can be used to target, acquire, reach, and retain customers. See ▶ Chap. 11 for further details on using social media to interact with customers.

Enterprise Management Social media platforms are also a useful way to interact with various actors in a firm's value network. Enterprise social media (ESM) is a specific type of social media platform that allows the employees, suppliers, partners, and other stakeholders of a business to collaborate and communicate with each other. It can be used to do many aspects of enterprise management such as research and development, recruitment, financing, crowdsourcing, and more. For example, many businesses use ESM to facilitate and streamline internal business affairs; see the article: "Maximizing the impact of enterprise social media."

> ### Maximizing the Impact of Enterprise Social Media
> Many leaders adopt enterprise social media (ESM) platforms as the cornerstone of their organization's internal digital transformation with the hope that employees will reap the highly desirable benefits of knowledge sharing, collaboration, and efficiency. Still, employees often get lost during these strategic shifts because of the technical and cultural disconnect between ESM and the rest of the internal IT systems and digital platforms that they use in their day-to-day job-related activities. Research shows that less than 50% of ESM platforms are actually used by employees on a regular basis.
>
> MIT Sloan Management Review's 2017 Digital Business Global Executive Study and Research Project made it clear that implementing systemic changes in how companies organize could cultivate digitally minded cultures and experiences. Here we explain why companies should not introduce ESM in the workplace as a siloed system but rather as a strategic component of an organization's digital portfolio and an integrated tool to support employees' daily work. Our insights are based on a field study of a multinational cosmetic company that implemented an ESM platform to connect more than 4500 employees, spread across 29 countries on five continents. ESM was added to an already tangled web of technologies meant to support communication and collaboration, and, at the outset, less than 30% of this organization's employees—and 8% of executives—contributed to ESM on a regular basis.
>
> #### Employees Lost in Digital Transitions
> As companies are attracted to the benefits of digitization, they ask their IT departments to equip employees with a rich digital portfolio that integrates platforms including team collaboration software, project management tools, chat-based software, internal knowledge management systems, and intranets.
>
> At the same time, most ESM platforms are cloud-based applications. For the first time, the responsibility for a technology in the workplace falls at least partially outside the scope of the IT department. Thus, non-IT managers are asked to lead

the cultural implementation of ESM in the workplace. However, in many situations, when ESM is adopted, leaders fail to articulate priorities for navigating the thicket of all the digital tools that employees are expected to use in their day-to-day, job-related tasks.

When employees are not given guidance on how to navigate the different platforms that form their organization's digital portfolio, they become lost in the digital transition. Paradoxically, connecting to ESM platforms requires disconnecting from existing patterns of communication and collaboration. For instance, one social media champion at the organization we studied cited the lack of interoperability between systems as the cause of employee frustration: "There is a competition in terms of digital tools, since the company offers other digital tools and email [applications] that are direct competitors to social media. I can [translate] my emails into tasks but I cannot do the same with social media." The disconnect between an organization's existing set of IT systems and newer, cloud-based technologies presents a very real hurdle to engaging employees on ESM. The cultural and technical solutions to this problem need to work in concert.

ESM as the Hub of Your Internal Digital Portfolio

From a technical standpoint, organizations should position ESM as the hub that connects IT systems, business applications, collaborative tools, and digital platforms. With proper integration, employees are able to access various platforms such as the corporate intranet site, email, directories, document-sharing tools, forums, blogs, and wikis directly from the ESM platform with little effort. Better information flows between ESM and other digital and IT systems will increase adoption and efficiency.

Organizations that implement stand-alone ESM platforms can also contend with their fragmented systems by using application programming interfaces (APIs) to integrate ESM with preexisting digital tools such as a corporate intranet site, mobile applications, messaging systems, and third-party web applications. ESM platforms like Salesforce Chatter, Microsoft Yammer, or Workplace by Facebook offer open APIs that enable interoperability between ESM and other information technologies. IT departments and developers can contribute to social media success by leveraging APIs to integrate ESM platforms with internal applications and systems that are critical to their employees' productivity. Developers can also customize ESM platforms for their employees by making it the focal entrance point to the employees' digital portfolio. This can enhance the functionality of the ESM platform and improve employees' comprehension of the platform as a working tool.

Demonstrate Leadership Buy-In and Showcase Best Practices

From a cultural vantage point, leaders need to articulate flexible principles that guide employees toward which digital platform is best used for which purpose and then extol unexpected uses of the technology that align with cultural aspirations.

For some employees, connecting to social media feels as if they are disconnecting from their jobs. Organizations should provide some early guidance as to how these tools can be used productively. For example, ESM platforms might be especially helpful for asynchronous brainstorming sessions with groups of geographically dispersed employees or for asking questions that the classic off-line network of employees cannot answer or that do not require an immediate answer. In contrast, email might be best for more formal communication on promotions, new organizational policies, and meeting agendas. Organizations should devise their own best practices for using digital tools, but some guidance at the beginning will help alleviate confusion for employees.

Leaders of these social media transformation initiatives should also watch out for unanticipated uses of ESM that match the values the organization aspires to embody and then extol these unforeseen uses in stories and examples. Thus, during early implementation, guidance along with flexibility for the unexpected will help employees realize ESM is a process and not an event. As implementation matures, highlighting social media champions can inspire the rest of the organization. These champions show fellow colleagues how to best navigate digital transformation and integrate social media in their daily practices and routines.

To deliver on its promise, ESM needs to be thought of as the hub of an organization's digital transformation. Organizations can seize this opportunity by carefully addressing any confusion this new implementation will cause employees and providing a clearer technical and cultural map of how to navigate ESM along with their existing digital tools.

Source: M. Charki, N. Boukef and S. Harrison, "Maximizing the impact of enterprise social media," *MIT Sloan Management Review*, 20 February 2018.

Technology Support s-Commerce is similar to e-commerce in some aspects. It is notable that social platforms are used initially for social interactions instead of commercial activities. Firms need to orient these platforms to be used for commerce by, for example:

- Creating a catalogue site in a Facebook homepage
- Adding a call-to-action feature into ads
- Linking direct shopping sites to posts
- Providing integrated payment gateways

To illustrate, Shopify allows stores sell directly in Facebook Messenger; for more details, see the article: "Shopify now lets stores sell directly in Facebook Messenger."

Shopify Now Lets Stores Sell Directly in Facebook Messenger

Shopify was early to bring its merchants the ability to converse directly with customers via Facebook Messenger, and now it is launching the ability to actually sell directly within messages between stores and customers. The integration works by giving customers a "Shop Now" option when they start a conversation with any Facebook Business Page store using Shopify's Messenger sales channel, which will bring up the merchant's entire product catalogue and let them tap through to browse and buy, completing purchases via Shopify's checkout portal, which actually operates completely within Messenger, so there's no round trip needed.

Shopify sees a lot of potential in using Messenger as a vector for direct sales, but the company acknowledges that it's early days yet for an entirely in-message shopping experience, especially in the North American market.

"From an end-consumer perspective, it's still pretty novel to think of messaging a business first when you want to interact with them, so that's going to take some time to catch up with some of the interactions that are common in Asia," explained Shopify product manager Brandon Chu in an interview. "The outcome is moving to an internet version of what retail used to be, where you walk into a store and share with a merchant some of your problems or the thing that you're looking for."

Still, Chu says that Messenger is a "very good complementary channel" for Shopify's various other channels, since it allows merchants to do things like send order status receipts to customers via the platform, which kicks off a direct relationship that could lead to things like direct purchases within the service further down the line.

"There are a few really important platform features that we're going to be taking advantage of in the months to come, to keep more of that purchasing flow in the chat," Chu notes when I ask about the future potential of shopping directly in Messenger.

The first is different payment options, which Messenger's 1.2 platform update enables, and the other is the use of web views, which uses a new feature that Messenger offers to let developers set the height of web views within conversations. Chu says this is actually key, because it means you can set a half-height web view that gives customers the info they're looking for from the merchant's online store while still keeping them visibly within the context of the conversation they were having via Messenger.

Chu also says they're designing their messaging tools to be as useful across various platforms as possible for merchants down the road but adds that Shopify sees Messenger as the clear leader right now in terms of reaching the highest number of people in the North American market.

Shopify is definitely a leader in e-commerce when it comes to exploring new platform options: recent launches include an iOS keyboard that acts as a comprehensive back-end toolkit for merchants who sell via various messaging and social apps. A bigger bet on Messenger seems smart, especially if the North American scene moves (as many are hoping it will) to more closely mirror the state of mobile in other markets, like Asia.

Source: Adapted from: D. Etherington, "Shopify now lets stores sell directly in Facebook Messenger," *Techcrunch*, 5 October 2016.

14.3 Structure and Characteristics of Social Commerce

s-Commerce is a new form of e-commerce, and so there are some distinctions between s-commerce and traditional e-commerce. To illustrate, with regard to household products, people have various shopping modes and purchase preferences. Traditional e-commerce is more analogous to a supermarket. People come and purchase goods based on their free will. The salesperson or shopping assistant in this case is more supportive and seldom tries to influence and push a buyer's purchasing process. s-Commerce is more similar to a socialized merchandising situation, for example, a tupperware party. People come and purchase goods based on interactions with others. The salesperson or shopping assistant in this case is usually active in conveying value to buyers. These two shopping scenarios offer distinct shopping experiences for shoppers, and firms need to structure and tailor their business to a relevant shopping scenario. In this chapter, we will specifically introduce the structure and characteristics of s-commerce.

14.3.1 Structure of Social Commerce

In general, s-commerce is structured by four layers (see ◘ Fig. 14.2): individual, conversation, community, and commerce.[2] Firstly, the most inner layer—individual—represents *identities* that are able to proliferate a wide variety of content including user profiles, UGC (user-generated content, it includes posts, comments, "like," "share," etc.), and context profiles. The second layer—conversation— represents *vehicles* which are used to deliver or exchange information and content through sharing or posting. This layer is most crucial for s-commerce because a conversation feature determines a significant difference between s-commerce and traditional e-commerce. s-Commerce involves conversations between two and more users. Next, the third layer—community—represents *places* where conversations are able to happen. Some e-commerce platforms adding s-commerce features have various brand forums or communities; therefore, here, we use a plural form of place. Eventually, the outer layer—commerce—represents *institutions* that allow users to complete purchases through s-commerce platforms. This layer is more related to structural institutions related to commerce activity. Its design and technical features determine how identities use vehicles to fulfill commercial activities in a certain place.

In summary, any s-commerce activity should have a four-layer structure. But not all platforms need to adopt all of the in-depth features or attributes shown in ◘ Fig. 14.2. For example, a traditional e-commerce site adding s-commerce features may emphasize the commerce layer, while a social media platform places more value on the conversation layer and the community layer.

---

2   This section is adapted from: Huang and Benyoucef (2013).

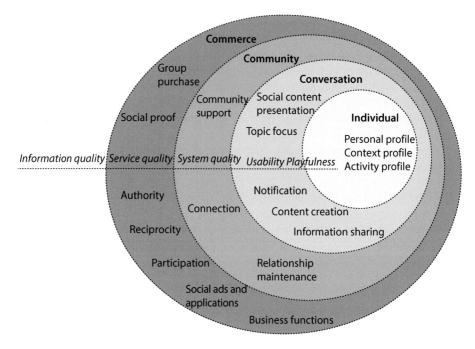

◘ Fig. 14.2   The structure of s-commerce. (Source: adapted from Huang and Benyoucef (2013), 253)

14.3.2   **Characteristics of Social Commerce**

s-Commerce is distinctly different to traditional e-commerce.[3] The major objective and activity of e-commerce is transactions. The content on e-commerce sites is mostly created by business users, and most of their contributions relate to their product and/or service descriptions. e-Commerce has a much wider targeting audience, and its selling channel is comparatively singular allowing shopping-related actions to be conducted inside the platform. In contrast to e-commerce, the major objective and activity of s-commerce are social interactions and user engagement. The majority of content on an s-commerce platform is generated by users, and their posts are typically related to their social lives. For example, commercial narratives on television are quite different from ones on social platforms. Commercial narratives on social platforms, at least in some extent, present themselves in a guised approach to create "digital intimacy" with audiences as if the storyteller (business employee) is a friend.

s-Commerce clearly targets a market segment based upon a person's social profile (including hobbies or interests). The social commerce selling channel usually is not singular. The fulfillment of a commercial activity is typically done via an online transaction system; however, social platforms usually do not have a system like

---

3   This section is adapted from: Turban et al. (2015).

this. Hence, in many cases, s-commerce is a mash-up of social platforms and e-commerce systems and many other platforms or systems.

These salient characteristics of s-commerce imply that social platforms can be used for informative purposes such as advertising. For example, Facebook, where advertising counts for more than 90 percent of its total revenue, now realizes that its advertising-based business model is problematic, and, to some extent, Facebook is exchanging its business reputation and user experience for money. Some businesses use Facebook to merchandise poor or low-quality goods, while users who are interested in these goods tap on the advertisement, leave Facebook and go to an external site, which is outside of Facebook's control. Facebook is not able to know users' perception, feeling, purchase security, and shopping experience on that site. Sometimes users may purchase poor or low-quality items which are not the same as their description in the advertisement. Poor online shopping experiences damage users' trust and confidence in Facebook by association. Facebook has noticed users' shopping experience on external sites that link to Facebook is of paramount importance for sustaining its business reputation and retaining loyal customers. It implemented several measures to tackle this issue, for example, allowing users to give feedback on advertisements (see the article: "Facebook cracks down on ads from e-commerce scammers flagged by new reviews").

Positive experiences when customers shop online are a "win-win" solution for all parties. They enable social platforms to retain billions of users and to profit from advertising. Advertisers improve users' online shopping experiences and build and cultivate a long-term relationship with customers—which has been proven in many cases. The only issues are, actually, related to technology, management, and cultural rituals:

- A social platform needs to manage huge amounts of external commercial sites. A social platform's natural insulation from external sites means that identifying the multitude of sites is very difficult, and the costs of doing so are difficult to track.
- If a social platform is going to be an Amazon-style e-commerce platform, even if external commercial sites were managed and controlled, the platform would run into similar problems that Amazon faces. For example, when a customer reports a delivery is damaged, it is difficult for Amazon to identify which party should be responsible for this: the seller may send a damaged product; the package may get damaged in the shipping process; or the buyer may mishandle and damage the product.
- Most importantly, shopping on social platforms is not as popular as on traditional e-commerce sites. Most shoppers still feel more comfortable with shopping directly on traditional e-commerce sites. When poorly delivered, s-commerce for social media platform users may feel like a friend suddenly selling to them at a purely social occasion. It is embarrassing because they may not want it actually but have to receive this commercial message due to their friendship. This "cultural ritual" resistance may be the most prominent factor inhibiting a social platform's strategic move to an s-commerce platform. It is very common in countries or regions where s-commerce is undeveloped.

Facebook Cracks Down on Ads from e-Commerce Scammers Flagged by New Reviews

Facebook is cracking down on shopping sites and others that bait and switch customers by delivering lower-quality products than what they advertised on the social network. Today, Facebook launches a new e-commerce review option inside its "Recent Ads Activity" dashboard that lets buyers give feedback about slow shipping times, weird smells, and junky merchandise.

Users are able to access the ads that they have clicked and provide feedback, by clicking on their Ads Activity, where they can also provide feedback on any ad they may have intentionally or unintentionally clicked on. Now, those responses will be tailored when they are related to ads that have resulted in a purchase, and they will also get fed back to advertisers as well as Facebook itself. Facebook is also expanding feedback options to more areas for those who have purchased items on the back of ads, for example, with prompts in their notifications. There appear to be two aims to the new feedback option. On the more optimistic side, for those advertisers who are selling but not managing customers' expectations well enough, they are able to get more information to modify their practices. On the more practical (and pessimistic) side, if a business receives a critical mass of bad feedback, Facebook will notify them with an ultimatum to improve. If they don't, Facebook will refuse to run their ads.

Facebook's efforts as an e-commerce platform are relatively young: it was only last week that it launched a way for those posting items in its community-focused marketplace to advertise them also in the News Feed; and in May, it expanded its Craigslist competitor also to include home services professionals. So, to make sure that its e-commerce advertising doesn't die on the vine, it has to boost trust, or else its 2.2 billion users might stop clicking its shopping ads for fear of getting burned.

"We've all had negative customer experiences with businesses," Sarah Epps, product marketing director for Facebook, said in an interview. "Sometimes they're hard to reach, late shipping items, or ship you low quality goods. What we hear from people is that bad shopping experiences cost them money and are really inconvenient. They're bad for people, bad for good businesses on Facebook, and they're bad for Facebook." There is another reason for making the experience better for both users and advertisers: there has been research that indicates that some companies, which have grown entire businesses on the back of selling items via Facebook ads, are now looking for alternative platforms after the ads started to become too expensive.

While policing the claims of every sketchy e-commerce vendor would be impossible, it can at least use negative reviews to choke off their traffic and absolve itself of profiting off their scams. Today's announcement is a start to balancing reliability with avoiding censorship or unscalable enforcement. In that regard, it's similar to the approach that Facebook has been taking with regard to offensive posts and outright fake news: rather than expecting or hoping that its algorithm can identify everything accurately, it's also trying out upvotes and downvotes on comments and currently works with third parties to fact check and flag news.

Facebook's move to let users' experiences shape how advertisers sell products—and in the worst cases whether they sell them at all—stems from 2 years back, when BuzzFeed first brought to light an ongoing issue among those who were clicking on Facebook ads for merchandise, specifically clothes, and getting products that were far from what they expected. Facebook says that it's taken 2 years to roll this out because of the nature of how things are purchased off the back of ads on Facebook.

Facebook was exploring this issue before it was surfaced by the press, from what we understand. The biggest challenge is that the activity was happening off Facebook, and the company has limited ability to understand what a user does once she or he leaves Facebook from an ad. So it took time to develop a feedback mechanism to solve the problem and make sure it was fair to all parties. The company already had policies in place that prohibit things like online scams, publishing ads with text that misrepresent products, and Facebook had already been proactive in enforcing against landing pages that do not represent an ad.

What's important to note here is that this is not a slam dunk, where banning advertisers or certain ads from Facebook is the inevitable outcome. Facebook says that it's just as likely that advertisers are making bad choices in how they present or run their businesses, not that they are intentionally misleading people. A bulk of the ads originally identified by BuzzFeed were found to be coming from companies out of China, pointing both to logistical and language challenges, among other issues.

"We give businesses time to act on the feedback," said Epps. "Of the hundreds of the businesses we've shared negative feedback with so far, many have taken steps to change. If they don't show improvement over time, their ads won't deliver to people's news feeds. The reaction from businesses has been positive so far. That's been surprising for us. There are some bad actors out there to scam people, but [most businesses do want to offer a good experience]."

Source: J. Constine, "Facebook cracks down on ads from e-commerce scammers flagged by new reviews," *Techcrunch*, 12 June 2018.

14.4 Value Creation on the Social Web

As we discussed in ▶ Chap. 11, online social platforms are a vital channel to reaching and interacting with customers. In the era of the social web, firms should not overlook the role of social platforms in creating value.[4] Here, we will introduce how marketers should change their mindset together with the evolution of web technologies and further discuss how value is created on the social web.

---

4   This section is taken, with permission from its publisher, from one of this book's co-authors research book: Martínez-López et al. (2016).

14.4.1   Evolution of the Marketing Approach

Web technologies are continually evolving. This technological evolution requires businesses to change their marketing mindset and to better organize value creation activities on the social web.

14.4.1.1 Marketing 1.0

Marketing 1.0 is characterized by the Web 1.0. As a refresher, the Web 1.0 phase was based on a system in which the information on a company's website was published, usually by the company itself, without any alteration for the type of consumer. These websites also had very limited feedback possibilities. Web 1.0 business websites were more than online catalogues; they were 24 hour-a-day stores, accessible from anywhere, and through which the company offered products and/or services in a unidirectional fashion (Maciá and Gosende 2010). They were dealing with an immature version of the Internet, where users were limited to passively surfing and were removed from "the action" (Caldevilla 2009). Therefore, Marketing 1.0 was based on selling products and services that a company manufactured for whomever wanted to buy them. Its primary objective was expanding and standardizing in order to reach lower production cost, have lower prices, and be more accessible to shoppers. Levels of success were measured through market share. In conclusion, this was the age of product-based e-marketing (Kotler et al. 2010).

14.4.1.2 Marketing 2.0

In the years between 2000 and 2010, an Internet-based dialogue took place in which a group of people tried to understand and explain how a new focus of company-client relationships could be created. It led to the conception of an excellent work outlining the end of the traditional company: Cluetrain Manifesto. This manifesto is based on the idea that markets are made up of conversations. It laid out the principles of the evolution from Marketing 1.0 to Marketing 2.0 and marked the evolution from a product-centric focus to people-centric focus, where message trumps image and experience trumps product (Cortés and Martínez-Priego 2010). This evolution is marked by three types of changes (Burgos and Cortés 2009):

Language Advertising ceased to be the most effective way of impacting clients, making way for the emergence of conversations between clients and between clients and companies or brands.

Base The client became the center of focus, not the website, product, or message.

Form The client was no longer a passive subject and became an active participant. The collection of applications that enable communication and interaction between users that forms the Web 2.0 platform is totally applicable to marketing (Villanueva 2011). Notably the web became ever-more important in the medium of marketing (Weber and Kauffman 2011). The social web was presented not only as a challenge for companies but also as an opportunity to interact with the market, learn about the needs and opinions of clients, and relate with them in a direct and personalized way (Constantinides and Fountain 2008). Therefore, the Web 2.0 promoted the creation of a collaborative network between individuals, which was founded and relied upon participation (O'Reilly 2005). One of the main advantages of the Web 2.0 was the availability of numerous cooperation tools to accelerate social interaction between people separated in time and space. Furthermore, due to its reticulated structure, open collaborative spaces and collective intelligence, it led to a new communication model based on "many-to-many" interactions. Accordingly, marketing, following in the footsteps of the evolution of Web 1.0 to Web 2.0, has changed from a model where the protagonist was a product on a company website to a user-centric model.

In summation, the Web 2.0 makes it possible for marketing to be centered around new relationship models in which consumers take on a fundamental role. In this way, consumers can share information, become tastemakers, vote to award or punish content, and/or create or share their information.[5] Because of this, some researchers believe that a new marketing model has begun, one that is more than just the traditional banner, search engines, social networks, or emails; this new marketing is social, viral, more creative, and can have its return on investment measured (Muñiz 2010). Other researchers have proposed that Marketing 2.0's principal characteristics are being interactive, flexible, democratic, viral directed, accessible, and fun (Payton 2009). Businesses that want to adopt this new model of marketing need to undertake a series of structural changes to adapt to version 2.0[6]:

From Individualism to Collectivism Currently, markets are conversations, meaning they are connected places in which clients are no longer passive subjects but have asserted themselves as active players that consume and create content. Therefore, the most collaborative, participatory, and interactive consumers become "prosumers" (producers and consumers of information). This forces marketing to move from being individually based to being collectively based.

From Advertisement to Conversation Today the market is saturated with advertisements, which is why businesses must use new methods for getting their message to clients, based on conversations and equality. To achieve this, businesses must go to the places where their clients are on the Internet (blogs, social networks, and more) or in whichever device they are using to connect (computer, mobile devices, and more).

From Self-Initiative to Client Initiative: Collective Intelligence Collective intelligence is understood as "the sum of knowledge and activities in a web setting that creates a final result superior to the sum of the individual intelligence or contributions."[7] Therefore, clients, groups, and society in general must form a part of the projects of a business.

---

5 F. Maciá and J. Gosende, op. cit., 2010
6 M. Cortés and C. Martínez-Priego, op. cit., pp. 16–24
7 M. Cortés and C. Martínez-Priego, op. cit., p. 18

From Project to Engagement   The product and/or service is the only way through which clients relate with a brand or company. Therefore, it is essential to promote the possibility of participating and interacting with the business's brands or products and/or services in a sensory fashion, to the client, facilitating experiences and engagement.

From Advertisement to Experience   In this context, the company must abandon persuasion and begin to attract customers through experiences.

From the Computer to the Use of Multiple Electronic Devices   In the current age, consumers are always connected through different electronic devices that offer the possibility of navigating, communicating, and being informed in any moment.

From Brochure to Recommendation   Recommendations, either from the company itself or from other users, accelerate the process of positioning and of purchasing.

From Egocentrism to Corporate Reputation   The Internet offers sufficient media to be able to manage the reputation of a company.

From Supposition to Web Analysis   The Internet provides companies with the necessary tools and indicators to gather information in real time about the behaviors of clients on the network.

In order to adapt to this new focus, companies should adjust the various marketing variables and strategies that the current market demands. To achieve this, businesses must think about marketing as a more global and strategic business concept and apply this philosophy across all business units.[8]

As some researchers point out, in this new marketing model, the vendors, instead of acting like broadcasting organisms, need to become aggregators of consumer communities, which is the true mission of marketing on the social web (Weber 2007). To do this, businesses have to stop transmitting messages to an ever-more indifferent public and start fostering participation on the social networks where the clients want to be. There are two necessary actions for aggregating clients. Firstly, businesses should offer complete content on their website and create commercial spaces that clients want to visit, and, secondly, they should participate and involve themselves in the public sphere. Furthermore, the marketing objectives on the social web will continue to be the same as always, although from a different perspective: attracting and retaining the client to take advantage of the business/consumer relationship. Therefore, marketing's new job consists of creating communities of interest, providing content, but also facilitating the creation of content by users.

It is important to encourage dialogue between the business and its consumers, as well as between the consumers themselves, to create engagement, positive "word of mouth" opinions and customer loyalty to the brand. A researcher analyzed the implications of the Web 2.0 and marketing at both a conceptual and operational

---

8   R. Muñiz, op. cit., 2010

level (Mazurek 2009) and found the potential to transfer a large amount of activities to the consumer, focusing exclusively on image and research, encouraging community members to participate and to create value. The researcher found that businesses could use tools that promote the new technologies to:

- Allow faster search times for, access to and exchange of information
- Allow the use of contacts and knowledge more efficiently
- Help companies hold on to their best employees and improve their job satisfaction
- Break down time and geographical constraints in order to improve communication between employees
- Reduce costs passed on to customers
- Improve productivity and competitiveness

14.4.1.3 Marketing 3.0

The most ambitious foreseeable evolution of the Internet is the potential for a semantically focused web that allows machines to speak to one another: a network that becomes a large, intelligent library with data flow programmed by users, transforming the Internet into a neuronal system, capable of self-awareness (Cruz 2007). Developers are trying to create a more intelligent, intuitive, open, efficient, and sensible Semantic Web that would be able to work with databases distributed across various systems (Cobo and Pardo 2007). Some authors refer to this goal as the Web 3.0 or the potential for a Semantic Web.

On the journey to this evolved web context, substantial changes are occurring in marketing, motivated by technological developments and giving rise to what is known as Marketing 3.0, the next stage in the evolution of marketing. This new marketing is characterized by the convergence of new technologies and the progressive change of consumers' shopping tendencies, which are influenced by the unlimited volume of information available through any device (Tasner 2010).

Some researchers have pointed out that while Marketing 1.0 was based exclusively around the product and unidirectional communication, Marketing 2.0 was based around the consumer and interaction, and Marketing 3.0 will consider the consumers' thoughts and demands in order to offer products based on values and emotions.[9] People view Marketing 3.0 as the value-oriented era, in which consumers are treated as human beings with hearts, minds, and spirits, working toward making the globalized world a better place. For their part, consumers will try to contact businesses that satisfy their deeper needs and that contemplate social, economic, and environmental developments in their mission, vision, and core values. Specifically, consumers will search for products and services that provide satisfaction not only on a functional and emotional level but also on a spiritual level. This vision of marketing, which is general, is not incongruous with the social web; it would be in line with the ultimate objective suggested by some researchers (Martínez-López and Sousa 2008) that organizations should include "contributing to customers" self-actualization in their marketing strategies.

---

9 P. Kotler, H. Kartajaya, and I. Setiawan, op. cit., 2010

Marketing 3.0 boasts consumer collaboration and participation as one of its basic pillars. It gives people the opportunity to express themselves and to collaborate with other individuals, through the creation and consumption of news, ideas, and entertainment. In this context, social media is key. Companies have been affected by the increased tendency toward collaboration, which decreases the control they have over their brands.

With this in mind, some researchers have argued that the role of consumers is being transformed (Prahalad and Ramaswamy 2004). Consumers are no longer isolated entities, but people connected with one another, who consciously make decisions and become active agents that provide useful information to businesses.

14.4.2 Co-creating Value on the Social Web

The previous ▶ Chap. 8 concluded with the idea that the value a consumer obtains does not depend solely on the product and/or service but also on the interaction at the moment of consumption (Ind and Coates 2013). This means that the value obtained by the customer depends on the quality of the interaction. Therefore, from this new perspective, the process of value creation is understood as a process shared between the business and the client. It involves considering the market with consumers (Cova and White 2010). This is the underlying focus in the context of the social web, where the control companies traditionally have had over the processes of value creation and marketing has been reduced in favor of the consumer control.

Clients or users are not necessarily passive receptors of the value offered by businesses. Now, thanks to the tools of the Web 2.0, they are informed, connected through networks, and have a higher degree of power that they have never had before, due to the possibilities afforded by search engines, participation platforms, an increased number of Internet-based interest groups, and the generalization of the technologies of social interaction. Clients, through the use of these tools, have learned how to make their opinions and ideas heard, and, therefore, achieve an active role in the process of value creation. This has happened largely without cost (Fisher and Smith 2011) and has benefited businesses as well (Pongsakornrungsilp and Schroeder 2011).

Some researchers have pointed out that businesses are adapting to this new scenario (Ramaswamy 2008). They are expanding the co-creation of value toward creating value for customers (Gyrd-Jones and Kornum 2013). In this regard, the experience of co-creation can be defined as a process that allows co-creative interactions in which people can enjoy significant and convenient participatory experiences that are tailored to specific consumers (Prahalad and Ramaswamy 2000). Specifically, there is a new context of value creation in which value is created through experiences (Prahalad 2004), and both businesses and customers are considered co-producers of not just goods and services but also of experiences and value.

Co-creation is a process that allows individual consumers to have a hand in designing future products, marketing messages and the sales channels through

14

which they will be available (Lenderman and Sánchez 2008). A dialogue, therefore, occurs between parties involved in an interactive process of mutual learning (Ballantyne and Varey 2006), in which the experience of co-creation itself takes on a relevant role. From this perspective, co-creation can be defined as "the participation of consumers along with producers in the creation of value in the marketplace" (Zwass 2010: p. 13). Therefore, the process of value creation is not competition exclusive to companies; value is co-created by the market's different actors that participate in the process online (Nenonen and Storbacka 2010). The co-creation of value is understood as being shared between companies and consumers.[10] Accordingly, the dominant role of companies has been eliminated, establishing equality between the various participants of co-creation, where organizations share their experiences in exchange for various benefits.[11]

According to the Service-Dominant logic (Lusch and Vargo 2006), the process of value co-creation produces significant benefits for companies. This is partly due to how it helps them understand consumers' opinions and uncertainties and partly due to improvements to the process of identifying the needs and desires of customers. However, some scholars have pointed out that the concept of value co-creation is currently overly abstract, both in theory and in practice (Grönroos and Ravald 2011). These authors have suggested that, even if it is accepted that customers are co-creators of value, the implications of this for customers and providers have not been explored.

Similarly, some researchers have affirmed the idea that value co-creation has materialized thanks to the confluence of various factors.[12] Some of these factors that are particularly noteworthy are the generalized use of the Internet, the orientation of companies toward services and experiences, and the inclination toward innovation and the boom of social, collaborative, and participatory technologies provided by the Web 2.0. From this same point of view, it is trustable that the elevated importance of the consumer's part in value co-creation has been strengthened by the Internet and even more so by the social web's ubiquity and accessibility.[13] Additional important aspects are networks of relationships, collaboration, forums, and interactive media. Some scholars have argued that collaboration is constantly growing between producers and consumers due to the new digital technologies that make the connection between them possible.[14] They confirm that these new tools are creating new ways of engaging in marketing processes, augmenting a change in mentality in relation to the role of consumers in experiences.

Therefore, it is reasonable that the rapid adoption of these digital tools is making new growth and innovation strategies possible in settings that are more complex, dynamic, and nonlinear, like those presented in this scenario (Pagani 2013). For example, some researchers think that companies are putting more trust into

---

10 D. Fisher, and S. Smith, op. cit., 2011
11 N. Ind, and N. Coates, op. cit., 2013
12 N. Ind, and N. Coates, op. cit., 2013
13 V. Zwass, op. cit., 2010
14 D. Fisher, and S. Smith, op. cit., 2011

public opinion and viral communications that are produced in these media as elements of corporate reputation and brand value (Arvidsson 2011). Furthermore, they are increasingly incorporating consumer participation in the creation of their products and innovations.

The basic elements of the value co-creation process in the context of the social web are connectivity, content, community, and commitment (Kucuk 2011). Co-creation can be characterized by four types of elements: common access, collective intelligence, virtual communities, and open innovation.[15] The participatory design and collaborative innovation, which have been enabled by new technologies such as virtual communities, have supported new possibilities for co-creation.[16] The new web context provides:

- Elements that facilitate co-creation
- Access to different media that make production possible
- Coordination of effort by involved parties
- Aggregation of disperse digital products
- The supplying and distribution of digital products

With this in mind, there are two distinct methods for enabling value co-creation in a virtual world, especially in online communities: sponsored co-creation and autonomous co-creation. Sponsored co-creation refers to those activities in which consumers create value by supporting the business model of the producers, at the request of said producers, for example, supporting ideas for new products. The activities of autonomous co-creation, on the other hand, are those in which the consumer creates value through their participation in actions that are voluntary and independent of any organization while still creating value for consumers (e.g., wiki development).

14.5 Monetizing Strategies for Social Platforms

A social platform could have various approaches to profit from its businesses. Basically, social platforms have two monetizing strategies: advertising strategies and commerce strategies (see ◘ Fig. 14.3). Here, we will introduce these two strategies, respectively.

14.5.1 Advertising Strategies

Advertising could be profitable for most online platforms. Its value logic is to increase traffic and public awareness for brands or sponsors. Traditional mass media such as radio, newspaper, and TV have proven this business strategy. For example, if a TV channel wants to boost its advertising revenue, it must increase its

---

15 V. Zwass, op. cit., 2010
16 N. Ind, and N. Coates, op. cit., 2013

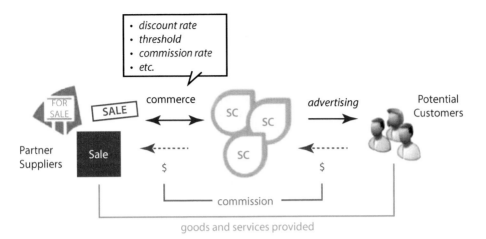

popularity, therefore letting advertisements reach a larger scale of audiences. Social platforms have adopted this monetizing strategy. This strategy consolidates the *free business model*. A free business model allows online platforms to run their business without directly charging platform users. People may consider why Facebook is able to offer instant social networking service for free. It is because advertisers and sponsors will pay Facebook. This strategy is suitable for online social platforms with significant network externality. The larger a platform's user network is, the more advertising revenue it attracts. A large user network indicates that advertisements are able to reach more targeted customers and exert more influence to build brand images or boost sales; hence companies or brands are more willing to place advertisements on influential and mainstream media platforms. On the other hand, this strategy can also directly monetize users who are willing to pay in order to get rid of all in-platform advertisements. For users who pay a subscription fee, social platforms will not push commercial notifications or send advertisements to their News Feed.

Traditional media companies also consider advertising effectiveness and how advertisements can be tailored to specific contexts (e.g., location). For example, a channel would tend to display advertisements that are suitable for its audience, e.g., displaying car advertisements in between sports programs. Some social platforms also adopt this trick. For example, any individuals or companies can display advertisements to their targeted customers on Facebook. Because Facebook collects user demographics and geolocation information (and more), it can distribute advertisements that target specific segments. Small advertising businesses even do not need to contact Facebook's advertising salesperson. They can select specific customer segments on Facebook, then customize advertising details such as time and numbers, pay, and then let the advertisements run. Some social platforms have also considered contexts where users run into an advertisement. They developed a special advertisement selling mechanism by identifying how an advertisement is tailored to ambient content that users are reading. If an advertisement aligns to other surrounding content, a social platform in that regard will charge less for it; otherwise, the advertising fee will be comparatively higher. For more detailed information on how Facebook monetizes its advertising business, please see this article: "How Facebook's ad system works." Note that the European Union introduced GDPR (General Data Protection Regulation) to protect the data and privacy of individuals, and it came into effect in 2018.

How Facebook's Ad System Works

In early September, Facebook revealed that it had identified about $100,000 in ads purchased on its social network by a Russian company linked to the Kremlin. Distributed between June 2015 and May of this year, more than 3000 ads added to evidence that Russia interfered with the 2016 presidential election.

Similar ad purchases by Russian agents were also uncovered on other Internet services like Google and Twitter. The online ads in question do not necessarily fit the traditional idea of advertising, and Facebook's ads are particularly unusual.

Are Facebook Ads More Subtle Than Other Ads?

Facebook's primary ad system plugs straight into the Facebook News Feed, the stream of information that serves as the primary interface for the social network. This system was created to deliver ads that could grab your attention as effectively as what Internet companies call "organic content—posts from your friends and family and other entities you are connected to on Facebook.

Indeed, ads are often the same as organic content, just with money behind them. "There is an ad-selling mechanism, but the ad itself isn't really an ad. It's content," said Ron Berman, a professor of marketing at the University of Pennsylvania's Wharton business school who studies online advertising, including the Facebook ad system. Facebook was part of a gradual but significant change in online advertising over the past decade. As more people have moved more of their online activity from PCs to mobile phones, the lines between ads and organic content have continued to blur, particularly on popular social networking service like Instagram, Twitter, and Facebook.

Why Did Mobile Phones Encourage This Change?

Mobile phones offer less room on their screens for ads. Usually, there is only space for a single column of information, and that must accommodate both ads and other contents. The result is that ads have moved into a more prominent position. Consider the Google search engine. If you type the word "Samsung" into Google on a laptop, a Samsung ad is likely to appear at the top of the screen, above the list of search results chosen by Google. But if you do the same thing on a typical smartphone, the ad is likely to take up the entire screen.

Responding to the screen limitations, Facebook went further. It created a new ad system that made ads an integral part of the News Feed, which dominates the screen on mobile phones.

14

What Exactly Is a Facebook Ad?

These are Facebook pages built by businesses and other organizations on the social network. Facebook allows businesses and other advertisers to serve pages straight into the News Feeds of people they had no other connection to, targeting their particular interests and behavior. As these pages appear, people can comment on them and "like" them, just as they can with anything else that shows up in their feeds. And if people click the like button, these pages will continue to show up in their feeds—and the feeds of their Facebook "friends"—for free.

How Closely Can Advertisers Target Ads?

On Facebook, people describe themselves and leave all sorts of digital bread crumbs that show their interests. Then Facebook matches these with other data it collects. Facebook's ad system provides ways to target geographic locations, personal interests, characteristics, and behavior, including activity on other Internet services and even in physical stores. Advertisers can target people based on their political affiliation; how likely they are to engage with political content; whether they like to jog, hike, or hunt; what kind of beer they like; and so on.

If advertisers provide a list for email addresses, Facebook can try to target the people those addresses belong to. It can also do what is called "look-alike matching." In this case, Facebook's algorithms serve ads to people believed to be similar to the people those addresses belong to.

How Does All That Happen?

Like Google and others, Facebook runs an instant digital auction for each ad placement, considering bid prices from many advertisers. An advertiser might bid $2 to place an ad in a particular situation. Then Facebook weighs these bids against how relevant the ad is to that situation. If an ad is relevant, the advertiser need not bid as high to win the auction. Unlike similar services, Facebook does not just consider how relevant an ad is next to the other available ads. It considers how relevant an ad is next to all other content, and it chooses ads based on how well they compete for attention with organic posts.

Aren't Ads and Content Supposed to Be Separated?

Google says it runs separate teams and separate technology for organic content and ads. The algorithm for organic content does not consider ads and vice versa. Facebook's arrangement is a little different because the ad auction considers organic content as well. Ads are also reviewed by a mix of algorithms and human moderators to determine if they are breaking company policies. Facebook recently said it would add 1000 more human moderators to the team that reviews ads.

What About Instagram and Twitter?

By the fall of 2015, the Facebook ad engine was also driving ads on Instagram, which the company had acquired 3 years earlier. Twitter works a bit differently from these services, but the dynamic is similar. Twitter ads are merely posts that business and others pay to place in the feeds of individuals who match certain criteria.

Is There No Separation from Regular Content?

As all these companies point out, paid advertisements are labeled ads or "sponsored" or "promoted" content. Facebook executives add that ads also usually include some sort of call to action, such as "liking" a page. Rob Goldman, Facebook's vice president of ads products, said in a statement that the people who manage content from regular users and people who manage ads coordinate their work but operate in separate organizations, with different goals and policies.

"Our goal is to make ads on Facebook just as useful and relevant as posts people see from friends and family," Mr. Goldman said. "But we also want people to know when they're looking at an ad, so we clearly label them as sponsored." But the line between ads and content has blurred in ways that may not be obvious. If you "like" an ad, for example, posts from the same account will turn up in your feed automatically, without paid promotion—and without the "sponsored" tags.

These posts are not just free advertising, Mr. Berman said, but also something that people see as more credible and that Facebook is more likely share in the feeds of these people's "friends." On a service like Facebook, the effect of an ad can extend well beyond what an advertiser paid for.

[...]

Mr. Berman said that published academic studies, including one of his own, indicated that people were more likely to share sensational content—content that generates an emotional response. That could include posts related to gun control, gay rights, or race relations. If an advertiser posts an ad that is widely shared, this is still more free advertising. And from the perspective of the Facebook ad engine, that is a relevant ad. This means the cost of the next ad goes down. And the cycle continues.

Adapted from: C. Metz, "How Facebook's ad system works," *The New York Times*, 12 October 2017.

14.5.2 Commerce Strategies

14

Traditional mass media platforms cannot replace social media platforms because of their low interactivity with consumers and low interoperability with e-commerce systems. For example, viewers cannot interact with television advertisements by tapping into the television screen to gather more relevant information or descriptions. Instead television advertisements usually indicate an order number or a purchase website address rather than provide a direct gateway to allow consumers to search for complementary accessories and compare one with another. In fact, allowing users to interact and access an e-commerce system is a valuable strategy for companies. High interactivity with consumers can increase consumer engagement and improve their memory recall of the advertising message, which eventually increases advertising effectiveness. High interoperability with e-commerce systems can reduce friction on consumers' path to purchase, allowing consumers to search, browse, compare, and purchase in an e-commerce system without hassle.

Many social platforms have adopted the special strategy rolling out buyable posts, messages, pictures, or short videos. The value logic is to embed commercial features into content and empower users to sell and buy products or services through content with in-built shopping features. This idea generates a new business strategy for social platform companies: building a digital business ecosystem and empowering anyone to profit from generating or distributing content, wherein companies can take a percentage from each sale. This strategy is more than just pushing ads or notifications allowing shopping. For example, YY, a Chinese social live streaming platform employed this strategy and boosted its net annual 2017 revenue to 3.6 billion Renminbi from 2.5 billion Renminbi in the corresponding period of 2016.

This social platform enables everyone to become a live streamer and interact with enormous audiences. It enables commercial features that allow streamers to exchange their show for in-app tips. For more details, see the article: "Apple legalizes and taxes in-app tipping for content creators."

Apple Legalizes and Taxes in-App Tipping for Content Creators

Apple has activated a new revenue stream that could foster communities of digital content creators around the world like those already thriving in China. Apple's newly published update to its App Store policies officially designates voluntary tipping via virtual currency as in-app purchases that Apple taxes 30 percent. By taking tipping out of the gray area, more app developers might institute digital tip jars as an alternative way to get creators paid without having to offer ad revenue sharing.

Chinese live streaming video apps like Yinke and Yizhibo have long embraced tipping, allowing viewers to tip or give virtual gifts to the stars they watch in exchange for extra attention from the performer or just as a show of gratitude. American live streaming apps like Facebook Live and Periscope don't offer tipping; instead, Facebook has begun letting broadcasters show ads in their streams and keep 55 percent of the revenue.

But last month, Apple cracked down on unofficial tipping, which sidestepped its 30 percent tax on in-app purchases by highlighting how the tips were donations rather than purchases. *The Wall Street Journal* reported Apple had told WeChat and other Chinese social apps to disable their tipping functions or be kicked out of the App Store. Previously, there was no formal rule from Apple about how tipping was classified. Now, Apple has instituted a legitimate way to tip. As part of the App Store policy update coinciding with the developer release of iOS 11, Apple writes: apps may use in-app purchase currencies to enable customers to "tip" digital content providers in the app.

This means developers can add tipping features without fearing repercussions from Apple, as long as they're willing to give the giant 30 percent. The gray area had kept tipping out of some popular apps who sought to avoid any tension with Apple. Now app makers can offer and promote tipping features with confidence. Native iOS tipping functionality could make it difficult for third-party tipping platforms to take root, though it could also spark a new trend of micropayments that are smaller than the typical $1 in-app purchase. The developers will have to determine whether they themselves take a cut of the tips or pass the full 70 percent on to the content creators. Passing on 50 percent while taking a 20 percent cut could unlock paths to monetizing video where ads can be interruptive or tough to match with unpolished footage.

On some platforms where 100 percent of the tips were passed through, creators might be a bit bitter about the change that will dock their earnings 30 percent. That's a big deal for stars who can pull in hundreds or even thousands of dollars per stream. But the institutionalization and potential explosion in popularity of in-app tipping could grow the pie of donations. Thanks to tipping, musicians, comedians, artists, e-sports athletes, and more risqué creators outside of China could be incentivized to make higher-quality digital content. And even if they don't take a cut, platforms that adopt tipping could see users flock to consume it.

Source: J. Constine, "Apple legalizes and taxes in-app tipping for content creators," *Techcrunch*, 9 Jun 2017.

In theory, a social platform that is adopting an e-commerce strategy can monetize its business customers and Internet consumers (see ◘ Fig. 14.4). As for business customers, a social platform can provide them targeted information related to their consumers, such as behavioral patterns and shopping habits. Business that want to access the information in aggregate (not identifiable to individuals) need to pay for it. Regarding Internet consumers, a social platform can provide them information and services offered by business customers, and it usually take as payment a percentage from each sale between business customers and Internet consumers

14.6 Building a Mobile Social Commerce Business

14

The success of s-commerce should also consider what is new in today's business world. Mobile is transforming all almost all e-business forms, and s-commerce is not an exception. Most social media members use mobile devices to browse their News Feed or tweet their moments of happiness. The usability and mobility powered by mobile devices enable users to create content and value anywhere and anytime, which is more advantageous than PCs. As we presented in ▶ Sect. 14.4, social platforms leverage the enormous power of users to co-create or co-produce content and value; hence platforms have to consider by which means users' value co-creation and content co-production can be facilitated or improved. Smartphones, for instance, are a useful vehicle to facilitate this value co-creation process. Many social media companies have rolled out app versions for their social platforms. Moreover, many of them are continually and specifically improving and innovating the user mobile experience. For example, smartphone cameras are a major tool for many users to create and share pictures or videos of their daily lives. Snapchat, a

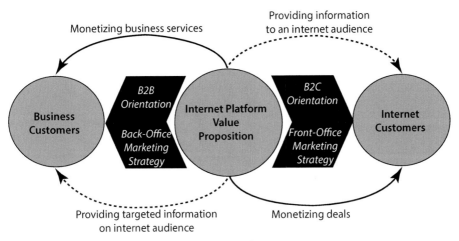

B2B&C
Business provider with benefits for Internet user

Monetizing business services

Providing information
to an internet audience

Business Customers

B2B Orientation

Back-Office Marketing Strategy

Internet Platform Value Proposition

B2C Orientation

Front-Office Marketing Strategy

Internet Customers

Providing targeted information
on internet audience

Monetizing deals

B2C&C
Business informediary with benefits for business partners

⬛ **Fig. 14.4** The monetising model of a social platform's commerce strategy. (Source: adapted from Muzellec et al. (2015))

social networking app, offers augmented reality lenses, or "masks," for its users to create novel and interesting pictures by placing virtual objects in the real world. At the same time, augmented reality-powered smartphone cameras allow users to virtually try on brands in reality (see the *Financial Times* article: "Snap adds 'buy' button to camera app in bid to lure advertisers").

Snap Adds "Buy" Button to Camera App in Bid to Lure Advertisers

Snap is adding a "buy" button to Snapchat's camera app, in the hope that *the combination of commerce and augmented reality* will lure new advertisers. The company is vying for leadership with many of its larger rivals in Silicon Valley—including Facebook, Google, and Apple—in the emerging market for augmented reality, where digital graphics are overlaid on a smartphone's camera to create special effects or place virtual objects. Many applications of AR have been seen as games or entertainment at best and gimmicks at worst.

But Snap is hoping to turn its playful face masks and virtual products, which are used by 70 m people every day, into real transactions by creating a more direct link to retailers' websites, videos, and app stores. The first brands to experiment with what Snap is calling "shoppable AR" include sports company Adidas, which promotes its Deerupt running shoes, and King, maker of the Candy Crush video games. Clairol, the makeup brand, will use Snapchat's AR camera to let users virtually try out its products.

Adding the ability to transact through Snapchat could give brands more confidence that their ads are giving a return on investment. "With this move, Snap is now providing brands with the opportunity to not just drive engagement with AR Lenses, but also seamlessly drive them to commerce with a new 'tap to visit' [a website] feature," said Chris Murphy, Adidas's US head of digital experience.

Martin Kon, a partner at Boston Consulting Group's TMT practice, likens AR today to the early days of the Internet or social media, when brands were still figuring out how best to use the new technology. "It's not just AR but rather the camera as the medium that we think is very exciting," he said. "A lot of people are saying that this is interesting, cool and fun, but we haven't yet figured out how this should fit into 'business as usual'."

Snapchat's AR platform could provide an alternative to developing a dedicated app using Apple's ARKit or Google's ARCore, Mr. Kon said. "What has been perhaps missing in the ecosystem and is now changing quite quickly is more standardised, readily available tools and services for advertisers," he said. Since Snap went public last year, Wall Street has become concerned that the company is not attracting new users fast enough as it struggles with increased competition from Instagram, the Facebook-owned photo-sharing app. That has put pressure on the company to find new sources of revenue that can generate more income from its existing audience.

After a brief spike when it reported better than expected earnings in February, shares in Snap have sagged. As it prepares to report its next quarterly earnings on May 1, Snap is looking to regain momentum with a series of new product announcements. Earlier this month, it introduced group video calling, allowing as many as 16 people to chat together, similar to rivals such as Houseparty, Google Hangouts, and Skype.

On Tuesday, it expanded its Lens Studio platform to allow anybody to create virtual "selfie" masks in just a few minutes. Although the tool is aimed mainly at consumers, it could also help smaller companies to market themselves within Snapchat using the new "shoppable" lens system. On average, more than half of Americans aged between 13 and 34 play with Snapchat's AR lenses, said Peter Sellis, Snap's director of revenue products. "Shoppable AR Lenses give brands a new way to leverage our unique scale."

T. Bradshaw, "Snap adds 'buy' button to camera app in bid to lure advertisers," *Financial Times*, 18 April 2018.

14.6.1   **The Concept of Mobile Social Commerce**

Kucukcay and Benyoucef (2014: p. 2) identified "mobile social commerce" as "the set of e-commerce activities performed in a mobile environment and enhanced by user-generated content." Mobile social (ms) commerce is not a mechanical combination of social and mobile commerce. Mobile-related features can add value to social commerce. Mobility injects two characteristics into s-commerce: convenience and instantaneity. Compared to online social media that can only be accessed via PCs, mobile social media supports people to friend each other anytime and anywhere, so that the use of online social networks is exponentially expanding. There is no denying that these two characteristics spark how social media permeates real social life. Advertisement notifications are able to reach targeted customers in a timely manner because social media users would not want to miss messages sent by their friends. Smartphone-powered social media can now record the physical presence of a business (e.g., a dedicated dish, a creative ad campaign, or a disappointing service environment) and create more vivid content such as pictures and videos which can be shared and distributed to a mass market on online social networks. Mobile empowers social media to better reflect and interact with the real world.

14.6.2   The Three Layers of Mobile Social Commerce

To implement ms-commerce in practice, firms need to consider three layers: a business model layer, a mobile layer, and a social layer.[17] Each layer plays an irreplaceable role and is articulated with others in creating an ms-commerce business.

Firstly, ms-commerce services a company's current business model. Based on the variety of e-business models, there are seven major business models that can be delivered through ms-commerce solutions.

(B1) e-tailer is where users can access, check inventory information, and place orders for desired items. This feature allows users to conduct direct commercial activities in the platform.

(B2) portal enables users to access various sources and information such as in-app search engines, news, shared content, and more. Firms are able to mix advertisements in various sources and content to advertise to users.

(B3) content provider is a prominent actor that creates and makes content available to audiences. Content is king in the era of social media, and content can be created from diverse sources such as firms, marketers, users, professionals, and more.

(B4) transaction broker refers to intermediaries that process transactions for users over the Internet. In an action chain of completing a purchase, users need to fulfill transactions somewhere. For example, Facebook and WeChat both rolled out its in-built payment methods, and for more details, see the article: "What are Facebook payments?"

What Are Facebook Payments?
In March, social media giant Facebook officially announced it was going to launch a new payment service through its messenger application. Users can now send friends money through the app for no cost after entering an optional PIN or touch ID for extra layers of protection.

---

17   This section is adapted from: I. E. Kucukcay and M. Benyoucef, op. cit., 2014.

What Are Facebook Payments?

Current Facebook users can link their debit card to the messenger app's settings section and send mobile peer-to-peer payments to their friends by striking up a conversation. Once two friends engage in dialogue, a "$" icon will appear above the keyboard. All users have to do is enter the amount they wish to transfer and select the pay option. Facebook payments users can also fund and complete transactions to third-party companies that advertise on the platform as well. Once the payment is successfully processed, Facebook transfers the value of the transaction to the developer offering the content the consumer wishes to purchase.

Users can only enter their debit card information because the company said it wanted to minimize and avoid fees as much as possible. Similar to bank transactions and deposits, payments could take up to three business days to go through. Facebook is looking to explore the popular mobile payments space and keep users on its site longer. According to its F8 developers conference in March, its messenger app was used by 600 million people worldwide.

What Does This Mean for e-Commerce Businesses?

For one, Facebook payments provide a direct link for your e-commerce business to the consumer. Since their debit card information is already linked to the platform, the payment is seamless and easy to use. Facebook is already a major advertising platform, and now that users can link their payment information to the social media outlet, they can make purchases more quickly and easily than ever before.

In addition to creating a seamless payment funnel for consumers, Facebook payments also open up a world of opportunities for its advertisers. Facebook already sells individuals' personal information to companies that market on its platform, and it is likely your e-commerce business can obtain individual card numbers and purchase history as well. By getting this information, your online business can better optimize its outreach to consumers, sending more relevant messaging and offers. This type of customized marketing approach may gross higher bottom-line gains as a result.

Source: Bigcommerce, "What are Facebook payments?," ▶ Bigcommerce.com, 2015.

14

(B5) market creator creates an online environment for buyers and sellers to meet and conduct online transactions.

(B6) service provider provides informative services to users. Services here can refer to a consultancy about a special issue, expertise, financial planning, and making available online the items, menus, promotions, and discounts at physical stores.

(B7) community provider offers an online environment where fans with similar interests can gather in one place to share views, pictures, videos, etc. Businesses can use these communities for branding or marketing activities.

The seven business models are underpinned by a second layer comprising the three elements of mobility:

(M1, M2) mobility and ubiquity enable users to access ms-commerce anytime and anywhere through wireless Internet and mobile operating systems. These two features also need businesses to deploy relevant infrastructure. For example, small business owners can print a QR code allowing in-store shopper to scan it and then friend their Facebook account and become informed about coupons and promotions.

(M3) context sensitivity detects a users' use and consumption context. It enables businesses to respect users' differentiation by increasing *personalization (M3.1)*, making content more *interactive (M3.2)* and offering *localized services (M3.3)* based on a users' geolocation information and smartphone usage.

Due to the popularity of the social web technologies, user generated content and online social interactions, there are new opportunities available for businesses. The six common social features below constitute the third layer of ms-commerce.

(S1) social shopping refers to online shopping conducted through social platforms. The platforms create a social atmosphere for online shopping where shoppers can interact with sellers and others. For more information on social shopping, please see the FT article: 'Retailers tap into social mobility'.

Retailers Tap into Social Mobility

The battle of the "buy" buttons is in full swing. With just 7 days to go until Christmas, this year is shaping up to be the first festive season that social shopping has taken off—as some of the world's biggest brands try to hook the connected customer. From Google and Facebook to Instagram and Pinterest, social networks have been experimenting with various ways of enabling consumers to buy items directly from their platforms, to generate additional revenue streams.

And it appears to be working. According to research by the Internet Retailer website, companies ranked in its Social Media 500 list grew their "social commerce" sales by 26 percent last year, to $3.3bn. This race to dominate social shopping is being driven by shoppers' increasing use of mobile phones in the buying process. "The smartphone is probably the biggest single tool that people are using for mobile holiday shopping," says Thom Blischok, chief retail strategist at Strategy&, the consulting arm of PwC. He estimates that about 60 percent of US shoppers will research products online on their smartphone over the holiday shopping season. And 40–45 percent will also use their smartphones to contact friends and family via social media about gifts.

Facebook has been testing a "buy" button with partner retailers on the Shopify ecommerce platform, so users can complete a purchase without ever leaving the site. Pinterest, the online scrapbook, also launched a "buy" button this year, partnering with Shopify and retailers who use another platform, Demandware. On the Pinterest site, "buyable pins" on product images include price information and the ability to make secure payments.

Kelly Graziadei, director of global marketing solutions at Facebook, says marketers have two social shopping objectives in the fourth quarter: first, they need to provide tools to boost awareness of their brands and promote specific products, and, second, they must demonstrate that using Facebook can lead to purchases in store as well as online. A rapid increase in video content on Facebook—some 8bn videos are now watched every day—has certainly helped retailers lure people to their online stores. So, too, has the opening up of Facebook-owned Instagram to marketers, who are now using the photo-hosting platform to create imagery reminiscent of glossy magazines.

Since last year's holiday season, Facebook has launched carousel adverts, a series of images that users can swipe to see more of, and dynamic product ads, which help marketers upload entire catalogues of goods. There are also new formats on Instagram including 30-second videos—the same duration as a television advert. Target, the US retailer, is now using almost all these formats on Facebook. On Instagram, J Crew, the mid-market fashion retailer, has uploaded its annual gift guide and is using "shop now" ads to speed users toward purchasing.

In the United Kingdom, some of the biggest retailers are also encouraging consumers to embrace social shopping—and rewarding them for interacting with their brands online. "It clearly will be the most impactful social shopping Christmas," says Patrick Bousquet-Chavanne, director of marketing and international at British retailer Marks and Spencer. Online retailer ASOS, which already connects with its tech-savvy customers on everything from Instagram to Snapchat and Periscope, is taking its engagement one step further, through a new loyalty card. Under the scheme, consumers will be rewarded every time they post a picture of themselves on Instagram in an ASOS outfit and use the hashtag #asseenonme.

Loyalty is no longer just about sales. M&S's new Sparks card also rewards shoppers on their interaction with the brand, for example, through online product reviews. "The more consumers are engaged with us in this digital era, the more valuable they are to M&S," says Mr. Bousquet-Chavanne. Robert Howard, a US-based digital partner at consultants Kurt Salmon, agrees that consumers are beginning to shop via the social networks. "We are going to see more and more of that over the next several years, as retailers embrace social media as a legitimate commerce channel," he says. "The social media sites will aim to get a slice of the pie." At the moment, social media platforms do not take a cut of the sales. However, Mr. Howard says: "I suspect that may change as social media sites try to determine how to monetise [social commerce]."

Some analysts, however, believe optimism about the rise of social shopping is misplaced. Scott Galloway, founder of research firm L2 and professor of marketing at New York University's Stern Business School, expects it will continue to underwhelm because social networks are for social activities, not shopping. "Social still plays a huge role in retail or a brands' business, but it's just not where the actual retailing gets done," Mr. Galloway says. He describes shopping on social media as the equivalent of talking to someone you has just been introduced to and finding that they try to french kiss you. "It is moving to a level of intimacy but it's skipping several steps," he warns. "It's skipping dinner and courtship."

Source: A.Felsted and H.Kuchler, "Retailers tap into social mobility," *Financial Times*, 17 December 2015.

(S2) ratings and reviews allow users to give feedback on items. This information is crucial for potential customers to evaluate choices.

(S3) recommendations and referrals support users to create shareable content about certain products or brands within their social network, which leads message receivers to another site.

(S4) forums and communities can retain consumers and foster brand loyalty by creating institutional occasions to facilitate user interactions. Firms can also seek and identify business opportunities through forums or communities.

(S5) social media optimisation (SMO) aims to attract customers by optimising content created by firms and how content is distributed on social platforms. SMO is a tactic to increase brand awareness and firm websites or apps' online traffic.

(S6) social advertisements and widgets are content created with playfulness and interactivity. These advertisements and widgets can be placed on social platforms to interact with consumers and increase consumer engagement.

In practice, any business model can add some (not all) features in the mobile layer and the social layer. It depends on how a firm selects and integrates features in outer layers to smoothly conduct its ms-commerce. Furthermore, we will introduce a real case[18] designing and applying the three-layer structure into practice.

CapitalBurger has three restaurants mainly sell burgers and drinks. In comparison to other restaurants, CapitalBurger is mostly handling customers coming during lunch time. To improve its lunch business, CapitalBurger developed an app. The app is used to provide various items on the menu and discount information. Users who have installed the app can use it to see today's menu and attain discount coupons.

The app adopted the three-layer design for ms-commerce. Within the inner layer, CapitalBurger is a *service provider* providing informative services related to available menus and items. In terms of the mobile layer, mobility, ubiquity and context-sensitivity features are added into the app. For mobility, the app is compatible with most mobile operating systems. As to ubiquity, users can ignore time and place and access to services anytime and anywhere. Context-sensitivity is realised via its three core features. Firstly, *localised service* is able to identify the location of customers and make the back-front system offer differentiated discounts varying time to time. For example, menu prices may be comparatively higher on weekends. Secondly, *personalisation* is to provide a discount offer relying on a customer's preferences of items in the menu, and his/her prior purchases or interactions in the app. Last, the *interactivity* feature is to push notifications to consumers and allow two-way communication between consumers and service providers.

The social feature in this case is to propagate promotional content throughout existing consumers' social networks. This example uses social media optimisation (SMO) to increase CapitalBurger's brand awareness among consumers' friends or followers. Consumers can use the app to share promotional content on their social media, and get a QR code for a discount in return. By implementing this three-layer ms-commerce, CapitalBurger can significantly improve

---

18 This case is taken from: I. E. Kucukcay and M. Benyoucef, op. cit., 2014, p. 3.

its business via successful use of ms-commerce. In summary, this case shows that ms-commerce is a feasible commercial scenario in practice. Businesses can consider how they should integrate mobile and social features into their business models.

Summary

- Firstly, this chapter presents reasons why businesses should adopt social commerce strategies. Any new strategy should be well studied before being officially adopted by businesses.
- Secondly, this chapter classified various social commerce activities. Basically, they involve social media marketing, enterprise management, and technology support.
- Thirdly, social commerce has a special structural frame and characteristics. Strategists need to consider these structural distinctions and characteristics when applying and deploying social commerce in practice.
- Fourthly, marketing is a major business activity on social platforms. With advances in technologies, marketing approaches and mindsets are evolving from marketing 1.0 to marketing 3.0.
- Fifth, this chapter delineates what value co-creation is on the social web.
- Sixth, advertising strategies and commerce strategies are two main strategies to monetize social platforms.
- Lastly, in terms of today's mobilized e-business, social commerce implementation should be in the mobile context. This chapter presented a three-layer design of mobile social commerce and presented a case to show that mobile social commerce is a feasible strategy in practice.

❓ Review Questions

1. Why should firms adopt social commerce strategies?
2. How many varieties does social commerce have? What is enterprise social media (ESM)?
3. What are the differences between social commerce and mobile commerce?
4. What is marketing 1.0, marketing 2.0, and marketing 3.0?
5. What strategies can firms employ to monetize social platforms?
6. What is mobile social commerce?
7. Discuss pros and cons of adopting social commerce strategies.
8. Select a social commerce platform in reality and analyze its structure and characteristics.
9. In terms of all approaches and mindsets of marketing, discuss how firms should handle the challenges and opportunities in this mindset-change evolution.
10. Exemplify cases of companies adopting mobile social commerce and evaluate whether their business is a success or not.

14

Notes and References

Arvidsson, A. (2011). Ethics and value in customer co-production. *Marketing Theory, 11*(3), 261–278.

Ballantyne, D., & Varey, R. J. (2006). Creating value-in-use through marketing interaction: The exchange logic of relating, communicating and knowing. *Marketing Theory, 6*(3), 335–348.

Burgos, E., & Cortés, M. (2009). *Iníciate en el marketing 2.0. Los social media como herramientas de fidelización de clientes*. La Coruña: Editorial Netbiblo.

Caldevilla, D. (2009). Democracia 2.0: La política se introduce en las redes sociales. *Revista Pensar la Publicidad, 3*(2), 31–48.

Cobo, C., & Pardo, H. (2007). *Planeta Web 2.0: Inteligencia colectiva o medios fast food*. Barcelona: Grup de Recerca d'Interaccions Digitals, Universitat de Vic.

Constantinides, E., & Fountain, S. J. (2008). Web 2.0: Conceptual foundations and marketing issues. *Journal of Direct, Data and Digital Marketing Practice, 9*(3), 231–244.

Cortés, M., & Martínez-Priego, C. (2010). El nuevo marketing y la figura del community manager. *Harvard Deusto Marketing y Ventas, 96*, 16–24.

Cova, B., & White, T. (2010). Counter-brand and alter-brand communities: The impact of web 2.0 on tribal marketing approaches. *Journal of Marketing Management, 26*(3–4), 256–270.

Cruz, M. (2007). Web 2.0 '¿Reconfiguración social o tecnológica?, Available at: http://www.red.com.mx/index.php?page/19

Fisher, D., & Smith, S. (2011). Cocreation is chaotic: What it means for marketing when no one has control. *Marketing Theory, 11*(3), 325–350.

Mazurek, G. (2009). Web 2.0 implications on marketing. *Management of Organizations: Systematic Research, 51*, 69–82.

Galer S. (2018, January 19). How much is 'too much time' on social media? *BBC Future*.

Grönroos, C., & Ravald, A. (2011). Service as business logic: Implications for value creation and marketing. *Journal of Service Management, 22*(1), 5–22.

Gyrd-Jones, R. I., & Kornum, N. (2013). Managing the co-created brand: Value and cultural complementarity in online and offline multi-stakeholder ecosystems. *Journal of Business Research, 66*(9), 1484–1493.

Hutchinson A. (2016, September 26). The evolution and future of social commerce [infographic]. *Social Media Today*.

Huang, Z., & Benyoucef, M. (2013). From e-commerce to social commerce: A close look at design features. *Electronic Commerce Research and Applications, 12*(4), 246–259.

Ind, N., & Coates, N. (2013). The meanings of co-creation. *European Business Review, 25*(1), 86–95.

Kim, D. (2013). Under what conditions will social commerce business models survive? *Electronic Commerce Research and Applications, 12*(2), 71.

Kotler, P., Kartajaya, H., & Setiawan, I. (2010). *Marketing 3.0. From products to customers to the human spirit*. Hoboken: Wiley.

Kucuk, S. U. (2011). Towards integrated e-marketing value creation process. *Journal of Direct, Data and Digital Marketing Practice, 12*(4), 354–353.

Kucukcay, I. E., & Benyoucef, M. (2014, September). Mobile social commerce implementation. In *Proceedings of the 6th international conference on Management of Emergent Digital EcoSystems* (p. 2). New York: ACM.

Lenderman, M., & Sánchez, R. (2008). *Marketing experiencial. La revolución de las marcas*. Madrid (Spain): ESIC.

Liang, T. P., & Turban, E. (2011). Introduction to the special issue social commerce: A research framework for social commerce. *International Journal of Electronic Commerce, 16*(2), 9.

Lusch, R. F., & Vargo, S. L. (2006). Service dominant logic: Reactions, reflections, and refinements. *Marketing Theory, 6*(3), 281–288.

Maciá, F., & Gosende, J. (2010). *Marketing online. Estrategias para ganar clientes en Internet*. Madrid: Anaya Multimedia.

Martínez-López, F. J., & Sousa, C. M. P. (2008). Marketing transformation to the new business environment. *International Journal of Business Environment, 2*(2), 101–115.

Muñiz, R. (2010). *Marketing en el siglo XXI*. Libro electrónico: Centro Estudios Financieros. Available at: http://www.marketing-xxi.com/marketing-presente-futuro.html

Muzellec, L., Ronteau, S., & Lambkin, M. (2015). Two-sided Internet platforms: A business model lifecycle perspective. *Industrial Marketing Management, 45*, 139–150.

Nenonen, S., & Storbacka, K. (2010). Business model design: Conceptualizing networked value co-creation. *International Journal of Quality and Service Sciences, 2*(1), 43–59.

O'Reilly, T. (2005). *What is web 2.0 design patterns and business models for the next generation of software*. O'Reilly. Available at: http://oreilly.com/web2/archive/what-is-web-20.html

Pagani, M. (2013). Digital business strategy and value creation: Framing the dynamic cycle of control points. *MIS Quarterly, 37*(2), 617–632.

Parker, S. (2017, February 13). 'What is social commerce and why should your brand care?' *Hootsuite*.

Payton, S. (2009). *Internet marketing for entrepreneurs. using web 2.0 strategies for success*. New York: Business Expert Press LlC.

Pongsakornrungsilp, S., & Schroeder, J. E. (2011). Understanding value co-creation in a co-consuming brand community. *Marketing Theory, 11*(3), 303–324.

Prahalad, C. K. (2004). The co-creation of value. *Journal of Marketing, 68*(1), 23.

Prahalad, C. K., & Ramaswamy, V. (2000). *Co-opting customer competent* (pp. 78–87). Boston: Harvard Business Working Knowledge Series.

Prahalad, C. K., & Ramaswamy, V. (2004). *The future of competition: Co-creating unique value with customers*. Boston: Harvard Business School Publishing.

Ramaswamy, V. (2008). Co-creating value through customers' experiences: The Nike case. *Strategy and Leadership, 36*(5), 9–14.

Tasner, M. (2010). *Marketing in the moment: The practical guide to using web 3.0 marketing to reach your customers first*. London: FT Press.

Villanueva, M. A. (2011) *Marketing de Relaciones en Internet. Análisis empírico de las empresas de Venezuela*, PhD Thesis, Universidad de Málaga, Málaga.

Weber, D. M., & Kauffman, R. J. (2011). What drives global ICT adoption? Analysis and research directions. *Electronic Commerce Research and Applications, 10*(6), 683–701.

Weber, L. (2007). *Marketing to the social web. How digital customer communities build your business*. Hoboken: Wiley.

Zwass, V. (2010). Co-creation: Toward a taxonomy and an integrated research perspective. *International Journal of Electronic Commerce, 15*(2), 13.

Recommended Key Reading

Turban, E., Strauss, J., & Lai, L. (2015). *Social commerce: marketing, technology and management*. Springer.

Martínez-López, F. J., Anaya-Sánchez, R., Aguilar-Illescas, R., & Molinillo, S. (2016). *Online brand communities: Using the social web for branding and marketing*. Heidelberg: Springer.

14

Unifying Channels to Reach Customers: Omni-Channel Strategies

Contents

© Springer Nature Switzerland AG 2020
T. Jelassi, F. J. Martínez-López, *Strategies for e-Business*, Classroom Companion: Business,
https://doi.org/10.1007/978-3-030-48950-2_15

> **Learning Outcomes**
>
> After completing this chapter, you should be able to:
>
> - Understand why firms take risks to launch omni-channel strategies
> - Learn three basic dimensions constituting an omni-channel system
> - Identify the major stumbling blocks for going omni-channel
> - Understand how firms mitigate and resolve channel conflict
> - Discern how firms use SoLoMo to organize and reach an omni-channel audience

■ Introduction

It is becoming more difficult for firms to reach and sell via a single channel, so many firms adopt multi-channel strategies to conduct commercial activities via various channels. From a strategic perspective, business leaders should broaden their vision from single channel management. They should picture a wider landscape of several integrated channels and overall firm performance. One or few channels may star in a business, and other channels could drag behind and jeopardize the overall performance. In this regard, businesses need a strategic, holistic, and systematic view of all channels, that is, omni-channeling. This view is key in the emerging conceptual approach of Marketing 4.0.

15.1 Why Should Firms Implement Omni-Channel Strategies?

Omni-channeling requires a holistic view on various channels. It is difficult to realize this in practice because each channel has its own characteristics and uniqueness. It is problematic to purely replicate and apply managerial approaches of one channel into other channels. For instance, online channels are distinct from offline channels. Even between various online channels, as discussed in ▶ Chap. 14, social media channels are distinct from standard unidirectional online channels such as traditional e-commerce sites. Today more and more companies are trying to implement omni-channel strategies, despite the difficulties and complications of doing so. For example, Alibaba invest heavily in an omni-channel approach, see the article "In China, Smart Retailers Are Looking Beyond O2O" below. Firstly, we will present reasons why companies are willing to do so.[1]

Today's Customers Are Cross-Channel Shoppers Customers can easily connect to the Internet anywhere and anytime. This connectivity makes it more effortless for customers to move across various channels. There are two emerging descriptions for customers' cross-channel behaviors. First is *showrooming* behavior. It refers to when a customer shops at a storefront but finally purchases relevant items online. In this case, the physical store does not generate direct purchases for that store; instead, it diverts customers from a physical channel to an online channel. From the lens of that store (a singular

---

1   This section is adapted from Criteo, 'Why Omni-channel is So Hot Right Now', ▶ *Criteo.com*, 10 April 2017; Chen et al. (2018).

channel lens), it is wasteful to create an attractive physical store when it does not lead directly to sales within that store. But from a holistic lens of a brand (an omni-channel lens), it could be of benefit to create a luxury and magnificent storefront even if customers finally make a purchase via another channel. The second emerging behavior is *webrooming*. It refers to a reverse situation in which a customer researches online but buys at a physical store. These two behaviors may explain why businesses invest in building websites, apps, physical stores, and other channels to drive activity and sales holistically. It makes sense for businesses to implement omni-channel strategies which align the brand of each singular channel to others.

Omni-Channel Entails Many Business Opportunities On the one hand, bricks-and-mortar businesses in today's market face a challenging environment. Customers are much more empowered by the Internet to choose where and how they purchase. Bricks-and-mortar business owners must consider how they can translate limited in-store traffic into purchases to override fixed costs such as store design and fit-out, rent, staffing, and more. However, online channels enable businesses to reach more customers and the transactional power of ecommerce cannot be underestimated. There are many opportunities for a physical business to adopt online channels to distribute and sell in-store goods. On the other hand, bricks-and-mortar stores can have inherent strengths such as tactile information access, and can offer experiences such as in-store events and the services of salespersons. It is difficult for online business to replicate these benefits. Bricks-and-mortar stores can be a crucial channel to interact directly with customers. In summary, an omni-channel strategy indicates potential incremental sales. An omni-channel strategy enables businesses to appeal to more shoppers (online) who may then buy in store (if within physical distance of one). Alternately, shoppers who visit a store may then go home or elsewhere and make a purchase online. Therefore, an omni-channel strategy should assess sales holistically (Konus et al., 2008).

Omni-Channel Underpins a Seamless Shopping Experience When channels are independent from each other, shoppers would inevitably run into fragmented shopping experiences. The idea of an omni-channel approach lies in creating a seamless shopping experience for cross-channel shoppers. Customers can effortlessly access online channels while in store. At the same time, online buyers can be informed about which store they can pick up purchases and peruse new products that are in store. Under an omni-channel scenario, the channel in which a customer finally purchases does not matter; it aims to reduce friction on a customer's path-to-purchase.

In China, Smart Retailers Are Looking Beyond O2O
The development of China's e-commerce sector has been unlike any seen so far, largely due to its mobile-first consumer base, adoption of new social commerce models, and the prevalence of digital payment systems in the country. One result of that development has been the growth of the online-to-offline retail sector, in which online consumers are given incentives to make offline purchases. This year, O2O e-commerce sales in China alone are expected to total RMB521 billion ($78.4 billion), according to iResearch Consulting Group.

But there are signs that merchants are attempting to move beyond the O2O model to embrace a concept that cannot be ignored in retail: omni-channel. According to a survey conducted by PricewaterhouseCoopers (PwC) last September, consumers are now doing more of their daily or weekly shopping on a mobile device than at a physical store. In fact, 52% of the digital buyers polled in China had shopped on a mobile device on a daily or weekly basis, compared with 46% who had done so at a brick-and-mortar store.

The inevitable tilt toward digital media by shoppers means that retailers and brands in China must move beyond O2O and invest in omni-channel, which allows customers to connect with merchants on their terms, when and how they want to."[Omni-channel] is an evolution of online-to-offline, moving from having an online store and driving traffic to an online store, or vice versa, to truly interconnecting online and offline," said Nishtha Mehta, founder of CollabCentral Consulting, a firm that specializes in omni-channel marketing.

e-Commerce giant Alibaba is a prime example of a once pure-play e-commerce platform that has come to see the necessity of establishing a real-world presence to maintain its growth. In January, the company spent as much as $2.6 billion to take Chinese department store chain Intime Retail Group private as part of an initiative it calls "New Retail." The move gives Alibaba the potential to remake offline retail using lessons learned from e-commerce, such as more efficient inventory management techniques.

In turn, stores supplement online retail offerings by giving consumers a physical location from which to pick up purchases. In-store shoppers can also use apps to make purchases, further blurring the line dividing online and offline retail. "The 'new retail' idea is that Alibaba is trying to build a network, an ecosystem," said Mehta. "They are trying to acquire different offline assets and a net of physical stores so that they can integrate with their online infrastructure and cloud computing data to provide a seamless integrated service."

Source: E-marketer, "In China, smart retailers are looking beyond O2O," ▶ *Emarketer.com*, 25 May 2017

15.2 The Conceptual Framework of an Omni-Channel System

15

Here we will introduce a conceptual framework of an omni-channel system.[2] Basically, omni-channeling has two key aims: firstly it informs consumers and various channel parties of the available channels and what is on offer where at what price. For example, a consumer may download the app of a business to ascertain whether a product is available in the nearest physical store, cheaper than paying delivery costs, and then purchase it via the app so that it doesn't sell out before they get to the store. Secondly, omni-channels provide consumers with seamless shopping experiences that integrate multi- and cross-channels. Put simply, firms need to increase the visibility and integration of multi- and cross-channels.

---

2   This section is adapted from: Saghiri et al. (2017).

15.2.1 Channel Visibility

Channel visibility refers to which extent a channel can be seen or noticed by people. Under an omni-channel scenario, consumers are aware of various channels: storefronts, websites, social media, call centers, catalogues, etc. By increasing channel visibility, a business can mitigate against a situation in which useful and available channels or offerings specific to those channels are not noticed or are misunderstood by consumers. Shared information—products, customer details, stock, returns, shipment details, and more—between channels is vital to address this issue. Channel visibility refers to:

- *Product visibility*: the sharing of product-related information such as product descriptions, ingredients, brands, and production dates, and more.
- *Demand visibility*: the sharing of demand information such as consumer choice preferences, purchases, demand amounts, and more. The sharing of demand information is crucial for various channel parties and agents to co-evolve. For example, salespersons in a physical clothing store may find that many shoppers leave without purchasing because the store has a shortage in larger sizes. This information can be shared and referred to suppliers and online vendors informing them to produce and prepare more large size stock or send excess stock in larger sizes to that physical store.
- *Order/payment visibility* refers transactional information in one channel to other channels parties. For instance, confronting diverse brands and products, some shoppers would prefer to select top selling items. Physical stores, with limited floor space, can analyze online transaction information to highlight in their store display the top selling items in their region.
- *Stock visibility* makes inventory status shareable across an omni-channel system. The sharing of stock information avoids a situation in which a customer finds a product out of stock on an online shopping site but actually can take one from a nearby physical store. Stock visibility is of paramount importance for supply chain management. Visible stock information can help upstream sellers and downstream buyers coordinate with each other to reduce wasteful spending and mitigate purchase risk caused by demand fluctuation across channels and within geographic channels.
- *Shipment/delivery visibility* aims to increase the transparency and traceability in delivery processes entailing shipment timing, location of shipped items, custom taxes, and more.
- *Supply visibility* means that customers and entities in the value chain can access the production, sourcing, and supply processes of a product. Increasing transparency on supply processes is of benefit to customers who are worried about safety and quality issues. This is necessary for specific goods, particularly food products. For example, there is rising demand in Asia for consumers to know where their food products come from. Called "traceability," this has led producers to implement new processes to mark their food so that people throughout the value chain can trace its source. Visibility of supply processes is also beneficial for reverse logistics to deal with return, used, and discarded products. For example, traceability approach enables faster, more thorough recalls of contaminated products.

15.2.2   An Integrated Omni-Channel System

Channel visibility cannot be fulfilled without a holistic integration of various channels, channel agents, and channel stages, as shown in ◘ Fig. 15.1 and described below.

Integration Among Channel Stages   Each channel has its hypothetical stages in completion of certain activities. The integration of channel stages allows consumers to continue, suspend, or cancel their order across various channel stages without complexity or frustration. For example, online shopping channels can save shopper's items in their shopping cart if they temporarily leave the site. Doing so saves shopper time. When they return to the site, they do not need to rebuild their shopping cart and can quickly check out and pay using saved payment details, to complete their purchase.

Integration Among Channel Types   This refers to the synchronization and cooperation among various channel types, which means that channels should be symbiotic with each other. This integration increases an omni-channel system's compatibility in which customers can continue, suspend, or cancel purchase actions at any channels.

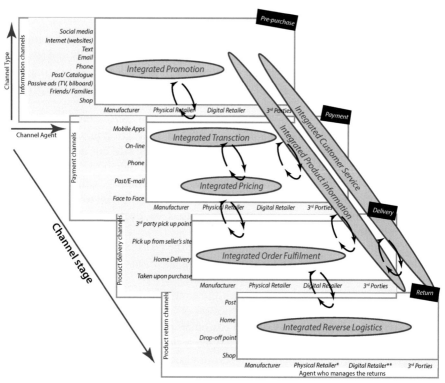

◘ **Fig. 15.1**   The integration of channel type, channel agent, and channel stage. (Source: adapted from Saghiri et al. (2017))

Integration Among Channel Agents   Businesses need to ensure various channel agents offer congruent information and services to customers. For example, a customer may feel satisfied after purchasing an item with a 30 percent discount but then becomes disappointed upon learning that online channels offer a 40 percent discount and free delivery.

The integration of these three dimensions underpins and structures an omni-channel system framework. Later in this section, we will specify what should be integrated in this framework.

Integrated Promotion   Businesses should offer congruent promotions across various channels simultaneously. This creates a congruent brand and marketing strategy for consumers. Marketing narratives such as an advertising image, slogan, and logo should match consistently. This means that promotions of one channel should be able to apply into other channels at the same time.

Integrated Transaction   This implies the congruence of transaction methods across various channels. Today's shopping routines are fragmented and flexible. Mobile devices enable shopping anytime and anywhere via various devices. A female shopper may add a dress into her shopping cart via a PC in office, then add a pair of trousers via a tablet at home, and finally make the purchase via her smartphone while on public transport. The integration of transactions allows consumers to complete a transaction across various channels, which requires that consumers' shopping and transaction-related data need to be securely shared and stored across channels in real time.

Integrated Pricing   Product prices should be congruent across various channels. This integration is most difficult to achieve in practice because channels have a diversity of cost structures. For instance, bricks-and-mortar channels include high upfront fixed costs such as rent, inventory carrying cost, store fit-out and more. The variable costs of online channels include network costs of online traffic, warehousing, website and app hosting and maintenance, shipment fees, and more. Online channels may also offer digital products that reduce costs. For example, rather than ship products, a business might instead email codes for 3D printing to a customer. The customer can then input the codes to a 3D printer and print (create) the product. Online channels need a higher selling price to break even on their variable costs, ceteris paribus.

The same pricing strategy across channels with distinct cost structures, to some extent, would damage certain channels' profitability. For this reason, a holistic and agile approach to pricing is required, and this can be a more complex undertaking.

Integrated Order Fulfillment   Integrated order fulfillment encompasses order placement, order preparation, order delivery, and other stages involved in an order fulfillment process. It requires the cooperation of various channels to fulfill orders. For example, under an integrated order fulfillment scenario, a customer placing an order online should be able to pick it up at a nearby store. This integration is more complicated in practice. It is related to, and influences, how enterprises organize and govern various bricks-and-mortar stores and online channels. As for the case we just mentioned of pricing disparity between online and physical stores, the physical store may have bought a franchise from its parent company and only uses the parent company's brand to do business. In this case, the nearby store may be dissatisfied with the low online price for that product and so may decide to remove it from its store.

Integrated Reverse Logistics   This refers to the integration and compatibility of various channels' to handle reverse logistics (product returns). Omni-channel companies can reap benefits from product returns because they customers may choose to return purchases to nearby physical stores, which increases in-store traffic. Furthermore, in-store traffic allows salespersons the opportunity to sell other products to the customer. When customers can return products to stores, they bear the cost of delivery, can merge the cost in with other benefits ("I was going to the shopping centre anyway") and also receive reimbursement more quickly.

In summary, this section provides a conceptual framework of an omni-channel system with three dimensions—channel stages, channel agents, and channel types. This framework is only conceptual because it is very difficult for businesses to fulfill and optimize all aspects of visibility and integration.[3] In practice, this framework may inform businesses who may adapt it to design their omni-channel system that is tailored to their customer segment and firm competencies.

15.3 Stumbling Blocks for Moving Toward Omni-Channel

Omni-channel strategies have many obstacles in reality. New adopters of this strategy should consider upfront these major obstacles for moving toward omni-channel, so that they may mitigate against their impact.[4]

Acquiring New Resources and Developing New Capabilities   Going omni-channel requires businesses to acquire new resources. For instance, Internet-only companies need to acquire resources and develop capabilities to build and operate physical businesses. This is a strategic drift that will change the market position and e-business model of a business. Bricks-and-mortar companies may need to launch their strategic move to e-business while distributing their goods online. This move certainly needs these businesses to invest time and resources into how to build and develop the new e-business. Encompassing both an online channel and an offline channel is challenging. An omni-channel approach is even more challenging because it requires the synchronization and synergy of various channels and touch points, in real time. The more complicated an omni-channel system is, the more difficult it is for a business to acquire new resources and new capabilities.

---

3   Saghiri et al. (2017) used a multi-case study to construct and validate this framework's three dimensions. In their case study, it found that no cases (Amazon, Argos, John Lewis, Ocado, Tesco, Westbridge furniture, Wren) can be the same as this framework.

4   This section is adapted from Lewis et al. (2014).

Reorganizations Going omni-channel requires companies to reorganize, redesign, and redeploy legacy physical and IT infrastructure. For instance, under a pure bricks-and-mortar business scenario, carriers from distribution centers (DCs) usually transfer products in cartons to all stores. By contrast, under a pure Internet business scenario, DCs in this case are usually breaking down products "just in time" in cartons into several items ready to be singly packed and shipped to individual customers. These two DCs have two different distribution methods; hence going omni-channel needs the business to redesign their DCs to comply with both distribution methods. Moving to an omni-channel requires companies to redesign an existing organization structure and supply chain in order to apply their offering consistently across various channels and support customers completing the purchase journey across the various channels. (See the article "The Challenges of Reaching an Omnichannel Audience.")

Measuring Channel Performance Performance is a critical metric in the decision about whether it is strategically worthwhile to invest in opening a new channel or closing a channel. Omni-channeling means viewing all channels as an entirety, but this creates the challenge of how to evaluate the performance of each channel. It is imperative for businesses to design a reasonable channel performance evaluation metric to identify the channels that are dragging the overall financial performance, and thus companies can either close those channels to reduce the complexity and cost of omni-channel management and improve overall performance. Or they may consider that non-financial benefits (brand reinforcement via experiences) contribute to reinforcing purchases in other channels. This is why a critical activity in omni-channel management is hybridizing, articulating, and integrating performance across all channels. It is difficult to design one metric to assess all channels. For instance, social media may be an optimal channel to reach target audiences and entice them to visit physical stores, yet it is inappropriate to use "sales" to compare channel performance between social media and bricks-and-mortar stores because social media does not generate sales per se.

The Challenges of Reaching an Omni-Channel Audience

Marketers are all pushing for an omni-channel, holistic view of their audiences, but that vision requires integrating audience insights from three core areas: TV, digital, and in store. And that poses substantial challenges.

"The integration of disparate data sets, systems, vendors and technologies poses obvious challenges. At many companies, the need for organizational overhaul is less obvious, yet also vital," said Lauren Fisher, principal analyst at eMarketer and author of the new report "Integrating TV, Digital and In-Store Data: The Pursuit of a True Omni-channel Audience."

A January 2017 poll of US digital marketing and media practitioners conducted by the Interactive Advertising Bureau (IAB) and the Winterberry Group found the greatest portion of respondents planned to devote time and attention to cross-channel measurement and attribution in 2017. Cross-channel audience identification and matching was also mentioned by nearly half of marketers.

"The No. 1 reason why clients are interested in cross-channel is they want to get out of focusing on silos and want to start looking at customers holistically and messaging them across all mediums," said Jared Belsky, president of digital advertising agency 360i. "They want to get out of their own siloed budgeting channels, like, 'This is my e-commerce budget,' or 'This is my in-store budget,' when it really should be, 'How do I use marketing dollars to move consumers through the funnel to buy more goods.'"

As most marketers have found, successful integration of TV, digital, and in-store data is only partially about combining all the necessary pieces. Navigating organizational and technology-driven obstacles is also a must. Without organizational cooperation—and in many cases, digital transformation—any efforts aimed at integrating technology and data are in vain.

"Integrating data sets is about a marketing organization's decision to invest in a data link of their own—a data infrastructure that pulls together the requisite data from all pieces of finance and marketing to different channels that are being managed across TV, digital, etc.," said Michael Cohen, head of data and analytics at Convertro, an attribution firm owned by AOL. "That one piece of an investment can take a couple of years for an organization to achieve. But then there's other work to be done, in terms of designing an organization that aligns with the underlying decision to support technology."

Organizational realignment around technology initiatives is as important as it is difficult. A Q2 2016 survey of business professionals worldwide conducted by Harvard Business Review Analytics Services found that in many instances, respondents said the highest barriers to company use of digital technologies had to do with organizational and people-based challenges.

"The biggest challenge marketers will have over the next 10 years is investing in the resources and people to make those systems work well together and cohesively on their behalf," said Joe Kyriakoza, vice president and general manager of automotive and TV solutions at Oracle. In the latest episode of "Behind the Numbers" eMarketer analysts Lauren Fisher and Yoram Wurmser talk about how well marketers are doing in their quest to integrate digital, in-store, and traditional media usage data.

Source: eMarketer, "The Challenges of Reaching an Omnichannel Audience,"
▶ *Emarketer.com*, 5 July 2017

15

15.4 Managing Conflicts Between Online and Offline Distribution Channels

Businesses that sell products through physical outlets using a sales force may fear that moving into online sales will cannibalize their offline sales.[5] Their argument is that the new online channel is not creating a new market or extra sales but merely siphoning off existing sales.

---

5 For a more extensive discussion of channel conflicts, see Bucklin et al. (1997).

To understand whether firms should fear distribution channel conflicts, they need to analyze how new online channels affect their offline channels and whether the various channels actually serve the same customer segments. For instance, companies may believe mistakenly that different channels are competing with one another when in fact they are benefiting from each other's actions. They may also believe that the loss of sales is ascribed to a new channel when, in reality, it results from the intrusion of a new competitor.

15.4.1 Understanding Conflicts in Distribution Channels

Conflict is inherent to almost all distribution systems, but what do we mean by conflict? One of its classic definitions refers to "a situation in which one channel member perceives another channel member(s) to be engaged in behavior that is preventing or impeding it from achieving its goals" (Stern and El-Ansary, 1992: p. 289). In this context, two specific dimensions should be emphasized: (1) a channel member perceives that its objectives are blocked or interfered by another channel and (2) there is an implicit assumption that the related conflict can negatively affect the relationship between channel members.

A conflict does not suddenly emerge from a channel relationship, but it is the result of a process. A typical structure of a multi-stage conflict process comprises[6]:

1. A *latent* conflict, when conflict sources are covered yet
2. A *perceived* conflict when there is a cognitive perception of some conflict aspects, but with no negative emotional effects yet in the members' relationship
3. A *felt* conflict that carries an emotional response (including anxiety or stress)
4. A *manifest* conflict which explicitly involves a behavioral evidence of conflict between members
5. The conflict *aftermath* which is the final consequence of the process, that is, the stage in which members face the conflict either by solving it or breaking up the relationship between them

Obviously, the existence of channel conflict affects the distribution channel's performance (in terms of efficiency and effectiveness). There are several theoretical approaches to this "performance-conflict" relationship, which can be grouped into two main views (see ■ Fig. 15.2): the *negative linear correlation*, or a higher level of conflict as performance decreases, and the *inverted-U curve*, which suggests that the level of conflict increases when the relationship performance between channel members is moderate while it increases at low and high levels. A third approach which is quite similar but superior to the negative linear model, is proposed by Duarte and Davis. It suggests that a conflict slowly increases as performance decreases until a certain threshold, where conflict is triggered. This model suggests that a conflict should be adequately handled when it is still at a low level, before it

---

6   See Pondy (1967).

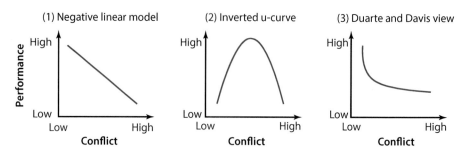

reaches a threshold level and escalates. This is an important issue for bricks-and-mortar businesses that consider adding an e-commerce channel. In order to avoid an online/offline channel conflict, businesses need to proactively and explicitly address related issues and take preemptive actions upfront. This subject is discussed in detail in the next section.

15.4.2   The Channel Conflict Matrix

The channel conflict matrix analyzes how traditional bricks-and-mortar retailers should react toward possible conflicts between their offline and online channels. There are two main dimensions that determine how to deal with possible channel conflict: (1) the prospect of destructive conflict between different channels and (2) the importance of the existing channel that is threatened by the new online channel.

The resulting matrix provides insights into how to deal with possible channel conflicts. The four quadrants of the matrix are now described:

Quadrant 1   If the prospect of destructive conflict between channels is high and the importance of the threatened channel is also high, then it is sensible to address the problem and find ways to reconcile the two channels. For instance, when Nordea Bank started its online banking operations, it was positioned clearly in Quadrant 1. Branch-based banking was threatened severely by the rise of the online channel, yet it was of great importance to the overall functioning of the bank. Contrary to many other banks, Nordea decided to integrate fully its online banking within its physical banking operations, thereby eliminating possible competition between the two channels. In fact, branch employees were enticed to move branch customers over to the Internet. Ultimately, the ability to leverage the branches to move customers to the Internet, thereby eliminating the need for expensive marketing campaigns, was one of the main reasons why Nordea was able to successfully gain a dominant position in the online banking world.

Quadrant 2   If the prospect of destructive conflict between channels is high and the importance of the threatened channel is low, then it is usually sensible simply to allow the threatened channel to decline.

15

Quadrant 3 If the prospect of destructive conflict is low but the importance of the threatened channel is high, then the latter's employees need to be reassured that they will not be affected. This is the case, for instance, with Tesco's bricks-and-mortar retail store network. In spite of the sudden increase of online sales through the ▶ Tesco. com channel, retail stores continue to play a major role. Thus, it is important to let employees know that the new channel does not present a threat to them. To alleviate fears of cannibalization, Tesco physical stores were credited with all sales that they fulfill, irrespective of channel. Similarly, when Ducati started selling motorcycles directly to consumers exclusively over the Internet, it was necessary to inform and placate the network of dealers and reassure them of their continuing importance. To back up this claim, Ducati identified the closest dealer to an online customer and then informed that dealer about the online transaction. The dealer could subsequently accept or reject to hand the motorcycle over to the online customer. In the case of acceptance, the dealer would receive a 10 percent commission of the total price, which was less than the average commission received on an in-store Ducati motorcycle sale. However, with online sales, dealers had no inventory management cost, no inventory risk, and no advertising or marketing costs. The goal of Ducati's online sales was not to cannibalize sales made through the offline channel; rather it was to reach and expand into hitherto untapped market segments (Jelassi and Leenen, 2003).

Quadrant 4 If the prospect of conflict between the online and offline channels is low and the importance of the threatened channel is also low, then the channel conflict is not important, and, therefore, it can be ignored.

❯ In summary, omni-channeling may be daunting for most businesses, but channel conflict can be managed and resolved.

For more strategies and advice for how businesses may alleviate their pressure and anxiety when transitioning to omni-channels, see the article "Stop Being Afraid of Channel Conflict."

Stop Being Afraid of Channel Conflict
For more than 20 years, brands have been wary of developing direct-to-consumer (D2C) e-commerce channels because of concerns the move may upset their retail partners. I still walk into meetings every day with companies worried about creating conflict between their sales channels.

And frankly, it needs to stop. Channel conflict has always been more of an internal fear than an external reality. Given the changing retail landscape, it is time for brands to come to terms with the fact that they need to develop D2C ecommerce channels or risk paying the price.

Reality Check
There is not a single country in the world today where retail has not been affected by people shopping online. Large retailers that were once household names are now closing stores. Even for retailers that remain open, the available shelf space for

brands to display key products is dwindling. The space to showcase a wider product range is shrinking even faster. With fewer and fewer customers walking through the doors of retailers, brands need to find new ways to develop relationships with their customers. A D2C e-commerce channel is the most effective way to foster those relationships while providing a valuable customer experience.

This is not meant as an attack on retail. Nor is it a suggestion that you should move away from retailers altogether—they remain an important route to market. Rather it is an honest assessment of the current landscape. Retail is not dead. And with innovations happening in the space, I foresee it continuing to be an important piece of the commerce puzzle. The increase in "buy online, pick up in store" activity demonstrates that brick-and-mortar stores still hold value for consumers. But at this point, physical locations simply cannot generate the revenue that brands need to stay viable. Given market conditions, building direct relationships with your customers through an aggressive D2C ecommerce channel is your most strategic play.

Communicating with Retailers

Again, I am not suggesting brands abandon retail altogether, but rather that they need to reevaluate retail's place in their overall sales strategy. It is important for brands to be open with their retail partners and have a conversation about the future of their partnership. This can be daunting for brands scared to lose the little shelf space they have. But it is ultimately a conversation that needs to happen for the sake of both parties.

You are never going to reach 100 percent agreement, because effectively we are talking about some level of competition. But there is room for understanding. Some retailers are already squeezing companies on margins, making it a race to the bottom for brands that continue to rely on those channels. The question then for brands nervous about upsetting retailers is what do you have to lose?

Effective D2C Channel Strategy

Just building a D2C channel is not enough to recoup lost revenue from declining retail sales. Brands need to create an engaging e-commerce destination that aims to develop long-term relationships with customers. By offering exclusive products online that are not available through retail channels, or bundling accessories online, brands can add value to their digital storefront without competing with retailers on price.

Research shows consumers will purchase products at a percent higher price point if they know they're getting a better experience. But brands have to make sure they are actually supplying that superior experience or risk losing the customer altogether. An effective D2C channel uses customer data to offer a personalized experience that adds value for the customer and ultimately forms a relationship that can be leveraged for future sales.

Yes, there is upfront cost to building a D2C channel. But the cost of not committing to a D2C strategy is even greater. Without a D2C channel, brands will fail to maintain control of their revenue streams, will not gather crucial customer data, and, most importantly, will fail to create meaningful relationships with their customers. Innovative products only get you so far, building strong consumer relationships will take you a lot further.

Source: T. Haycocks, "Stop Being Afraid of Channel Conflict," *Digital River*, 30 March 2018

15.5 Devising an Omni-Channel Strategy Hybridizing Social/Local/Mobile (SoLoMo)

Social media, location-based services, and mobile technology are three main forces to achieve omni-channeling. In this section, we will illustrate why SoLoMo is necessary for omni-channeling and what components constitute SoLoMo in practice.

15.5.1 Why Do We Need SoLoMo?

An omni-channel strategy with mobile, social, and local (SoLoMo) elements is not wishful thinking. It resonates with traditional approaches how businesses reach and interact with consumers. For example, when stepping into stores, customers find a salesperson may actively interact with them and select products in store that may suit them. Businesses have always known the importance of creating a conversational, context-aware, and convenient situation in which customers have a fantastic shopping experience, and, at the same time, the business can optimize the benefits of customer satisfaction and loyalty. In the digital era, mobile apps, social media, and smartphone-powered location-based services enable businesses to create this situation remotely. For example, many apps have evolved their advertising display mechanism to display advertisements that are consistent with the sex, location, and browsing history, and more, of each specific customer.

On the other hand, businesses have been trying to embed brands into customer's minds via various traditional advertising and branding approaches such as TV, radio, media coverage, flyers, and more. With compliance to privacy and data regulations within each country, SoLoMo aims to create a ubiquitous environment for branding via images and advertisements. In this environment, customers will experience consistent marketing narratives across devices and platforms. They may find friends discuss a brand on social media; their smartphone will then push advertising notifications related to that brand; and brand-related content is mixing with other content on their most visited websites. SoLoMo-based omni-channeling may not be able to present consistent images and narratives simultaneously, but is possible to reach and provide customers with a ubiquitous environment to fasten brand memory and build brand images. For a SoLoMo example, see the article "Case Study: Samsung Goes SoLoMo for Smart TV Product Launch."

Case Study: Samsung Goes SoLoMo for Smart TV Product Launch

From early October through mid-November 2012, Samsung, through its agency Starcom Worldwide, ran a social-mobile advertising campaign that targeted shoppers based on location. Using location-based advertising technology from JiWire, the brand and agency sought to get consumers out of their homes and into physical retail stores to experience the Samsung TV.

With the Smart TV launch in fall 2012, Samsung introduced motion control and voice control features. The challenge was not only to create consumer demand for an entirely new TV category but also to get consumers to experience the TV in person. Based on Samsung's consumer research, 86% of people who bought a Samsung Smart TV first experienced the product at retailers. The brand's research also indicated that online reviews and word of mouth heavily drove smart TV purchases, so the goal became to drive consumer awareness of Samsung's new product by getting people to experience it in stores. Then the hope was they would be compelled to share their experience with friends and family.

An idea to wrap the campaign around the Angry Birds mobile game led Samsung to the campaign strategy it decided to pursue. Samsung partnered with Angry Birds to demonstrate how motion and voice control work on the Samsung Smart TV. The campaign goal was to get consumers in stores and playing Angry Birds on big TVs to experience firsthand the motion and voice control.

"We [decided] to leverage a SoLoMo [social, local, mobile] experience, especially since smartphone users so commonly leverage social networks on their mobile devices," said Erica Chen, associate global director at Starcom Worldwide. Mobile technology platform JiWire delivered location-specific ads to consumers' mobile phones—only when they were within the particular stores or within a 5 mile radius of a store. The ads included the name and address of the closest store so shoppers could access directions from their current location with one click.

"We know people are more likely to be active and spontaneous when they are already on the go," Chen said. "Or even better, when they are already near the retail destination." The ad encouraged users to visit local retail stores to experience Angry Birds on the Samsung Smart TV. The ads also incorporated check-in buttons so that consumers could share, with their friends and followers, their location and the experience of being in the store playing Angry Birds on the smart TV. By checking in, users could enter a sweepstakes to win a Samsung Smart TV.

Samsung hoped these calls to action would motivate consumers to share their experience. Measuring consumer engagement—engagement with the ad, click-throughs, the number of consumer actions, as well retail store traffic—Starcom reported that the campaign results outperformed their expectations. Starcom and Samsung also measured social engagement through Facebook check-ins, social sharing, sweepstakes entries, and in-store experience surveys.

"By leveraging hyper-location targeting, we were able to talk to consumers while they were already close to the stores," Chen said. "This hugely increased the likelihood of them actually taking an action while in the store."

Source: eMarketer, "Case Study: Samsung Goes SoLoMo for Smart TV Product Launch," ▶ *Emarketer.com* [website], 3 June 2013

15

15.5.2 Omni-Channeling Through a Social/Local/Mobile (SoLoMo) Approach

A conceptual framework for omni-channeling by SoLoMo includes social, mobile, and local channels. Each channel (stations, e-commerce sites, m-commerce sites, and catalogues) resonates with other channels forming an entire circle by integrating SoLoMo. These channels are connected and reconciled to serve well-defined target customer segments.

In order to help readers understand detailed components of this framework, we break down its structure into the following parts.7

Social Media   Businesses have various social media platforms to reach customers and convey information related to their physical stores, e- and m-commerce sites, and online catalogues. The social media sites include, but are not limited to, Snapchat, WeChat, Twitter, Instagram, Facebook, Twitter, YouTube, Sina Weibo, LinkedIn, Pinterest, and more. For example, marketers can create an enterprise Facebook account using various Facebook features such as Profile Page, Store Page, and News Feed to reach customers.

Local-Based Services   Local-based services can be provided via social networking sites, PC apps, and mobile apps that are able to access a user's geo-location information. It also includes in-store digital solutions such as iBeacon technology and store-based terminals that give shoppers access to location-based online services. Location-based services can be linked to online ordering which supports "Click &Collect" (customers can place an order online and pick it at a nearby store) and "Same-Day-Delivery" where nearby stores can ship or deliver goods ordered online at the same day or even within an hour (for a premium fee).

Mobile Technology   Mobile-related offerings are much wider. Mobile devices can link customers to online shopping sites, social media, and even physical stores. Mobile apps, for instance, can enable customers to shop anytime and anywhere. Mobile social media, as mentioned in ▶ Chap. 14, is dominating the digital time of today's Internet users. Augmented reality-powered apps can place virtual objects into reality, for example, allowing furniture shoppers to put a virtual sofa into their living room. Most importantly, mobile devices can link online and offline channels. For example, QR codes are 2D codes containing digital content such as e-coupons, pictures, information, competitions, websites, and more. Stores can publish these QR codes anywhere such as at checkout counters, billboards, flyers, electronic screens, and more. Consumers can use their smartphone to read these codes to access the digital content and take a picture of them to share with friends.

In summary, SoLoMo represents today's three most prevailing vehicles to integrate multi-channels and materialize an omni-channel strategy. But omni-channeling does not mean that opening more channels definitely leads to higher performance

---

7   This section is adapted from: Yumurtacı Hüseyinoğlu et al. (2017).

or competitive advantage. On the contrary, omni-channeling may dilute a firm's current advantage or high performance by distracting management from their strategic focus. Through the lens of customers, information overload caused by omni-channel merchandising or advertising may also jeopardize customer loyalty and shopping experiences. SoLoMo strategies are complex, sensitive, and require vigilant monitoring.

Summary

- Firstly, this chapter presented reasons why firms should implement omni-channel strategies.
- Secondly, this chapter provided a framework of an omni-channel system. An omni-channel system needs to increase channel visibility and channel integration. This chapter detailed channel integration encompassing channel types, channel agents, and channel stages.
- Thirdly, this chapter discussed three major stumbling blocks on the journey to omni-channel.
- Fourthly, this chapter categorized channel conflicts and offered contingent solutions for each type of channel conflict.
- Lastly, SoLoMo represents three dominant vehicles to integrate various channels. This chapter shed light on how companies should devise their omni-channel strategy by SoLoMo.

Review Questions

1. Why should firm consider about omni-channeling?
2. What are major obstacles to moving toward omni-channel?
3. What are the three dimensions of channel integration?
4. How should firms handle with different channel conflicts?
5. What is SoLoMo? Why is it important for omni-channeling?
6. Exemplify one or two real cases employing omni-channel strategy.
7. Among all the difficulties in implementing omni-channel strategy, which one is most difficult for companies? Why?
8. Apply the framework of an omni-channel system into a real case, and analyze and evaluate its omni-channel strategy.
9. Design a simple omni-channeling campaign via SoLoMo.

15

References

Bucklin, C., Thomas-Graham, P., & Webster, E. (1997). Channel conflict: When is it dangerous? *McKinsey Quarterly, 3*, 36–43.

Duarte, M., & Davis, G. (2003). Testing the conflict-performance assumption in business-to-business relationships. *Industrial Marketing Management, 32*(2), 91–99.

Jelassi, T., & Leenen, S. (2003). An e-commerce sales model for manufacturing companies: A conceptual framework and a European example. *European Management Journal, 21*(1), 45–46.

Konus, U., Verhoef, P. C., & Neslin, S. A. (2008). Multichannel shopper segments and their covariates. *Journal of Retailing, 84*(4), 398–413.

Pondy, L. R. (1967). Organizational conflict: Concepts and models. *Administrative Science Quarterly, 12*, 296–320.

Stern, L. W., & El-Ansary, A. I. (1992). *Marketing channels* (p. 289). Englewood Cliffs: Prentice-Hall.

Yumurtacı Hüseyinoğlu, I. Ö., Galipoğlu, E., & Kotzab, H. (2017). Social, local and mobile commerce practices in omni-channel retailing: Insights from Germany and Turkey. *International Journal of Retail & Distribution Management, 45*(7/8), 711–729.

Further Reading

Chen, Y., Cheung, C. M., & Tan, C. W. (2018). Omnichannel business research: Opportunities and challenges. *Decision Support System, 109*, 1–4.

Lewis, J., Whysall, P., & Foster, C. (2014). Drivers and technology-related obstacles in moving to multichannel retailing. *International Journal of Electronic Commerce, 18*(4), 43–68.

Saghiri, S., Wilding, R., Mena, C., & Bourlakis, M. (2017). Toward a three-dimensional framework for omni-channel. *Journal of Business Research, 77*, 53–67.

The Strategic Approach of the World's Biggest e-Tailing Companies: Amazon and Alibaba

Contents

© Springer Nature Switzerland AG 2020
T. Jelassi, F. J. Martínez-López, *Strategies for e-Business*, Classroom Companion: Business,
https://doi.org/10.1007/978-3-030-48950-2_16

Learning Outcomes

After completing this chapter, you should be able to:

- Understand the importance of learning from Amazon and Alibaba
- From different aspects learn how Amazon and Alibaba strategize their e-business
- Get a practical understanding of strategies for e-business

▪ Introduction

As management scholar Peter Drucker (1986: p. 14) said: "Management is practice. Its essence is not knowing but doing. Its test is not logic but results. Its only authority is performance." There is little point in discussing business and strategy without including exemplars of how it works in practice. A strategy could be successful under certain circumstances, and it also can become a failure under other conditions. This chapter will describe, compare, and contrast Amazon and Alibaba, which are two major e-businesses in the world today. Their sustained success and lucrative businesses can help us understand e-business in practice by exploring their strategic choices.

They are both e-commerce platforms, but Amazon also brands its own products and sells them directly, and Alibaba has a strong payments processing capacity (Alipay). While both are global, they are strongest in specific regions. In this chapter, we firstly describe the lessons that businesses can learn from Amazon and Alibaba. Secondly, we separately analyze their e-business practices. The last section concludes by highlighting the practical implications of the strategic moves made by Amazon and Alibaba.

16.1 Why Can We Learn from Amazon and Alibaba?

Amazon and Alibaba are two phenomenal e-business giants. We can learn a lot from them. Firstly, they have sustained spectacular growth. Below are some financial indicators (see ◘ Table 16.1) that reflect their dominance of the United States and Chinese markets.

There is no doubt that Amazon and Alibaba have generated a widespread consumer understanding of, and confidence in, e-business. They are frequently cited by academics and analysts around the world as "best practice" in e-business strategies at the corporate, business unit, and operational levels.

Secondly, many lessons could be learned about business competition from their actions. Companies cannot ignore these two companies when launching their e-business strategy. Between them, Amazon and Alibaba dominate markets in most countries of the world (see the article: "Why Amazon is eating the world"), and their global platforms enable trade between countries. When a business undertakes e-business, it would typically consider how to leverage Amazon and Alibaba to promote and grow the reach of their products and/or services; avoid direct competition; and avoid others using the Alibaba or Amazon platforms to undercut pricing

16

◘ **Table 16.1** Financial indicators of Alibaba and Amazon

	Alibaba	Amazon
Predominant e-business type	B2B	B2B; B2C
Launch	1999	1994
IPO	2014	1997
Volume of sales (items per annum, 2015)	14.5 billion	5 billion
Packages delivered per day, 2015	12 million	3 million
Biggest annual shopping day	Singles Day (2018 $17.49 billion)	Cyber Monday (2018 $3.39 billion)
Payment processing	Alipay 400 million frequent users	Pay with Amazon 33 million users
e-Commerce revenue (US$, year to 30 September, 2018)	$42.4 billion	$197.6 billion
e-Commerce operating income (US$, year to 30 September, 2018)	$10.9 billion	$4.3 billion
Stock market performance (percent price growth, January 2016–December 2018)	90 percent	150 percent
Market value (USD, September 2018)	$427 billion	$1 trillion
Potential e-commerce market size 2020 (US$ equivalent)	China - $1.7 trillion	USA $632 billion

Sources: adapted from N. Rossolillo, "Better Buy: Alibaba vs. Amazon," Motley Fool, 15 December 2018

for similar products and/or services. Amazon and Alibaba have created an enormous online marketplace for everyone, which, at the same time, has increased price competition (because buyers will always select the cheapest offer for the same product), and it empowers anyone to imitate or clone profitable and valuable products.

Lastly, Amazon and Alibaba clearly show what e-business strategies look like in practice. Amazon and Alibaba are both pioneers, "best practice benchmarks," and dominate many e-business domains. They created two e-business empires encompassing almost all aspects of e-business from C2C to B2B. Not only should new e-businesses consider Amazon and Alibaba's pioneering strategic moves and their dominant economies of scale, they largely influence how consumers complete online purchases and set consumers expectations for how other businesses sell to them (in the same way).

Why Amazon Is Eating the World

[...] Instead of just writing about our "internal" news, I wrote about the impending apocalypse in the broader world of retail. More specifically, I included some thoughts on Amazon and why their commanding lead is only going to get larger. Amazon is the most impressive company on earth, and I think it is one of the least understood. [...].

It is the fact that each piece of Amazon is being built with a service-oriented architecture, and Amazon is using that architecture to successively turn every single piece of the company into a separate platform—and thus opening each piece to outside competition. [...].

The most obvious example of Amazon's SOA structure is Amazon Web Services. Because of the timing of Amazon's unparalleled scaling—hypergrowth in the early 2000s, before enterprise-class SaaS was widely available—Amazon had to build their own technology infrastructure. The financial genius of turning this infrastructure into an external product (AWS) has been well-covered—the windfalls have been enormous, to the tune of a $14 billion annual run rate. But the revenue bonanza is a footnote compared to the overlooked organizational insight that Amazon discovered: By carving out an operational piece of the company as a platform, they could future-proof the company against inefficiency and technological stagnation.

In the 10+ years since AWS's debut, Amazon has been systematically rebuilding each of its internal tools as an externally consumable service. A recent example is AWS's Amazon Connect—a self-service, cloud-based contact center platform that is based on the same technology used in Amazon's own call centers. Again, the "extra revenue" here is great—but the real value is in honing Amazon's internal tools.

If Amazon Connect is a complete commercial failure, Amazon's management will have a quantifiable indicator (revenue or lack thereof) that suggests their internal tools are significantly lagging behind the competition. Amazon has replaced useless, time-intensive bureaucracy like internal surveys and audits with a feedback loop that generates cash when it works—and quickly identifies problems when it does not. They say that money earned is a reasonable approximation of the value you are creating for the world, and Amazon has figured out a way to measure its own value in dozens of previously invisible areas.

But this much is obvious—we all know about AWS. The incredible thing here is that this strategy—in one of the most herculean displays of effort in the history of the modern corporation—has permeated Amazon at every level. Amazon has quietly rolled out external access in nooks and crannies across their entire ecosystem, and it is this long tail of external service availability that I think will be nearly impossible to replicate.

The broadest example of this is the Fulfillment by Amazon (FBA) program. If you've ever ordered a product from Amazon that says "Sold by {Company} and Fulfilled by Amazon," you have seen FBA in action. With FBA, Amazon allows third-party sellers to ship bulk inventory to Amazon—Amazon stores this inventory (which the seller still owns) in Amazon's fulfillment center, ships the product to the Amazon customer when the order is placed, and even handles all of the returns and customer service. The rates are incredibly competitive. And FBA is not limited to items sold on Amazon—sellers also can use Amazon's "multi-channel fulfillment" option to ship non-Amazon orders to the seller's customers. An example of this would be if Hydro Flask operated their own separate e-commerce store on Shopify—when a customer places an order on the Shopify store, Hydro Flask can send the order to FBA (you guessed it—via an external API), and FBA will ship it directly to the customer.

The benefit for Hydro Flask is obvious. They can have the product manufactured in China and use a freight forwarder like Flexport to ship the product directly from the factory to Amazon's warehouse—and thus avoid the headache (and overhead) of operating their own warehouse. For Amazon, the surface benefits are numerous: (a) better utilization of excess capacity, (b) increased shipping volume/leverage with UPS/FedEx, and (c) revenue from the fulfillment services (which, combined with marketplace commissions and "other third-party seller services," totaled a whopping $6.4 billion in Q1 2017—or 25 percent of Amazon's total revenue). […]

It is a relatively clean, abstracted, service-based interface that is "owned" by a separate team—a team with responsibilities to external customers. Bezos has imbued a sense of customer worship within Amazon ("Earth's most customer-centric company"), and Amazon has three distinct groups of customers to worship: e-commerce shoppers (► Amazon.com), developers (AWS), and sellers (Amazon Marketplace/FBA). […]

The key advantage that Amazon has over any other enterprise service provider—from UPS and FedEx to Rackspace—is that they are forced to use their own services. UPS is a step removed from backlash due to lost/destroyed packages, shipping delays, terrible software, and poor holiday capacity planning. Angry customers blame the retailer, and the retailer screams at UPS in turn. When Amazon is the service provider, they're permanently dogfooding. There is nowhere for poor performance to hide. Amazon has built a feedback loop as a moat, and it is incredible to watch the flywheel start to pick up speed.

Amazon has committed to this idea at a granular level. Even when it comes to services that cannot be sold, Amazon is still making a push to expose the services externally. The perfect example of this is Amazon's Marketplace Web Service (MWS) API—this is the set of services that Amazon Marketplace sellers can use to programmatically exchange data with Amazon. Amazon built out a service that they call the "Subscriptions API," which gives the seller instant notification of any price change by any competitor—including Amazon itself!

Amazon is externally exposing the tools it uses to set its own prices in order to guarantee that the price listed on Amazon is as low as possible for the customer. This has spawned a whole ecosystem of third-party price optimization tools called "repricers," which use the MWS API to automatically respond to price changes in order to maximize sales for the marketplace seller (the WSJ published a great piece on this back in March, aptly likening it to high-frequency trading). The beauty here is that Amazon does not care if a seller undercuts Amazon's price—Amazon takes a 12–15 percent commission on the sale regardless and then collects FBA fees to boot.

I could go on and on with examples. I am on the email list for updates from AWS, Amazon Marketplace, Amazon's Vendor Program, and a handful of customer-facing programs—they are systemically productizing the entire company, honing what works, fixing what does not, and killing off everything else. [...]

Amazon will only be brought down by an anti-trust case (though that's a long way off, given that they only have a small percentage of total retail volume today) or a paradigm shift in how we consume physical products—the scenario that comes to mind is widespread adoption of massively immersive VR combined with intravenous nutrition (Soylent in 20 years) and universal basic income, which would obviate the need for physical products altogether. But that's a ways off too.

Adapted from: Z. Kanter, "Why Amazon is eating the world," *Techcrunch*, 15 May 2017

16.2 Amazon

16.2.1 An Introduction to Amazon

Definition

I very frequently get the question: 'What's going to change in the next 10 years?' And that is a very interesting question; it's a very common one. I almost never get the question: 'What's not going to change in the next 10 years?' And I submit to you that that second question is actually the more important of the two — because you can build a business strategy around the things that are stable in time. ... [I]n our retail business, we know that customers want low prices, and I know that's going to be true 10 years from now. They want fast delivery; they want vast selection. It's impossible to imagine a future 10 years from now where a customer comes up and says, 'Jeff, I love Amazon; I just wish the prices were a little higher,' [or] 'I love Amazon; I just wish you'd deliver a little more slowly.'[1]

–Jeff Bezos

Founder, President, CEO, and Chairman of the Board of Amazon

Amazon is a global e-commerce and cloud computing company founded by Jeff Bezos in 1994 and headquartered in the United States.[2] In 2017, it is the second largest Internet company worldwide by annual revenue and accounts for 74.1% of total e-commerce sales in the United States.

Amazon is a customer-centric company. Its businesses are across diverse industries from e-retailing to physical stores to video streaming and secure online stor-

---

1   See Z. Kanter, 2017 "Why Amazon is eating the world," *Techcrunch*, 15 May 2017.
2   Section 16.2.1, 16.2.4, and 16.2.5 are adapted from: J.Batistich, "Understanding ▶ Amazon. com," 15 May 2017. Available at: ▶ https://www.ami.org.au/imis15/librarymanager/ understandingamazon-170515004436.pdf.

age and potentially into pharmaceuticals and health insurance. Despite the diversity of sectors, locations, and services that Amazon offers, its business model is, and has always been, centered on an obsession with customers.

The multinational businesses of Amazon include:

Amazon e-commerce marketplace. Amazon began as an online bookstore via ► Amazon.com and today still sells books there and also via other online platforms that it has acquired (Book Depository, AbeBooks, ComiXology, and Audible). It also now publishes books directly (Amazon Publishing). ► Amazon.com then expanded to offer other goods by third-party vendors. This was followed by offering fair-priced "private label" goods that are sold exclusively on ► Amazon.com, either with an Amazon brand or with a third-party brand.

As in October 2018, there were 120 private label brands on Amazon including nappies, clothing, snack foods, bed and bath products, and even furniture. For example, Amazon Fresh allows customers to order healthy and fresh vegetables online. Vendors selling on ► Amazon.com can choose to either handle delivery logistics and customer services themselves, or Amazon can handle them (Fulfillment by Amazon - FBA). Amazon charges a percent commission on all goods sold, and the commission is higher for private label sales.

Fulfillment by Amazon (FBA). FBA is a representative Amazon service. Sellers can store their stock in Amazon's fulfillment centers, and when an order is placed via ► Amazon.com, Amazon will pick, pack, and ship products to buyers and handle any customer service issues. Amazon charges a higher FBA fee on goods sold using for this service.

Amazon private label. The private label covers two different types of products. Amazon sells its own branded products (e.g., Amazon Elements baby wipes) or sells products with third-party brands that are exclusive to Amazon. When a third party purchases goods directly from a manufacturer and then sells exclusively through Amazon and uses FBA, they do very little apart from ordering goods with an Amazon delivery address.

How Amazon Plans to Dominate the Private Label Market

Amazon already has the loyalty of 100 million Prime members, a most dedicated audience that paid $99 for the privilege, though soon it will go up to $119 per year. Now it wants to go even deeper with the 68% of Americans who own pets. Amazon just launched its own private label brand of dry dog food called Wag, which is reputedly the first of a major expansion of the company's pet products business. Amazon is getting into pet products in a serious way after its AmazonBasics line of pet carriers and beds generated some $2 million in sales last year, according to a report by One Click Retail. Now Wag dog food joins the party of the estimated $30 billion pet food market, which accounts for the largest share of the $72.1 billion Americans spent on their pets last year.

Wag dog food competes in the premium dog food segment, with meat being its primary ingredient and lentils added as binder instead of grains, as is typical in mass brands. Priced at $44.99 for a 30 lb. bag, it undercuts the price of Blue Wilderness brand, another meat-first, grain-free line, which sells for $49.99 for a 24 lb. bag on Amazon. Both brands are delivered via Prime.

Wag is adding to some 80 private label brands in Amazon's arsenal to capture a dominant share of the private label business, estimated by Nielsen to account for nearly 1 in every 5 items sold in US supermarkets during 2016. That totals an estimated $150 billion in supermarket sales, as value-yearning consumers no longer feel the stigma of buying store brands.

Private Label Is Where It's at

In today's "paradox of choice" consumer economy, characterized by consumers confronted with too many choices in most any category under consideration for purchase, private label brands make the selection process simple and smart.

Shoppers already trust the retailer that they are patronizing, so they confidently extend that trust to buying their private label brands. That those private label brands are cheaper than the national brands is another good reason, especially with the knowledge that private label products today are often manufactured by the same companies that make the name brands and to virtually identical quality standards. That is why Cadent Consulting Group predicts that private labels will "steal" as much as $64 billion from the nationally advertised brands in the next 10 years, rising from 17.7% of the CPG/food market in 2017 to 25.7% in 2027. The group further predicts that Amazon, including its Whole Foods 365 Everyday Value brand, with an estimated $2 billion in sales added to Amazon's $2 billion grocery private label sales in 2017, will grow to $20 billion by 2027.

Amazon's Plans for Private Label Dominance

A recent study by Gartner L2 delves more deeply into Amazon's ambitious private label brand strategy across all its offerings, which in sheer numbers is led by its home-grown clothing, shoes, and jewelry brands, accounting for 86% of Amazon's private label brands. In that study, the authors ask the provocative question, "Do first-party and third-party sellers have any hope in competing against Amazon's private label brands?"

The answer clearly is "not much," as Amazon has aggressively moved into garden/outdoor, grocery, health/household, home/kitchen, as well as its cross-category everyday commodity essentials, AmazonBasics, which are only available to Prime members. The study concludes, "Brands need to accept that private label will play an increasingly important role in Amazon's overall strategy, particularly in categories where Amazon goes head-to-head against traditional retailers."

AmazonBasics Is Its Ace in the Hole

The Gartner L2 study also reveals that AmazonBasics is the big winner in its private label business. While only 3 of Amazon's ~ 80 private brands include "Amazon" in their name, these represent nearly 25% of the company's private label products. This suggests, the report states, that "they represent an outsize role in Amazon's private label strategy," noting that the number includes its Whole Foods 365 house brand. "AmazonBasics has cannibalized assortment from Amazon's non-branded private brands over the years," the report continues, finding that Amazon-branded labels typically sell for less than the comparable non-Amazon-branded products.

16

By playing both sides of the Amazon-branded and non-branded private label business, the study concludes, it "allows Amazon to identify promising private label products for its more valuable branded-label business." Of note, its new Wag dog food straddles the line by adding Amazon to its official brand name, "Wag Dry Dog Food by Amazon."

Amazon Is in the Catbird's Seat

Amazon has established itself as people's default product search engine. According to research firm Survata, some 49% of consumers' first product search starts on Amazon, and for the other 36% of product searches that start on Google or another search engine, a goodly percentage are going to point to an Amazon listing first. And the Survata study doesn't separate out the preferences of Amazon's most loyal Prime members, who I suspect have an even greater likelihood to turn to Amazon first.

These findings about where consumers' product searches begin highlights the Gartner L2 finding that "Amazon operates more like a traditional search engine than a traditional retailer." Amazon knows even better than Google what customers want and need and when they are likely to need the product again for replenishment.

That big data puts Amazon in the catbird's seat when it comes to deciding what products are its best candidates for the next private label branding opportunity and further how to slot their home-grown products into their captive search engine to pull the best prospective customers, most especially its Prime members. It is ironic that so many companies, having gotten onboard Amazon in their search for new customers and broader distribution, are now effectively colluding with Amazon to give their business over to it. Amazon holds all the cards, and at the rate it is going, there doesn't seem a way to stop its juggernaut.

Source: P. N. Danziger, "How Amazon plans to dominate the private label market," *Forbes*, 6 May 2018

Amazon Marketing Service (AMS) ▶ Amazon.com is one of the world's highest-traffic websites that appeal to a worldwide audience of online shoppers. AMS monetizes the Amazon platform traffic by offering advertising to Amazon vendors. AMS can place advertisements for vendors' products on ▶ Amazon.com and create a frictionless path-to-purchase: customers click on the ads to the product page and complete a purchase. AMS offers a variety of pay-per-click marketing solutions for Amazon vendors.

Amazon Prime Prime represents a premium membership that offers benefits across the Amazon ecosystem. Prime members pay an annual subscription to access premium services such as free 2-day delivery, streaming video and music, Twitch Prime, free unlimited photo storage, special discounts, and other offers including 30-minute earlier access to "Lightning Deals." Other benefits include the Amazon Dash Buttons (automated replenishment of used household goods). Prime is well-known for the media and games streaming service, for which Amazon also funds and creates content (films and television series). Only Prime subscribers can access it, and they also pay an additional fee to access premium content.

Amazon Web Services (AWS)   AWS offers on-demand cloud computing services to companies and governments. The initial impetus for AWS was that Amazon had spare server capacity and decided to offer it to businesses as a service. The approach was influenced by the concept of Software-as-a-Service (SaaS). AWS is now a world leader in cloud computing-based services, with its current market share being equal to the aggregated share of its competitors (including Microsoft and Google among others). AWS allows users to use their browser to log in, configure, and use virtual systems offered by Amazon. It has grown to be a core part of Amazon, providing cloud-based infrastructure to hundreds of thousands of businesses in 190 countries.

Kindle   Amazon's successful e-reader, the Kindle, was launched in 2007 solely as a device with a non-glare screen for reading digital books. It aligned to Amazon's strategy for online book sales. Since then the Kindle has added new features. The Kindle marked Amazon's first step into hardware. From there it created the Fire tablet, television (from streaming media), mobile phone and operating system, and, although they met with mixed market success, lessons learned from the Fire initiatives informed development of Echo, Alexa, and home security systems.

Amazon Echo and Alexa   Amazon Echo is a smart speaker developed by Amazon. It can connect to a voice-activated virtual assistant Alexa. Customers can use Alexa via the Echo device that is connected to Wi-Fi, to perform tasks in their home. For example, a person may ask Alexa to turn on the radio, to play an audiobook, or to provide weather, traffic, and other real-time information. The Echo device also can connect to other smart devices and so acts as a "command center." Users can install third-party apps such as weather programs and audio features.

16.2.2   Business Model of Amazon

As mentioned in ▶ Chap. 5, business models show how a business creates, delivers, and captures value at a strategic level. The business model canvas is a well-known tool to visualize a business model, and in ▶ Chap. 5, we used it to analyze Amazon's business model for its online marketplace, which remains a core part of the Amazon value proposition. This section will expand to Amazon's other major businesses after a quick recap of the Amazon marketplace.[3]

Amazon Marketplace   Through the ▶ Amazon.com marketplace, Amazon helps vendors worldwide to sell goods (B2B) and also sell goods directly (B2C). The value proposition to vendors is that through Amazon, they can reach a global market. By

---

3   This section is adapted from: Investopedia, "The Difference between Amazon and Alibaba's Business Models," ▶ *Investopedia.com*, 2 August 2016.

outsourcing logistics to Amazon, vendors avoid the cost of holding slow-moving stock and the effort and cost of logistics. Amazon does not charge vendors any fixed or upfront fees for using its platform, instead it takes a percentage of revenues from each sale. Additional services, including logistics and advertising within search results, incur additional fees.

The Amazon private label dual strategy of Amazon-branded goods and goods sold exclusively through Amazon benefits Amazon in several ways. Amazon ensures private label products have more exposure on the site. They are prominently placed in search results, thus increasing potential sales. Through economies of scale, they can aggressively compete on price. Thirdly, Amazon receives a higher percentage of revenue from each sale. Fourthly, it increases the range of goods available on Amazon. These benefits also pressure other vendors to purchase more advertising on Amazon.

The other Amazon marketplace of note is Amazon's purchase of the bricks-and-mortar store Whole Foods in the United States. Amazon has absorbed Whole Foods into its online grocery products (for the United States only) and is using the physical Whole Foods stores to experiment with cashless payments and other omni-channel initiatives.

Kindle   Amazon's e-reader, the Kindle, was launched in 2007 solely as a device with a non-glare screen for reading digital books. It aligned to Amazon's strategy for online book sales. Since then the Kindle has added new features and continues to form part of the portfolio of Amazon hardware. Through both the Amazon website and the Kindle, various digital content creators can engage in the production and distribution of digital content and applications. For example, readers of Kindle need to purchase or pay a subscription fee for paid books.

Amazon Prime   Amazon Prime also represents a premium membership to every service that Amazon offers, notably faster delivery for Amazon orders in certain urban locations. In a form of cross selling to grow its membership, Prime (video streaming) members can access free 2-day or same-day delivery on physical goods purchased through Amazon. This includes online groceries via Amazon Fresh (including discounted Whole Foods goods) which may require an upgraded "Prime Fresh" membership.

Amazon Prime is also known as its platform for streaming content. Only Amazon Prime subscribers can access Amazon Prime content (television shows, films, games) via the Prime platform. In addition, they may also pay an additional amount to access premium content (e.g., first release blockbuster shows). Amazon Studios also funds and creates new content (games, films, and television series) for the Prime platform. It also owns Twitch.tv—the world's leading social video platform and community for gamers and video game culture.

This is something that another prominent media streaming company, Netflix, cannot offer because it is a "stand-alone," "pure play" business. In April 2018, Amazon reported the worldwide number of Prime members reached 100 million. However it is estimated that only 40 percent of Prime members watch Prime shows every week (Nath, 2018), so this figure includes Prime members who may not be active on the platform, rather they may be Prime grocery customers who may also use it for occasional-specific transactions (to view a first release blockbuster) rather than regular media streaming. As mentioned previously, the average annual subscription to Prime costs $119, plus specific (discounted and premium) purchases.

Amazon Web Services (AWS)   AWS enables business customers to rapidly grow the scale of their computing capacity with ease. By using AWS, companies do not need to invest upfront in hardware infrastructure such as a physical server farm, which suits customers who cannot predict the scale of their data storage requirements. AWS uses a subscription model and bills each customer based on the capacity of storage used over a specific duration.

Amazon Smart Speaker Echo and Voice-Activated Assistant Alexa   Amazon, Google, and Apple are transitioning their digital platforms into digital ecosystems (see the article titled "Creating a digital ecosystem that benefits your business" in ▶ Chap. 5), and their smart home devices are a core device to do this. Through them, a customer can access multiple apps from other providers. Once a consumer is using multiple products and/or services within the ecosystem of one business, they have "high switching costs." For example, it becomes harder for the consumer to leave because it means changing multiple services, passwords, and payment methods. Via Alexa, a customer simply needs to talk, and it recognizes their voice and commands. For example, to swap to Apple's voice-activated command assistant, "Siri," a consumer would need to reprogram it and learn a new operating system (IoS).

Echo and Alexa also represent Amazon's strategic step forward in artificial intelligence (AI) and machine learning (ML). The Alexa voice-activated assistant can learn and evolve from human-computer interactions, see the article "Amazon pours resources into voice assistant Alexa" for more details on Amazon's strategy for AI and ML.

Amazon Pours Resources into Voice Assistant Alexa

When Amazon launched Alexa, its intelligent voice assistant, it did so on the back of an embarrassing failure. The company's attempt to make a success of a smartphone called the Fire had flopped, forcing a $170 m write-down in late 2014. Analysts called it one of the worst phones made. The end of the Fire Phone seemed to dash Amazon's hopes of developing its own mobile platform. At the time when Apple had the iPhone and Alphabet had its ubiquitous search engine, Amazon was desperate to find ways to reach customers directly without going through a rival tech company.

Although few expected it at the time, Alexa has given Amazon precisely the entrée it had been seeking with the Fire Phone—just in a different format. Instead of asking users to interact with a screen, Alexa is entirely voice based. The initial Alexa product, the Echo speaker, was launched just 2 weeks after the Fire Phone write-down and became the first voice-controlled speaker to have mass public appeal. In the 2 years since its release, Alexa has spread like wildfire, and the voice service is now integrated into dozens of home gadgets, including refrigerators and, soon, cars.

Amazon hopes that Alexa Voice Services, the digital mind behind the assistant, will become ubiquitous wherever voice commands are used. The company has succeeded in unlikely business areas before, most notably with Amazon Web Services, its cloud computing business. Launched 10 years ago, AWS exploited its first-mover advantage and is now the biggest cloud computing provider in the world. Replicating that success with Alexa will not be easy, but Amazon has already put big resources behind the effort. To encourage adoption, the company sells its Alexa devices at a loss—pricing them between 10 and 20 percent less than the cost of the hardware, according to an estimate from Evercore. The company has never disclosed how many Alexa-enabled devices it has sold.

Amazon also gives Alexa Voice Services away for free, meaning a developer can integrate Alexa into any device with a speaker and microphone. And there is an Alexa Fund that gives grants to developers to work on new applications for the platform. The company has also been pouring resources into Alexa at an ever-faster pace. Evercore estimates that Amazon lost about $330 m on Alexa in 2016, including net losses on the devices as well as personnel costs, and that this figure will nearly double to exceed $600 m this year. Amazon is advertising openings for more than 500 jobs in its Alexa team as it seeks to expand. (The company has also promised to add 100,000 new jobs, mostly warehouse positions, in the United States by mid-2018.)

The strategic imperative for Amazon is clear: Alexa is its chance to own the operating system in this new medium, voice. "It's kind of like trying to become the Google for voice or the Windows for voice," said Mark Mahaney, analyst at RBC. "I think Amazon is just running away with this market." He points to two places where voice interactions are most convenient: the home and the car. In the home, Amazon can strengthen its ties to customers and of course make it easier for them to shop on Amazon and listen to Amazon Music. This presence in the home dovetails with Amazon's recent effort to expand its grocery business, Amazon Fresh. "It is kind of Amazon's Trojan horse into the refrigerator," said Mr Mahaney. He estimates as many as 10 m Alexa devices were sold in the recent holiday quarter.

These direct retail opportunities are only part of the picture, however. Owning the popular voice operating system puts Amazon in a powerful position, allowing it to act as the gatekeeper for third-party applications and customer data. So far, Amazon has taken an open approach toward third-party apps, or "skills," that integrate with Alexa. Spotify and Pandora are available through Alexa, even though they compete directly with Amazon's music service. Customers can also use Alexa to order Domino's Pizza—even though it competes with Amazon's restaurant delivery service in many cities.

This approach has been reassuring to companies that are planning to partner with Alexa. Ford, the carmaker, set itself a simple task when it came to picking a giant tech company with which to forge an alliance: find one that was unlikely to end up being a direct competitor. That was a large part of the thinking behind the carmaker's announcement last week that it will use Alexa in its cars from the middle of this year. The arrangement is a breakthrough for Alexa, giving it a place in car dashboards for the first time. It also caps an early lead over Google and Microsoft in the race to bring voice-activated intelligent agents into devices of all types.

> Perhaps even more important is what the Ford alliance may say about future competition: the e-commerce company is finding an open door among hardware makers that see it as a neutral partner, at the time when Silicon Valley's ambitions are casting a long shadow over many different industries. Others in the car industry feel like Ford. "It's more difficult to work with someone when you don't understand what their objectives are," said Carlos Ghosn, chief executive of Nissan and Renault, in a reference to Apple and Alphabet.
>
> Amazon, on the other hand, has been clear about its intentions. "Some companies have already decided — these companies like Amazon and Uber — [and] you want to work with them, because they know where they're going," said Mr Ghosn. "And where they're going is not a threat to you." Amazon has also learned the all-important art for a technology platform company of expanding its ecosystem by making Alexa easier for developers to incorporate in other products.
>
> "We've seen Alexa become a much more robust ecosystem than it was two years ago," said John Rhee, North American general manager for UBTech, a maker of humanoid robots that last week announced an integration with Alexa. With free use of the voice assistant bringing a new dimension to their products, hardware makers such as UBTech have been happy to let Amazon use their devices to extend its e-commerce reach into new places. Both Ford and UBTech, for instance, said that adding things to a shopping list—and pushing sales through Amazon—will be a natural thing for their own customers to do when talking to Alexa. "It's symbiotic," said Mr Rhee. [...]
>
> Adapted from: L. Hook, R. Waters and T. Bradshaw, "Amazon pours resources into voice assistant Alexa," *Financial Times*, 17 January 2017

16.2.3   Amazon's Success Factors

Examining a successful exemplar such as Amazon provides useful insights for entrepreneurs and businesses. Businesses can learn from its strategic moves and evolve their business strategy accordingly to either copy it, leverage off it, or defend against it. Entrepreneurs can use the example of Amazon to conceptualize and design their own strategies. If their proposed strategies are influenced by the example of Amazon, it may improve stakeholder confidence.

But, when planning strategies, businesses should prioritize their own competitive advantages and context, because Amazon is a unique, well-established company that dominates the global market. Tim Brown[4] suggests Amazon has six key success factors:

— *Offering a vast selection of products.* This is a significant competitive advantage in comparison with other rivals. Amazon is an ideal shopping destination where shoppers can find favorite products or select from a vast variety of choices. From the lens of Amazon, this strategy will broaden their market segments, and vendors wanting to compete with others have to improve their offerings.

---

4   This section is adapted from: T. Brown, "Why is Amazon so successful? Learn these 6 keys to Amazon's success," *Hookagency*, 6 January 2018.

- *Free shipping and returns*. Shipment costs are typically an additional cost borne by customers, and products sometimes get lost or damaged in transit. When goods are damaged or lost, customers deal with both couriers and the seller, and it typically spoils the online shopping experience. Amazon identified free shipping and returns as an easy way to differentiate themselves from other e-commerce companies. They invested in logistics and delivery to reduce the customer concerns about shopping online. This removed a major barrier to online shopping for mainstream consumers.
- *Overnight delivery*. Waiting for deliveries can irritate online shoppers. Amazon addressed this by offering overnight delivery at a fair price. This allowed Amazon to target customers who seek convenience and more immediate gratification or who leave shopping until "the last minute."
- *A consumer-centric marketplace*. The Amazon marketplace is a market with low barriers of entry allowing any vendor to sell merchandise online. This then increases the number of sellers and so intensifies competition between vendors in the marketplace. When stepping into a physical marketplace, customers may be able to select from dozens of choices, but in online marketplaces like Amazon, there are hundreds or thousands vendors merchandising products in the same category. Amazon created a consumer-centric marketplace, where customers could not only easily compare prices but also write reviews on products to help other customers around the world in their purchasing decision. One-star ratings on Amazon can damage a vendors' reputation and diminish their sales, and so vendors improved their responsiveness to customer complaints. Amazon may have pioneered in the concept of social commerce in a mass market.
- *Excellent leadership*. Amazon is not the only company using the above factors, or they are factors that can be copied. However, Amazon is distinguished from other e-businesses by the excellent leadership capability of Jeff Bezos. He has infused a unique culture and long-term vision into Amazon and has shaped it into a global dominant e-commerce company (see the article: "10 ways to think like Jeff Bezos").

10 Ways to Think like Jeff Bezos
What does it take to make $100 billion? Ask Jeff Bezos. The entrepreneur became the richest man on the planet by turning Amazon into the world's largest online retailer. This kind of success doesn't happen by accident. It comes with the right mindset. It is one you can adopt, too. [...]

1. Make Decisions with 70% of the Information
It is valuable to be informed. But as Bezos explains, "Most decisions should probably be made with somewhere around 70% of the information you wish you had. If you wait for 90%, in most cases, you're probably being slow." For example, Prime Now was launched 111 days after it was conceived. Were there bumps and turns along the way? Sure. But fast decision-making is how you get ahead of the competition. If you wait for perfect information, it's too late.

2. Ignore the Competition

Many businesses get caught up in what others do. More often than not, this causes them to copy their competition. In reality, serving the customer should always come first. This is how you innovate and succeed. As Bezos explained, this is how Amazon Prime came to be. "Even when they don't yet know it, customers want something better, and your desire to delight customers will drive you to invent on their behalf. No customer ever asked Amazon to create the Prime membership program, but it sure turns out they wanted it."

3. Take the 10% Chance

Bezos once said, "Given a 10% chance of a 100-times payout, you should take that bet every time." Those aren't impossible odds! You need to make bold business decisions to achieve big success. You will not always succeed, but you can still learn things to help you achieve that big payout in the future. For example, Amazon Marketplace failed in its first two launch attempts. The third time, it worked. It has since grown to contribute to almost half of Amazon's sales.

4. Do Not Be a Blockbuster

Being successful now doesn't mean you'll be relevant in the future. Look at what happened to Blockbuster video. Pay attention to what's happening so you can drive change, rather than react to it. As Jacob Munns, CEO of Boomsourcing, explains, "You can never assume your industry will stay the same forever. If you don't innovate, someone else will — and you'll get left behind." Looking forward is how Amazon became successful. Jeff Bezos recognized the potential for personalizing e-commerce and made that his focus. Amazon has continued to innovate and change to stay relevant and successful.

5. Develop a Distinct Culture

Amazon has a distinct culture that has attracted both criticism and praise. While this culture will not work for all companies, it works for them. As Bezos explained in a shareholder letter, "Someone energized by competitive zeal may select and be happy in one culture, while someone who loves to pioneer and invent may choose another. The world, thankfully, is full of many high-performing, highly distinctive corporate cultures. We never claim that our approach is the right one – just that it is ours." Find what makes your business culture unique. Think about what it means to be a great manager versus a good manager. Then recruit people who fit into that mold.

6. Don't Let Process Kill Progress

Too big companies let process kill progress. Amazon, despite its size, still shows a willingness to experiment. For example, look at their constant tests and experiments with Amazon Prime. They've introduced free same-day delivery and even 1-hour delivery with Prime Now. There's been the introduction of Prime Video and Prime Day. A willingness to tinker has led to even greater growth in Prime membership. You should always look for ways to innovate instead of getting letting bureaucratic processes slow you down.

7. Take It All Apart

Disrupting traditional business practices helped Bezos bring Amazon into frui-tion. This allowed him to create a new way to deliver goods when so many com-petitors tried it before him. Elon Musk took a similar approach, taking apart a Mercedes Benz before designing Tesla's cars. Bezos has now inspired a new gen-eration of entrepreneurs to do the same. This includes Forbes 30 Under 30 hon-oree Taylor Offer who learned from Bezos when founding FEAT Socks. "We analyzed the sock industry and questioned why companies relied so heavily on retail outlets," he said. "Instead, we saw an opportunity to sell socks through social media. It was a crazy idea at the time, but has lead to millions of dollars in sales." What everyday ideas can you "take apart" so you can discover ways to do it better?

8. Ditch the Bureaucracy

Start-ups are full of innovation and fast-paced decisions. But as businesses grow, they often get slowed down by bureaucracy. This kills innovation. As The New York Times explains, "[devolving] from a ruthless predator to a sluggish bureaucracy… is exactly what Bezos doesn't want to happen to Amazon. He wants it to always have the feel of a startup." Maintaining a startup mentality is essential for staying on the cutting edge.

9. Become a Master of Failure

Fear of making bad decisions often keeps companies from innovating. But as Bezos has said, "If you're good at course correcting, being wrong may be less costly than you think." Learn to fail fast and cheap, and correcting bad decisions won't be a problem. This will help you learn and achieve better results in the future. Felix Odi-gie, CEO and founder of Occasion Station, adds, "Any failure is an opportunity to build toward bigger and better things. Why did that product fail? How could I have done better? Find answers to these questions and learn from them to set yourself up for success with your next endeavor."

10. It's All About the Long Term

"It's all about the long term" is a phrase that appeared in Bezos's first letter to Amazon shareholders. As Bezos explained, all decisions would need to "consis-tently [reflect] this focus." Everything from investment decisions to growth plans to hiring took a long-term outlook. It paid off for Amazon. Take a long-term approach. You will make smarter decisions and achieve lasting (rather than tempo-rary) success.

Following these tips will not necessarily earn you $100 billion like Jeff Bezos. That's okay. With this proactive, forward-thinking mindset, you will still set your-self up for a more lucrative future with your own business ventures.

Adapted from: J. Youshaei, "10 ways to think like Jeff Bezos," *Forbes*, 19 December 2017

16.2.4 Amazon's Current Strategies

In general, Amazon is employing five major strategies to sustain competitive advantage.

Expand marketplace. Amazon may expand into emerging markets such as India.

Develop key platforms. Amazon Marketplace, Prime, and Amazon Web Services are core e-business cash cows of Amazon. Amazon is further developing the voice-assisted assistant Alexa and is foraying into content creation via Amazon Studios and attempting to construct an omni-channel system via Amazon Fresh (groceries) and Go (cashless physical stores).

Improve customer experience. Amazon views customers as the company's most precious asset. It continually updates and improves products, services, and platforms in order to provide the very best customer experiences.

Reinvest in efficiencies. Amazon opposes bureaucratic processes and maintains a culture of agility and process improvement.

Develop an enterprise culture. Amazon is well-known for its explorative, ambitious, consumer-centric, and learning culture.

16.2.5 Amazon's Future Strategic Decisions

Strategy needs to continually evolve in response to internal and external dynamics. Amazon is very different today to the online bookstore in 1994, and it cannot ensure it will still be operating in 2034. To embrace the future, the company has stated it will make the following strategic moves:

Corporate restructure. Amazon aims to become a matrix organization to highlight its different market-facing business units and internal capabilities.

Strengthen its global supply network and fulfillment infrastructure. For example, a subsidiary of Amazon China was awarded an ocean shipping license from the US government (Hahn, 2016).

Strengthen local fulfillment. Amazon has stated it will collaborate with retailers to leverage their physical distribution networks to strengthen local fulfillment. For example, in 2018, Amazon added six new fulfillment centers in India (Business Line, 2018).

Cultivate and expand private label brands.

Offer financial services to Prime members.

Grow Amazon Fresh services by partnering with local supermarkets to roll out more Amazon Fresh services. In the future, the Amazon Fresh business may be integrated with Amazon Dash for automated replenishment (Page, 2015).

Expand Amazon Go. Offer cashless streamlined self-service instore shopping (Bonnington, 2018).

Gain market leadership for voice activated assistants. Commercialize and monetize Alexa-based platforms through, for example, paid product recommendations (Hirsch and M. Castillo, 2018).

Become a leading content creator/distributor via Amazon Studios.

Strengthen Amazon Web Services. Add more services and capacity.

Succession planning and leadership development. Amazon, with Jeff Bezos, faces "key person risk," that is, if he were to leave, Amazon risks would increase. To mitigate this, another two CEOs have been appointed of key business units (Mac, 2016).

16.3 Alibaba

16.3.1 An Introduction to Alibaba

> **Definition**
>
> "Our philosophy is that we want to be an ecosystem. Our philosophy is to empower others to sell, empower others to service, making sure the other people are more powerful than us. With our technology, our innovation, our partners — 10 million small business sellers — they can compete with Microsoft and IBM. Our philosophy is, using internet technology we can make every company become Amazon."[5]
>
> Jack Ma
> Co-founder and Executive Chairman of Alibaba Group

Alibaba is an e-commerce, retail, Internet, and technology conglomerate that operates across many sectors. As in May 2018, its market capitalization was just below that of Facebook and higher than Chinese e-business giant Tencent. The company's major businesses are[6]:

Retail Commerce in China   Alibaba owns China's largest e-commerce marketplaces for consumers to purchase products, Taobao for consumer trading, and China's largest third-party platform for brands and retailers, Tmall. Taobao focuses on C2C commerce, while Tmall focuses on B2C commerce. Alibaba provides the platform for e-commerce but offers no fulfillment logistics services; the seller must arrange delivery of goods purchased through these platforms.

Wholesale Commerce in China   Alibaba runs a wholesale commerce platform in China, ▶ 1688.com, that targets China's B2B markets. Numerous vendors and small business owners use this website to source and replenish their inventory.

Ant Financial   Ant Financial is an affiliate of Alibaba that offers Alipay, the world's largest mobile and online payments processing platform. Alipay is typically used in all Alibaba transactions by consumers. It is similar to PayPal but is integrated closely within Alibaba platforms so it is seamless, fast, and secure.

---

5   See A. Balakrishnan, "Jack Ma explains the difference between Alibaba and Amazon: 'Amazon is more like an empire,'" ▶ *CNBC.com*, 18 January 2017.
6   This section is adapted from: Alibaba, *Annual and Transition Report (foreign private issuer)*, 2017.

Global Retail Commerce   Alibaba runs AliExpress which enables consumers around the world to buy products directly from sellers in China at significantly cheaper prices than similar products on other e-commerce platforms. Many physical products that are sold via e-commerce platforms that operate in other regions were originally made in China, and so AliExpress cuts out middle operators. In April 2016, the company purchased Lazada which operates e-commerce platforms among South Asian countries.

Global Wholesale Commerce   Alibaba operates ▶ Alibaba.com allowing buyers worldwide to buy from manufacturers and brands in China.

Cloud Computing   Alibaba Cloud is China's largest provider of public cloud services (as measured by revenues). Alibaba Cloud contains a series of cloud services from elastic computing to big data analytics.

Mobile Browser   Alibaba offers a free mobile UC browser by acquiring UCWeb in 2014. This browser is one of the top three in the world by market share. UCWeb also offers other mobile services such as news feeds, mobile search engines, and mobile web navigation.

Entertainment   Alibaba acquired Youku Tudou, a Chinese entertainment and media platform that allows users to post and access video content via multiple devices. Youku Tudou is similar to Google's YouTube in that it is a digital entertainment ecosystem that leverages a mass market of content creators who want to share their content and access the content of others.

Innovative Initiatives   Alibaba continually experiments to build new ecosystems and refine existing ecosystems. For example, AliOS is an operating system that is similar to IoS, and it operates across devices including automobiles, mobile phones, and televisions. Another example is DingTalk, a business collaboration platform for real-time communication, business collaboration, and workflow management.

To summarize, Alibaba provides an online ecosystem that creates value for all participants by taking advantage of their innovative IT resources and capabilities. For more information on Alibaba's businesses, see the FT article: "Alibaba profits surge 83% powered by online shopping."

16

Alibaba Profits Surge 83% Powered by Online Shopping

Chinese e-commerce giant Alibaba has soundly beaten market expectations with an 83 percent increase in quarterly operating profit to Rmb16.58bn ($2.5bn) powered by online shopping. "Once again, we have delivered an outstanding quarter," said Daniel Zhang, chief executive. Analysts' consensus forecast for the 3 months to the end of September had been Rmb15.4bn, according to Bloomberg.

   The US-listed company also raised its already optimistic projections for full-year revenue growth to between 49 and 53 percent, due to the consolidation of loss-making logistics business Cainiao. It had previously guided for growth of 45–49 percent, which was comfortably beaten by the latest quarter's 61 percent year-on-year increase. In September, the company increased its stake in Cainiao from 47 to 51 percent. Cainiao, which will be consolidated from the current quarter, lost $273 m in the 3 months to the end of September.

Alibaba shares have more than doubled this year to give it a market capitalization of $477bn. The rally has left even its surging US tech peers in the shade. The company founded 18 years ago by former English teacher Jack Ma made its name as an e-commerce site along the lines of eBay but has since morphed into a business that spans video streaming, cloud services, and, through affiliate Ant Financial, payments. Cloud computing revenues doubled to $447 m, with clients ranging from Dutch technology company Philips to domestic liquor producer Kweichow Moutai, but the group reported negative earnings before interest, tax, and amortization margin of −5 percent.

However, commerce remains Alibaba's cash engine, generating adjusted earnings before interest, taxes, and amortization of $4bn in the quarter. Alibaba makes money through advertising and commissions from companies including Mondelez and Procter & Gamble, which use its Tmall site to sell wares such as snacks and nappies. Mr Zhang said Alibaba was unconcerned by losses in areas such as cloud computing and digital entertainment. "We are not in a hurry to monetise young businesses," he said. Rather, these are about building an ecosystem that keeps users entertained—and spending—for longer.

Alibaba expanded its monthly active user numbers by 20 m in the quarter to 549 m in September. Steven Zhu, senior analyst at Pacific Epoch, commented: "They have the power to subsidise all these money-losing businesses and if they can penetrate [users'] lives then they can become moneymaking in the future."

Costs and capital expenditure also continued to rise. The results can also be interpreted as vindication of Alibaba's concept of "new retail" that aims to reduce barriers between online shopping and buying from physical stores, for example, by using data gleaned from online browsing and buying to improve shop layout.

Source: L. Lucas, "Alibaba profits surge 83% powered by online shopping," *Financial Times*, 2 November 2017

16.3.2 Business Model of Alibaba

Alibaba uses a simple intermediary business model[7] because it does not own any warehouse infrastructure and goods move directly from supplier to customer. The intermediary model has allowed Alibaba to grow rapidly and with agility, because it does not carry massive fixed cost infrastructure. As of 2018, Alibaba has nearly 30 separate business units that specifically target market opportunities including B2B commerce, B2C commerce, C2C commerce, mobile payments, and cloud business. Each business unit has a unique strategy with different objectives for each target market.

---

7 *Investopedia*, op. cit., 2016

As an intermediary, the key customer segment of Alibaba is its online vendors, and the value proposition it offers to vendors is a highly targeted mass market of shoppers. Taobao is Alibaba's core service, and vendors and buyers do not pay any fees to complete transactions on this platform. Instead, Alibaba incurs revenues from paid placements—advertising fees paid by vendors to place their product prominently in search results. Alibaba has created a self-reinforcing business eco-system, motivating small business owners to pay more advertising to place their products ahead of others in search results. Doing so creates more sales, which increases revenues for vendors. The value logic of Alibaba is predicated on its scale of reach to a mass market: the more powerful online vendors are, the larger profits the platform creates, and thus vendors will rely more on the platform and be more willing to nurture the platform and pay for paid placements. Many platforms offered by Alibaba follow this logic, that is, they aim to create a lucrative platform and design suitable incentive systems and supportive policies to attract both vendors and shoppers.

16.3.3 Alibaba's Success Factors

In this section, we will point out Alibaba's success factors. Understanding how Alibaba has succeeded may provide insights to businesses who aim to enter the Chinese and other Asian markets.[8]

Focus on Small Enterprises   Alibaba is a loyal follower of the Long Tail theory.[9] The company believes that the Internet economy is not dominated by oligopolies but rather by numerous small- and medium-sized businesses. Alibaba's major platforms, 1688, Taobao or ▶ Alibaba.com, are designed to serve small businesses and to help them grow and evolve.

Special Profit Model   Unlike most e-commerce companies monetizing platforms by charging admission fees and taking a percentage from each sale, Alibaba has a special profit model. The company mainly profits from advertising, which accounts for 57% of total revenue. Another major revenue source (25% of total revenue) is based on data analytics of consumer behaviors. Alibaba does not charge for transactions and allows worldwide sellers to register for free. This strategy has helped Alibaba to attract eight million active sellers (representing the largest online market in China, which is the largest Internet economy in the world). The breadth of sellers means customers can use Alibaba's markets to buy almost everything they want. The business logic behind the model is simple, reducing transaction costs of online purchas-

---

8   This section is adapted from: X.Pavie, "Seven reasons for Alibaba's ground-breaking success," *BBN Times*, 10 May, 2018.

9   As described in Sect. 11.4. See also M. Krasinski "The Long Tail Effect theory in practice explained" ▶ *MilosKrasinski.com*, n.d. Available at: ▶ https://miloszkrasinski.com/the-long-tail-effect-theory-in-practise-explained/.

ing. According to Transaction Cost Economics,[10] admission fees and transaction fees are positively associated with transaction costs which could inhibit transaction behaviors.

Building Credibility   In spite of low entry barriers, Alibaba places great importance on assessing the credibility of online vendors. Firstly, vendors need to certify and verify their identity information and business license. Secondly, all transactions are saved by system and can be traced and retrieved by sellers and buyers. Thirdly, Alibaba has its own payment system operating payments under its control. It provides an institutional guarantee for buyers because their payments will not be directly transferred to sellers until they confirmed the order. Alibaba provides a buyer protection for China's buyers, which allows buyers to return products in 7 days without any reasons. Lastly, Alibaba also values customer feedback and comments. The company built a credibility evaluation mechanism to allow buyers to rate vendors on factors including product description, service attitude, and shipment. Alibaba will clearly indicate vendors with lower credibility in the same product category.

Cultivating Quality Customer Services   Alibaba aims to offer a decent shopping environment and customer services. It has an instant messaging application for seller-buyer communication. Except for some new platforms such as AliExpress, online shoppers are able to instantly communicate with online sales clerks. The clerks are trained by Alibaba to be respectful of customers.

Creating and Seizing Business Opportunities   It is widely known that it usually is a quiet season in the lead up to Christmas, Alibaba created the Singles Day on November 11, a special shopping festival for singles to celebrate online shopping. The event grew into a national shopping day, and in 2018, shoppers spent the equivalent of $17.49 billion in one day, a world record.

Offering an Integrated Ecosystem   Alibaba expanded its core competence to other businesses. The company provides customers across its business units with advertising services and founded a payment company called Ant Financial to finance numerous online vendors. To streamline and integrate consumer purchasing, it developed a mobile payment app, Alipay, for users to make payments anywhere and anytime, which is the nexus of its omni-channel system.

Excellent Leadership   Jack Ma is a reputable business leader who founded and grew Alibaba. Ma, an English teacher, conceded that he has "no idea on management and technology" but knows that he can employ people who have expertise and knowledge in relevant domains. The role of leadership is to acquire and allocate

---

10 For details on Transaction Cost Economics, see M. Ketokivi and J.T. Mahoney, "Transaction Cost Economics as a Theory of the Firm, Management, and Governance" *Oxford Research Encyclopedias, Business and Management*, October 2017. Available at: ▶ http://oxfordre.com/business/view/10.1093/acrefore/9780190224851.001.0001/acrefore-9780190224851-e-6.

talented employees into suitable businesses. The business philosophy behind Alibaba is influenced and shaped by Ma's personality, for example, he reportedly values altruism more than egoism. This is similar to the concept of "shared value" coined by Michael Porter.[11] Jack Ma thinks that if a company shows concern and respect for society, it will ultimately gain from what it gives. For more information on Jack Ma's leadership philosophy, see the article: "How Jack Ma's 'crazy' management style built a technology empire."

16

How Jack Ma's "Crazy" Management Style Built a Technology Empire

More than 100 years ago, Rudyard Kipling wrote those words before the world had shrunk back into a new Pangaea, reconnected by fiber-optic lines, global supply chain networks, and global brands.

Alibaba and its kinetic leader Jack Ma have blended the best of Western and Chinese technologies, culture, and management to create the world's largest e-commerce company and perhaps soon to be biggest and most diversified global technology enterprise. The company's Sept. 19 IPO raised more than $20 billion and gave Alibaba a market cap of $240 billion. It also made Jack Ma, already the richest man in China, one of the wealthiest men in the world with a net worth of more than $18 billion.

Alibaba is not just an e-commerce company. While its three main platforms Taobao (a consumer-to-consumer company), Tmall (a business-to-consumer firm), and ▶ Alibaba.com (a business-to-business operation) generated more than $250 billion in transactions and $7.9 billion in revenue in 2013 in China, the company also has interests in electronic payments, cloud computing, streaming entertainment, supply chain infrastructure, and investment funds. It is poised to expand its technology interests and platforms on a global basis.

So how did a former English teacher from Hangzhou, known as "Crazy Ma" because of his unorthodox management philosophy, build one of the most valuable companies in the world in just 15 years? He did it by blending the best of Western and Eastern technologies, operational practices, and management styles. The following are four elements of Ma's management style that entrepreneurs and small business owners can follow to build the next Alibaba.

1. Be like Forrest Gump

Jack Ma relates to the naive innocence with which the character Forrest Gump approaches life. Ma watches his favorite film Forrest Gump over and over and over again. Indeed Ma never let himself get down, even when he made $15 a month as a teacher while supplementing his income peddling on the street. Nor did he become discouraged when KFC, a hotel, and the police turned him down for jobs. He kept on believing that if someone sticks to his principles and works hard, anything was possible. Like Forest Gump, Ma has always seen the world and its possibilities almost as if through the eyes of a child, believing technology could be

---

11 See M.E. Porter "Creating Shared Value," *Harvard Business Review*, January–February 2011.

magic and life truly a box of chocolates—but one that a person never knows what he will get inside.

Successful entrepreneurs do not let setbacks get them down, and they see both what's impossible and possible, but the difference is that they focus only on the possible.

2. Innovate on the Shoulders of Giants.

Ma has consistently understood that innovation is not always synonymous with invention. Like Steve Jobs, who did not invent the digital music player, and Bill Gates, who did not invent computer operation systems, Ma built his most successful properties on the foundations of what came before. For example, eBay had long been established as the largest and most successful consumer-to-consumer e-commerce site in the world when Ma launched Taobao.

What Ma did was adapt the concept specifically for China, knowing that culture, history, philosophy, and mindset were as important to success as functionality. That is why he included a real-time chat function on Taobao, so that buyers and sellers could build a relationship and trust and negotiate in real time. In China, every transaction is personal. To be like Jack Ma, entrepreneurs should believe that pure invention is not necessary to be an innovator.

3. Soar with Eagles

Jack Ma has surrounded himself with the smartest and most capable and innovative executives and managers he could find. He never believed that he was an expert at everything and that as a founder he had earned the right to micromanage every aspect of his business. At a time when it was very unusual, Ma was open to bringing in foreign executives to further his goal of blending East and West. He also befriended Jerry Yang, co-founder of Yahoo, and Masayoshi Son, chairman of Japanese telecom giant SoftBank. Both were early investors in Alibaba and helped the company grow more quickly. Yahoo and SoftBank were repaid handsomely on IPO day. Entrepreneurs need to let others have control and should do what is right for their business not their ego.

4. Take Your Business but not Yourself Seriously

Ma has worked hard from day 1 to build a unique culture at Alibaba. Yes that sounds like a cliché and old-fashioned management speak, but it has proved to be one of the most important factors in Alibaba's success. Ma has built a culture of participation, inclusion, and fun. He exhibits high energy and is outspoken, fun-loving, and charming. He has ensured that all those personal traits have become company traits and is well-known for singing karaoke with employees, holding company retreats for 15,000 (focused on fun not work), and dressing in outlandish outfits when addressing management.

He has created an atmosphere such that Alibaba employees treat him like a combination of father figure, inspirational guru, and band leader. The result is a super loyal, hardworking group of executives, managers, and employees who would follow Ma to the ends of the Earth. It's of paramount importance that entrepreneurs build a brand and culture simultaneously and not take themselves too seriously. None of this was an accident. Ma spent years studying Western culture, management concepts, and successful businesses, took what he needed, and left the rest. He combined that with his love and understanding of China's culture and consumption habits to create an all-encompassing technology success that is positioned to become the first truly global Chinese brand.

Ma has proved through his unique management style for Alibaba that East and West can meet and when they do, something beautiful can come of it.

Source: M. Zakkour, "How Jack Ma's 'crazy' management style built a technology empire," ▶ *Entrepreneur.com*, 29 September 2014.

16.3.4 Alibaba's Current Strategies

Here, we will delve into Alibaba's current strategies to further understand the company.[12]

Making It Easy to Do Business Everywhere   In the past, most of China's SMEs focused on local businesses. Their development was constrained by geographic and market isolation. This phenomenon still exists in today's China, particularly rural areas and undeveloped regions. However, Alibaba has targeted this problem since its launch. Jack Ma recognized that the Internet can powerfully break through physical limitations caused by geographic- and market-related factors.

This is a winning strategy for various parties. For local SMEs, Alibaba not only provides a free platform for them to sell, but it also invests in local e-commerce infrastructure (such as fulfillment centers) and provides accessible financial services for farmers (Ant Financial). For local governments, e-commerce adoption can contribute to the vibrancy of a region economy and generate tax income. Alibaba's reach to remote areas can increase its platform's network externality and economies of scale, which ultimately enhances the company's competitiveness and platform influences. In countries such as China, where private companies rely on a good relationship with the government, this strategy is of paramount benefit for Alibaba because it enables access to more political resources and reinforces its political network.

Be Sustainable to Generate Revenue   As mentioned previously, Alibaba makes earnings primarily from advertisements and also from memberships and data service fees. It is crucial for the company to maintain a good relationship with sponsors and members. It is unlikely for the company to roll out private brands like Amazon, particularly in the B2C marketplace Tmall, because those advertisement sponsors, brands, and retailers may be wary of direct competition with those private brands. It is akin to a situation in which a referee has to master a game as well as wants to act as a

16

---

12 This section is adapted from: R. Yazdanifard and M.T.H. Li, "The Review of Alibaba's Online Business Marketing Strategies which Navigate Them to Present Success," *Global Journal of Management and Business Research*, 2014, vol. 14, no. 7, pp. 33–37.

player in the game, which definitely could jeopardize the fairness of the game. On the other hand, Alibaba is also exploring new revenue sources such as providing more value-added services for customers.

Strengthening Domestic and Expanding Global Markets Alibaba currently dominates its domestic market, and China's e-commerce competition is intensive. ▶ JD.com, the second largest e-commerce company in China, entered the Fortune 500 list in 2016, 1 year earlier than Alibaba. ▶ JD.com, as one of Alibaba's major rivals, is similar to Amazon. The company has numerous distribution centers in China and sells private label products. Based on its enormous logistics infrastructure, it has unbeatable velocity in picking, packing, and shipping products. It rolled out 24 hours delivery service via its powerful logistics network. Moreover, Tencent, another Internet giant in China who operate the WeChat platform, collaborated with a new social commerce venture, Pinduoduo, to create a social commerce platform that integrates with WeChat. In 2017, Pinduoduo had 1.08 million active daily users—still behind Taobao's 3.29 million daily users but just capping ▶ JD.com's 1.05 million (Bhandari, 2018). This new rival forced Alibaba to offer a Taobao Special Offer Edition to counterattack.

16.3.4.1 Alibaba's Future Strategic Decisions

Founder Jack Ma envisioned Alibaba's world dominance. Alibaba aims to sell $1 trillion in gross merchandise value (GMV) by 2020 and, by 2036, have two billion customers worldwide and represent the fifth largest economy whose total sales are just behind the GDP of the United States, China, Japan, and the EU (Wang, 2017). AliExpress is the online marketplace that will target global growth.

The following are indications of Alibaba's future strategic decisions[13]:

Entry into Offering Logistics to Vendors In 2016, Alibaba created the Cainiao Network—a logistics business unit—in collaboration with five logistics businesses, a warehouse construction business, warehouse management business, and line-haul business. Alibaba owns a 43 percent stake in the Cainiao network, and it suggests Alibaba may begin to increasingly offer logistics services to vendors.[14]

Entry into the Smart Car Market Alibaba is experimenting with innovative cars in collaboration with China's largest automaker SAIC Motor Corp. SAIC will design and develop physical cars, and Alibaba will design the operating systems and other cloud-based services within the cars. This new business signals Alibaba's interest in the Internet of Things, where the company can exert their talent in IT and e-business.

---

13 This section is adapted from: A.L. Deutsch, "What's Next For Alibaba?", *Investopedia*, 25 March, 2015.
14 For more details, see C. Luo, "One Platform to Rule Them All: The Brains Behind Cainiao Network (PI)" *e-Commerce IQ*, 7 December, 2016. Available at: ▶ https://ecommerceiq.asia/cainiao-logistics-southeast-asia/.

Incubating a Financial Behemoth   Shopping online in China is fraught with perception of poor security and the validity of sellers. To combat this, Alibaba's financial affiliate, Ant Financial, created one of China's most popular mobile payments methods—Alipay. Security is paramount to Alipay, and Alipay also protects buyers in the event that sellers do not deliver the goods. In January 2018, Ant Financial was valued at $60 billion, just outranked by Uber ($69 billion), as the world's second largest unicorn. Ant Financial intends to undertake an IPO, and if so, it will boost Alibaba's pre-tax earnings up to 37.5%.

Foray into Social Media   China's social media market is dominated by Tencent and Sina. Alibaba has released a niche social media network "DingTalk," which focuses on social and business networking services for SMEs. The company also invested into the popular social media platform Snapchat.

Offering Cloud Computing Services in America   Alibaba has listed on the New York Stock Exchange and may enter the United States cloud computing market, where Amazon Web Service (AWS) holds the dominant market share.[15] In July 2015, Alibaba made a $1 billion investment into Aliyun cloud computing services, a company with plans to enter the United States market. In the meantime, Alibaba has established cloud computing servers in East and South Asia and the Middle East and plans to directly establish its first satellite department in Silicon Valley. It may need to overcome political barriers to offering server storage in the United States, before it can target a market dominated by AWS.

Building an Omni-Channel System   Similar to Amazon Go and Amazon Fresh, Alibaba has been experimenting with an omni-channel system that unifies online and offline channels. New Retail is an Alibaba business unit that opened a cashless supermarket, Hema, that allow customers to place an order online and also to physically visit the store. As in January 2019, there were 100 Hema supermarkets in 19 cities in China, and Alibaba aims to continue the rapid growth in the number of Hema supermarkets.

16.4 The Contrasts and Lessons of Amazon and Alibaba

16.4.1 Distinctions Between the Amazon and Alibaba Marketplaces

Both Alibaba and Amazon offer e-marketplaces, and both enjoy strong brand names. Alibaba is a pure platform, whereas Amazon is a platform plus fulfillment services. The differentiation between Alibaba and Amazon derives from many aspects including business models, culture, politics, technology, and markets.

---

15 At the same time, Amazon tried to enter the China market and failed. In 2018 Amazon diverted its focus to the India market (see P. Fuhrman, "Alibaba Grabs The IPO Money But The Future Belongs To Jeff Bezos And Amazon China," *Seeking Alpha*, 10 September 2014, and Bloomberg, "After losing China, Jeff Bezos really wants to win in India," *India Times*, 6 March, 2018).

If Amazon is analogous to a digital supermarket, Alibaba is similar to a digital shopping mall. Alibaba's primary focus is on vendors, whereas Amazon's primary focus is consumers. Vendors are also Amazon's customers, but it has demonstrated that they are secondary to consumers, notably Forbes[16] mentions "Amazon wants a bigger piece of its suppliers' profit margins to purportedly pass on to its customers in the form of lower prices." Amazon is obsessed with offering competitive prices and products for shoppers. This obsession, and the pricing transparency on Amazon, forces vendors to reap smaller profit margins on products sold; however, this may be mitigated by a higher volume of sales due to the global scale of Amazon.

Definition

Alibaba is not a company for consumers [...] I knew that we didn't have the right DNA to become a consumer company. The world is changing very fast, and it's hard to gauge consumers' needs. Small businesses know more about the needs of their customers. We had to empower our power sellers and our SME's to support their customers. –Jack Ma

---

Definition

We have so many customers who treat us so well, and we have the right kind of culture that obsesses over the customer. If there's one reason we have done better than of our peers in the Internet space over the last six years, it is because we have focused like a laser on customer experience, and that really does matter, I think, in any business. It certainly matters online, where word of mouth is so very, very powerful. –Jeff Bezos[17]

Alibaba has created many highly targeted markets, whereas Amazon focuses more on its main marketplace—▶ Amazon.com (and country variants). The Alibaba approach minimizes shopper frustration from seeing products that cannot be delivered to them. Furthermore, the onus is on the vendor to supply goods to customers. In comparison, shoppers on Amazon may sometimes purchase products, go to the checkout, and then find they cannot be delivered.

In Alibaba's ecosystem, shoppers would only see products that can be delivered to their address, and Alibaba bears no responsibility for logistics. Amazon aims to reduce this friction by further investments to improve its local fulfillment capabilities worldwide. Indeed, there is a growing trend of Amazon private label vendors who source goods made in China via the AliExpress platform and then place them on Amazon as a private label product (exclusive to Amazon) and use Amazon FBA to handle the logistics of ordering from AliExpress and supply to customers on the Amazon platform. These private label vendors profit from arbitrage of goods made cheaply in China and sold directly via Amazon to developed markets.

---

16 In A.M. Do, "Jack vs. Jeff: The two biggest e-commerce billionaires in the world are total opposites," *TechinAsia*, 24 October 2014
17 Both quotes are from A.M. Do, op. cit.

As mentioned in ▶ Chap. 2, ▶ Amazon.com initially thought that it could focus solely on the customer interaction aspects of its business and outsource to external providers all activities that would have required substantial investment, including logistics and distribution activities. However, ▶ Amazon.com learned that to guarantee a high level of reliability and speed, it had to operate its own warehouses filled with robotics, a fleet of airplanes, and delivery trucks (and drones), which in turn increased the required fixed cost capital investment. Setup costs for a warehouse averaged $50 million, and operating costs were also significant. In order to finance these infrastructure investments, ▶ Amazon.com was forced to issue more than $2 billion in bonds. In contrast, China's Alibaba does not own any warehouse infrastructure,[18] and goods move directly from supplier to customer. But this may change. The absence of a physical logistics infrastructure makes Alibaba's business model very easy to copy, whereas Amazon dominates its markets, and its scale of infrastructure cannot be copied easily, making Amazon's business nearly impossible to replicate.

Alibaba's strategic direction is shifting toward becoming a pure technology company,[19] whereas Amazon continues to focus on the supply of goods and services to consumers in a variety of ways that include innovative technologies.

Another difference between Alibaba's business model and Amazon's is their profit orientation. Alibaba focuses on its profit margins within each sale. Amazon focuses on smaller profit margins with a higher volume of sales. This is explained further in the article: "Why Alibaba is more profitable than Amazon."

Why Alibaba Is More Profitable than Amazon

Alibaba and Amazon are in the right business at the right time. And they both have their own formulas of success that have delivered hefty returns to their stockholders. Alibaba shares have gained 63.97% in the past 12 months and 146.15% over the last 2 years, while Amazon's shares have gained 67.76% and 121.44% over the same period.

While it's unclear which of the two companies will deliver better performance to its stockholders in the long run, one thing is clear: Alibaba's formula of success consistently beats Amazon's in a key metric, operating margins. In the most recent quarter, Alibaba's operating margin was 31.25%, while Amazon's was 2.31%.

Simply put, Alibaba's business model is more profitable than that of Amazon due to a key difference in the ways the two companies approach and monetize e-commerce. Amazon's approach is to bring Walmart's scale cost savings online.

"Amazon's approach in the United States was essentially to move the 'Walmart economy' online, creating a large retailer based on a high-volume, low-cost model that relied on massive scale and technology to create cost savings," explains Porter

16

---

18 Alibaba's creation of the Cainiao network business unit suggests Alibaba may begin to offer logistics services to vendors.

19 A.M. Do, op. cit

Erisman, author of Six Billion Shoppers (New York: St. Martin's Press, 2017). And it passed them on to consumers at razor-thin margins. Alibaba's approach, by contrast, is to bring collective entrepreneurship online, a network business model that turns the vendors who list their products with its Taobao site to entrepreneurs.

In a sense, Alibaba's approach to e-commerce is similar to eBay's model. "eBay's approach was to move the yard sale economy, online, creating a market for used goods and collectibles," notes Erisman. "But Taobao's was to move the mom-and-pop economy online, where small retailers could open stores to sell new products." That's a better formula for success than that of Amazon. Collective entrepreneurship helps Alibaba become rich by turning hundreds or even millions of people into entrepreneurs, lifting them out from poverty, and making some of them rich, too.

This model works particularly well in countries like China, which is by far the largest Internet market in the world—twice the size of the US market. Still, Alibaba's model charges no listing fees and has no warehouses to maintain inventories, making it very likely to be copied by others—much easier than Amazon's model. That's especially the case in China's Internet economy, which is highly competitive, with new competitors appearing quickly and eroding operating margins. [...]

Adapted from: P. Mourdoukoutas, "Why Alibaba is more profitable than Amazon," *Forbes*, 6 May 2018

On the surface, the leadership styles of Jeff Bezos and Jack Ma are distinctive. Anh-Minh Do highlights this contrast with two quotes[20]:

Definition

There were three reasons behind our success. They were very valid points. First, we had no money. Second, we didn't understand technology. Third, we never planned.

Jack Ma

Definition

Any company that wants to invent on behalf of customers has to be willing to think long-term. And it's actually much rarer than you might think. I find that most of the initiatives that we undertake may take five to seven years before they pay any dividends for the company [...] It requires and allows a willingness to be misunderstood.

Jeff Bezos

---

20 A.M. Do, op.cit

16.4.2   Lessons of the Amazon and Alibaba Business Models

Jeff Bezos has said that Alibaba uses an advertising model, and Jack Ma has said Amazon is an e-commerce company which Alibaba isn't: "Alibaba helps others to do e-commerce. We do not sell things.[21]" This highlights the different value propositions of Amazon and Alibaba. Amazon's shoppers are their most valuable customer segment. Alibaba considers online vendors and other businesses as their most lucrative customer segment. It is meaningless to evaluate the correctness of each strategy because they have been proven to successfully fit their target markets.

Today's companies can learn a lot from Amazon and Alibaba. This point is even true for non-digital natives who plan to enter e-business markets. Key lessons include:

The Nature of e-Business Is Service   The two companies view e-business as a strategic way to serve customers. E-business is a service; it does not produce any tangible objects per se. It allows users to complete activities remotely and conveniently. On the other hand, e-business success depends on a company's ability to identify, develop, and use business opportunities for new services. Amazon identified shoppers' willingness to purchase cheap and convenient products. Alibaba found SMEs need a platform to merchandise and promote goods.

A Firm Should Clearly Know Who Its Customers Are   Customers are not interchangeable with users. Firms capture value from customers who are willing to pay. Amazon views shoppers as their most important customers, while Alibaba values online vendors. A clear definition of the target customer segment is critical to a company's e-business success, because strategies and business models for e-business cannot be well designed unless a company understands who its customers are and then devise specific strategies and business models to serve them.

Strategizing e-Business in Contexts   It makes no sense to talk about strategizing e-business without a thorough consideration of the contexts (environment) in which a business operates. As two companies that were founded in the 1990s, Amazon and Alibaba both have achieved sustainable success, but their path to success was very different and was affected by many social, cultural, and political factors. For example, Alibaba's "collective entrepreneurship" may be easier to succeed within an Eastern culture context that emphasizes social and collective affairs. However, globalization largely facilitates the convergence of worldwide businesses. ▶ JD.com, whose operating models are similar to Amazon, has sustained great success in Eastern Asian countries and even challenges Alibaba's lead position.

---

21   Source: C. Riley, "Alibaba is not the Amazon of China," *CNN Business*, 16 September, 2014

Entrepreneurial Spirit Drives e-Business Growth Today's e-business world is not like that of the 1990s. Even giants like Amazon and Alibaba are facing constricted growth of markets and profits as business cycles and political environments turn. This is a major reason why these two companies highlight the role of innovation and are expanding their core businesses to omni-channels and artificial intelligence. Sustainable e-business growth requires companies to update their e-business technology and services regularly, as well as to be ready for new competition that arises in today's sectors without borders.

Summary
1. It is worthwhile to learn from two e-business giants: Amazon and Alibaba.
2. This chapter provided a synthesized understanding of Amazon and Alibaba from various dimensions. The two companies offer similar e-business services, such as e-commerce, cloud computing, artificial intelligence, and omni-channel businesses. Yet their business models and strategies are quite different.
3. Amazon and Alibaba, as two e-business exemplars, provide many practical lessons on e-business. Firstly, e-business is all centered on service. Secondly, how customer segments are defined can significantly influence a company's strategy formation. Thirdly, strategy should vary with contexts and be created to fit each company's characteristics. Lastly and most importantly, entrepreneurial spirit drives e-business growth.

? Review Questions
1. Why should we learn from Amazon and Alibaba?
2. What is the major difference between Amazon and Alibaba?
3. What do you project in the future for Amazon and Alibaba?
4. Use your own words to describe what e-business is.
5. Share your opinions and views with classmates on Jeff Bezos and Jack Ma and discuss what makes a successful e-business entrepreneur.
6. Illustrate which factor is most critical to e-business success.

References

Bhandari, B. (2018). *'Taobao launches bargain app to rival Pinduoduo'*, sixth tone.
Bonnington, C. (2018). *'Why Amazon is opening more of its futuristic, cashier-free convenience stores'*, Slate.com.
Business Line. (2018). *'Amazon doubles storage space, delivery station network'*, Thehindubusinessline.com.
Drucker, P. F. (1986). *Management: Tasks, responsibilities, practices* (p. 14). New York: Truman Talley Books.
Hahn, L. (2016). *'Amazon (AMZN) stock boasts 3 powerful growth engines'*, InvestorPlace.
Hirsch, L. & Castillo, M. (2018). *'Amazon has big plans for Alexa ads in 2018; it's discussing options with P&G, Clorox and others'*, CNBC.com.
Mac, R. (2016). *'After Jeff Bezos hands out promotions, Amazon now has three CEOs'*, Forbes.

Nath, T. (2018). '*Hulu, Netflix and Amazon Prime Video Comparison*', Investopedia, Available at: https://www.investopedia.com/articles/personal-finance/121714/hulu-netflix-and-amazon-instant-video-comparison.asp
Page, V. (2015). '*How Amazon fresh works*', *Investopedia*.
Wang, Y. (2017). '*Can Alibaba realize its global ambitions?*', *Forbes*.

Further Reading

Investopedia. (2016). '*The Difference between Amazon and Alibaba's Business Models*', *Investopedia.com*.
Pavie, X., '*Seven reasons for Alibaba's ground-breaking success*', *BBN Times* 2018.
Yazdanifard, R., & Li, M. T. H. (2014). The review of Alibaba's online business marketing strategies which navigate them to present success. *Global Journal of Management and Business Research, 14*(7), 33–37.

16

Strategic Trends for e-Business

Contents

© Springer Nature Switzerland AG 2020
T. Jelassi, F. J. Martínez-López, *Strategies for e-Business*, Classroom Companion: Business,
https://doi.org/10.1007/978-3-030-48950-2_17

Learning Outcomes

After completing this chapter, you should be able to:

- Have a general understanding of what will fundamentally change and revolutionize e-business in the future
- Understand a novel business model based on blockchain
- Understand how a company should design a roadmap to apply artificial intelligence and machine learning into business
- Understand the various applications of augmented reality and virtual reality in shipment
- Identify the business value of fast delivery and picture the future of drone and robot shipment
- Have a broad understanding of China's e-commerce practices and potential opportunities
- Know the benefits that e-commerce can reap by adoption of cloud computing services
- Be aware that video will play a more and more important role in digital marketing
- Understand that returns of online purchases are a critical issue for global e-commerce and identify potential opportunities and threats entailed in returns

■ **Introduction**

e-business is evolving along with progresses in technology innovations. In today's competition environment, companies cannot ignore those disruptive forces to build and sustain competitive advantage and improve strategy performance. This chapter will provide a landscape of strategic trends for e-business. Businesses should consider how to manage these trends, seizing potential opportunities and devising strategies for next-generation e-business.

In this chapter, we will first discuss strategic trends from a holistic view. And we will specifically introduce nine strategic trends and illustrate their impacts on e-business.

17.1   An Overview on Strategic Trends for e-Business

E-Business is dynamic and evolving along with advances and innovations in the combination of IT and business.[1] Today's e-business has influential impacts on physical business. It is estimated that e-commerce accounts for 56 percent of in-store sales. Online retail commerce represents 10 percent of total retail revenue in the United States, and the figure grows every year up to 15 percent. It is predicted that e-business will play an increasingly more important role in the economy.

17

---

1   This section is adapted from Absolunet, "10 Ecommerce Trends for 2018," ▶ *10ecommercetrends. com*, 2018.

The concept of e-commerce is evolving too. Today's e-commerce is more than online shopping. It can reach across almost all industries and sectors. Businesses that are not using digital technologies to transform their business are typically under pressure.

» With the popularity of mobile devices, social media, and smart technologies, mobile commerce, social commerce, and ubiquitous commerce are no longer just spoken about; they are applicable and reliable in practice.

This section will present strategic trends and frontiers in today's e-business world.

The Digital Transformation of Bricks-and-Mortar Retail On the one hand, increasingly more customers have *showrooming* and *webrooming* behaviors. On the other hand, it is worthwhile for retailers to reap benefits from digital transformation, for example, but analyzing online sales. In the future, more physical stores will attempt to transform their business by adding digital services, such as supporting online ordering, allowing users to pick up and return goods at store, and working as a showroom for Internet-only products.

The Consumerization of B2B e-commerce B2B e-commerce clearly has bright prospects. It is estimated that the scale of B2B e-commerce in the United States may reach revenues of US$1.1 trillion and represent 12 percent of all sales by 2020 (more than US$6 trillion worldwide). Today's B2B e-commerce platforms are as user-friendly as B2C e-commerce platforms. For example, B2B e-commerce platforms typically provide a customer-focused, simple, and effective ordering process. e-Commerce giants Amazon and Alibaba are blurring the border between B2B and B2C. For example, in 2017, Amazon Business revealed that the company had one million "Amazon Supply" subscribers. Amazon Business accumulated more than 30,000 sellers and achieved US$1 billion in sales revenue in its first year with a 20 percent monthly growth rate. In the same year, Alibaba's wholesale commerce achieved more than US$4 billion in sales revenue, an approximately 40 percent year-on-year growth rate.

Augmented Reality (AR) and Virtual Reality (VR) AR will be employed by more brands allowing users to put items virtually into the real world. From apparel to furniture, AR technologies enable consumers to visualize what a real object will look like in a virtualized reality. In the past, shoppers usually evaluated an object by reading a text or graphic description. These days AR can improve the customers' pre-purchase experience by helping them to ensure items are suitable. This also reduces product returns (which are a major problem for e-commerce). VR provides users virtualized real experiences. Although the Internet has been offering virtual experiences since its inception (e.g., Second Life), the use of VR technology within e-commerce is improving its ability to represent reality. If so, there is potential to create a new virtual world for mass markets.

Digital Success Becomes Measurable   New forms of performance data are becoming available. For example, historically it was challenging to measure the conversion (purchase) rate of digital advertising. This was a disincentive for traditional businesses to adopt digital advertising. However it is now measureable, due to:

- Advances in data analysis techniques and capacity
- The combination of e-payments, social media, POS (point-of-sale) systems, checkout systems, and geo-location information
- New performance evaluation methods

Businesses can now gauge the extent to which expenditure on digital advertising converted into sales. They can invest in digital advertising with more confidence and decisiveness.

A Cashless World with Mobile Payments   In Chap. 13, we have pointed out that m-payment approaches have a wide range of applications in practice. Remote m-payment and proximity m-payment both have a huge potential impact on business. In a nutshell, m-payment technologies will further simplify payment processes and drastically increase the volume of payments made via mobile devices. Google, Samsung, Apple, Starbucks, Paypal, and Alibaba, among many others, are developing and expanding their global m-payment market, doubling or even tripling their customer base. This reflects customer preferences for convenience.

Reaching Customer More Precisely Via Artificial Intelligence (AI) and Machine Learning (ML)   AI and ML technologies enable businesses to shift from "one-to-many" marketing to "one-to-one" marketing. Machines can learn from user behavior data, identify patterns, and complete personalized actions such as making recommendations. For example, Netflix divides its 93 million users into 1300 "taste communities" with similar taste in movies and dramas. Based on this segmentation, it then pushes personalized content for each user.

Blockchain is Disrupting Traditional e-commerce   Blockchain is a decentralized information technology. Its operation does not depend on an intermediate or a middle operator. This novel characteristic could fundamentally change how e-commerce works. Specifically, e-commerce businesses that profit from intermediary fees are challenged by emerging blockchain-based online marketplaces. This technology will largely remove friction and intermediary fees involved in online transactions. Furthermore, it has potential to protect and verify the authenticity of physical goods, which is useful to insurance companies and potential purchasers of those goods. This is discussed in more detail in sect. 17.2.

17

The Internet of Things (IoT)   IoT allows the Internet to interact with ubiquitous objects and individuals. In previous chapters, we discussed the role of IoT in various contexts such as supply chain management, inventory management, human-computer interactions in physical settings, and the "sharing economy." IoT is an enabler for businesses to digitalize their business operations.

Cloud Computing Cloud computing enables businesses and individuals to access high-speed and ubiquitous computing capability without carrying or deploying cumbersome servers or computers. Cloud technology also generates special web-based business models in which businesses can host and manage the data of others, such as Amazon Web Service and Alibaba Cloud service.

Returns are A Major e-commerce Challenge It is strategically imperative for e-commerce businesses to manage returns. It is estimated that at least 30 percent of all online purchases are returned to vendors, which represents a major logistics cost. Businesses cannot oppose returns—they typically have legal and customer service requirements to accept returns. But there are some strategic solutions to minimize the cost and improve convenience. For example, some omni-channel businesses allow customers to return online purchases in their physical stores, which may offer opportunities to increase in-store traffic and repair the damaged relationship with customers. Furthermore, staff may potentially hear of defects involved in current products through conversations in-store with customers who are returning those goods.

17.2 Blockchain

Blockchain is a new technology that is revolutionizing many sectors and businesses (see the FT article: "Blockchain explainer: a revolution only in its infancy").[2] According to a survey of 1053 global executives, some 43 percent of respondents regard blockchain as one of their top strategic targets.[3] Blockchain means that a computer network can store data and transactions on a distributed transaction ledger. Each time an actor performs an action, it leaves a "proof of work" or block on the ledger. Due to all blocks and proofs being supervised by all parties, it is almost nearly impossible to alter the record of transactions that has been stored and distributed via the network. In this case, blockchain-based networks do not need a gatekeeper or a middle operator.

How does blockchain reshape e-commerce? Imagine there is a shopper and a vendor on a blockchain-based marketplace. The shopper places an order online, which generates a block and a "proof of work" on the marketplace by which the vendor confirms the order and prepares for shipment. The shopper then makes payment (and does not have to use specialist e-currencies such as Bitcoin), which generates another block and "proof of work" recorded by the marketplace. The vendor confirms the payment and ships the item to the shopper, which again generates a block and "proof of work" saved by the marketplace. Eventually, the shopper receives the item.

---

2 This section is adapted from A.Suja, "Everything You Need to Know about Bitcoin and Blockchain in E-commerce," *Ecommerce Platforms*, 23 October 2017.

3 Source, "2018 Global blockchain survey," Deloitte, 2019. Available at: ▶ https://www2.deloitte.com/us/en/pages/consulting/articles/innovation-blockchain-survey.html

The process does not involve other economic agents apart from a buyer and a seller. It is quite different from traditional e-commerce, which could involve a platform operator, one or two transaction service operators, a payment insurance provider, and more, who all need to obtain benefit from the transaction.

Blockchain-based e-commerce has its pros and cons. Through the lens of transaction cost economics, this form of e-commerce has lower transaction costs due to the absence of gatekeeper and middle operator. Exchanges are based on each party's integrity and reciprocity. On the other hand, the blockchain commerce model has to handle similar disputes as per traditional e-commerce. For example, a buyer may receive damaged products and want to return them, while a seller may think poorly of the buyer and consider them as dishonest because the seller double-checked products before shipment. In this case, there is no third party responsible for addressing the dispute. In serious or large transactions, legal action may be the only option, which tends to be avoided because it increases transaction costs (time and financial costs).

Blockchain Explainer: A Revolution Only in Its Infancy

The word blockchain has been the equivalent of financial fairy dust in recent weeks, adding tens of millions of dollars to the market value of companies, including former camera pioneer Kodak Eastman, which have announced a project involving the technology or simply added it to their names. However, technologists and executives warn that blockchain technology is still developing and the high-profile name changes, and often giddy reactions in the stock market are far removed from the real-world experiments.

What Is a Blockchain?

It is an electronic database of transactions, whereby new deals are added to the chain and then stamped and protected with a mathematical equation. The database is shared among hundreds of other computers, or "nodes" on the network, to make it virtually impossible for one agent to change it. These nodes use their computing power and compete to verify and decode the latest transaction. This is then appended as a "block" to the chain. Its ability to offer a verifiable, immutable public record is what attracts many advocates.

"It can do for the nearly free and frictionless transfer of assets what the internet did for the nearly free and frictionless transfer of information," says Jonathan Johnson, an executive at ▶ Overstock.com, an online retailer that accepts payment in virtual currencies.

How Is It Being Used?

Its chief use is as the system behind most of the hundreds upon hundreds of virtual coins that are being created, stored, and traded online—of which Bitcoin is the best-known. Estonia uses distributed ledgers for the public to follow court, legal and democratic procedures. But interest in its potential is far greater, generating

17

great discussion at the recent World Economic Forum in Davos. Some countries, such as Russia and China, are interested in creating their own virtual currencies. Sectors from pharmaceuticals to shipping and agriculture are looking at it as a way to streamline record-keeping and improve inventory management through tracking systems.

Financial markets are among the most enthusiastic adopters. Equity funding into companies building on blockchain technology hit $1bn last year, across 215 deals, according to data from CB Insights, a research group. Ventures such as the bank-backed R3 consortium have raised more than $100 m. Crédit Agricole, the French lender, on Thursday took a small equity stake in Setl, the UK blockchain technology developer. Many institutions—including bulge bracket banks and fund managers—hope that a real-time ledger could automate their creaky and expensive back office systems, saving them millions.

Several test cases are planned, such as the effort by Australia's stock exchange to replace its system for clearing and settling trades with blockchain. CLS, the world's largest currency settlement service, is drawing up plans. Setl has more than 20 institutions on its Iznes record-keeping platform for European funds. "People who are working with us trust us. We're seen as a really specialist market," says Peter Randall, chief executive of Setl.

What Are Its Limitations?

Development is slow while institutions become accustomed to blockchain technology's biggest features—that the records are public but the owner of the digital currency is anonymous and therefore untraceable. Many are creating their own "permissioned" distributed ledgers, where only those with authorization can access the network. Some are exploring ways to build privacy options into the technology—for example, the ability to mask certain parts of the data such as trade or customer information.

"Right now any kind of corporate blockchain initiative is using multiple platforms and coins and building their own proprietary technology on top of it," says Jalak Jobanputra, founder of New York-based venture capital fund Future/Perfect Ventures. "There isn't anything off the shelf right now that works for these consortia."

It has also been held back by the troubled reputation of its associated asset, Bitcoin. The anonymity afforded to Bitcoin users means it has been used to enable money laundering and organized crime. Some experts have questioned whether the technology can be scaled to process thousands of deals and payments per second that other electronic systems routinely handle. As the market develops, watchdogs are also weighing up new specific regulations targeting the technology. "There is a lot of focus on the potential conflict between blockchain and data protection laws," says Sue McLean, a partner in Baker McKenzie's IT and commercial practice division. [...].

Adapted from H. Murphy and P. Stafford, "Blockchain explainer: a revolution only in its infancy," *Financial Times*, 2 February 2018.

17.3 Artificial Intelligence/Machine Learning

AI and ML analytics tech are not expensive to mid-market businesses. Businesses can afford up-to-date AI and ML technologies to find a new roadmap to building competitive advantage. It is not exaggerative to link AI and/or ML with competitive advantage, which is needed in an environment where physical retail stores are closing as consumers increasingly shift online. Under such a competitive survival environment, businesses need to embrace technology innovation to boost revenues.

Accenture Strategy (2018) identified that 44 percent of consumers are using some types of virtual assistants such as Apple Siri, Facebook M, or Amazon Echo; one-third use once a day; and many consumers may not notice the existence of AI and ML and use it every day. Digital content, interactions, and product prices are provided or calculated by AI and ML technologies used by many businesses including Facebook, Google, and Uber (see the article: "Will AI be the future of retail?"). However, fewer than 20 percent of retailers have deployed AI and/or ML; and of those who do use it, approximately 40 percent do not have necessary skills, techniques, cultures, and leadership. Put simply, despite AI and ML entailing enormous potential, businesses do not know how to turn new technologies and ideas into fruition. The journey from AI adoption to business success encompasses five evolving stages that are now discussed.[4]

Adopting AI   Considering the analytic capabilities and business opportunities provided by AI and ML, businesses should consider them as a strategic priority that can improve the productivity of their workforce and business.

Providing Conversational and Personalized Experiences   AI and ML can be implemented together with new technologies such as bot technologies, IoT, AR, and VR, to improve personalization and the customer experience. When implemented effectively, AI and ML can help diminish the physical and psychological distance between a business and a customer, as described in Sect. 14.4 which glanced at the use of AI and ML on reaching and interacting with customers.

Managing Data Instead of Being Managed by Data   Digital transformation generates data as well as hazards. Some data may be inaccurate, distorted, and false, which if relied upon could result in incorrect tactics and execution deviation. Businesses should not rely on data and analytic technologies alone, without separately verifying findings through alternate means. This is a key reason why humanlike robots or systems cannot replace humans for tasks that require in-depth judgment.

Reorganizing Legacy Systems and Business Infrastructure   AI and ML adoption will increase the dependence of a business on information systems. But their prior legacy systems and organizational infrastructure may not adapt. To ensure the success of

17

---

4   This section is adapted from Accenture Strategy, *Redefine your company based on the company you keep*, 2018. Available at ▶ https://investor.accenture.com/~/media/Files/A/Accenture-IR/investor-toolkit/accenture-techvision-2018-tech-trends-report.pdf

new digital-dependent operations, businesses should reorganize systems and infrastructure and tailor their legacy systems and organizational processes to optimize their investment in new systems.

Approaching Internet of Thinking   A deep fusion of AI and/or ML and other technologies within a business, working in sync with a trained workforce and physical objects, can contribute to a higher degree of business IT maturity. Internet of Thinking (IoTk) refers to adding humanlike thinking into this deep fusion. In the realm of IoTk, human, technology, objects, and broader society can collaborate beyond physical constraints such as space and time, whereby cyber-physical-social systems are interlocked and articulated. Put simply, it refers to a smart interconnection of all relevant elements (Ning et al., 2016). Businesses that have implemented AI and many other collaborative technologies become an *intelligent enterprise*. For example, Land O'Lakes, an agriculture company, has embedded smart tractors that help to make variable planting decisions as they work, finally boosting yields by three to five times. Likewise, some businesses have adopted "conscious" surveillance cameras. These are used for "smartly" detecting differences outside of set norms for actions that are performed by a human or an animal, for example, if certain actions are performed too slowly or quickly. Within compliance to privacy regulations, this additional information gives businesses intelligent security in real time.

Will AI Be the Future of Retail?

[…] While there has been plenty of innovation in retail, a few consumer technology trends stand out to these VCs: increasing real-time demand for products, the rise of AI-powered conversational interfaces (e.g., Facebook Messenger, web chat, and voice assistants like Alexa), and highly personalized online shopping via subscriptions and services.

- *More demand for real-time product delivery*: Beth Ferreira and Scott Friend emphasize increasing consumer demand for immediacy. "Consumers want what they want, when they want it, no matter where it comes from," said Ferreira. This was validated by the recent acquisition of Shipt by Target, which demonstrates the growing appeal of same-day (or same-hour) delivery and the need to have customer service available 24/7. Friend added, "This real-time consumer demand is also driving consumers to search for internationally sold products. This requires retailers to find new solutions like Flow.io that help them sell and deliver products efficiently across borders."
- *The rise of AI-powered conversational interfaces*: When I inevitably realize that one of my gifts has not arrived at its desired destination on time this holiday season, I'm going to want that fixed immediately. How can retailers staff customer service for shoppers like me? According to Janie Yu, "Retailers can use AI-powered conversational interfaces [like Facebook Messenger or Alexa] to answer routine questions and supplement human customer support with chat-based shopping." Friend envisions a bigger opportunity for AI in retail as an enhancement to customer service associates in-store. "Imagine you're walking into a Home Depot," Friend

says, "what if you could simply use your voice to ask the Home Depot app where the product you want is located and have it show you exactly where it is on a store map? You could avoid sales associates altogether." Despite AI's clear limitations today, as the technology improves and its applications feel progressively more human, its role in retail will only become more robust.

— *Increasingly personalized online shopping*: Alex Taussig believes the way people shop is changing, opening a path for more personalized shopping experiences. "Take apparel subscription services, like Stitchfix, which uses sophisticated algorithms to curate boxes of personally picked items," noted Taussig "customers no longer need to think about the clothes they buy because the services get smarter based on what the customer keeps and what they return." "Or, consider service-driven experiences like Laurel & Wolf and Modsy," Taussig added, "they help retailers sell furniture by starting the experience with design services that allow customers to envision how the products will look in-home." Looking 10+ years into the future, the VCs see the consumer trends of today fueling tomorrow's technology. The current real-time demand will get a boost from advancements in 3D knitting technology and autonomous vehicles, and AI will continue to evolve, powering nearly every personalized shopping and customer experience.

— *3D knitting enables personalized shopping in real time*: Yu believes part of the demand for real-time product delivery will be serviced by 3D knitting. As 3D knitting technology gets more sophisticated, stores and/or online retailers can produce custom apparel in the customer's exact size in a matter of hours. This phenomenon will bring manufacturing back onshore as it requires less labor and closer customer proximity.

— *Autonomous delivery of people to stores*: With autonomous vehicles already test-driving the roads, Taussig knows this is key to meeting consumers' real-time demand. Through cheaper and more convenient transportation of people to stores, autonomous vehicles could seriously boost retail traffic, especially in urban areas.

— *(Much) smarter shopping*: AI already powers product selection and personalizes entire experiences from end-to-end. Yu knows this power will only grow stronger, faster, and smarter over time. Personally, I am not one to wear a uniform of gray hoodie sweaters like Mark Zuckerberg. I like variety in my wardrobe but hate the process of shopping or choosing what to wear. If I could wake up and have the computer check my calendar before picking the perfect outfit according to my day's meetings, I would be thrilled. According to Yu, that future is much closer than we think.

While there is a lot of uncertainty about what the future has in store, the winner, in the end, will be the consumer. With more personalized products available in near real time and little effort required by the consumer to choose or even know what they want, traditional retail, as we know it, is over. Say goodbye to the days where consumers browse through malls on rainy Saturdays. Tomorrow's shoppers will 3D knit her outfit or have it delivered autonomously to her house.

Source adapted from V.Sonsev, "Will AI Be The Future Of Retail?," *Forbes*, 15 December 2017.

17

17.4 Augmented Reality (AR)/Virtual Reality (VR)

When powered by AR and/or VR, digital can interact with reality. It is estimated that the VR-/AR-generated revenue will be worth US$60.55 billion by 2023, with a compound annual growth rate of 40 percent in the 5 years to 2023.[5] There are three key trends in AR and/or VR, and they are discussed below[6]:

- *VR and/or AR hardware sales account for more than 50 percent of total revenue.* This is akin to the early phase of mobile devices, wherein most sales of its revenue came from hardware sales such as smartphones and tablets. The service revenue of VR and/or AR will grow as demand from business markets' increases.
- *AR will eventually produce more revenue than VR.* In 2017–2018, VR-generated revenue mainly depended on video games and paid content. But revenues in this segment will be surpassed by AR when it is applied into more business operations such as shipment, healthcare, product design, and field management.
- *The United States will contribute most revenue in the years up until 2020.* The United States, Western Europe, and Asia Pacific (excluding Japan) markets account for 75 percent of global revenue. There is a high likelihood that the US market will grow most rapidly.

VR and AR Are Quite Different VR mainly provides users a virtual environment generated by VR devices. In most cases, users need to wear some VR devices such as VR glasses, VR goggles, and VR headsets. For example, users can wear VR goggles to experience a virtual concert. Contrarily, AR overlays the real environment wherever a user is, with digital content. Pokémon Go, for instance, in 2016 was one of the world's best-selling games, allowing players worldwide to capture virtual pets in their surrounding environment. VR provides lifelike "real experiences," which are still virtual and digital, while AR enables users to digitally interact with real world by providing an overlay over the local environment. VR focuses on virtual features, and AR highlights mobility and interactivity in a real environment. AR and VR can be incorporated and integrated in practice. Engineers can embed some AR features into VR wearables that can generate virtual content and also support interactions with reality.

The two technologies have many applications in business helping companies reduce manual errors, improve staff efficiency, and field management performance.[7]

---

5 Source, *Augmented Reality Market by Offering (Hardware (Sensor, Displays and Projectors, Cameras), and Software), Device Type (Head-Mounted, Head-Up, Hand-held), Application (Enterprise, Consumer, Commercial, Automotive), and Geography—Global forecast to 2023*, Markets and Markets, July 2017. Available at ▶ https://www.marketsandmarkets.com/Market-Reports/augmented-reality-market-82758548.html

6 The three key trends are adapted from *The virtual and augmented reality market which will reach $162 billion by 2020*, Business Insider Intelligence, 22 August 2016. Available at ▶ https://www.businessinsider.com/virtual-and-augmented-reality-markets-will-reach-162-billion-by-2020-2016-8/

7 The applications of AR/VR in business are adapted from A. Arnold, "How AR and VR Are Revolutionizing the Supply Chain," *Forbes*, 29 January 2018.

AR can Improve Order Picking Processes   Workers at transport logistics business DHL have been employing AR technologies to accelerate order picking processes and to avoid mistakes. Previously order pickers used documents or a hand-held scanner to pick and place packages on trucks. Now workers wear a pair of smart glasses when picking orders and are able to see where they should put packages on trucks. Moreover, the AR glasses can display picking lists for workers and indicate and suggest an efficient route through the warehouse. AR improves this process by reducing processing errors and accelerating the velocity of order picking. This application is also beneficial for novice pickers who are less experienced in picking orders and filling the storage space in trucks.

VR and AR Powers Field Management   Multinational businesses may have various branches, affiliates, facilities, distribution centers, and warehouses worldwide. However some sites are not staffed by management, especially in remote places. VR and AR enable managers to control locations and activities remotely. By using VR- and/or AR-based visual tools, managers can access a real-time picture of any place at any time. By doing so, they can avoid production disruptions caused by the absence of key leaders.

VR Makes Delivery Processes More Secure and More Efficient   Receiving damaged products is frustrating for most buyers. In reality, delivery workers endure a variety of challenging situations and difficulties when delivering items. They must work efficiently to complete all delivery tasks in due time. However, packages are quite diverse: some need to be kept in a low-temperature environment; some are very fragile and can be easily damaged; some need to be delivered on time; otherwise they go bad or expire. DHL delivery drivers usually have to pull over and manually check cargo several times when shipping packages. However, VR can provide a solution to this. VR can display key information on the windshield such as routes, road, and traffic information. Delivery drivers can use the information to select a secure and fast route to accomplish shipping tasks. The VR will display potential dangers for them. For example, if the cargo temperature is approaching a dangerous threshold, this information will be displayed on the windshield to inform the delivery driver. VR can also help delivery drivers to access package information before they touch packages. Packages can be attached with readable images for VR devices. VR devices can read and push information such as weight, content, and special instructions (e.g., "be careful, this is fragile") to handlers. This application allows drivers to know how to handle with each package in advance.

17

AR and Facial Recognition Can Make Delivery More Secure   When it comes to delivering packages to a specific person, traditional methods are to ensure one's identity and collect a signature. Upon approval from a customer, an image of a customer can be saved in a database. Then, AR and facial recognition technologies can be used by delivery workers to match the recipient's face with the database image. This approach ensures the package is sent to the right hands. It is comparatively more secure than traditional IDs or signatures, which can be easily replicated.

AR and VR in Consumption Settings   AR and VR have various applications in consumption settings. For example, AR enables consumers to virtually put on a piece of clothing, and VR can create a virtual immersive shopping environment for shoppers. For example, in 2016, Alibaba issued a futuristic VR app that included a virtual mall; through the virtual mall users could access bricks-and-mortar shopping experiences at home. For more information on AR and/or VR in a consumption setting, see the article "In retail, AR is for shoppers and VR is for business."

In Retail, AR Is for Shoppers and VR Is for Business

In some of the coverage of augmented and virtual reality, it feels like there are efforts to make it a "versus": AR vs. VR, like one has to win and the other has to lose. But even though the most basic fundamentals of the technologies are similar—a graphical overlay that is directed at a single user's experience and that moves according to the physical movements of the user—they're actually very different technologies.

While both can feel immersive, only one (VR) is definitely immersive, as in, the goal is to minimize other inputs. The visor eliminates other visual inputs and often comes with headphones to control auditory inputs. In the Samsung 837 Experience in New York, VR users stand on platforms that vibrate or rock, to give movement inputs as well. Studies are starting to show that people accept VR inputs with the same visceral reactions as real life, bringing new dimensions of care to people with post-traumatic stress disorder to phobias to end of life.

AR, on the other hand, requires interaction with reality—it is an overlay of virtual onto the physical world, with the intent of creating interesting interactions between the two. Eliminating other inputs actually reduces what AR can deliver. So it should not be a case of AR versus VR, like VHS vs. Beta, but just because one technology is good for one application does not mean the other will work just as well. Which is why, in retail, it seems to be shaping up that AR will have more consumer applications, while VR will have more management applications. Here's a roundup of some of the innovations in each.

AR for Consumers
What Does It Look Like in my Home?

This kind of AR technology overlays products in the consumer's home setting, so that they can see if it looks good or will fit or get a better sense for if it will go with pieces the consumer already owns. Consumer electronics have been onboard with enabling "what's the best sized TV for my space" (which someone will have to then wisecrack "the biggest you can afford to put there") for years. It could easily be the oldest application of AR in retail. Home furnishings retailers have jumped onboard as well, with companies like IKEA and Wayfair letting you figure out if you really like that sofa. You can even digitally test out paint colors on your walls without having to break out any paint.

What Does It Look Like on Me?

Retailers also have rolled out consumer-facing applications that let them virtually try on clothing, makeup, and accessories. Memomi, a smart mirror technology company, has developed solutions that support all three scenarios, from sunglasses to sundresses. Neiman Marcus has been testing a clothing-oriented version of the technology. Sephora has a virtual makeup app. Jura lets you try on virtual watches on your wrist. The list goes on and on and doesn't look like it will stop any time soon—aside from the conversion rate benefits of making consumers feel comfortable about a purchase, there is a lot to say these days about any technology that helps reduce return rates from consumers making purchase mistakes.

Tell Me More About This Product/How to Use This Product

Brands want to reach consumers at the shelf, and combining products at shelves with consumers' phones will help them do that. Be on the lookout now for Sauza and Hornitos bottles in your local liquor store, which will offer an augmented reality experience around Cinco de Mayo, provided in partnership with Shazam. These experiences can focus on the practicalities of how to use the product or recipe ideas or can be fun, entertaining branded experiences that cut through the clutter of traditional shelf-edge advertising.

VR for Business Users

Store Design

For retail, nothing is more asset intensive than the decision to remodel or redesign a store layout. Virtual reality has already been around for a while to help businesses visualize store layouts and potential traffic issues, but as the technology becomes more accepted, it is becoming a greater part of testing consumer acceptance, A/B testing different format options, and more. It is far cheaper to build out a virtual store than a real one, and the feedback retailers get about virtual store designs is close enough to what they would get in a physical environment as to make no difference.

Shelf/Assortment Layout

Retailers have been using VR for shelf and assortment layout and packaging performance tests for even longer than for store design.

Contextual Store Walks/Real-Time Views of Store Performance

Where VR is entering new territory in terms of business use is around the application of analytics to a VR experience. For an executive sitting in headquarters, there is nothing that helps you stay in touch with where the business is at than walking a store, but most important is the ability to "walk" through far-flung stores or drop into any store in the chain—virtually—and see how it is doing. Posting analytics through a VR interface that is driven off of the actual store design provides a lot of important context and can potentially surface connections between things like product categories that are physically proximate, which might not be easily found from a chart or a graph. This is much more cutting edge than some of the shelf layout or store design, but it's definitely coming to retail—there are just too many advantages to being able to dive into the performance of a store, in the context of that store's layout—to have this not someday be a staple of how a retail executive team evaluates performance.

> Just because AR is tending toward consumer experiences and VR toward business use in retail does not mean that the respective technologies are exclusive in their applications. I am certain there will be a shoppable VR experience soon, if I just have not missed it already. There is the London bar that offers a VR experience of the Scottish Highlands while you sip whiskey. And there are AR overlays for retailers too, like planogram compliance AR tools that show what is right, what is wrong, and what is missing. And I am sure there are many more innovations to come on all fronts, as we are really just in the early days of both AR and VR acceptance and use, both in businesses and among consumers. But in the end, for an office-bound executive, VR is going to shine light into parts of the business that an executive does not get to see often enough, like far-flung retail stores, while AR will more ably serve consumers looking to interact with real products in a digital way.
>
> Source N. Baird, "In retail, AR is for shoppers and VR is for business," *Forbes*, 26 April 2017.

17.5 Same-Day Delivery and Last-Mile Fulfillment

Fulfillment can add value to e-commerce and become a competitive advantage. Imagine shoppers place an order online and receive products a couple of hours later; this would be considered a decent shopping experience. It is why people are increasingly buying goods online rather than in physical stores, and so e-commerce is taking a larger percentage of people's regular spending. Fast delivery services such as same-day delivery or second-day delivery are offered on this premise.

❯ Businesses should be aware that offering same-day delivery is not just a speed issue; it has potential to change their business model.

Same-day delivery accelerates stock turnover. Compared to 1-week or longer delivery time frames, same-day delivery does not leave much downtime for production. Product lines may need to adjust to more fragmented orders and create smaller batches of deliverables more often. For example, under a 1-week delivery scenario, local retailers may need to replenish store stock weekly. However, by offering same-day delivery, retailers may need to replenish their stock daily.

Imagine a customer placed an order at night, and then the package is shipped from overseas and arrives the next afternoon. Customers may be astonished by the velocity of delivery that is, more importantly, offered at a very reasonable price. Fast delivery could be a competitive advantage for an e-commerce business whose delivery cannot be profitably matched by rivals. Fast delivery requires extensive logistics infrastructure and an international labor force. E-Commerce giants such as Amazon and ▶ JD.com have their own logistics system. Amazon offers Fulfillment by Amazon (FBA); ▶ JD.com runs its proprietary logistics service JD Fulfillment. These companies leverage their advantage in economies of scale and logistics management to coordinate online orders and shipments holistically.

Last-mile fulfillment relies heavily on a labor-intensive logistics system, which is an exhausting and costly process in terms of labor and time. To tackle this issue, many logistics companies have experimented with drone and robot delivery (see the FT article, "Amazon makes first commercial drone delivery"). For example, in 2017, Amazon established its drone delivery R&D in Cambridge (Lomas, 2017). Domino's Pizza trialed the use of robots to deliver pizzas in inner-city suburbs (Kolodny, 2017). Technology innovation enables businesses to effortlessly handle the last-mile delivery, reduce labor costs, and improve the efficiency of deliveries.

Amazon Makes First Commercial Drone Delivery

Amazon has used a drone to deliver a bag of popcorn to an address in rural England, in the first commercial outing for a technology that is the US group's boldest step toward automating deliveries. The snack was delivered last week, along with a TV streaming stick, to the back garden of a customer identified as Richard B, who the company on Wednesday said had placed the order 13 minutes earlier.

A drone several times larger than a Frisbee took off with its payload from a modified shipping container that Amazon has built to serve the two customers who are taking part in the trial. Both live in a five square mile area covered by special rules put in place for the trial, which Amazon has agreed with the UK Civil Aviation Authority. The service is available 7 days a week during daylight hours, although CAA rules require flights to be paused during inclement weather. […].

Amazon's prototype delivery drones can carry a shoebox-sized container weighing up to 5lbs (2.3 kg). A video posted online showed the device navigating its way over hedgerows and fields without human intervention, before closing in on a landing pad marked with what looks like computer-readable code planted on a customer's lawn.

United Kingdom regulators have been among the most permissive in the world in allowing tests of self-flying vehicles, although they insist that Amazon stations human watchers along the route to intervene if the drone appears likely to make a dangerous mistake. Amazon has been flying unmanned vehicles in selected British suburbs at altitudes of up to 400 ft. since July, when it won permission from the government to operate its vehicles under real-world conditions, beyond the confines of an airfield or shooting range.

A key focus of Amazon's research has been "sense and avoid" technology that allows its drones to perceive obstacles in their path. While some analysts question whether Amazon's delivery drones will be commercially feasible, the company's research fits a pattern of increasing investment in logistics and transportation networks. The company expects to offer the "Prime Air" service to dozens of customers in Cambridge shire in the coming months, before inviting hundreds more to participate in the tests.

Source, Adapted from M. Vandevelde, "Amazon makes first commercial drone delivery," *Financial Times*, 14 December 2016.

17

17.6 E-Commerce in China

Statista (2017) predicts that e-commerce in China is growing at approximately 17.4 percent growth per annum, while growth in the United States is slower. In the online fashion sector, it is predicted that China will dominate the world market by 2021 with revenues worth US$285 billion per annum. Amazon currently leads the market in Europe and in the United States. Yet it has not yet broken into the Chinese e-commerce market.[8] China, with its growing middle class market, has a potentially high-growth e-commerce market. This should be attractive to global business leaders, and the next section will dissect China's e-commerce market.[9]

There are many reasons why historically Western businesses have failed in China. One reason is that markets are complex and heavily regulated, and the regulation of imports, foreign investments, and businesses can change quickly. Intellectual property rights are also not automated protected in China (Hedley, n.d.), and there are stronger firewalls (Mueller, 2017). Secondly, the consumer and business cultures are very different to the West. Businesses tend to establish long-term relationships with partners, so any market entry can take long lead times. Advertising that may work in Western cultures may not appeal to Chinese consumers, so foreign businesses typically must adjust their advertising campaigns for the China market.[10] For this reason, joint ventures with local businesses are a common and successful market entry strategy.

China's B2C e-commerce market. China's B2C e-commerce market is a duopoly, which is very different to Western markets. For example, B2C sales on Amazon only account for a very small percentage of Western B2C e-commerce sales. In contrast, sales of Alibaba's Tmall and ▶ JD.com represent approximately 80 percent of China's B2C markets. The two platforms integrate most brands and retailers in China to sell directly. On the other hand, customers in Western countries are used to searching for specific brands via search engines such as Google. They may complete purchases in a variety of platforms: on a brand's direct selling platform or website; via Amazon or eBay; or via market specific sites such as Net-A-Porter. Western B2C e-commerce markets are more diverse.

---

8 After initially failing in its market entry strategy for China, Amazon refocused on India with a market entry strategy based on AI. For more details see R. Bhatia, "Amazon's India Strategy—Consolidating Its Empire On The Back Of Artificial Intelligence," *Analytics India Magazine*, 27 February 2018; M. Sawhney, "7 Ways Amazon Is Winning By Acting 'Glocally' In India," *Forbes*, 30 April 2018.

9 The key differences between China and Western e-commerce are adapted from Retex, "The 7 Key differences between Chinese and Western e-commerce," ▶ *Retexspa.com*, 6 December 2017.

10 Source: J. Brookfield, "How Western companies can succeed in China," *The Conversation*, 20 October 2016. See also: C. Prange (ed.), *Market entry in China*, Switzerland, Springer International Publishing, 2016. For an example of the failure of a Western advertising campaign, see R. Williams, "Dolce & Gabbana Is Still Paying for Insulting Chinese Women" *Bloomberg*, 7 March 2019.

This difference is caused by many factors. One of them is Alibaba's business model. Alibaba was an e-commerce pioneer, the first to create a market in China and so "defined" online shopping there. Customers can purchase almost everything on its platforms, and, most importantly, retailers and brands do not pay intermediary fees to Alibaba. The business model infused the concept "one-stop shopping" into the Chinese culture and Alibaba's Tmall helped numerous small- to medium-sized enterprises to effortlessly establish their online distribution channel. It shaped and characterized China's B2C e-commerce.

China's M-Payment Market   Paypal dominates e-payments in Western markets due to its early entry into the market; however Paypal failed to increase its impact and expand into m-payments, which now has been largely captured by Apple Pay and Google Pay. Alibaba's Alipay has led China's e-payment market since its inception and, most importantly, offers free m-payment services ahead of many other competitors to also capture that market. Tencent's WeChat Pay commenced operations in 2014 and leverages its scalable user base and integrates m-payment services into its social networking services, thus allowing users to transfer funds to friends easily and quickly. The two companies have also prepared for m-payments in physical settings and offer m-payment services earlier than other rivals, to create and capture the bulk of China's m-payment market. Mobile apps in China may use proprietary m-payment methods, but they must be compatible with WeChat Pay and Alipay, because that is what consumers use.

China's Single's Day   Black Friday, Cyber Monday, and Prime Day are major sales events in the United States. E-Commerce companies, online vendors, and brands prepare for them and the sudden spike in sales that they generate. In 2018's Singles' Day, it is estimated that Alibaba sold 213.5 billion yuan (US$30.8 billion) worth of goods, including US$2 billion within the first 2 minutes of the day (Rapoza, 2018). ▶ JD.com leveraged off Alibaba's promotion to also sell RMB 159.8 billion (US$23 billion) in goods over an 11-day festival that included Singles' Day (Russell, 2018). Singles' Day has grown into a worldwide shopping day that attracts shoppers from nearly 200 countries or regions worldwide and who place more than 200 thousand orders per second (Liu, 2018).

Delivery Times   Customers are typically highly satisfied with the delivery speed of Amazon and many other e-commerce companies. Yet shipments within China are, on the whole, faster. JD and Tmall generally offer free next or 2-day delivery.

17

Responsive Customer Service   As discussed in Chap. 16, China's e-commerce competition is intense. For example, a few minutes delay in replying to a customer enquiry may result in loss of that customer. China's e-commerce platforms focus on the provision of a responsive customer service. Most have integrated an instant messaging window that allows shoppers to interact with either human customer service staff or smart chatbots (usually after hours).

Cross Border e-commerce China's mature e-commerce markets have cultivated a market of global shoppers. China's customers purchase luxuries and import merchandise through online channels that enable them to access the best import prices. Consumers in a few countries may avoid shopping overseas. This may be due to cumbersome and high-cost shipping services. For example, the processes for international parcels in the United States, driven by additional security measures, have increased the complexity and cost of delivery to and from that country. Amazon, with its own logistics capability, can absorb and manage this internally, but other suppliers, such as Etsy and eBay, pass the cost onto customers.

17.7 The Internet of Things (IoT) and e-Commerce

New technologies such as AI, ML, AR, and VR are promising, but none of them are directly related to the Internet. In contrast, the Internet of Things (IoT) can be defined as a technology that deeply combines objects with the Internet (via sensors). It is estimated that 61 percent of European companies are investing in IoT, and over 50 percent of new business processes and systems will use IoT-based solutions by 2020 (Infographics22, 2017). At that time, it is predicted that the world will have 50 billion IoT devices connected (For more details on IoT's bright future, see the article, "The Internet of Things (IoT) will be massive in 2018: here are the 4 predictions from IBM").

IoT can create an ubiquitous environment for e-business and e-commerce.[11] If an object is powered by the Internet, it could be armed with new features such as interactivity and immediacy. IoT powers objects and devices to support frictionless and ubiquitous commerce. Users can make payments via diverse IoT-powered devices or objects. As such, u-commerce is not an illusion but a reality.

Everything Connected In 2017, Mastercard launched a "Commerce for Every Device" campaign to transform almost everything from cars to home appliances into a platform for shopping. It partnered with Samsung to develop IoT-connected fridges. Customers in the United States can use their IoT-connected fridge to purchase goods from supermarkets. Likewise, financial giant Visa leveraged IBM's cloud service to allow consumers to make payments via wearables and vehicles. In automobile industries, Toyota, BMW, Nissan, and Hyundai are considering how automobiles can include in-car IoT-based devices and services such as a virtual voice assistant that is similar to Microsoft's Cortana and Google Home and in-car voice payment systems. A 2017 study of 1000 senior executives from the world's leading automotive companies[12] found that:

---

11 This section is adapted from T. Alford, "The emergence of IoT commerce," *Editions Financial*, 24 August 2017; Ib-admin, "Future of e-commerce business with Internet of Things (IoT)," *Industry Buying*, 13 October 2017.

12 Source, Global Automotive Executive Study 2017, KPMG, v.18, 2017 Available at: ▶ https://assets.kpmg/content/dam/kpmg/xx/pdf/2017/01/global-automotive-executive-survey-2017.pdf

- Approximately 76 percent of executives believed that an IoT-connected car with value added services can produce more revenue than ten regular cars.
- Around 80 percent of automobile leaders view data generated from IoT-connected devices or services as a critical driver of future business models.
- 83 percent predicts that companies can profit from it.

Collaboration is Key   Collaboration may be critically important to IoT-based e-commerce. Amazon's Dash Button is a good example. When a customer presses the button, Amazon processes an order automatically, sends a message to the customer, deducts money from the customer's payment account, and, finally, arranges shipment. This process requires a company to collaborate with different parties across various sectors from online vendors to logistics companies. In practice, these Dash Buttons should be intelligent to a user's context of use. For instance, it should be able to identify a playful child who repeatedly presses the button rapidly and send an alarm to the host. In short, a successful IoT application requires a harmonious collaboration between humans, objects, information, and the Internet.

All Eyes on Experiences   Companies that are integrating IoT within their business should aim to enhance the customer experience. IoT-based devices can work with many other technologies and features such as AI, ML, and other predictive technologies, so that these objects and devices can more accurately identify customer needs and perform specific actions. All of these center on satisfying customer demand and improving the customer experience in ways that differ from traditional solutions. In reality, the failure of many IoT solutions may be attributed to not meeting customer expectations, such as poor usability and limited functions.

17

> **The Internet of Things (IoT) Will Be Massive in 2018: Here Are the Four Predictions from IBM**
>
> I had the chance to speak to Bret Greenstein, VP of IBM's Watson IoT Consumer Business, who highlighted four key trends. Interestingly three of those trends were around convergence with other distinct yet highly correlated technologies. This underlines the principle that data is the fundamental ingredient of digital transformation. The technologies predicted to make big waves in the coming year—including IoT, artificial intelligence, blockchain, and edge—are all methods of collecting, analyzing, and storing information.
>
> *AI Will Make the IoT Smarter and More Productive to Work with*
>
> Artificial intelligence (AI) is undoubtedly the buzzword of the moment—everyone is talking about it, but a lot of people still aren't quite sure what it is. According to Greenstein, however, 2018 is the year that understanding of its role as the brain running IoT systems will spread. As more and more devices become connected and capable of speaking to each other, AI—deep learning, natural language processing, image recognition, and neural-network-driven decision-making—will help them to understand each other and us.

"In the early days you could do IoT in your home in a lot of different ways and there were a lot of wires and a lot of hard-code – mobile apps came later, but it was still an isolated experience that doesn't really feel connected", Greenstein tells me. "AI is helping to bridge that gap – now we are seeing automakers and hotels and other companies trying to create more integrated experiences and using AI to better understand and interact with people."

More CPU Power Will Be Spent at the Edge

Pushing processing power to the "edge"—the front-facing elements of the IoT such as cameras and sensors which traditionally passively collect data to be processed in the cloud—brings a number of benefits and opportunities. Movement toward greater exploitation of this technology is a key trend for 2018 too, says Greenstein. "Suddenly there are cameras that can not only see, they can understand the image, and microphones which can listen – that's increasingly being pushed to the edge."

As well as ensuring only useful data is passed back to the cloud, edge computing can benefit other considerations such as privacy. Greenstein gives an example of a system in a home care setting, where cameras or microphones could be trained to look out for signs which could indicate a resident is in danger, without impinging their privacy.

"In this scenario, you might use cameras to tell if someone is recovering well, if their gait is normal or they are walking a little slower than they should be. But also you can pick up sounds like breaking glass, things falling or water spilling. And because the processing is done at the edge, we maintain privacy because nothing is sent to the cloud unless something bad happens."

Blockchain Adds Immutability and Integrity to IoT Transactions

Blockchain and the IoT in many ways seem built for each other. Blockchain—a distributed and encrypted digital ledger—is well suited for recording details of the millions of transactions which take place between IoT machines. It is only recently that the idea of convergence between these technologies has been widely talked about, though. Greenstein tells me that though the partnerships are not yet public, IBM is working in "multiple industries" with clients on bringing them together and hinted that more details are very likely to emerge in 2018.

"What people missed about blockchain, because they were so focused on the financial side of things, which is the obvious use case," he tells me, "is that all of this IoT data, particularly in supply chains or where things move between owners, requires all of that data to be stored in some kind of unchangeable record."

Much of the interaction on the IoT takes place between robots, often with little human oversight. Blockchain records offer security, as only those with the encryption keys can edit or amend the sections they are entitled to. In addition, copies of the record are split between multiple (often thousands) of physical locations, so no one party has centralized control to manipulate it.

Massive Growth of IoT in Manufacturing and Industries

Augmentation is the keyword here—and the vision here is that smart, connected tech will continue to help humans in skilled and manual tasks. This will be done by giving them access to context-sensitive insights that answer specific questions about specific things at the right point in time. "There's no question the industrial side of IoT is growing rapidly. [At first] everyone thought it was about the sensors – but we are getting to the point where it is the insights and interactions with people. In a way, it is kind of supercharging manufacturing operators and people who do maintenance on machines by providing real-time data and real-time insights."

Fruits of this convergence can be seen moves toward "smart documentation" with huge numbers of technical manuals and procedure guides being ingested by AI engines in order to be able to provide real-time assistance. "So people ask a question – they do not have to look through the manual anymore," explains Greenstein. "They can ask their manual 'is this the right setting for the tire pressure.'"

In 2018 we are likely to see this trend taken further with the inclusion of a greater number of external data sets into the mix. So in theory not only will your manual tell you the correct tire pressure, it will make adjustments based on the weather or other operating conditions the machine will be facing at that moment. Greenstein tells me "So we combine the manual with live data and say 'this is the right thing to do right now, in your situation.' This is going to be really cool in customer services, by the way, as well as manufacturing."

Source B. Marr, "The Internet of Things (IoT) will be massive in 2018: here are the 4 predictions from IBM," *Forbes*, 4 January 2018.

17.8 Cloud Computing and e-Commerce

Cloud computing refers to delivering and saving data, information and using on-demand computing analytic technologies and resources through the Internet on a virtual network of servers.[13] The opposite is retrieving, using, and analyzing data on a hardware-based server or a PC. Cloud computing can generate many benefits to e-commerce. By 2020, more than 100 billion devices and sensors will access data via the cloud; almost 85 percent of all online computing, data storage, and e-commerce activities would probably be conducted under a "cloudy" environment (Infintrix Global, 2018). Google, Amazon, Baidu, Alibaba, and many other Internet companies have adopted cloud computing and built new cloud-based business models (see the article, "Google is winning the cloud war").

Cloud computing has a significant impact on the growth of e-commerce. Many e-commerce companies have adopted or plan to embrace cloud computing for the following reasons.

Scalability Traditional servers can offer steady and consistent services but have limited computing capacity and capability. When they are powering websites and receive a sharp increase in traffic, the sites can potentially suddenly shut down or freeze as the number of visitors increases. By contrast, cloud computing enables e-commerce

---

13 This section is adapted from Bigcommerce, "What is cloud computing?," ▶ *Bigcommerce.com*; Techtalk, "How Cloud Computing is Shaping E-commerce," ▶ Techtalk.com, 29 May 2018.

applications to respond consistently to diverse demand scenarios and settings. The capacity can expand and contract seamlessly. As such businesses can increase their e-commerce scale and confidently invite numerous consumers to visit their site. For example, Magento with POWER8 is a cloud service that provides a scalable computing capacity and capability for e-commerce. It can help companies cope with peak times and various demands.

Speed   Online shoppers can now easily abort online purchases which force them to wait for website responses. Speed is a crucial factor in a shopping site's service quality. According to a study, if a webpage cannot load within 3 seconds, 40 percent of people will shut it down and leave. This point is even true for e-commerce giant Amazon, which achieves 1 percent growth in revenue for every 100 millisecond speedup of its site (Einav, 2019). Cloud computing can offer e-commerce businesses high-speed data transmission and access.

Collaboration and Flexibility   The Cloud can provide data access and management authority for all parties. This is advantageous for today's businesses that confront dynamic markets and emerging opportunities and threats. For example, upstream and downstream parties in a supply chain can collaborate with each other to optimize offerings for end users by adjusting data shown on their websites such as prices and stocks.

Less Sunk Cost   Most cloud computing services are charged on use consumption, as such they represent variable costs for businesses. It is different to invest and create a proprietary IT infrastructure for equivalent utility. Upfront investments for infrastructure such as purchasing and building a server farm are a sunk cost for future business. Strategists should balance each strategy to construct their e-business. It is hard to tell which scenario is absolutely superior in practice. However strategists should be aware that use of cloud-based servers is an asset-light strategy that leaves more options for a business when it cannot scale up or contract with agility to meet future growth expectations.

Consumerization of B2B e-commerce   Today's B2B commerce markets involve more frequent transactions, often in smaller order or "just in time" ordering. Retailers tend to purchase smaller batches of stocks and require manufacturers to offer more customized products. Cloud-based, collaborative, flexible, and shareable platforms can adequately respond to the trend of "consumerising" B2B e-commerce. Retailers can communicate with manufacturers via cloud-based platforms and make purchases as if they are purchasing on a B2C e-commerce platform.

> **Google Is Winning the Cloud War**
> Google's secret weapon is simple—its roots. While there is no denying Amazon Web Services is conquering market share, since we here at Quantum Metric are Google Cloud Platform customers (and have used AWS in the past), I have seen firsthand how Google is actually winning the cloud war. It may seem counterintuitive when looking at what many consider to be the primary indicators (i.e., revenue,

number of customers, lists of services). But looking beyond these, to where the battles are being fought, lie the true dynamics behind who is the ultimate cloud champion.

Cloud Roots

The foundation of each major cloud service best individually defines and differentiates them. In 2006, Amazon was the first to deliver a cloud offering based on an e-commerce platform. Following suit in 2010, Microsoft made Azure generally available, with expertise earned through hosting SQL server and exchange platforms. Later in 2010, Google released its cloud, rooted in delivering a diverse set of the largest scale platforms in the world. A whopping 25% of Internet traffic is served on Google's network, and most Internet users take for granted how Google delivers seemingly effortlessly at scale.

What precipitates out of delivering at cloud scale is where the magic of Google Cloud is born. From services such as Google search, Gmail, Adwords, and Google Analytics, Google engineering has perhaps the best understanding of how to deliver an unparalleled digital experience to the masses. Think about it: When was the last time you Googled something and it did not work? Or tried logging into Gmail and it took longer than a few milliseconds? While Amazon undoubtedly has a seamless shopping experience, delivering one service versus multiple types of services at a much more extensive reach is very different.

Best of the Basics

Commodity cloud services are the fundamentals, including the basic services of computers (i.e., CPU, memory, storage, and networking). Because they are so ubiquitous, it is easy to downplay their worth. Many cloud developers focus on completing a task, and most do not worry much about operations or large-scale deployments. Thus, the "little" details about how fast memory or disk access turn out often to be an afterthought—if even contemplated at all. The running belief, which is based in truth, is that generally you can simply buy your way out of a performance issue. But this simply is not the way to approach cloud.

Google engineering shines in these commodities, with services such as GCP's maximum sustained disk read/write performance more than triple that of AWS, dollar for dollar. Network maximum throughput is a staggering 2 Gbps/CPU on Google Cloud vs. a maximum of 0.3 Gbps/CPU on Amazon. When you have the fastest disks, speediest networks, and the quickest memory access, the services you run are faster and more cost-efficient.

Security

Over 60% of enterprise executives surveyed site security as the primary barrier to cloud adoption. Google recently announced its latest cloud security innovations. Beyond the laser beam-protected data centers (no kidding), Google heavily invests in security engineering. For example, the latest hardware generation at Google Cloud has an embedded custom-designed security chip that uniquely identifies the hardware and cryptographically validates the BIOS and OS to prevent tampering and unauthorized hardware. This detailed security-first approach is empowering cautious enterprises, such as the financial services industry, to more rapidly embrace the cloud.

17

Architecting Cloud: Less Is More

As companies like Apple have demonstrated, sometimes less is more, and getting the right level of flexibility is critical. For example, Azure's limited flexibility around basic services provides a rigid and sometimes odd assortment of compute configurations, including fixed memory and vCPU choices. This leads to an overall sense that the enterprise must fit a predefined cloud mold instead of the cloud fitting the enterprise. Amazon's seemingly endless array of services can feel like a menu of items at chain restaurants, where a lengthy assortment of items can be purchased but few masterpieces are served.

In contrast, offering a short list of necessary and flexible building blocks can enable cloud architects to model the right patterns on cloud design, without the complexity of dozens of moving parts. Google delivers the 3-star Michelin menu, where there's a curated list of services to help architects focus on design essentials with full customization down to vCPUs and memory.

Cloud Commodity Pricing

Before comparing cloud services, most CIOs look at the bottom line: price. There is no denying the big three are in a race to the bottom, and prices are dropping. With price cited as a primary decision factor, Google's monthly computer pricing is cheaper than with what AWS and Azure offer:

8 vCPU x 32 GB Instance x 100GB Storage/100GB Backup

- GCP: $214.92/month (Custom-8-32)
- AWS: $299.99/month (m5.2xlarge)
- Azure: $309.06/month (D8-v3)

Developer Adoption Challenge

Building a next-generation cloud does not mean enterprise customers begin streaming in effortlessly. Amazon and Microsoft have a tremendous lead in cultivating developers, and available talent is a serious consideration when choosing a cloud provider. Trends demonstrate rising GCP developer traction, but Google will need to continue to invest in developer evangelism to jump ahead.

Winning the War

With its 7-year head start, Amazon has won the early battles by default. Amazon's market share will lead for the upcoming years, as enterprises do not have the luxury of switching clouds rapidly. However, with no resistance from enterprises to embrace a multicloud approach, the door is open for competition. Google's recent wins with Disney, HSBC, Colgate, Verizon, Home Depot, and eBay are proving its strong hand and ability to attract some of the largest brands across industry verticals.

There is a long road ahead for the cloud war to be played out, as only a small percentage of potential enterprise projects have shifted to the cloud. Google's $30 billion investments and recent announcement surpassing $1 billion of quarterly cloud revenue have shown it is a strong contender. While it may have lost a few early battles, with its foundation in massive-scale delivery across multiple services, quality products, and low pricing, I think Google is strategically poised to win the cloud war.

Source M. Ciabarra, "Google is winning the cloud war," *Forbes*, 9 May 2018.

17.9 Video Marketing

Video is growing in terms of consumer content preferences. Filming is commonplace, enabled by smartphone cameras that allow people to create clips, stream, and livestream and even create films. More than other content types such as text and audio, video can record and present interesting stories around us. Most importantly, in comparison to text, images, or audio, it is easier for videos to "go viral" via online channels.[14] According to Hubspot[15]:

- Video is estimated to account for over 80 percent of all web traffic by 2019.
- Commercial emails with a piece of video can enhance their click-through rate by 200–300 percent.
- Adding videos on commercial webpages can improve conversion rates by 80 percent.
- 90 percent of customers say product videos are of benefit to their purchase decision-making.
- According to YouTube, mobile video consumption has a 100 percent annual growth rate.
- 87 percent of digital marketing campaigns have adopted video content.
- It is estimated that one-third of people's digital time is watching videos.
- Video advertising expenditure represents over 35 percent of all online advertising expenditure.

Considering video is growing in favor among Internet users, businesses can create value from it in the following ways.

Video Content Promotes Brand Recall   Videos are more visual and auditory than pure text and images, so they can more easily create a longer-term memory in customers. This memory in relation to brands or products can eventually convert into sales. Customers may also share videos with friends to reach more potential customers. In practice, video marketers should contemplate and design videos in conjunction with brands or their marketing purposes. For example, video making can adopt fonts, color, slogans, and narrative styles that align with advertisements and business logos. In this way videos can reinforce customer memories of a brand.

Videos can Increase Website Traffic   In the era of the Internet, online traffic is important to e-business. Given a general conversion rate, the number of visitors can largely determine how much value a business can generate from its e-business. It is estimated that 65 percent of enterprise customers visit a company's website after watching a branded video. Video should not be underestimated when a business contemplates its branding and marketing strategy.

17

---

14 This section is adapted from M. Bowman, "Video Marketing: The Future of Content Marketing," *Forbes*, 3 February 2017.

15 Source L. Kolowich, "16 Video marketing statistics to inform your 2019 strategy," *Hubspot*, 29 March 2019. Cited in M. Bowman, ibid

Videos can Perform Well on all Devices   Video can perform well across diverse platforms, from smartphones to PCs. Unlike apps and websites, almost all platforms can play videos. Consumers receive these videos in different ways. On small smartphones they are personal, whereas in the cinema they are viewed socially. Businesses should primarily think of video as a simple and effective vehicle to reach various customers and users.

Video can Reinforce Brand Messages   Video should not be omitted when businesses design brand messages. Businesses may focus energy and funds in designing logos, images, and commercial stories but should also remember that video, while not mandatory, can make their branding narratives more vivid and attractive and can reinforce a brand's identity, if well designed.

Video Generates "Shares"   The social web empowers everyone to create content for themselves and others. It is reported that video is shared 1200 percent more than both links and text combined; and 92 percent of people who have consumed mobile videos are willing to share them with others. "Shares" are a crucial value co-creation and co-production mechanism for socialized online platforms. Video has the potential to be an essential component of viral marketing.

Considering the benefits of video, businesses should not undervalue its role in today's digital marketing. For example, videos can be integrated with mobile shopping settings (see the article: "Tictail's new Instagram, video and sticker tools are shaking up mobile shopping").

Tictail's New Instagram, Video, and Sticker Tools Are Shaking up Mobile Shopping

Words are dead. Even photos are on their way out. Video is the new way to sell products, says Tictail co-founder Birk Jernström. "Gen Z entrepreneurs, they do not care about writing product descriptions, they leverage the camera and, specifically, video to show off every aspect of their products," the Forbes 30 under 30 member explains.

This is why today he is unveiling a new raft of video features specifically catered to Tictail's young mobile-first shoppers and sellers. You may know the Swedish start-up already: with tens of thousands of brands from 140 countries onboard, it is the marketplace to shop emerging design across sectors like fashion, homeware, and art—and when it secured a $22 million round in 2015, it set a new fundraising record for Europe.

Now its trendsetting sellers can record videos and post them to Tictail (where they will be prioritized over photo posts), and they can add filter-like stickers (e.g., to indicate that an item has free shipping or is a limited item).

They can also post their content directly to Instagram with its own unique Tictail link to ensure shopping across platforms is "as short and as seamless experience as possible." "It is a way to further allow people to communicate and express themselves," says Jernström of the new tools. "Creating filters that are e-commerce specific will allow our entrepreneurs to use their cameras to create shoppable content that can be posted on Instagram or Snapchat or Facebook or any other social network."

Steering the Video Revolution

It's not surprising that Tictail is at the front of the shoppable video trend. Jernström was first inspired to start the business to help his non-tech mum sell her art online, so he has always prioritized good UX. "It is in our DNA is to make selling super simple and fun so that anyone can use it and start selling and realize their dreams," he says.

Millennials and Gen Z sellers make up 62% of Tictail's entrepreneurial community, and 65% use mobile to run their business. It is not just sellers that love their mobiles either: 70% of Tictail traffic and sales comes from mobile (well above the industry average of 40%), and 30% of Tictail's traffic comes from Instagram.

Considering that experts like Goodvidio believe putting A video on a product detail page causes visitor engagement to rise 340% and makes visitors feel 85% more likely to purchase; this spells good fortune for both Tictail and its emerging brands. And the company, which already serves the United States, the United Kingdom, France, Germany, Sweden, and Spain, is already going in "a very strong direction" in terms of revenue (it anticipates reaching profitability in early 2019).

What Is Next for the Industry?

While other apps, like eBay or Depop, have focused on consumers buying and selling from each other, Birk says that Tictail beckons the start of an age where businesses start acting more like consumers.

"The biggest advantage they have over giants like H&M and Zara is that they can have and nurture a relationship with their consumers and act as consumers themselves," he adds. His prediction is not so bright for online retailers who fail to move with the times. "They will die in the future if they are not part of a marketplace," Jernström warns, noting that today's mobile-first consumers are using fewer and fewer apps.

"Why would you still live in a world where you have to go between sites, rather than going to content aggregators like Instagram?" he asks. Written descriptions may not pack punch for online sellers anymore, but words like those still hurt.

Source K. Knowles, "Tictail's new Instagram, video, and sticker tools are shaking up mobile shopping," *Forbes*, 8 May 2018.

17.10   Returns Rates of Online Purchases

E-Commerce may be able to replace traditional commerce by taking a larger share of the retail market. But e-commerce has significant weaknesses too.[16] It is estimated that worldwide returns of online purchases reached an astonishing US$642.6 billion in 2017. The return rate of online purchases is 25–40 percent, while that of purchases at bricks-and-mortar stores is around 8 percent (for more information,

---

16 This section, including statistics, is adapted from Paazl, "E-commerce returns rates—how much is coming back?," ▶ *Paazl.com*, 1 November 2017.

see the article, "The ticking time bomb of e-commerce returns"). In other words, online sales figures are not as powerful as they appear when the return figure is subtracted from them.

Customers that decide to return purchases have various reasons: product defects, poor quality, sizes that fit poorly, and alternatives with lower prices elsewhere. 23 percent of all returns are because buyers reportedly received wrong items. 22 percent are because these items did not reach buyers' expectations—the items look different to how they appear online. This can be attributed to enhanced imaging (such as photoshopped images) and other forms of impression management to influence consumer perceptions of an item. In extreme cases the enhancements become unrealistic. 20 percent of returns are caused by damages during shipping. Many sellers try to mitigate this problem through improved packaging which, at the same time, creates environmental problems (plastic pollution and non-biodegradable waste). The prosperity of e-commerce should not build on environmental costs.

"Wardrobing" is viewed as a form of shoplifting. It occurs when consumers purchase a product with a plan to return it after using it. Many e-commerce platforms offer return policies that allow consumers to return purchases without any reasons within a specified time period. To some extent, the policies have facilitated wardrobing behavior. Wardrobing is not an issue that solely affects fashion brands. It is reported that the return rate of TVs will drastically increase after the World or European championship of football. In 2016, it was estimated that returns cost retailers in the United Kingdom £60 billion per year, one-third of which was derived from online purchases (Ram, 2016).

In spite of the problems caused by returns, free returns are important to sellers. 68 percent of consumers say that they are more likely to purchase online when returns are free. People cannot access all of the product information when purchasing online because they cannot trial the item in real life. A lack of information causes uncertainty in decision-making. Free return policies provide a security guarantee for customers who are uncertain and hesitant to purchase. Therefore, an appropriate and smooth return process is important. Customers should be able to receive a full refund if the item is returned undamaged. When returns and complaints occur, it highlights the role of the e-commerce platform, which often can ensure that the interests of both buyers and sellers are protected in dispute resolutions.

Over 60 percent of people who return an item to a bricks-and-mortar store eventually purchase another product. This figure is interesting. Returns of online purchases can also create in-store traffic and therefore have the potential to translate into sales. Returning purchases from online channels to offline channels is beneficial for customers. As online vendors usually do not cover the shipping cost of returns, returning to local bricks-and-mortar stores can "save money" for customers. Offline return channels provide a way for businesses to repair jeopardized customer relationships and to sell in-store products. It is reported that 95 percent of customers who are satisfied with the return policy and process of a business are willing to purchase again from that business; and 82 percent of buyers returning items actually repeat purchases (Bowman, 2017).

In a nutshell, returns of online purchases have pros and cons or rather cons that be turned into pros. The large number of returns has a significant impact on e-commerce. Businesses should consider their return policies and design streamlined processes and channels to optimize the customer experience, minimize frustration, protect against fraud, and transform returns into new purchases.

The Ticking Time Bomb of e-Commerce Returns

Returns have long been the nemesis of many retail brands. When a product is returned or exchanged, not only does the retailer experience incremental supply chain costs, but often the item cannot be resold at the original price owing to damage, wear and tear, or obsolescence/devaluation given the passage of time—particularly an issue with fashion or seasonal merchandise. As I laid out in my 2018 retail predictions last month, the mounting cost of returns is a growing and scary problem for many retailers that simply cannot go unchecked much longer. As e-commerce continues to grab share, it is going to get worse—perhaps considerably—before it gets better.

We Have Created a Monster

Over the years, I have worked for two retailers with significant catalog businesses. I have also been the chief operating officer for a furniture brand. We worried about returns, which could often run in excess of 30% in certain product categories—quite a lot.

Of course, back in the day, outbound shipping was rarely free, and free returns and exchanges were virtually unheard of. Today, as the direct-to-customer business is almost entirely e-commerce-driven, free shipping is nearly ubiquitous, and "hassle-free" returns and exchanges are increasingly common. So not only has the average net per-item cost of handling a return gone up, we have made it so easy to return and exchange products that frequently customers will order three or four of the same item in different sizes or colors to be sure they get one item that works.

By design, whether we like it or not, as retailers have become more customer-responsive, they have driven return and exchange rates higher; at the same time the cost of those returns has escalated. Whoops.

And It Is only Getting Worse

It is probably no shock that return rates for products purchased in physical stores are typically less than products purchased online—often radically so. As e-commerce captures a growing share of all retail sales, omni-channel brands that have high return rates and high return handling costs find themselves in the unenviable position of seeing their marginal economics deteriorate—what I refer to as the "omni-channel migration dilemma"—as their online business grows.

Conversely, for some "digitally native" brands that were starting to experience an unsustainable rate of returns, this has been a huge motivator for opening their own brick-and-mortar locations. Moreover, given Amazon's hyper-growth and its (and the US Postal Service's) willingness to massively subsidize delivery, many brands feel they have to maintain free shipping and liberal returns policies simply to remain competitive. None of this is all that new, but for many brands, it is fast becoming a huge issue.

17

Something Has to Give

Rumors abound that even Amazon is starting to worry about the escalating cost of returns and exchanges. Of course, as long as it continues to be valued based on growth instead of profitability, there can be no assurances of any major changes anytime soon. Yet we are seeing some small shifts.

Last week, LL Bean announced a change to its (some would say ridiculously) liberal return policy. A number of retailers have quietly been raising their average minimum order sizes to qualify for free shipping or implementing more restrictive measures, including processes to combat fraud. New technology is being deployed to try to minimize returns upfront. And some retailers are waking up to the fact that their physical stores can actually be assets and are encouraging online shoppers to return and exchange products in their brick-and-mortar locations. It turns out that not only is it typically cheaper to handle returns in a physical store, but consumers often make incremental purchases when they come in.

While Amazon has added to the problem, there are dozens of other venture capital-funded pure plays that have made free and easy returns a centerpiece of their value proposition. The good news (for traditional retailers, not consumers) is that it is increasingly clear that many are having difficulty profitably scaling and are not viable enterprises over the long term. As more of them fail completely, scale back, or get acquired by a traditional retailer, the pressure to maintain unsustainable pricing and policies will subside. I predict we will see a lot of this activity over the next year or so. Whether this will have a dramatic effect on mitigating the escalating costs remains to be seen.

A Delicate Balance

Legacy retailers like Neiman Marcus, Nordstrom, and Lands' End have made liberal return policies a key part of their value proposition for decades. Newer brands—think Bonobos, Zappos, and dozens of others—have leveraged hassle-free returns and exchanges as a key component of their growth story. Now it is increasingly hard to put the genie back in the bottle.

Brands that seek to materially lessen the blow from the unsustainable cost of returns will have some harsh realities to deal with, not the least of which is that research shows consumers will often shun retailers that do not maintain generous policies. Chances are that any brand that decides to revert back to "the good old days" may suffer from first-mover disadvantage.

But let us be clear. While some brands have the financial wherewithal to absorb the greater and greater hit—or will mitigate the costs in a way that does not materially impact the customer experience—most cannot. And when the bomb finally goes off, we should all be prepared for a fair amount of collateral damage.

Source S, Dennis, "The ticking time bomb of e-commerce returns," *Forbes*, 14 February 2018.

Summary

- First, this chapter provided a landscape of strategic trends for e-business.
- Second, this chapter introduced that blockchain is a decentralized data transmission and storage technology. It has a distinct working mechanism.
- Third, AI and ML are inspiring and hold great potential for future e-business. But businesses need to fully integrate them and develop a roadmap toward the "Internet of Thinking."
- Fourth, AR and VR have various e-business applications, particularly in making delivery processes smarter and more intelligent.
- Fifth, fast delivery is becoming a necessity for online shopping. But in practice it requires a cost-intensive and labor-intensive infrastructure. As such, businesses are planning to use drones and bots to replace their labor force.
- Sixth, there is no doubt that China has an enormous e-commerce market where tremendous opportunities lie.
- Seventh, cloud-based e-business has significant differences from traditional e-commerce. Businesses may reap many benefits from cloud computing, but they also should be aware of issues such as data privacy and loss of control.
- Eighth, video is playing a crucial role in people's digital lives. Video is beneficial for branding and marketing, embedding messages within the brand memory of customers.
- Last, returns of online purchases are a "ticking time bomb" for e-commerce business, though businesses should notice returns can bring about in-store traffic and many other benefits. It is a major challenge that businesses need to cope with.

❓ Review Questions

1. What are the strategic trends for e-business?
2. How does blockchain work?
3. How do AR and VR influence a delivery process?
4. What benefits can companies reap from cloud computing?
5. What are the pros and cons of returns?
6. How should companies cope with strategic trends?
7. What are the differences between China's e-commerce and the West's?
8. How should marketers design a video to let advertisements go viral?

17 References

Bowman, M. (2017). 'Video marketing: The future of content marketing', *Forbes*.

Einav, Y. (2019). 'Amazon found every 100ms of latency cost them 1% in sales', *Gigaspaces*.

Infintrix Global. (2018). 'How E-Commerce Can Benefit from Cloud Technology?', *Infintrixglobal.com*.

Infographics22. (2017). 'The internet of Things and E-commerce', *Iot.telefonica.com*.

Kolodny, L. (2017). 'Domino's and starship technologies will deliver pizza by robot in Europe this summer', *TechCrunch*.

Liu, C. (2018). 'Online sales bringing a world of opportunity', *China Daily*.

Lomas, N. (2017). 'Amazon beefs up drone delivery R&D in Cambridge', *TechCrunch*.

Hedley, M.. (n.d.). 'Entering Chinese Business-to-Business Markets: The Challenges & Opportunities', *B2B International*. Available at: https://www.b2binternational.com/publications/china-market-entry/

Mueller, S. (2017). 'Doing Business in China: Eight Important Considerations When Entering the Chinese Market', *Ming Labs*. Available at: https://medium.com/ming-labs/doing-business-in-china-eight-important-considerations-when-entering-the-chinese-market-1302b2b4e53a

Ning, H., Liu, H., Ma, J., Yang, L. T., & Huang, R. (2016). Cybermatics: Cyber–physical–social–thinking hyperspace based science and technology. *Future Generation Computer Systems, 56*, 504–522.

Ram, A. (2016). 'UK retailers count the cost of returns', *Financial Times*.

Rapoza, K. (2018). 'Alibaba's 'Singles Day' sales record a symbol of an unstoppable China', *Forbes*.

Russell, J. (2018). 'Alibaba rival JD sees singles' day revenue jump 27% thanks to offline push', *TechCrunch*.

Statista, e-Commerce: China vs. the US, (2017). Available at: https://www.statista.com/study/46935/e-commerce-china-vs-the-us/

Further Reading

Absolunet. (2018). '10 Ecommerce Trends for 2018', *10ecommercetrends.com*.

Bigcommerce. (n.d.). 'What is cloud computing?', *Bigcommerce.com*.

Sonsev, V. (2017). *'Will AI be the future of retail?', Forbes*.

Suja, A. (2017). 'Everything you need to know about Bitcoin and Blockchain in ecommerce', *Ecommerce Platforms*.

A Roadmap for E-business Strategy Implementation

This part proposes a roadmap for e-business strategy implementation; it addresses the following issues:

Vision

- Objectives
- Value creation
- Target segment(s)
- Influential factors
- External partners
- Organisational model
- Revenues and costs model
- Strategy alignment

Contents

A Roadmap for e-Business Strategy Implementation

Contents

© Springer Nature Switzerland AG 2020
T. Jelassi, F. J. Martínez-López, *Strategies for e-Business*, Classroom Companion: Business,
https://doi.org/10.1007/978-3-030-48950-2_18

Learning Outcomes

After completing this chapter, you should be able to:

- Explain the nine steps of the e-business strategy formulation roadmap
- Link the individual steps of the roadmap to the different parts of the e-business strategy framework
- Understand the main business and management issues involved in each stage of the e-business strategy formulation roadmap

■ Introduction

To help you as an executive, manager, or manager-to-be and to develop and implement an e-business strategy for your company, this chapter proposes a roadmap consisting of the following elements:

1. Vision
2. Business objectives
3. Customer value creation
4. Market segmentation and targeting
5. Influential factors
6. Vertical boundaries
7. Organizational model
8. Revenue and cost model
9. Strategy alignment (see ◘ Fig. 18.1)

After having presented the e-business strategy framework in the course of the previous chapters, what is the purpose of this implementation roadmap? The e-business strategy framework described previously outlines the key elements of strategy formulation from a structural perspective. The goal of this chapter's roadmap is to propose the different steps involved in setting up and implementing an e-business strategy from a process-oriented perspective.[1]

Despite their different perspectives, the roadmap and the strategy framework are closely interrelated. On the one hand, this roadmap aims to provide you with a practical way to develop an e-business strategy. On the other hand, the cross-references to the more extensive e-business strategy framework allow you to reference back depending on your previous knowledge and the specific organizational situation you are addressing. The depth of the analysis obviously depends on the issue. If you do not choose carefully where to drill deeply into the detail and where to skim the surface, you increase the risk of over-analyzing issues of relatively low importance while overlooking other issues of critical importance.

---

1 For an excellent discussion of different forms of strategy formulation processes, see C. Christensen and M. Raynor, *The innovator's solution*, Boston, Harvard Business School Press, 2003, pp. 217–234.

◻ Fig. 18.1   The roadmap for e-business strategy implementation addresses nine interrelated issues (Source adapted from Jelassi et al. (2014a))

18.1 What Is the Mission of Our Company?

As mentioned above, the mission presents the starting point of strategy formulation. It reflects the strategic intent of the firm and points to its desired future state.[2] As examples, consider the following mission statements by some of the companies featured in the case studies section of the book:

> **Definition**
>
> We will be valued as the leading financial services group in the Nordic and Baltic financial market with a substantial growth potential. We will be in the top of the league or show superior profitable growth in every market and product area in which we choose to compete. We will have the leading multi-channel distribution with a top world ranking in e-based financial services and solutions.[3] – Nordea Bank

> **Definition**
>
> We seek to be Earth's most customer-centric company. We are guided by four principles: customer obsession rather than competitor focus, passion for invention, commitment to operational excellence, and long-term thinking.[4] – ► Amazon.com

> **Definition**
>
> Google's mission is to organize the world's information and make it universally accessible and useful. – ► Google.com

> **Definition**
>
> Alibaba Group's mission is to make it easy to do business anywhere and the company aims to achieve sustainable growth for 102 years. We enable businesses to transform the way they market, sell, operate and improve their efficiencies. We provide the technology infrastructure and marketing reach to help merchants, brands and other businesses to leverage the power of new technology to engage with their users and customers and operate in a more efficient way.[5] – Alibaba

2 See also R. Grant, *Contemporary Strategy Analysis*, Malden MA, Blackwell, 2003, pp. 29–30, and G. Johnson, K. Scholes and R. Whittington, *Exploring Corporate Strategy*, seventh edition, New Jersey, Prentice Hall, 2005.
3 Source, Nordea annual report summary, 2005, p. 7.
4 Source, ► Amazon.com, Annual Report 2018, Part I, Item 1.
5 Source Alibaba "About—overview" website, 2019.

> **Definition**
>
> Facebook's mission is to give people the power to build community and bring the world closer together. People use Facebook to stay connected with friends and family, to discover what's going on in the world, and to share and express what matters to them.[6] – Facebook

> **Definition**
>
> Our mission is to be the world's favorite destination for discovering great value and unique selection. We give sellers the platform, solutions, and support they need to grow their businesses and thrive. We measure our success by our customers' success. – eBay

The goals of formulating a company's mission are threefold. As is shown below, mission statements typically address one to three key questions of "where" and "how" a business wants to compete, as well as "why" it wants to do so (see ◘ Fig. 18.2):

Definition of Business Scope (Where?)   On a very broad level, this question addresses the areas, both on a regional and product basis, in which a firm wants to compete. This decision is essential because it indicates how to prioritize the resource allocation. For example, the business networking platform Xing explicitly stated in its initial mission statement that the company wants to be "an everyday online and live resource—across all countries, languages and industries," which is, admittedly, a very broad definition of its business scope. As at 2019 its revised mission statement now limits itself to the German-speaking countries.

◘ **Fig. 18.2** A mission statement serves multiple different purposes (Source adapted from Jelassi et al. (2014b))

---

6   Source Facebook Investor website, 2019.

Definition of Unique Competencies (How?) This questions addresses, also on an overarching level, which competencies a firm wants to develop and exploit. For example, the mission statement of LinkedIn says it wants "to connect the world's professionals to make them more productive and successful." In doing so, LinkedIn explicates the different types of capabilities that need to be developed in order to fulfill the mission.

Definition of Values (Why?) Values reflect the core principles that guide and direct the organization and its culture. Presenting emotional values that the firm identifies with inspires others and strengthens their loyalty and involvement in their work. In addition, the definition of values helps to establish ethical standards of which behavior is acceptable and unacceptable. For example, the values of financial services provider Intuit are:

- It starts with caring and giving back.
- Integrity without compromise.
- A passion for what we do.
  A bold approach to delivering awesome products that drive amazing results.

By addressing these three dimensions and providing broad guidelines, mission statements serve as a starting point during strategy discussions, because the ideas laid out in these statements serve as a shared understanding for reflection, reaching consensus, and they help to define priorities for the strategic agenda. In addition, ethical standards that are made explicit in the mission statement direct and empower employees.

However, developing a powerful mission statement that will be supported by all members of an organization over many years presents a challenging task. On the one hand, it needs to consider the specific characteristics of the company and its employees. On the other hand, it also needs to incorporate the broader context within which the company operates. To address this, strategists might ask questions such as:

- What are the major recent technological developments that we can leverage in the future?
- How are demographics changing in our society and what does this mean for our company in the long term?

For a structured approach to formulating these types of questions, it is helpful to analyze the different dimensions of the macro-environment, which were outlined in ▶ Chap. 3.

18.2 What Are the Objectives for Our e-Business Strategy

While a mission statement is important to establish the direction of your company, it is equally important that you select parameters to measure the success of your efforts toward achieving the vision. These parameters are the quantifiable objectives, which can include measures such as revenues, market share, profits, and customer satisfaction level.

Depending on the type of mission statement, the objectives will differ. Yet all of them should have in common the fact that they can be measured and quantified. Only then can they provide goals for the employees to strive for, and only then is it possible to track progress and make adjustments along the way in order to achieve the objectives.

Consider the example of the retail company Central Group. This company aimed at building the first holistic digital ecosystem and being the largest omnichannel operator in Thailand, which would provide Central Group with a healthy growth path, with online sales accounting for over 15 per cent of the group's overall revenue within 5 years.

Examples of quantifiable objectives include:

- Improve the sales conversion rate by eight percent.
- Reduce the time it takes to complete online orders by six percent (measured by data analytics).
- Reduce website management costs by ten percent (measured by staff time and financial costs).
- Improve customer satisfaction by implementing chatbots (measured by feedback surveys).

18.3 What Value Do We Want to Offer Through Our e-Business Strategy?

18.3.1 What Type of Competitive Advantage Do We Aim for?

When answering this question, you need to determine why customers would want to buy your products or services. They could do so because of low prices or high quality, or both.

If your company decides to compete primarily on price, you need to strive to become a cost leader within your industry. The low-cost airline easyJet is a prime example of a low-cost leader. The Internet is an integrated part of the company's strategy because it allows easyJet to cut out expensive ticketing offices and sales agents.

The other option is to strive for a differentiation advantage vis-à-vis rivals. You can achieve this, for example, by offering high levels of convenience, a broad product selection, high service quality, or a superior brand name. Additionally, you can leverage information that is already available in your organization to create benefits for your customers.

Regardless of which of the two options you choose, it is important to create a strong fit between different activities by:

1. Aiming for consistency among them
2. Ensuring reinforcement between activities to increase customer benefits
3. Optimizing overall efforts so as to reduce costs

Finally, you can also aim at achieving both cost leadership and differentiation advantages at the same time, as ▶ Amazon.com and ▶ Tesco.com have achieved in their respective markets. However, doing so entails the risk of getting "stuck in the middle," where you possess neither a cost nor a differentiation advantage vis-à-vis rivals.

The likelihood of outpacing your competitors along both the price and differentiation dimensions improves if you find ways to open up new and attractive market spaces. For example, you can break out of traditional ways of conducting business by looking across substitute industries, strategic groups, complementary products, or unrelated industries.

18.3.2 How Much Breadth Do We Want to Have in Our Product and Service Offerings?

In addition to the type of competitive advantage that you want to provide to customers, the second key dimension of the value you offer to your customers relates to the breadth of products and services that you want to offer. This breadth depends to a large extent on the target market segment(s) that you want to serve. If your company wants to achieve broad coverage, you will, in all likelihood, need to offer a broad variety of products to meet the needs of different customer segments. This is the case, for example, with the car manufacturer Volkswagen, which offers different models covering all target segments. If, on the other hand, your target segment is very narrow with well-defined preferences, as is the case with, for example, Ducati, then it is advisable also to limit the number of products offered. When thinking about an extension of scope, you need to consider the trade-offs involved. The opportunities are increased market reach and sales, while the risks include a possible loss of internal focus and a dilution of the brand name from a customer perspective.

In addition to a company extending product scope by itself, it can also leverage the Internet to establish partnerships with complementors. Here, the critical question is, What else would your customers want to buy in addition to the products and services which are currently offered? For example, the online travel agency ▶ ebookers.com has links on its website that point to weather reports, currency exchange information, car rental services, and travel insurance. As another example, ▶ Amazon.com went beyond the ▶ Amazon.com vision statement mentioned above. It invited all types of retailers to sell their products on its online platform (including new and used books) including those who might be in direct competition with its own product offerings.

18.4 What Are the Customer Segments to Target and What Is Our Value Proposition for Each Segment

Closely linked to value creation is the decision about who your customers should be. Deciding on a target market entails two steps. Firstly, you need to select criteria for dividing your potential market into segments. The chosen criteria will have a significant impact on the segmentation outcome. For example, you can segment markets according to customer types (niches within consumer, corporate and governmental/public-sector customers) or according to age or income.

Based on the market segmentation, you need to decide which segments to target with products and services that are tailored specifically to a segment's needs. Consider how some of the companies featured in the case studies section of this book have chosen their target segments. ▶ Tesco.com, for example, focused initially on targeting upper-income shoppers with its online grocery service. Subsequently, it expanded into mass market segments. Forbes magazine targets "business leaders and affluent consumers" (Forbes, 2019).

18.5   What Factors Do We Need to Consider when Implementing e-Business Strategies?

Here we discuss the main factors that companies should consider in terms of organizational capabilities, resources, adhocracy culture, and top management support when dealing with their e-business strategies.[7]

The implementation of e-business strategies means the materialization and application of Internet- or digital-based computing and communications to manage external and/or internal business processes. Because implementation of e-business strategy can largely determine strategic performance, it is necessary to analyze factors that may influence strategy implementation. This analytical approach can lead managers to holistically foresee potential obstacles or barriers which their strategic implementation process might have, and thus managers can preempt them. Research shows numerous influential factors such as financial and technological resources, the top management team, e-business infrastructure, organization culture and values, and more. Below, diverse significant factors are described together with their relevance to e-business.

18.5.1   Organizational Capabilities

Organizational capabilities comprise organizational learning capabilities and knowledge management capabilities. Furthermore, organizational learning capabilities are composed of training availability, technical expertise, and knowledge level. To some degree, organizational capabilities represent the extent to which an organization can implement successful e-business strategies. Organizational capabilities could be the most important factor for superior performance in e-commerce. Within this context, organizations must have the relevant skills and capacity to adopt new technology and embrace new forms of e-business. Therefore, both learning and knowledge management capabilities play a crucial role in the implementation process. By exerting these two capabilities, personnel may more readily adopt the new technology and understand the value of executing the e-business strategy. This section will rationalize each factor later on.

18

---

7   Contents of this section are adapted from MM. Migdadi, M.K.S. Abu Zaid, O.S. Al-Hujran, and A.M. Aloudat, "An empirical assessment of the antecedents of electronic-business implementation and the resulting organizational performance," *Internet Research*, 2016, 26(3), 661–688.

On the other hand, knowledge management capabilities focus on establishing knowledge repositories and developing a knowledge sharing environment to implement the e-business strategy. The importance of knowledge management capabilities suggests that e-business firms are usually more knowledge-intensive than traditional businesses. In the context of e-business, research showed that knowledge acquisition and knowledge diffusion may significantly influence e-business implementation success (Yeh et al., 2012). Thus, an efficient and effective knowledge management capability—which is composed of knowledge acquisition, knowledge application, and knowledge sharing—is important for a successful implementation of e-business. Each factor that influences the degree of organizational capability is described in more detail below.

Learning Capabilities   E-business strategies are concerned with much more than simply displaying products online or fulfilling e-commerce transactions. They may also reshape old business models and the traditional value creation and capture process, and they may create more value and higher revenues. Research stated that companies with an open mind toward external input have a higher likelihood to develop information sources not only for the availability of new technologies but also for their effective usage (Theodosiou and Katsikea, 2012). Therefore, learning capabilities play a crucial role in the formal implementation process of the e-business strategy.

Training Availability   This refers to the efficient amount of training that is made available to adopters or users of a technology. Training is a planned and holistic effort to modify or develop knowledge, skills, capability, and expertise through learning processes in order to achieve certain performance targets. Managers should be aware of the importance of investing in employee training and user training. Training programs help the company to develop personnel with the necessary and sufficient skill sets that—when applied—transfer them into superior e-business functionalities to create and capture the e-business value. Hence, organizations that allocate training resources to develop skills for e-business are more likely to implement e-business strategies.

Technical Expertise   This represents the organizational level of technology-related expertise. This construct refers to the specific skills to develop technology capabilities, such as the skills to merge the bricks-and-mortar channel with online channels. Technical skills can be a promoting factor that helps companies to reshape the value chain by highlighting the central and leading role of e-business. Empirical evidence shows that e-business is more likely to achieve success in businesses where general IT skills and relevant expertise exist (Ghobakhloo and Tang, 2011). For example, e-business specialists can help a business to smoothly implement an e-business strategy by matching their specialized expertise to projects. In theory, firms with high levels of technical expertise also have greater reliability in the technical aspects of e-business and contribute to firm performance.

Knowledge Level   This refers to the familiarity of a firm employee with e-business and technology. If employees are aware of new technologies, they typically show a greater capability of handling new technology.[8] For example, employees who are more familiar with Internet use would feel more comfortable communicating with clients via Internet-based platforms. Moreover, with a high level of knowledge in e-business and technology, a firm is more likely to get the superior performance of e-business strategy implementation.

Knowledge Acquisition   This refers to the business processes that use existing knowledge and capture new knowledge. Research suggests that firms where personnel are able to acquire valuable knowledge have a higher likelihood of implementing and benefiting from e-business (Lin, 2008). The implementation of e-business strategy needs to embed internal and external processes for business operations (Argote et al., 2003). This includes identifying relevant knowledge in the external environment and transferring it for appropriate use within the organization.

Knowledge Application   This represents the absorption of knowledge generated in the phases of acquisition and sharing, so it can be applied to businesses and other activities. Research shows that businesses that tend to implement e-business systems also improve their ability to apply knowledge (Chong et al., 2007). Consequently, businesses that show a higher tendency to adopt new technology are firms that keep improving their application of knowledge (Chong et al., 2014). Hence, businesses that emphasize and improve knowledge application have more chances to successfully implement e-business strategies.

Knowledge Sharing   Online platforms can allow business personnel to communicate and cooperate with consumers, suppliers, and others via the sharing of data, information, and knowledge. Knowledge sharing is regarded as a factor that enhances e-business performance (Lin and Lee, 2005). e-Collaboration tools are becoming routinely used between supply chain members. The literature on the effectiveness of information systems suggests that managers should be aware that a knowledge sharing culture plays a crucial role in successful knowledge management (Damodaran and Olpher, 2000).

18.5.2   Resources

The implementation of an e-business strategy requires financial and technical human resources and infrastructure. Here, e-business strategies are analogous to other strategies such as organization strategies, market strategies, and business strategies. They inevitably deplete types of resources in organizations. When assessing the optimal strategic option, and before implementing e-business strategies, strategists must holistically consider the resource needs and their availability for each option.

---

8   M. Ghobakhloo and SH. Tang, op. cit., 2011.

For an example, see the article "How drones are changing mining" and the *Financial Times* article Prospecting for profits as "Minetech" seek it's moment which concerns how technologies and data mining are changing the processes and resource requirements in businesses.

BHP Billiton Reduces Dull, Dirty BHP Billiton Reduces Dull, Dirty, and Dangerous Tasks

The mineral commodities sector competes primary on price, and so operational cost efficiencies are vital to ongoing success.

The mining and resources sectors employ staff to work in harsh climates and where they may be exposed to dirt and stifling heat. The work can be tedious, and companies invest heavily to prevent injuries, for example, through regular blood testing of staff, training, and protective clothing. Mine sites are typically remote, so companies may use a practice called "fly in fly out"—where they fly staff to the site and who then live onsite for a duration of about 3 weeks before being flown home for a week off. Dangerous and dirty tasks in the mining sector that were typically labor intensive are now being done by drones. Using technologies to replace tasks that are dear (high-cost), dull, dirty, and/or dangerous is an easy business case to make.

For example, BHP Billiton is a global mining company that uses remotely controlled drones in its mine sites. In 2015 a small local pilot was undertaken on a remote mine site where drones were fitted with military-grade cameras to provide real-time aerial footage and 3D maps. Staff who were based off site could operate the drones to survey and ensure the land is clear before blasts, to track post-blast fumes, to monitor other hazards, and to measure stockpiles. Data was relayed online and analyzed via a supercomputer. Typically these activities would have been undertaken on the ground or in planes by staff. The test showed that drones were more time efficient, safer, and significantly cheaper.

Following the pilot BHP established a remote control center with supercomputers in a capital city. Staff there remotely operate drones across mine sites around the world and analyze the surveillance data for faster decision-making. Where miners previously undertook dirty and dangerous work on the mine sites, now there are fewer staff at the mine site whose roles are to physically operate and maintain the drones and coordinate their use with the remote control center.

BHP Head of Production for Mining BMA, Frans Knox, said that with drones:

» we now gather more information about our sites than ever before. We can more quickly and accurately measure our stockpiles, review compliance to design against mine plans and understand where we need to make changes to improve safety or boost productivity … Technology will change the nature of work … for example, with drones capable of delivering samples from site, surveyors will spend less time gathering data in the field and more time interpreting it.

BHP Heritage Manager Daniel Bruckner said:

> » the bigger picture is what this technology allows us to do that could never have been done before, and for us that means being able to share and preserve cultural heritage that might otherwise have been lost … We're now able to share all our footage with local Aboriginal groups, and they're excited about that possibility.

Building on this success, BHP is implementing drones in other areas of its supply chain. For example, drones may undertake safety inspections in its ocean freighters, particularly in freighter holds where access is potentially hazardous, physically difficult, time-consuming, and oxygen may be low. Furthermore drones fitted with infrared cameras can view cracks in the hold much earlier than the human eye.

Adapted from Knox (2017).

Outside Inspiration: Robots and Data Mining

Greg Lilleyman, Rio Tinto's head of technology and innovation, has looked outside the mining industry to think about the mine of the future.

The company has taken inspiration from how Formula One uses sensors to monitor their engines, as well as from the waste industry's use of technology to help sort ore, he says.

The Anglo-Australian company has put over 70 autonomous trucks into use in its mines and is in the process of automating its railway in its Western Australian iron ore operations.

The operating costs of automated trucks are 13 percent lower, Mr Lilleyman says: "That's a significant cost improvement just on that one investment in one technology in a single mine."

The company is now looking at advanced analytics: "I think the secret is how you use data to turn it into useful information and bring insights you wouldn't be able to see without the very sophisticated algorithms and analytics that we're now capable of building."

Mr Tafazoli admits low-level jobs in poorer countries could be threatened, but Mr Lilleyman says that although there may be fewer people in the mines in future, that could lead to a broader, diverse workforce.

"I certainly try to describe my mine of the future as not just robots running a mine in a remote location with no people, but more [like] the transition of the banking industry. There's still people working in that bank, they're just doing different jobs."

Excerpt from Sanderson (2016).

18.5.3 Adhocracy Culture

This implies that the business is a dynamic, entrepreneurial, and risk-taking workplace that promotes experimentation and innovation and enables the adoption of e-commerce (Senarathna et al., 2014). Adhocracy cultures forge innovation and risk-taking. Furthermore, the organizational support for risk-taking and motives for creating new ideas hasten the process of e-business adoption (Moon and Norris, 2005). Cultivating an adhocracy culture that supports the implementation of e-business strategy is an important consideration for businesses because e-business will not realize its full potential unless employees are empowered to respond to opportunities and challenges within the evolutionary progress of the e-business environment. Therefore, businesses that display the cultural characteristics of adhocracy are more likely to achieve e-business success.

18.5.4 Top Management Support

This refers to the involvement, enthusiasm, motivation, and encouragement of top management toward the implementation of e-business strategy. Their support is an indication of organizational readiness for e-business. At the same time, the support and positive tone set by top management helps to define the role of e-business in the whole organization. Their explicit support and positivity can overcome barriers such as:

Employees' resistance and/or negative perceptions about the e-business strategy. With repeated reinforcement, the explicit support of senior firm leaders can strengthen cultural norms that emphasize the value of e-business strategies. Therefore, securing the explicit support of senior leaders in the firm is crucial. For example, see the *Financial Times* article on Facebook below.

> **Facebook Hires Nick Clegg as Head of Global Affairs**
>
> Facebook has hired Nick Clegg, the former UK deputy prime minister, to head its global affairs and communications team as it faces escalating problems over data protection and the threat of greater government regulation.
>
> His recruitment will be as much of a surprise to the British political establishment as it will be to Silicon Valley, where few European politicians enjoy a high profile in the insular tech industry. In a post on Facebook, Sir Nick said he felt Facebook must tackle the thorny questions about how technology is affecting society "not by acting alone in Silicon Valley, but by working with people, organizations, governments and regulators around the world to ensure that technology is a force for good."
>
> Sheryl Sandberg, Facebook's chief operating officer, said Sir Nick was a "thoughtful and gifted leader" who "understands deeply the responsibilities we have to people who use our service around the world." She also acknowledged the need for Facebook to bring in new blood to help it manage its many issues. "Our company is on a critical journey. The challenges we face are serious and clear and now more than ever we need new perspectives to help us through this time of change."
>
> The decision by Facebook to hire Sir Nick, a former European Commission trade negotiator and member of the European Parliament, suggests the company is trying to boost its connections in Brussels, where Facebook is facing escalating battles over data privacy, online disinformation, and hate speech.

> The former deputy prime minister may be seen as an unusual choice for the role, given his limited experience in US politics. Nonetheless, as the first external recruit to Facebook's senior leadership team since the 2016 US election, Sir Nick could help to stem criticism that Mr Zuckerberg has been too insular and made few changes to his inner circle.
> *Source* adapted from Parker and Nuttal (2018).

18.6   Should We Implement Our e-Business Strategy Alone or with External Partners?

When deciding on the degree of integration of e-business activities, you need to analyze the value chain again and decide which e-business activities to perform in-house and which ones to outsource to external providers. The main reasons that favor in-house to "make" decisions include strong linkages between individual activities within the firm and high transaction costs. "Buy" (outsourcing) decisions may be more suitable when there are high economies of scale, high capital requirements, specialized know-how, and in the higher efficiency of the open market.

As the ▶ Tesco.com case study illustrates, the right "make-or-buy" decision can be a major source of competitive advantage. Tesco's historical success resulted partly from its ability to find the right balance between activities that are sourced from external providers, thereby reducing costs, and activities that the company performs in-house to ensure differentiation from other competitors.[9] Consider, for example, Tesco Direct's internal development of a media center for a team of 40 experts including designers, photographers, and publishers.

18.7   What Organizational Structure Should Our e-Business Activities Have?

Choosing the appropriate organizational structure for e-business activities is vitally important. At one end of the spectrum, this would mean completely integrating the e-business activities into your existing organization. At the other end of the spectrum, it would mean setting them up as an independent entity or spin-off.

The benefits of spinning off e-business activities include factors such as greater focus, a faster decision-making process, and a higher degree of entrepreneurial culture. The Internet moves into a maturity phase, with improving valuations of online companies and an increasing volume of IPO activities. Access to venture capital might increasingly motivate firms to spin off online operations.

The overall trend is to integrate e-business activities into the existing operations of a business. By doing so, companies can leverage their established brands to attract customers to the online channel, as is illustrated through the examples of Ducati and Tesco. Additionally, it becomes possible to provide multichannel offerings, where customers can choose between the online and offline interaction, depending on their

18

---

9   C. Christensen and M. Raynor, op. cit., 2003, pp. 170–171.

individual preferences and needs. This opens up the opportunity for cross-promotions, shared information systems, and integrated customer services, where customers can, for example, return products purchased over the Internet to a physical store.

18.8   What Is Our Cost and Revenue Model?

The final and most critical issue to address concerns the financials of e-business activity. To identify them, analyze your business model in terms of both the cost structure and the revenue structure.[10]

18.8.1   What Is the Cost Structure of Our e-Business Activities?

To determine the cost structure, you need to consider the individual parts of the value chain—such as production, IT, marketing, sales, and after-sales service—and analyze their underlying cost drivers. This entails asking questions such as:
- "How will costs evolve as the scale of operations increases?,"
- "How can we use the Internet to lower costs across the value chain?"

As the focus of investors has shifted toward the profitability of e-business ventures, it has become much more important to control costs. Ultimately, the cost structure of your e-business venture determines the gross profit margin that your company must earn in order to cover overheads and generate profits. However, if you start out with high costs (e.g., high fixed costs or marketing expenses), then this limits your spectrum of business opportunities. Obviously, your cost structure dictates the types of revenues you need to generate in order to achieve the desired profitability. For example, with a cost-intensive infrastructure in place, it is generally difficult to justify targeting small markets (although these may be very promising), since they are unlikely to generate enough revenues to cover costs. In addition, you will also find it more difficult to adjust your e-business strategy if market realities do not meet your expectations.[11]

To determine the required scale, you need to analyze the (expected) cost structure of your e-business activities. This entails an analysis of each activity of the value chain and its underlying cost drivers. If fixed costs are high, as is the case with physical property, you will need to operate with high economies of scale—high production and sales—to distribute the fixed costs among more units. Ultimately you should aim to reduce the total cost per unit. Your operations need

---

10 The term "business model" has been widely used, entailing many different elements. To keep things simple, we decided to include only costs and revenues in it. For a more extensive definition of the business model concept, see D. Straub, *Foundations of Net-Enhanced Organizations*, New York, John Wiley, 2004, pp. 237–239.

11 For an insightful discussion of how companies should manage their cost structures during different stages of growing a new business, see C. Christensen and M. Raynor, *The Innovator's Solution*, Boston, Harvard Business School Press, 2003, pp. 216–231.

to be sufficiently large in order to benefit from the cost reduction brought about by scale effects.

Beware, however, that scale effects are achieved only if your company is also able to generate the required sales volume. Many companies during the early Internet boom years ramped up operations very quickly in order to achieve economies of scale. However, they did so without first having understood the underlying economics and customer demand. After having developed expensive proprietary technology platforms and putting into place vast physical warehouse infrastructure, it became impossible for Webvan to adapt their strategy to meet different market conditions.

18.8.2   What Is the Revenue Structure of Our e-Business Activities?

In order to determine the revenue structure of e-business activities, firstly analyze the different options for generating revenues. The latter depend on the type of business and can include the following sources:

- Advertising revenues and usage fees, as is the case in P2P e-commerce
- Information posting and transaction fees, as is the case in C2C e-commerce
- Hosting service fees, membership fees, transaction fees, and/or (monthly) subscription fees, as is the case in B2B e-commerce
- Transaction fees, advertising revenues, and subscription fees, as is the case in B2C e-commerce

In addition to analyzing revenue sources, assess the sustainability of the business model, which depends to a large degree on the customer's ability to bargain down prices, intensity of competition, substitute products, and barriers to entry.

In order to sustain revenues, consider the following two options, which are not mutually exclusive. The first option is to "reinvent" continuously e-business activities to stay abreast of changes and avoid being pushed out of the market. As the Internet matures, it becomes less likely that fundamental changes will overthrow established business models. Nowadays, the rise of Internet-based start-up companies[12] that revolutionize ways of doing business using the Internet is still possible but becomes more unlikely as the technology matures and e-business applications become established and used widely.

The second option is to aim at creating customer lock-in, which can be achieved through the following means:

- By setting up *customizable websites* where customers can adapt the company's website to their own needs. For example, in virtual worlds,[13] customers can construct their personal virtual world including building infrastructure and creating inhabitants. As another example, at ► Tesco.com, online shoppers can store their shopping list for future purchases.

18

---

12 For example, Google, ► Amazon.com, Facebook, and eBay.
13 For example, Second Life or Kitely.

- By leveraging *data-mining techniques* to analyze customer information (age, gender, income, etc.), clickstream patterns, past purchases, and comparisons with other like-minded customers. The information gathered via data mining can then be used to make specific targeted service and product offerings based on individual preferences. Numerous companies, including Nordea and Tesco which are featured in the case studies section of this book, have used data-mining techniques extensively to strengthen customer loyalty.

- By leveraging *network effects*. To do this, find ways in which the product or service becomes more valuable for customers as the overall number of customers increases. The most popular way of achieving this is to set up social networking communities in which online users have the opportunity to interact with one another on topics that are of special interest to them.

18.9 How Should We Align Our Physical-World Strategy with Our e-Strategy

Assessing how to align online activities with offline ones is only relevant for those companies that are already running physical operations and now want to expand into the online world. The alignment of a company's physical-world strategy and its e-strategy requires strategic decisions to be made on issues such as branding, product/service offering, pricing, IT, and omni-channel management. The guiding question here is, for each one of these issues, what should we do regarding our physical operations and our Internet operations? For example, with regard to branding, should we name our Internet activity after our physical-world brand (e.g., ► Ducati.com at Ducati, ► Tesco.com at Tesco), or should we use a different brand name (e.g., ► ooshop.fr at Carrefour)?

Regarding channel management, when adding an online channel, firstly determine how to align it with the existing physical channel. This includes addressing the following three issues:

1. What products/services to offer online compared with what has been offered offline?
2. What should the pricing strategy be for goods sold online?
3. How can any potential conflicts between the online and offline channels be preempted and/or proactively addressed?

Regarding the online offering, although it can consist of the same product/service range that is offered offline, most often it is either:

1. A totally different portfolio of goods (e.g., ► Ducati.com where the company sells new, limited edition motorcycles, apparel, and accessories that cannot be found at physical dealerships)
2. A combination of new products/services and some of the existing offline offering (as is the case on ► Tesco.com where online customers can find grocery items which are also available in stores and at the same time financial, travel, and legal services that are only offered online)

To assess what pricing strategy to use for products and/or services sold across online and offline channels, there are three main options (as illustrated below in the context of, e.g., Internet-based grocery retailing):

- Apply online the *same product prices* as in stores (as ▶ Tesco.com does in Britain) to convey the message that the value is elsewhere than in price savings.
- Charge *lower prices* online (as Alcampo.es did in Spain) to attract, through this financial incentive, a large number of online shoppers and quickly build a critical mass of customers.
- Charge *higher prices* (the way Ahold did in the Netherlands) to reflect the extra costs involved in order fulfillment and packing and delivery of the goods.

In financial services, Nordea has used a differentiated pricing strategy. Customers pay a significantly lower fee for a given banking transaction if it is carried out online rather than in a physical branch office of the bank. This approach has helped Nordea to attract customers to its Internet-based banking services.

If the offline and online channels compete for the same customer group, it will likely result in a conflict because of cannibalization effects. If the offline channel is expected to remain important and the likelihood of a channel conflict is high, then it is essential to address this potential conflict early on and to find ways to reconcile the interests of the two channels. This can be achieved, for example, by creating one unified profit center or, as in the case of Ducati, by providing dealers with a financial incentive if they support the online direct sales channel.

Summary

Firstly, the chapter suggested in broad terms a roadmap for e-business strategy formulation.

It then described in detail each of the nine steps involved in this roadmap and illustrated them through examples and some of the case studies contained in this book. These steps consist of:

1. Defining a vision
2. Setting up quantifiable business objectives
3. Deciding on the specific customer value to create
4. Selecting the target market(s) and customer segment(s)
5. Considering factors that could influence the strategy implementation
6. Deciding on the vertical boundaries for the e-business activity (should it be carried out internally or in partnership with external organizations?)
7. Defining the organizational structure of the e-business activity (including scale and scope)
8. Establishing a business model that outlines the expected cost and revenue structure of the e-business venture
9. For companies that are adding clicks to bricks, aligning their e-business strategy with their physical-world strategy

18

? **Review Questions**

1. What are the nine steps involved in the e-business strategy formulation roadmap?
2. What strategic issues does a company need to address when adding clicks to bricks?
3. What factors should a company consider to successfully implement the e-business strategy?
4. What possible decisions can a company make regarding branding and goods pricing across channels?
5. What options does a company have for solving the online/offline channel conflict?
6. What possible revenue streams can a company consider for its e-commerce activities?
7. Illustrate the nine steps of the e-business strategy formulation roadmap through a real-world example that you are familiar with.
8. What challenges do traditional companies face when moving from bricks to clicks?
9. Assess which influential factor could be the most critical factor for the e-business strategy implementation? Why?
10. Critically assess the three broad pricing strategies for goods sold online, which are outlined in ▶ Sect. 18.9.
11. Choose an e-business activity of your own, and formulate it through the nine steps of the e-business strategy roadmap.

References

Argote, L., McEvily, B., & Reagans, R. (2003). Managing knowledge in organizations: An integrative framework and review of emerging themes. *Management Science, 49*(4), 571–582.

Chong, C. W., Chong, S. C., & Wong, K. Y. (2007). Implementation of KM strategies in the Malaysian telecommunication industry: An empirical analysis. *Vine, 37*(4), 452–470.

Chong, A. Y. L., Ooi, K. B., Bao, H., & Binshan, L. (2014). Can e-business adoption be influenced by knowledge management? An empirical analysis of Malaysian SMEs. *Journal of Knowledge Management, 18*(1), 121–136.

Damodaran, L., & Olpher, W. (2000). Barriers and facilitators to the use of knowledge management systems. *Behavior and Information Technology, 19*(6), 405–413.

Forbes. (2019). The largest & most influential audience. *Forbes Media*, New Jersey. Available at: https://www.forbes.com/forbes-media/platforms/magazines/

Ghobakhloo, M., & Tang, S. H. (2011). Barriers to electronic commerce adoption among small businesses in Iran. *Journal of Electronic Commerce in Organizations, 9*(4), 48–89.

Jelassi, T., Enders, A., & Martínez-López, F. J. (2014a). *Strategies for e-business: Creating value through electronic and mobile commerce: Concepts and cases* (p. 301). Harlow: Pearson Education.

Jelassi, T., Enders, A., & Martínez-López, F. J. (2014b). *Strategies for e-business: Creating value through electronic and mobile commerce: Concepts and cases* (p. 302). Harlow: Pearson Education.

Knox, F. (2017, April 19). How drones are changing mining. *BHP.com* [website]. Available at: https://www.bhp.com/media-and-insights/prospects/2017/04/how-drones-are-changing-mining

Lin, H. F. (2008). Empirically testing innovation characteristics and organizational learning capabilities in e-business implementation success. *Internet Research, 18*(1), 60–78.

Lin, H. F., & Lee, G. G. (2005). Impact of organizational learning and knowledge management factors on e-business adoption. *Management Decision, 43*(2), 171–188.

Moon, M. J., & Norris, D. F. (2005). Does managerial orientation matter? The adoption of reinventing government and e-government at the municipal level. *Information Systems Journal, 15*(1), 43–60.

Parker, G., & Nuttal, T. (2018, October 20). Facebook hires Nick Clegg as head of global affairs. *Financial Times.*

Sanderson, H. (2016, March 1). Prospecting for profits as "Minetech" seeks it's moment. *Financial Times.*

Senarathna, I., Warren, M., Yeoh, W., & Salzman, S. (2014). The influence of organization culture on e-commerce adoption. *Industrial Management & Data Systems, 114*(7), 1007–1021.

Theodosiou, M., & Katsikea, E. (2012). Antecedents and performance of electronic business adoption in the hotel industry. *European Journal of Marketing, 46*(1/2), 258–283.

Yeh, C. H., Lee, G. G., & Pai, J. C. (2012). How information system capability affects e-business information technology strategy implementation: An empirical study in Taiwan. *Business Process Management Journal, 18*(2), 197–218.

Further Reading

Chaffey, D. (2011). *Presents general questions related to e-business strategy processes and implementation in e-business and e-commerce management* (pp. 235–306). FT/Prentice Hall.

Christensen, C., & Raynor, M. (2003). Provide a detailed account of how to choose different strategy development processes depending on the type of innovation at hand. In *The innovator's solution* (pp. 214–231). Boston: Harvard Business School Press.

Migdadi, M. M., Abu Zaid, M. K. S., Al-Hujran, O. S., & Aloudat, A. M. (2016). An empirical assessment of the antecedents of electronic-business implementation and the resulting organizational performance. *Internet Research, 26*(3), 661–688.

Palmer, D., & Stoll, M. L. (2013). Offer a detailed analysis of the ethical issues associated with e-business in 'Ethics in e-business: Emerging issues and enduring themes'. In F. J. Martínez-López (Ed.), *Research handbook on e-business strategic management*, Series PROGRESS in IS. Springer.

Venkatraman, N. (2000). Suggests a five-step approach for developing e-business strategies: 'Five steps to a dot-com strategy: How to find your footing on the Web'. *Sloan Management Review, Spring*, 15–28.

18

Case Studies

Contents

Digital Transformation at Axel Springer

Contents

Research Associate Ivy Buche prepared this case under the supervision of Professor Mikołaj Jan Piskorski as a basis for class discussion rather than to illustrate either effective or ineffective handling of a business situation. Copyright © 2016 by IMD —International Institute for Management Development, Lausanne, Switzerland (► www.imd.org). No part of this publication may be reproduced, stored in a retrieval system, or transmitted in any form or by any means without the prior written permission of IMD.

© Springer Nature Switzerland AG 2020
T. Jelassi, F. J. Martínez-López, *Strategies for e-Business*, Classroom Companion: Business, https://doi.org/10.1007/978-3-030-48950-2_19

■ **Introduction**

In 2016, Axel Springer was one of Europe's largest media houses, with numerous regional and national print publications, including *Die Welt* and *Bild*, two of Germany's best-known newspaper brands (see ▶ Box 19.1 and ◘ Fig. 19.1 for company information). At the turn of the millennium, the company experienced declining revenues and profitability mainly due to digitization of the publishing industry. In response to these problems, CEO Mathias Döpfner decided to break away from the company's reliance on print and embarked on an internationalization and digital transformation strategy in 2002. The goal was to become the leading digital publisher in Europe.

Box 19.1   An Introduction to Axel Springer
Axel Springer in 2015

Axel Springer was a leading digital publisher in Europe and a pioneer in paid subscription offerings. The company had two flagship brand families in Germany—*Die Welt* (national newspaper) and *Bild* (daily tabloid newspaper along with a variety of targeted magazines). *Bild* was Europe's biggest daily newspaper with the widest reach in Germany commanding 75.6% share of newsstand sales.[1] The company delivered journalistic content to Internet users, readers, viewers, and advertising customers via digital, print, and TV channels. It owned 160 online services, 120 apps, and many holdings across Europe. Axel Springer was family-owned, with over 52.4% majority stake controlled by Friede Springer, the founder's widow. In December 2015, it had a market capitalization of €5.5 billion with presence in 40 countries through subsidiaries, joint ventures, and licenses, supported by an employee base of over 15,000 (including 6846 working outside Germany).

In the financial year ending December 2015, the company generated total revenues of €3294 million with earnings before interest, taxes, depreciation, and amortization (EBITDA) of €559 million.[2] Income from outside Germany made up 47.8% of annual revenue. Axel Springer had embraced digitization as an opportunity for growth and succeeded in establishing itself as a digital publisher—about 62% of total revenues and 70% of EBITDA was generated by its digital businesses. Its core *Bild* and *Die Welt* brands had over 384,000 digital subscribers. Across all its online platforms, Axel Springer reached over 200 million unique digital users.[3] Axel Springer's business portfolio comprised (i) paid models which offered content for paying readers and users; (ii) marketing models which generated income streams from advertising customers on the basis of reach-based or performance-based marketing; (iii) classified ad models where revenue was generated by online platforms for jobs, real

---

1   Axel Springer. Annual Report 2015.
2   Axel Springer. Annual Report 2015.
3   "Axel Springer buys Business Insider for $343m." *The Guardian*. 29 September 2015.

19

estate, cars, and other classified ads; and (iv) services and holdings which included all activities related to the production and distribution of the company's newspapers and magazines, including three printing plants and logistics. The increase in 2015 revenues was driven by growth in the classified ad models and marketing models.

Axel Springer Group (key figures)				
Continuing operations	2015	2014	2013	2012
Total revenues in € millions	3295	3038	2801	2737
Digital media revenue share	62%	53%	48%	42%
EBITDA in € millions	559	507	454	499
EBITDA margin	17%	17%	16%	18%
Digital media EBITDA share	70%	72%	62%	49%
Consolidated income in € millions	279	251	230	259
Earnings per share, adjusted in €	2.22	2.01	1.81	2.20
Dividend per share in €	1.80	1.80	1.80	1.70
Total dividend in € millions	194	178	178	167
Free cash flow in € millions	300	244	246	297
Total assets in € millions	6505	5558	4774	4808
Equity ratio	39%	42%	47%	47%
Average number of employees	15,023	13,917	12,843	12,080

Source: Based on Axel Springer Annual Report 2015 and 2014

Axel Springer transferred its strengths from the traditional print business to the online world of paid content, classified advertisements, and marketing businesses. By 2016, the company had repositioned itself as a truly digital media company with the majority of its revenues and profits coming from digital media. However, along with these opportunities came new challenges:

- Monetizing journalistic content remained tough. Should Axel Springer continue to invest to increase the number of paying digital subscribers?
- Should Axel Springer remain true to its journalistic core while deriving greater revenues and profits from online classifieds and digital advertisements?
- How should Axel Springer prepare for competition with digital giants, such as Facebook and Google while continuing to make investments in mobile advertising, one-to-one marketing, and increasing integration with corporate customer relationship management systems?

Axel Springer Group Structure

Axel Springer Group

Paid models	Marketing models	Classified Ad models	Services/holding
National • BILD Group • WELT Group **International** • Switzerland[1] • USA • France • Austria[2] • Russia[3] • Spain • Belgium ──────── **Ringier Axel Springer media** • Poland • Hungary • Slovakia • Serbia	**Reach-based marketing** • Idealo • aufeminin • Bonial • Smarthouse • finanzen.net **Performance marketing** • Zanox/Digital Window	**Jobs** • StepStone • Totaljobs • Saongroup • YourCareerGroup • Jobsite **Real estate** • SeLoger • Immonet/ Immowelt • Immoweb **General/other** • LaCentrale • @Leisure • Meinestadt.de • Yad2 • CarWale[4]	• Printing plants • Logistics

1. As of 1 January, 2016, part of joint venture – Ringier Axel Springer Schweiz company

2. Sold in August 2015

3. Sold its activities in Russia in October 2015

4. Sold in December 2015

Revenue by segments

Total revenue €3,294.9 million (FY end December 2015)

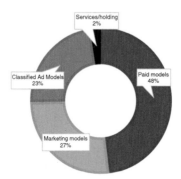

❑ **Fig. 19.1**   An introduction to Axel Springer. (Source: Compiled from Axel Springer annual report 2015)

19.1 **Company History**

Axel Springer had come a long way since its founding in a garage-like facility in Hamburg in 1946 by publisher Hinrich Springer (66) and his son Axel (34), a reporter and journalist.[4] Within a decade, the company launched ten publications and emerged as a major publishing group in Germany.[5] Axel Springer was a widely known advocate of German reunification and called on the East German authorities to "open the gate" to the West through his newspapers. In 1959, he went on to lay the foundation stone for a new headquarter building right beside the border of the Soviet-occupied sector of Berlin, which later became the route of the Berlin Wall.[6] He was strongly opposed to the notion of a divided Germany. By the time the building opened in 1966, Axel Springer had acquired significant political clout by controlling the publication of 39% of newspapers and 18% of magazines in Germany. Its newspapers had a strong conservative slant, which aroused opposition from left-wing groups and liberals that went as far as bombing company headquarters in 1972. Soon after, Axel Springer sold off several publications and even considered selling his entire publishing business. However, the company regained its stature and went on to list on the Frankfurt Stock Exchange in 1985. After the listing, Axel Springer passed away, and control of the company passed on to his wife, Friede Springer.

In the wake of German reunification, Axel Springer's newspapers became more centrist in their political view, and the company started to expand into France, Poland, Russia, Spain, and Switzerland. In 2002 a new CEO was appointed, who was tasked with transforming the company from print publisher to a digital media company. Mathias Döpfner had been the editor-in-chief of *Die Welt* and a member of the executive board, responsible for the multimedia and the newspaper divisions. Döpfner sketched out his mission as follows:

» Printed newspapers will survive longer than some people expect, but it is not a growing business. We have to realize the fact that in the world of younger readers printed newspapers do not exist anymore. This does not mean that they do not read, they simply use other ways of viewing news or entertainment on other technical devices. Is that bad news for us? No! Because our core competence as a publisher is not the printing itself, but the content. Therefore, the real challenge is not to protect printed papers to make them survive as long as possible, but to emancipate the idea of a newspaper from paper.[7]

---

4 Axel Springer website, ▶ http://www.axelspringer.de/en/artikel/The-Company_42994.html, accessed 15 February 2016.
5 Publication titles: *Nordwestdeutsche Hefte, Hörzu, Hamburger Abendblatt, Bild, Bild am Sonntag, Die Welt, Welt am Sonntag, Das neue Blatt, B.Z.*, and *Berliner Morgen-Zeitung*. Some of these publications were bought be Axel Springer.
6 "50 years Axel Springer Building Berlin – Unveiling of the Balancing Act sculpture by Stephan Balkenhol." Axel Springer Press Release, 25 May 2009.
7 Alain Elkann interview with Mathias Döpfner. 3 December 2014.

19.2   Early Attempts at Digitization

By 2002, Axel Springer's traditional business models had come under immense pressure reflecting declining advertising revenues and shrinking subscriptions. Alexander Schmid-Lossberg, Head of Corporate Human Resources, explained why:

» When a plane went down in the Hudson River, radio stations, television and newspaper companies sent out reporters. They took pictures and wrote about the event, and you learned what happened in the evening news or the next morning. Today, there are many people on the spot who report immediately via Twitter or blogs. The news is out at the same time as when the event happens, and that news is free, which makes it hard for any publisher to create profit both offline and online. So it is not surprising that many publishers end up giving away content for free.

Despite these concerns, executives at the company strongly believed that this was a temporary state of affairs and that in the end, readers would pay for content. This led Axel Springer to focus on improving the quality of its content and rolling it out across digital properties. The company also decided to monetize its offerings in the digital world in the same way as it had done in the analog world, by relying on: (1) the paying reader, (2) marketing (advertisers bought access to the reader), and (3) the classified advertisements. Döpfner believed that the company could become the leader in each of these three segments because it had knowledge of how these audiences and markets worked.

Unfortunately, Axel Springer's efforts were insufficient to achieve the company goals, with newspapers and magazines accounting for 72.9% of turnover and the digital business contributing 8.1% by 2007 (Schultz et al. 2013). To accelerate the execution of its strategy, Axel Springer made a bid to buy Germany's largest commercial broadcaster ProSieben satellite TV network. However, the deal was blocked by German antitrust authorities, as the company already had too much media market power in the country (Stone and Silver 2015). The inability to broaden its distribution scope led the company to accelerate the digital transformation efforts in its content business.

19.3   Accelerating Content Digitization

The management decided to begin this accelerated process by releasing a new digital version of its *Bild* tabloid. The previous version, launched in 2001 as a joint venture with Deutsche Telekom, had been run by a separate editorial and management team. Axel Springer took over the stake from Deutsche Telekom and invested heavily to relaunch *Bild.de* in December 2007. The move spawned serious opposition from the editor-in-chief and managers of *Bild* who saw the move as a creation

19

of competition for the printed version and a serious drain of resources. Schmid-Lossberg summarized the sentiments:

>> Are you crazy? We are killing our proven business model. We don't believe in it. We have margins of more than 20% with all our newspapers, magazines. Digital business is less than 1%. Why bother? There will never be success.

Furthermore, Axel Springer was locked in by trade unions which fiercely defended the traditional business model. Despite the opposition, the transformation process went ahead. Digitization of the print brand was completely centralized, and the digital journalistic offerings were developed jointly in-house by the IT team, journalists, marketers, and strategy planning departments. To strengthen buy-in from across the organization, Döpfner solicited senior management engagement in several ways. He added multimedia to the directive of each division and leveraged committed managers to promote the new strategy internally. He also openly accepted the fact that self-cannibalization of print would occur in the short term. Andreas Wiele, President of Marketing and Classified Ad Models, explained:

>> We told people "Cannibalize yourself, it doesn't hurt as much," and "Be in charge of your own destruction and your migration to the digital world." Otherwise, we would have winners and losers within the company, the ones that managed the growing digital business and the ones that managed the declining print business, respectively, but they would never have cooperated.

The operations were organized differently for *Bild* and *Die Welt*. At *Bild*, two separate teams were established for the digital platform and the print segment. The overall business was run by a person with a digital background, while the editor-in-chief was a former print person. At *Die Welt*, the company decided to create a unified editorial team, combining print, digital, and TV content production. Working together at one newsroom, the team held conferences to decide what would be put on the print and/or on the online edition, as well as topics that would be combined with supporting TV stories. The transition was not without challenges. To begin with, an online team was formed with 30 to 40 journalists, while 400 journalists continued working on print. Both teams were integrated in 2009, and it was only in 2012 that the company adopted a *digital-first* approach with regard to the journalist team and revamped it so that the majority of the storytellers moved to a bigger team on the digital side with a small dedicated team of 15 who worked purely on print.

The investments, coupled with organizational changes, allowed *Bild.de* to become Germany's largest content portal, largely by attracting the younger, more urban, better educated, and higher-income readers, who would not buy a tabloid at a physical kiosk. This alleviated the cannibalization concerns and helped the company to push on with the digital transformation initiatives.

In 2009, Axel Springer moved to monetize its digital business by launching its first paid content premium offering. The initiative included pay-for-service apps for

Bild and *Welt* on the iPhone and the iPad, available for download as exclusive sub-scriptions. For instance, users could exclusively read the PDF versions of print issues of the two newspapers the previous evening before they were published the following day. Users could also get breaking news and the latest sports results on their devices.[8] Other services launched by Axel Springer as part of this premium initiative included the online national soccer league game BILD.de Super-Manager and the *Welt am Sonntag* emag, the new digital magazine from Germany's biggest premium Sunday newspaper. By the end of 2010, Axel Springer had launched 15 paid content offerings including "freemium" models for both paid and free content from the newspapers *Hamburger Abendblatt* and *Berliner Morgenpost* among others.[9] Döpfner commented:

» Our experiment with paid-content offerings has begun to yield positive results after only one year. It is still too early to make a definitive assessment of users' willingness, over the long term, to pay for journalistic content in the digital world. And of course, the revenues are still rather small compared with the print business; but we have gotten off to a successful start.[10]

19.4   Digitizing the Classified Advertising Business Through Acquisitions

In 2004, Axel Springer started to realign its business portfolio to include various types of online marketing and classified ads for jobs, real estate, travel, and used cars. Many analysts felt that Axel Springer was late to the game (Weverbergh n.d.). For example, at that time Norwegian competitor Schibsted had already entered the digital classifieds business. As classified ads generated the highest margins in physical newspapers, the digital move meant cannibalization of the existing business. However, Axel Springer realized that pure online players were already disrupting the market and it was at risk of being left behind. The key question for the company was how to pivot from print to digital classifieds—an area where the company lacked competence.

To meet this challenge, Axel Springer engaged in a number of acquisitions of late-stage start-ups that had demonstrated a clear track record, had revenue-proven business models, were EBITDA-positive, and promised significant growth potential. Axel Springer chose to enter markets that it understood very well to mitigate potential risks. The company started acquiring a large number of affiliate market-

---

8   The BILD app cost 79 cents for the first 30 days, after which users could choose between two different subscription models: the BILD app with the next day's print issue available for €3.99 per month; without PDF, the app cost €1.59 per month. The WELT app was available in the first month for €1.59, thereafter for €4.99 per month with the PDF version or €2.99 per month (without PDF).

9   "Premium Initiative for digital paid-content offerings: Axel Springer offers positive interim assessment after the first year." *Media Impact.* 8 December 2010.

10   Ibid.

ing, online classifieds, and digital footprint-tracking companies that were big enough to "move the needle for Axel Springer." A senior executive explained:

> To establish online marketing activities and the classifieds offerings out of a print environment was absolutely impossible. To have somebody who is playing in the digital real estate business world is quite different from having distributors of newspapers or magazines. You not only need deep market knowledge on the marketing side, but you need also the technological competence. You need to know about programming, search engine optimization and be an expert on online marketing. These were competences that we didn't have.

19.4.1 Classified Ads Business

Axel Springer's first major acquisition was that of StepStone Germany, a job listing portal, in 2004, followed by a majority stake in 2009 in its parent company Oslo-based StepStone ASA, a leading international online recruitment and talent management solutions company. This enabled Axel Springer to get a hold on the fast-growing European market of online job portals. It then invested in scaling up these enterprises across new markets and new customer groups by channeling all listings from *Die Welt*, *Hamburger Abendblatt*, and *Berliner Morgenpost* to StepStone, which allowed the company to move up from being a distant second to ▶ Monster.com to become the largest player in Europe. StepStone's stellar trajectory was a learning for Axel Springer in terms of understanding the speed of the online jobs market and seizing the consequent growth opportunities. In 2012, the company expanded its stronghold by acquiring Totaljobs, the largest online recruitment business operating seven job boards in the United Kingdom, from Reed Elsevier.

By then Axel Springer had moved into first gear with its acquisition strategy. It looked to the real estate classified ad market to broaden its online offerings. In 2011 and 2012, it acquired ▶ SeLoger.com, the market leader in real estate listings in France, and Immoweb, the Belgian market leader in real estate classifieds. These acquisitions allowed Axel Springer to leverage synergies and share best practices with its own German property portal immonet.de.

In 2012 Axel Springer Digital Classifieds was established as a 70:30 joint venture between Axel Springer and global growth investor General Atlantic with the aim of continuing its growth offensive in the digital classifieds area. All the above-mentioned online classifieds businesses were subsequently consolidated under this newly formed entity.

19.4.2 Marketing Business

The marketing business was another area where the online space presented huge advantages over the existing print business model. Axel Springer categorized this segment into performance-based and reach-based marketing services. In 2007 Axel

Springer acquired Berlin-based Zanox to tap into the rapidly growing market of performance-based online marketing. Zanox offered advertisers, e-commerce companies, and online shop operators an Internet-based platform for effective affiliate marketing, search engine management, email marketing, online shopping, and customer loyalty programs. With subsidiaries in nine countries, Zanox's online marketing services were used by an international network of over 1 million sales partners including 1800 MNCs. A senior executive explained that Axel Springer sought out Zanox because its business model was completely the opposite to its own marketing model:

» If you publish one advertisement in *Bild*, you reach 12 million people. From a broad perspective you know that it works, but you don't have a clue about the real outcome. However, the advertiser pays, say €400,000 for one page, and then he has to wait and see what happens. Under the performance marketing business model, the advertiser only pays if an actual sale is completed. So, that is the opposite end of our spectrum. And it is the promise of the internet to make everything measurable. If we want to be able to deliver the whole value chain for advertisers, we have to start at the very other extreme.

Going forward, all Axel Springer's performance marketing activities were bundled within Zanox. For example, Zanox acquired Dutch affiliate marketing network M4N (in 2011) and leading British affiliate network Digital Window (in 2010), thereby securing a leading market position in the Benelux countries and the United Kingdom, respectively. Having secured a broad base of companies, Axel Springer focused upon developing them organically, enlarging them step-by-step in terms of new markets or new target groups, thus building a strong network.

At the same time, Axel Springer started to build its e-commerce portfolio by acquiring Berlin-based Idealo, a price comparison portal. Post-acquisition, Idealo started expanding into new markets and extending its range of services into the travel sector with new sites such as flug.idealo and hotel.idealo. From 2006 to 2013, Idealo's revenue and EBITDA grew at 38% CAGR; it became the number one price comparison platform in Germany and had a strong presence in Austria, France, the United Kingdom, Italy, Spain, and Portugal. In another move to increase market share, in 2011 Axel Springer acquired majority stakes in two companies. The first was kaufDA, Germany's market leader for online brochures and mobile couponing, which distributed digitized advertising brochures from retailers on a regionalized basis, mainly via mobile devices. Subsequently, these services were also rolled out in France (Bonial France), Spain (Ofertia), Russia (Lokata), Brazil (Guiato), and the United States (Retale). The second was Berlin-based Visual Meta GmbH, which operated shopping portals in Germany (LadenZeile. de) and in six other European countries (e.g., ▶ ShopAlike.co.uk). A senior executive shared:

» The classified ad business remains the largest profit generator as before. The difference is that it used to be under the brand of the newspaper as a physical object. Now it has moved to the digital space which is better for everyone – for the consumer, for the agent, and also for the owner of the platform because it's

19

a fast-growing, high-margin business. We have focused on the three biggest segments – real estate, jobs, travel and cars, and also a little bit on general classifieds – just like it was in the newspaper space. But digital classified ads has become a standalone business model, completely sustainable on its own.

Axel Springer's strategy was to make big-ticket investments in companies that were already market leaders. However, it made the conscious decision not to take a 100% stake in every acquisition; mostly it took a majority stake, while the founders or strategic partners held the rest and stayed on board. A senior executive noted:

» We were always skeptical when founders came to us and wanted to make a complete exit. Instead, we liked the concept when founders came to us and said, "I have set up something really nice here. It's really working well, but I want to go international now. I need a strong partner with financial capacity. I need attachment to a network. And I'm ready to give away a majority."

Axel Springer followed a philosophy of entrepreneurial freedom and did not replace a new CEO or CFO to enforce integration with its existing business. Corporate influence was only limited to governance, compliance, and tax, while HR preferred to play a consulting role. Therefore, the acquired entities ran their own operations fairly independently. Since the founder and the management remained onboard, they followed through with their vision for growth.

The same went for developing a common technological platform for the newly acquired businesses. Despite significant cost synergies of doing so, Axel Springer chose not to force one on the start-ups to avoid distracting them from their growth focus. In fact, Axel Springer followed the same strategy for internal development, thereby avoiding centralized IT innovation and development. For example, it launched new iPhone and iPad applications with different teams and agencies to ensure rapid growth, iteration, and scaling.

Furthermore, the company sought to create an internal headhunting service helping the newly acquired companies source talent from other Axel Springer companies as well as from outside the firm. With time, the service started focusing on proactive hiring for roles such as search engine optimization (SEO) managers, sales managers, and account managers. This worked well within the competitive landscape in Berlin, where candidates did not apply openly anymore but waited to be approached. These joint efforts also allowed the corporate center to gain further insights into the acquired companies and rectify whatever was going wrong or make an early exit in case of nonperformance.

The strategy paid off handsomely, with Axel Springer's revenue from digital activities increasing from €24 million in 2006 to €1.2 billion in 2012—the digital business contributed 37.2% of the total revenue (Boston 2014). Indeed, in 2012 Axel Springer's digital activities led by the classified ad and marketing businesses brought in more revenue than its newspapers. Axel Springer with its Internet subsidiaries was counted among Germany's leading online businesses, next to industry giants like Amazon Deutschland, online and catalogue retailer Otto Group, and eBay Deutschland. By 2015, Axel Springer had spent a total of €4 billion on 220 acquisitions (*see* ◘ Table 19.1 for th*e company's major acquisitions*).

□ Table 19.1   Axel Springer's major acquisitions

Selected acquisitions up to 2015		
Company Year and price	**Description**	**Details**
Idealo.de 2006 €30.3 million	Largest online price and product comparison search engine in Germany Over 1 million products and 4500 online retailers	Idealo was a profitable company. Post-acquisition, Idealo revenues expanded at a CAGR of 39% till 2013. It expanded into new markets (France, Italy, Spain) and new services in the travel sector with sites such as flug.idealo and hotel.idealo
Zanox 2007 €214.9 million	A leading service provider for performance-based online marketing	Profitable since launch in 2000 2006: Revenue = €107 million, EBITDA = €8 million; No. of employees = 275
aufeminin 2007	Europe's leading women's network of online portals on trends and fashion, beauty, fitness, health, and psychology Founded in 1999 in Paris	Presence in eight countries, enjoying number one positions in France, Germany, Italy, Spain, Belgium, and Switzerland and number two position in the United Kingdom. 2006: Revenues = €13.4 million, EBITA = €7.3 million
StepStone 2009	International provider of e-recruiting via online job boards and talent management software Founded in 1996 in Oslo, Norway	One of the pioneers of online job boards in Europe 2008: Revenues = €123.5 million, EBITDA = €15.7 million
SeLoger 2011 €633 million	Leading French real estate portal Operated six property portals Founded in 1992	Its portfolio consisted of 1.1 million online property ads with 3.1 million unique users and 14.1 million visits per month
kaufDa 2011	German market leader for online brochures and mobile coupons; retailers advertised their products/ services on the mobile and stationary Internet Founded in 2009	With more than 80 partners, the kaufDA network reached over 11 million users in 12,000 German cities and towns. kaufDa had a gross media advertising volume of €8 million in 2010 and generated more than 25% of revenue on mobile devices (Butcher 2011)
Totaljobs 2012 €132 million	Largest online recruitment business in the United Kingdom Founded in 1999, employing 340 staff and operating seven job boards in 2012	The group's platforms saw more than 7 million unique visitors per month making over 4 million applications. In 2011 Totaljobs Group profitably served more than 24,000 UK companies
Immoweb 2012 €127.5 million	Leading online property portal in Belgium Founded in 1996	About 140,000 real estate listings and over 2.4 million unique visitors every month

19

◼ **Table 19.1** (continued)

Selected acquisitions up to 2015

Company Year and price	Description	Details
Jobsite 2014 €110 million	Online jobs portal Founded in 1995 in Hampshire, UK	Operating job board ▶ jobsite.co.uk along with brands including ▶ CityJobs.com and ▶ eMedCareers.com
Business Insider 2015 $343 million	Founded in 2007 as a web-only publication in the United States. By 2015 it had seven additional editions in the United Kingdom, Australia, and Singapore 325 employees, 50% journalists	Post-acquisition, Business Insider was launched in three regions—Germany, the Nordics, and Poland
Immowelt 2015 €131 million	Third largest real estate portal in Germany	Subsequently, Axel Springer's existing real estate portal Immonet (second largest in Germany) was merged with Immowelt

Source: Compiled by author from public sources

19.5 Reducing Analog Footprint

By 2013, the market conditions for print media had deteriorated further, forcing the *Financial Times Deutschland* and the *Frankfurter Rundschau* to file for bankruptcy. Axel Springer's print offerings also continued to see a decline in readership, circulation, and advertising rates, leading Döpfner to sell many regional newspapers, including its founding dailies, the *Abendblatt* and the *Berliner Morgenpost*; two women's magazines; *Bild der Frau*, the largest women's weekly in Germany; and five television magazines, such as *Hörzu*, to Funke Mediengruppe for €920 million pre-tax. In the fiscal year 2012, these publications jointly generated €512.4 million accounting for about 15% of group revenues and contributed €94.8 million to group EBITDA (Sheahan 2013).

This move sparked sharp criticism both inside and outside the company. For example, when the board invited all employees to announce that they were going to sell these traditional newspapers and magazines, the executives were booed, while the workers' council was applauded when it harangued the managers. Schmid-Lossberg recalled:

» This was a tough meeting. People were crying. They were disappointed. They felt hurt and humiliated. But sadly this was the only way to go given what was happening with the markets.

Consolidation and cost-cutting followed, and about 1000 employees left Axel Springer to join the Funke Mediengruppe with effect from 1 May 2014.

19.5.1   Building Subscriber-Based Digital Brands

By selling the print newspapers at a time when they could still fetch favorable prices, nearly 10 times the EBITDA pre-tax multiple, Axel Springer could invest the proceeds into its digital projects, focusing on its *Bild* and *Die Welt* brands as well as on online classified property and recruitment advertising.

For example, in September 2012, it launched a paywall for the *Die Welt* website to become the first publisher to experiment with paid-content offerings (Miller 2013). The paywall offered an allowance of articles before charging for access. A year later, in June 2013, the company established a paywall for *Bild*—some of the tabloid's popular stories and other content on computers, tablets, and smartphones were made available only to paying customers. The new, pay-for-use area on the website was called BILDplus, providing three different packages: BILDplus Digital for €4.99 per month (web, smartphone and tablet apps), BILDplus Premium for €9.99 per month (web, smartphone and tablet apps, and e-paper editions), and BILDplus Komplett for €14.99 per month (web, smartphone and tablet apps, e-paper editions, and the printed newspaper).[11] For an extra €2.99, Bild also provided video highlights of Germany's Bundesliga national soccer league matches.

By 2015, the number of digital-only subscribers to *Bild* and *Die Welt*—about 384,000—was still dwarfed by their combined weekday print circulation of 3.8 million. Regardless, Döpfner referred to the digital subscriber figures as "a nice start" but not something "we can be happy with at all" (Slater 2015). Therefore, investments continued in the digital growth of these brands, mainly in hiring social media experts, video editors, and reporters who provided a higher inventory of video content. Döpfner stated:

» Content has not been a very attractive business in the digital world in the last 10 years. For this reason, our investment in digital content brands won't, in the next one or two years, be the most profitable investment with regards to immediate contribution to the bottom line. But they will be, in the next three to five years, the fastest-growing and the most value creating element in our portfolio.[12]

19.5.2   Turning Its Attention to Early-Stage Investments

In 2013, Axel Springer teamed up with Plug and Play Tech Center, a leading start-up investor and accelerator based in Silicon Valley, to form the Axel Springer Plug and Play Accelerator in Berlin to help budding start-ups in media-related fields. Three times a year, the company ran a 3-month program, providing start-ups with seed investment of €25,000, office space in Berlin, coaching, workshops, networking events, and more.[13] The accelerator received hundreds of applications, half of

---

11 "BILDplus launched successfully: 152,493 digital subscriptions after six months." Axel Springer Press Release, 11 December 2013.

12 Q&A with Mathias Döpfner at Q4 2014 Axel Springer SE Earnings Call – Final. 4 March 2015.

13 Axel Springer Plug and Play Accelerator. ► http://www.axelspringerplugandplay.com/about/, accessed 15 September 2015.

19

which were from outside Germany, mainly Eastern Europe and Israel. The program ended with the Demo Day, where start-ups pitched in front of an elite audience of local and international venture capital firms for additional funding. Axel Springer owned 5% of the company, and its rule was to continue investing into the companies only if they were able to get external lead investors, i.e., approval from the market. Within 2 years, the accelerator provided 56 promising digital entrepreneurs with opportunities through its network in Europe and the Plug and Play Tech Center in the United States.

Axel Springer frequently sought to leverage the start-up assets for mutual benefit. For example, Blogfoster—a marketplace for long tail advertising—had a large network of fashion bloggers in Germany, while Axel Springer had business relations with all of the big fashion brands, which were keen to advertise on blogs. Joerg Rheinboldt, CEO of Axel Springer Plug and Play, shared:

>> Before, Axel Springer had been unable to connect with the blogs in a frictionless way. Blogfoster built a self-service, self-optimizing platform for bloggers and small- to medium-sized websites where they could choose the kind of advertising (the banners, the style, quality) they preferred for their sites. By connecting with Axel Springer, Blogfoster gained speed and growth in ways that they could not have done otherwise.

In other cases, however, Axel Springer invested in companies working on emerging technologies without immediate commercial application. One such company, for example, was developing a bitcoin bookkeeping solution that could subsequently be used by Axel Springer's customers to pay for its products.

Separately, Axel Springer also invested in two incubators of early-stage companies: (i) Project A Ventures, which specialized in Internet, mobile, and online advertising technology start-ups, and (ii) Lakestar II, which specialized in disruptive, technology-enabled start-ups. When dealing with incubator start-ups, Axel Springer held a much higher equity stake and was very closely involved in the development of the new company.

19.5.3 Expanding Horizontal and Geographical Footprint

In December 2013 Axel Springer bought N24 Media GmbH, a German TV news channel, and placed it within the WELT Group. The goal was to combine the print and digital operations of *Die Welt* with N24's digital newsroom and video operations, creating one of Germany's largest multimedia companies. The editorial team of WELT Group was expanded to include the N24 digital editorial team. The new joint editorial team would produce journalistic content for both brands.

In 2015 Axel Springer made a bid for the *Financial Times* newspaper from Pearson PLC, but it lost out to Japan's Nikkei Inc., which paid £844 million for it. In the previous year, Axel Springer had also tried to take a majority stake in Forbes Media LLC, which was sold to Hong Kong's Whale Media Investments for more than $300 million. The company ultimately succeeded in acquiring English-language online news site *Business Insider* for $343 million in September 2015,

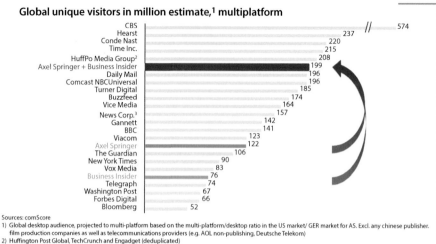

Global unique visitors in million estimate,[1] multiplatform

Sources: comScore
1) Global desktop audience, projected to multi-platform based on the multi-platform/desktop ratio in the US market/ GER market for AS. Excl. any chinese publisher. film production companies as well as telecommunications providers (e.g. AOL non-publishing, Deutsche Telekom)
2) Huffington Post Global, TechCrunch and Engadget (deduplicated)
3) Total News Corp. Online, Dow Jones & Company and Fox News

◘ Fig. 19.2 International Digital Publishers (July 2015). (Source: Based on Comscore via Axel Springer. "Axel Springer acquires Business Insider." Investor/Analyst Conference Call, New York, 29 September 2015)

which expanded Axel Springer's total worldwide digital audience to nearly 200 million, ranking it as the sixth largest digital publisher globally in terms of reach (*refer to* ◘ Fig. 19.2 *for the ranking*). In the same year, the company launched the European version of *Politico*, drawing on a joint venture with Washington-based political news outlet with the same name. It also went on to acquire majority stakes in New York-based social video news publisher *NowThis Media* (catering to 18- to 34-year-olds, producing short videos about trending stories) and Silicon Valley-based web magazine *Ozy*. These acquisitions were a vital part of Axel Springer's strategy to broaden its global reach, diversify its English-language offerings, and expand its commitment to innovative digital journalism.

Axel Springer further announced a partnership with Samsung launching *Upday*, an aggregated news content app for Galaxy devices featuring curated content for Samsung customers. *Upday* would offer access to a range of news content combining "need to know" information selected by a local market editorial team and "want to know information," an algorithm-based service tailored to customers' individual interests. *Upday* had 50 employees, with one-third on the editorial operations. Initially *Upday* was made available in Germany, and Poland followed by a full-service launch in more regions in early 2016.

19.6 Human Resource Transformation

As Axel Springer was transforming its strategy, Döpfner believed it was equally important to change the company culture at all levels. To help the top executives understand the possibilities offered by digital transformation, he wanted the top team to learn and adopt from Silicon Valley. In 2012, the editor-in-chief of *Bild*,

19

the chief marketing officer, and the founder of Idealo went together to Silicon Valley for a year to network and identify new trends and ideas to transform their businesses. A year later, the entire top management team of 70 went on an experiential trip to Silicon Valley. Schmid-Lossberg recalled:

> » We could see how companies like Apple, Google, and Airbnb work, what the atmosphere is, what they do, what could be adapted. But one could likewise see what should never be adapted because not everything in Silicon Valley is fitting to the European culture. So, people were proud of their own culture to some extent, but they opened up for shifting and adapting. At the end, everyone took home something. The trip also turned out to be a major team building exercise that helped to blur the boundaries between the print and the online executives. Everyone wore jeans and hoodies, flew in economy class, and stayed in a small hotel in the Tenderloin district of San Francisco, where they had to share rooms with each other, which led to endless discussions on who would share with whom. The entire experience turned out to be an eye opener and fun.

Subsequently, a follow-up fellowship program was established, so any employee with a creative idea could apply to go to Silicon Valley for about 6 weeks. On their return, they had to present their findings and tangible results to the board, which approved the next steps. As such, the company always had three people in Silicon Valley throughout the year.

To cascade the cultural change throughout the organization, Axel Springer embarked on an aggressive plan for educating its workforce on opportunities afforded by the digital transformation. For example, employees were able to attend "Media Powerhouse" a 2-day activity comprising four to five sessions each day on a variety of digital topics. A board member opened the forum, and presenters could belong to Axel Springer, its subsidiaries, or other affiliates. Employees could also follow the sessions on their laptops from their offices. They could also watch a variety of 2- to 3-minute informational videos, called Buzzword Decoders, to help them understand the ins and outs of the digital world. A senior executive explained:

> » If you ask people at our company's developmental stage now, do you know what a search engine optimizer does? Or what does cross media storytelling mean? Or what does paid services mean and how does it work in detail with the applications and the payment ways? People would not dare to say no, because thousands of people have clicked on these and I think it is a very easy way to get people on board.

In addition, Axel Springer rolled out a series of drop-in courses and events to enable employees to acquire digital knowledge and connect with others who were interested in the same topic. Some of these educational opportunities, such as the Early Bird Café, took place at breakfast and allowed employees to meet people from other business divisions. Others happened during lunch, such as the Learning Lunch series, where employees were able to learn about personal branding or how to use social media, or the Pizza CONNECTion, which brought 100 or more employees together to discuss topics, such as the future of soccer in the digital world with the discussion being led by the chief editor of *Sport Bild* and the manager of *Transfermarkt.de* (a portal where one could bet on transfers of players). Employees could also attend Best Practice Clubs which let employees with similar interests, such as 3D printing, to get together and discuss the opportunities afforded by new technologies.

Once an employee developed a new idea through these meetings, she or he could present it to Talent Campus, a group of 150 employees who specialized in digital acceleration. Once the idea received support, members of the Talent Campus worked on it for 2 days to develop it into a project proposal and presented it to the employee. If the proposal worked, then the employee took it up for further development and implementation.

As all of these changes were taking place, it was also important for Axel Springer to communicate its human resource transformation and reposition its employer brand in the hope of attracting more digitally savvy employees. This was done by launching video campaigns on YouTube which poked fun at Axel Springer's image among digitally minded potential employees and signaled openness to change. Other campaigns used humor to portray Axel Springer as successfully combining the cultural environment and freedom of start-ups with the advantages of a proven business model.

To accelerate these changes, Axel Springer also hired many new employees while letting go of some of the old ones. By 2015, only 3000 out of 15,023 employees hailed from the pre-digitization period, while the number of employees involved in printing declined from 3000 to 700.

19.7 Cultural Transformation

Despite the substantial human resource changes, much was to be done to transform Axel Springer's culture, and its top executives focused on three cultural challenges.

First, there was wide belief in the company that it should become less concerned with perfection and more obsessed with agility and speed to market, to be faster than any competitor. Schmid-Lossberg explained what this meant in terms of the corporate culture:

» How easy is it to kill an idea, to kill a project, if you demand perfection? In the digital world, we should dare to go out to our customers, to our internal customers, even to the board, with great ideas keeping in mind that time to market, time for presentation, is fast.

Second, it was important for the managers to change their focus from internal organization to outside environment to connect with experts outside the company and also with other departments to get fresh ideas and solve business issues. One senior executive commented:

» There may be disruptive business solutions in the market and you have to think radically in terms of products or employee competencies. Questioning your own methods daily is easily said but difficult to live up to.

19

Third, the senior management of Axel Springer believed that managers across the corporation should be less concerned with annual goal-setting and monitoring progress and instead emphasize inspiring the team and leading them with purpose to get them to become creative. It was equally important to managers to collaborate across the organization. To support these efforts, Axel Springer introduced Microsoft Office 365 and encouraged employees to share documents, find experts dispersed across the organization, and collaborate in joint project rooms. One high ranking executive opined:

» You cannot hold back ideas any longer. You have to share or you will be asked by your colleagues, "Why are you not contributing? Why are you not part of these discussions? Are you not interested?" So, there is pressure created from the bottom on management to position themselves and not to hide in a political environment.

19.8 Going Forward

Döpfner envisioned a future for Axel Springer that was international, English-speaking, and entirely digital. He stated:

» If modern journalism is not a real need of the society, a real request of the consumer and a real business, monetized by readers, advertising and new sources of revenue, if that is not the case, then forget about journalism. Then we cannot do it, and nobody else will do it. That's why it is so important to fight because you cannot tell me that great storytelling and information, independent, critical information, and great entertainment is not a need....I think it an everlasting desire of mankind, and it is up to us to define what we are doing for the digital consumer. (Doctor 2015)

Making this reality profitable, however, required answering numerous questions:

— *Globalization*: From 2010 to 2015, print circulation for Europe's newspaper industry had fallen a combined 21.3%, compared with 8.5% in the United States, according to the World Association of Newspapers and News Publishers. Publishers had pushed to expand readership on computers and mobile devices, but the potential was often limited as audiences in Europe were fragmented along national and linguistic borders. Further, the economic downturn in Europe was of concern, especially for a company intending to make big investments in new business areas. Should Axel Springer continue to look for some bigger acquisitions in diverse geographies to create a stronger global presence?

— *Monetizing the journalistic content*: The print business was being subsidized by the digital marketing and classified ads businesses which were driving revenue and EBITDA. As print losses continued and the digital-only prices were no more than a quarter of the print ones, overall revenue from content continued to decline. Recent developments, such as the growing importance of Facebook in delivering journalistic content, made these concerns even more salient (*refer to* ▶ Box 19.2 *for competitor information*). While Facebook enabled publishers to get between 70% and 100% of revenue from ads delivered against certain types of journalistic content, many in the industry were worried that Facebook would soon start eating into these revenues, shrinking the pool of available revenues even further. Thus, while the company believed that brand and content mattered, it was less clear whether revenue economics would work out and what steps should be taken to capture value.

Box 19.2   Competitors (2015)

In the digital world, publishers faced an ongoing distribution war with different types of players: producers of mobile devices, telecom companies, and large tech players. Individual news brands and news apps were no longer the primary point of contact for news; rather they were raw material, feeding into broader platforms. Media companies from Germany (including Axel Springer) and France met European officials with proposals to regulate Europe's digital economy. With Google attracting attention and ad revenue that once funneled to publishers, they were lobbying to strengthen copyright rules and limit Google's power. For example, in late 2014 Spain passed a robust law making compensation of publishers by search engines and aggregators compulsory. Axel Springer's competitors could be classified as:

- E-commerce players: such as ▶ Amazon.com's venture—Amazon Publishing—launched in 2009 providing tools for on-demand publishing to authors along with access to the Amazon store.
- Tech monopolies: such as Google, Yahoo, and Apple, which provided a unified user experience and owned the customers. The rift between publishers and Google became most public in April 2014 when in an open letter Döpfner criticized the tech company's dominance over many aspects of how people and companies used online services. He was especially opposed to Google's policy of showing snippets from several large German newspapers without paying for the right to post them. He stated, "Once you reach a certain market domination like Google, or hold a quasi-monopoly status, transparency and fairness in competition becomes more important; and, in the case of Google, the fairness of search criteria."[14] However, Google argued that it directed huge volumes of readers to news sites. In June 2015, Apple announced an improved app, News (replacing its Newsstand), a personalized magazine with a wide range of news stories and sources. The News app would algorithmically compile stories from the world's biggest media organizations. Apple partnered with several large publishers including CNN. Participating news outlets would keep 100% of the money they made by selling ads attached to their articles (Stelter 2015). But they would cede some control over the news reading environment to Apple.
- Online news providers: such as CNN, Reuters, and *The New York Times* which were providing free content.

19

---

14 Alain Elkann interview with Mathias Döpfner. 3 December 2014.

- Traditional competitors: such as Germany's Bertelsmann, the largest media conglomerate in Europe, which posted revenue of €17.1 billion and operating EBITDA of €2.49 billion in 2015 supported by over 117,000 employees in 50 countries worldwide. The Norwegian media group, Schibsted, was the owner of the largest newspapers in Sweden and Norway and a pioneer and a strong contender in the online classified advertisements space globally (ranked third after eBay and Nasper). In 2015 the company reported operating revenues of NOK15,117 million (€1574 million) and gross operating profit (EBITDA) of NOK2016 million (€210 million). It had diversified away from the printed newspaper business such that classified advertisement accounted for nearly 40% of revenues and 80% of operating profits (Mance 2016).

Source: Author

- *Analytics*: Axel Springer had to move toward connecting customer data from reading to shopping and build a data warehouse that would be fundamental to its future digital strategies. Döpfner explained:

» In the old world, three things [reader payment, local commerce in the form of display advertising and classifieds] were all encapsulated in one product, the paper. Now they are independent entities. So what's the linkage among digital reader revenue, digital ad revenue and digital classifieds? The link today isn't paper. It's data. And it is entirely up to us to figure out how to capture value from it. (Doctor 2015)

References

Boston, W. (2014, February 10). In Axel Springer's bid for Forbes, a German player steps out. *Wall Street Journal*.

Butcher, M. (2011, March 2). *Axel Springer acquires majority stake in kaufDa mobile coupons startup for $40 million*. www.techcruch.com.

Doctor, K. (2015, April 7). What are they thinking? The eight principles for transforming Axel Springer. *Politico Media*.

Mance, H. (2016, January 12). Schibsted digital drive rewrites script for squeezed press groups. *Financial Times*.

Miller, B. (2013, October 23). Axel Springer shares its 3 pillars of growth in the digital age as INMA European Conference begins. *Conference Blog*. http://www.inma.org.

Schultz, S., Steinmetz, V., & Teevs, C. (2013, July 26). Sell-off: Newspaper giant turns back on journalism. *Spiegel*.

Sheahan, M. (2013, July 25). Axel Springer sheds oldest print titles in $1.2 billion deal. *Reuters*.

Slater, J. (2015, August 14). Axel Springer CEO Mathias Doepfner steps boldly into the future of media. *The Globe and Mail*.

Stelter, B. (2015, June 9). Apple's "News" app stokes fear among journalists. *CNNMoney*.

Stone, B., & Silver, V. (2015, August 6). Google's $6 billion miscalculation on the EU. *Bloomberg*.

Weverbergh, R. *Strategy: how Axel Springer calculated and then bought its way to European digital dominance*. http://www.whiteboardmag.com.

Dallara Automobili: Transforming a Racing Legend

Contents

Giovanni Ravano, Maurizio Seletti, and Fabio Tremolada (IMD EMBA2016) prepared this case under the supervision of Benoît Leleux, S. Schmidheiny Professor of Entrepreneurship and Finance, and Tawfik Jelassi, Professor of Strategy and Technology Management, as a basis for class discussion rather than to illustrate either effective or ineffective handling of a business situation. Copyright © 2016 by *IMD—International Institute for Management Development*, Lausanne, Switzerland (▶ www.imd.org). No part of this publication may be reproduced, stored in a retrieval system, or transmitted in any form or by any means without the prior written permission of *IMD*.

© Springer Nature Switzerland AG 2020
T. Jelassi, F. J. Martínez-López, *Strategies for e-Business*, Classroom Companion: Business,
https://doi.org/10.1007/978-3-030-48950-2_20

20

■ **Introduction**

Italy, March 2016. Andrea Pontremoli looked proudly through his office windows at the new building now soaring over the headquarters of Dallara Automobili SpA in Varano de Melegari, a scenic village near Parma, Italy. It was almost 9 years to the day since he had left his position as CEO of IBM Italy and joined the adventure of one of the most peculiar race car manufacturers in the world. This had not been an entirely rational decision: He had simply not been able to resist the call of passion. His instincts had warned him that it would not be an easy ride. Change was already in progress at Dallara and more was on its way, sooner rather than later. It would be his job, with the help and support of Gian Paolo Dallara, the company's legendary founder and president, to steer this ship in the right direction and get it ready for more turbulent times to come. During his stay in office, he had already orchestrated a profound transformation of the company, but he was starting to wonder if Dallara Automobili was ready for the next batch of changes. In effect, Andrea and Gian Paolo had decided to invest most of the company's earnings into a new R&D center that would enable Dallara to compete with the best in carbon fiber technology and its applications.

Practically, a number of strategic questions occupied his mind: Should Dallara Automobili stick to its original vocation and focus on the car racing business? Should it fully embrace the transformation and become a new company? Moreover, a new venture in Formula 1 (F1) was about to start: Was Dallara really up for the game?

20.1 Gian Paolo Dallara: The Birth of a Giant

In 1959, upon graduating in aeronautical engineering from Milan's Politecnico University where he won the best "Student in Aerodynamics" award, Gian Paolo joined Ferrari to work on vehicle dynamics, handling, and wind tunnel tests. A talented engineer, Gian Paolo had a communicative passion for cars, but his attraction was really to the more competitive aspects of building the best racing car and winning races. A photo of Gian Paolo Dallara with Enzo Ferrari can be seen in ◘ Fig. 20.1. Over the following 11 years, he joined some of the world's most glamorous car racing manufacturers in a constant search for excellence, moving from Ferrari to Maserati, Lamborghini, and De Tomaso. His thirst for racing was never completely quenched, but the years proved invaluable in terms of learning. These top-end producers gave him the chance to hone his skills in car handling, dynamics, and aerodynamics techniques. He was also able to experience firsthand different angles of the car industry. While at Maserati, he was offered the chance to contribute to the company racing team, which included prestigious pilots such as Bruce McLaren and Roger Penske. In his own words, this is where he "really caught the racing bug once and for all."[1]

---

1   G. Schittone. *Dallara, It's a Beautiful Story."* Milan: Automobilia, 2011

■ **Fig. 20.1** Gian Paolo Dallara with Enzo Ferrari. (Source: Dallara website)

■ **Fig. 20.2** Gian Paolo Dallara (top left) with the team that built the Miura. Gian Paolo working at Maserati (left) and with Frank Williams (top right). (Source: ► www.dallara.it)

A few years later, while at Lamborghini, Gian Paolo had the opportunity to work on the company's "24 Hours of Le Mans" car racing project, which ultimately did not materialize. However, he was named chief engineer on the team that ultimately gave birth to the Lamborghini "Miura," which quickly became an iconic vehicle.

Finally, with De Tomaso, he designed his first F1 chassis for the Frank Williams Racing Team 1970 season. Unfortunately, Ford acquired De Tomaso and subsequently lost interest in F1, but the F1 experience proved life-defining for Gian Paolo. Photos of Gian Paolo Dallara can be seen in ■ Fig. 20.2.

By 1971 Gian Paolo had become an Italian reference in aerodynamics, car handling, and race chassis engineering. It was time for him to achieve his ultimate objective: Create his own company to fulfill his racing dream.

20

» In any other activity you never know if you're the best. But working with race cars, every Monday after the race, you realize if there's someone better than you are. Also you have the chance the next weekend to compete again and try to be the first. Nothing beats that in terms of feeling![2]

20.2 Dallara Automobili (1972–2007)

Dallara Automobili SpA was founded in 1972 in the hills near Parma, Italy. Racing was the company's sole focus. Gian Paolo had become convinced that success in racing cars was built on three fundamental pillars: the car structure and weight, the engine, and the pilot. Leaving aside the pilot's competence, the key performance drivers were the racing car's weight (about 35%), aerodynamics (about 50%), and engine power (about 15%). Dallara Automobili decided to focus its energy and resources on weight, aerodynamics, and handling since it could rely on other iconic Italian brands (such as Ferrari, Maserati, and Lamborghini) to deliver top-class engines.

As an engineer, Gian Paolo naturally organized his company's resources around the engineering process: concept design, studying aerodynamics and vehicle dynamics, prototype manufacturing, aerodynamic tests (mostly wind tunnel), final manufacturing, and track tests.

The process was inherently iterative, even though each cycle was long and expensive. Iterations were key to improvements, and Gian Paolo's unique talent laid in his ability to reduce their number. A picture of Dallara's core competencies within its development process can be seen in ◘ Fig. 20.3.

In the years that followed, the company pioneered the use of carbon fiber composites in racing cars (1978), establishing Dallara Automobili as a top innovator. This was a disruptive step that led to lighter, stiffer, and safer cars and to the first victory in the F3 Italian championship (1980). In 1985 Dallara was the first company to create a wind tunnel with moving belt for 25% scale models. A second experience in F1 (1988–1992 BMS Scuderia Italia) was mildly successful for Dallara but invaluable in terms of learning. It also proved to Gian Paolo that there was a need for niche technology suppliers to serve large manufacturers in search of visibility and recognition on the racing track.

By the mid-1990s, Dallara had established a solid name for itself but was still seeking new territories to roam. The company continued to refine its capabilities in pursuing innovation, opening up in 1995 its new wind tunnel for 50% scale models. Dallara expanded its geographic reach, providing chassis and complete racing cars for several championships around the world, often beating local competition in their captive markets, such as for the UK F3 series or IndyCar Series in the United States.

By 2000 the company had reached the pinnacle of car racing by following a simple recipe: win on the track. It had won every major title in Formula 3 (F3) and

---

2   G. P. Dallara, Interviewee, *President and Founder.* [Interview]. 29 October 2011

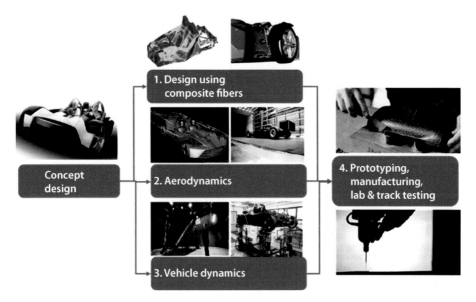

◘ Fig. 20.3   Dallara's core competencies within its development process. (Source: Dallara Automobili SpA)

won races in GP2 and IndyCar, not to mention in GT series. The company blossomed out of these racing successes. It was retained as the sole chassis supplier for GP2 in 2005 and for the IndyCar and GP3 series soon after.

In parallel, Dallara tried to capitalize on its unique engineering skills by providing specialized engineering services to car manufacturers. A flagship project was Volkswagen's commission in 2001 to create the carbon monocoque of what became the fastest and most exclusive sports car in the world, the Bugatti Veyron. It was the first "over one million dollars" and "over 400Km/h" production car ever (*refer to* ◘ Table 20.1 *for a glimpse of Dallara's achievements since 1972*). The Veyron proved a shocker to the automobile world, pioneering dozens of leading-edge technologies, many borrowed from the world of aeronautics, which later made their way into more common models.

20.3 The Succession Challenge

By 2007 Dallara Automobili was established as a brand in the industry, with 107 employees, no debts, revenues in excess of €30 million, and net profit margins of 12–15%, not to mention a pristine reputation in F3, GP2, and IndyCar. Strategically, it had made a deliberate choice to focus almost obsessively on its racing heritage and not to deviate from it, leveraging its unique expertise and know-how to participate in specific projects like the Bugatti Veyron, the Alfa Romeo 8C (2007), or the "track-day" KTM X-Bow (2007). It avoided moving into the adjacent "design" space to compete with the likes of Giugiaro, Bertone, or Pininfarina or to compete head to head with the likes of Lotus, McLaren, and Ferrari in producing luxury sports cars.

20

◨ Table 20.1   A Short History of Dallara Automobili SpA

1972		**Founded, first prototype SP1000**	
	1977	First competition car (Wolf Can Am)	
	1978	First F3 car	
	1980	First F3 Victory (Italian Championship)	
	1982	Lancia LC1 Chassis built by Dallara with an open cockpit, Engine is a 1425 cc straight-4 Lancia unit with a single turbocharger. Martini racing ran the program with Martini & Rossi colors	
	1983	Lancia LC2	
1984		**First wind tunnel with moving belt**	(25% of real size)
	1987	Dallara F3000	
	1988	F1 car Scuderia Italia Ford provided engines, Dallara provided the chassis	
	1991	New Dallara headquarters	
1993		**F393 and first F3 successes** Dallara designed and manufactured the chassis and the monocoque of this all-winning car	
	1995	New wind tunnel	(50% of real size)
	1996	Ferrari F50 GT1	
	1997	Dallara IR7	
1998		**First victory in the Indy car**	(and first Indy Car)
	1999	F1 project for Honda	(aborted)
	2000	Audi TT DTM	
2001		**Bugatti Veyron** Dallara provided chassis and aerodynamics studies and carbon fiber monocoques	
	2002	Formula Super Nissan	
	2004	Maserati MC12 project With Maserati and Ferrari, Dallara designs MC12 chassis	
	2004	Potential partnership with Midland to create an F1 car for 2006	(project abandoned)
2005		**Exclusive supply of GP2 cars**	
	2007	KTM X-Bow Dallara designed the chassis, including carbon fiber body, and first production run of cars	

◘ Table 20.1	(continued)		
2007		**Pontremoli joined Dallara Automobili as CEO and Investor**	
	2008	New wind tunnel	(60% of real size)
2008		**Exclusive supply of IndyCar series**	(fusion of Indy Car and Champ Car)
	2008	Licensed to run in the Grand Am race	
	2008	Supply of Volkswagen ADAC	
2009		**Exclusive supply of GP3**	
2010		**Creation of the driving simulator**	
	2010	F1 car Hispania Racing Team	
	2011	New GP2 cars generation	
2012		**Dallara IndyCar factory United States** Dallara IndyCar factory is a multifunctional center for research and development A twin simulator is currently installed in the IndyCar Factory	
	2013	New Generation of GP3 cars	
	2013	Alfa 4C Carbon fiber chassis provided by Dallara (as was the case with the 8C Competizione)	
	2014	Dallara Super Formula	
	2015	Renault RS01 Carbon body made by Dallara for a weight of less than 1100 kg and an engine over 500 hp., it can reach a top speed of over 300 km/h. The Renault Sport RS 01 will be part of the World Series by Renault in the Renault Sport Trophy, springboard for the GT and Endurance championships.	
2015		**Construction of a new R&D center**	(for industrialization of composites)

Sources: Dallara Automobili website (▶ www.dallara.it), accessed 4 December 2015; Dallara Wikipedia Page (▶ https://it.wikipedia.org/wiki/Dallara), accessed 30 November 2015

Yet, Gian Paolo was now 70 years old, and the question of "what next" was coming up. It was as much a question of succession as one of strategy. The company was dominating its market, except perhaps in F1, so growth was going to be an issue going forward. Moreover, the current business model was also showing its limits: The fast-paced changing cycles of the industry (typically 3–5 years), driven by innovation and changes in racing regulations, were producing unstable earning streams with violent peaks and troughs (*for financial details, refer to* ◘ Fig. 20.4).

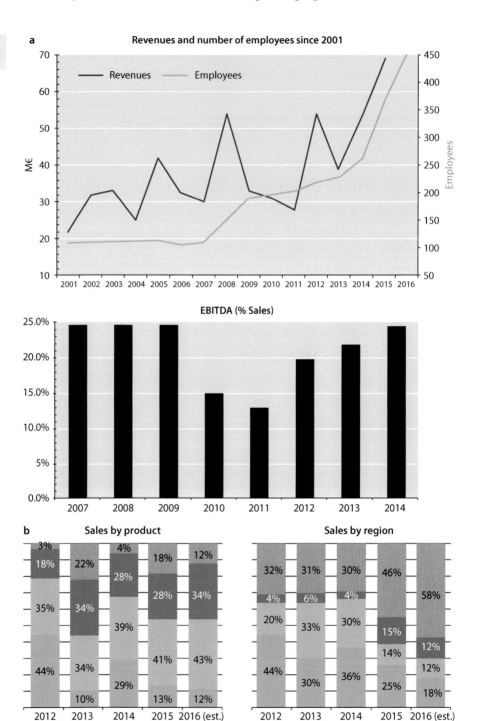

For years, Gian Paolo had been courting a close friend to succeed him. They came from the same valley in Northern Italy, their values were similar, and they both had a great deal of respect for and were dedicated to innovation. However, Andrea was also a successful executive as president and CEO of IBM Italy. It took quite a bit of cajoling to convince him to consider a career change, but the racing genetics could not be tamed for long. He resigned from IBM in October 2007 and joined Dallara Automobili as its CEO and minority investor.

Reactions to the appointment were muted. Many observers saw it as an impossible "marriage," but Gian Paolo begged to differ. He would continue to provide the engineering vision, the network, and an unparalleled understanding of the race industry. Andrea would bring his organizational and business expertise as well as his ability to rethink the company's innovation strategy for long-term survival.

20.4 Andrea Pontremoli's First Steps

As an outsider to the industry, Andrea had to rely on Gian Paolo's leadership for the racing part of the business. He focused his attention on matters that he could understand and improve quickly.

20.4.1 Culture Shift

Dallara Automobili's success resided in the visionary and innovative thinking of Gian Paolo and a handful of charismatic engineers. To ensure a sustainable future, Pontremoli knew he had to institutionalize this knowledge by organizing the wealth of experience of these few men and transferring it into a culture supported by clear processes. A photo of Andrea Pontremoli can be seen in ◘ Fig. 20.5. Furthermore, historically the focus had been on innovation and delivering the best possible product without much consideration for other aspects of the business. It was craftsmanship at its best and possibly at its worse!

◘ **Fig. 20.5** Andrea Pontremoli. (Source: Dallara website)

20

Andrea sought professionals with expertise in industrialization and organization, mostly automotive specialists familiar with defining and applying recognized industrial processes (Lean, Six Sigma, etc.). "Spare parts" was a typical example. These essential components often took a long time to manufacture and proved costly. Demand was erratic during off-peak years, so mistakes in inventory management could be costly. Prior to Andrea's arrival, the ability to standardize spare parts, reduce their number, and speed up the manufacturing process was at best a secondary consideration in the design phase. He turned this around quickly, making Lean Design a key program, even before Lean Manufacturing was initiated.

20.4.2 Process Modernization

Andrea also helped the company map and upgrade its processes and information flows. From his years at IBM, he understood how the computational aspect of the business could be a source of competitive advantage. The intent was clear: institutionalize the capabilities and improve and/or shorten the decision-making processes. Powerful systems and strong IT infrastructure would enable Dallara Automobili to do more with less, jump start steps and ultimately reduce costs. The ultimate goal was to turn Dallara from a product or service company into a true knowledge-based company.

Andrea introduced supercomputing power that permitted computational fluid dynamics (CFD), i.e., software-enabled simulation of the behavior of a moving object immersed in a fluid. CFD replicated the air flows around a vehicle in all conditions and could influence the design of a car from its early stages. CFD helped parameterize and frame the talents of Gian Paolo and a few disciples, turning their design skills into rigorous processes and parameters that could be transmitted to younger engineers. It also restricted the need to validate prototypes in the wind tunnel, which would only be used for final testing to confirm the correlation between simulation and reality (*refer to* ◘ Fig. 20.6 *for the full development process*). As a term of reference, while in 1992 a session in the tunnel would bring a 20% improvement in aerodynamics, today 20 sessions would only bring a 1% improvement, thus showing the importance of a simulation tool to reduce time and costs.[3]

20.4.3 Vision and Structure Changes

Andrea soon realized that the company structure would not support the needed changes, in particular leveraging the know-how to address external clients' needs. Historically, this had been done on an ad hoc basis and on specific projects such as the Bugatti Veyron or the Alfa Romeo 8C. The core business remained car racing.

---

3   A. Berzolla, Interviewee, *COO*. [Interview]. December 2015

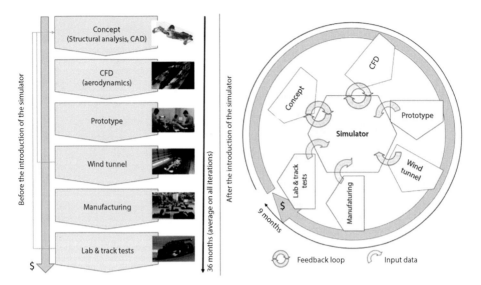

◘ Fig. 20.6 The car development process before and after the introduction of the simulator

It was time to realign the structure with the new company vision, which was going to be built on two solid pillars.

First, it was critical to capitalize on Dallara Automobili's existing capabilities—which included aerodynamics, vehicle dynamics, car design, and prototyping as well as carbon fiber composites—and to expand its engineering services to the mainstream car segment. The main goal was to improve revenue stability for the years when racing car demand was low (typically between two cycles of regulatory changes). A photo of Andrea Pontremoli and Gian Paolo Dallara can be seen in ◘ Fig. 20.7.

Second, it was equally essential to maintain its technological leadership in areas that were critical to succeed in car racing, mostly weight control, aerodynamics, and vehicle dynamics/handling. Both pillars would require continuous innovation, which could be done by taking up "uncomfortable" challenges that did not necessarily come from Dallara's quasi-monopolistic status in the competitions.

Andrea and Gian Paolo redesigned the company structure to reflect the new vision. They launched a matrix organization whereby Dallara Automobili was split into two formal divisions (Car Racing and Engineering Services). These intersected on transversal specialized resources, which would be allocated to either division on a need basis. Each division would independently source the competences and people required according to project specifications.

20.4.4 Network Externalities: Toward a Cluster Economy

Gian Paolo contributed to building a unique network of specialized manufacturers. However, the new vision also required revamping and upgrading the network to meet the latest needs. In its existing iteration, the system was really a network of

20

▣ **Fig. 20.7**   Andrea Pontremoli (left) and Gian Paolo Dallara (right) at the Geneva motor show in 2015. (Source: Dallara website)

craftsmen specialized in a particular component. Inevitably, as Andrea modernized the processes, the production cycles and the know-how concerning the product engineering or the "cluster" would have to change. Andrea had recognized early on the value of a cluster economy model for small companies (*refer to* ▣ Fig. 20.8 *for an illustration of the cluster economy model in the Motor Valleys around the London Oxford Airport in the UK*). Not dissimilar to what happened in Silicon Valley for the hi-tech sector, he deeply believed in the value of an extremely connected pool of people and know-hows covering all aspects of the motorsports and car racing industry. This cluster would constantly raise the bar on innovation through the openly competitive nature of the network itself. How else could a small company of 100 or so employees nourish the innovation required to offer engineering services to brands like Ferrari or Volkswagen?

20.5 Innovation-Driven Change

In 2007 the Fédération Internationale de l'Automobile (FIA), the organization created to represent the interests of motors sports, unwittingly brought about an important industry pivot. That year, in an effort to slash F1 teams' spiralling costs, the FIA began imposing severe testing restrictions, and over the following two seasons, it implemented even harsher testing restrictions. The FIA's decisions pushed all F1 teams to invest in driving simulators in order to circumvent track testing restrictions.

20.5.1 Simulator to the Rescue

Dallara was not involved at all in F1, but Ferrari, as a long-standing partner, convinced it to enter the simulator journey to reduce costs across the board. The project thus started as a joint effort between Dallara and Ferrari, which contracted

◘ Fig. 20.8 The Motor Valleys and the cluster economy model. (Source: Oxford Airport Website; Motorvalley website. ► http://www.motorvalley.com/motor-valley)

20

Moog Industrial Group to provide the motion system, the dome, and the control center for a leading-edge F1 simulator. A photo of Dallara and the Simulator can be seen in 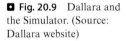 Fig. 20.9.

Simulators were not really a novelty. Major automotive and aerospace manufacturers had been using them for years to test vehicles and to train pilots. But Dallara's approach was more ambitious. It aimed to use the simulators to help develop new cars and improve time to market by reducing the prototyping steps. While Ferrari was satisfied with giving its F1 pilots a sophisticated tool to develop their skills, Dallara was more interested in the software used to run tests, with the goal of giving its engineers or those of its clients a tool to test their ideas (*refer to* ☐ Fig. 20.10 *for more details*). Clearly, the simulator was an essential enabler of Dallara's new vision, with innovation (and cost reductions) at its core.

20.5.2 Designing the Beast

IBM's experience came in handy for the development of the new simulator. Dallara Automobili opted for an open-source platform rather than a proprietary system like Ferrari's. The design brief was to build a simulator to allow pilots to practice and engineers to test mathematical hypotheses before they became physical prototypes, to test specific components, whether existing or not in a given car setting, and to experiment with handling setups for different tracks and weather conditions.

The development did not go smoothly. Dallara engineers were race car specialists, not IBM IT developers. While they relished a good scientific challenge, this was way beyond their capabilities. After scratching their heads for a while, they pretty much gave up on the software redesign.

Not easily discouraged by a setback, Andrea recognized the constraints and hired ten freshly minted graduates from a select IT engineering program. They had

☐ **Fig. 20.9**   Dallara and the Simulator. (Source: Dallara website)

no industry experience but plenty of enthusiasm for the task at hand. As he recalled in an interview[4]:

» They didn't know that it was impossible and therefore they just did.

The simulator ultimately went live in the middle of 2010.

20.5.3 Moving the Lines

The simulator proved its value when it came to innovation. Dallara's standard loop process of concept, design, prototype, test, and iteration rapidly became obsolete. The simulator allowed the team to squeeze the concept-design-test part of the cycle into a single stage, drastically reducing the number of prototypes produced and shrinking the time to market for a new vehicle from 3 years to 9 months (*refer to*  Fig. 20.10 *for the impact of the simulator on Dallara's development process*).

Expensive physical prototyping and wind tunnel tests quickly became a sort of final validation of what had been developed and tested virtually and fine-tuning only. The new approach proved extremely efficient, fast, and cost-effective. As Andrea stated:

» The simulator allowed Dallara Automobili to make mistakes faster, improving dramatically the learning curve.[5]

☉ Fig. 20.10   Dallara simulator

4   A. Pontremoli, Interviewee, *CEO*. [Interview]. 7 November 2015
5   A. Pontremoli, Interviewee, *CEO*. [Interview]. 7 November 2015

20

At the time the simulator was introduced in 2010, approximately 50% of the company's workforce was involved in producing prototypes. This ratio fell dramatically with the new approach.

20.5.4 New Tools, New Organization... New Strategy?

While the simulator dramatically affected Dallara's processes, shortening cycles and lowering costs, it also generated new opportunities that warranted a rethink of the company. Gian Paolo and Andrea discovered that the business model they had imagined around the simulator was not the only feasible one. As the company started to accumulate data and precise mathematical models of cars, components, and tracks, opportunities emerged to sell that knowledge to OEMs to test specific components, existing or not, in diverse road conditions and stresses. A suspension manufacturer could now test its new concept on various tracks and in different weather conditions for thousands of kilometers before even building a physical prototype of the new suspension. The new product's 3D design file could be uploaded onto a USB drive, plugged into the simulator, tested for hours, and improved rapidly. Cost and time savings were huge.

This opened up a completely new direction for Dallara Automobili, essentially as a sophisticated provider of simulation testing services. The underlying business segment was very much untapped (*refer to* ◘ Fig. 20.11 *for how McLaren changed its business model and role in the industry along similar lines*).

20.5.5 Leading the Local Cluster

With a firm belief that a strong local network makes all the difference, Andrea actively contributed to building a stronger Motor Valley cluster in Italy. He invested selectively in the industrial tissue of the region and pushed the boundaries a bit further. The company promoted the development of the required skills through educational programs and event sponsorships that attracted talents to the region. The region itself as well as the new generations recruited by the company would

◘ **Fig. 20.11**   The McLaren digital transformation

eventually substitute the founder's talent with organizational know-how. In Andrea's words, the idea behind this is simple:

» They can clone your product but not the territory (…). It's better to have visibility on our competitive environment rather than wait for some external player to disrupt it without us even noticing. Our competitors are not brands but other territories. Actually only one: the region around Oxfordshire in the UK, where there's Lotus, Catheram, McLaren, Williams, Mercedes, Red Bull, Force India and many others.[6]

(*Refer to* ◘ Fig. 20.8 *for the competitive landscape.*)

20.5.6 Global Dominance

While building the new income streams, Dallara Automobili expanded its traditional business too, capitalizing on the upgraded capabilities and the competitive advantage of the simulator.

20.5.6.1 Indianapolis Motor Valley

In 2012 a new 9500 m^2 factory opened in Indiana (United States) as a joint venture between Dallara and the State-funded IndyCar Experience. Indy cars were manufactured there, and visitors could indulge in an "edutainment" center where two-seater racing cars can lap the world-famous Indianapolis circuit with a passenger.[7]

The facility, strongly backed by the State of Indiana, not only supported the racing industry but also proved to be a development center around which a new Motor Valley-like ecosystem was assembling. Ultimately, the Indiana Governor's aim was to promote and improve the overall economy of the State. A second simulator was installed within the factory, a perfect twin of the original one in Italy.

20.5.6.2 Super Formula

A recent request to improve a popular existing racing car championship in Japan, previously known as Formula Nippon and now promoted to Super Formula, was met in 9 months as a digitally simulated new vehicle. The demand was to raise performance while relying on a smaller and less powerful engine and introducing electrically assisted steering to meet the feebler body strength of Japanese pilots. A pilot was sent down to Italy to test the car in the simulator. The pilot drove in sequence the digital renditions of both the original and the new vehicle, improving his typical lap time in the former stage by a full second in the latter. This proved the quality of the simulation and the value of the new car design. Dallara received the mandate to build the car prototype.[8]

---

6   A. Pontremoli, Interviewee, *CEO*. [Interview]. 7 November 2015
7   Dallara Automobili Website. ► www.dallara.it (accessed 4 December 2015)
8   A. Pontremoli, Interviewee, *CEO*. Interview. 7 November 2015

20

❑ **Fig. 20.12**   Haas F1 2016 car chassis, built by Dallara in Italy. (Source: Michael Potts. M. Potts on Flickr, taken at 2016 winter testing in Barcelona, Creative Commons license CC BY-SA 2.0)

20.5.6.3 **Formula E**

Dallara was selected as the supplier of the carbon fiber monocoque chassis of the Spark-Renault SRT 01E, the first electric car to be homologated by the FIA and built by the French Spark Racing Technologies. In the 2014/2015 Formula E Season, all racing teams retained the Dallara chassis. Virtual models of the electrical drivetrain and other components were also run through the simulator to evaluate their potential performance on the track.

20.5.6.4 **Formula One**

In 2016, Dallara returned to the F1 Circus with the newly formed Haas Racing Team. In an interview, Andrea hinted to the fact that the car would benefit from extensive work on the simulator.[9] A photo of Haas F1 2016 car chassis can be seen in ❑ Fig. 20.12.

20.6 **The Future**

By 2016 Dallara Automobili employed over 380 employees, and its revenues approached €70 million. Since 2007 it had tripled the number of employees and doubled its sales, while the headcount in production had barely increased.[10] Its track record remained impressive, even though it had never raced directly as a proprietary team. The company was pushing along three distinct areas:

— *Engineering services*: The new capabilities generated a fresh stream of revenues, with new opportunities beyond the car racing industry. OEMs were now both a new category of clients and a great learning opportunity.
— *Carbon fiber R&D*: It built a new facility next to its headquarters to further develop its industry-leading carbon fiber capabilities. It was due to be completed in 2016 at a cost of over €10 million. The new center would truly move composites manufacturing from craftsmanship to an industrial level. Carbon fiber and other composites were in high demand in the automotive and transportation industries.

---

9   A. Pontremoli, Interviewee, *CEO*. Interview. 7 November 2015
10   A. Pontremoli, Interviewee, *CEO*. Interview. 7 November 2015

- *F1 again*: With Team Haas, Dallara was again challenged to provide innovative solutions to an F1 contender. It looked promising, having already collected a few points during the first races of the 2016 season.

All three paths were rich in promises and could take the company into new territories. However, Andrea and Gian Paolo still had many questions to resolve. Were these directions compatible and leveraging each other? As a small firm, resources were still constrained and choices had to be made to balance opportunities and resources. What would this mean for Dallara's overall strategy? Was this significantly changing the company's profile? Was it time to revisit the business model and envision new approaches for the future? Finally, the digital transformation brought about by the simulator venture was still in its infancy, yet the world was abuzz with "big data" dreams. Should Dallara embrace this movement and try to capitalize on it? If so, how could this be done?

Many thoughts and no lack of excitement for years to come…

Cluster economies generally arise around three main elements:

- An infrastructure that is favorable to a certain business
- A suitable culture
- An economic/know-how opportunity

In the case of the UK Motorsport Valley, after WWII, a lot of aerospace engineers found themselves with unused skills for building fast, lightweight vehicles, as well as unused flat airfields (like Silverstone) where such vehicles could be tested and raced. With the arrival of TV and satellite came the publicly available show, which attracted even more engineers and small companies to the region. "If you were serious about motor racing, you had to be in that area, so teams and suppliers started to move there to form a hub of industry," said BBC F1 technical analyst Gary Anderson.

Being in the proximity of universities (Cranfield and Oxford) also meant a continuous fresh supply of talents, and the industry eventually became large enough to push schools to integrate specific courses dedicated to motor sports. According to a 2013 review of the Motorsport Industry Association, the UK Motorsport Valley employed more than 41,000 people in over 4300 companies for overall revenues of approx. £9 billion.[11]

The origins of the Italian Motor Valley were much older with a presence already in the early 1900s of companies like Bugatti. Maserati and Ferrari established their companies in the 1920s. Interestingly the area has integrated another cultural element that is typically Italian, tourism. This is becoming an important source of revenue for the region with "food-wine-motor" tourist packages promoted by the region and the local operators.[12]

---

11 Motorsport Industry Association, "Some Highlights of the 2013 Review of the Motorsport Valley Business Cluster," MIA, 2013
12 Motorsport Industry Association, "Some Highlights of the 2013 Review of the Motorsport Valley Business Cluster," MIA, 2013

20

Even though it is hard to compare two clusters in terms of figures (as there are multiple ways of computing the industry), they look extremely similar, including in terms of size. Ferrari alone generates worldwide revenues of €2.76 billion, just as much as Maserati, while Lamborghini's turnover increased to €629 million.[13]

The simulator software is based on the concurrent real-time system based on RedHawk Linux® and DYMOLA physical modeling tool open platforms; it can handle up to 65,000 variables relating to the physics of the car, the pilot, the track, the weather conditions, etc. The finer the tuning of the parameters, the more it allows Dallara's engineers to run quasi-perfect experiments. It is possible to keep the same set of variables and change only one single feature to see how it impacts the car performance. This is not possible in the real world. Imagine a pilot testing two sets of tires on two different laps. From one lap to the other, there are so many things that can change beyond the tires (temperature, asphalt conditions, side wind, humidity, and so on), and each of them will impact the overall performance. In the virtual world of the simulator, it is possible to isolate the impact of a single variable or component on the overall car performance. This allows R&D on a specific part to move quickly toward production.

Development using the simulator is done in two phases. First the mathematical models are benchmarked against actual values collected from real races and the inputs of the drivers (Driver-in-loop, an actual driver behavior influences the outcomes of the simulation in ways that are not possible to simulate by computer). Once the driver obtains the same results in the virtual vehicle as in the real one, the models are validated, and it is possible to start tweaking them (a particular component for instance) to improve their performances (hardware-in-the-loop, a virtual vehicle is simulated to test an actual specific subcomponent, like an ECU).

As the simulator shows such improvements, the revised component can be sent to production and tested in real life.

Another important aspect of being capable of simulating new conditions is that the output of the simulation can be used, in quasi real time, to influence the outcome of ongoing races.

The driving simulator control room (top) at Dallara Automobili's headquarters and a partial view of a simulation as seen by the driver (left) (Source: *Dallara Magazine* n°27).

McLaren has been known for its obsession in F1 for measuring parameters and collecting data. It makes the telemetry systems for all its F1 competitors, along with the computerized engine control units for F1, IndyCar, and Nascar. When a McLaren car is on the track, more than 120 sensors transmit a torrent of information on tire pressure, torque, temperature, and downforce. During the race season, McLaren engineers run thousands of simulations, testing components, settings, and strategies. Once a race starts, the simulation continues and is fed with data from the track. The predictive power of the simulating software is used to adapt the race strategy in quasi real time: pit stops, decisions on tires, or fuel quantities are

---

13   FCA Group, "Annual Report 2014," FCA Group, 2014; VW Group, "Annual Report 2014," VW Group, 2014

all suggested by the system, from McLaren headquarters to wherever in the world the race is taking place.

The company decided that the highly specialized expertise it developed in data analysis, simulation, and what it calls "decision support" was something that businesses outside the world of racing would profit from and pay for. Five years ago, McLaren launched a consulting firm called McLaren Applied Technologies (MAT), under the leadership of Geoff McGrath, an engineer who started his career in the oil and gas industry and later moved into telecommunications.[14] Among MAT's various customers, Heathrow Airport used its software to manage air traffic and runway schedules, taking into account real-time weather condition data, delays, traffic, etc. Specialized,[15] the North American bikes manufacturer, relied on MAT's experience to turn the machine into a high-end bike simulator, encoding within the mathematical model the bike rider's characteristics which, with the rider representing up to ten times the weight of the bike itself, dramatically influence the final performance.[16]

---

14 J. Medeiros, "How McLaren uses F1 tech to help global companies reinvent themselves," Wired UK, 7 July 2015.
15 See Specialized's company website: ▶ https://www.specialized.com/us/en.
16 D. Bennet, "What Can the McLaren Racing Team Teach the Rest of Us?," Bloomberg Businessweek, 2 October 2014.

DBS Transformation (a): Becoming a World-Class Multinational Bank

Contents

Researcher PC Abraham prepared this case under the supervision of Professor Seán Meehan as a basis for class discussion rather than to illustrate either effective or ineffective handling of a business situation (Copyright © 2017 by IMD – *International Institute for Management Development*, Lausanne, Switzerland (▶ www.imd.org)). No part of this publication may be reproduced, stored in a retrieval system, or transmitted in any form or by any means without the prior written permission of *IMD*.

© Springer Nature Switzerland AG 2020
T. Jelassi, F. J. Martínez-López, *Strategies for e-Business*, Classroom Companion: Business, https://doi.org/10.1007/978-3-030-48950-2_21

21

■ Introduction

1 August 2013. Piyush Gupta, CEO of DBS, had just announced that the bank was walking away from its bid to acquire Indonesia's Bank Danamon. This was a major setback to the bank's plans to expand its presence in Asia's growth markets.

Looking back, however, he was still satisfied with the results of the transformation he had initiated on joining the bank in November 2009. A lot had been achieved and a lot remained to be done. The once underperforming bank was now performing well. Progress had been made on all three central objectives—getting strategic alignment, fixing the plumbing (ensuring the operational and technological architectures supported effective and efficient management decision making), and getting the culture right. The bank had aligned around the goal of being the Asian bank of choice, was about two-thirds of the way toward fixing operations and technology issues, and was about one-third of the way along in terms of changing its culture. With DBS's transformation journey well underway, it was this, rather than the setback to the expansion plans that Gupta chose to focus on now.

DBS had not materially increased its presence in the small and medium-sized enterprise (SME) or mass affluent markets in the Asian growth markets of China, India, and Indonesia, where DBS already had a footprint. With the high costs, regulatory uncertainty, and scarcity of suitable targets, acquisitions might no longer be a viable path to growth. He felt it was time to reconsider the bank's overseas growth strategy.

He was also concerned by the growing threat fintechs represented. They were beginning to compete with banks to deliver many of the same services without expensive branch networks or legacy technology issues. He believed they would be formidable competitors within 5–10 years, and doing nothing in the face of that development could be fatal. DBS needed to assess its position against the rising fintech tide and reflect this in its strategy.

DBS's executive board was meeting later that day to discuss these two key questions. Making the right call on these issues would be critical to the bank's future.

21.1 Company Background

DBS Bank was set up as the Development Bank of Singapore by the government in 1968 to provide loans and financial assistance to industries promoted by the Economic Development Board. It became Singapore's dominant bank in November 1998 when it acquired POSB Bank (the Post Office Savings Bank), which had a strong consumer banking franchise. The bank began expanding internationally in the late 1990s. It made two large acquisitions in Hong Kong: Kwong On Bank in 1999 and Dao Heng Bank in 2001—and acquired Bowa Bank in Taiwan in 2008. It also focused on growing its operations in China, India, and Indonesia. It changed its name to DBS Bank in 2003 to reflect its growing international presence. By 2009, the bank's international operations accounted for 40% of its income and 43% of its net profit. Hong Kong accounted for about half of this, and the bank's presence in other international markets was small (refer to ◻ Table 21.1 and ◻ Fig. 21.1).

DBS was run by civil servants until mid-1998, when John Olds joined as CEO from JP Morgan. Between 1998 and 2009, the bank was led by four CEOs—mainly investment bankers—and therefore run more like an investment bank than a commercial bank. Observers felt this explained a lack of strategic consistency and clarity and accounted for some now questionable moves such as its expansion into the Middle East and the West Coast of the United States. In November 2009, Morgan Stanley characterized the 2000–2009 period as DBS's lost decade, highlighting underperformance in Hong Kong, limited growth options in South and Southeast Asia, below market returns compared to its Singaporean peers, poor risk management, and perceived weak service and brand.

◻ **Table 21.1** Company financials[a]

	2009	2010	2011	2012
Balance sheet (S$ billion)				
Total assets	258.6	283.7	340.8	353.0
Customer loans	130.6	152.1	194.7	210.5
Total liabilities	229.1	250.6	307.8	317.0
Customer deposits	183.4	193.7	225.3	242.9
Total shareholders' funds	25.4	26.6	28.8	31.6
Income statement (S$ billion)				
Total income	6.60	7.07	7.63	8.06
Profit before tax	2.54	3.33	3.73	4.16
Net Profit	2.04	1.63	3.04	3.81
Financial ratios (%)				
Net interest margin	2.02	1.84	1.77	1.70
Cost to income ratio	39.4	41.4	43.3	44.8
Return on assets	0.79	0.60	0.97	1.10
Return on shareholders' funds	8.4	6.3	11.0	12.7
Loan to deposit ratio	71.2	78.5	86.4	86.7
Non-performing loan rate	2.9	1.9	1.3	1.2

Source: DBS Annual Reports
[a]US$1 = S$1.22 (31.12.2012)

PERFORMANCE BY MARKETS

OVERALL STRATEGY
Continue to grow in six key markets of
Singapore, Hong Kong, China, Taiwan,
Indonesia and India.

Korea
1 branch

China
29 branches
1 representative office

Japan
1 branch

India
12 branches

Hong Kong
55 branches

Taiwan
41 branches

Macau
1 branch

Philippines
1 representative office

Thailand
1 representative office

Vietnam
1 branch
1 representative office

Malaysia
1 branch
1 representative office

Singapore
89 branches

Indonesia
43 branches

As of 31 December 2012
Branches include sub-branches and centres.
DBS also has branches and outlets in London, Los Angles, Dubai and
a representative office licence in Myanmar. In addition, DBS Vickers has
offices in Singapore, Hong Kong, Indonesia, Thailand, UK and US.

Over

250

Branches across Asia

◘ **Fig. 21.1**   DBS's presence in Asia. (Source: DBS 2012 Annual Report)

Piyush Gupta joined DBS as its CEO in November 2009. Over 27 years with Citibank, he held various senior management roles across Citi's corporate and consumer banking businesses, including Head of Strategic Planning for Emerging Markets and Regional Director for Global Transaction Services for Asia Pacific and, immediately prior to joining DBS, was CEO for Southeast Asia, Australia, and New Zealand.

21.2 DBS in 2009

Gupta was energized by the opportunity to revive DBS and transform it into a world-class multinational bank. DBS was not achieving its full potential. Market share erosion at home and lack of progress and presence in overseas markets, apart from Hong Kong, were symptoms of greater challenges. DBS, in 2009, lacked a compelling strategy, an effective and efficient operational architecture, and a performance culture. This could be changed.

The bank's operational architecture had been negatively impacted by a succession of overseas growth initiatives—its five overseas markets operated as independent silos. DBS was, in effect, multiple banks with multiple cultures, policies, and systems. Its leaders, however, realized changing this would be a significant challenge. Operations and technology were:

> **Definition**
>
> …in a disastrous state, with no real metrics, no clear targets of where you wanted to be, and zero aspirations around customer service. —Dave Gledhill, Head of Group Technology and Operations

This was costly. Wait times at the branches and call centers grew longer and ATMs frequently ran out of cash. Earlier efforts to fix operations had failed. When Dave Gledhill joined in 2008, DBS was already 3 years into a 2-year core banking refresh with an estimated further 3 years to go and costs running to S$300 million[1]—50% over budget. It was consuming all the group's resources and blocking progress on everything else. Gledhill also felt that the bank did not have world-class resilience and had weak disaster recovery capabilities.

Independent of any decisions about DBS's future direction and strategy, these complex operational issues would need to be resolved. Gupta foresaw a lot of change and wondered whether the organization was up to the challenges this would bring. On the positive side, he perceived that his new DBS colleagues were highly collaborative. However, even though professional bankers had run DBS for more than a decade, he worried that its culture remained bureaucratic and risk averse:

> **Definition**
>
> Things went up to committees who forwarded them to [other] committees. —Piyush Gupta, DBS CEO

Based on his 27 years at Citibank, Gupta felt each of these challenges could be addressed and that there was enough low-hanging fruit to be able to significantly improve the bank's performance. Now he needed to create consensus around a transformational program.

---

1 US$1 = S$1.44 (31.12.2008).

21.3   Turning DBS into a World-Class Multinational Bank

21.3.1   The Strategic Vision

In early 2010, Gupta led a 3-day offsite for the bank's management committee to determine what its strategy should be. The group quickly agreed on the key elements, which were formalized and communicated through the "DBS House."

The overarching goal was to make DBS the Asian bank of choice for a rising Asia. It would have a presence in Southeast Asia, Greater China, and South Asia and be the only Asian bank in a set of multinationals including HSBC, Standard Chartered, and Citibank serving the region. It would have comparable presence but be much more agile.

DBS would continue to be a universal bank in Singapore while focusing on three lines of business outside Singapore: corporate, SME, and affluent banking. On the corporate side, DBS would cross-sell to existing clients. To make inroads with SMEs and the mass affluent, it would build on the capabilities of the existing Singapore- and Hong Kong-based teams.

The colleagues prioritized putting in place three enablers for the new strategy. The strategy would put customers at the heart of the banking experience—an area that management were well aware was a challenge. As it looked internally, it would reform management processes, performance orientation, and culture. In addition, it would support both with a stable, reliable, unified technology, and infrastructure.

The new strategy led directly to DBS exiting the retail mass market outside Singapore—given regulatory constraints and funding and infrastructure costs, it concluded that a presence in this market was impossible to justify. It also prompted the private banking group to rethink how best to access the vast wealth "hidden" in the consumer banking division. It placed wealth management within consumer banking and developed a single platform to serve all affluent customers. Finally, the Institutional Banking Group developed its trade finance and cash management capabilities to take advantage of underserved Singaporean businesses, and the space created as Continental European banks reduced their exposure to Asia[2] and the opening up of China from 2010 onward (trade account and Renminbi).

21.3.2   An Efficient and Effective Operational Architecture

Soon after joining the bank in 2008, Gledhill killed the core banking refresh in Singapore and Hong Kong. By then, there were quicker and cheaper alternatives to fix the original problems and support the rollout of the bank's priorities. Instead he refocused its technology resources on achieving consistency of systems and processes across the bank (refer to ◘ Fig. 21.2). The technology project became one

---

2   Total lending dropping from a peak of $455 billion in June 2008 to $356 billion by the end of 2011.

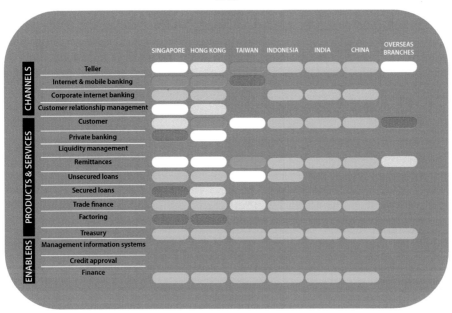

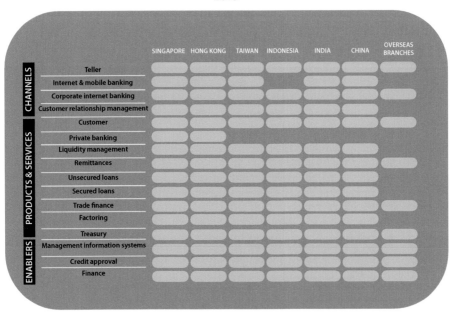

■ Fig. 21.2 DBS technology – 2009 versus 2013. (Source: Company information)

that supported business transformation and enabled customer service improvements and performance management.

Gledhill set two goals for operations—to either eliminate control issues or improve them by 50% and to improve productivity by reducing the time spent on operations by a million hours. It eventually exceeded both of these goals comfortably. He made a conscious decision not to set goals for cutting costs by a given percentage:

> **Definition**
>
> People try to explain why it does not apply to them, or they cut the important people, who can do change and make improvements. You are left with a crappy process and you can't improve because you fired all the people that could improve it. Instead, we set positive, aspirational goals that everyone could contribute to and celebrated the hell out of everything that we achieved. —Dave Gledhill, Head of Group Technology and Operations

---

At the outset, reliable performance measurement was impossible, as there were no metrics or data. This was resolved by putting over a thousand instrumentation and measurement points in place to provide customer performance data. With this information, the operations team used a dashboard/heat-map to identify and address problem areas. It was, however, imperative to rethink how exactly it got to workable solutions because the legacy way of working was ineffective:

> **Definition**
>
> If an operations person wanted to change something, they talked to control who sent them to compliance, who told them to talk to audit who sent them to legal. You got the runaround because no one would make a decision. —Dave Gledhill, Head of Group Technology and Operations

---

To overcome this, Gledhill implemented 5-day Process Improvement Events (PIEs) to address priority challenges. Colleagues capable of addressing all the issues and making decisions about the way forward came together to create a cross-functional team. On day 1, they mapped the current state of the process. On day 2, they decided what the future state would look like. On day 3, they presented the proposed new process to the key stakeholders, who were required to make an immediate decision on the changes required. The remaining 2 days were used to document the future state of the process and prepare an action plan for getting there. Perhaps the most striking example of how these PIEs became central to the way DBS implemented its new strategy was its move to put customers at the heart of the banking experience.

Harnessing the existing hunger to enhance the customer experience, Gupta established and chaired the Customer Experience Council to drive, support, and oversee transformation efforts. It was here that the bank set a goal of reducing the number of customer hours by 100 million. Customer hours measured the length of time that a customer had to wait for something—for example, to get a credit card. Using PIEs, it took out 250 million customer hours over 4 years. As transformation ramped up, the bank was running around 50 PIEs annually.

Many of these PIEs were motivated by RED, which originated from the strategy off-site and was developed and refined over the subsequent months, during which they benefited from inputs of the Singapore Airlines service quality team. Colleagues felt that, as a goal, DBS should be *R*eliable, *E*asy to deal with, and *D*ependable.

21.3.3 Changing the Culture

Three levers were central to the bank's intended culture change: People, PIEs, and Process.

Gledhill set about reshaping the Technological and Operations Group, infusing new talent and perspective. He brought in people from multinational banks who thought and operated differently with a view to positively influencing the group's sense of performance orientation. In the process, he realized not every one of the existing team would fit his vision for what the group needed to become and consequently parted company with several managing directors and senior vice presidents.

In enabling the mission-critical customer transformation, hundreds of senior colleagues experienced the empowerment implicit in PIEs:

> **Definition**
>
> We agreed if implementing an idea would improve customer experience, we should go ahead and do it. This started to make a difference to the bureaucracy. There were people at the coal face willing to take some chances, so we started building a bit more individual accountability and individual responsibility for doing things. This had a greater impact than the many workshops and town hall meetings we conducted. —Piyush Gupta, DBS CEO

PIEs led to a subtle change in discourse. RED became part of the bank's culture and language, with everything being evaluated based on whether it was RED or not.

As the work of employees was reengineered, there was deep respect for the new processes that had emerged from the PIEs. Employees had a chance to directly impact the bank's existing processes and achieved new performance levels resulting from the new processes. They came to trust them, rely on them, and follow them enthusiastically. As a result, colleagues were clear about what was expected and could move forward with confidence. The bank's scorecard set out the key corporate objectives, and this was cascaded down so that people knew what they needed to achieve.

21.4 Emerging Challenges

21

As Gupta looked back in August 2013, he felt that the bank had made considerable progress since he came on board as CEO in November 2009. DBS had achieved strategic alignment around the goal of becoming the Asian bank of choice and was about two-thirds of the way to fixing its technology and operations issues and about one-third of the way to changing its culture. However, the bank faced some challenges that it needed to address.

21.4.1 The Rise of the Fintechs

By 2013, financial technology companies (more popularly known as fintechs) were becoming visible, and DBS was beginning to think about how it should react to them. While the reach of fintechs in Singapore was still limited, the story was very different in China, where companies like Alibaba were beginning to compete with banks.

Alibaba was China's leading e-commerce platform. Alipay, which it had set up in 2004 to provide payment services to its buyers and sellers, was China's leading online payment provider. In 2008 Alibaba started offering micro-loans to its sellers in cooperation with two banks that provided the funding—China Construction Bank and the Industrial and Commercial Bank of China. In 2010 Alibaba began making micro-loans to its sellers independently by establishing its own small loan companies that secured licenses from local governments. In May 2013, Alibaba launched a consumer credit service that provided overdraft services to Alipay users. In June 2013, Alipay launched Yu'e Bao, a money market fund. (Refer to ❏ Fig. 21.3)

> ┌─ **Definition** ───┐
>
> Alibaba scared the living daylights out of us. They were raising money, making payments and making loans with zero branches and completely electronically. They were reaching millions of people. We knew that the change in our industry was upon us, that the discontinuity had arrived. —Piyush Gupta, DBS CEO

DBS knew that it was only a matter of time before fintechs would disrupt banking in its key markets of Singapore and Hong Kong. Moreover, the rise of nonbank competitors rapidly encroaching into the financial services value chain prompted Gupta to challenge what success meant:

❏ **Fig. 21.3** Alibaba in 2013

In Progress → Fully Implemented

Definition

If my competition is Alibaba, I will lose. Being a world-class multinational bank will not be good enough. If we want to succeed, we will have to be an Alibaba, which means a complete rethink of where the bar needs to be and what kind of bar. —Piyush Gupta, DBS CEO

21.4.2 Achieving Critical Mass in the Big Asian Markets

By August 2013, it was clear that the bank's expansion efforts in China, India, and Indonesia were not working out relative to the ambitions set (refer to ◘ Figs. 21.4, 21.5, and 21.6). Reasonable returns depended on achieving critical mass, yet building a reasonably sized branch network was difficult, and this was holding back the development of the SME and consumer businesses, consequently extending the payback period materially.

DBS had considered growing through acquisitions in these countries, but found that the regulatory hurdles were too great. It came close to acquiring Bank Danamon in Indonesia, but had to walk away after Indonesia put new rules in place limiting it to a 40% ownership stake. Making significant acquisitions was even harder in China and India because foreign banks were generally limited to an ownership stake of 20% and 10%, respectively.

With acquisitions proving so challenging, DBS had three options in these countries. The first was to retreat. DBS could choose to be a universal bank in Singapore and a niche corporate bank in the other countries in which it operated. Many multinational banks (including Citibank and HSBC) had chosen to pull out of countries in which their operations were marginal, and this would be a reasonable choice for DBS in these markets given its lack of success there.

◘ **Fig. 21.4** China country profile (2013)

21

■ **Fig. 21.5**   India country profile (2013)

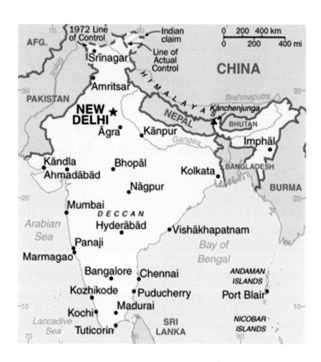

■ **Fig. 21.6**   Indonesia country profile (2013)

The second option was to pick one of the three countries and double down on branch expansion there in order to achieve critical mass in SME and mass affluent banking. This was similar to the strategy HSBC had implemented in the Pearl River Delta region of China where it opened a large number of branches.

The third option was to build a digital bank. This had been tried earlier during the "Internet 1.0" era in the late 1990s and early 2000s. Many digital banks were created at this time, but the only one that survived was ING Direct in Germany and Australia. However, as DBS evaluated this strategy, it felt that the digital world was much more mature in 2013. There had been tremendous changes in consumer behavior, important technological developments, and Internet and mobile penetration that had transformed expectations and, at the same time, transformed the business opportunity for banking services. Gupta felt it was time to have another serious attempt to build a digital bank. When DBS looked around the world to see if there were any successes, it found several, including mBank in Poland. It also, of course, had the example of Alibaba in China.

If DBS decided to build a digital bank, it would need to decide whether to do so in a pure form, with no branches (as Alibaba was doing in China), or to opt for a hybrid strategy, whereby it also opened some branches (as mBank had done in Poland). If it decided on a hybrid strategy, it would have to determine the right mix between branches and digital:

Definition

There is some tipping point at which you enter into the consideration set of the consumer. Is that tipping point 50 branches in your city? Is it like Prada, where you need three or four flagship stores and that already gets you to the tipping point? Or is it zero like Alibaba? —Piyush Gupta, DBS CEO

The answer was not clear.

■ History

Alibaba was founded by a group of 18 friends and acquaintances, headed by Jack Ma, in Hangzhou, China in 1999. The company began operations with an English language website (▶ Alibaba.com) that matched small exporters based in China with international buyers. This was followed by the launch of a Chinese language platform (▶ 1688.com) for wholesale trade between small Chinese businesses in 1999; its first consumer platform, ▶ Taobao.com, which became China's top e-commerce platform, in 2003; Tmall, an upmarket consumer platform for the Chinese market that focused on top-quality branded products, in 2008; and AliExpress, a global consumer platform which enabled Chinese exporters to sell directly to consumers all over the world, in 2010. The company also launched the Taobao Mobile App, which became China's most popular mobile commerce app, in 2010.

The company established a number of supporting services including Aliwangwang, an instant messenger service connecting buyers and sellers; Alimama, an online marketing platform that offered marketing services to sellers; and Alibaba Cloud Computing, which handled the traffic volume and data management needs of the company and offered services to third parties and to its sellers.

By June 2013, Alibaba was the world's largest e-commerce company, with 185 million active buyers on its e-commerce platforms in China. The gross market value transacted on its Chinese e-commerce platforms in the quarter ending June 2013 was RMB 345 billion.

21

■ **Financial Services**

Alibaba set up Alipay in 2004 to provide an escrow service to its buyers and sellers. Buyers transferred payments for purchases to Alipay, but the payment was only released to sellers after the buyers had verified that they were satisfied with the products. Over time, Alipay also began providing services to third-party platforms and merchants. By 2013, it was the largest third-party payment services provider in China with an estimated 300 million active users and an estimated market share of close to 50%.

Alibaba started its SME Loan business in 2010 to provide credit to the buyers and sellers on its e-commerce platforms. It employed proprietary models that used buyer and seller transaction data to assess creditworthiness. Loans were made through lending vehicles licensed by local governments. As of mid-2013, estimates put the number of borrowers the company was serving at more than a quarter of a million, with an estimated total loan portfolio of over US$1 billion.

The company launched Yu'e Bao, a money market fund, in 2013 and positioned it as a way for its buyers and sellers to earn a good return on their cash reserves. The initial signs were encouraging and it looked as if this would be successful.

Source: Form F-1 filed with US SEC, May 2014; Company Website; Analyst Reports; Press Reports

■ **General**

- GDP, $8.5 trillion; per capita GDP, $6263 (2012 data)
- Population—1.36 billion, world's largest; urban population is over half of total
- Median age—37.1 years
- Nominally Communist government
- Mandarin is the main official language, with a number of other languages prevalent
- Land area—slightly smaller than the United States
- Internet penetration, 45.8%; mobile penetration, 88.7%

■ **Banking Sector**

- Bank credit totaled an estimated $10.7 trillion at the end of the first quarter of 2013 and had grown rapidly over the last several years.
- The five largest commercial banks, all of which were state-owned, dominated the banking sector. Their market share had dropped from 78% in 2003 to 44% at the end of 2012.
- There was a large informal financial sector, which catered to the needs of small private firms that found it difficult to obtain loans from the banking sector.
- Foreign banks in China had less than 2% share of total banking assets. Regulatory constraints, especially a 20% upper limit on equity ownership in domestic banks, made it difficult for them to achieve scale.
- Companies like Alibaba had begun to offer financial services using digital-only models. However, they were still marginal players. Alibaba had a loan portfolio of around $1 billion while ICBC had $1.6 trillion in loans.

Source: US Central Intelligence Agency; World Development Indicators, The World Bank; The Chinese Financial System – An Introduction and Overview. Douglas J. Elliott and Kai Yan. John L. Thornton Center Monograph Series, Number 6, July 2013; Analyst Reports; Press Reports

- **General**
- GDP, $1.82 trillion; per capita GDP, $1444 (2012 data).
- Population—1.28 billion, world's second largest; urban population is one-third of total.
- Median age—27.6 years.
- Secular democracy.
- 15 official languages; English widely spoken.
- Land area—slightly more than one-third of the United States.
- Internet penetration, 15.1%; mobile penetration, 70.8%.

- **Banking Sector**
- Non-food gross bank credit totaled INR 49.6 trillion ($878 billion) as of end May 2013. Bank credit had been growing at double digit rates in the 5 years to May 2013.
- Fewer than 400 million people in India had a bank account in 2013, and many accounts were dormant. An estimated 90% of transactions were cash based.
- Private sector banks had raised their market share to 21% in 2013 (from 12% in 2000) at the expense of public sector banks (whose share dropped from 80% to 73%) and foreign banks. Their share was projected to increase further to 32% by 2025.
- The market share of private banks in digital banking was at least twice their overall market share. Digital banking was projected to grow rapidly as smartphone penetration increased.
- The Reserve Bank of India (India's central bank) had eased entry into the banking sector. It was open to new business models which would promote financial inclusion.

Source: US Central Intelligence Agency; World Development Indicators, The World Bank; Reserve Bank of India; Analyst Reports; Press Reports

- **General**
- GDP, $918 billion; per capita GDP, $3701 (2012 data).
- Population—251 million; urban population is about half of total.
- Median age—29.9 years.
- Secular democracy.
- Bahasa Indonesia is the official language; several other languages prevalent.
- Land area—slightly more than three times the size of Texas.
- Internet penetration, 14.9%; mobile penetration, 114.2%.

21

- **Banking Sector**
- Bank loans in Indonesia totaled IDR 2708 trillion ($281 billion) at the end of 2012 and had grown more than 20% per year in the previous 2 years.
- Indonesia's top four banks—Bank Mandiri, Bank Rakyat Indonesia, Bank Central Asia, and Bank Negara Indonesia—accounted for almost half of total bank loans.
- Bank Central Asia (BCA) dominated digital banking, accounting for the bulk of digital transactions (by value) of customers of the top four banks.
- Bank Indonesia (Indonesia's central bank) had issued regulations in May 2013 allowing the country's top four banks to pilot branchless banking services by partnering with retail outlets and mobile operators to pilot mobile financial services.
- In 2012 Bank Indonesia had issued new regulations restricting the ownership stake a foreign bank could take in a local bank to 40%, except with special approval.

Source: US Central Intelligence Agency; World Development Indicators, The World Bank; Analyst Reports; Press Reports

DBS Transformation (b): Going Digital and Creating a 22,000-Person Start-Up

Contents

Researcher PC Abraham prepared this case under the supervision of Professor Seán Meehan as a basis for class discussion rather than to illustrate either effective or ineffective handling of a business situation. Copyright © 2017 by IMD—*International Institute for Management Development*, Lausanne, Switzerland (► www.imd.org). No part of this publication may be reproduced, stored in a retrieval system, or transmitted in any form or by any means without the prior written permission of *IMD*.

© Springer Nature Switzerland AG 2020
T. Jelassi, F. J. Martínez-López, *Strategies for e-Business*, Classroom Companion: Business, https://doi.org/10.1007/978-3-030-48950-2_22

22

■ **Introduction**

It had been a busy week in India for Piyush Gupta, CEO of DBS. The launch of DBS digibank in India on 26 April 2016 had gone well, and the months leading up to it, although intense, suggested the transformation of DBS from a world-class multinational bank to a 22,000-person start-up was well on track. The digibank team had delivered on time, leaving Gupta optimistic that they would achieve their ambitious new business targets. But was this enough? Ant Financial, the 3-year-old financial services spin-off from Alibaba, had just announced another successful funding round that valued it at US$60 billion. It already had a banking license in China, its payments arm had 451 million active users, and its wealth management business boasted $760 billion assets under management.

As his flight to Singapore reached cruising altitude, Gupta asked himself whether DBS had gone far enough, fast enough. And, crucially, was it fit to compete, win, and grow in a world in which the financial services landscape was changing beyond recognition?

22.1 Making Banking Joyful

The board were persuaded by Gupta's argument, in late 2013, that the competitive set it needed to understand and address was the so-called fintech space. This was a diverse space with three types of players emerging: start-ups, spin-off financial institutions, and evolutions of Internet platforms. In general these were often start-ups initially focused on one product market; they were founded by experienced bankers, staffed heavily by technology experts, and heavily backed by private equity. Among them were Qudian, Oscar, Atom Bank, and Avant. Other fintechs were established by one or more major financial institutions—for example, Lufax (backed by Ping An, a major Chinese insurer) and ZhongAn (established by Ping An, Tencent, and Alibaba). And lastly there were the Internet platforms that entered the space with enormous numbers of customers in their ecosystem, most of whom were engaging in a financial transaction (buying or selling goods or services)—most notable among these was Ant Financial, founded and owned by Alibaba. Ant operated far beyond facilitating e-commerce—it created an ecosystem where customers could invest, secure loans, make reservations for taxis/movies/travel/dining, chat, and consume digital entertainment and news. The board were satisfied with the transformation journey. They liked the direction and the approach, and they could see progress. Further, the bank's financial performance remained robust (refer to ◘ Table 22.1). They supported Gupta 100% as he pivoted from the earlier transformational ambition of creating a world-class multinational bank to that of becoming a 22,000-person start-up.

As the senior management embraced this mandate, they stepped back to situate the strategy, the ongoing transformation, and, indeed, the enterprise in the context of its purpose. Gupta reflected that consumers and business customers did not care about banking per se; rather they cared about accomplishing their own underlying objectives, be it buying a home or a car or educating their kids or, for businesses, securing a credit facility to enable a significant trade. But he and his colleagues felt it was not enough to be a bank that could address such basic needs. They needed

■ Table 22.1 Company financials[a]

	2012	2013	2014	2015
Balance sheet (S$ billion)				
Total assets	353.0	402.0	440.7	457.8
Customer loans	210.5	248.7	275.6	283.3
Total liabilities	317.0	364.3	400.5	415.0
Customer deposits	253.5	292.4	317.2	320.1
Total shareholders' funds	31.7	34.2	37.7	40.4
Income statement (S$ billion)				
Total income	8.06	8.93	9.62	10.79
Profit before tax	4.16	4.32	4.70	5.16
Net profit	3.81	3.67	4.05	4.45
Financial ratios (%)				
Net interest margin	1.70	1.62	1.68	1.77
Cost to income ratio	44.8	43.9	45.0	45.4
Return on assets	0.97	0.91	0.91	0.96
Return on shareholders' funds	11.2	10.8	10.9	11.2
Loan to deposit ratio	83.1	85.0	86.9	88.5
Non-performing loan rate	1.2	1.1	0.9	0.9

Source: DBS Annual Report 2015
[a]US$1 = S$1.41 (12.31.15)

to go further in a world in which banking was a chore—something that had to be done, but that people did not look forward to doing. DBS should work to make banking per se "invisible," seamlessly integrated with customers' everyday activities, fitting into their lives on their terms—helping them live life, not getting in their way. Achieving this would be a real game changer:

Definition

If you could make banking joyful, you could really be very distinctive. If you can deliver on joyful banking, then you will be a very different kind of company.
—Piyush Gupta, DBS CEO

The management team revisited their transformation journey with this changed mandate and heightened clarity as to DBS's purpose. They agreed DBS would need to focus on and drive change to transform three key elements: technology, the customer journey, and culture.

22.1.1 Fixing the Technology

As a result of recent efforts, common systems and processes were in place throughout DBS, and, although functional, more improvements were needed to make them fit to compete effectively with the rising fintechs:

> **Definition**
>
> Fintechs are nimble and quick. They have a completely different technology architecture, allowing them to think in terms of turnaround times, cycle times and end-to-end customer experiences that are exponentially different from those of a bank. —Piyush Gupta, DBS CEO

A key enabler in the DBS transformation was building a middleware layer on top of the core banking platform using service-oriented architecture and an application programming interface (API) framework. This allowed DBS to easily and quickly create plug-and-play links, both within the bank and with external partners, making it possible to develop and roll out new products at a faster pace (refer to ◘ Fig. 22.1). It also allowed the bank to implement straight-through processing (STP), whereby the majority of transactions could be completed electronically (without human intervention). Transactions were completed instantaneously —a big differentiator compared with the other local banks in Singapore:

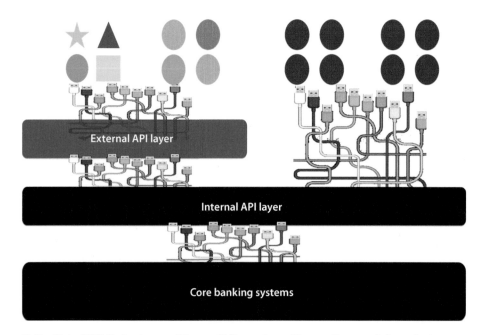

◘ **Fig. 22.1** DBS Technology—adding a middleware layer. (Source: Company information)

> **Definition**
>
> Our digital journey has been inside out. A lot of other banks say, "Let's create a great app." Their user experience is sometimes better than ours, but there is no STP. You can't actually trade. They will tell you what funds to buy, but you can't actually execute. We might take a little longer, but we want to do it right.
> —Tan Su Shan, Group Head of Consumer Banking & Wealth Management

22.1.2 Rethinking the Customer Journey

DBS had fixed many of the basics. Long queues and ATMs without cash were generally a thing of the past. Now, DBS moved forward on three tracks to make banking joyful.

First, it redesigned its customer interactions to make them faster, easier, and more pleasant. For example, it redesigned branches so that customers could sit down while waiting to be served and also implemented a system that allowed customers to obtain a queue number before visiting a branch so they could be notified by SMS a few minutes before their turn.

Second, it sought to seamlessly embed itself in customers' lives. The *DBS Home Connect* mobile app provided customers with helpful and relevant inputs to help them in their decision-making (e.g., recent transaction prices and amenities available at different locations) as well as information on home mortgages. Food and beverage entrepreneurs were offered an F&B *Starter Package* including both banking (a bank account and working capital support) and technology (point-of-sale and back-office) solutions.

Third, in a departure from the traditional approach in which assumptions about process failures informed the operations support remit, it embraced "design for no ops." Operations would be digitized and automated wherever possible to improve completion times and lower failure rates—and costs. Its Internet and mobile banking platforms enabled customers to carry out most transactions without visiting a branch or phoning the call center. Further, "design for customer struggle" insisted the bank's systems flagged up, in real time, when customers had a problem. This allowed for a refreshing level of proactivity. For example, if a credit card transaction approval was being refused, DBS could send an SMS explaining why this had happened and what to do next, so that the customer did not need to contact the call center.

22.1.3 Rewiring Mindsets Toward a Start-Up Culture

If DBS was to compete successfully with fintechs, it would need to cultivate a culture that:

> **Definition**
>
> …embraces innovation, decisiveness, entrepreneurship and nimbleness, one that places the customer's perspective at the center. —Piyush Gupta, DBS CEO, 2014 Annual Report

22

The bank's drive to improve customer experience changed its culture by exposing staff to new tools and ways of thinking and working. In 2013 it began experimenting with customer journey projects, redesigning how customers interacted with the bank to complete a specific task. It introduced the concept of human-centered design thinking, which involved deeply understanding customer needs, rapidly prototyping and iterating possible solutions, and finally implementing the chosen solution. The bank decided to go with a model of integrating innovation into the businesses, instead of setting up a stand-alone unit. As such, the Innovation Group provided guidance, but the work was done by the business units themselves.

In 2014 the bank set a target of a hundred customer journeys and conducted over a thousand "looking" activities—including customer interviews, surveys, and immersion—to understand consumers better. It set up a new human-centered design lab and trained 700 staff in human-centered design. It partnered with A*STAR[1] to support its use of big data. In 2015 the bank trained all 250 managing directors in customer journey techniques and asked each of them to lead a customer journey project. As a result, DBS had more than 300 customer journey projects running in 2016 in every part of the bank. Thousands of bank staff across functions, levels, and geographies were involved in these projects, which pushed them to think and act differently.

As part of its digital immersion programs, DBS conducted 15 hackathons in 2015. Teams consisted of three members from a start-up and three from different DBS levels and geographies. After an initial 2 days' training of DBS members, the team worked for 3 days to solve a business problem. They developed concepts, talked to customers to get feedback, and then decided whether to pivot or persevere. Once they had decided on a concept, they had to codify and test it and develop a business case. The objective was to be able to pitch to the business after 3 days.

DBS conducted over a thousand experiments in 2015, in which teams used the new tools to try and find solutions for business problems. More than a hundred prototypes were developed across the bank as a result. The bank also established start-up accelerators, which allowed bank staff to interact with people who had very different mindsets. These programs touched about 2000 staff throughout the bank in 2015, and an increase to 5000 staff in 2016 was on track:

Definition

Collectively, these activities supported a mindset shift – the self-belief that we are the best bank in the world. To be the best bank in the world, you have to be willing to do things differently, and the bank's staff is beginning to fundamentally get this. —Neal Cross, Chief Innovation Officer

---

1   A*STAR—Agency for Science, Technology and Research—was established by the Singapore government to support Singapore's economic growth and enhance the lives of both the community and the industry.

Innovation activities were initially focused on external customers, but over time they began to address internal customers and employees. The Innovation Group's biggest client in 2016 was human resources, and they also worked with finance and compliance and fisk.

22.2 DBS digibank: India's First Mobile-Only Bank

As DBS proceeded to drive change in technology, customer journey, and culture, it was imperative that it push ahead in the market at home and in overseas markets (China, India, and Indonesia) where it sought to grow. It rejected the option of becoming a niche corporate bank in these markets because it felt that to be meaningful, it should serve the mass SME and retail market. Regulatory hurdles made growing through acquisitions difficult. Cost constraints made building out the branch network in any one country unattractive. DBS recognized that while a digital-only strategy would not guarantee success, it became the preferred route to market overseas. The investment was manageable and failure would not imperil the bank.

DBS decided to attempt this first in India and to go with a pure mobile-only model because the digital infrastructure was available in the country. The Indian government had begun rolling out the Aadhaar card to provide a unique identifier to every Indian resident, which meant companies could use it to authenticate potential customers digitally and remotely (refer to ▶ Box 22.1).

Box 22.1   Aadhaar and the India Stack

Aadhaar

The Indian government first identified the need to provide a unique identity number to each Indian resident in 2000 as a tool to efficiently deliver welfare services and monitor government programs. The Unique Identification Authority of India (UIDAI) was set up in 2009, and Nandan Nilekani (who had formerly led Infosys, one of India's most successful IT services firms) was appointed its chairman with cabinet minister rank.

The UIDAI began rolling out the Aadhaar, a 12-digit unique identification number, to all Indian residents in 2009. It collected a set of demographic information (including name, verified date of birth or self-declared age, gender, and address) and biometric information (including fingerprints, iris scans, and facial photographs) from each person who received an Aadhaar. Enrolled individuals could also provide a mobile number and an e-mail address if they chose to do so. UIDAI used the collected information to ensure that each Aadhaar was unique and that no individual had more than one.

By the end of 2013, the UIDAI had enrolled 300 million Indian residents in the program, and by early 2016, the number exceeded a billion.

22

The India Stack

Using the Aadhaar database as the foundation, the government built a digital infrastructure consisting of a set of application programming interfaces (APIs) that it referred to as the India Stack. The government and businesses could use this infrastructure to develop and deliver presenceless, paperless, and cashless services digitally. It had five key elements:

- *Aadhaar Auth* was a web-enabled service through which the identity of enrolled individuals could be authenticated using their Aadhaar, individual demographic information, and either their fingerprints or an iris scan.

- *Aadhaar eKYC* could be used to electronically verify an individual's identity, address, date of birth and gender, as well as an e-mail address and mobile phone number if he or she had chosen to provide this information to the Aadhaar database.

- *Aadhaar eSign* allowed enrolled individuals to electronically sign a form or document anytime, anywhere, and on any device.

- *Unified Payment Interface* (UPI) enabled individuals who had linked their bank account to their Aadhaar to send and receive money from their smartphones using just their Aadhaar, without entering bank-specific account numbers and passwords.

- *Digital Locker* allowed organizations to deposit electronic copies of documents and certificates directly into the digital lockers (dedicated cloud storage space linked to Aadhaar numbers) of individuals who had signed up for this service. Individuals could then give other organizations access to these documents electronically.

Source: ► www.indiastack.org

22.2.1 Creating the Platform

DBS set up a separate group to create the digibank India platform so that it could think differently and not be constrained by the bank's established norms:

Definition

We put them in a separate building. We looked at how a tech company would operate. Dave Gledhill spent time in Silicon Valley and we copied shamelessly. We got into agile and lean, co-located people, went to a completely different style of working. —Piyush Gupta, DBS CEO

The group set a stretch goal of designing the platform to operate with 10% of the staff that a normal banking operation would require. The bank had to completely rethink every aspect of banking operations and make some tough decisions:

> **Definition**
>
> We had to get everybody's buy-in that what we can't digitize, we won't do. Cheques are very big in India, but they were manual so we decided not to offer them. There was massive discussion and disagreement before this was settled. —Dave Gledhill, Head of Group Technology and Operations

The platform had three key features. First, the account opening was completely paperless and electronic, with customer authentication being done using biometrics and the Aadhaar card. DBS partnered with a popular national café chain allowing potential customers to visit any of over 500 designated outlets to complete the authentication process. Second, customer service was delivered through an artificial intelligence-driven virtual assistant developed in partnership with Kasisto, a US-based fintech. Third, it used a dynamic soft token security system embedded in the customer's smartphone which was much more secure than inputting one-time passwords received via SMS. The bank opted for a completely branchless model.[2]

In mid-2016 digibank India had 35–40% the headcount of a traditional bank and only 10% of the normal headcount required for onboarding customers. Maintaining this discipline, however, was challenging. Some at the bank were already advocating moving away from a pure mobile-only model and offering an Internet-based platform. This would address customer concerns about accessing their account if they had a poor mobile connection.

22.2.2 Launching DBS digibank India

DBS launched DBS digibank India in April 2016 with the objective of reaching 5 million customers and INR 500 billion (about S$10 billion) deposits within 5 years. With Sachin Tendulkar, a popular Indian cricket star, as its brand ambassador, it targeted the 125 million English-language speakers with a smartphone.

The bank's first challenge was to get customers to download the app and use it as an e-wallet. This did not require the customer's identity to be authenticated, and the process could be completed almost instantaneously. Once funded the e-wallet could be used to pay utility bills and top up prepaid mobile phone accounts. It came with a virtual Visa card for online purchases. Once customers started using the e-wallet, the bank's next task was to get them to convert it to a savings account, which required them to complete the authentication process.

India's digital banking space was likely to be very competitive. First, India's major private banks were taking steps to ensure that they dominated this space. The largest, HDFC Bank, had built up its mobile platform allowing customers to carry out over 75 different kinds of transactions. Second, the government had

---

2 ▶ https://www.dbs.com/digibank/in/features.html

issued a banking license to Paytm, the owner of India's most popular mobile wallet (40% owned by Alibaba and Ant Financial). Other licenses were issued to telecom companies, including Vodafone M-PESA and Airtel. Third, easy access to the India Stack would make it easy for fintechs to build and launch product offerings (refer to ▶ Box 22.2).

22

Box 22.2   India's Changing Digital Banking Landscape

India's banking landscape had changed significantly, with the market share of public sector banks declining from 80% in 2000 to 73% in 2013. The Reserve Bank of India (India's central bank) had predicted that the market share of public sector banks would fall further, to 63% by 2025, and many observers felt that the drop would be even steeper. India's private banks had been particularly successful in the digital space, accounting for almost 60% of the value of mobile banking transactions in March 2016, about three times their 20% share in the overall banking market.

The leading private banks had spotted the digital opportunity early and had decided to take advantage of it. HDFC Bank, the largest of these, had set out to transform itself into a digital bank after its CEO, Aditya Puri, visited Silicon Valley in the summer of 2014. He came back convinced that his bank should disrupt itself rather than waiting to be disrupted by others. Since then, the bank had launched a number of innovative products in the digital space, including a 10-second loan and a digital banking platform for SME customers. Mobile and Internet banking accounted for over half of the bank's transactions in early 2016. It had built up its mobile banking platform so that customers could carry out over 75 different types of transactions.

The Reserve Bank of India had opened up the banking sector by issuing 23 new banking licenses in 2014 and 2015. Two were universal bank licenses; 11 were for payment banks, which were limited in the deposits they could accept and focused more on payment and remittance services and distributing financial products; and 10 were for small finance banks, which focused on serving SMEs. One of the payment bank licenses had gone to Paytm, India's most popular mobile wallet in which Alibaba and Ant Financial had a 40% equity stake. Payment bank licenses had also been issued to telecom companies including Vodafone M-PESA and Airtel, which was India's largest mobile telecom company.

The creation of the India Stack (refer to ▶ Box 22.1) was likely to increase competition in the mobile payments space, with 29 banks having announced plans to offer payments solutions using the Unified Payments Interface. The India Stack would also make it easier for fintechs to develop and launch innovative financial products, so competition from these companies was likely to increase.

Source: ▶ www.indiastack.org; Reserve Bank of India; Analyst Reports; Press Reports

22.3 Emerging Challenges

22.3.1 Singapore: Are We Doing Enough?

In Singapore, which accounted for over 60% of DBS's income, the initial results from its digital transformation had been encouraging. It had developed significant new income streams, most notably from DBS Remit, an online overseas funds transfer service that had almost doubled the bank's cross-border remittance traffic since it was introduced in 2014. Costs had begun to decline, with call center volumes falling 10–15% in the previous year (with headcount dropping from over 600 to less than 500 as a result) and branch traffic declining by 4–5% over the same period. DBS was confident that these trends would continue and had told analysts that it expected its cost-income ratio to be below 40% (from 45% in 2015) in 5 years.

Despite these achievements, the growing presence of fintechs was worrying. For example, Gupta felt that Alibaba was getting further ahead of DBS (refer to ◗ Exhibit 22.1). The bank needed to maintain its change momentum in order to stay competitive.

> **Exhibit 22.1 Alibaba in 2016**
> Alibaba had gone from strength to strength since 2013. The number of active buyers on its e-commerce platforms in China had increased from 172 million in the first quarter of 2013 to 423 million 3 years later. The gross market value (GMV) of transactions had more than doubled from RMB 294 billion to RMB 742 billion over the same period, and the share of mobile transactions in total GMV had increased from 11% to 73%. Alibaba's initial public offering (IPO) on the New York Stock Exchange had taken place in September 2014 and was the biggest in the world at the time, raising $25 billion.
>
> Ant Financial, under which Alibaba aggregated all the financial services it provided, was spun off as a separate entity in 2011. Alibaba had sold its SME loan portfolio to Ant Financial in the run-up to its IPO. Ant Financial had raised $4.5 billion in funding in April 2016 at a valuation of over $60 billion.
>
> Alipay, which provided payment services to both Alibaba and third-party merchant customers, had benefited from the growth of e-commerce and mobile commerce in China. By March 2016, it had a market share of 43% of China's online payment market and 52% of its mobile payment market. It supported 451 million consumers, who were served by over 10 million merchants. Alipay had also started to move into the offline payments space and supported over 300,000 merchants as of March 2016. It had also started expanding internationally to cater to Chinese travelers and could be used to pay at about 70,000 merchants globally, which it planned to increase to 1 million merchants within 3 years.

Yu'e Bao, a money market fund that the company had launched in June 2013, was China's largest by March 2016, with RMB 760 billion in assets under management and 152 million active users. It had started offering other wealth management products as well. Ant Financial had teamed up with Tencent Holdings to form China's first online-only insurance company in 2014 and had acquired a majority stake in Cathay Insurance.

Ant Financial had ramped up its efforts to lend to SMEs by setting up MYbank, a private online bank, in June 2015, and the bank had made over 20 million loans by March 2016. The company had also moved into consumer finance by launching Ant Check Later, which offered consumer loans in the RMB 1 to RMB 30,000 range on Alibaba's e-commerce platforms. The eligibility of individuals for loans was decided based on a credit rating provided by Sesame Credit (also launched in 2015), which used big data technology to analyze consumer spending data from both online and offline sources. During Singles Day on 11 November 2015, Ant Check Later had provided credit for over 60 million purchases made on Alibaba's e-commerce platforms.

Source: Form 20-F for the year ended March 31, 2016 filed with US SEC; Company Website; Analyst Reports; Press Reports

22.3.2 Growth Markets: Will the Digital Bank Strategy Work?

Credit Suisse estimated the Indian consumer and SME loan markets would grow from US$600 billion to US$3020 billion over the next decade. DBS digibank India had huge potential if it could compete effectively. The fact was that the India Stack was available to all comers. The Reserve Bank of India, India's central bank, was making it easier for companies to procure banking licenses—in 2015 it had issued 2 universal banking licenses, 11 payment bank licenses, and 10 small finance bank licenses. Competitors were well managed, well resourced, and technologically advanced.

DBS planned to launch a digital bank in Indonesia in 2017 that was similar to its Indian venture. It would be up against Indonesia's leading banks such as Bank Central Asia (the leading private bank) and Bank Mandiri (the leading public sector bank), which were determined to protect their turf. In addition, telecom companies such as Indosat had built a presence in mobile financial services.

DBS faced a dilemma in China. Given the existence of players like Ant Financial and Tencent, which had established a commanding lead, it did not feel that the strategy it was pursuing in India and Indonesia would work. It would need to look at other ways to penetrate this market:

Definition

What works in a market where there is a window of opportunity cannot work in a market where the window has been gone for 2 or 3 years. —Piyush Gupta, DBS CEO, 2016

Digital Business Transformation in Silicon Savannah: How M-PESA Changed Safaricom (Kenya)

Contents

Researcher Stephanie Ludwig prepared this case under the supervision of Professor Tawfik Jelassi as a basis for class discussion rather than to illustrate either effective or ineffective handling of a business situation. Copyright © 2016 by IMD – *International Institute for Management* Development, Lausanne, Switzerland (▶ www.imd.org). No part of this publication may be reproduced, stored in a retrieval system, or transmitted in any form or by any means without the prior written permission of *IMD*.

   Unless otherwise referred to in footnotes, facts used from this case study were retrieved directly from information received through a direct interview by the case study authors with Safaricom's CEO Bob Collymore as well as from the Safaricom website, including Safaricom's annual reports available at ▶ http://www.safaricom.co.ke.

© Springer Nature Switzerland AG 2020
T. Jelassi, F. J. Martínez-López, *Strategies for e-Business*, Classroom Companion: Business,
https://doi.org/10.1007/978-3-030-48950-2_23

■ **Introduction**

The view had changed since Bob Collymore, chief executive officer of Kenya's leading telecom operator, made his first helicopter flight over Nairobi, when he moved there 6 years earlier. Soaring up into the sky, he still remembered the excitement he had felt when he got his first bird's-eye view of the city that would soon become his home.

Taking a sharp right toward Ngong city outskirts, he pondered the professional journey he started when he took over Safaricom from his predecessor Michael Joseph in November 2010. Just like Nairobi over the previous 6 years, Safaricom had changed significantly under his leadership. Overall, it had been quite an ascent, but there were also some challenges and failures along the way. Much as he had done during his inaugural flight, Collymore kept his eye on the horizon and was not shy about taking calculated risks.

23.1 Safaricom and M-PESA

Most people probably did not think of Kenya as an innovation and technology hub. However, in 2007, this sub-Saharan African country became the birthplace and launch pad of M-PESA, a transformative mobile phone-based platform for money transfer and financial services. Operating under the slogan "Safaricom, Transforming Lives," Kenya's incumbent telecom operator offered voice, data, enterprise solutions, and M-PESA-based financial services for retail customers, small businesses, and government. As the biggest telecommunications company in East and Central Africa, Safaricom had over 25 million subscribers to whom it offered more than 100 different products via 200,000 touch points.

Services included:
- Person-to-person
- ATM withdrawal
- Lipa na M-PESA
- Lipa na M-PESA Online
- Bulk payments
- Bank to M-PESA and vice versa
- M-ticketing
- Lipa Karo
- M-PESA prepay Visa card
- International money transfer (IMT)
- M-Shwari

Since its launch, M-PESA had enjoyed exponential growth, and Safaricom had registered 94% of its customers on the M-PESA platform. Of these 23 million customers, close to 17 million were 30-day active M-PESA users (*refer to* ◼ Fig. 23.1).

23

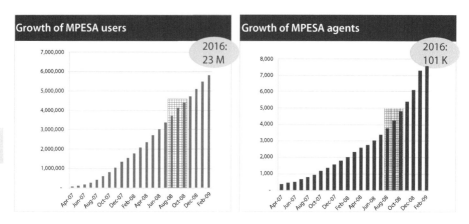

□ **Fig. 23.1**   Constant growth of M-PESA users and agents from 2007 to 2016. (Source: FSD Kenya)

Safaricom held a market share of 66% in a market with 89% mobile penetration,[1] and M-PESA was by far the most used mobile financial service. In late 2015, M-PESA's average monthly value of person-to-person remittances reached KES 101 billion (US$1 billion). It had become ubiquitous in the daily lives of millions of Kenyans due to a range of services that included money deposits and withdrawals, remittance deliveries, bill payments, and microcredit provisions.

While M-PESA had developed very quickly and disrupted traditional financial services, Safaricom kept using its proven business development and marketing approaches and continued to build a strong and trusted brand. M-PESA had started as a mere remittance service allowing customers to send money to each other via text message and enabling them to cash in the electronic value at agents across the country (*refer to* □ Fig. 23.2). In the 9 years since it had launched, Safaricom had constantly expanded this service in volume and quality (through add-on features and easier mobile account management options).

Users could choose from a large array of Safaricom products and partners (*refer to the box on the left*). Besides an increasingly dense network of Kenyan partners, Safaricom built a global network of money transfer services, which allowed customers abroad to send money to Kenya from over 100 countries.[2]

Products were marketed through a very large physical distribution network (100,744 agents in 2016), which had been rolled out nationally from the start and expanded over the years (*refer to* □ Fig. 23.3). To develop a critical mass of agents and customers, M-PESA's business model incurred significant upfront costs, and this was one of the reasons many mobile money deployments failed in the early days. According to a McKinsey report, to make mobile money viable, operators

---

1   Communication Authority of Kenya, March 2016, cited in Safaricom Annual Report 2016

2   Safaricom Blogger, October 2015. More information can be seen at: Safaricom Blogger, Oct 2015, Money Transfer service partners include for example MoneyGram and Vodacom Tanzania, Safaricom, ▶ http://www.safaricom.co.ke/blog/9-reasons-why-kenya-runs-on-m-pesa/ [Oct 2016].

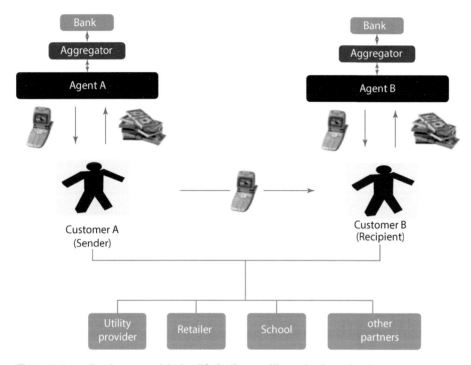

◘ Fig. 23.2 m-Remittance model (simplified). (Source: Illustration by authors)

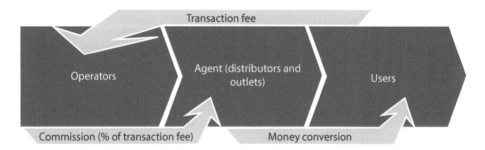

◘ Fig. 23.3 Value chain and roles of selected M-PESA players. (Source: Ludwig 2010)

like Safaricom had to sign up at least 15–20% of the addressable market in the first place, which Safaricom managed to do in the first couple of years.[3] In 2015 it became Kenya's largest distribution network across sectors! M-PESA's success was also due to its ability to grow its customer base and network of agents simultane-

---

3 Beshouri/Gravråk, January 2010. More information can be seen at: Beshouri, Christopher P. and Jon Gravråk, January 2010, capturing the promise of mobile banking in emerging markets, McKinsey&Company, ► http://www.mckinsey.com/industries/telecommunications/our-insights/capturing-the-promise-of-mobile-banking-in-emerging-markets. [Oct 2016].

23

ously, which allowed it to achieve 1000 transactions per agent per month on average. Managing the float between agents in rural and urban areas, which showed different remittance dynamics, remained a challenge. e-Commerce was later added as an extra offering through the online platform, thus opening up a whole set of new opportunities.

Safaricom set a pricing strategy for M-PESA, which had not changed much over the previous 9 years, in spite of increasing inflation. Through segmented pricing, Safaricom succeeded in attracting young customers, who represented the high-growth market segment. It provided them with the Blaze tariff suited to their needs. To increase trust and loyalty, it offered refunds for dropped calls, which used to be an issue but now accounted for less than 0.3% of total calls. However, for low-income people (who constituted the largest user segment), the prices remained quite high.[4] Competitors came up with simpler price structures (*refer to* ◘ Fig. 23.4) and were generally more affordable.

Nearly a decade after its launch, M-PESA had drastically changed Kenya's economic landscape.[5] It transformed the banking and telecom sectors in Kenya and facilitated operations for thousands of small businesses. It had become a role model worldwide for inclusive business practices that were aimed at integrating low-income segments into the main economic stream and offering them value-added services. Besides providing a faster, secure, and more convenient means of remittance and payment, M-PESA also massively contributed to financial inclusion in Kenya (*refer to* ◘ Fig. 23.5).[6]

M-PESA's success paved the way for many other mobile financial services around the world. Its impact in Kenya put mobile money services on the map and encouraged, as of August 2016, the take-up worldwide of more than 282 mobile money services.[7] Most of these services were rolled out in developing markets, with most deployments taking place in sub-Saharan Africa, where the traditional banking sector remained underdeveloped and the less-affluent, high-volume segments

---

4   Riaga, May 2016. More information can be seen at: Riaga, Odipo, May 2016. The three Safaricom overpriced products that generated the Shs 38.1 billion in profits, Kachawanya, ► http://www.kachwanya.com/2016/05/17/the-three-safaricom-overpriced-products-that-generated-the-shs-38-1-billions-in-profits. [August 2016].

5   According to CGAP (2014), referencing the Kenyan Central Bank, mobile money contributes to 6.6% of the total National Payments System's throughput value (including both gross and retail) but a staggering 66.6% of the total National Payments System's throughput volume. This means that M-PESA is important, but does not necessarily pose a systemic risk (Brian Muthiora (GSMA), September 2014). More information can be seen at: Muthiora, Brian, Sept 2014, New infographic: Mobile money and the digitisation of Kenya's retail payments systems, GSMA, ► http://www.gsma.com/mobilefordevelopment/programme/mobile-money/new-infographic-mobile-money-and-the-digitisation-of-kenyas-retail-payments-systems [Aug 2016].

6   About 75% of Kenyans are now formally included. This signifies a 50% increase in the last 10 years (FSD 2016).

7   GSMA Mobile Money Deployment tracker: ► http://www.gsma.com/mobilefordevelopment/tracker

CICO Transactions by Provider (Registered Customer only)							
Service	Transaction Amount US$*	M-PESA	Equited	Airtel Money	MobiKash	KCB Mob Bank	Orange Money
Cash In	$10	Free	Free	Free	Free	Free	Free
	$50	Free	Free	Free	Free	Free	Free
	$100	Free	Free	Free	Free	Free	Free
Cash Out	$10	$0.27	$0.25	$0.25	$0.25	$0.20	$0.25
	$50	$0.66	$0.45	$0.45	$0.45	$0.33	$0.45
	$100	$1.10	$0.75	$0.75	$0.75	$0.55	$0.75

*1US$=Kes101

Money Transfer Fees - Within Networks							
Service	Transaction Amount (US$)	M-PESA	Equitel	Airtel Money	MobiKash	Orange Money	KCB Mobile Banking
P2P Transfers	$10	$0.15	Free	Free	$0.30	$0.30	$0.33
	$50	$0.60	Free	Free	$0.30	$0.30	$0.33
	$100	$0.85	Free	Free	$0.30	$0.30	$0.33

Money Transfer Fees - Across Networks												
Service	TX Amount (US$)	M-PESA	Equitel		Airtel Money	MobiKash		Orange Money		KCB Mobi Bank		
		To Other Network $	To Other Banks and Airtel	To Any M-PESA Line	To Any Network	Own A/c to M-PESA	To Any M-PESA line	To Other Networks	To Other Banks	To Equity A/C	To Any M-PESA Line	To Other Banks
P2P	$10	$0.48	$0.44	$0.44	Free	$0.55	$0.77	$0.7	$4	$0.4	$0.55	$0.77
	$50	$1.32	$0.61	$0.61	Free	$0.55	$0.77	$0.9	$4	$0.4	$0.55	$0.77
	$100	$2.01	$0.61	$0.61	Free	$0.55	$0.77	$1.55	$4	$0.4	$0.55	$0.77

Pricing Structure Compared to Competitors

Fig. 23.4 Pricing structure compared to competitors. (Source: ▶ http://www.helix-institute.com/blog/competition-kenyan-digital-finance-market-mobile-money-part-1-3)

were not served. Global telecom operators, such as Vodafone (Safaricom's mother company), led the way and launched similar deployments across countries, thus leveraging regional networks and experience. Nevertheless, most of these rollouts had nowhere close to M-PESA's success. As many struggled to scale up their service,

23

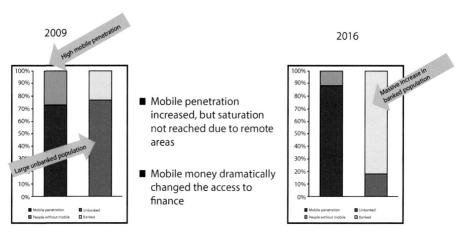

❑ **Fig. 23.5** Mobile penetration and financial inclusion rates in 2009 and 2016 in Kenya. (Source: FSD Kenya 2009 and 2016)

it became clear that there was not one single successful formula because country specificities played a major role.[8] Often, large banks and global third-party providers collaborated with telecom operators to provide more comprehensive products. M-PESA and other mobile financial services were no longer stand-alone products but rather formed part of a digital business ecosystem.

23.2 M-PESA Spurred Safaricom's Digital Business Transformation

By offering mobile phone-based financial services via M-PESA, Safaricom ventured into a new market segment, and M-PESA's growth had a significant impact on the company's revenues and business model. Safaricom managed to stay ahead of the competition by constantly diversifying the product and extending it into new market segments. A strong technology backbone proved to be as important as leadership and a lean organizational structure. Without continuous human resource development, Safaricom would not be able to tackle growth areas such as leveraging big data and digital innovations.

8   Gerdeman, Sep 2015. More information can be seen at: Gerdeman, Dina, September 2015, 6 Lessons From Mobile Money Ventures In Developing Countries, Forbes, ► http://www.forbes.com/sites/hbsworkingknowledge/2015/09/28/6-lessons-from-mobile-money-ventures-in-developing-countries/#2c79b17125d4, [July 2016].

23.2.1 **Extending Safaricom's Business Model**

> **Definition**
>
> M-PESA released us from reliance on traditional telecom products. We do not feel the same pressure as many of our counterparts do because we have this other thing, which is now delivering more than 20% of the company's revenues. – Bob Collymore[9]

M-PESA was originally developed as a means of increasing customer loyalty, not necessarily as a profit generator. However, over time, M-PESA had significantly changed Safaricom's revenue streams and strategic priorities. In 2015 voice service revenue accounted for 54% of total revenues and grew by a mere 4%. By contrast, non-voice service revenues, which accounted for 42% of total revenues, sustained continued growth, with a 27% increase to KES 68.8 billion (US$700 million), driven mainly by mobile data and M-PESA (*refer to* ☐ Figs. 23.6, 23.7 *and* 23.8).

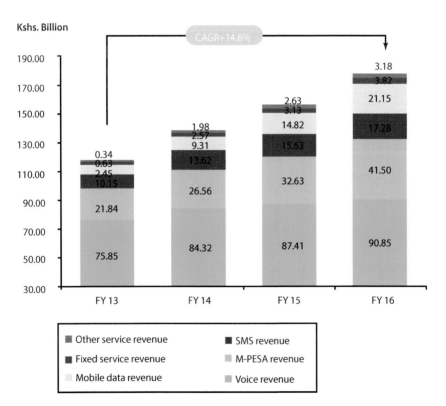

☐ **Fig. 23.6** Overview of Safaricom's performance—service revenues. (Source: Safaricom Annual Report 2016)

---

9   Unless indicated, all the quotes by CEO Bob Collymore were made during the authors' interview with him in August 2016.

23

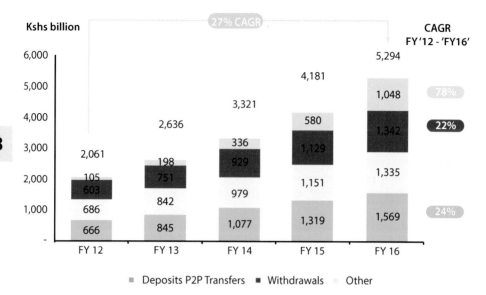

● **Fig. 23.7** Overview of Safaricom's performance—M-PESA value transacted 2012–2016. (Source: Safaricom Annual Report 2016)

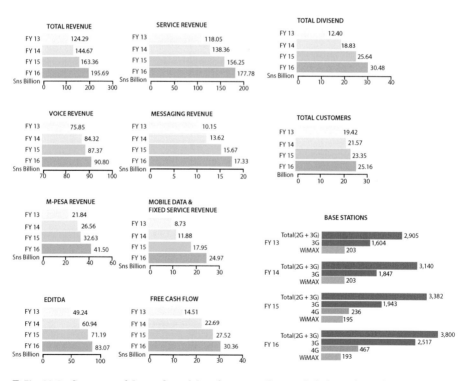

● **Fig. 23.8** Summary of 5-year financial performance. (Source: Safaricom Annual Report 2016)

M-PESA facilitated the purchase of Safaricom's core voice service product anytime and anywhere, with 41% of airtime purchases[10] going through the mobile wallet. Through its value proposition of sending and receiving money via mobile phone, Safaricom skimmed transaction fees from both senders and receivers. By providing this additional service, it reduced churn while improving customer engagement and lifetime value, thus saving on opportunity costs. However, the real game changer was the launch of Lipa na M-PESA (pay with M-PESA) supported by the M-PESA platform, which opened up the digital platform to third-party providers.

23.2.2 Diversified Service Increasingly Plugging in Third Parties

In the first years following its launch and despite numerous shortcomings (including misuse cases), M-PESA already had a relatively high customer adoption rate. To overcome any issues, features and services were incrementally added to the original core product, including:

- Hakikisha: A service to confirm, before completing a transaction, the name of the money receiver (when sending money) and the agent's name (when withdrawing money).

As people gradually started using M-PESA for everyday financial transactions, Safaricom supported them in keeping track of their income and expenditure through an enhanced M-PESA account management service, provided free of charge:

- More transactions required more oversight: The M-Ledger app produced a financial journal of M-PESA transactions by scanning existing M-PESA SMS messages and creating a database with their content.
- Since businesses mainly used a PC for their financial transactions, M-PESA statements could be received not only on a mobile phone but also via email.
- Handling various invoice numbers and due dates was difficult. Bill Manager made it possible to save and paid invoices through a single transaction (rather than separate transactions), remembered the paid invoices and the bank account numbers that were used, and reminded users of bill payment due dates.
- Traditional cash-based chamas[11] experienced issues with unreliable fund collection from members. The M-PESA Chama Account assisted saving groups/chamas to collect funds from group members more conveniently and securely.

---

10 Transfers between businesses and persons started in 2009. M-PESA's average monthly value of person-to-business transactions is KES 23.5 billion (US$232 million).

11 Chamas, locally also called merry-go-rounds, are saving groups, mostly attended by women, who collect funds (saving without interest) together in order to achieve group savings goals (like receiving a loan because a collective is seen as more reliable than an individual) or individual savings goals (like cashing out group savings for business investments) (Ludwig 2010). More information can be seen at: Ludwig, Stephanie, 2010: Socio-economic impacts and creative usage of mobile financial services among low-income micro-entrepreneurs. Evidence from an ethnographic field research in Kenya. Thesis. Vienna: University of Vienna, Austria.

- Physically collecting funds from banks was often made difficult by the limited number of bank branches, the opening hours, and long queues. The KCB M-PESA account was a paperless mobile-based bank account only for M-PESA users offering interest on savings (2% per annum) and loans (2–4% per month).
- Bank to M-PESA and M-PESA to bank allowed access to money in users' accounts any time through Unstructured Supplementary Service Data (USSD).[12]

Over the previous decade, M-PESA's service offerings had become more sophisticated and highly diversified, catering to a larger and more segmented client base. By 2016 Safaricom offered a wide range of mobile financial services through M-PESA, including:

- *M-Shwari*: A paperless banking service that allowed customers to open a bank account via a mobile phone without having to visit a bank branch or fill out forms. It made it possible to move money in and out of an M-Shwari savings account and to credit an M-PESA account at no charge. Furthermore, customers could save as little as KES 1 and earn interest on it. This cash was moved into the savings account via the M-PESA menu. M-Shwari also enabled access anytime to a micro-credit product (loan) of a minimum of KES 100, which was credited to the M-PESA account instantly. This was further enhanced through the M-Shwari Lock Savings Account, which allowed customers to save for a specific event such as a wedding. The funds were kept in the account until the maturity date, which the customer fixed when opening the account.
- *International Money Transfer*: Users could receive funds from abroad, including East Africa and countries with a large Kenyan diaspora like the United States, the United Kingdom, Continental Europe, and the UAE. This service was free of charge for the receiver since the sender bore all fees. It was developed in partnership with money transfer service companies such as Western Union and MoneyGram. Over the previous year, international money transfers had increased 64% to KES 13.1 billion (US$130 million).
- *Government (P-2-G) Transactions*: Safaricom facilitated payments for e-government services. Because government e-payment transactions had challenges on their own, the potential of citizens' online payments had not been fully leveraged, partly due to a weak (e-)governance system. Collymore was aware of the challenge of working with the public sector, especially since he represented the private sector in the government's anti-corruption campaign.
- Safaricom was also active in two main public sector areas:
  - It supported building inclusive, public-private value chains. For example, in the agricultural sector, it deployed M-PESA for an agriculture-based economic development project. Through an app, it enabled the efficient use of fertilizers and provided the government with farmers' data in order to under-

---

12 Unstructured Supplementary Service Data (USSD), sometimes referred to as "Quick Codes" or "Feature Codes," is a protocol used by GSM mobile telephones to communicate with the service provider's computers. Unlike Short Message Service (SMS), USSD messages create a real-time connection during a USSD session. The connection remains open, allowing a two-way exchange of a sequence of data. This makes USSD more responsive than services that use SMS.

stand their fertilizer needs better. The app was linked to an electronic voucher—prepaid by the government—which farmers could redeem at fertilizer companies for the quantity they needed according to the app.

- Mobile money was increasingly being used worldwide for humanitarian causes, especially during crises such as Kenya's drought or bordering civil wars. The Kenyan government, together with international donors, used M-PESA to deliver cash assistance to people. More specifically, Safaricom worked with the UN World Food Programme to provide electronic vouchers via a mobile phone to people in Dadaab, the world's largest refugee camp.

23.2.3 Going Online

> **Definition**
>
> Safaricom … practically more or less own[s] m-commerce in Kenya courtesy of over 18 million [in 2013] M-PESA users. – Moses Kemibaro, Digital Services Blogger and Founder of Dotsavvy[13]

Lipa na M-PESA (pay with M-PESA), developed by Safaricom, was an add-on to mobile money for purchasing goods and services. It offered private and business users a number of functionalities: (1) Pay Bill was a cash collection service that allowed organizations to collect money regularly from customers through M-PESA; (2) Lipa Kodi linked landlords with bill numbers to facilitate rent payments; (3) the eCitizen government services portal provided a link to M-PESA payment; and (4) Buy Goods which allowed business owners to receive payments for goods and services via M-PESA. In 2013 businesses started registering their Lipa na M-PESA till numbers, which uniquely identified each business. By 2016, 100,000 organizations in Kenya had registered as Lipa na M-PESA merchants, out of which about 44,000 were active for 30 days. In March 2016, payments reached KES 20 billion (US$200 million).

Through M-PESA, users could pay for supermarket groceries as well as website hosting, domain name registration, online purchases, etc. They could also pay online for goods and services, including Uber Kenya, SportPesa, and mCHEZA football bets, as well as utility bills such as KPLC electricity, water services, and DSTV.[14] The emergence of online shopping sites such as OLX, N-soko, Rupu, Bid or Buy, Jumia, and Cheki further strengthened Lipa na M-PESA and vice versa.[15]

---

13 Kemibaro, November 2013. More information can be seen at: Kemibaro, Moses, Nov 2013, 3 e-commerce things Safaricom could be launching in 2013, Electronic Blogger, ▶ http://www.moseskemibaro.com/2013/11/30/3-e-commerce-things-safaricom-could-be-launching-on-the-4th-december-2013/ [July 2016].

14 Read more on ▶ http://www.mpesacharges.com/

15 Daily Nation, December 2013. More information can be seen at: Daily Nation, Dec 2013, Safaricom launches online payment system, Nation Media Group, ▶ http://www.nation.co.ke/business/Safaricom-launches-online-payment-system/-/996/2098922/-/isds0f/-/index.html [August 2016].

Since the launch of the platform, Kenyans increasingly worked online since they could be paid through M-PESA or other competing platforms (such as Equitel Kenya). Thus, Safaricom generated 27% growth, mainly because of the uptake of Lipa na M-PESA.

23.2.4 Competition Within and Across Sectors

> **Definition**
>
> We are removing barriers of financial inclusion. We are targeting telcos to compete on data, SMS, voice and all levels of money transfer.[16] – James Mwangi, Chief Executive Officer, Equity Bank

Telecom operators, mobile virtual network operators (MVNOs), banks, and other financial transfer providers—such as Airtel through Airtel Money, Finserve through Equitel, Tangaza Pesa, MobiKash, and Orange through Orange Money—were in fierce competition early on when they realized the market impact of the new service. For example, telco Airtel tried to beat Safaricom on price but failed due to Safaricom's strong brand. With an agent network one-tenth the size of that of Safaricom, Airtel aimed to increase its agent network. To avoid losing customers to competitors, Safaricom had built up switching costs for customers and competitors. From a competitor's perspective, however, this inhibited healthy competition because Safaricom was using its market power to lock customers in.

Since the emergence of mobile financial services, banks and telecom operators had started moving into each other's markets. Safaricom's partnership with Commercial Bank of Africa (CBA) on the M-Shwari platform and a similar agreement with Kenya Commercial Bank, on KCB M-PESA, had created two mobile phone-based platforms that allowed M-PESA users to save as well as to obtain micro-loans. Also, many banks relied on M-PESA to support their customers in depositing, withdrawing, and borrowing money as well as transferring funds or settling bills.

On the banks' side, in 2015 Equity Bank—one of the largest banks in East Africa—launched its own MVNO, Finserve Africa Limited,[17] trading as Equitel for its mobile banking service. It ran on Airtel's telecom network and therefore served as a value addition for Airtel Money. The latter worked with different banks and mobile money services. Bank account holders used Equitel for free, but they were charged to use M-PESA.[18] Furthermore, Equitel used an extremely thin SIM card (0.1 mm) that could be placed over a standard SIM card, thus creating a dual-

---

16 Mohammed, July 2015. More information can be seen at: Mohammed, Omar, July 2015, The battle between Africa's mobile phone companies and banks is a boon for financial inclusion, Quartz Africa, ▶ http://qz.com/462044/the-battle-between-africas-mobile-phone-companies-and-banks-is-a-boon-for-financial-inclusion/ [August 2016].

17 It is a wholly owned subsidiary of Equity Group.

18 Masinde, July 2016. Read more about Equitel on ▶ www.equitel.com

SIM effect. Even though Safaricom claimed that the technology could compromise its M-PESA customers' login security, Kenyan regulators eventually approved the thin-SIM technology.[19]

Most banks used M-PESA to transfer cash between users and themselves. To avoid the associated costs, the Kenya Bankers Association (KBA) launched the test version of a mobile money transfer platform and set up the Integrated Payments Service Ltd (IPSL) company in August 2016. The platform allowed lenders to make inter-bank fund transfers at subsidized rates without having to use M-PESA. IPSL, like M-PESA, operated under the National Payment System (NPS) guidelines and was expected to reduce customers' transaction costs while maintaining the proceeds earned with banks. IPSL complemented the KBA's existing clearinghouse and offered a person-to-person (P2P) money transfer platform linked to five main bank channels: mobile banking (USSD and mobile application), internet banking, ATM, branch front office, agency banking, and point of sale (POS).[20]

A month earlier, in July 2016, Safaricom decided to tap into a new market—payment cards, which annually handled KES 1.3 trillion (US$ 12.8 billion) in transactions. It launched trials for a new debit card linked to its Lipa na M-PESA payment platform. Still in its pilot stage, the card was intended to challenge commercial banks for card commissions.[21]

From an ecosystem perspective, with the above moves, competition had entered a bigger league. Industry leaders were cooperating with each other in their competition against another industry—while competition remained fierce within the sectors.

In addition, new regional competitors emerged. BitPesa, founded in 2013, was a universal payment and trading platform for Africa headquartered in Nairobi. It provided an online platform to convert digital currency such as bitcoin into local African currencies and offered transfers to and from 7 different mobile money networks and over 60 banks in Nigeria, Kenya, Uganda, and Tanzania.

---

19 Karuga, July 2015. More information can be seen at: Karuga, Edwin, July 2015. What is Equitel and How Does it Work? blog post, ▶ http://blog.calculator.co.ke/what-is-equitel-and-how-does-it-work/ [July 2016].

20 Techmoran, May 2016. More information can be seen at: Techmoran, May 2016, Kenya Bankers Association Launches its Interbank Transaction Switch to Take On M-Pesa, ▶ http://techmoran.com/kenya-bankers-association-launches-its-interbank-transaction-switch-to-take-on-m-pesa/ [Jul 2016].

21 "Operating on the Near Field Communication (NFC) technology ecosystem, Safaricom's M-PESA debit cards and point-of-sale (POS) terminals will allow consumers to pay for goods and services much quicker on the 'tap-and-go' basis. It was best suited for 'high-volume, low-value transactions that are typically paid for with cash (pdf).' A transaction occurs when an NFC-enabled mobile handset is placed near a POS terminal, typically over distances of up to 10 centimetres. The current payment set-up using M-PESA is much slower as it requires users to follow through several stages before a transaction is completed. In a typical set-up like the cashier's till at a supermarket, a buyer is required to input the till number, the amount of money due, the M-PESA PIN and then wait for the transaction to be completed." (Masinde, July 2016). More information can be seen at: Masinde, Joshua, July 2016, Mobile money giant M-Pesa is getting its own debit card to compete with banks, Quartz Africa, ▶ http://qz.com/734842/mobile-money-giant-m-pesa-is-getting-its-own-debit-card-to-compete-withbanks/?utm_medium=social_media&utm_content=page_post&utm_campaign=1031&utm_term=&utm_source=facebook&wmc=1031 [Aug 2016].

☐ **Fig. 23.9**   M-PESA advertisements 2009 and 2016. (Source: Safaricom 2009 and 2016)

Other global players entered the market as well, as friend or foe. Visa Inc., the world's largest payments network, introduced a mobile phone application to enable cashless transactions in Kenya, where the majority of wireless payments were made through Safaricom. Visa worked on launching in other African countries.

23.2.5 Revamping Customer Segmentation

Safaricom continued using a people-centered communication approach, which highlighted how the product's core benefits could enhance people's lives. While early ads had focused on urban to rural transactions, recent ads shifted the focus from the low-income segment to medium-/higher-income layers[22] as new services were targeted to suit different customer profiles (*refer to* ☐ Fig. 23.9). At its start, M-PESA's early adopters were mainly high-income, educated men living in cities and sending money to rural areas.[23] By filling a market gap overlooked by banks, M-PESA became an alternative financial service for the poor segments of society. By 2016, Safaricom targeted the majority of the Kenyan adult population (about 85%), thus cutting across customers' social strata, geographical locations, and the like. It provided services to end consumers, businesses, and government.

Definition

We had a bit of a challenge where we had people using Safaricom by default just because it's big. It's there. The challenge is how to make all these 25 million people love you. – Charles Wanjohi, Head of Customer Segmentation, Safaricom

---

22 Compare, for example, the "Relax, you've got M-PESA" ad from 2013 (▶ https://www.youtube.com/watch?v=g1IqjY88YuM) with the first "Send money home" ad (▶ https://www.youtube.com/watch?v=4vV24gz3DpY).

23 Pulver et al., 2009. This profile is in line with research from South Africa (Ivatury/Pickens 2008). More information can be seen at: Pulver, Caroline/Jack, William/Tavneet, Suri (2009): The Performance and Impact of M-PESA: Preliminary Evidence from a Household Survey, FSD Kenya.

In an attempt to achieve this, the company had been going through a transformation over the previous year. It was focused on becoming a "consumer-led" business. This meant using data and research to organize marketing, distribution, customer service, and product offerings around niche markets.

The company had begun more heavily targeting Kenya's various regions over the previous year. These ranged from pastoral communities to the coast where most of the country's Muslims lived or tribes that preferred their own language over Kiswahili or English. Safaricom's consumer segments were inspired by those of global consumer brands and were based on four categories. These were further divided into 16 sub-segments, such as the "young flashers"—entry-level professionals eager to show off their newfound wealth. Categories were based on average spending—or average revenue per user (ARPU)—education level, age, and less tangible factors like their "attitude to life."

23.2.6 Multichannel Customer Engagement to Strengthen Loyalty

Although telecom operators and MVNOs competed for market share, most customers remained loyal to Safaricom thanks to the features of its M-PESA offering[24]: service quality, availability, price, innovation, trust, and government ties. Customer loyalty was also correlated with customers' switching costs.[25] Safaricom received several brand awards including Kenya's most influential brand[26] and Kenya's most admired brand.[27]

Safaricom relied on a large network of over 200,000 customer touch points, including those staffed by M-PESA agents and airtime sellers. It fostered customer communication by providing live chat online, customer hotline centers, and support and sharing via social media channels (Facebook, Twitter, Google+, Instagram, blog, and YouTube). The company launched its own My Safaricom app, which integrated online support and account management, as well as a Safaricom M-Ledger app focused on M-PESA account management. In 2015 users were able to receive M-PESA e-statements free of charge. Safaricom also directed customers to self-service channels, which provided information without having to contact a

---

24 A study indicated that 86% of respondents were loyal Safaricom customers because of the influence of M-PESA (Mutunga, 2012). More information can be seen at: Mutunga, Joshua, 2012, The Influence of Mobile Money Transfer in sustaining customer loyalty at Safaricom Limited, University of Nairobi, ▶ http://erepository.uonbi.ac.ke/handle/11295/12863 [August 2016].

25 This was somewhat confirmed by a non-representative study, which suggested that 69% of Safaricom users perceived service delivery as a factor affecting customer loyalty, 75% of respondents mentioned that switching barriers hindered them from migrating to competitors, 75% viewed Safaricom as customer focused, and 71% found Safaricom well protected by the government.

26 Ipsos Research 2015, cited in Kubania, March 2016. See Kubania, Jacqueline, March 2016, Safaricom ranked Kenya's top influential brand, Daily Nation/Nation Media Group, ▶ http://www.nation.co.ke/news/Safaricom-ranked-Kenya-top-influential-brand/-/1056/3128368/-/ur00r8/-/index.html [August 2016].

27 Internally commissioned research performed by Millward Brown, cited in Safaricom Annual Report 2016.

customer care agent. In 2015 it increased the use of web self-care, which enabled customers to manage their own mobile account, instead of calling customer service.

Safaricom used various loyalty schemes to improve customer stickiness: the Bonga loyalty program for its core business (One Bonga Point for every KES 10 spent on voice calls, SMS or data) and the Lipa na M-PESA Fuel Loyalty Program for fuel purchases using M-PESA (1 minute of airtime for every KES 500 of fuel bought). For its newer M-Shwari product, Safaricom incentivized stronger adoption through a kind of lottery (Stawisha na M-Shwari), which improved users' chances of winning if they increased their use of loans and savings.

Loyalty could be further encouraged by better quality service—resolving customers' concerns speedily. One way to go about this was to have knowledgeable customer service representatives available[28]; another way was to get to know the customer in depth and being aware of the current issue so that next to real-time support could be provided.

23.2.7 Ensuring a Strong IT Backbone and More Digitized Processes

For any telecom operator, the network was the core of the business on which products and services were developed and delivered. Safaricom had to improve its network and IT capabilities to cope with its bigger customer base and larger service offering. In 2015 it invested over KES 32 billion (US$300 million) in telecom infrastructure, covering 78% of the population with 3G and 95% with 2G services.[29] An independent evaluation revealed that Safaricom had the best telecom network in Kenya. When it launched 4G, Safaricom became the first mobile telecom operator in the whole sub-Saharan region to provide this technology. It focused on improving the following core activities: network coverage, 3G enhancement and additional spectrum, own fiber projects, network stability, modernization and optimization, as well as upgrading the M-PESA platform. Safaricom opened a KES 20 million (US$200,000) data center in Western Kenya to improve the efficiency of data center organization and installation, as well as network equipment maintenance in the North Rift region. It also aimed to handle increased data processing needs as analytics applications were further developed. Such upgrades were also needed. Especially in early 2008, when the service was still freshly launched, M-PESA had attracted more customers than expected, which led to network congestion (mostly during peak times such as Friday nights), resulting in money transfer delays of several days.

In 2015 Safaricom relocated an upgraded server version of the M-PESA platform from Germany to Kenya in order to improve transaction speeds and allow

28 Kihara/Ngugi, 2014. More information can be seen at: Kihara, Allen and Dr. Gordon K. Ngugi, 2014, Factors influencing customer loyalty in telecommunication industry in Kenya, International Journal of Social Sciences and Entrepreneurship, Special Issue 2, ► http://www.ku.ac. ke/schools/business/images/stories/research/dr_ngugi/factors_influencing_customer_loyalty_in_ telecommunication_industry_in_kenya.pdf [August 2016].

29 Safaricom already had the widest network coverage in the country, with over 3200 base stations, nearly half of them 3G-enabled.

its development partners to better link to the platform via secure application programming interfaces (APIs). M-PESA was simple to use and device agnostic[30] and so was the API, provided through web services' open interfaces over standard protocols. Unlike the old platform where many workarounds were required to automate payments, developers and other third-party providers were able to connect directly to the M-PESA platform.

23.2.8 Organizational Structure and Leadership

Ten years earlier, Safaricom had an organizational structure that was typical of a large, national telecom operator—with silos and lacking high-efficiency standards. In 2013 Collymore changed the way the company operated. He created customer-focused strategic business units (SBUs), streamlined the supporting corporate center, delegated some of the CEO's decision-making responsibilities, and reduced the number of his direct reports by half. The leaner organizational structure consisted of three revenue centers (i.e., financial services, enterprise business, and consumer business) and nine functional positions (*refer to* ◘ Fig. 23.10).

> **Definition**
>
> The process [of management restructuring] upon which we have embarked is absolutely necessary for our journey towards a Safaricom 2.0. – Bob Collymore, 2011[31]

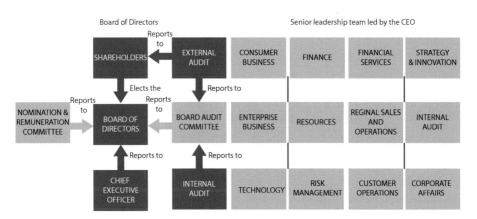

◘ **Fig. 23.10** Structure of Safaricom's executive leadership. (Source: Safaricom Annual Report 2016)

---

30 It worked the same way on the latest iPhone as it did on older devices like the Nokia feature phone.
31 CIO East Africa, March 2011. More information can be seen at: CIO East Africa, March 2011, Safaricom restructures top level management, ▶ http://www.cio.co.ke/news/main-stories/Safaricom-restructures-top-level-management [Aug 2016].

Some employees were let go and replaced by new staff, ready to embrace change. This included two senior executives: the CTO and the CIO. These changes were also rumored to have addressed corrupt practices.[32] Both senior positions were consolidated into one: Thibaud Rerolle became Technical and IT director. While this position managed most technology investments and hardware, the financial services director was in charge of, among other things, the marketing of M-PESA.

In August 2016, Safaricom hired Rob Webb, who had a banking and payment background, as the new director of financial services. He was a co-founder of PesaPoint, an agent network, and was recruited from Equity Bank to replace Betty Mwangi-Thuo who left Safaricom mid-2016 after nearly a decade in the post. She presided over Safaricom's mobile money division and was listed in 2010 as one of the world's top 10 women in the mobile sector and in 2013 as one of Africa's 20 most influential women in technology.[33]

Furthermore, to break down siloed approaches between divisions, Safaricom recruited a young technology-savvy man to serve as a bridge between the senior finance and technology positions. In addition, new positions/teams were created, such as customer segmentation, whose head was hired from competitor Airtel to start the department in 2015.

> **Definition**
>
> The telecom mindset is not the right mindset for the innovative space that we need to be operating in. We need to think of breaking off elements of the company to start to think and act like start-ups. Not only to attract the right people, also to attract the right relationships. – Bob Collymore

Safaricom clearly faced the challenge of building strong relationships with smaller developers who did not fully trust large brands. The recruitment of some entrepreneurial staff in the financial services area infused the company with a start-up mentality to better relate to the developer community. Safaricom aimed to have the best of two worlds: the "exploit" ability of a well-established company and the "explore" mindset of the new entrepreneurial recruits.

23.2.9 Human Resources Requirements for Becoming a Digital Platform Company

As a result of the drastic increase in mobile data, online financial services, and related data analytics, executives and staff needed to have capabilities not only to leverage these markets but also to foster them.

---

32 Alai, March 2011. More information can be seen at: Alai, Robert, March 2011, Safaricom 2.0 Launch See The Sacking Of Two Senior Employees, Blog TechMtaa, ► http://www.techmtaa. com/2011/03/23/safaricom-2-0/ [Aug 2016].

33 Mobile Communications International (MCI) and ► http://www.itnewsafrica.com/2013/08/afri-cas-most-powerful-women-2013/

Definition

I don't believe that the leadership, including me, really fully understands what the capabilities and needs are [for this new digital era]. We are in the process of learning what we don't know and learning about the skills that we need to identify and recruit. – Bob Collymore

---

While Safaricom aimed to maintain and develop its human resources, requirements had significantly changed in recent years. Collymore therefore released staff who were unable to adapt and recruited people with different capabilities than his predecessor Michael Joseph would have recruited 10 years earlier. He was especially looking for people with distinct data analytics skills. Although Collymore himself grew up in the telecom business (after leaving painting to pursue a corporate job), he was no longer looking for typical telecom competences. He wanted to recruit specialized data professionals from various industries. Having been brought up in Guyana himself, he also looked beyond Kenya's borders to recruit from a global talent pool.

23.2.10 Data Analytics in High Demand as Platform Businesses Thrive

---

Definition

We don't want to do everything in one go, because I describe it like buying a Ferrari when all you know so far is how to ride a scooter. We have to learn how to do this. The technical capabilities are there, but the human resources are not yet. So we are in the process of trying to recruit and indeed develop a skill set before we get too far down that road. We will probably become a leader in data analytics over the course of the next 18 to 24 months. – Bob Collymore

---

As Safaricom consistently moved more into data analytics, it required additional IT and HR capabilities to spur its advancement. In 2016 it hired Flytxt, a Dutch firm specialized in big data and mobile consumer analytics, to work on better monetizing mobile consumer data in order to generate revenues. The mother company, Vodafone, had achieved enhanced revenues through two other engagements with Flytxt and thereby also improved the customer experience through personalized and contextually relevant engagement with clients. Flytxt worked across Africa with other major telecom operators such as MTN.[34]

---

34 Kariuki, February 2016. More information can be seen at: Kariuki, James, Feb, 2016, Daily nation/ Nation media Group, Safaricom taps big data analytics to grow revenues, ▶ http://www.nation. co.ke/business/corporates/Safaricom-in-deal-to-monetise-customer-data/-/1954162/3089494/- /12u5jbp/-/index.html [August 2016].

As big data increasingly defined the game, Safaricom teamed up with Nokia's "Customer Experience Management (CEM) on Demand" in a bid to improve the customer experience. The CEM big data solution allowed the telecom operator to derive real-time insights from network, customer, and revenue touch points to provide proactive customer care, resolve network issues, and prioritize capital expenditure. The Nokia CEM on Demand solution could collect over 214 billion data points daily, generated from voice, SMS, and M-PESA traffic. It was piloted over the previous year in one region of Kenya and made it possible to retrieve subscriber records for customer care more quickly (from 2 to 6 hours to 15 minutes), obtain customer satisfaction scores for the entire network in near real time (from 30 days), and define the root causes of service degradation (from 24 hours to 10 minutes). Overall, it helped put network-related issues in context, with a real-time understanding of customers' problems.

Before long, Safaricom would not only be able to enhance its decision-making and customer service but also directly monetize the wealth of data it was generating. Soon telecommunications and mobile transaction data, triangulated with other data sources from other parties including web searches (e.g., Google) or social media (such as Facebook), could be used to analyze the behavior patterns of both users and societal groups at large.

23.2.11 Start-Up Business Diversifying Safaricom's Revenue Streams

Through its online payment platform, Safaricom entered the e-commerce space 6 years after M-PESA's launch. e-Commerce growth had been slow in Kenya due to the lack of an accessible and secure payment system. The Lipa na M-PESA online platform closed this gap. For Collymore:

>> M-PESA is at the heart of the innovation culture that has developed in Kenya and came about because of the proper platform, the payment platform that M-PESA has provided. Kenyans largely feel they are at a more innovative leading edge than many of our African counterparts and it is because of the success of M-PESA that people identify with it – and with the fact that Kenyans are into business development and have been prepared to take the logical leapfrogs – and that kind of set the table.

Such advancements transformed people's perceptions of Safaricom as a technological leader. M-PESA not only showed the potential of mobile money in developing markets such as Kenya but also contributed to developing Kenya as the (East) African technology hub, nicknamed Silicon Savannah. In recent years, Nairobi had attracted numerous start-ups, many of which could realize their digital business because of the now available payment method. Without M-PESA, the market was not able to support online businesses as they lacked core infrastructure, i.e., a reliable payment channel to enable a viable business cycle. Thus, M-PESA not only transformed Safaricom's business model but also contributed to a more integrated online and offline economy in Kenya and beyond.[35]

Definition

M-PESA is a liberating product. It opened a space where most other telecom companies are not. M-PESA is a catalyst for other things such as finding educational solutions, agricultural solutions, and health solutions. It allows us to work in partnerships with people with whom we would otherwise not work. – Bob Collymore

---

One of Safaricom's partnerships was with M-KOPA, a Kenyan solar energy company, founded in 2011, that delivered home solar systems in Kenya, Tanzania, and Uganda to mainly rural, poor customers. Customers paid a deposit (basically a credit) of KES 3500 (US$35), used the system at home, and paid KES 50 (US$0.50) a day over a year to own the solar system. Payment could be made via M-PESA.

By working closely with developers and start-ups to link them with the mobile payment system, Safaricom held the main resource and the network; it also held the main payment channel. Until recently, it had been selling these resources as a service, cashing in on user and transaction fees.

Safaricom's first digital service was in the transport sector, as Kenya's public transportation system was massively underdeveloped and taxi services were comparatively expensive. Dubbed "Little," the service was basically a local competitor for Uber—which had recently launched in Kenya—with a few add-ons. Little gave drivers a larger percentage of the fare, provided Safaricom Wi-Fi inside the car, provided live GPS-enabled maps for pickups, and integrated the M-PESA payment platform while allowing cash payment as well. It was changing the industry considerably, and traditional providers were dropping their prices.[36]

Safaricom continued to fund innovations through its Spark Fund. It also invested in Sendy, a last-mile package delivery and logistics start-up. Through products like M-TIBA—a healthcare product delivered in partnership with the PharmAccess Foundation and CarePay—the company was creating a new case for mobile health platforms. It also continued working with Eneza Education to offer access to quality education through a mobile-based platform known as Shupavu 291.

---

35 Compared with technologically more "mature" countries, Kenya is leapfrogging technologies one after another at a very fast pace. Technological innovation is therefore very time sensitive (not too early or too late). It also requires a company to be highly adaptive to the business environment, which still has a number of hindering factors such as unreliable infrastructure or security concerns.

36 Read more on Little in blog posts, for example, on ▶ www.techcrunch.com

23.3 New Horizons

23

Definition

[My aim is to] turn the company into a platform company, rather than a pipe company. A platform company means that you have more industries that rely on services that you are providing. We believe that the platform we have is able to improve efficiency of delivery, reduce costs and, very importantly, in an environment like ours, add more transparency and reduce corruption. – Bob Collymore

---

M-PESA did not only transform the market; since its launch in 2007, it had significantly transformed Safaricom. It allowed Safaricom to venture into a business area as a first mover—an outright first comer in Kenya and one of only a few worldwide. This new product had allowed Safaricom to outpace the competition as it maintained its grip on the market and its dynamics. With a strong business ecosystem built around the M-PESA service, Safaricom had been able to develop over the years from a bread-and-butter telecom business to an aspiring platform built around mobile financial services.

However, there were still challenges ahead as competition in the telecom and banking sectors intensified and rival companies became more aggressive. Safaricom still led the market, but it had recently lost market share. Although M-PESA moved funds for banks, it could break away if IPSL launched its interbank platform.

As he zoomed in on the airfield and the nearby helicopter landing pad, Bob was convinced that to stay ahead of the pack, Safaricom had to expand its M-PESA digital platform geographically and to continuously innovate its offerings, but what sectors should it focus on? Back on solid ground, Collymore looked forward to leading his company towards new horizons (◗ Exhibit 23.11).

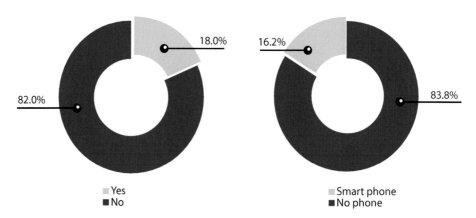

◗ **Exhibit 23.11**   Access to Internet (left) and use of smart phones (right) in Kenya. (Source: FSD Kenya 2016)

Appendix

Background Information 1: Safaricom CEO's 2016 Statement on Annual Performance and Strategic Focus (Adapted Extract)

The annual results were a result of our continued focus on the three strategic pillars: putting customers first, providing relevant products, and enhancing operational excellence. This resulted in an 8% growth of our loyal customer base, generating strong financial and commercial performance.

We realigned our sales and operations teams to be independently managed in six regions, with the sales and network teams in each region reporting to their respective region heads. Additionally, investments of KES 32.1 billion in our network led to improved data speeds and voice network quality. Independent drive tests commissioned by Safaricom in March 2016 to measure key quality metrics such as dropped calls, call setup success, voice quality, and data speeds indicate that our network delivers the best voice quality and faster data services than our competitors.

Mobile penetration in Kenya now stands at 89.2% as at 31 March 2016 with Safaricom having a subscriber market share of 65.6%. Our market share was reduced partly due to a change in internal reporting policy, which aligned our customer number reporting methodology to that of our competitors. We now report total customers as those contributing to revenues in the last 90 days.

Service revenue grew by 13.8% to KES 177.8 billion. Voice service revenue, which now represents 51.1% of our service revenue, grew by 3.9% to KES 90.8 billion. Non-voice revenue representing 48.9% of service revenue up from 44.1% last year grew by 26.3% to KES 87.0 billion.

Messaging revenue grew by 10.6% to KES 17.3 billion due to an increase in the number of SMS users benefiting from affordable SMS bundles and targeted promotions. Mobile data revenue grew at 42.7% driven by a combination of a 21.5% increase in 30-day active mobile data customers to 14.1 million, an increased uptake of data bundles and a growth in smartphone penetration.

In March 2016, we had 7.9 million customers on 3G- and 4G-enabled devices, of which 0.7 million were 4G handsets. Fixed service revenue grew by 22% to KES 3.8 billion because of an increased number of fixed service customers to 10,490 up 21.6%. We now have 1,018 commercial buildings and 1,795 homes connected to high-speed fiber.

M-PESA revenue grew by 27.2% to KES 41.5 billion driven by a 19.8% growth in 30-day active M-PESA customers to 16.6 million and a 17.5% growth of our M-PESA agent footprint to 100,744. Lipa na M-PESA payments made at 44,000 merchant outlets in March 2016 grew by 74% to KES 20 billion.

Contribution margin improved by 1.1% points to 66.7% attributed to lower growth of direct costs at 10.0% compared to a 14.1% growth in total revenue excluding construction revenue.

Operating expenses as a percentage of total revenue excluding construction revenue was unchanged at 22.1% despite a 9.8% depreciation of the Kenya shilling in the financial year under review. We continue to explore cost reduction opportunities with efforts focused on lowering transmission costs, network-operating costs (including fuel), and IT operational costs.

The business delivered encouraging results and continued to create value for our shareholders, supported by growth across all our revenue streams and focus on cost efficiency, resulting in an EBITDA margin of 44.6%, which was a 0.9 percentage point improvement.

Free cash flow grew by 10.3% to KES 30.4 billion despite the significant supplier payments for [building] the National Police Security Network.

Background Information 2: Safaricom Chairman's 2016 Statement on Kenyan ICT Market (Adapted Extract)

In the year under review, Kenya's gross domestic product (GDP) grew by an estimated 5.6% in 2015 compared to 5.3% in 2014. The performance was driven by a stable macroeconomic environment and significantly improved performance of agriculture, construction, finance, insurance, and real estate sectors. This was despite inflationary pressures and volatility in foreign exchange rates.

The ICT sector grew by 7.3% in 2015, which was lower than the 14.6% growth achieved in 2014. The growth in 2015 was because of resilient expansion in the mobile telephony network and increased uptake of Internet services. We remain confident that the sector is on course to attain the Vision 2030 target of contributing 10% to the country's GDP by 2017. The telecommunications sub-sector continues to be a significant contributor of this growth, with Safaricom and other players supporting economic growth.

In March 2016, inflation was at 6.45%. In the period under review, the foreign currency exchange market improved and the local unit stabilized at KES 101.33 to the US dollar compared to a high of KES 105.29 recorded in the first half of the financial year.

In light of the strong financial performance, the Board recommended a dividend of KES 30.48 billion, an increase of 18.9% from previous year. This is once again the largest dividend in Kenyan corporate history.

Source: Safaricom Annual Report 2016

References

Ivatury/Pickens. (2008). *Mobile phone banking and low-income customers. Evidence from South Africa*. Washington: CGAP.

Ludwig, S. (2010). *Socio-economic impacts and creative usage of mobile financial services among low-income micro-entrepreneurs. Evidence from an ethnographic field research in Kenya*. Thesis. Vienna: University of Vienna, Austria.

DBS Transformation (C): The World's Best Digital Bank

Contents

Researcher PC Abraham prepared this case under the supervision of Professor Sean Meehan as a basis for class discussion rather than to illustrate either effective or ineffective handling of a business situation. Copyright © 2017 by *IMD—International Institute for Management Development*, Lausanne, Switzerland (► www.imd.org). No part of this publication may be reproduced, stored in a retrieval system, or transmitted in any form or by any means without the prior written permission of *IMD*.

© Springer Nature Switzerland AG 2020
T. Jelassi, F. J. Martínez-López, *Strategies for e-Business*, Classroom Companion: Business,
https://doi.org/10.1007/978-3-030-48950-2_24

■ **Introduction**

Since CEO Piyush Gupta and his colleagues reset DBS's vision and strategy and commenced its transformation in 2009, DBS doubled both its top and bottom lines (*see* ◘ Table 24.1—*Company Financials*). The accolades and awards it received in 2016 suggested it had successfully transformed to become a world-class multi-national bank and was well on its way to becoming a 22,000 start-up (see full list of accolades and awards ▶ https://www.dbs.com/awards/default. page). This included being recognized by *Euromoney* as the World's Best Digital Bank:

24

◘ **Table 24.1**   Company financials (US$1 = S$1.41 (12.31.15) and US$1 = S$1.44 (12.31.16))

	2012	2013	2014	2015	2016
Balance sheet (S$ billion)					
Total assets	353.0	402.0	440.7	457.8	481.6
Customer loans	210.5	248.7	275.6	283.3	301.5
Total liabilities	317.0	364.3	400.5	415.0	434.6
Customer deposits	253.5	292.4	317.2	320.1	347.4
Total shareholders' funds	31.7	34.2	37.7	40.4	44.6
Income statement (S$ billion)					
Total income	8.06	8.93	9.62	10.79	11.49
Profit before tax	4.16	4.32	4.70	5.16	5.08
Net profit	3.81	3.67	4.05	4.45	4.36
Financial ratios (%)					
Net interest margin	1.70	1.62	1.68	1.77	1.80
Cost to income ratio	44.8	43.9	45.0	45.4	43.3
Return on assets	0.97	0.91	0.91	0.96	0.92
Return on shareholders' funds	11.2	10.8	10.9	11.2	10.1
Loan to deposit ratio	83.1	85.0	86.9	88.5	86.8
Non-performing loan rate	1.2	1.1	0.9	0.9	1.4

Source: DBS Annual Report 2015 and DBS Performance Summary, Financial results for the Fourth Quarter ended 31 December 2016 and For the Year 2016

Definition

Leaders in digital banking talk about the difference between digitizing aspects of a bank and creating a truly digital financial institution. DBS is doing this better than any other bank. It is demonstrably the case that digital innovation pervades every part of DBS, from consumer to corporate, SMEs to transaction banking and even the DBS Foundation. – Clive Horwood, editor of Euromoney magazine (Source: cited in DBS 2016 Annual Report)

Now, Gupta believed it was time to leverage the bank's growing digital, customer-centric, and cultural capabilities so that DBS would lead the market in "Making Banking Joyful."

24.1 Making Banking Joyful: Three-Pronged Approach

24.1.1 Embracing Digital

For DBS being digital goes beyond customer interfaces, such as digital apps or mobile/Internet banking. It has reengineered its middle- and back-office technologies and processes. With its common platform of services and APIs, it can integrate best-in-breed technologies, thereby moving faster on the front end. It continues to adopt the practices of global technology companies: constantly experimenting, automatically scaling, and rapidly bringing new features to market. It is embracing microservices and cloud technology to be nimbler and more fintech-like. It was one of the first banks in Asia Pacific to partner with Amazon Web Services to create a hybrid cloud environment for rapid capacity and functional changes.

24.1.2 Embedding Itself in the Customer's Journey

DBS believes banking should be seamlessly interwoven into a customer's everyday life. It has focused on customers' "jobs-to-be-done." For example, previously, a home buyer might have interacted with the bank only when she identified a dream home and was in need of a mortgage. Today, DBS seeks to understand customers' needs from the start, beginning with the house-hunting process, identifying pain points, and addressing these long before any banking is done. To be effective, journey thinking involves research and interviews, business case development, conducting experiments, and prototyping, before a new product or process is rolled out. Many employees have been trained in journey thinking and human-centered design. Today, over 300 journeys are being run across the bank. These journeys involve collaborations across business and support units, as well as across geographies, engaging a large part of the organization.

24.1.3 Creating a Start-Up Mindset

To familiarize employees with relevant technologies and embrace experimentation, entrepreneurship, and innovation, DBS created immersion programs such as hackathons, where employees work with start-ups to develop solutions to business challenges. It also embraced and institutionalized the practices and methodologies common among global technology companies. In an industry-first move in the region, it trained management at all levels in human-centered design and user experience while adopting agile ways of working. This helped the bank accelerate the rollout of its digital offerings. In addition to the 1000 plus experiments it has conducted since 2015, DBS conducts its own incubator/accelerator programs providing firsthand exposure to the start-up mindset. Over 400 start-ups were engaged in 2016 as part of these programs.

In addition, it adapted its infrastructure. Many offices are now entirely open plan with dedicated spaces such as social hubs for networking as well as innovation and journey "laboratories." In 2016, it launched DBS Asia X—a 16,000 sq ft space in Singapore, dedicated to designing iconic customer experiences and fostering greater collaboration with the fintech ecosystem. All these allow employees to become immersed in new technologies, a start-up culture, agile methodology, and other digital working concepts. The bank has also established a technology hub in India dedicated to developing technology and intellectual property, rapidly scaling up its in-house capabilities.

DBS appointed Neal Cross as DBS's first Chief Innovation Officer in April 2014. His remit is to work with the businesses and corporate functions to drive innovation, supporting the many teams engaged in projects to enhance customer experience and better engage with customers digitally. He orchestrates an ecosystem of collaborators and fills the role of innovation advocate in the bank. He was named the world's "most disruptive Chief Innovation Officer" in the Talent Unleashed Awards in August 2016.

24.2 Outcomes

24.2.1 Customer Reach and Acquisition

In 2016, 25% of wealth customers and more than 60% of Singapore SME customers were acquired via digital channels. In India, DBS launched digibank, the country's first mobile-only bank to penetrate the retail banking segment. The bank has acquired more than one million digibank customers in its first full year.

24.2.2 Efficiency

DBS's cost-income ratio improved two percentage points to 43%, due in part to improved productivity arising from digitalization initiatives. In particular, fewer manual processes have enabled the bank to support higher business volumes with the same level of resources. For example, digibank India uses one-fifth of the resources required in a traditional bank setup.

24.2.3 Data Analytics

DBS has leveraged analytics for various purposes, for example, providing contextual offers and advice to customers, reducing ATM downtime, predicting and preventing trade fraud, and lowering employee attrition.

24.3 The Future

Piyush Gupta was pleased with the progress on the three platforms of transformation: strategy, operational architecture, and culture. The latter, culture, he concedes is particularly challenging, but he was very encouraged that now at least half of DBS staff had embraced the kind of ambition, behavior, and reflexes one tends to associate with start-ups: entrepreneurial, innovative, and actively rethinking the business and all its processes from bottom-up and from inside-out. In Gupta's view, this is how banking must evolve:

Definition

The disruption experienced by bookstores, music and telecommunications is going to happen in banking. We need to be as nimble and agile as the technology companies. We must operate effectively in a completely disruptive world, where consumer behavior is changing and technology allows you do things fundamentally differently. – Piyush Gupta, CEO DBS

In this future, increasingly occupied by fintechs and techfins disrupting industry after industry, he saw a key role for banks like DBS that embraced a new way of thinking and working. Banks bring with them very specific and valuable experience and skills especially managing risk and balance sheets over credit cycles.

Definition

When you bring our innate and inherent strengths together with those of the new competition I think you have a good basis for competition. – Piyush Gupta, CEO DBS

AccorHotels' Digital Transformation: A Strategic Response to Hospitality Disruptor Airbnb

Contents

Researcher Valerie Keller-Birrer prepared this case under the supervision of Professor Tawfik Jelassi as a basis for class discussion rather than to illustrate either effective or ineffective handling of a business situation. Copyright © 2017 by *IMD – International Institute for Management* Development, Lausanne, Switzerland (▶ www.imd.org). No part of this publication may be reproduced, stored in a retrieval system or transmitted in any form or by any means without the prior written permission of *IMD*.

© Springer Nature Switzerland AG 2020
T. Jelassi, F. J. Martínez-López, *Strategies for e-Business*, Classroom Companion: Business,
https://doi.org/10.1007/978-3-030-48950-2_25

■ **Introduction**

AccorHotels, Europe's leading hotel group, was going through a major digital transformation initiated by its CEO, Sébastien Bazin. A relative newcomer to the hospitality industry, the private equity investor was shaking up the traditional strategy of a large hotel chain and disrupting AccorHotels' business model.

Bazin was transforming the group at breathtaking speed, yet believed AccorHotels was not changing fast enough to keep up with the changes occurring in the hospitality industry. New digital players had entered the market and were challenging the conventional hospitality approach. In particular, the emergence of the sharing economy—with the start-up Airbnb in the lead—had created a major challenge if not a threat to established hotel chains. The San Francisco-based accommodation rental company had turned a simple idea, renting an air mattress in your living room, into a US$30 billion company in just 8 years. More than a short-term, real estate rental company, Airbnb had become a societal phenomenon appealing to a new generation of travelers.

Although the new digital players' business model was considered one of the most significant trends to shake up the hospitality industry in recent years, established hotel chains showed little reaction. They maintained healthy growth rates and experienced little impact on their bookings. Bazin, however, quickly realized that the new sharing economy players represented a threat to the business model of existing hotel chains and firmly believed that Airbnb should be taken seriously. After joining the Accor Group in 2013, he set out to drastically transform the 50-year-old hotel chain with the aim of turning it into an active player in the new hospitality economy able to compete head-on with the industry's digital disruptors. AccorHotels embarked on a far-reaching digital transformation that affected its corporate culture, organizational structure, value proposition, and overall business model.

Had AccorHotels reacted fast enough to the industry changes and was the business transformation initiated by Bazin enough to compete with the new sharing economy giant Airbnb? Could a large, asset-heavy company become a dynamic and agile organization? Bazin believed the only way forward was to stop "watching the world passing by" and fully embrace the sharing economy. Was he right to develop an acquisition strategy of digital platforms to be on a par with Airbnb or should he stick to his core competence of managing and running hotels?

25.1 The Hospitality Industry

25.1.1 The Traditional Hospitality Industry

The hotel industry had been growing for 7 consecutive years since the 2008–2009 global financial crisis and was expected to reach revenues of $550 billion by 2016.[1]

---

1 "The Global Hotel Industry and Trends for 2016." ► *Hospitalitynet.org*, 18 December 2015. ► http://www.hospitalitynet.org/news/4073336.html (accessed 14 June 2017).

25

It benefited from a strong growth in demand as the number of people traveling around the world for business or leisure continued to grow and was expected to increase by 4% in 2016 from its 2015 level of 1.2 billion travelers worldwide (Escobar 2016). This was matched by a growth of 4%, or 420,000 additional rooms, in the global branded supply since 2011, reaching a total of 9.9 million rooms and apartments.[2] (*Refer to* ◘ Fig. 25.1 *on global hotel industry revenues from 2008 to 2016 and* ◘ Fig. 25.2 *on the annual growth rates of hotel chains supply.*)

After a decade of relative stability in the global ranking of hotel groups, several merger and acquisition operations in 2015 and 2016 brought about significant changes. Marriott with the acquisition of Starwood Hotels & Resorts became the biggest player worldwide and the first to surpass the one million-room mark. It was followed by Hilton Worldwide, InterContinental Hotels Group (IHG), Wyndham (with the acquisition of Dolce), Jin Jiang Hotels, and AccorHotels with the acquisition of Fairmont Raffles. (*Refer to* ◘ Fig. 25.3 *for the global hotel groups' ranking by number of rooms*). Despite this industry concentration, and with the exception of the Americas, the hotel industry remained extremely fragmented, with the majority of hotels still held by independent hoteliers.

Hotel chains depended heavily on the high-end categories: the upscale and luxury segment represented 59% of revenues, while the midscale range remained an important contributor with 27%. However, the economy and budget segment, representing only 14% of revenues, was the only segment showing some decline, with average daily rates down by 0.2% compared to an overall increase of daily rates of 1.9%.[3]

Note: Revenoe in txllions of U.S. dollars.

◘ **Fig. 25.1**   Global hotel industry revenue (2008–2016). (Source: ▶ http://www.hospitalitynet.org/news/4073336.html)

---

2   "Worldwide hotel chain supply: Global chain supply confirms growth." ▶ *Hospitality-on.com,* 7 June 2016. ▶ http://hospitality-on.com/en/news/2016/07/07/worldwide-hotel-chain-supply-global-chain-supply-confirms-growth/ (accessed 14 June 2017).

3   "Worldwide hotel industry: New growth in hotel results despite the Asian slowdown." ▶ *Hospitality-on.com,* 7 June 2016. ▶ http://hospitality-on.com/en/news/2016/07/07/worldwide-hotel-industry-new-growth-in-hotel-results-despite-the-asian-slowdown/ (accessed 14 June 2017).

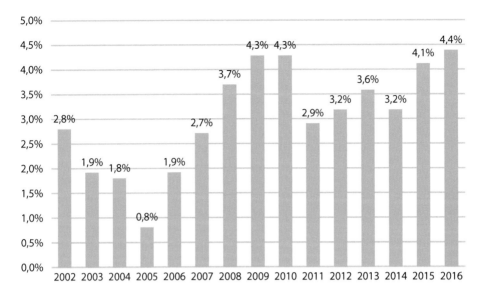

● **Fig. 25.2** Annual growth rates of hotel chains supply. (Source: ► http://hospitality-on.com/en/news/2016/07/07/worldwide-hotel-chain-supply-global-chain-supply-confirms-growth/)

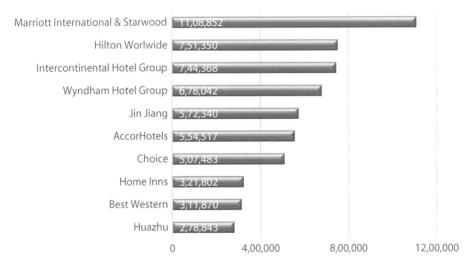

● **Fig. 25.3** Global hotel group ranking by number of rooms (2016). (Source: ► http://hospitality-on.com/en/news/2016/04/08/global-hotel-ranking-top-10-what-does-the-future-hold-after-the-marriott-starwood-merger/)

25.1.2 The Digital Disruption of the Hospitality Industry

For half a century, the hospitality industry had mostly been unchallenged. The majority of big hotel chains were created between 1942 and 1965 and were able to grow exponentially, with little competition, until 2000. A first disruption took

25

place in 2005, with the emergence of new digital players: online booking platforms such as Expedia, which replaced physical travel agencies. A second disruption took place a few years later with the rise of price comparison websites, such as KAYAK, and rating sites, such as Tripadvisor, which facilitated customers' selection decisions. According to Bazin, by 2016, 80% of online traffic was going through ▶ Booking.com and Expedia, while 80% of the recommendations were in the hands of Tripadvisor (Ting 2016). Yet, these two disruptions triggered little reaction from the hotel industry.

The third disruption occurred with the emergence of the sharing economy, a marketplace built around the sharing of resources (e.g., a room, a service, a skill, or a car), mostly between private individuals. All transactions were coordinated through the internet, mainly as a temporary exchange. This practice quickly evolved into a profitable business model thanks to pioneering start-ups, such as Airbnb (for sharing accommodation) and Uber (for sharing a car). Many other companies also emerged in the sharing economy, such as Fon (a Wi-Fi sharing service), Holidog or DogVacay (pet sitter communities), and TaskRabbit (for hiring people to do small tasks or jobs).

The high market capitalization of some shared economy companies and the amount of funds they were able to raise clearly showed that these new players were to be taken seriously. After Marriott and Hilton, Airbnb already represented one of the primary values in the industry, even if this was not recognized since the company had not yet been introduced on the stock exchange[4] (*refer to* ◘ Fig. 25.4 *for Ranking of Major Hotels Groups and Digital Companies by Company Value*). While Airbnb was the pioneer of the sharing accommodation sector, it was quickly followed by other start-ups around the world, such as Homestay, Bedycasa, and Onefinestay, to name just a few.

- **Did the Sharing Economy Represent a Threat for the Hotel Industry?**

According to Yves Lacheret, senior Vice President of new business integration at AccorHotels, "The hotel industry underestimated the third hospitality revolution: The rise of the sharing economy."[5] Hotel group leaders initially doubted that the sharing economy represented a competitive threat. Hilton CEO Chris Nassetta said in October 2016 that Airbnb was not "a major threat" to his company's business (Bryan 2016). Many industry players considered Airbnb a competitor but not a threat, assuming that sharing platforms were bringing in new customers, as had low-cost airlines in the passenger air transportation industry 10 years earlier. Hoteliers believed it was possible for both hotels and sharing platforms to grow without stealing customers away from each other—a belief that was supported by the strong growth rates in the traditional hotel industry since the economic crisis.

---

4   "Financial ranking of groups: "Muscle-flexing among hotel & digital travel industry leaders." ▶ *Hospitality-on.com*, 7 June 2016. ▶ http://hospitality-on.com/en/news/2016/07/06/financial-ranking-of-groups-muscle-flexing-among-hotel-digital-travel-industry-leaders/ (accessed 14 June 2017).

5   All quotes from Yves Lacheret are based on an interview conducted by the authors on 18 April 2017.

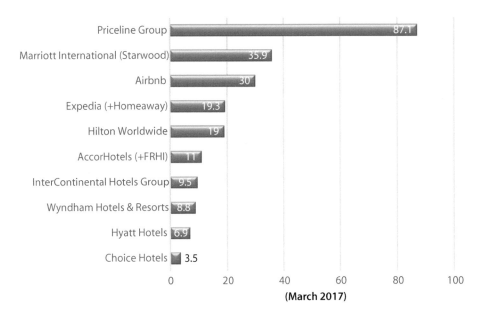

■ **Fig. 25.4** Ranking of major hotels groups and digital companies by company value. (Source:
▶ https://finance.yahoo.com)

Major hotel chains catered to luxury business travelers, while initially Airbnb
operated in the economy segment since it offered a cheaper alternative to budget
travelers. A Boston University study conducted in Texas confirmed that the sharing
economy indeed had a negative impact on budget revenues. It found that each 10%
increase in supply on Airbnb caused a decrease of 0.37% in monthly hotel revenues, in particular among low-end hotels (Zervas et al. 2016).

25.2 Airbnb

Based in San Francisco, Airbnb was a privately owned accommodation rental
company. It enabled hosts around the world to list and rent out their properties or
rooms to guests who used the website to find a place to stay—from a shared room
in an apartment to a whole villa or castle. Nathan Blecharczyk, CTO and co-
founder of Airbnb, described the concept of Airbnb: "Airbnb allows travelers to
stay in someone else's home. We make it as easy to book someone else's home as it
is to book a hotel." (World Economic Forum 2016)

25.2.1 History

In 2007, roommates Brian Chesky and Joe Gebbia started AirBed&Breakfast in
their San Francisco apartment. Their idea was to make a few extra dollars by facilitating accommodation rentals. The two friends provided three inflatable mat-

tresses and a homemade breakfast to guests who were unable to find alternative accommodation in the city during a design conference. In 2008, Nathan Blecharczyk joined the two co-founders, and ▶ Airbedandbreakfast.com was subsequently launched. The start-up initially struggled to convince investors of its business potential and was relaunched at the 2008 Democratic National Convention in Denver (Colorado) based on the idea that the shortage of hotel rooms would push people to look for alternative accommodation options.

This was a turning point for the start-up. It had the opportunity to join a prestigious start-up accelerator where the co-founders spent 3 months improving their business plan. The website name was shortened to ▶ Airbnb.com, and in April 2009, the start-up finally found an investor, Sequoia Capital. From then on, the company started to grow, and in 2011, 4 years after the first air mattress guests, it covered 89 countries, had its first international office in Hamburg (Germany), and hit one million online bookings. That same year, a further funding of $112 million pushed the value of the company to over $1 billion, making Airbnb a "unicorn"[6] in Silicon Valley. By the end of 2016, 8 years after it was formally launched, Airbnb had three million listings, including 3000 castles and 1400 treehouses in more than 65,000 cities and 191 countries. Its market value was estimated at $30 billion, making it the second most valued start-up company in the world, behind Uber ($68 billion). Airbnb had become a key player in the hospitality industry, with a value just below the $35 billion market cap of Marriott International, the world's largest hotel chain.[7] Blecharczyk described the unique growth of Airbnb at the 2016 WEF:

> » We started it eight years ago and nobody thought it was a good idea back then. The obvious thought was, "Why would you allow a stranger to stay in your home?" So, fast-forward eight years, to date, 70 million guests have stayed in a stranger's home, just 40 million last year alone (World Economic Forum 2016).

25.2.2 Key Figures

Being privately owned, Airbnb did not disclose its detailed financial performance. However, it was estimated that its revenues had grown from $250 million in 2015 to $1.7 billion in 2016, with a target of $2.8 billion in 2017 and $8.5 billion by 2020. Airbnb recorded profits for the first time in 2016 with $100 million earnings before interest, tax, depreciation, and amortization. The company was expected to be profitable again in 2017, with $450 million in EBITDA and had a target of $3.5 billion by 2020 (Mikey 2017). (*Refer to* ◘ Fig. 25.5 *for Airbnb revenue growth and forecast.*)

6 A unicorn is a start-up with a value of US$1 billion or more.
7 "Marriott International Market Cap." ▶ *Ycharts.com* 23 March 2017. ▶ https://ycharts.com/companies/MAR/market_cap (accessed on 23 March 2017).

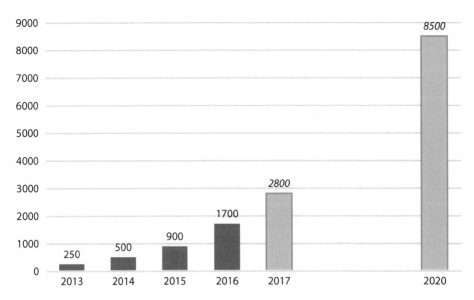

❏ **Fig. 25.5** Airbnb revenue growth and forecast in million USD (2013–2020). (Sources: 2013 and 2015 data: ► http://www.inc.com/linkedin/sramana-mitra/billion-dollar-unicorn-airbnb-continues-soar-sramana-mitra.html; 2014: ► https://www.quora.com/How-much-revenue-is-Airbnb-making; 2016, 2017 and 2020 data: ► http://www.valuewalk.com/2017/02/airbnb-expects-2-8b-2017-revenue-8-5b-2020/)

25.2.3 Business Model

- **Product**

Airbnb defined itself as "a trusted community marketplace for people to list, discover, and book unique accommodation around the world." The start-up provided the platform to facilitate the transactions but was not the provider of the ultimate service —the accommodation. As Blecharczyk explained: "The hosts are micro entrepreneurs and we're giving them a hospitality toolkit, facilitating the search, the payment, the standards." (World Economic Forum 2016) A central piece of Airbnb's success model was a simple equation: disappointment equals expectation minus reality (McMillin 2016). To manage expectations, Airbnb ensured that each listing offered an accurate portrayal of the amenities, and the type of experience guests would find, by listing the accommodation's advantages as well as potential negative aspects. Airbnb strongly believed that high-quality pictures would make a key difference, and professional photograph services were provided in most cities free of charge. In Paris, for example, 50% of Airbnb apartments featured professional photographs.[8]

Full transparency was what fueled the community and ensured high satisfaction rates. Throughout the application process, hosts and guests could find reviews

---

8   "Accor vs Airbnb – S. Bazin et O. Grémillon aux Mardis de l'ESSEC." ► *Youtube.com*, 28 March 2015. ► https://www.youtube.com/watch?v=Q3gwLlVhMMs (accessed 14 June 2017).

and social media connections to build trust among users. Using Airbnb's online reputation system, both hosts and guests provided feedback at the end of each stay with guests rating the accommodation's features such as location, cleanliness, convenience, etc. Mapping and destination pictures further helped customers find the right accommodation. Airbnb had an excellent mobile presence that described and mapped nearby attractions and services from any connected device.

- **Pricing**

Airbnb generated revenues by charging hosts a 3% service fee to cover the cost of processing payments, and guests a 9–12% service fee for each reservation they made. The company provided a dynamic pricing tool that offered hosts pricing recommendations based on available demand, supply, features, and amenities of the accommodation (Mitra 2016).

- **Customer Experience**

Beyond providing a platform to find accommodation, Airbnb offered its users an authentic experience, a way to discover out how it felt to live like a local. The younger generation was not interested in many of the services big hotels offered; they preferred to be in a cool neighborhood with bigger rooms, more space, and possibly a kitchen. More than just a platform to find a place to stay, Airbnb had become a trendy movement, a new lifestyle.

The Airbnb concept appealed to young, leisurely travelers willing to consider more adventurous accommodation options. More than a third of Airbnb users were under 30 years of age, compared with 16% for online travel agencies. Due to its sharing economy mindset, verification system and high customer satisfaction, Airbnb users showed high levels of loyalty and satisfaction (Huston 2015). Beyond the unique experience, part of the appeal was that Airbnb offered a cheaper alternative to a hotel room. In San Francisco, for example, the 2015 average daily rate of Airbnb accommodation was 18.8% lower than that of a hotel room.[9]

25.2.4 Challenges

Airbnb's exponential growth came with some challenges. Various reports began to emerge of theft or damage to property as well as increasing complaints from neighbors about disturbances, noise, and damage. One growing concern was the start-up's negative impact on the housing market, as landlords were reported to kick out long-term tenants to maximize their income by renting apartments to Airbnb customers, thus converting apartment buildings into what essentially became illegal hotel rooms. These unlawful professional landlords were putting an important strain on rental prices. The rapid growth of Airbnb listings led to the "corporatiza-

---

9 "Airbnb – Statistics & Facts." ▶ *Statista.com*. ▶ https://www.statista.com/topics/2273/airbnb/ (accessed 14 June 2017).

tion" of the offering, with an increasing number of listings coming from other hospitality companies and providers of multiple properties, including hotels, real estate agents, and serviced apartment providers.

Following these concerns, city authorities started to issue laws to protect the housing market and tenants. Since existing regulation did not cover accommodation provided by the sharing economy, Airbnb found itself in a regulatory gray area. Related discussions were particularly heated in New York City, where Airbnb's growth was particularly strong. A bill was signed in 2016 to fine tenants or landlords who rented out unoccupied flats for less than 30 days. Other cities followed suit, including Berlin and London, where restrictive rent rules were introduced. Airbnb's response to such new regulation was to proactively work with city authorities to find a compromise with policy makers before restricting regulations were issued. Seventy lobbyists were said to be working for Airbnb in the United States, trying to get favorable legislation passed to benefit the company.

Another source of conflict, and hoteliers' most frequent criticism of Airbnb, was the way it was taxed compared with hotels. While hotels had to pay occupancy and sales taxes, Airbnb was not subject to occupancy tax laws and was not paying local governments' sales tax. The company was working with governments across the world to explore ways to facilitate occupancy tax collection in as many locations as possible.

25.2.5 Expansion

- **Targeting the Business Sector**

For years, hoteliers had claimed that Airbnb and hotels did not compete for the same customers, since hotels catered to business and luxury travelers, while Airbnb appealed to budget and leisure travelers. This changed when Airbnb adapted its offer to appeal to the highly profitable business travel segment, the bread and butter of hotels. *Airbnb for Business* was launched in 2015 and included a central billing system, a dashboard for HR representatives, as well as billing and reporting tools.

"Business travel ready" lodgings had to meet various criteria, such as high customer ratings, 24/7 access to the property, an entire home or apartment, Wi-Fi, and a laptop-friendly workspace. In July 2016, Airbnb announced a partnership with three of the world's biggest corporate-travel bookers (American Express Global Business Travel, BCD Travel, and Carlson Wagonlit Travel), thus putting Airbnb properties on the list of options for employees when booking a business trip.

By the end of 2016, Airbnb's new focus seemed to be paying-off. Data from Concur, a travel-expense firm, showed that the number of business travelers expensing Airbnb accommodation had grown 44% in the second quarter of 2016 compared with a year earlier, driven by small- and mid-sized businesses as well as tech and academic companies. Airbnb estimated that about 10% of its bookings were for businesses travel rather than pleasure (Gulliver 2016), with customers including Google, Morgan Stanley, ▶ Salesforce.com, SoundCloud, and Vox Media.

■ **Future Outlook**

Airbnb did not stop at growing its core business, and targeting business travelers, it had big plans for further expansion. In March 2016, it was able to raise $1 billion to provide fresh funds for expansion, bringing the total funds raised from investors since it started in 2008 to more than $3.5 billion and further delaying any prospect of an initial public offering (Hook 2017a). In an effort to diversify its services, Airbnb began to develop a flight-booking service to compete with leading travel-booking sites, like Expedia and Priceline.

In February 2017, Airbnb made its biggest acquisition, spending about $300 million to acquire Luxury Retreats. With 4000 properties around the world, this Canadian company specialized in high-end rentals such as Richard Branson's Necker Island, which could accommodate 34 guests and cost $80,000 per night for the whole island (Hook 2017b). The deal gave Airbnb access to the highly profitable luxury market to appeal to elite travelers while also enabling it to offer Luxury Retreats' concierge service to its other customers.

AccorHotels was reported to have also bid for Luxury Retreats. Although AccorHotels' cash offer was bigger, Luxury Retreats chose Airbnb partly because its founder, Joe Poulin, had foreseen keeping more control with Airbnb (Zaleski and De Vynck 2017). Clearly, AccorHotels' and Airbnb's paths were increasingly crossing as they seemed to play more and more in the same field.

25.3 AccorHotels Group

25.3.1 History

AccorHotels was a French multinational hotel group headquartered in Paris. Its history started in 1967, when two friends, Paul Dubrule and Gérard Pélisson, opened their first Novotel in Lille Lesquin, in the North of France. Five years later, they started the international expansion of Accor with the opening of the first Novotel abroad, in Neuchâtel, Switzerland. Then in 1974, the first economy hotel, Ibis, was opened in Bordeaux. A year later, the company started to expand through acquisition with the purchase of 3-star chain Mercure, followed by the takeover of the 4-star Sofitel brand in 1980. In 1983, the Accor group was created, with a total of 440 hotels and 35,000 employees in 45 countries. Forty years after it was started, AccorHotels was present in 95 countries, employed 240,000 people, and owned, operated or franchised 4100 hotels for a total of 570,000 rooms. Its portfolio comprised 20 internationally renowned brands, from luxury hotels to economy lodgings. (*Refer to* ◘ Fig. 25.6 *for AccorHotels global presence, and* ◘ Figs. 25.7 *and* 25.8 *for an overview of AccorHotels brands and portfolio structure*).

25.3.2 Key Figures

In 2016, AccorHotels revenues were up 0.9% at €5631 million, and EBIT was up 4.6% at €696 million. Net profit at €266 million had grown 8.1% compared to 2015,

Fig. 25.6 AccorHotels global presence. (Source: ► http://www.accorhotels.group/en)

thus outpacing revenue growth. The group considered itself the biggest hotel operator in the world, as it operated 75% of its 4100 hotels directly, an approach that significantly differed from many of its US competitors, like Marriott and InterContinental, which were mostly franchisers. (*Refer to* **Fig.** 25.9 *for AccorHotels revenue and net profit growth from 2011 to 2016.*)

25.3.3 Corporate and Digital Transformation Under New CEO Sébastien Bazin

Since 2005 AccorHotels had witnessed a high turnover among its top leadership, with four different CEOs at its helm in 8 years. In 2013, Bazin was appointed with the objective of driving the company's stock price up. Bazin had a private equity background and came from a Los Angeles-based private real estate investment firm, Colony Capital, which was a major investor in AccorHotels. He headed up Colony Capital's European branch and led several acquisitions in the hospitality sector, including Fairmont and Raffles.

According to Lacheret, the start of Bazin's role at the helm of the Accor group coincided with a rupture in the group's strategy. A relative newcomer in the hospitality industry, Bazin was the first hotelier to acknowledge the risk the new industry disruptors represented for the hotel business. He firmly believed that traditional hotels had to fundamentally change their business model if they wanted to be able to compete with the new players. The new CEO quickly set out to completely transform the group with the goal of giving Accor the means and capabilities to embrace the disruptive changes taking place in the industry. He observed:

25

◘ **Fig. 25.7** Overview of AccorHotels brand portfolio. (Source: Company information)

Luxury and upscale segment: The goal of this segment, with 510 hotels and 129,000 rooms, was to improve service excellence and develop flagship hotels in cities with a view to enhancing brand value. This segment included the high-end luxury hotels Raffles, Fairmont, Sofitel Legend, the luxury hotels SO Sofitel and Sofitel, the accommodation rental company Onefinestay, as well as the upscale hotels MGallery by Sofitel, Pullman, Swissotel, Grand Mercure, and The Sebel

Midscale segment: The aim of the 1281 midscale hotels with 196,000 rooms was expansion and innovation to bolster the range and brand differentiation. It encompassed Novotel, Suite Novotel, Mercure, Mama Shelter, and Adabio

Economy segment: Finally, the objective of the economy segment was to take the Ibis brand family's success to the next level to cement its leadership with Ibis hotels and Adagio Access. This segment included 2318 hotels offering 255,000 rooms

Brand	Owned		Fixed lease		Variable lease		Variable lease on EBITDAR		Managed		Franchised		Total	
	Hotels	Rooms	Hotels	Rooms	Hotels	Rooms	Hotels	Rooms	Hotels	Rooms	Hotels	Rooms	Hotels	Rooms
RAFFLES	0	0	0	0	0	0	0	0	11	1 927	0	0	11	1 927
FAIRMONT	1	593	1	769	0	0	0	0	71	27 618	1	258	74	29 238
SOFITEL	16	2 681	4	1 199	3	419	1	150	93	24 673	3	1 196	120	30 318
PULLMAN	5	1 119	5	1 219	4	810	2	1 339	81	23 968	22	6 762	119	35 217
MGALLERY	2	219	5	578	3	432	0	0	34	3 841	44	3 846	88	8 916
SWISSOTEL	0	0	3	2 123	2	468	0	0	22	8 129	4	1 273	31	11 993
GRAND MERCURE	0	0	0	0	0	0	0	0	26	8 024	15	1 096	41	9 120
THE SEBEL	0	0	0	0	0	0	0	0	12	1 074	14	702	26	1 776
Upscale	24	4 612	18	5 888	12	2 129	3	1 489	350	99 254	103	15 133	510	128 505
NOVOTEL	49	10 595	34	6 975	78	13 590	9	1 645	166	40 176	112	16 238	448	89 219
NOVOTEL SUITES	1	118	6	971	11	1 396	0	0	5	637	9	806	32	3 928
MERCURE	31	5 381	42	6 897	47	7 443	4	614	194	31 177	429	44 382	747	95 894
ADAGIO	2	207	9	992	6	732	1	336	32	3 881	4	437	54	6 585
Midscale	83	16 301	91	15 835	142	23 161	14	2 595	397	75 871	554	61 863	1 281	195 626
NO BRAND	1	62	1	51	0	0	0	0	20	2 966	13	1 495	35	4 574
Multibrand	1	62	1	51	0	0	0	0	20	2 966	13	1 495	35	4 574
IBIS	107	16 387	83	11 380	132	19 615	43	7 692	168	31 376	555	52 291	1 088	138 741
IBIS STYLES	6	734	12	1 027	7	1 304	3	696	58	10 061	281	22 322	367	36 144
IBIS BUDGET	65	6 970	78	8 636	59	6 698	13	3 430	43	6 269	312	23 513	570	55 516
ADAGIO ACCESS	0	0	5	467	1	160	1	156	40	4 122	0	0	47	4 905
HOTELF1	20	1 455	0	0	158	12 579	0	0	0	0	59	3 830	237	17 864
FORMULE 1	0	0	0	0	0	0	0	0	9	1 286	0	0	9	1 286
Economic	198	25 546	178	21 510	357	40 356	60	11 974	318	53 114	1 207	101 956	2 318	254 456
Total	306	46 521	288	43 284	511	65 646	77	16 058	1 085	231 205	1 877	180 447	4 144	583 161

◘ **Fig. 25.8** AccorHotels portfolio as of December 2016. (Source: Company information)

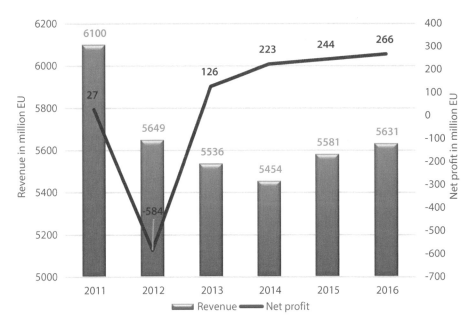

Fig. 25.9 AccorHotels revenue and net profit growth 2011 to 2016. (Source: Company information)

» Accor is in the middle of a revolution (…). For 50 years, we have been doing things very well, but from now onwards we are going to do things differently.[10]

AccorHotels' ambition was to reinvent the hospitality profession and become the world's industry benchmark, so it could offer a unique experience to its guests, employees, and partners. The group's new strategy was based on several pillars: two fields of expertise (HotelServices and HotelInvest), a new brand name (AccorHotels*)*, and a new promise (Feel Welcome*)*. In order to compete with the new disruptive players, the group would go through a major digital transformation that would make it more customer centric. It would be supported by a transformation of AccorHotels' corporate culture as well as its organizational structure. Finally, a strong focus was put on expansion, through acquisitions and participation as well as through internal innovation.

- **Two Fields of Expertise: HotelServices and HotelInvest**

In November 2013, AccorHotels redefined the group's structure: its two core competencies, hotel operator/franchisor and hotel owner/investor, were reorganized into two strategic divisions. By clearly distinguishing its two businesses, the group hoped to acquire the resources to develop its hotel projects with greater efficiency

---

10 "Sébastien Bazin (AccorHotels): "Nous allons faire mieux qu'Airbnb." ► *Frenchweb.fr*, 20 July 2016. ► http://www.frenchweb.fr/sebastien-bazin-accorhotels-nous-allons-faire-mieux-quairbnb/251095 (accessed 14 June 2017).

and flexibility and enhanced profitability. Each unit represented a value creation lever: HotelServices was the operator and franchisor of 4100 hotels operated under the group's brands. Of the 4100 hotels managed by Hotel Services, 1183 were owned by HotelInvest, the property owner and investor. HotelInvest's mission was to streamline and manage the existing assets through disposals and acquisitions. In July 2016, AccorHotels announced "Booster," a plan to divest the real estate ownership in its HotelInvest to new investors, a process that was expected to yield $5 billion by 2017. These funds would give AccorHotels greater financial resources to speed up growth.

- **A New Brand Name and a New Customer Promise: Feel Welcome**

In June 2015, the hotel chain was rebranded AccorHotels to uphold its hospitality business and increase its visibility by connecting it to its digital platform ► AccorHotels.com. The group also adopted a new slogan "Feel Welcome," which illustrated the group's passion for hospitality and the hotel industry profession.

- **Digital Transformation: Leading Digital Hospitality**

Bazin strongly believed that in order to compete with the new hospitality players, AccorHotels had to reinvent digital hospitality by becoming more technology oriented. He explained:

» Airbnb is a technology company and its mission is to become a hospitality company. For AccorHotels, it's the other way around: It has been in the hospitality business for 50 years and needs now to become a technology company.[11]

In October 2014, AccorHotels launched a 5-year digital transformation plan named "leading digital hospitality" for which €225 million was allocated—a big investment for AccorHotels. This digital transformation plan, covering 2014 through 2018, was based on three building blocks: a common mobile app for all hotels, a strong focus on the customer, and various tools to streamline the customer experience. More than 100 digital experts were hired to help the company in its digital transformation.

The group's online booking platform, ► AccorHotels.com, was already well established with 329 million visits a year. Available in 28 languages, the platform was not only accessible to all AccorHotels brands but also to independent hotels. One-third of Accor's sales were booked through the internet and 12% via mobile devices. In 2015, AccorHotels launched a single mobile application, Mobile First, common to all Accor hotels, with the objective of increasing mobile bookings to 35% and, within 5 years, having half of its direct bookings made via mobile.[12] By 2016, AccorHotels' mobile application already showed a users' increase of 40%.

11 "Accor vs Airbnb – S. Bazin et O. Grémillon aux Mardis de l'ESSEC." ► *Youtube.com*, 28 March 2015. ► https://www.youtube.com/watch?v=Q3gwLlVhMMs (accessed 14 June 2017).► https://www.youtube.com/watch?v=Q3gwLlVhMMs

12 "Transformation numérique d'Accor: vraie stratégie ou sauve-qui-peut?" ► *Frenchweb.fr*, 27 February 2015. ► http://www.frenchweb.fr/transformation-numerique-daccor-vraie-strategie-ou-sauve-qui-peut/184968 (accessed 14 June 2017).

One of the objectives introduced by the new CEO was for AccorHotels to become much more customer centric. As he put it:

>> The only thing that matters is the customer. For years, we had it all wrong; we were focusing on the product and the brand. We are going to listen to what customers want, why they are going to Airbnb, and why they go to other brands.[13]

Bazin believed that customer retention was driven by experience and the memories customers retained about their hotel stay. A key factor influencing the customer experience was the level of interaction the hotel had with guests, together with its ability to use information to improve the customer experience. AccorHotels developed a customer experience model that described the entire travel experience in seven steps: (1) the dream, (2) selection, (3) booking, (4) planning the trip, (5) traveling and staying, (6) sharing the experience, and (7) loyalty. The group's objective was to be present through the whole journey and in particular increase its presence before and after Step 5. (*Refer to* ◘ Fig. 25.10 *for AccorHotels' customer experience model.*)

One way for AccorHotels to become more customer centric was to leverage its customer database, through a project that was called "Voice of the Guests." According to Bazin, most companies had useful customer data but were unable to use it. The objective of "Voice of the Guests" was to enable AccorHotels to extract information from the customer database and use it to offer tailor-made services for each customer.

◘ **Fig. 25.10** AccorHotels customer experience model. (Source: Company information)

---

13 "Sébastien Bazin (AccorHotels): "Nous allons faire mieux qu'Airbnb." ► *Frenchweb.fr*, 20 July 2016. ► http://www.frenchweb.fr/sebastien-bazin-accorhotels-nous-allons-faire-mieux-quairbnb/251095 (accessed 14 June 2017).

Various tools were introduced to improve the customer experience at every step to ensure a "seamless journey": "one-click" booking, online check-in (similar to airlines' online check-in), and paperless payment, to name just a few. The plan also included an electronic membership card to the loyalty program "Le Club AccorHotels," which covered every brand of the group in every country worldwide and had, in 2017, around 25 million members.[14]

In order to speed up its digital transformation, in October 2014, AccorHotels acquired Wipolo, a web and mobile platform that managed trip itineraries, linking them with Facebook and Twitter. It then acquired in April 2015 Fastbooking, France's leader in the direct digital marketing of hotels. Fastbooking served more than 3500 hotels, mostly in Europe and Asia, with a website builder, a channel manager, digital marketing campaigns, and a business intelligence software.[15] Fastbooking was also open to independent hotels that were not part of the AccorHotels Group, which was, according to Lacheret, "going to transform AccorHotels into an e-marketplace." The group hoped to have 10,000 hotels on its platform within the next few years.

■ Cultural Transformation

AccorHotels was competing with lean digital disruptors that were fast, flexible, and very dynamic. It therefore had to become flatter, faster in decision-making, and more agile. This meant fundamentally changing managers' and employees' mindsets. In order to drive innovation, management had to accept the prospect of failure. According to AccorHotels deputy CEO, Sven Boinet, "the biggest challenge is to transform middle management as they are the most resistant to change. People at AccorHotels need to change the way they think. It's hard to become disruptive."[16] The human factor was central to the hospitality industry. With 240,000 employees, 56% under 35 years of age, AccorHotels was committed to the training and development of its employees, encouraging them to express themselves and become self-reliant, bold, and collaborative.

To support the group transformation from the inside, in early 2016, AccorHotels moved its international headquarters to Issy-les-Moulineaux, just outside Paris. Designed with the objective of reinventing the way AccorHotels employees should work together, the new building featured innovative work spaces and technology that allowed high connectivity anywhere in the building. Describing the new premises, Boinet remarked:

---

14 "Communiqué: Accor engage sa transformation digitale « Leading Digital Hospitality »." ▶ *Tendancehotellerie.fr*, 31 October 2014. ▶ http://www.tendancehotellerie.fr/articles-breves/communique-de-presse/4236-article/accor-engage-sa-transformation-digitale-leading-digital-hospitality (accessed 14 June 2017).

15 "Accor acquires FastBooking, a B2B hotel tools provider." ▶ *Tnooz.com*, 17 April 2015. ▶ https://www.tnooz.com/article/accor-acquires-fastbooking-a-b2b-hotel-tools-provider/ (accessed 14 June 2017).

16 All quotes from Sven Boinet's are based on a presentation at IMD Alumni Paris on 18 April 2017

» In the new building, there are open office spaces for everybody, including the CEO. Microsoft is right down the road. The change to open space is brutal. The idea is to foster communication among employees.

- **Corporate Transformation: Driving Innovation**

Challenging and disrupting codes at AccorHotels, which had not launched a new brand in 30 years, were also part of the digital plan. Bazin was committed to changing the legacy culture of the company and disrupting the traditional hotel approach. His objective was to create a group in which 30% of activities were new, and 70% came from the classical hotel business within 5 years: "In the coming years, we intend making a third of our HotelServices revenue by targeting professions with which we were not associated over the last 50 years.."[17] Dedicating resources to innovation and development—almost like an R&D department—was something new in the hotel industry, as Lacheret explained:

» Manufacturing companies spend 4% to 7% of their revenues in R&D investment, but service companies like hotels do not invest in R&D. AccorHotels is going to set money aside to invest in research and development, though this is really not in the company's DNA.

In order to drive these changes, flexible structures were created within AccorHotels's heavy top-down hierarchy—a new position, a new committee and a new team:

- - **Chief Disruption and Growth Officer**

In April 2016, Bazin hired Thibault Viort, a 42-year-old serial digital entrepreneur, as Chief Disruption and Growth Officer, a newly created C-level position. Lacheret outlined the objective of the position: "the goal is to push AccorHotels to change, adapt faster and speed up decision making processes." Prior to joining AccorHotels, Viort had created, among others, Facebook's first online games. In his new position, he was expected to identify new growth opportunities in order to foster the emergence of new entrepreneurs within and outside the group, oversee investments or acquisitions in emerging activities, as well as reinforce interactions with start-ups. Bazin explained: "We are looking at start-ups that are developing state-of-the-art technologies following two angles: either to improve hotel performance or to enrich customer experience." (Hamdi 2016)

- - **Shadow Comex**

AccorHotels was the first major French group to create a Shadow Executive Committee staffed by six women and six men aged between 25 and 35 years, representing seven nationalities. Boinet saw them as a "think tank for innovation projects." These millennials met every 2 months to evaluate new projects and were

---

17 "Our ambitions." ► *AccorHotels.com.* ► http://www.accorhotels.group/en/group/our-ambitions (accessed 14 June 2017).

involved in strategic decisions. They contributed to making AccorHotels more attentive to digital natives and played a key role in AccorHotels' cultural transformation. This successful idea received the 2016 gold award for digital innovation (category: company optimization) and was quickly replicated at the country-level throughout the group.

▪▪ Marketing Innovation Lab

Innovation at AccorHotels was mainly the result of in-house creativity. To foster this, the Marketing Innovation Lab was setup, which focused on the creation of new lifestyle brands aimed at millennials.

▪ AccorHotels Disruptive Ideas

Millennials, the tech-savvy generation born after 1980, were rising up as the new global travelers and were expected to become the biggest single group of hotel customers by 2020. They had high expectations for hotels, wanting contemporary design, high-quality amenities, smart technology, and a locally inspired ambiance. To meet the demands of millennials, hotel offerings had to evolve, with a focus on design, experience, and perceived value. An outcome of AccorHotels' digital transformation and its newly created structures was a pipeline of disruptive ideas, targeted at millennials and embedded in the digital economy.

▪▪ Mama Shelter

In 2014, AccorHotels purchased a 35% stake in Mama Shelter, a chain of trendy hotels and restaurants created by Serge Trigano (founder of Club Med) and designed by Philippe Starck. The hotel's aim was to offer travelers what it described as "urban retreats" in a typical and often non-touristic neighborhood. More than hotels or restaurants, Mama Shelter was a living space, popular, fun, and friendly, where guests felt at home thanks to the kindness and family attitude of the teams that run them.

▪▪ Jo&Joe

Created by AccorHotels' Marketing Innovation Lab, "Jo&Joe" was the first brand created by the group since Bazin had joined the company in 2013. Jo&Joe was a groundbreaking hospitality concept that combined digital experience with living areas designed for locals as well as young globetrotters. Targeted at millennials, the new lifestyle brand was described by the company as an "open house," a unique environment that blended the best of private rental, hostel, and hotel formats. The first Jo&Joe opened in Hossegor, France, in March 2017, and the group was aiming at 50 Open Houses by 2020 in fashionable destinations around the world (*refer to* ◘ Fig. 25.11 *for more information on the Jo&Joe concept*).

▪▪ New Food and Beverage Strategy

Part of the shake-up strategy that Bazin started in 2013 was to reorient its food and beverage division. With the proliferation of smartphones, it had become easier for customers to find alternative restaurants, and by 2017, only 20% of hotel guests took a meal in the hotel. By redesigning its food and drink products to meet the

Accommodation: Jo&Joe includes different accommodation types such as a modular sleeping area that guests share, private sleeping accommodation in rooms and apartments for two to five people with a private bathroom and possibly a kitchen area, or out-of-the-ordinary accommodation (OOO) that includes yurts, hammocks and caravans for groups of up to six people.

Social interaction spaces: Jo&Joe provides spaces to encourage social interaction, such as a bar that is highly visible from the street to draw locals, a collaborative kitchen where guests can cook for themselves or for each other, or a "Happy House" area where guests can do their laundry, relax, cook, or unwind, just as they would if they were at home.

Location: Jo&Joe is located in urban city-center locations "close to public transport and less than 15 minutes away from the major points of interest."

Mobile app: A mobile app that connects guests, Jo&Joe staff members, and locals alike serves as a "social accelerator."

◘ **Fig. 25.11** *Jo&Joe Concept. Accommodation*: Jo&Joe includes different accommodation types such as a modular sleeping area that guests share private sleeping accommodation in rooms and apartments for two to five people with a private bathroom and possibly a kitchen area or out-of-the-ordinary accommodation (OOO) that includes yurts, hammocks, and caravans for groups of up to six people *Social interaction spaces*: Jo&Joe provides spaces to encourage social interaction, such as a bar that is highly visible from the street to draw locals, a collaborative kitchen where guests can cook for themselves or for each other, or a "happy house" area where guests can do their laundry, relax, cook, or unwind, just as they would if they were at home *Location*: Jo&Joe is located in urban city center locations "close to public transport and less than 15 minutes away from the major points of interest." *Mobile app*: A mobile app that connects guests, Jo&Joe staff members, and locals alike serves as a "social accelerator." (Source: Company information)

demands for more local and personalized experiences, the group was hoping to draw in diners, and in particular to appeal to the millennial generation, which had been courted by Airbnb.

■■ Community Services to Locals

Also part of the group's digital transformation was to expand AccorHotels' presence in the digital economy while at the same time discovering new ways to make the most of its existing assets. Bazin wanted to change the way people interacted with his hotels and expand services beyond hotel guests. A pilot was launched in early 2017 to offer a choice of daily services to residents who lived close to hotels, for example, assistance with simple tasks such as holding packages or keys, picking up dry cleaning, or recommending the best services nearby. The underlying platform providing and managing these local services would be AccorHotels' loyalty program, ▶ Le Club AccorHotels. The model would allow AccorHotels to increase return on buildings that, during the day, had little activity. Bazin summarized the idea:

» There is a "thin digital layer" that can be applied to under-used assets, in a similar way to how Airbnb was formed to become the service between hosts and guests. (…) AccorHotels will try to find a way of "bringing the neighborhood into the hotel."[18]

■ Growth Through New Activities via Acquisitions

The last element of AccorHotels' new business strategy was expansion. The company aimed at becoming a key player in the hotel luxury segment and the world's leading luxury private rental provider.[19]

■■ FRHI

In July 2016, AccorHotels acquired Fairmont Raffles Hotels International (FRHI), which included the brands Fairmont, Raffles, and Swissôtel. Luxury was the most profitable as well as fastest-growing customer segment, and these iconic brands were a major addition to AccorHotels' hotel portfolio while also strengthening the group's position in North America.

---

18 "Accor has eyes on other digital layers for hotels." ▶ *Tnooz.com*, 18 October 2016. ▶ https://www.tnooz.com/article/accor-has-eyes-on-other-digital-layers-for-hotels/ (accessed 14 June 2017).

19 Other acquisitions included 25 hours (acquisition of 30% of its capital), Banyan Tree (5% stake), BHG (integration of 26 hotels), Rixos (50% interest in the joint venture management company), AvailPro (full acquisition to create the European leader of digital services for independent hotels), VeryChic (digital platform for the private sale of luxury hotel rooms and apartments, cruises, breaks, and packages), Potel et Chabot (40% of the share capital), and Noctis (AccorHotels and the FCDE in exclusive talks to acquire 100% of the latter's minority interest in Groupe Noctis).

▪▪ Squarebreak

In February 2016, AccorHotels acquired for €3 million a 49% stake in Squarebreak, a company created in 2013 that rented out luxurious homes with hotel services in France, Spain, and Morocco. In 2015, Squarebreak had more than 250 listings and aimed at reaching 600 in 2016 and 1000 in 2017 (Harmant 2016a).

▪▪ Oasis Collections

Also in February 2016, AccorHotels acquired a 30% stake in Oasis Collections, an American marketplace for private rentals with hotel services. The company was launched in Buenos Aires in 2009 and had 1500 properties in 18 destinations in Latin America, the United States, and Europe. Oasis Collections complemented the private rentals with additional hotel services and amenities, including concierge services and access to members' club venues (Vidalon 2016).

▪▪ Onefinestay

In April 2016, AccorHotels acquired ▶ Onefinestay.com for €148 million and planned to invest another €64 million to help the start-up expand in 40 new markets (Harmant 2016b). Onefinestay was launched in London in 2009 and specialized in upmarket accommodation. As of April 2016, it employed over 700 people and had 2500 exclusive homes in its assortment covering selected European and North American cities. It emphasized hotel services delivered by local guest services teams available around the clock. Its patented "Sherlock" keyless entry technology, consisting of a physical device and a smartphone app, enabled secure keyless access to Onefinestay homes.

▪▪ John Paul

In November 2016, AccorHotels acquired for $150 million 80% of John Paul, the world leader in the concierge market. The company's founder kept the remaining 20% and continued to serve as CEO. John Paul offered premium customer and employee loyalty services to three million clients, mostly in the banking, car, travel, and luxury sectors. John Paul's concierges were available 24/7 to cater to their customers' requests, from the simplest to the most extraordinary, anywhere around the globe. Founded in 2007, John Paul employed a workforce of 1000 people across five continents. In 2016, the company had revenues of $60 million and an EBITDA margin of 15% to 20%. It aimed to achieve 2017 revenues of $80 million and hoped to double sales to $170 million by 2018 (Vidalon 2016).

▪▪ Travel Keys

AccorHotels announced in February 2017 that it had begun negotiations for the acquisition of Travel Keys, an Atlanta-based private vacation rental broker. Founded in 1991, Travel Keys was an elite travel broker with a luxury collection of over 5000 upscale villas across more than 100 destinations around the world. It offered professional vacation planning and 24/7 concierge services. The transaction was expected to close in the second quarter of 2017 (Ting 2017).

25

25.3.4 **Challenges Ahead**

AccorHotels had recognized early the potential threat that the sharing economy presented for the hotel industry. Bazin actually believed that "the industry had not reacted quickly enough to these changes" and that "it had been a mistake not to have become an investor in Airbnb in the past." (Ahmed and Moore 2015) Over several years, the two business models grew in parallel, seemingly without threatening each other. However, they started to converge as Airbnb adapted its offering to appeal to business travelers, while hotel groups entered the sharing economy. AccorHotels' digital transformation was well under way, but would it be enough for the hotel giant to become an agile player able to effectively compete against Airbnb? What else could Bazin do to strengthen and speed up his group's transformation? How would AccorHotels look in the near-to medium-term future? Deputy CEO Sven Boinet was quite optimistic since he firmly believed that over the next 10 years, hotel supply would not be enough to meet the continuously increasing demand, as he concluded: "we work in an industry that is blessed by the gods!"

References

Ahmed, M., & Moore, M. (2015, June 29). Hyatt and Wyndham invest in home-sharing rivals to Airbnb. FT.com. https://www.ft.com/content/27bfc262-1b4c-11e5-8201-cbdb03d71480. Accessed 14 June 2017.

Bryan, B. (2016, January 10). Why Airbnb doesn't spell doom for the hotel business... yet. Businessinsider.com. http://uk.businessinsider.com/airbnb-is-not-threat-to-hotels-yet-2016-1?r=US&IR=T. Accessed 14 June 2017.

Escobar, E. (2016, June 27). The sharing economy: Concepts and lessons for hospitality. Hospitalitynet.org. http://www.hospitalitynet.org/news/4076818.html. Accessed 14 June 2017.

Gulliver. (2016, November 4). Business travelers will be hit hardest by the crackdown on Airbnb. Economist.com. http://www.economist.com/blogs/gulliver/2016/11/lets-down. Accessed 14 June 2017.

Hamdi, R. (2016, April 25). Bazin seeks startups to accelerate AccorHotels transformation. Forbes. com. https://www.forbes.com/sites/hamdiraini/2016/04/25/bazin-seeks-startups-to-accelerate-accorhotels-transformation/#29c099274a8e. Accessed 14 June 2017.

Harmant, O. (2016a, February 18). AccorHotels investit 3 millions d'euros dans les villas de Squarebreak. Frenchweb.fr. http://www.frenchweb.fr/accorhotels-investit-3-millions-deuros-dans-les-villas-de-squarebreak/229040. Accessed 14 June 2017.

Harmant, O. (2016b, April 5). AccorHotels s'offre Onefinestay, un « Airbnb du luxe », pour 148 millions d'euros. Frenchweb.fr. http://www.frenchweb.fr/accorhotels-soffre-onefinestay-un-airbnb-du-luxe-pour-148-millions-deuros/236712. Accessed 14 June 2017.

Hook, L. (2017a, March 9). Airbnb completes $1bn fundraising to support expansion. FT.com. https://www.ft.com/content/0fde09e0-04ef-11e7-ace0-1ce02ef0def9. Accessed 14 June 2017.

Hook, L. (2017b, February 9). Airbnb poised to buy exclusive vacation villas specialist. FT.com. https://www.ft.com/content/2873d952-eef7-11e6-ba01-119a44939bb6. Accessed 14 June 2017.

Huston, C. (2015, June 24). Airbnb poses long-term threat to online travel sites like Priceline. Marketwatch.com. http://www.marketwatch.com/story/airbnb-poses-long-term-threat-to-online-travel-sites-like-priceline-2015-06-23. Accessed 14 June 2017.

McMillin. (2016, October 3). 2 reasons why Airbnb is achieving so much success. Pcma.org. http://www.pcma.org/news/news-landing/2016/10/03/3-reasons-why-airbnb-is-achieving-so-much-success#.WKsJoX-UJb0. Accessed 1 Mar 2017.

Mikey, T. (2017, February 16). Airbnb expects $2,8B in 2017 revenue, $8,5B By 2020. Valuewalk.com. http://www.valuewalk.com/2017/02/airbnb-expects-2-8b-2017-revenue-8-5b-2020/. Accessed 14 June 2017.

Mitra, S. (2016, August 23). Here are the numbers behind Airbnb's staggering growth. Inc.com. http://www.inc.com/linkedin/sramana-mitra/billion-dollar-unicorn-airbnb-continues-soar-sramana-mitra.html. Accessed 14 June 2017.

Ting, D. (2016, August 5). AccorHotels CEO to the hotel industry: 'You have an obligation to be bold.' Skift.com. https://skift.com/2016/08/05/accorhotels-ceo-to-the-hotel-industry-you-have-an-obligation-to-be-bold/. Accessed 14 June 2017.

Ting, D. (2017, February 5). AccorHotels to buy private vacation rental platform travel keys. Skift.com. https://skift.com/2017/02/05/accorhotels-to-buy-private-vacation-rental-platform-travel-keys/. Accessed 14 June 2017.

Vidalon, D. (2016, July 27). AccorHotels buys concierge group to counter Airbnb challenge. Reuters.com. http://www.reuters.com/article/us-accorhotels-m-a-johnpaul-airbnb-idUSKCN1070XW. Accessed 14 June 2017.

World Economic Forum. (2016 January 21). Davos 2016 – A new platform for the digital economy. Youtube.com. https://www.youtube.com/watch?v=-pFRIlgEdl0. Accessed 14 June 2017.

Zaleski, O., & De Vynck, G. (2017, February 16). Airbnb acquires luxury retreats, beating out expedia, Accor. Bloomberg.com. https://www.bloomberg.com/news/articles/2017-02-16/airbnb-buys-vacation-home-management-company-luxury-retreats. Accessed 14 June 2017.

Zervas, G., Proserpio, D., & Byers, J. W. (2016, November 18). *The rise of the sharing economy: Estimating the impact of Airbnb on the hotel industry.* http://people.bu.edu/zg/publications/airbnb.pdf. Accessed 14 June 2017.

Disruptive Change at Bossard with SmartFactoryLogistics.com?

Contents

EMBA Candidates Celine Relecom, Mikhail Efimov, and Maria Kokontseva prepared this case under the supervision of Professor Stefan Michel as a basis for class discussion rather than to illustrate either effective or ineffective handling of a business situation. Copyright © 2017 by *IMD—International Institute for Management* Development, Lausanne, Switzerland (▶ www.imd.org). No part of this publication may be reproduced, stored in a retrieval system, or transmitted in any form or by any means without the prior written permission of *IMD*.

© Springer Nature Switzerland AG 2020
T. Jelassi, F. J. Martínez-López, *Strategies for e-Business*, Classroom Companion: Business, https://doi.org/10.1007/978-3-030-48950-2_26

■ **Introduction**

As Tee Bin Ong, Bossard's vice president of sales and marketing, headed to the strategy meeting with Bossard's management team and board, his expectations were high, and he was excited about the prospects. He had invested a substantial amount of time preparing for the meeting on "Smart Factory Logistics," where the evolution of Bossard's strategy around the "smart factory" and its implementation would be discussed. One of the key strategic questions was whether Smart Factory Logistics would be the trigger for Bossard's digital transformation or an important differentiator for Bossard's value proposition. The newly created website ► www. SmartFactoryLogistics.com would point in this direction. A third option was pointing in a very different growth direction, i.e., using the technology that was established by a fastener distributor to enter completely new markets with no connection to the fastener industry, e.g., hospitals.

Bossard had grown from a family-owned hardware store in Zug, Switzerland, in 1831 to a global leader in fastening technology in 2016. It was a pioneer in the use of SmartBin technology and other sensors. Its competitive advantage was significant, but competitors were catching up.

With the advent of the Internet of Things (IoT), new business models and bases of competition were appearing. Bossard was benefiting from this trend because some of its customers wanted to be relieved of the hassle of dealing with C-parts—the inexpensive nuts and bolts that were critical to the manufacturing process. While Bossard had been using Smart Factory Logistics services before they were fashionable, the current hot topic in the company was "What's our next step in IoT?"

Some of Bossard's competitors were attempting to copy its SmartBin system, and while Bossard had more than 15 years of experience with the product, a proprietary network solution, and a strong track record of reliability and proven performance, it was only a question of time before competitors would bridge the gap in product quality. As a result, Tee Bin and his team believed that 2016 was the time to make their next move.

26.1 Bossard Group: Background

Bossard was founded as a family-owned hardware store in Zug, Switzerland, selling fastening products, such as bolts, screws, nuts, rivets, etc. (*refer to* ◘ Fig. 26.1). Over the years, the business expanded regionally and then nationally and eventually evolved into a global leader in fastening technology in Europe, the Americas, and Asia Pacific with more than 2000 employees in over 26 countries. Its product selection comprised more than one million different items, with 2016 sales of CHF 695 million and earnings before interest and taxes (EBIT) of CHF 78.5 million. With an EBIT margin of 11.3%, it was about twice as profitable as the average competitor (*refer to* ◘ Fig. 26.2). In June 2017, Bossard issued a positive profit warning to its shareholders that announced a 15% increase in sales and a 30.5% increase in EBIT year-to-date. Between 2012 and 2017, the company's share price more than quadrupled after stock analysts rated the shares as "undervalued" and increased the share target price several times (*refer to the price/earnings ratios in* ◘ Fig. 26.3).

Fig. 26.1 Typical fastening parts sold by Bossard. (Source: Bossard Catalogue)

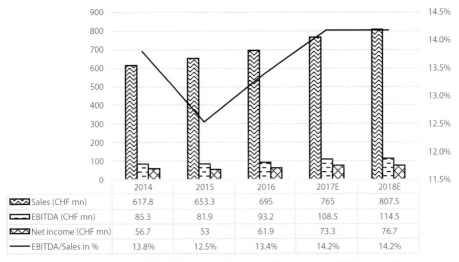

	2014	2015	2016	2017E	2018E
Sales (CHF mn)	617.8	653.3	695	765	807.5
EBITDA (CHF mn)	85.3	81.9	93.2	108.5	114.5
Net income (CHF mn)	56.7	53	61.9	73.3	76.7
EBITDA/Sales in %	13.8%	12.5%	13.4%	14.2%	14.2%

Sales (CHF mn)   EBITDA (CHF mn)   Net income (CHF mn) ——— EBITDA/Sales in %

Fig. 26.2 Bossard financials 2014–2018. (Source: Bossard Annual Report 2016)

	2014	2015	2016	2017E	2018E
Price/Earning (PE) adjusted	7.7	15.1	14.1	17.6	16.8

Fig. 26.3 Bossard financials 2014–2018e. (Source: Bossard Annual Report 2016 and Baader Helvea Equity Research)

With a unique global footprint that included more than 70 service locations, 35 logistics centers, and 10 application engineering laboratories around the world, Bossard provided the production sites of industrial companies around the world with fastening technology products and offered associated services with consistently high-quality standards and standardized systems and processes.

Bossard's main customers were John Deere, Tesla, Bombardier, Alstom, Emerson, Grundfos, Schneider Electric, Siemens, ABB, GE, Honeywell, and Roche. Among its key clients, Tesla appeared to be very promising in the long run. Bossard started working with Tesla in 2010 as the sole supplier of all its fastening solutions, including the logistics. Following the signing of a US$140 million 3-year contract with Tesla on 12 March 2014, Bossard invested in a dedicated distribution center for Tesla.

26.2 Global Fastening Industry

The global fastening industry was evaluated at $72 billion, and it was expected to experience significant growth over the next 6 years due to the increasing demand for fasteners in the automotive industry. The construction industry in emerging markets including China, Brazil, Russia, Poland, the United States, and India was also expected to further increase the demand, and it was anticipated that increasing consumption in electrical and electronics, aerospace, machinery, and MRO (maintenance and repair operations) applications would also fuel the growth of the fastener market over the forecasted period. In addition, rising motor vehicle demand was expected to propel the need for fasteners by automotive original equipment manufacturers (OEMs). By 2020, the global market for industrial fasteners was forecasted to reach over $100 billion,[1] with further growth expected (*refer to* ◘ Fig. 26.4).

Fastening products were considered "C-parts": in general, they were not expensive, but they were critical to the manufacturing process. Producers of home appliances, for example, could use several hundred different fasteners for one appliance. The quality of fasteners was of utmost importance, as errors in choice or defects in quality could have disastrous consequences, e.g., a plane crash.

It was essential that all the needed parts were in stock, as just one out-of-stock nut could lead to a production outage. On average, fasteners, or "C-parts," made up 15% of the total costs; the remaining 85% came from development, procurement, testing, inventories, assembly, and logistics. This chain of events added costs to the entire fastening ecosystem. Experience in the industry had shown that cost savings of 50% or more could be achieved in the logistics and engineering areas, which could significantly impact the total cost of the end product.[2] Recognizing this, Bossard focused on the creation of solutions designed to reduce the total cost of ownership (TCO).

26.3 Bossard's Early Innovations

As early as the 1980s, Bossard began supporting its clients at the earliest stages of engineering design to select the best fastening solutions to optimize both the quality and safety of the final products as well as the cost of production, taking into account inventory management, manufacturing, and maintenance. Through its sales network, it had developed close relationships with its main clients, so it began offering to analyze their whole C-parts logistics and supply chain to identify oppor-

1 "Report: Industrial Fastener Market Tops $81b by 2018" ▸ *GlobalFastenerNews.com*, 15 November 2012 ▸ www.globalfastenernews.com/report-industrial-fastener-market-tops-81b-by-2018-global-fastener-news-usa/ (accessed 19 July 2016)

2 ▸ www.bossard.com/en/how-we-add-value/the-rule-of-15-85.aspx (accessed 10 October 2017)

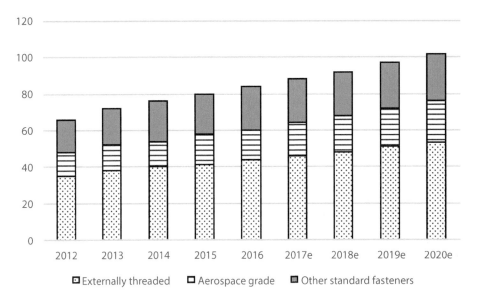

□ Fig. 26.4 Global industrial fasteners market revenue, by product, 2012–2020 (USD Billion). (Source: "Industrial Fasteners Market Analysis by Product, by Application and Segment Forecasts To 2020." *Grand View Research*, May 2015 ► www.grandviewresearch.com/industry-analysis/asia-industrial-fasteners-market (accessed 21 July 2016))

tunities for optimizing their production processes. The company knew how to identify the hidden potential of their customers' production processes and boost their productivity, which, in turn, improved their TCO. The company analyzed sourcing, design, engineering, logistics, handling, ordering, quality inspection, stocking, and assembly; helped its clients map value streams and go lean; save production time; and reduce inventory. Clients could even use an online TCO value calculator on Bossard's website to estimate their savings potential.

Since the 1990s, Bossard had experimented with different solutions to relieve its clients of some of the burden of managing C-parts, including developing solutions that simplified ordering. SmartBin was a fully automated reordering system that took the Kanban[3] approach to the next level. SmartBin, which consisted of a combination of Kanban bins and especially developed weight sensors, constantly checked current stock levels. When the minimum stock level was reached, the predefined order quantity was shipped automatically. Depending on the level of service, the parts were forwarded to the client's warehouse or directly to the point of use.[4] SmartBins, which were a key element of Bossard's logistics advantage, allowed Bossard to help its clients optimize the supply processes, i.e., reduce supply complexity, excessive activity, and inventories, increase throughput, and provide data analytics.

---

3   Kanban is a set of manufacturer processes developed in Japan to optimize the flow of goods, reduce or eliminate warehouse inventory, and facilitate just-in-time production.

4   Bossard's website ► www.bossard.com/en/smart-factory-logistics/systems/smartbin-intelligent-logistics-system.aspx (accessed 10 October 2017)

In 2014, Bossard introduced a wireless enabled mobile solution called SmartBin Flex. The following year, SmartLabel was introduced. SmartLabel triggered the ordering of a pre-specified amount of product by pressing on a labelled button. With these two innovations, orders could now be triggered directly at the point of use. In order to provide a meaningful and integrated service to its clients, Bossard developed a platform called ARIMS that integrated all orders placed to Bossard as well as orders from its clients to their other providers. All of this enabled Bossard to implement the Smart Factory Logistics Concept, whereby computer systems monitored the physical processes and made decentralized decisions. Through the Internet of Things (IoT)—a term that had not yet been coined—Bossard communicated and cooperated with participants in its clients' value chains in real time and offered its services. With this holistic view, called "proven productivity,"[5] the company positioned itself as a real partner for its clients (*refer to* ◘ Figs. 26.5 *and* 26.6).

By 2015, Bossard's sales force was well trained in using IoT solutions to provide vendor-managed inventory (VMI). However, with the competition increasingly developing similar approaches or alternatives, VMI was no longer a differentiator; it was increasingly considered a given in the industry. However, Bossard's service offer, with the analytics and optimization potential it provided, was still one step ahead. But Bossard's management team had to consider its next moves in order to maintain and develop its strategic advantage. The hot topic at Bossard was the possible next step the company could develop in the field of IoT. What would be the next wave of automation? How could Bossard best create and capture value from developments in this field?

Process	Conventional	Bossard Smart&Lean	Explanation
Realization of need	$$	$	Not necessary with SmartBin
Inquiry	$$$	$	1x per delivery period (e.g. yearly)
Orders	$$$		
Receiving	$$	$	Not needed when shipping to Point-of-Use
Quality inspection	$$		
Material handling in factory	$$	$	Not needed when shipping to Point-of-Use
Storing	$		
Warehousing costs	$$$	$	Not needed when shipping to Point-of-Use
Preparing goods for shipping	$$$	$	Not needed when shipping to Point-of-Use
		Savings:	
$=costs		$$$$$ $$$$$ $$$$$	

◘ **Fig. 26.5** Bossard's logistics value proposition: lowering total cost of ownership (TCO). (Source: Bossard's website ▶ www.bossard.com/en/smart-factory-logistics/potential-savings.aspx (accessed 5 November 2016))

---

5   See the "proven productivity" concept explanation at ▶ www.youtube.com/watch?v=vKATZ5Gxx-8&feature=youtu.be

Your current situation		Changes you would like to see in the Future	
Number of Articles	500		
Turnover	100000		
Number of Locations Supplied	3		
Number of Deliveries	52	Number of Deliveries	26
Number of Suppliers	3	Number of Suppliers	1
Stock Inventory Turnover	3	Stock Inventory Turnover Rate	6

Operating Sequence	Cost Basis	Without Logistics System	Changes you would like to see in the Future
Requirements	75	2250	75
Orders	75	3900	0
Goods Receipt	10	520	0
Storage	8	12000	0
Warehousing Cost (%)	12	2000	1000
Provision of Goods	6	27000	0
Annual Inventory Cost	5	2500	0
Accounting Monitoring and Payments	75	3900	900
Reset		**Total Cost** 54070	**Reduced Cost** * 1975 (96.35% Savings)

❏ **Fig. 26.6**   Bossard's total cost of ownership online calculator. (Source: Bossard's website ► www. bossard.com/en/smart-factory-logistics/potential-savings.aspx (accessed 5 November 2016))

26.4 **The Potential of the Internet of Things**

Definition

Everyone has fallen in love with the term Internet of Things and the technology involved, without understanding what it really means. – T. K. Kurien, Executive Vice Chairman, Wipro Limited, during the round table on Internet of Things in Davos in January 2016[6]

---

6   "The Internet of Things Is Here." *World Economic Forum*, 22 January 2016. ► www.weforum. org/events/world-economic-forum-annual-meeting-2016/sessions/the-internet-of-things-is-here (accessed 20 March 2016)

According to the McKinsey Institute, the potential economic impact—the effect of IoT on the economy—of having "sensors and actuators connected by networks to computing systems," otherwise known as the Internet of Things (IoT), could be as high as $11 trillion a year by 2025. It included changes in business revenue, business profits, personal wages, and/or jobs and companies needed to be prepared for it. The projected global revenue of the "Internet of Things" from 2007 to 2020 was expected to grow from €750 million to €8,200 million (*refer to* ◻ Fig. 26.7).

IoT presented a unique technology transition that was impacting everyone's lives and would have huge implications for the supply chain. By itself, IoT would generate $8 trillion worldwide in value at stake over the next decade. From this amount, supply chain and logistics alone would comprise $1.9 trillion in value. This was a very promising indication of the potential profits that could be gained by utilizing IoT in the logistics industry. According to Zebra Technologies, in a study conducted with Forrester Research, 65% of respondents had deployed IoT technologies in their enterprises in 2014, compared to only 15% in 2012.

According to SAP, the number of connected devices was expected to exceed 50 billion by 2020 (Wellers 2015). These connected devices, which allowed companies better visibility into their operations, would transform not only how logistics providers made decisions—how goods would be stored, monitored, routed, serviced, and delivered to customers—but also operational health and safety practices. They had the potential to influence the entire value chain, including warehousing operations and freight transportation. Inventory management optimization was expected to be one of the most important potential markets for the industrial IoT. McKinsey stated that the market for operations optimization (machinery performance adjust-

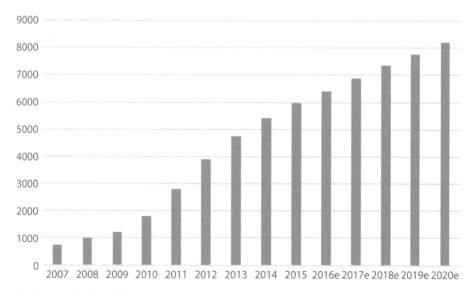

◻ **Fig. 26.7**   Projected global revenue of the "Internet of Things" from 2007 to 2020. (Source: Myers (2016))

ment based on the sensor's data) would have a potential value of more than $633 billion per year in the factory setting in 2025 and the market for predictive maintenance (using sensors for continuous monitoring of machinery in order to avoid breakdowns) would be $630 billion per year.[7]

IoT provided an opportunity for companies to significantly improve their operational innovation and excellence. Analysts and industry experts called this opportunity Industry 4.0, Smart Manufacturing, Smart Factory, or Brilliant Factory. No matter what it was called, these smart, connected operations were moving companies closer to operational excellence. The components, equipment, and production units of the connected, smart factory would use predictive analytic tools to identify problems in real time.

The logistics industry was among the first adopters of IoT technologies in operations. While many of these technologies, such as wireless connectivity and sensors, had already been used in logistics applications, the full potential of IoT was yet to be fully exploited.

McKinsey forecasted that inventory optimization measures such as those proposed by Bossard could save from 20% to 50% of a factory's inventory carrying costs.[8] IoT could also drive optimal asset utilization; by connecting machinery to a central system, it was possible to monitor all assets in real time. Connected assets would also enable predictive maintenance for warehouse transport systems, and factories could benefit from predictive maintenance for their machines.

IoT was also expected to provide the next level of visibility and security for freight transportation's track and trace by using telematic sensors in trucks and multi-sensor tags on items. These sensors would transmit data on the location and condition of the goods. Another interesting supply chain example—the so-called last-mile delivery—used IoT to connect the logistics provider with the end recipient in an efficient way. The connected fridge—a well-known example—tracked the expiration dates of products, detected when resupply was needed, and ordered more online automatically. Sensors could also detect when a retailer was low on stock and automatically place an order, which would result in lead-time and out-of-stock reductions.

These automatic replenishment and anticipatory shipping solutions were resulting in implications for logistics providers. Certainly, particular conditions were required to benefit fully from IoT. Facilities with IoT sensors and actuators, short-range and long-range data communications networks with sufficient reliability and capacity, data analytics capabilities, data security and confidentiality, and, of course, skilled human resources and the appropriate organizational structure were all required to take full advantage of IoT technologies.

IoT was presenting different stakeholders with unprecedented opportunities. Technology suppliers could develop new systems and create new sources of reve-

---

7   "The Internet of Things: Mapping the value beyond the hype." *McKinsey Global Institute*, June 2015

8   "Industry 4.0: How to navigate digitization of the manufacturing sector" *McKinsey & Company*, April 2015

nue. To build competitive advantage in the IoT market, they needed to create a distinctive technology, distinctive data, software platforms, or end-to-end solutions. Businesses adopting IoT systems could improve their operations and get rich insights for data-driven decision-making. In a survey entitled "Manufacturers Rely on Big Data Analytics" "more than two-thirds of respondents (68%) said they are currently investing in data analytics, and 50% said they believe their companies are right on track in their use of data analytics. 15% said they believe their companies are ahead of the curve as it relates to data analytics usage." (Johnson 2016)

26.5 Time to Make a Move from Products to Services

IoT was expected to provoke the appearance of new business models and bases of competition, both for the companies that were using IoT systems and for those that supplied IoT technology. While Bossard had been using Smart Factory Logistics services before they were fashionable, Tee Bin and his team believed that 2015–2016 was the time to make their next move. Competitors were attempting to copy Bossard's SmartBin system, and despite Bossard's 15-plus years of experience, its proprietary network solution, and strong track record of reliability and proven performance, it was only a matter of time before competitors would bridge the gap in product quality.

Over time, Bossard had acquired valuable knowledge about its clients' behavior and needs. They had observed a trend among customers who aspired to be relieved of the hassle of dealing with C-parts. These clients wanted to not only reduce the risk associated with choosing the correct engineering parts but also improve their efficiency through automated ordering and delivery of inventory. For the most advanced clients, they simply wanted to be completely relieved of managing C-parts by completely outsourcing them. As a result, Tee Bin thought:

The implication for the company would be to shift the focus of the value proposition from products to service. Then it would not be fasteners that the company would sell, but a service package that would allow our client company to optimize, and even fully outsource, its inventory management.

Through direct measures of inventory utilization at the point of use, Bossard's system helped companies avoid the order variations caused by delays and human behavior that were important drivers of inefficiencies in inventory management. Moreover, the analytics in the system were able to predict its client's future needs, unbiased by human estimations, and consolidate the data from all clients for optimization of its own purchases to suppliers.

Tee Bin's team proposed three levels of service packages—entry, advanced, and premium—to shift the focus of the value proposition from products to services. It would not be fasteners that the company would sell with the service as an additional free bonus but a service package allowing the client company to optimize, and even fully outsource, its inventory management based on Bossard's engineering competencies, IoT platform, and big data analytics. The offer was appealing and the value proposition unquestionable. However there were many obstacles to overcome if Bossard was to successfully bring this service to market.

The first challenge required an internal change. For more than 10 years, Bossard's sales force had used their expertise in engineering and the automated SmartBins as differentiators to sell fasteners. The introduction of the new product suite generated skepticism internally. Over the years, the sales force had developed strong relationships with buyers in client companies. However, buyers were not incentivized to optimize the total cost of ownership; instead, they merely sought to reduce the cost of supplies. In order to engage in a conversation about total cost of ownership and global factory efficiency, the sales force had to approach the management level of the company. It was only at this level that the value could be truly discussed.

This implied a significant change in the sales approach and training. Bossard's top management team, including Tee Bin himself, was ready to participate actively and to travel to meet and engage personally with the sales force to drive the change. Moreover, many of Bossard's clients were long-time partners, and managing the transition could be challenging. Resistance from the buyers in client companies was a risk, particularly if Bossard was the first to embrace this new approach.

26.6 From Smart Factory to Smart Ecosystem: ▶ SmartFactoryLogistics.com

Reflecting on the first discussions and attempts to sell the IoT-enabled inventory management service to the clients, Tee Bin realized that if Bossard could provide its clients with inventory planning, then huge volumes of data would be available to them. Tee Bin thought:

To plan inventory, Bossard would need to get and analyze on a regular basis the statistical data: clients' sales, stocks levels, their returns and damages. With our IoT-enabled SmartBins we could already partially collect the data. And this was an incredible amount of information that could be used for analysis and creating a C-part replenishment plan for our clients!

Many businesses had been transformed through the power of data-driven insights. In supply chain, thanks to the vast number of IoT-enabled technologies already implemented in processes, unprecedented amounts of data could be captured from different sources. Researches shared that more than one-third of executives reported being engaged in serious conversations about implementing analytics in the supply chain and three out of ten already had an initiative in place to implement analytics.[9] The increased amounts of data—termed big data—that were both structured and unstructured were inundating businesses on a day-to-day basis. But it was not the amount of data that was important; it was how organizations made use of the data. Big data could be analyzed for insights that led to better decisions and strategic business moves. According to experts, capitalizing on the value of big

---

9   "Big Data Analytics in Supply Chain: Hype or Here to Stay?" *Accenture Global Operations Megatrends Study*, 2014

data in logistics offered massive potential to optimize capacity utilization, improve the customer experience, reduce risk, and create new business models.[10]

To move forward, Bossard would need its clients' projected sales and their forecasts to plan inventory. However, although manufacturing companies were able to forecast their net sales and profitability in the short and long term, almost all of them had difficulty forecasting inventory volumes. With thousands of stock keeping units (SKUs), manufacturing companies always struggled to convert their value plans into the volume plans that predicted how many pieces they would produce and sell. And even if they could roughly estimate the volume, what was absolutely impossible for most of them was decomposing these volumes by SKU or at least by SKU groups. Usually the accuracy of such forecasts was extremely low, and it created difficulties for suppliers of the components who based their replenishment plans on that data.

Tee Bin knew of cases where most of the IoT data collected was not used, and the data that was used was not fully exploited. A critical challenge was analyzing the flood of big data generated by IoT devices for prediction and optimization. With this in mind, Tee Bin believed that this data would allow Bossard to predict its clients' demands. If they had IoT-based smart services, why not use them as a key source of big data that could be analyzed to capture value. Bossard could provide demand planning services for its clients. It could also actively integrate the data into the business processes via analyses and further processing to build the datability competence—the ability to use data. As a consequence, Bossard's core competence would be inventory optimization. Once it received the analyzed data, it could enhance it by:

- Strategic forecasting—long-term forecasting of clients' demands
- Strategic network planning—long-term demand forecast of transport capacity
- Operational capacity planning—short- and mid-term capacity planning, which leads to optimization of manpower and resource utilization and scaling
- Clients' product portfolio optimization advisory—a comprehensive view of customer requirements, past sales, and stock to aid the understanding of which products are in low demand
- Market intelligence—supply chain monitoring data to be used for market intelligence report creation (*refer to* ◘ Fig. 26.8 *for a stepwise approach*).

◘ **Fig. 26.8** How IoT can improve the customer's manufacturing process. (Source: Authors)

---

10 "Logistics trends radar." *DHL Customer Solutions and Innovation*, 2016

This new challenge had the potential to completely change Bossard and bring it to a new level. But was it the right time for this? Was Bossard ready for this or should it consider this as an option for the future?

26.7 Key Developments in IoT for Bossard's Smart Factory Logistics

For some of Bossard's clients, this type of offer would only make sense if Bossard could consolidate supply inventory management with all of its suppliers. Therefore, ARIMS 4.0, an integrated cloud-based system was developed, which enabled the automated management of inventory and delivery, both from Bossard and third-party suppliers.

To ensure competitiveness in this arena, and taking into consideration value distribution in the IoT eco-system defined by McKinsey, Bossard was making the necessary investments in developing its solution, mainly acting at the following three levels:

1. Software platform development: SmartBin was a proven and robust solution for C-part inventory management, unique on the C-parts market. However, in order to keep the leading position, investment in continuous software updates was required, especially to ensure adequate security levels and algorithm performance. In a context of fast progress in technology in domains such as artificial intelligence and machine learning, strong efforts on market intelligence had to be maintained to ensure it remained relevant by incorporating the right technology elements.
2. Application development: To provide additional value for its customers, Bossard was considering additional investments in analytic tools development. These applications, developed as tools linked to the SmartBin software platform, could be adjusted in accordance with the particular customers' requirements. One example was a mobile application developed to help workers manage refills of inventory at the production site by optimization of their trajectory inside the client factory.
3. Integration with upper level systems: With many giants investing in IoT-driven smart inventory management, such as GE, Cisco, and even IBM, Bossard realized that to have a chance of surviving the competition, its solution had to be compatible with any other system that the client company had in place.

Although Bossard was mainly planning to use analytics to optimize its own logistics processes management rather than provide general logistics dashboards to clients, it would provide clients with data about their C-parts/fasteners. Clients could integrate this information into their "general" dashboards.

Therefore, the challenge for Bossard would be the integration with upper level Smart Factory Logistics software platforms, which would be responsible for the overall automation and optimization of the whole manufacturing process. The integration interfaces for the inventory IoT platforms, such as Bossard's SmartBins, had not yet been standardized. Thus the SmartBin could become an industry standard for inventory parts and could induce interest from different industries.

Developing a partnership with RWTH Aachen University for co-development in imagining the future of smart factories was fully consistent with Bossard's strategy. Bossard was indeed selected by the university with its logistics system as a partner for its "Industry 4.0" demonstration factory.

26.8 Will ▶ SmartFactoryLogistics.com Lead to Disruptive Change?

Historically, Bossard developed advanced logistics solutions to lower the customers' TCO and, consequently, sell more fasteners. Moving to a service model based on Smart Factory Logistics was a strategic shift because the revenue model would change from selling screws to getting paid for savings (*refer to Bossard's dedicated website* ▶ www.SmartFactoryLogistics.com). However, as a pioneer in Smart Factory Logistics, Bossard's management team considered deploying the technology outside of its core market, i.e., equipment manufacturers.

Possible markets for replicating the IoT-driven smart inventory management service offer were hospitals, nursing homes, and other care institutions. Pressure on costs had long been negligible, but it was starting to rise. Public hospitals had a huge opportunity to improve efficiency and limited know-how in this domain. In most hospitals, purchasing was done centrally, and inventory stocked in warehouses. Direct deliveries from manufacturers were much more costly than using distributors that were also investing in lowering the hassle and time to reorder items.[11]

Nurses in each ward regularly checked the remaining amount of supplies and placed manual orders in the hospital system when necessary. Similar to factories, a large assortment of many items needed to be managed, and stockouts created significant problems during operations. Aging and cumbersome IT interfaces and interruptions in their availability to patients made this task particularly time consuming and unrewarding.

The much more competitive (and potentially more eager for efficiency-improving solutions) private clinic market was consolidating with large groups of clinics active in the field. Nursing homes were probably the most affected by cost pressure, with strict control by the state on prices linked to the subsidy system.

McKinsey assumed that IoT-based inventory optimization could reduce inventory costs significantly in hospitals. It estimated that using automated replenishment systems to restock medical supplies could produce savings of $1–$4 billion

---

11 "Hospital Procurement Study." *PwC, 2012* ▶ www.hida.org/App_Themes/Member/docs/Hospital_Procurement.pdf (accessed 4 October 2017)

dollars for hospitals around the world by 2025. In total, they estimated that IoT-based inventory optimization could create value of $98–$342 billion dollars per year.[12]

So, if small supplies such as bandages, syringes, needles, and basic medicine could be assimilated to C-parts, how could an automated inventory management system fit into the complex logistics of a hospital? And how could Bossard convince the first clients to try the system?

References

Johnson, D. (2016, November 1). Manufacturers rely on big data analytics. *Industry Safety & Hygiene News.* www.ishn.com/articles/105193-manufacturers-rely-on-big-data-analytics. Accessed 7 Nov 2016.

Myers, J. (2016, July 21). Explainer: The Internet of Things. *World Economic Forum.* www.weforum.org/agenda/2016/07/the-internet-of-things-explained/. Accessed 1 Nov 2016.

Wellers, D. (2015, November 27). Is this the future of the Internet of Things? *World Economic Forum.* www.weforum.org/agenda/2015/11/is-this-future-of-the-internet-of-things/. Accessed 10 Oct 2017.

---

12 "The Internet of Things: Mapping the value beyond the hype." *McKinsey Global Institute*, June 2015

Mary Barra and the Lyft Investment: Leading GM into the Sharing Economy Through Acquisitions

Contents

IMD EMBA 2017 graduates Tareq Ayub, Dario Donnini, Saidah Gomez and Riccardo Tediosi prepared this case under the supervision of Professors Carlos Cordon and Tawfik Jelassi as a basis for class discussion rather than to illustrate either effective or ineffective handling of a business situation. Copyright © 2018 by *IMD – International Institute for Management Development*, Lausanne, Switzerland (► www.imd.org). No part of this publication may be reproduced, stored in a retrieval system, or transmitted in any form or by any means without the prior written permission of *IMD*.

© Springer Nature Switzerland AG 2020
T. Jelassi, F. J. Martínez-López, *Strategies for e-Business*, Classroom Companion: Business, https://doi.org/10.1007/978-3-030-48950-2_27

■ **Introduction**

> **Definition**
>
> We're going to disrupt ourselves, and we are disrupting ourselves, so we're not trying to preserve a model of yesterday. And when you think of the assets the company has – the scale, the control of the vehicle platform, the ability with embedded connectivity, the knowledge we have of just every aspect of the vehicle and how we're putting it together now – I think there's a lot of plus signs, and we can lead. — Mary Barra, CEO, General Motors[1]

In January 2014, Mary Barra took over as the first female CEO of General Motors, which celebrated its 100th anniversary in 2008. She rose to the CEO role after joining the company in 1980 as a co-op student. During her time at GM, she saw the company go through extreme economic fluctuations, from a world-class brand with record sales to ▶ Chap. 11 bankruptcy and the subsequent $50 billion US government bailout that positioned the company for a new future. Since Barra's takeover, the company had bought back the last government-owned stock and was back on its feet.

27.1 Emergence from Bankruptcy

Since recovering from bankruptcy in 2009, GM had vastly improved upon its sales and overall performance. A strategic move to reduce the number of brands it had in the market increased the density of penetration and helped the company focus on target segments instead of attempting to capture every available market. In addition, the timing of the drop in fuel prices and relatively low-cost financing options gave a boost to consumers' appetites for spending on automobiles (*see* ❏ Fig. 27.1: *US Total Vehicle Sales*).

In 2015 GM posted solid sales numbers by selling 9.8 million vehicles globally, representing $145.9 billion in annual revenues. Models like Buick, Chevrolet, Cadillac, and Opel/Vauxhall performed strongly, and the company fared well in its North American market with a 5.4% increase in sales revenues over 2014. GM's North American market share of the automotive industry, which included Canada and Mexico, was 17.3%, and collectively the industry saw an increase of light vehicle sales from 1 million units to 17.5 million.

The company made significant internal improvements by successfully restructuring and renegotiating complex labor contracts with labor unions that had previously cost it billions in losses. These new agreements resulted in reduced pension obligations.

Despite these performance improvements, investors with a long-range view were seeing disruptions to the automotive industry on the horizon. The rise of car-

---

1   DeBord, Matthew. General Motors CEO Mary Barra: "We are disrupting ourselves, we're not trying to preserve a model of yesterday." *Business Insider*, 16 November 2015. ▶ http:// uk.businessinsider.com/general-motors-ceo-mary-barra-were-going-to-disrupt-ourselves-we-are-disrupting-ourselves-were-not-trying-to-preserve-a-model-of-yesterday-2015-10?r=DE&IR=T

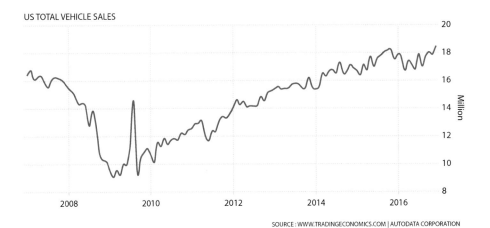

US TOTAL VEHICLE SALES

SOURCE : WWW.TRADINGECONOMICS.COM | AUTODATA CORPORATION

☐ **Fig. 27.1** US total vehicle sales. (Source: "US Total Vehicle Sales." *Trading Economics*, 2017. ▶ www.tradingeconomics.com)

sharing and ride-sharing services in the United States and the race to produce autonomous vehicles were posing significant threats to the traditional manufacture-financing-sale-repair business model.

In 2016 GM's market share in the United States dropped from 17% to 15%. Analysts anticipated that this decline would continue as more and more cars were being consumed by a shared business model. Barra saw traditional and non-traditional competitors making swift moves around her in a race to be the first and best positioned in the next incarnation of the automotive industry. On 5 January 2016, she led her company to invest $500 million in the ride-sharing platform Lyft, a smaller rival to Uber.

Like executives from other leading manufacturers within the automotive industry, Barra was faced with uncertainty as it was difficult to predict the extent to which disruption would impact her business.

27.2 Constantly Shifting Consumer Preferences: A Reality for All Companies

> **Definition**
>
> We are here to earn customers for life.[2] — General Motors, Corporate Strategy

Personal mobility needs were rapidly changing. Present-day sales figures indicated a healthy appetite for ownership (*see* ☐ Fig. 27.2: *GM Market Share 1980–2008*);

---

2 General Motors website. ▶ http://www.gm.com/investors/corporate-strategy.html. Accessed 30 October 2018.

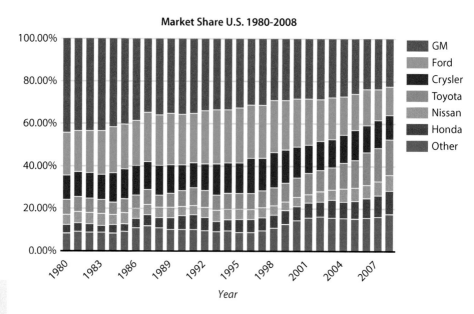

Market Share U.S. 1980-2008

☐ **Fig. 27.2** GM market share 1980–2008. (Source: Motor Intelligence. ▶ http://www.motorintelligence. com/)

however, long-term sustainability was not guaranteed, particularly within urban areas where consumers were moving away from traditional car ownership.

From a market perspective, there were three levels of car ownership defined by the region in which the owner lived. Those living in urban areas (urban drivers) faced challenges with respect to population density, parking, heavy traffic congestion, and higher insurance costs. Compared to their urban counterparts, those who lived in the suburbs (suburban drivers) lived in less densely packed areas, faced less traffic congestion, had few issues with parking, and centered their driving activities on work, family activities, and childcare (i.e., taking children to and from school, soccer practice, etc.). Finally, those who lived in remote areas faced little traffic congestion or parking challenges.

Under the traditional car ownership model, GM had maintained a strong focus on performance factors such as speed and consumption levels. Establishing financing options to facilitate ownership had also been an important component in ensuring customer satisfaction. For example, the company launched its financing business called General Motors Finance (GMF) in 2010. In 2015 the business generated annual revenues of $6.4 billion, representing 4.2% of total revenues.

Traditional customer expectations were not just limited to performance features. Features that were once deemed attractive, such as air conditioning and multimedia systems, were now viewed as mandatory, and attractive options like connectivity, which enticed customers today, may not be sufficient to entice them tomorrow. Rapid changes in technology and consumer expectations were making it difficult for original equipment manufacturers (OEMs) to develop offerings in pace with consumer demand.

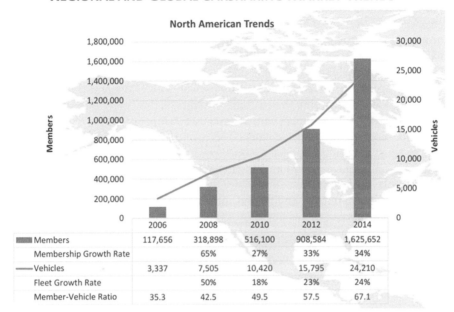

REGIONAL AND GLOBAL CARSHARING MARKET TRENDS

North American Trends

	2006	2008	2010	2012	2014
Members	117,656	318,898	516,100	908,584	1,625,652
Membership Growth Rate		65%	27%	33%	34%
Vehicles	3,337	7,505	10,420	15,795	24,210
Fleet Growth Rate		50%	18%	23%	24%
Member-Vehicle Ratio	35.3	42.5	49.5	57.5	67.1

Fig. 27.3 Regional and global carsharing market trends. (Source: Shaheen, Susan and Adam Cohen. "Innovative Mobility Carsharing Outlook: Carsharing Market Overview, Analysis, and Trends." *Transportation Sustainability Research Center – University of California, Berkeley*, Winter 2016. ▶ http://innovativemobility.org/wp-content/uploads/2016/02/Innovative-Mobility-Industry-Outlook_World-2016-Final.pdf. Accessed November 52,018)

The evolution of consumer preferences, led by millennials, was driven by two key components: urbanization and a strong desire to remain connected. Vehicle ownership rates were slowing due to the desire of this emerging segment to favor "experiences" over ownership. Facts showed that private-car ownership was declining; in the United States, for example, the share of young people (16 to 24 years) who held a driver's license dropped from 76% in 2000 to 71% in 2013,[3] while there had been over 30% annual growth in car-sharing members in North America and Germany over the last 5 years (*refer to* ▶ Fig. 27.3: *Regional and Global Car-sharing Market Trends*). According to Navigant Consulting,[4] global car-sharing services revenue would approach US$6.2 billion by 2020, with over 12 million members worldwide.

---

3   "Eight disruptive trends shaping the auto industry of 2030." *Automotive World*, March 18, 2016. ▶ www.automotiveworld.com/analysis/eight-disruptive-trends-shaping-auto-industry-2030/. Accessed 30 October 2018.

4   "Carsharing Services Will Surpass 12 Million Members Worldwide by 2020, Forecasts Navigant Research." *Marketwatch*, 22 August 2013. ▶ https://www.marketwatch.com/press-release/carsharing-services-will-surpass-12-million-members-worldwide-by-2020-forecasts-navigant-research-2013-08-22. Accessed 5 November 2018.

Consumers, particularly those living in urban and suburban areas, had always had access to shared mobility services like taxis and public transportation; however, their appetite for the current iteration of shared mobility was a different phenomenon that Barra's GM team had to master to remain relevant in the future. Companies like Uber, the largest ride-sharing platform by number of connections at 1 billion and a valuation of $68 billion (December 2016), had been in operation for less than 10 years, which paled in comparison with GM's century-old business; however, it led in gathering the customer insights of this emerging segment.

Like traditional customers who favored ownership, customers in this emerging segment were looking for price, safety, and comfort. However, they were also looking for short wait times, service network coverage, and minimum associated costs (i.e., insurance and parking) and to eliminate other heavy obligations associated with vehicle ownership like maintenance, insurance contracts, service, and repairs. They cared less about the engine and more about entertainment, service, and an Internet connection.

27.3 Modern Automotive Trends Were All About Digital Enablement

The rapid-fire changes in today's competitive landscape were forcing Barra to think beyond the traditional value chain and shift to an ecosystem mindset in which unlikely actors were playing key roles in shaping the future.

These changes were triggered by the development in emerging markets, the accelerated rise of new technologies, environmental and sustainability policies, and changing consumer preferences around ownership. Digitization, new energy sources, increasing automation, sharing platforms, and new business models had revolutionized other industries, and questions were being raised within the automotive sector. The new world was a mashup of digital, millennial demographics, global economic movements, and tech-savvy enterprises collectively forcing the transformation (and disruption) of established companies that had previously failed to imagine threats from non-traditional sources. This new world posed a threat to GM despite its past successes and the strength of its brand.

27.3.1 Realigning to Green Energy

Stricter emission regulations, lower battery costs, more widely available charging infrastructure, and increasing consumer acceptance were creating new momentum for the penetration of electrified vehicles (hybrid, plug-in, battery electric, and fuel cell).

One pioneer and the best example of energy disruptors was Tesla Motors with its ability to upgrade the capabilities of electric vehicles via software downloads, which made its cars more valuable to their owners over time. The Tesla Model S, the world's first premium electric sedan, was built from the ground up to be 100% electric. The Model S has redefined the very concept of a four-door car. With room for seven passengers and more than 64 cubic feet of storage, the Model S provided the comfort and utility of a family sedan while achieving the acceleration of a sports car: 0 to 60 mph in about 5 seconds.

In addition to a shift to green energy, GM was forced to examine two aspects of the new world that were simultaneously impacting the automotive industry—intelligent cars and on-demand consumption (sharing economy). Both of these had a symbiotic relationship. On-demand consumption changed the way cars (as products) were acquired and intelligent cars lessened the dependence on human beings while adding more mobility.

27.3.2 Intelligent Vehicles

Intelligent "connected" vehicles were at the forefront of automotive industry's innovation agenda. While autonomous (driverless) vehicles were the first thing to come to mind when we think about intelligent vehicles, the impact was much broader. Intelligence referred to the integration of robotic activity (driving) and artificial intelligence (contextual decision-making).

It was the "intelligence" in the vehicle that delivered hassle-free experiences to owners (or operators) by providing advanced insights related to maintenance and other services like routing or emergency by being constantly context-aware. The same intelligence enabled green energy consumption by replacing fossil fuel with batteries that could be managed. These cars were able to alter the entire transportation infrastructure for cities; from public services, to fuel sites, parking infrastructure, insurance policies, etc.

A study conducted by the Organization for Economic Cooperation and Development (OECD) showed that shared self-driving fleets could deliver the same mobility with significantly fewer cars. In a city that had a good public transport system and was primarily serviced by ride-sharing companies operating self-driving (intelligent) cars, 90% of cars could be removed from streets.

While the consumer and efficiency benefits were substantial, there was an economic impact as well to both the cities and financial institutions that relied on supply chain financing as well as payment systems. Intelligent vehicles opened limitless options for business models that integrated the ecosystem external to the automotive industry for the purpose of delivering customer outcomes.

Definition

The significance of intelligent connected vehicles not only lies in the upgrading of automobile products and technologies, but also in the reshaping of the overall structure and value chain of the automobile and related industries.[5] — Hao Fei, Deputy General Manager of Zebra Technologies.

---

5 Ran, Yu. "Intelligent cars: The future of transportation." *Chinadaily USA*, 1 October 2016. ▶ usa.chinadaily.com.cn/china/2016-10/01/content_26954886.htm. Accessed 30 October 2018.

That was a big deal for automotive manufacturers—making intelligent vehicles required a different set of capabilities that delivered software-led technology innovation. The model also required a rethink of the company's channel strategy so that it could ensure the necessary growth and required margins.

27.3.3 Sharing Economy Was Taking Off

Digital technologies had changed the way people lived, worked, traveled, consumed, and shared things with one another, as well as how businesses operated. Consequently, the power was shifting from organizations to networks of people and communities, which had given rise to the sharing economy. According to *The Economist*, the value of the sharing economy was estimated to reach $250 billion by 2030.

Consumers tended to use their cars as all-purpose vehicles, whether they were commuting alone to work or taking the whole family to the beach. It could be that in the future, they would want the flexibility to choose the best solution for a specific purpose, on demand and via their smartphones.

As on-demand services and intelligent car technology matured and got widely adopted—urban drivers would see ride-sharing as an appealing option, while suburban areas would value a combination of ownership and sharing options. The remote areas were less dense and would most likely stick to ownership.

> **Definition**
>
> The whole idea of owning a car, parking it for $1,000 a month and letting it sit there 90 percent of the time is just ludicrous.[6] — Julia Steyn, GM's Vice President of Urban Mobility Programs.

Coupled with intelligent vehicles, the sharing economy would open opportunities for owners and operators since opportunities extended beyond matching supply and demand when fully or semi-autonomous vehicles could locate demand without being requested.

27.3.4 Move to Digital Engagement

Another industry trend that companies had to face was the move to digital engagement, which allowed cars to become platforms for drivers and passengers who could use their time in transit on other personal activities. The associated digital

---

6   Wernle, Bradford. "Why GM is embracing car sharing." *Automotive News*, August 3, 2016.
   ▶ http://www.autonews.com/article/20160803/OEM06/160809907/why-gm-is-embracing-car-sharing. Accessed 6 November 2018.

services could reinvent existing business models, change the auto ecosystem, and redesign customer engagement and expectations.

Brands like Uber had rewritten the rules of the market through digitalization. Instead of owning car fleets, it signed up private drivers willing to provide rides and connected them with paying passengers via its app. In just over 6 years, Uber was able to surpass the valuation of industry giants GM and Ford, as well as "traditional" transportation companies like Hertz and Avis.

27.4 Lessons from Past Innovation Successes and Failures

GM's leadership in the automotive industry was well recognized. The company had pioneered several market-leading innovations that had shaped the automotive industry both in domestic and international markets. Despite GM's impressive credentials, its journey had been a collection of decisions that had led to successes and failures. A pattern had emerged that told a story about its ability to innovate, disrupt, and adapt. These historical lessons could indicate how the company, under the guidance of Barra, adapted to the new emerging threats.

From creating the industry's first electric start engine in 1912, to four-wheel brakes in 1956, through the industry's first catalytic converter in 1975, GM's investments in research had earned it a reputation as the industry's most innovative brand. This had played a significant role in maintaining customer loyalty.

The most recognized innovation from GM was OnStar, the first product to realize the vision of the connected car 20 years ago, by providing security and service for its customers—that is 20 years before the concept of the connected car became an industry phenomenon. The OnStar product was a subscription-based service that offered owners of GM vehicles capabilities such as automatic incident response, turn-by-turn navigation, remote diagnostics, and roadside assistance in several countries in North and South America as well as Europe.

One of the primary reasons this product was deemed a success is that the CEO maintained a relentless position for disrupting the business while taking on the risk of an uncertain outcome. Chet Huber, who ran the program, made the following statement: "If you try to do something profoundly disruptive within a large company, the core business will probably smother it unless the CEO purposefully ensures otherwise."[7]

An example of a failed innovation was the Saturn brand, which was created in response to the introduction of low-cost Japanese vehicles. This defensive play targeted a broad market and lacked focus. GM had failed to do what it did best—listen to the voice of the customer—and produced and marketed vehicles to "everyone" without keeping its customer segment in mind. The inability to recognize the flaws in this defensive strategy led the company to continue production of the brand, though largely unprofitable. The capital expenditures related to building

---

7 "Lessons from Running GM's OnStar." *Forbes*, 4 March 2013. ▶ https://www.forbes.com/sites/hbsworkingknowledge/2013/03/04/lessons-from-running-gms-onstar/#74155ea33151. Accessed 6 November 2018.

a new Saturn facility and the operating costs were upward of $5 billion throughout the brand's life span, yet sales of the vehicle failed to cover production operating costs. By 2000, Saturn was losing $3000 on every car it sold.

27.5 GM Invests in the Ride-Sharing Company Lyft

As growth across traditional segments was no longer certain, GM recognized the need to capture growth through different sources, which required substantial research and understanding of the new service-based business model. The urgency to act was enhanced by the swiftness with which traditional and non-traditional competitors were collaborating and partnering in open and scalable ecosystems. These moves pointed to a recognition that in future, it was expected that cars would be commoditized and personalized mobility services would dominate.

In response to this emerging picture of a different future, Barra made the decision to find a way to accelerate GM's participation in the new services-based model. The company was far too focused on stabilizing its operations relative to its traditional business. GM's initial attempt was to fully acquire the young ride-sharing company called Lyft. When that attempt failed, GM resorted to a 9% stake in exchange for a seat on the board held by GM President, Dan Ammann, and a partnership to develop a network of self-driving, on-demand cars. This move complemented the company's investment in Maven (acquisition and merger of Zipcar and Sidecar together with their intellectual property portfolio that included "e-hailing" patents), an on-demand vehicle service that allowed customers to rent GM vehicles for an hourly fee.

Lyft operated in US markets and was founded in 2012 by Logan Green and John Zimmer. It was defined as "a peer-to-peer transportation platform that connects passengers who need rides with drivers willing to provide rides using their own personal vehicles.[8]"

It was heavily reliant on the use of a mobile app for smartphones. Private car owners signed in and announced their availability to transport ride sharers. Individuals looking for a ride could request a Lyft driver and car while directly paying for the ride and providing driver's feedback in a seamlessly integrated digital process.

Drivers became service providers for Lyft with flexible working hours and earned hourly rates from $10 to $30 per hour (average $11.5 per hour) depending on the time of the day.

Lyft primarily operated in urban areas and was a much smaller outfit than Uber, the industry leader. Investors were showing increasing interest in the ride-sharing concept, which helped Lyft accomplish its biggest fundraising round in 2016. In addition to GM's $500 million investment, the Saudi Prince Al-Waleed's Kingdom Holding Company, Janus Capital Management, invested $500 million (*refer to* ◘ Fig. 27.4: *Lyft Fundraising Rounds*).

---

8 "Lyft." *Crunchbase*. ► www.crunchbase.com/organization/lyft#/entity. Accessed 30 October 2018.

LYFT–Funding Rounds (11) –$2.61 billion			
Date	Amount/Round	Lead Investor	Investors
April 2017	$600M/Series G	–	5
October 2016	Undisclosed amount/Secondary Market	–	1
December 2015	$1B/Series F	General Motors	10
May 2015	$150M/Series E	Icahn Enterprises	8
March 2015	$530M/Series E	Rakuten	8
April 2014	$250M/Series D	Coatue Management	9
May 2013	$60M/Series C	Andreessen Horowitz	3
January 2013	$15M/Series B	Founders Fund	6
September 2011	$6m/Series A	Mayfield Fund	4
August 2010	$1.2M/Seed	FLOODGATE	4
		K9 Ventures	
July 2008	$300k/Seed	Fb Fund`	1

Source: Crunchbase.   <www.crunchbase.com/organization/lyft#/entity>

◘ **Fig. 27.4**   LYFT fundraising rounds

In September 2016 Lyft co-founder John Zimmer declared to the press:

» In the U.S. alone, two trillion dollars is being spent on car ownership, and cars are being used only four percent of the time. This makes no sense. So, what's happening here is that there's no bigger opportunity to create economic value in the country than changing that fact. And that means there are a lot of people that want to take part in that.[9]

And according to Ammann, GM's president:

» GM is now pretty well positioned to pursue a strategy of expanding its presence in ride sharing and ride hailing, and in the long term, develop services that use autonomous vehicles to provide customers with transportation. A ride sharing network is the logical first place to deploy driverless technology.[10]

GM recognized Lyft as a "platform" company that had the opportunity to create a "network effect." In this context the platform was the customer engagement technology that allowed them to connect with services offered by the platform. Other

9 Steinmetz, Katy. "Lyft Cofounder Lays Out His Vision of the Driverless Future." *Time*, 18 September 2016. ► http://time.com/4495768/lyft-cofounder-john-zimmer-self-driving-cars/. Accessed 6 November 2018.

10 White, Joseph. "GM president: Pieces in place to develop ride sharing, autonomous cars." *Reuters*, 1 June 2016. ► http://ca.reuters.com/article/businessNews/idCAKCN0YN5NF?pageNumber=1&virtualBrandChannel=0. Accessed 6 November 2016.

"platform" companies like Alphabet (widely recognized as Google), Apple, Facebook, Amazon, LinkedIn, Airbnb, Netflix, Uber, Twitter, GitHub, and Alibaba created a competitive edge by enabling "network effects" both as a competitive edge and an innovation resource. Network effects were their "secret sauce" for success. Technically, economists said network effects—also known as "network externalities"—exist when a product's or service's value to users increases as the number of users grow. The more users participate, the more quickly value can be generated. And the more value created, the more users and innovative uses would materialize. That virtuous value cycle simultaneously disrupted and transformed companies. Value could exponentially increase as costs grew only marginally. This made the economics of "network effects" combinatorially compelling.

This interest in Lyft would play a significant role in determining the staging and pacing of Barra's moves when it came to deploying the company's services of the future. Barra had set a clear direction for GM by stating, "Our goal is to disrupt ourselves and own the customer relationship beyond the car."[11]

Internally, GM faced challenges vis-à-vis the culture and capability shift required to achieve the level of responsiveness necessary to compete in the digital economy or "disrupt" themselves. In contrast, startups would find ways of turning their constraints into strengths. With a small budget and limited time, startups were forced to operate with a great sense of urgency. They were often able to out-maneuver large corporations because of their speed in bringing new ideas to market and their nimbleness in adapting to market needs. To compete with startups, large organizations had to be inspired by them.

To overcome GM's legacy inertia, Barra was spearheading a fundamentally different approach to innovation, one that would draw upon the playbook of startups mentioned earlier. It boiled down to adopting a concept called "venture thinking," an entrepreneurial mindset that looked to drive innovation and growth. Venture thinking organizations aimed to be nimble when testing potential solutions to problems. They created well-articulated hypotheses and tested them through a sequence of small experiments directly in the market.

There were many examples of companies who had operationalized "venture thinking" by acquiring mature startups, setting up divisions in Silicon Valley or exchange partnerships for cross-industry sharing. GE, as an example, had built a major presence in Silicon Valley where it was building a world-class software backbone, Predix, and integrating it into most of its products and services. Automotive industry players like Ford, BMW, Mercedes, and Volkswagen were all following suite.

Under Barra's guidance, GM had been making significant investments in innovation by deploying research centers in the United States and Canada. It had also invested in establishing a presence in Silicon Valley and was helping create an emerging transportation ecosystem. The GM "innovation centers" focused on developing software-based capabilities for future GM products and searching for appropriate investments and partnerships.

---

11 White, Joseph. Exclusive: "GM to tap into connectivity, expand car sharing services – CEO."
► www.reuters.com/article/us-gm-ceo-idUSKCN0RS2K420150929. Accessed 30 October 2018.

As the digital economy centered on customer experience, the key to getting impact from the research within the context of "venture thinking" was getting good insights from real data. While data could be collected from GM's own services and products being deployed in their cars, the real value of venture thinking would come from intersecting additional insights.

Tesla, as an example, utilized a great deal of data collected from its cars. This had changed the conversation on the type of personalized experience car owners (drivers and passengers) could expect from an automaker. Tesla had taken a lesson from Apple, Alphabet, Facebook, and Amazon, four companies that were obsessed with connecting pieces of data and using it to better understand their consumers and tailor their services to provide the right experience. It was this personalized experience that Tesla offered that had allowed it to build a brand that delighted its customers.

Toyota for its part had invested in a small stake in Uber to gain insights into how consumers used the ride-sharing platform. In October 2016, the company announced that it invested $10 million in Getaround, a San Francisco-based company that had developed a peer-to-peer car rental platform in 2009. Car owners rented out their vehicles to peers in their network for a predetermined period of time. Those seeking transportation could maintain possession of the vehicle for more than one journey, unlike those using Lyft or Uber.

GM's launch of Maven in early 2016 was itself proving to be an intelligence-driven move leveraging the WhatsApp app for data collection. The platform was both a customer service tool and a tool used to get feedback and field questions from customers, who in turn would provide insights into customer experiences and preferences. From a "network" perspective, the insights from the number of people using WhatsApp (acquired by Facebook) would define the value pivots of the GM service.

Definition

We believe it's important in the car sharing experience for the passenger and customer to feel like it's your own vehicle.[12] — Julia Steyn, GM VP, Urban Mobility Programs

---

As mobility services were playing an increasingly important role in automotive solutions, companies that offered such services had become ideal partners to automotive makers.

As noted earlier, the network of platform integrations could give rise to new business models and revenue streams that complemented the existing business model and over time could become the core business. When the users became the platforms' most valuable assets, they extended the reach via application programming interfaces (API) to other partners or product integrations, and this could cause rapid expansion of value.

---

12 Lunden, Ingrid. "GM Unveils Maven, Its Big New Play in Car-Sharing Services." ▶ https://techcrunch.com/2016/01/20/gm-unveils-maven-its-big-play-in-car-sharing-and-other-new-ownership-models/. Accessed 30 October 2018.

As an example, in March 2016, Ford created a subsidiary called Ford Smart Mobility Company to "design, build, grow and invest in emerging mobility services." According to the company's website, the newly formed company was "part of Ford's expanded business model to be both an auto and mobility company,"[13] thus, revealing to investors and competitors alike the direction the company had taken. In September 2016, Ford Smart Mobility acquired the ride-sharing service called Chariot with the strategic motive to extend Ford Smart Mobility by leveraging Chariot.

Similarly, in January 2017, Honda unveiled its NeuV (New Electric Urban Vehicle) concept car designed for the ride-sharing market. Owners could monetize downtime of this self-driving vehicle by "lending it" out to the ride-sharing market while not in use. Owners could also sell the remaining energy generated by the electric vehicle back to the grid.

A key movement by GM's competitor was that in January 2017, Daimler and Uber reached an agreement to commence work on an autonomous taxi business model in which Daimler would provide a self-driving fleet and operate vehicles for the ride-hailing platform. In addition, in late 2017, Daimler, along with Audi and BMW, obtained a majority stake in HERE, an open location service provider. HERE was developing technology that facilitated semi-autonomous driving by allowing connected cars to gather real-time data on the surrounding environment.

27

One of the biggest assets GM got as part of the Sidecar acquisition was the system and method for determining an efficient transportation route. A Sidecar patent detailed how to use mobile phones to coordinate on-demand transportation. GM had also decided to offer Uber drivers via its Maven service—another channel opportunity for several of its remaining brands.

Similarly, GM's recent investment stake in Lyft was an opportunity to leverage its Express Drive program to provide GM vehicles to drivers who did not own ride-sharing-ready vehicles. These investments and partnership were opening up new channels (while exploratory) for GM that could become sustainable channels for its new cars as well as a secondary market for ex-lease or fleet cars.

Definition

When a GM car is sold, it is good for GM, when someone uses a Maven, GM gets a piece of that, too. When a Lyft driver picks up a customer in an Express Drive vehicle in a GM car, we're getting a little piece of that, too. I think General Motors is really ahead of the curve. Nobody has a crystal ball, but if there is going to be this change or evolution in the automotive industry, it's nice to have all these options available to a company this size. — Maven COO, Dan Grossman[14]

---

13 "Ford Smart Mobility LLC established to develop, invest in mobility services; Jim Hackett named Subsidiary Chairman." Ford, 11 March 2016. ▶ https://media.ford.com/content/fordmedia/fna/us/en/news/2016/03/11/ford-smart-mobility-llc-established%2D%2Djim-hackett-named-chairman.html.Accessed October 30, 2018.

14 Etherington Darrell. "How GM's Maven car sharing service got to over 4.2 M miles driven in 7 months." *TechCrunch*. ▶ https://techcrunch.com/2016/08/24/how-gms-maven-car-sharing-service-got-to-over-4-2m-miles-driven-in-7-months/. Accessed 30 October 2018.

27.6 **Where to Next?**

GM had positioned its innovation across four categories: electric vehicles enabled by the Bolt product, autonomous cars supported by GM's Cruise Control acquisition, connected cars supported by On, which was the next generation of GM's flagship OnStar product, and sharing supported by Maven. It must be noted that there was a difference between the services that Maven provided and what Lyft provided even though both fell under the "sharing economy" umbrella. Maven was a "car-sharing" service while Lyft was a "ride-sharing" service. Establishing strong synergies between all four categories was key for GM to address the digital economy; collectively, they could provide data insights and offer opportunities for new revenue streams.

While Barra exercised her options for capitalizing on the Lyft investment, Lyft continued to form partnerships with other players and potential competitors within the ecosystem. In May 2017, it entered into an agreement with the Alphabet-owned Waymo to develop self-driving cars.[15]

With only a 9% stake, could Barra leverage the Lyft investment such that it could have a sufficient impact toward leading her company through this transitional period in the automotive industry?

With the sharing economy rapidly becoming mainstream, Barra was forced to reevaluate GM's value across the car buyer's journey. Whether this triggered a complete departure from the manufacture-financing-sale-repair business model or led to so some form of co-existence with augmented and emergent business models was an open question.

With so many new players entering the automotive space and creating an ecosystem of interconnected services, there was a higher risk of diluting the value over a larger base and diverting it from the traditional market leaders (◘ Table 27.1).

---

15 Fingas, Jon. "Lyft and Waymo work together on self-driving cars." *Engadget*, 14 May 2017. ▸ www.engadget.com/2017/05/14/lyft-and-waymo-self-driving-car-partnership/. Accessed October 30, 2018.

▣ Table 27.1 LYFT – funding rounds (11) – $2.61 billion

Date	Amount/round	Lead investor	Investors
April 2017	$600 M/series G	–	5
October 2016	Undisclosed amount/secondary market	–	1
December 2015	$1B/series F	General Motors	10
May 2015	$150 M/series E	Icahn Enterprises	8
March 2015	$530 M/series E	Rakuten	8
April 2014	$250 M/series D	Coatue Management	9
May 2013	$60 M/series C	Andreessen Horowitz	3
January 2013	$15 M/series B	Founders Fund	6
September 2011	$6 m/series A	Mayfield Fund	4
August 2010	$1.2 M/seed	Floodgate	4
		K9 Ventures	
July 2008	$300 k/seed	fbFund	1

Source: Crunchbase. ▶ www.crunchbase.com/organization/lyft#/entity

27

Turkcell (A): How to Respond to Digital Disruption?

Contents

Researcher PC Abraham prepared this case under the supervision of Professor Tawfik Jelassi as a basis for class discussion rather than to illustrate either effective or ineffective handling of a business situation. Copyright © 2018 by IMD – *International Institute for Management Development*, Lausanne, Switzerland (▶ www.imd.org). No part of this publication may be reproduced, stored in a retrieval system or transmitted in any form or by any means without the prior written permission of *IMD*

© Springer Nature Switzerland AG 2020
T. Jelassi, F. J. Martínez-López, *Strategies for e-Business*, Classroom Companion: Business, https://doi.org/10.1007/978-3-030-48950-2_28

■ **Introduction**

5 April 2015. Kaan Terzioglu, Turkcell's CEO, was in a pensive mood on his fifth day on the job. He had just received his first WhatsApp call, which highlighted the challenge his company—Turkey's largest mobile communications provider—was facing from over-the-top (OTT) service providers. Of Turkcell's 35 million mobile subscribers, 10 million were WhatsApp users.

The 4.5G spectrum auctions, where the company would be competing against Vodafone and Turk Telekom, were approaching in August. Turkcell needed to decide whether to bid aggressively to maintain its market leading position or to bid less aggressively to acknowledge a more competitive and less profitable future.

Turkcell had remained solidly profitable and its revenues in Turkey had increased by 10% from the first quarter of 2014 to 2015. Voice revenues in Turkey had dropped by 4%, though an increase in data revenues of 46% had more than counterbalanced this. Intense competition with Vodafone and Turk Telekom made it difficult to increase prices.

Turkcell faced significant internal challenges. Mobile and fixed-line communications were run by separate companies, which made it difficult for Turkcell to present one face to the consumer and react effectively to the converging telecom market. The organization was top-heavy with too many managers at all levels. Despite all this, the feeling within the company was that there was no compelling need for change because it was number one among mobile telecoms and profitable.

Turkcell's international operations had been hit by currency devaluations in Ukraine and Belarus. International operations were a mixed bag including both subsidiaries and minority stakes.

As the new CEO, Kaan knew that he had a window of opportunity to make significant changes. He wondered where he should start.

28.1 Turkcell's Founding and Early History

Turkcell began operations in 1994 and was Turkey's first mobile telecommunications provider. While two competitors (Vodafone and Turk Telekom) had entered the mobile telecommunications space subsequently, Turkcell had remained the dominant player. The company had also entered fixed-line communications in Turkey through a subsidiary—Superonline—which began operating in 2005.

Turkcell had also expanded internationally. It had been operating since 1999 through a wholly owned subsidiary in Northern Cyprus. It had been present in Ukraine since 2005 through a 55% stake in a local telco, and it had acquired an 80% stake in a telco in Belarus. It had also been operating since 2010 as a virtual telecom operator in Germany. It also had a presence in Azerbaijan, Kazakhstan, Moldavia, and Georgia through a 41% equity stake in Fintur, which had subsidiaries in these countries.

28.2 Turkcell in April 2015

28.2.1 Turkcell Turkey

Turkcell's operations in Turkey, which accounted for 91% of its total revenues in Q1 2015, were performing well. Looking back, Seyfettin Saglam, the company's executive vice president for human resources, explained:

» When Kaan came here, Turkcell was a shining star in the Turkish market. It was modern and innovative; it was a technology company.

Turkcell was the leader in mobile communications in Turkey and the second largest telco after Turk Telekom. Revenues in Turkey had increased 9.5% year on year in local currency terms in Q1 2015. The company's overall profitability was high, with a gross margin of 38.6% and earnings before interest, taxes, depreciation, and amortization (EBITDA) margin of 31.1%. Voice revenues had dropped by 4% year on year, but a 46% increase in data revenues had more than compensated for this. The growing adoption of smartphones was driving increases in mobile data consumption (see ◘ Figs. 28.1, 28.2, 28.3, and 28.4).

Mobile subscriber numbers had dropped by half a million, from 34.8 million to 34.3 million, because of the regulatory constraints that Turkcell faced as the dominant mobile operator. However, this drop hid some good news; while the number

CONSOLIDATED FINANCIAL RESULTS			
TRY MILLION[1]	Q1 2014	Q1 2015	Growth YoY %
Revenue	2,855	2,978	4%
EBITDA[2]	887	927	4%
EBITDA Margin	31.1%	31.1%	-
EBIT	488	533	9%
Net Income	359	141	(61%)

HIGHLIGHTS OF THE FIRST QUARTER

- Record high first quarter revenue and EBITDA, improved EBIT performance
- TRY1.78 dividend per share, TRY3.9 billion in total distributed for years 2010 -2014
- Net income impacted by FX losses in international subsidiaries

◘ **Fig. 28.1** Turkcell group: financial highlights. (Source: Turkcell Results Presentation Q1 2015)

Q1 2015 *TRY MILLION[1]*	TURKCELL TURKEY[2] YoY %		TURKCELL INTERNATIONAL[3] YoY %		OTHER SUBSIDIARIES [4] YoY %	
Revenue	2,711	*10%*	193	*(38%)*	75	*7%*
EBITDA	831	*8%*	53	*(34%)*	43	*15%*
EBITDA Margin	*30.7%*	*(0.4pp)*	*27.5%*	*1.6pp*	*57.1%*	*3.8pp*
EBIT	481	*6%*	11	*n.a*	40	*15%*
Net Income	779	*40%*	(656)	*n.a*	18	*(15%)*

- Strong growth in Turkcell Turkey, mainly on growth in broadband and mobile services
- Net income of Turkcell Turkey grew by 40% to TRY779 million mainly due to FX gain
- Turkcell Intl net income was impacted by TRY1,008 mn FX losses due to devaluation

◻ **Fig. 28.2**   Turkcell group: overview of business lines. (Source: Turkcell Results Presentation Q1 2015)

28

TRY MILLION	Q1 2014	Q1 2015	YoY %
TURKCELL GROUP	2,855	2,978	*4%*
TURKCELL TURKEY[1]	2,475	2,711	*10%*
CONSUMER	1,930	2,122	*10%*
CORPORATE	487	532	*9%*
WHOLESALE	70	71	*2%*
TURKCELL INTERNATIONAL	311	193	*(38%)*
OTHER SUBSIDIARIES[2]	70	75	*7%*

◻ **Fig. 28.3**   Turkcell group: revenue breakdown. (Source: Turkcell Results Presentation Q1 2015)

of less profitable prepaid subscribers had declined by 2 million, the number of more profitable postpaid subscribers had increased by 1.5 million. Average revenue per user (ARPU) was increasing, which had led to revenues rising despite the decline in subscriber numbers. Fixed-line penetration was also increasing, and total fixed-line customer numbers had reached 1.3 million (*refer to* ◻ Fig. 28.5).

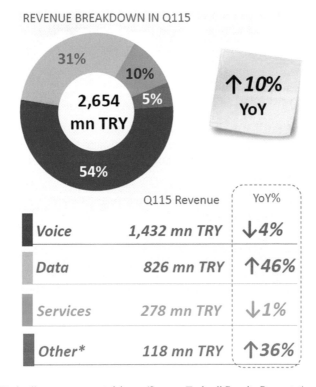

REVENUE BREAKDOWN IN Q115

31%
10%
2,654 mn TRY
5%
54%

↑10% YoY

	Q115 Revenue	YoY%
Voice	1,432 mn TRY	↓4%
Data	826 mn TRY	↑46%
Services	278 mn TRY	↓1%
Other*	118 mn TRY	↑36%

◘ **Fig. 28.4** Turkcell group: segment drivers. (Source: Turkcell Results Presentation Q1 2015)

SUBSCRIPTION

	QoQ NET ADD	TOTAL
MOBILE	↓370K	34.3 mn
POSTPAID	↑313K	15.5 mn
PREPAID	↓684K	18.7 mn

FIXED	↑80K	1.3 mn
FIBER	↑41K	776K
TV*	↑40K	~100K
ADSL	↑39K	496K

ARPU

ARPU (TRY)	Q1 2014	Q1 2015	Growth YoY %
Mobile blended	21.0	22.7	8.1%
Postpaid	36.3	36.9	1.7%
Prepaid	10.8	11.3	4.6%
Fixed residential**	47.2	47.1	(0.2%)

7 *TV subscribers are also included in total fiber subscribers
**Fiber and ADSL blended

◘ **Fig. 28.5** Turkcell group: subscriber numbers and ARPU levels. (Source: Turkcell Results Presentation Q1 2015)

Investment analysts had noticed Turkcell's good performance in Turkey, as the following comment from BNP Paribas in February 2015 demonstrated:

» In line with its profitable growth strategy, Turkcell remained focused on expanding the post-paid customer base (from 40% in 2013 to 44% in 2014) and increasing smartphone penetration (from 30% in 2013 to 40% in 2014). Both mobile data and fiber broadband segments continue to be the main drivers of revenue growth.[1]

Despite this outwardly rosy picture, several executive officers felt that revenues were not increasing rapidly enough given the large capital investments the firm was making. As Gediz Sezgin, Turkcell's executive vice president in charge of network technologies, explained:

» Traffic was increasing a lot but revenues not that much. We had to make large capex investments, but revenues were not going up in proportion.

Customers' stronger use of mobile data was driving increases in traffic and forcing Turkcell to make large capital investments to keep up. At the same time, intense competition with Vodafone and Turk Telekom made it difficult for the firm to raise prices commensurately.

28

28.2.2 **Organization and Culture**

Turkcell faced several organizational issues in Turkey in Q1 2015. First, the organization was complex, which made it difficult for it to move quickly and react to changing market conditions. As Banu Isci Sezen, who was co-head of human resources at the time, explained:

» There were a lot of companies and functions. Because of this, there were a lot of silos and it was hard to execute. When there was an issue, a lot of people had to come together and try to make a common decision.

Turkcell was responsible for mobile communications and its subsidiary, Superonline, for fixed-line communications. Each of these companies had its own management teams and systems. This made it difficult and time consuming for the firm to react effectively to the increasing convergence in the telecommunications space because every move required agreement from both management teams. In particular, Turkcell was finding it difficult to present a single face to the customer and enable the sales force to sell offers that encompassed fixed-line and mobile communications.

Second, the organization was top-heavy, with too many managers at every level. As Seyfettin put it:

» At that time, there were too many leaders and also too many followers.

---

1   Turkcell. 19 February 2015. Toygun Onaran. TEB Investment/BNP Paribas

This manifested itself in a span of control of five (with managers at all levels having an average of five direct reports). There were many cases of managers who had only two or three people reporting to them.

Third, a common data set was not used across the organization, which made it difficult to build consensus and move forward. Serkan Öztürk, Turkcell's executive vice president for IT and customer experience, illustrated this with a story:

> At one of our CXO meetings, the CEO asked how many customers we had. The chief sales officer said 1 million; the chief marketing officer said 1.5 million, and I said 1.2 million. We were all right, but we were all using different criteria. One of us was including active customers only. One of us was not including prepaid customers. One of us was including everyone. It was an easy question, but we could not answer it in a consistent way.

Because a common data set did not exist, there was a temptation to manipulate the data so that it showed what you wanted it to show. This increased conflicts between different groups within Turkcell.

Finally, there was no sense within the organization that it faced major issues or that significant change was required. Turkcell was number one in mobile communications in Turkey, and it was profitable and growing. While there were concerns among some top executives that revenues were not growing as fast as they should, the organization as a whole did not see this as a major concern.

28.2.3 **International Operations**

Turkcell's operations outside Turkey accounted for only 9% of its total revenues in Q1 2015. International revenues had declined 38% from the first quarter of 2014 because of currency devaluations in Ukraine and Belarus (*refer to* ◘ Fig. 28.6).

Astelit, Turkcell's subsidiary in Ukraine, accounted for the bulk of its international exposure. Ukraine's economy shrank in 2014 because of the Ukrainian crisis, but, despite this, Astelit's revenues had increased 18% in local currency terms, and its EBITDA margin was similar to that of Turkcell's operations in Turkey. Astelit was Ukraine's third largest mobile operator with 13.7 million subscribers and a revenue market share of 17%. The crisis in Ukraine remained unresolved at the end of the first quarter of 2015.

BeST (Belarusian Telecommunications Network), Turkcell's subsidiary in Belarus, had been loss-making for a number of years and was in financial trouble. Revenues had been flat in local currency terms year on year. It was the third largest mobile operator in Belarus with 1.4 million subscribers. The economy had shrunk in Q1 2015, and the World Bank was forecasting that this would continue.

Kuzey Kibris Turkcell (KKTCELL), Turkcell's subsidiary in Northern Cyprus, was the leading mobile carrier and had 400,000 subscribers in the first quarter of 2015.

Turkcell Europe had operated as a virtual telecom operator in Germany serving the Turkish community and had 300,000 subscribers in the first quarter of 2015. Turkcell had signed a marketing cooperation agreement with Deutsche Telekom

ASTELIT PERFORMANCE				BeST PERFORMANCE*			
UAH MILLION	Q114	Q115	YoY%	*BYR BILLION*	Q114	Q115	YoY%
Revenue	899	1,059	18%	Revenue	176	177	1%
EBITDA	288	327	14%	EBITDA	4	0	(90%)
EBITDA Margin	32.0%	30.9%	(1.1pp)	*EBITDA Margin*	2.3%	0.2%	(2.1pp)
EBIT	70	115	63%	EBIT	(63)	(150)	138%

HIGHLIGHTS OF ASTELIT

- UAH/USD continue to devalue 49% QoQ
- Revenue market share increased by 4pp to 17% in 3 yrs
- Awarded the most efficient frequency at 3G auction

HIGHLIGHTS OF BeST

- BYR/USD devaluated 24% QoQ
- Discontinuance of inflationary accounting
- Exploring our strategic options

▫ Fig. 28.6 Turkcell international: Ukraine and Belarus operations. (Source: Turkcell Results Presentation Q1 2015)

under which the customers and operations of Turkcell Europe were transferred to it in January 2015.

Fintur's subsidiaries had 13.1 million subscribers in Kazakhstan, 4.6 million in Azerbaijan, 2.1 million in Georgia, and 1.1 million in Moldova.

28.3 Emerging Challenges

28.3.1 The 4.5G Auction

The 4.5G spectrum auction, which was expected to be held in August 2015, was only a few months away. Turkcell needed to decide how aggressively it should bid for spectrum.

In the 3G spectrum auction, in November 2008, Turkcell had outbid Vodafone and Turk Telekom to win the largest spectrum, allowing it to maintain its dominance in Turkey's mobile communications market. Turkcell had bid €358 million for the 40-megahertz band, while Vodafone had bid €250 million for the 35-megahertz band, and Turk Telekom had bid €214 million for the 30-megahertz band. The 3G auction had thus raised a total of €822 million for the Turkish government.

The amounts at stake in the 4.5G auction were likely to be much larger. A total bandwidth of 390 megahertz was being put up for auction, and the government had set a minimum price of €2.3 billion for the frequency packages it was making available. The amounts that the three main players would have to bid would therefore be much larger than they had been in 2008.

Turkcell's networking division was advocating for the firm to bid aggressively in the auction and acquire the largest spectrum possible. Gediz explained why:

» We felt that a superior network infrastructure was a must for providing superior service to customers.

However, acquiring a large spectrum would mean incurring a large capital cost because network infrastructure costs would approximately equal spectrum costs.

It was expected that mobile data demand would increase rapidly once the three telcos had rolled out higher speed 4.5G networks. Given that all three telcos would be making large capital investments, there was the risk that they would focus on market share gains at the expense of maintaining prices at reasonable levels.

28.3.2 Competition from OTT Service Providers

The first WhatsApp call that Kaan received on his fifth day as Turkcell's new CEO had highlighted the challenge that telcos were facing from OTT service providers:

» The day I got my first WhatsApp call, I felt that one more castle was going down. I felt that there was something wrong with our industry. These are our customers, and in a typical telco relationship, there is a 32-minute limit because an average customer makes 17 minutes of calls and receives 15 minutes of calls. While smartphone penetration was increasing, and customers were spending more time on smartphones, we were not getting our fair share.

Kaan felt strongly that telcos were not being proactive enough in exploiting the new opportunities that were becoming available:

» As the world built trillion-dollar digital economies, telcos were mostly silent. They were like people waiting at the bus station and always missing the bus and never buying a ticket. They had their own definition of their industry and thought that all these OTT players were serving some other people rather than their customers. There are typically 10–30 applications on a smartphone. Three of these are embarrassingly primitive and these come from telcos – contact database, dialer and SMS. There have been no changes in these apps – it is almost like a religious taboo!

He felt that Turkey needed to take back control of its data from the OTTs:

» Everyone says that data is the new oil. When you take the oil out of the ground and put it in a barrel, it is $75 per barrel. But when you export that oil, people will buy it and create millions of dollars of compounds out of it after refining it. Data is exactly the same thing. Raw data is $2.50 per gigabyte, but if you process it and turn it into digital services or into analytics, then it is worth billions. Turkey was suffering from this. Of the data created in Turkey, 96% was kept and processed outside Turkey, and the outcomes in the form of digital services were sold back to Turkey.

In Q1 2015, Turkcell already had some digital services but was not sure what to do with them, as Murat Erkan, executive vice president in charge of sales, said:

» Digital services already existed – we had Turkcell Music, Bip, TV+, Lifebox and Dergilik.[2] We had all these products, but we were not investing in them. Bip was a simple messaging platform. We had about 100,000 downloads and even Turkcell employees were not using it! We had created it just to be able to say that we had a messaging service.

There were differences of opinion within Turkcell as to how the organization should react to the increasing presence of OTT service providers, as Murat explained:

» When Kaan joined the company, those were the challenges. Should we compete with OTTs and if so, how to do it? Most of the telcos will say, "You are wrong Turkcell; you should not do this." So, what should we do? You can say that I will be a utility company. But it is not easy to sustain this because we are paying billions for infrastructure and people are not using our voice services anymore.

While Kaan was mulling over his options, he noted that Turkcell had a resource that it could draw on if it decided to compete head to head with the OTTs. As he explained:

28

» One of the first things I noticed was that we had about 750 engineers in the company. This was a regulatory requirement – we had to invest in R&D.

---

2 Turkcell Music was Turkcell's Spotify equivalent which was later renamed Fizy; Bip was an instant messaging service like WhatsApp; Dergilik was an online publishing platform; and Lifebox was a personal cloud service.

Turkcell (B): From a Telecom Network Operator to a Customer Experience Provider

Contents

© Springer Nature Switzerland AG 2020
T. Jelassi, F. J. Martínez-López, *Strategies for e-Business*, Classroom Companion: Business,
https://doi.org/10.1007/978-3-030-48950-2_29

■ **Introduction**

14 March 2018. Kaan Terzioglu, Turkcell's CEO, and his top team had spent Capital Markets Day with global investment analysts celebrating the firm's achievements.

Over the last 3 years, the company had transformed itself from a network operator selling undifferentiated data and voice services in Turkey into an experience provider that provided messaging, music, TV, search, and other services to its customers. This had culminated in the launch of its Lifecell digital brand in Turkey in September 2017. This had turbocharged its revenue growth, which reached 23% in 2017.

While there was room for Turkcell to grow its core consumer business in Turkey, it would also rely on opportunities in digital services, the corporate market, and in new business areas including energy, finance, healthcare, and automotive to sustain future growth.

Turkcell had rationalized its international portfolio, taken steps to make its subsidiaries in Ukraine, Belarus, and Northern Cyprus financially stable, and was moving forward with the same digital operator strategy as in Turkey.

The company planned to grow internationally by franchising the digital operator model it had pioneered in Turkey to telcos worldwide. Kaan felt this would increase the company's valuation given the valuation of global over-the-top (OTT) companies.

Turkcell's growth plan raised questions. Did the firm have the management bandwidth to move into so many new business areas in Turkey? Would it be able to grow internationally using the franchise model? The answers were not clear.

29

29.1 Turkcell Turkey: From a Network Operator to an Experience Provider

Turkcell's financial and operational performance had improved tremendously in the 3 years since Kaan had become CEO (*refer to* ❏ Fig. 29.1). Revenue growth had hit 23% in 2017, and the firm's earnings before interest, taxes, depreciation, and amortization (EBITDA) margin now exceeded 35%. The average revenue per user (ARPU) levels had increased significantly, and mobile churn had dropped to a low of 20.5%.

Kaan had transformed the company's strategy, organization, and culture. This had required moving quickly and taking difficult steps in the face of internal opposition and external skepticism. Implementing these changes had been challenging for the organization, but the payoff had been worth it.

29.1.1 Creating the Impetus for Change

In June 2015, Turkcell's executive team set three new goals for the company: (1) to be the number one converged telco in Turkey, (2) to be a regional leader, and (3) to have some globally relevant services.

FINANCIAL

- Record top line at 17.6Bn TL, up 23.4% yoy
- EBITDA at 6.2Bn TL, up 34.8% yoy
- Highest EBITDA margin of past 9 years: 35.3%
- 3.0Bn TL dividend distributed

OPERATIONAL

- Annual mobile churn at 20.5%, lowest of the past decade
- 36.7Mn subscribers in Turkey, with 1.5Mn net adds
- 87% 4.5G subscriber penetration
- 242K Lifecell subs by Feb.18

Revenue, EBITDA and EBITDA Margin

Annual Mobile Churn Rate

Fig. 29.1 Turkcell 2017 Performance. (Source: Turkcell Results Presentation Q4 2017)

Changing the company's focus from mobile telecoms to converged telecoms (including both mobile and fixed) created the impetus for change that the company had lacked before, as Kaan explained:

>> Turkcell has a very proud culture. It cannot accept that it is not number one. We were obviously the number one mobile telecom operator in Turkey. I said, yes, we are number one in mobile telecoms, but we are not number one in total telecoms. Turk Telekom is bigger than us. I said we are number two, but we are going to be number one in three years.

Over time, the company's strategic focus moved increasingly toward digital services. In 2016, Turkcell set itself the objective of becoming an OTT company with telco capabilities. In 2017, the goal changed to becoming the world's first digital operator, which heightened the impetus for change.

29.1.2 Changing the Organization

One of the first moves that Kaan made in his first month as Turkcell's CEO was to simplify the organization (*refer to* ◻ Fig. 29.2):

>> We went from being an asset class organization to being a functional organization. We had two companies, a fixed and a mobile operator, each with its own management team. We reorganized based on that and created an executive team of nine people.[1]

---

1   Turkcell subsequently added 2 members to the executive team taking it to 11.

Executive Officers

1. Kaan Terzioglu, Chief Executive Officer
2. Bulent Aksu, Executive Vice President –Finance (CFO)
3. Ismail Butun, Executive Vice President–Marketing
4. Serhat Demir, Executive Vice President–Legal and Regulation
5. Murat Erkan, Executive Vice President–Sales
6. Seyfettin Saglam, Executive Vice President–Human Resources
7. Ilter Terzioglu, Executive Vice President–Strategy
8. Aysem Ertopuz, Executive Vice President–Digital Services and Solutions
9. Serkan Öztürk, Executive Vice President –Customer Experience and Information
10. Gediz Sezgin, Executive Vice President –Network Technologies
11. Ali Turk, Executive Vice President–Supply Chain Management

General Managers

1. Nihat Narin, General Manager –GlobalTower
2. Mehmet Cantekin, General Manager–Turkcell Ozel Finansman
3. Ismet Yazici, General Manager–Ukrayna Lifecell
4. Harun Maden, General Manager –KKTCell
5. Erkin Kilinç, General Manager –Turkcell Energy Solutions
6. Eren Eygi, General Manager–Azerinteltek
7. Dina Tsybulskaya, General Manager –Life (BEST)
8. Çağatay Aynur, General Manager -Turkcell Global Bilgi
9. Barbaros Özdemir, General Manager –Lifecell Ventures & Turkcell Europe
10. Banu İşçi Sezen, General Manager–Turkcell Academy
11. Ayşe Melike Kara, General Manager-Turkcell Payment & E Money Services
12. Ahmet Sezer, General Manager–Inteltek
13. Adem Duman, General Manager –TFS Turkcell Finansman

Source: Company information

☐ **Fig. 29.2**   Turkcell top management. (Source: Company information)

With the new structure, implementing strategies aimed at exploiting the increasing convergence in telecoms became much easier since each of the executive vice presidents had responsibility for both mobile and fixed telecoms.

Turkcell was top-heavy with too many managers at every level. The company moved quickly to address this issue as Seyfettin Saglam, executive vice president of human resources, explained:

» Our span of control was five and the CEO gave me a target to increase this to eight. We eliminated many EVPs, directors and managers. In one year, our management size dropped from 780 to 550 and our span of control became eight. The turnover rate in Turkcell was 10%, which was enough for transformation. I froze recruitment and relied mainly on natural attrition.

29.1.3 **Changing the Culture**

The organizational changes that Turkcell made in 2015 created a lot of stress since there had been a lot of change and employees were not sure how it would affect them personally. To address these issues, Kaan began to communicate his vision to the employees directly. In June and July 2016, the company organized all-hands meetings with all the functions. Kaan sat in front of each group, talked for 10 minutes about the company's strategy, and then invited questions. These interactive sessions helped to build understanding and trust within the organization.

The company took a number of steps to change its culture. First, it moved to a more participatory process for strategy formulation as Kaan explained:

» We had a visioning and strategy planning process which covered every individual in the company. We asked them a basic question: What does success look like three years out? Then let's go back to today and see what we need to do to get there. We did this through surveys with the employees, and workshops with the managers and directors. We do this every year.

Second, Turkcell implemented a number of initiatives when it moved its headquarters in August 2015 to a modern, open-plan office building, as Seyfettin explained:

» When we moved to this building, we changed everyone's location, and everybody started to see everybody else. For some critical issues, we conducted surveys – for example, what time will we start work in the morning. People voted on this and they chose 7:30 am because of the road traffic. We said that, one day a week, you can work from anywhere. We gave up control of entry and exit times – people can come and go as they want.

Third, the company started using self-managed cross-functional agile teams (*refer to* ◻ Fig. 29.3) as Serkan Öztürk, executive vice president for customer experience and information technologies, explained:

» There are more than 50 squads which have product managers and scrum masters. It is useful for younger employees because they like to work together, with analysts, developers and testers all in one team. The business guys are also part of this. They can see defects and can easily change the prioritization of requirements.

Developers

Product
Owner

Testers

Agile
Development
Methodology

Business
Analyst

Architect

Scrum
Master

Build Engineer

- **50** squads

- Virtual Agile Office

- **150+ project** with agile transformation

◻ **Fig. 29.3**   Use of agile teams. (Source: Turkcell Capital Markets Day 2018 Presentation)

Agile teams started with IT but had since spread to other parts of the organization. In 2018, Turkcell had more than 100 agile teams and planned to increase this to 200 in 2019. Turkcell employees were also using Bip, the company's instant messaging platform, to facilitate collaboration. The company had also experimented with internal crowdsourcing.

Fourth, Turkcell broadened access to training to equip its staff with the skills they needed, as Banu Isci Sezen, general manager of Turkcell Academy, explained:

» We created six programs with Udacity which are related to our future strategy: introduction to programming, machine learning, artificial intelligence, data analysis, business analysis, and data foundations. These are difficult, technical programs in English – you have to work at least two hours a day and create projects. We opened these programs with a big event where Kaan said that employees needed to prepare for the future by learning new skills; he expected these competencies from marketing, sales and HR people as well as from engineers, and he would follow the performance of the staff taking these programs and reward them. Employees were happy because they can get a Udacity certification. 1,200 employees (out of a total of 4,000) signed up for these programs which are continuing.

29.1.4 Becoming the Number One Telco

Turkcell focused on three key areas in its quest to be Turkey's largest telco: (1) acquiring spectrum, (2) increasing smartphone penetration, and (3) transforming its sales channels.

Turkcell decided to bid aggressively for spectrum at the 4.5G auction in August 2015. It acquired 172.4 MHz of spectrum for €1.62 billion. Its competitors were less aggressive—Turk Telekom spent €995 million and Vodafone €778 million. After the auction, Turkcell had 234.4 MHz of spectrum, while Turk Telekom had 175 MHz and Vodafone had 139.8 MHz. Turkcell also decided to make the investments needed to roll out 4.5G quickly across the country to get the most mileage from its spectrum investment.

These decisions meant that Turkcell's network infrastructure was superior to that of its competitors—it was able to provide gigabit speeds to its customers which its competitors could not. This was key as Ismail Butun, executive vice president of marketing, explained:

» I think the difference between good networks and bad networks is more obvious now because it is all about video. You have to be fast – even a three second lag is too much. So, an important criterion when you choose your operator is network quality. That is basic, and you build everything on top of this. If this basic feature is not there, you fail.

Turkcell set up a consumer finance company in 2015 to increase smartphone penetration. According to Bulent Aksu, the company's chief financial officer (CFO):

» In order to monetize our investment in 4.5G, we needed to increase data consumption and smartphone penetration. We established a consumer finance company to finance the smartphone requirements of our subscribers. We have sold 5 million smartphones and smartphone penetration among our subscribers has risen to 72%. We are transferring every quarter one million subscribers to 4.5G from 2G and 3G – ARPU levels among 4.5G subscribers are 1.5 times those of 2G and 3G subscribers.

Turkcell began the process of transforming its retail sales channels by reducing its street presence, as Kaan explained:

» We had 14,000 outlets with Turkcell logos. Today, there are 1,400 exclusive Turkcell shops and another 4,000 with our logos. We deleted more than 10,000 logos on the street because we believe that the brand is stronger if it is present only where it adds value.

The company invested in the remaining outlets to improve the customer experience (*refer to* ◖ Fig. 29.4) as Murat Erkan, executive vice president of sales, explained:

» We changed the shop layout so that customers feel that this is a digital company; this is a place where I can buy digital stuff. We introduced certification for the staff and we provide a lot of benefits for them such as health and life insurance. As a result, staff turnover dropped from 72% to 28%. They stay with the company, their knowledge is higher, they treat the customer better. We digitalized all the sales processes and gave tablets to the salespersons, so they can go through the sales journey with the customer and everything is transparent.

29.1.5 Becoming an Experience Provider

Turkcell decided to position itself as an experience provider rather than a supplier of network services as Gediz Sezgin, executive vice president of network technologies, explained:

» We did not want to sell minutes (of voice) or gigabytes (of data) or SMS – we wanted to sell services. Instead of selling raw data, we wanted to sell processed data. It was hard to compete with the other operators by selling minutes or gigabytes or SMS because everyone used the same technology and provided almost the same service. But we were able to differentiate ourselves by providing valuable services like Fizy, Bip and Lifebox.[2]

This required competing head-on with global OTT companies such as WhatsApp and Spotify in Turkey. Turkcell already had digital services in 2015, but they were rudimentary and not good enough to compete with the offerings of the global OTT companies. The company decided to refocus its research and development (R&D) team from telco technologies to improving its digital services. It also set up

---

2   Fizy was Turkcell's music service and was similar to Spotify; Bip was an instant messaging service like WhatsApp; and Lifebox was a personal cloud service.

STANDARDIZED TURKCELL STORES

END-TO-END DIGITALIZATION

29

DIGITALIZED SALES CONVERSATIONS : «MORE»

Following the customer and product based sales journeys

❏ **Fig. 29.4** Transformation of retail sales outlets. (Source: Turkcell Capital Markets Day 2018\ Presentation)

a new digital services and solutions group to spearhead the development of digital services and the spread of the digital operator model internationally.

The company built features into its suite of digital services that it could offer as a telco, but which the global OTTs could not offer as Aysem Ertopuz, executive vice president of digital services and solutions, explained:

>> We are using the capabilities we have as an operator to build features into our services that OTTs cannot match. For example, Bip will provide a second telephone number and will map your home number to Bip. Only a licensed operator can do this!

It also emphasized local content in services like Fizy, the music service, where this was important to local subscribers.

Turkcell started as the underdog in digital services. This was especially the case with Bip, its instant messaging platform, because WhatsApp had a strong presence in the Turkish market, with large numbers of regular users who already belonged to many WhatsApp groups.

The company decided to move to selling bundles that included voice, data, and digital services as Bulent Aksu explained:

>> We are not selling data, SMS and voice services to our subscribers. We are selling them music services, TV services and messaging services. We do not split the data part and the digital services part but sell these to our subscribers in one bundle.

Turkcell made it more attractive for subscribers to use its digital services (e.g., Bip or Fizy) by structuring its packages so that the mobile data used for this purpose was essentially free. In contrast, subscribers needed to pay for mobile data if they wanted to use the services provided by global OTTs such as WhatsApp and Spotify.

Turkcell also ran special promotions designed to increase the downloads and usage of its digital services. Ismail described one example:

>> We ran a promotion called "Surprise Point." You can participate in this through Bip. There is a map that pops up within Bip, which shows where we have installed gifts (e.g. one gigabyte of mobile data) in different places across Turkey. So, you go to that place and you try and grab the gift. This increased the downloads and the active usage of Bip.

In September 2017, the company launched Lifecell, its digital-only brand, in Turkey. Lifecell packages were digital only with no standard mobile voice minutes or SMS included. Subscribers could instead use Bip to make telephone calls and send instant messages. Lifecell packages also provided access to Turkcell's suite of digital services.

Turkcell's digital services had made significant progress as a result, with the number of active users increasing rapidly (*refer to* ◘ Fig. 29.5).

29.1.6 **Digitalizing the Company**

Turkcell began the process of digitalizing the company towards the end of 2015, as Serkan explained:

>> Kaan asked me to create a dashboard on which he could follow some metrics such as number of customers, number of acquisitions and number of downloads. We created a pilot within two weeks and he really liked it. Now we have reached more than two thousand metrics on the dashboard. It was really important. It was the first time that our executives could see what was going on. In the beginning, it was with a one-day lag, but within six months, we had moved to real-time monitoring.

29

* The download figures are as of December 2017.
** Includes users who utilised the zero rating benefit of Dergilik magazines and newspapers via browser.
*** Yaani download figures are as of February 2018.

◨ **Fig. 29.5** Turkcell digital services in 2017. (Source: Turkcell Annual Report 2017)

The dashboard covered the key KPIs for each corporate function and for ten major projects that the company was executing. It allowed executives to drill down for more detail (*refer to* ◘ Fig. 29.6).

Kaan actively promoted the use of this digital dashboard, and it soon became a critical tool for the whole company. In every meeting, Kaan started to push the CXOs to use the dashboard. He was usually at his office by 6:30 a.m., and he would use the dashboard to send out annotated excerpts to executives with his questions and comments. This pushed them to go deeper in their analysis. He could also check whether executives were using the dashboard, and if they were not, he pushed them to do so. Everyone knew that it was his main source of information.

Kaan felt that the digital dashboard had changed the culture of the firm because everyone had access to a common, accurate data set:

» The dashboard is hooked up to the system so everyone sees the same numbers. Nobody bullshits, nobody comes up with fake reports or power point slides which are manipulated. People understand that this is a numbers place and, when something is asked, you need to go back to these numbers. When someone says, no this is the wrong number, I say this is the right number, make this number right, change whatever is making this number wrong. This has changed the culture of the company.

◘ **Fig. 29.6** The digital cockpit. (Source: Company information)

29.2 Building the International Business

The performance of Turkcell's businesses outside Turkey had improved significantly because of the actions that it had taken (*refer to* ◘ Fig. 29.7).

In June 2015, Turkcell acquired the 45% of Astelit that it did not already own from its partner for $100 million and restructured its debt to put it on a more stable financial footing. The company adopted a strategy in Ukraine that was very similar to its strategy in Turkey. The company was rebranded as Lifecell, and its stores were modernized. Turkcell publicized the new brand and said that it would be creating more customer value. It launched 4.5G in Ukraine, and its market proposition was that it had the best 4.5G network. By adding digital services, the company was able to increase prices and ARPU levels.

Turkcell had restructured the debt of its subsidiary in Belarus in 2015 to stabilize it financially. It had established a 3G network in 2009 and was in talks with the only local telecom company with a 4G license to partner with it to offer 4G services. Its strategy there was also to position itself as an experience provider. The company had set up a technology group of about 200 engineers who worked on developing and testing digital services.

Northern Cyprus was a small market that was culturally very similar to Turkey. As Kaan explained, Turkcell had been using it to test new concepts such as a digital-only brand which was later launched in Turkey:

» We launched our digital only brand Lifecell for the first time in Cyprus. Lifecell achieved 1% market share, the ARPU was 50% higher, and the churn rate was one-third of Turkcell in Cyprus. When number portability started in Cyprus, Lifecell was the only winner. Cyprus is a test market for us. We test a lot of new ideas there.

Turkcell owned a 41% equity stake in Fintur which had subsidiaries in Azerbaijan, Kazakhstan, Moldova, and Georgia. In 2016, the company along with its partner

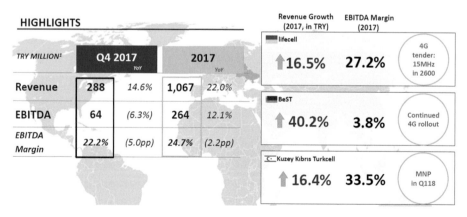

◘ **Fig. 29.7** Turkcell International in 2017. (Source: Turkcell Results Presentation Q4 2017. Note: Lifecell is Turkcell's subsidiary in Ukraine, BeST in Belarus, and Kuzey Kibris Turkcell in Northern Cyprus. A 4G tender was held in Ukraine in March 2018—Lifecell was awarded a license. MNP (mobile number portability) was implemented in Northern Cyprus in January 2018)

Telia decided to exit these markets and put the four subsidiaries up for sale. Fintur had divested its subsidiaries in Azerbaijan and Georgia in 2018 and was looking for buyers for its subsidiaries in Moldova and Kazakhstan.

29.3 Keeping the Growth Going

Maintaining its high growth rate was a strategic imperative for Turkcell, and it was pursuing growth opportunities both in Turkey and internationally.

29.3.1 Growth Opportunities in Turkey

Turkcell could grow revenues from its consumer business by moving mobile subscribers from 2G and 3G to 4.5G because it had found that this typically increased ARPU levels by 50%. It had more than doubled 4.5G subscriber numbers from 15 million in Q2 2016 to 31 million in Q1 2018. By the end of 2017, 15 million subscribers had 4.5G smartphones, and the company was migrating the rest at the rate of about 1 million per quarter (*refer to* ◘ Fig. 29.8). The launch of the new Lifecell digital brand had the potential to grow the number of mobile subscribers. There was potential to grow fixed-line broadband subscriber numbers from the current relatively low levels.

There were two potential avenues to increase revenues from digital services. First, Turkcell could increase the number of paying subscribers, which was important for services like Dergilik (publishing), Fizy (music), and TV+. Second, there were opportunities to monetize the platforms that Turkcell had created through advertising, as Aysem explained:

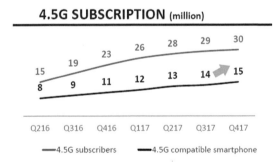

◘ **Fig. 29.8** 4.5G Adoption trends. (Source: Turkcell Results Presentation Q4 2017)

» Altogether, our services have been downloaded 100 million times. I am now sitting on top of an amazing data set, with my telco insights about people plus the footprint they have on these services. If you match this data together, there are all kinds of value propositions.

The company had developed and launched a search engine, Yaani, which it saw as the cornerstone of its efforts to grow digital advertising, as Aysem explained:

» I can create a lot of value for small and medium businesses. A good search engine needs great localization. That is how Yaani will compete because it speaks Turkish, understands the semantics, and understands the geography of Turkey.

Business services accounted for about one-fifth of Turkcell's revenues in Turkey, with connectivity accounting for the bulk of this and solutions for a small proportion. As Murat Erkan explained, the company was emphasizing solutions when selling to corporations:

» We don't sell stand-alone mobile solutions because the competition can drop their price. We compete on value. We defined 11 verticals to focus on. We went deep down. We hired people who understand these verticals, who can speak the same language as the customers. They know what is in their mind, what wakes them up at night. We know their business. We provide solutions for their business instead of selling IT or communications.

29   Turkcell felt that there would be big opportunities in healthcare and education and was making a big push in these sectors, as Murat Erkan explained:

» The government has established big city hospitals which consolidate everything in one place. Each of them is a billion-dollar hospital. We tendered for the digital part of this – IT, automation systems, some business operations like customer call management. Education could also be big. When we give tablets to students, we can work with them to provide digital services as well. The SIM card is owned by us and the services are provided by our data center, so we can add more services and make more money.

Turkcell was also moving into a number of new business areas. In 2017, it launched a mobile payments platform, Paycell, and was using this as the basis of an e-commerce model that Internet users could use to buy and pay for products and services online.

The company had launched an energy solutions company in 2017 and was targeting one million customers by 2020. It planned to focus on premium solutions such as uninterrupted energy and smart home solutions.

In November 2017, Turkcell became part of a consortium of five Turkish companies that aimed to produce a national car. Turkcell's objective, as Serkan who represented it in this venture explained, was to partner in technology development:

» We will be a shareholder with a 19% share in the project. We would like to participate in software development, AI [artificial intelligence] and connectivity. The car will be electric, and our target is 2022. The company will have a separate R&D group and we will support them.

Turkcell was also preparing for the transition to 5G networks which it believed would bring new opportunities, as Serkan explained:

» 5G is coming and our infrastructure already supports this. We should be ready for the Internet of Things and machine-to-machine communications. We are creating some use cases in key sectors – healthcare, agriculture, automotive, energy, education, and finance. We will use our data centers and we are bringing in partners from other countries.

29.3.2 International Growth Opportunities

Turkcell's strategy for growing internationally had changed significantly since 2015. The company had looked at turning Fintur into a wholly owned subsidiary and at acquisition opportunities in the Middle East but decided not to pursue these. People asked Kaan why the company was not acquiring anything since it had said that it wanted to be a regional leader. Kaan's response was that the global environment had changed in ways that made it difficult to own a telco in another country. In 2016, the company decided that instead of making acquisitions, it would focus on a digital strategy that would allow it to expand internationally with less investment.

The company's international strategy was informed by Kaan's view that every country should develop and control its digital economy:

» I think every country has to develop its own digital economy. There should be clouds in every country, and every country's cloud should be running the digital economy of that country.

Turkcell decided to expand internationally by franchising its digital operator model to other telcos rather than attempting to grow these internationally by itself. As Kaan explained:

» We felt that there were many other telcos that could benefit from our model, so we set up Lifecell Ventures (a 100% owned subsidiary in the Netherlands) whose objective is to take these technologies and the business model to other countries.

Lifecell Ventures was promoting two models for collaborating with international telcos, as Barbaros Ozdemir, general manager of Lifecell Ventures, explained:

» For established telcos, we will work with them to add a digital only brand as we have successfully done in Turkey and in our international subsidiaries. We will take a share of the revenues generated by this new business as well as fees for any services we provide (e.g. project management and business consultancy). For greenfield operations, we will work with them to build a digital only operator. Our role will include licensing our digital services as well as assistance with project management and business consultancy. It may also include a management contract where we depute a few senior managers from Turkey for the first few years to help them to get started after which we would hand the management back to them. In return, we would get an up-front one-time payment, a share of the revenues and fees for the services we provide.

Lifecell Ventures had publicized its offerings at the Mobile World Congress in Barcelona. As a result of this, it was now working with a greenfield operator in Asia and an established operator in the Caribbean. Barbaros felt that there was significant growth potential but was conscious of the human resource challenges:

» We have some project managers but their number and experience level need to be increased. We will also need software architects and business consultants. We will need to build up these resources in Turkey so that we can meet the needs of our international clients.

Aysem felt that Turkcell would have to develop new capabilities to make this strategy work since other telcos would need a high level of support from it:

» We will have to go there and show them how to do this. This will require some kind of consultative selling. We will need to figure out the operations side of it. In this type of business, you don't make money from selling the boxes but from the services you provide. We will have to figure out what will happen after the sale.

Despite the challenges, Kaan felt that international growth would be significant and would have a big impact on Turkcell's market capitalization:

» Ideally in a decade, one-third of our revenues will come from outside Turkey. Products like Bip and Fizy could become global franchises and could have valuations in the billions of dollars. It is possible that more than half our valuation will come from our international operations in the future. The digital services we are building today could be more valuable than Turkcell as a national Turkish operator.

29

Nestlé: Developing a Digital Nutrition Platform for Japan

Contents

IMD EMBA graduates Sunil Prabhakaran Vimala, Ashraf Kordy, Roman Podkolzine, and Hitoshi Ode prepared this case under the supervision of Professor Tawfik Jelassi as a basis for class discussion rather than to illustrate either effective or ineffective handling of a business situation. Copyright © 2018 by *IMD—International Institute for Management Development*, Lausanne, Switzerland (▶ www.imd.org). No part of this publication may be reproduced, stored in a retrieval system, or transmitted in any form or by any means without the prior written permission of *IMD*

© Springer Nature Switzerland AG 2020
T. Jelassi, F. J. Martínez-López, *Strategies for e-Business*, Classroom Companion: Business, https://doi.org/10.1007/978-3-030-48950-2_30

- **Introduction**

> **Definition**
>
> Every company needs to learn how to navigate in the new digital world. The digital nutrition platform helps Nestlé understand the opportunities, pitfalls and possible impacts of digital technologies on nutrition, so that we learn, adapt and build our own approach and strategy. — Valerio Nannini, Senior Vice President for Strategies and Performance at Nestlé

The Nestlé Institute of Health Sciences (NIHS), a specialized biomedical research institute, was part of Nestlé's global research and development (R&D) network. Over the last few years, the Institute had developed a platform that combined the processing and analysis of macro data (e.g., lifestyle, diet, and activity) and bioinformatics to create predictive models of health and disease. Nestlé's ambition was to achieve the following:

- Build scientific platforms to elevate the role of nutrition in people's healthy lifestyles.
- Create knowledge to better define and target appropriate nutrition.
- Apply these insights to the future of targeted nutrition for health maintenance.[1]

Valerio Nannini, the driving force behind this initiative, was aware that, from a commercial standpoint, there were several possible ways of bringing the digital nutrition platform to life and eventually turning it into something that was genuinely beneficial to its consumers and to the company. Among the options he pondered were using the platform to enable R&D to search for new and winning products; deploying the platform to enhance the direct distribution of new or existing Nestlé products, thereby aligning the portfolio and creating new consumption patterns for customers; or partnering with powerful online or device manufacturers that could help Nestlé gain insights into new or future products?

30.1 Bringing Digital Nutrition Solutions to Life

In support of Nestlé's strategy to develop digital nutrition solutions, the company announced a strategic partnership with Samsung in 2016 to collaborate on the Internet of Things and nutrition to advance digital health. At the time, Stefan Catsicas, Nestlé's chief technology officer (CTO), said:

> We are delighted to enter this collaboration with a global leader in the field of sensor technologies. It will advance our Nutrition, Health and Wellness strategy to support people who want to live a healthier lifestyle.[2]

---

1   Nestle Institute of Health Sciences website. ▶ www.nestleinstitutehealthsciences.com/discover/home
2   Nestle Institute of Health Sciences website. ▶ www.nestleinstitutehealthsciences.com/news/newsinstitute/nestl-and-samsung-to-collaborate-on-digital-nutrition-and-health

Young Sohn, president and chief strategy officer (CSO) of Samsung Electronics Co., Ltd., said:

> ›› We're excited about the breakthroughs this collaboration will bring. Today, we live in an era of smarter living brought about by the convergence of technology and life science. It's an era where the data from smart sensors and devices in our daily life, such as mobile phones, wearables, and smart refrigerators, can help us to understand our nutrition and activity and to guide us toward a healthier lifestyle.[3]

There were other examples of Nestlé joining hands with leading technology partners to bring digital nutrition solutions to life. In September 2017, Nestlé launched its own artificial intelligence platform in partnership with the Chinese e-commerce platform ▶ JD.com. A device called Nestlé XiaoAI aimed to meet the needs of the increasingly digitally savvy Chinese consumers.[4] This was Nestlé's first attempt at launching a digital nutrition assistant and China's first family-nutrition smart speaker that used artificial intelligence. The device integrated smart speaker technology with nutrition and health knowledge and was built into ▶ JD.com's best-selling DingDong smart speaker system.

According to Nestlé Greater China chairman and chief executive officer (CEO), Rashid Aleem Qureshi:

30

> ›› China is Nestlé's second-largest market globally, and over the 30 years we've been operating here, we've strived to keep our finger on the pulse of the consumer. This innovative business model is part of a global trend to go beyond traditional products with "digital services" that add new layers of value: convenience, entertainment and education for healthier living.[5]

In May 2018, Nestlé also announced a partnership with technology firm Xiaomi[6] to use technology and digital nutrition to address the increasing needs of China's aging population. As Angelo Giardino, CEO of Milk, Ice Cream, and Industry Sales at Nestlé China, explained:

> ›› The efforts to embrace digital tools is to engage more with daily consumers among the middle-aged and elders in China, as they are frequent users of internet and mobile devices for social, gaming and entertainment content. The platform is also a two-way communication for Nestlé to better understand their consumers through data collecting.[7]

---

3   Ibid.
4   "Nestle, ▶ JD.com unveil China's first AI nutrition assistant." ▶ ChinaDaily.com.cn, 20 September 2017. ▶ www.chinadaily.com.cn/business/tech/2017-09/20/content_32233912.htm. Accessed 15 October 2018.
5   Ibid.
6   Zhuoqiong, Wang. "Nestle partners with Xiaomi to provide seniors better nutrition." ▶ China-Daily.com.cn, 17 May 2018. ▶ www.chinadaily.com.cn/a/201805/17/WS5afd255ca3103f6866ee904a.html. Accessed 15 October 2018.
7   Ibid.

Elaborating further on Nestlé's efforts to put customer service experience at the heart of its new digital offerings, Pete Blackshaw, Nestlé's global head/digital innovation and service models, said:

» At a broad level, voice, chatbots, smart assistants, smart kitchens – they all fall into what I call the "concierge economy." How do you provide a reinvigorated customer-service experience for consumers? I think voice falls into that: it's both utility and it's entertainment. And, for us, it's a potential service layer that sits on top of our brand.[8]

In another example, Tom Buday, Nestlé's global head of marketing and consumer communications, spoke of how Nestlé has increasingly used digital technology to add layers of incremental service around its existing nutritional products:

» An example of adding service layers is Milo, a chocolate-malt beverage product. We recently launched a fitness tracker that links to an app that parents can use to monitor their eating and nutritional intake and to provide recommendations to parents on how to achieve balanced diets, while having the child involved in friendly competition with their friends, through sports tips and augmented reality.[9]

Nestlé was experimenting in the digital world and finding that the digital strategy employed depended on where in the world it was used. As Nestlé CEO Mark Schneider explained in a 26 September 2017 investor seminar:

» The way we live and work with the internet is quite nuanced as you go from country to country. … The Asian way of using the internet is quite different from the European or American one, and hence, what we're committed to is developing the tools, very aggressively demanding from our management teams that they use these tools, but also being flexible when it comes to how exactly they are being applied in each market.[10]

Because all these ways differed from one another strategically and involved several possible choices, a hard decision had to be made about which path to pursue. Thus, the big question that Nestlé faced was how to bring its digital nutrition platform to life. Would it use the platform to enable its R&D to search for new and winning products? Would it deploy the platform to enhance the direct distribution of new or existing Nestlé products, aligning the portfolio and creating new consumption

---

8   "How Nestlé is tapping voice tech." *WARC*, 19 February 2018. ▶ www.warc.com/newsandopinion/news/how_nestl%C3%A9_is_tapping_voice_tech/40061. Accessed 15 October 2018.
9   Vizard, Sarah. "Nestle's global head of marketing on why he hates 'data-driven marketing.'" *Marketing Week*, 26 September 2016. ▶ www.marketingweek.com/2016/09/26/the-global-marketing-head-of-nestle-on-why-he-hates-data-driven-marketing/. Accessed 15 October 2018.
10 Gelski, Jeff. "Nestle taking country-specific digital approach." *Food Business News*, 28 September 2017. ▶ www.foodbusinessnews.net/articles/10661-nestle-taking-country-specific-digital-approach. Accessed 15 October 2018.

patterns for customers? Or would it partner with powerful online or device manu-facturing players that could help Nestlé gain insights into new or future products?

In searching for a pilot market for the platform, Valerio turned to Japan, an impor-tant market for Nestlé. Characterized by a high proportion of elderly people and a high awareness of healthy food among all generations, Japan was also where Nestlé was pursuing several business-to-customer (B2C) and business-to-business (B2B) initia-tives. These initiatives were testing the adoption of new digital technologies and where possibilities for new commercial venues were emerging thanks to increased e-commerce penetration, a booming health food industry, and expanded use of medical data.

30.2 Japan's Aging Population: A Pressing Issue for the Nation—A Unique Opportunity for Nestlé

The problem of aging populations was not uncommon; however, the problem in Japan was extreme. In 2014, 25% of people in Japan were 65 years or older, and this percentage was expected to reach 38.8% by 2050. In 2018, Japan's ratio of the population over the age of 65 was the highest in the world, and reducing medical expenses was a pressing issue for the nation (*refer to* Exhibit 30.1).

As people increasingly stayed active into their later years, older people were seeking to maintain good physical and cognitive capabilities. In addition, as more and more people experienced obesity, allergies, and noncommunicable diseases, the general attitude toward health and wellness had become more holistic and included physical, mental, and spiritual well-being.

Japan's public authorities faced great financial constraints in sustaining the popu-lation's health benefits and were making important efforts to increase the popula-tion's awareness of healthy lifestyles, including healthier eating. For example, the 2005 Basic Law of Food Education introduced food and nutrition education with a program that taught children how to select food that was beneficial to their health. The 2008 "Metabo Law" required those between the ages of 40 and 74 years to have their waist measurements taken as part of an annual physical exam.

Consumers' awareness of healthy food was also stimulated by the quality of publicly available information. In particular, the Japanese National Institute of Health and Nutrition maintained a database (at ▶ hfnet.nlh.go.jp) for consumers and producers that contained information regarding health foods and functional foods (foods that make health claims) that had been evaluated by the authorities; current and past health issues associated with the intake of both types of food; information on food and food components; and scientifically proven information on food and food components (Gupta 2016).

As a result, people of all ages in Japan were increasingly aware of the importance of prevention to a healthy lifestyle as they aged, and this awareness was being reflected in their consumption patterns. For example, according to a 2017 report by Suntory Beverage and Food, the rate of growth in consumption of products defined as food for specific health uses (FOSHU), especially drinks making health-benefit claims, was highest among younger consumers; more than half of males (51.4%), 44.5% of females in their 20s, and 42.9% of females in their 30s consumed FOSHU

30

beverages. However, in terms of volume, the largest segment of Japanese consumers was the elderly. In 2015, customer segmentation in Japan was as follows[11, 12]:

- About 35% of private households had only one person, up from about 28% in 2000.
- 25% were defined as the healthy elderly, who were aged 65 years or more, retired, and had a pension-based income and children or grandchildren.
- 7.5% were defined as wealthy and active consumers, aged 44–52 years, working, progressive, enjoying luxury, and wanting to maintain a healthy life.
- 6.5% were defined as single, young, aged 20–34 years, and working but earning low incomes.
- 5.5% were defined as baby boomers, aged 61–63 years, recently retired, independent, enjoying their lives but having low incomes.
- 1.2% were defined as high-income consumers in no particular age group who enjoyed luxury and sophistication.
- Single career women of about 40 years old who are active and have hobbies.

It was clear from the above that the growing aging population and the high overall awareness of healthy food across all generations represented unique opportunities for nutrition, health, and wellness companies. As Nestlé and other food companies in Japan knew, multiple local producers were already offering products with nutritive elements—functional food—which presumably benefitted consumers' health. In addition, Japan's regulations on consumer health foods were actually quite supportive of the food industry. They had been adapted recently, which enabled the healthy food market to experience even higher growth.

Exhibit 30.1 Japan's Demography and Greater Societal Adoption of Healthy Foods

Japan: The world leader in healthy life expectancy

《National average life expectancy data for Japan》

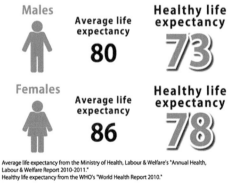

Males						
Average life expectancy **80**	Healthy life expectancy **73**		#1.	Japan	76
			#2.	Switzerland	75
			#3.	Italy	74
Females			#3.	Australia	74
Average life expectancy **86**	Healthy life expectancy **78**		#3.	Sweden	74
			#3.	Spain	74
			#26.	United States of America	70
			#39.	China	66

Average life expectancy from the Ministry of Health, Labour & Welfare's "Annual Health, Labour & Welfare Report 2010-2011."
Healthy life expectancy from the WHO's "World Health Report 2010."

Source: Independent Body National Test. ▶ www.jiritsutairyoku.jp/foreign/index_en.html

---

11 "Nutraceuticals and food supplements sector in Japan—Opportunities for European producers" EU-Japan Centre, 2016.
12 Note that numbers do not add up to 100 as the segments are not exhaustive.

30.3 Japan's Regulatory Framework Supports Healthy Food

Japan's Pharmaceutical Affairs Law prohibited labeling that indicated medicinal or pharmaceutical effects on any product other than drugs, and food producers were expected to strictly respect these labeling and advertising constraints so that consumers would not expect products to have drug-like effects or to make health claims. In addition to this, Japan had a fully functioning regulatory system for food that did make health claims, and this regulatory system provided a clearly defined operational framework for producers of nutriments that claimed health benefits (*refer to* Exhibit 30.2).

Japan was among the first countries in the world to regulate and legally recognize "functional" health food or "food with health claims," by introducing in the early 1980s the first FOSHU regulation. This regulation addressed the claims of health benefits and reduction of disease risk provided by dietary ingredients. Such claims were strictly supervised and could be displayed only after validation by a governmental body, the Directorate General of the Consumer Affairs Agency (CAA). FOSHU regulation was updated by the 2002 Health Promotion Act, which aimed to address the needs of the aging population. The number of health benefits that could be claimed by FOSHU foods was limited to 14, and clinical trials had to be conducted before the claims could be submitted for approval.

In addition, in 2001, the regulation of "food with health claims" (FHC) evolved with the adoption of the "foods with nutrient function claims" (FNFC) label. This label could be freely used if a product satisfied the standards for minimum and maximum daily levels of consumption for a precise, limited list of authorized vitamins and minerals.

However, the FOSHU regulation proved to be too stringent for producers, and, as part of Prime Minister Abe's regulatory reform plan, a third category was created in 2015. It was called the "foods with functions claim" (FFC). The registration process for FFC was faster and more affordable than FOSHU because FFC claims did not require clinical trials before approval; their producers only needed written evidence (which was defined as scientific information on safety and functionality) to make health-benefit claims. In particular, the FFC system allowed companies to display the product's specific health benefits (functionality) and the associated area of the human body on retail food packaging. The FFC system was comparable to an approach in the United States called the Dietary Supplement Health and Education Act of 1994.

Besides these three categories of FHC, Japanese regulations had an additional category—food for special dietary uses (FOSDU). This food was dedicated to a particular dietary use, including infant formulas or formulas for lactating or pregnant women. FOSDU foods had to be approved by the Ministry of Health, Labour and Welfare (MHLW).

The full picture of Japanese regulation of healthy food follows in ◘ Fig. 30.1:

The introduction of the FFC category stimulated the growth of Japan's market for functional food. In the year following adoption of the category, more than 440 claims were approved,[13] and this number had doubled to 847 by May 2017. In contrast, only 1271 FOSHU products had been approved between 1991 and 2016. The FFC category provided a favorable framework for small- and medium-sized companies because it eliminated the need for lengthy, costly approval procedures before a specific health claim could be added to a product's label. As a result, competition in the health food industry increased.

The speed of growth in the healthy food segment seemed very encouraging for producers. But what could be said about behavior patterns in Japan?

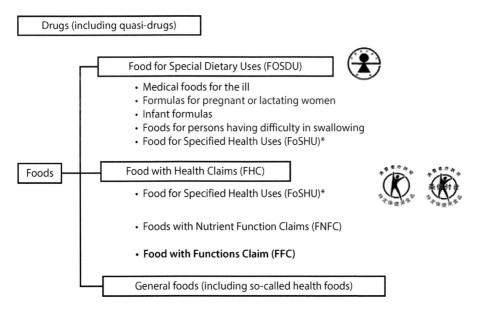

◘ **Fig. 30.1** Definitions of food and pharmaceuticals in Japan. (Source: Adapted from Gupta, Ramesh Chandra. *Nutraceuticals: Efficacy, Safety and Toxicity*. Amsterdam: Elsevier/Academic Press, 2016)

---

13 Scattergood, Gary. "Japan moves beyond Foshu: Over 400 products approved under new health claims regime in last year." ► *NUTRAingrediants-asia.com*, 9 October 2016. ► www.nutraingredients-asia.com/Article/2016/10/10/Japan-moves-beyond-Foshu-Over-400-products-approved-under-new-health-claims-regime-in-last-year. Accessed 15 October 2018.

Exhibit 30.2 Regulatory Environment for Functional Health Foods in Japan

	Drug	Food			
	Prescription drug, OTC drug (Including quasi- drug)	FHC			General Food
Products taken orally		FNFC	FOSHU	FFC	So-called health food
Applicable foods to each category →					
Efficacy/ Function Claims	1. Diagnosis, treatment, cure or prevention of disease. 2. Structure/ function claim on the body	Nutrient Function Claim for vitamins, minerals, etc. (Structure/ function claims)	1.Specified health effects (Structure/ function claim) 2. Disease risk reduction	Specified health effects (Structure/function claim)	Not permitted
Approval system of Labeling	Approval system by the government before selling	Fixed claims for each nutrient decided by the government decides . (Neither registration nor notification are necessary.)	Approval system by the government before selling	Notification system under food business operator's own responsibility	—

Japanese regulation of health food

Source: Update of the Japanese Regulation for Health Food, IADSA, April 2016
► www.fas.usda.gov/data/japan-retail-foods-1

Classification of FOSHU

Category	Description
FOSHU	Foods contain a functional ingredient with sufficient scientific evidence to support a health claim
Qualified FOSHU	Foods with health function which are not substantiated by scientific evidence that meets the level of FOSHU or foods with certain effectiveness but without established mechanism of action for the function
Standardized FOSHU	Foods meet the standards and specifications established for foods with sufficient FOSHU approvals and accumulation of scientific evidence
Disease-risk reduction FOSHU	Reduction of disease risk claim is permitted when reduction of disease risk is clinically and nutritionally established in an ingredient, currently for foods containing calcium of folic acid only

Source: Preventive Nutrition: The Comprehensive Guide for Health Professionals, 2010

Classification of FOSDU

Four categories of FOSDU
Medical foods for the ill

Single foods:	*Packaged meals (meals prepared for one serving,*
Low-sodium foods	*consisting of several foods):*
Low-calorie foods	Sodium-reduced meals
Low-protein foods	Meals for diabetes
No/low-protein and	Meals for liver disease
high-calorie foods	Meals for adult obesity
High-protein foods	
Allergen-removed foods	
Lactose-free foods	

Formulas for pregnant or lactating women
Infant formulas
Foods for the elderly with difficulty in masticating and/or swallowing (dysphagia)

Source: Adapted from "Nutraceuticals and food supplements sector in Japan: Opportunities for European Producers," EU-Japan Centre, 2016

	Part of body and claims	Main functional substance	Total No. of cases	%
1	Reduce fat absorption, triglyceride, visceral fat, BMI or obesity	Licorice ext., EPA, DHA, EGCg, Rosehip ext. Lycopin	183	46.3
2	Help eye functions or eye sight, Protect macular health	Lutein, Astaxantine, Bilberry ext.	44	11.1
3	Regulate gastrointestinal tract or movement of bowels	Bifidobacterium,	37	9.4
4	Improve skin condition (moisturizing)	Hyarulonic acid, glucosylceramide from rice,	23	5.8
5	Keep blood pressure normal	Sardine peptide,	19	4.8
6	Moderate blood sugar absorption	Wheat albumin, *Salacia reticulata* ext., Indigestible dextrin, α-Linolenic acid	17	4.3
7	Support Joint, muscle strength, walking ability	Glucosamine, Collagen	15	3.8
8	Ease mental stress or tension	L-theanine, GABA,	14	3.5
9	Ease physical fatigue, Improve physical condition	Reduced CoQ10, Litchi ext., L-theanine,	12	3.0
10	Support sound sleep or good quality of sleep at night	L-theannine, Glycine	10	2.5
11	Improve accuracy of memory as cognitive function	Ginkgo ext.	8	2.0
12	Others (bone health, blood flow, body temperature, etc.)	Soy isoflvone, β-cryptoxanthin	13	3.4
	Total		395	100

Illustration of FFC health claims, April 2016
Source: Update of the Japanese Regulation for Health Food, IADSA, April 2016
► www.fas.usda.gov/data/japan-retail-foods-1

Illustration of FOSHU health claims, April 2016

Examples of health claims	**Functional ingredients**	**No. of FOSHU**	**Share %**
Helps maintain good gastrointestinal condition	Oligosaccharides, dietary fiber, *Lactobacillus*, *Bifidobacterium*	408	33.7%

Examples of health claims	Functional ingredients	No. of FOSHU	Share %
Good for those who have high serum cholesterol/are concerned about serum triglycerides	Soy protein, peptides, MCTs, dietary fiber, plant sterol/ stanol (esters), coffee polyphenols	301	24.9%
Good for those who have high blood glucose levels	Dietary fiber, albumin, polyphenols, L-arabinose	210	17.4%
Good for those who have high blood pressure	Peptides, glucosides, amino acids	126	10.4%
Helps maintain dental health	Xylitol, polyols, tea polyphenols, CPP-ACP	102	8.4%
Helps improve absorption of calcium minerals Good for those who have bones health	CPP, CCM, oligosaccharides, heme iron, MBP, vitamin k2, soy isoflavonoids	63	5.2%

Source: "Regulatory Framework on Nutrition Labelling and Health Claims in Japan," Symposium on Health/Function Claims in Foods, 2016

30

30.4 Consumer Choices and Habits

Japan's long period of economic stagnation—the low or negative GDP since the beginning of the 1990s—had made Japanese consumers increasingly price-conscious. However, data showed that Japanese households prioritized spending on food compared to other items. According to 2015 statistics from the Ministry of Economics, Trade and Industry (METI), food represented 26% of the average monthly household expenditure.

As ◘ Fig. 30.2 shows, over the last 10 years, despite the slowing of consumption, healthy food expenditures increased. What was driving consumer choices in this important segment? According to the Yano Research Institute (2014), choice drivers included the following[14]:

- Efficacy of health food data.
- Positive past experiences.
- Types of health benefits.
- Brand and content of the key functional ingredients.
- Country of origin of the product.
- Naturalness: non-artificial, naturally derived ingredients and simple or minimal processing.
- Brand name.
- Price.
- Product safety.

14 Not ordered.

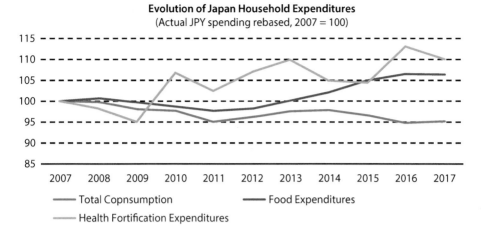

○ Fig. 30.2 Japanese household consumption, food and health fortification expenditures. (Source: Japan National Statistical Office, 2018 ► http://www.stat.go.jp/english/data/kakei/156time.html)

The list of drivers highlighted the preoccupation of Japanese consumers with the quality of products and the availability of precise, accurate information about them. Therefore, the right mix of information and communication was key to market success. Brand was also important when it came to framing what drove consumers' choices for particular health food products.

Other factors that were important to Japanese consumers included product innovation and the aesthetics of presentation. Elderly people were also eager to purchase products that could be opened or consumed easily (e.g., using just one hand).

Finally, Japanese people were increasingly integrating smartphone use into their daily lives, as shown by the growing success of online shopping and the use of smartphones during store-based purchasing (*refer to* Exhibit 30.3). Though consumption had slowed over the last 10 years, healthy food expenditures had increased, and having an online presence was becoming an essential part of marketing strategies in Japan.

E-commerce was slower to catch on in Japan than in other countries because of Japan's population density, its well-developed networks of convenience stores and drugstores, its delayed proliferation of smartphones, and, particularly, its brick-and-mortar retailers' and manufacturers' slow shift to digital strategies. However, the competition in e-commerce was increasing; e-commerce was becoming a major factor in reshaping distribution channels that had the potential to contribute to an eventual disruption of health food distribution in Japan. Food and beverage sales via the Internet were JPY 1.2 trillion (US$11.1 billion) in 2014, JPY 1.3 trillion (US$10.8 billion) in 2015, and JPY 1.45 trillion (US$13.2 billion) in 2016. Also, in 2016, the food, beverage, and alcohol category had the highest sales of all e-commerce categories.[15]

---

15 "Japan Retail Foods." *USDA Foreign Agricultural Service*, 29 December 2017. ► www.fas.usda.gov/data/japan-retail-foods-1. Accessed 15 October 2018.

Since Japan lagged behind other developed countries in terms of e-commerce development, developers of nutrition platforms needed to ponder the effects of the low adoption rate of mobile phones among the elderly, especially when they assessed the potential for gathering relevant consumer and health data via this channel. Collecting health-related data on Japan's elderly was a serious issue, but a recent reform dealing with the availability of medical data made the situation very different.

Exhibit 30.3 Smartphone Adoption and Use in Japan

Japan's adoption rate: Among the lowest in Asia

Country	Smartphone adoption rate %	
	Q42016	Q42015
Singapore	83	82.5
Hong Kong	81	75
South Korea	80	77
Australia	80	79
Taiwan	76	70
China	71	68
Myanmar	70	66
Malaysia	69	63
Thailand	65	58
New Zealand	63	53
Philippines	57	42
Indonesia	50	39
Japan	46	43
Sri Lanka	41	29
Vietnam	34	28
India	31	24
Pakistan	23	17
Bangladesh	28	22
Asia	51	45

Source: GSMA Intelligence

30

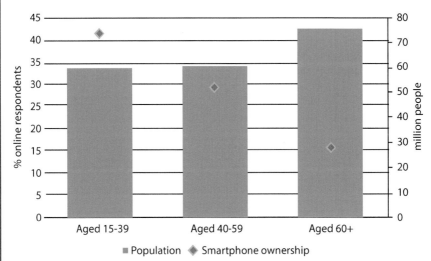

Japan's population and smartphone usage

■ Population ◆ Smartphone ownership

One reason for the lower adoption rate in Japan was that only 28% of the respondents aged 60 years or older owned personal smartphones according to Euromonitor International's 2016 Global Consumer Trends Survey.
Source: Gordon, Lydia, and Yuri Gorai. "Three Reasons Why Japan Is Falling Behind in Mobile Commerce." *Euromonitor International*, 22 April 2017. ▶ https://blog.euromonitor.com/three-reasons-why-japan-falling-behind-mobile-commerce/. Accessed 19 October 2018.

30.5 Evolution of Availability and Use of Medical Data

Japan was a pioneer and leader in the invention of high-tech equipment, but for a long time, it trailed other countries in exploiting medical data and medical data platforms. In 2018, the penetration of electronic medical records (EMRs) stood at 98% of hospitals with 600 or more beds and 50% of hospitals with fewer than 200 beds. Despite the availability of EMRs, in most cases, the data was not mutually compatible because the codes used for illnesses, pharmaceuticals, and other items differed for each vendor and medical institution due to independent development and system customization. In addition, stringent regulations limited access to and use of this data.

However, this situation was about to change dramatically.[16] First, in August 2016, the Japanese National Hospital Organization (JNHO) finalized a standardized storage format and codes for EMRs.

---

16 New trends in healthcare x ICT, Nomura, 2017.

Second, in April 2017, a new law for next-generation healthcare was approved, enabling medical information, including patient data held by medical institutions, to be provided to outside parties, including pharmaceutical companies, following anonymization by an authorized company that met the standards for protecting personal information. Essentially, this opened the door for the use of big data technology in the Japanese healthcare industry.

Third, individual healthcare IDs were being created by construction of a database that covered illnesses and individual treatment histories from birth to death. This database, called the Person-centered Open Platform for well-being (PeOPLe), integrated all basic health and medical data on individuals, including EMRs, pharmaceutical prescription records, and health checkups by local authorities. The full-fledged adoption of healthcare IDs was planned for 2020, following trials in 2018 and a gradual introduction.

Furthermore, the adoption of telemedicine was low in Japan because the elderly preferred to receive care in their homes and to have family members physically involved in their care. However, the ongoing changes to medical data access and use had the potential to spur a revolution in digital health platforms, including portals and mobile apps.

Nestlé in Japan, as well as other producers, was aware that these changes could represent a true opportunity for food and drink producers to exploit data, either to conceive new "health food" products or to propose nutritive formulas matching the nutritive needs of individual patients. Interestingly, there was a big concentration in terms of actors on the IT side of the reform: the "big four" EMR data integration companies, Fujitsu, Software Services, CSI, and NEC, together controlled 76% of hospitals' EMR data services.[17] Such concentration among service providers was worth exploring for possible partnerships regarding clinical data access and management.

But what about the economics of the health food industry and the clinical nutrition market in Japan?

30.6 Rapidly Evolving Market Structure and Distribution Channels

In 2016, the total value of all sales in Japan of retail food and beverages (F&B) was JPY 52.2 trillion (US$474.9 billion). Also, in 2016, the functional food market size in Japan was estimated to be close to JPY 2 trillion (US$19.5 billion). In the same

---

17 Nomura, from Gekkan Shin-Iryo, 2016 white paper on medical-equipment systems, November 2017.

year, the market size of FOSHU was about JPY 600 billion (US$5.85 billion).[18] As ◻ Fig. 30.3 shows, between 2013 and 2015, functional packaged goods and functional beverages had roughly the same amount of sales.

The most important distribution channels for health food were non-store ones, including mail order, door-to-door sales, and online and television shopping (refer to ◻ Fig. 30.4).

The surprising prevalence of the door-to-door sales channel was due to the high fragmentation of the Japanese retail food sector, the high number of specialty/semi-specialty stores, and, most importantly, the fact that the need for functional products and dietary supplements varied with the individual consumer's situation. For example, Yakult Honsha, a company with a 23% market share in functional dairy products, had created a network of "Yakult Ladies" or door-to-door representatives, who operated a nationwide home-delivery system that met customers face-to-face to explain how lactobacilli worked. This network was considered to have been the driving force behind Yakult's success in increasing its sales volumes since 2007.

	2013	**2014**	**2015**
Beverages	730	781	783
Health foods	709	720	721
Dietary Supplements	173	172	171
Total	**1,612**	**1,673**	**1,675**

◻ **Fig. 30.3** Total value of the health food market in 2013–2015 (JPY billion). (Source: Adapted from Fuji Keizai H/B Marketing Handbook no. 3, 2015)

Sales Channels Market Size	FY 2014		FY 2015		FY 2016 (Prospect)		FY 2017 (Forecast)	
	Market Size	Market Share	Market Size	Market Share	Market Size	Market Share	Market Size	Market Share
Door-to-door sales	235,000	32.6%	234,000	31.5%	232,000	31.0%	231,000	30.4%
Mail order sales	299,000	41.5%	309,100	41.6%	318,400	42.5%	331,000	43.5%
Pharmaceutical channel	96,700	13.4%	107,530	14.5%	106,500	14.2%	106,600	14.0%
Food store channel	26,500	3.7%	26,900	3.6%	27,200	3.6%	27,300	3.6%
Health food channel	15,600	2.2%	16,800	2.3%	15,400	2.1%	14,820	1.9%
Other channels	48,000	6.7%	49,200	6.6%	49,700	6.6%	50,200	6.6%
Health Food Market Size (Total)	**720,800**	**100.0%**	**743,530**	**100.0%**	**750,000**	**100.0%**	**761,820**	**100.0%**

◻ **Fig. 30.4** Health food market in Japan by sales channel (Market size is based on the shipment value at the manufacturers). Source adapted from Yano Research Institute chart, 2017. ► http://gij. aots.jp/u/market/dai853i7ajw6ci?sf_culture=en

18 Yamamoto, Osamu. "The Japanese food industry." *The Patent Lawyer*, 2016. ► www.yuasa-hara.co.jp/wp-content/uploads/2016/10/The-Japanese-Food-Industry.pdf. Accessed 15 October 2018.

Among store-based retailers, drugstores had been the fastest-growing channel since 2000. However, more recently, e-commerce had increased in importance. So far, the penetration rate of e-commerce was only about 2.3% for food and beverage, compared to 30% for home appliances and 34% for office supplies and stationery.[19] Yet, the growing competition among the incumbent players and e-sales giants was likely to change this picture.

The competition among the three emerging e-commerce leaders—Rakuten, Yahoo Japan, and Amazon—was becoming especially fierce (*refer to* Exhibit 30.4), but it had not yet led to substantial differentiation. To achieve this differentiation, e-commerce platforms in Japan were interested in partnerships with manufacturers. The winning platform in Japan would succeed due to its ability to accurately match its products with consumers' wants and to accurately develop and improve its products based on consumer feedback.

The functional food market was fragmented, and no single leader could be identified. Instead, various companies were performing in their respective segments. Thanks to its strong presence in probiotic drinkable yogurt, Yakult Honsha, with its 23% market share, was the leader in functional packaged food in 2015. Meiji was the second largest (13%), followed by the Lotte Group (7%). Coca-Cola Japan had a strong presence in functional sports drinks with its Aquarius brand and was the 2015 leader in functional beverages, holding a 21% market share. Also, in 2015, Otsuka Holdings Co. Ltd. had a 19% market share, followed by Suntory Beverage and Food Ltd., which had a 14% market share.[20]

It is notable that in addition to the retail health food market described, there was a substantial medical nutrition market in Japan. According to Greg Behar, the CEO of Nestlé Health Sciences, Japan was the world's second-largest nutrition food market for medical institutions after the United States, with a market size of about CHF 2 billion (about JPY 250 billion).[21] This market was dominated by specialist suppliers, and the three leaders were Abbott Japan, Otsuka, and Ajinomoto. Hospitals comprised the primary distribution channel.

Exhibit 30.4 E-commerce Platform Players in Japan

Primary e-commerce players in Japan

	1. Yahoo! Japan.	Rakuten	Amazon
Paid memberships			
	Yahoo premium member	Rakuten premium member	Amazon prime member
Price	¥499 per month	¥3900 annual	¥3900 annual, ¥400 per month

---

19 METI e-commerce market survey, quoted by JP Morgan, February 2018.
20 "Functional Foods and Beverages in Japan." Agriculture & Agri-food Canada, 2016.
21 According to an interview with Greg Beard, CEO of Nestlé Health Sciences, Nikkei Business Online 23 February 2015.

Main benefits	Yahoo! Shopping/LOHACO: Points 5x. Yahoo Auction: Capable of submitting auction items. Flea market product fee savings. Popular restaurant coupons. Some free movies and comics. Purchase reassurance warranty, travel cancellation compensation. Unlimited smartphone backup capacity. Yahoo Box: Uploads up to 1GB every 2 weeks.	Delivery point compensation. No-charge delivery: 2× points. Rakuten premium card number—free for 1 year. Rakuten TV, Rakuten Travel, Rakuten Books, Rakuten kobo: Points 2×. Member-only coupons.	Same-day express delivery, express delivery, delivery time designation: No charge. Prime Video: Unlimited view of some content. Prime Music: Unlimited listening to over one million songs. Amazon Pantry discount pricing. Participation in member-only limited-time sale events. Twitch Prime, link with US service. Prime Photo: Unlimited capacity.

Credit cards

	Yahoo! JAPAN card	Rakuten card	Amazon classic card
Annual fees	Free	Free	Free in the first year; free in subsequent years if used once
Points	T Points Yahoo! Shopping/LOHACO 3% Other purchases: 1%	Rakuten Super Points Rakuten Ichiba purchases: 4% Other purchases: 1%	Amazon points Amazon purchases: Typical 1.5%, Prime member 2%. Other purchases: 1%

Mobile services

	SoftBank Mobile Y! Mobile	Rakuten Mobile	
Main benefits	Yahoo! Shopping/LOHACO usage: SoftBank users: Points + 10×. Y! Mobile users: Points + 5×. Extra +5× for enjoy pack member contracts. Yahoo Premium Unlimited Use.	*Rakuten member discount*: Plan S: 9 months of no charges for the basic fee (3-year contract). *Diamond member discount*: Super Hodai monthly fee ¥500 discount (1 year). Rakuten Ichiba points + 1×.	

Source: "New Retail: Integration of Online and Offline," JP Morgan, 2018. ▶ https://markets.jpmorgan.com/. Accessed 19 October 2018

Amazon Japan: Already ranks seventh in sales—Total transaction volume already five digits

	Company	FY-end (yy/m)	Sales (Yen mn)	% y-y
	▶ Amazon.com (consolidated)	16/12	14,794,420	27.1
1	Aeon	17/2	7,811,110	1.1
2	Seven & i HD	17/2	7,718,855	2.1
3	FamilyMart Uny HD	17/2	3,977,067	na
4	Lawson	17/2	2,122,861	4.9
	Amazon Japan (estimated GTV)	16/12	1,881,020	17.5
5	Yamada Denki	17/3	1,563,056	−3.1
6	Isetan Mitsukoshi HD	17/3	1,253,457	−2.6
7	Amazon Japan (net sales)	16/12	1,174,637	17.5
8	J. Front Retailing	17/2	1,108,512	−4.7
9	Fast Retailing	16/8	1,033,058	6.8
10	Takashimaya	17/2	923,601	−0.6

30

Notes

An exhibit commission of 18% is assumed for Amazon Japan's total transaction volume. GTV stands for "gross transaction volume."

Source: "Retailing: Initiating coverage of 12 large cap retailing stocks," Nomura, September 2017.

30.7 Nestlé in Japan

Nestlé had a continued presence in Japan and offered a broad range of products. According to the most recent publicly available information (2011), powdered and liquid beverages (including Nescafe) represented 60% of company sales, while Nestlé Professional/Nestlé Health Science/Nespresso amounted to 14% of sales (the third category being confectionary at 10%). Thus, Nestlé Health Sciences' products were strategically important for the company in terms of business volume. The opening in 2014 of a new line in the Kasumigaura factory,[22] which specialized in medical nutrition products, highlighted the important role that Nestlé played in this product segment.

---

22 "Production Starts at Nestlé's Kasumigaura Factory". ▶ www.nestlehealthscience.com/news-room/press-releases/Inauguration-of-dedicated-product-line-for-Nestl-Health-Science-Japan. Accessed 15 October 2018.

In organizational terms, the business operations of Nestlé Health Sciences in Japan were divided into three main areas.[23] The first was specialized products for consumers, which were health foods that could be purchased in retail stores. The second was nutritional foods for medical institutions, which were used in hospitals and other related establishments for conditions such as cancer, obesity, and allergies, and many products were already used for actual treatments. The third area was the field of new nutritional food for therapeutic purposes, which had evolved rapidly in the past 3 years. Nestlé was conducting clinical trials to investigate nutrition sources that could be utilized for the treatment of certain diseases, such as Alzheimer's. Nestlé's key medical nutrition brands sold in Japan included Isocal®, Resource®, and Peptamen®, which were used by hospitals and nursing homes across the country.

Regarding its sales strategy, in recent years, Nestlé actively focused on a market that could be described as a combination of medicine and food, i.e., the healthy food market, while also exploring new sales channels and innovative digital solutions. In doing so, Nestlé aimed to create additional touch points with customers and to increase engagement with them.

30.7.1 Nestlé Products for Consumers

Regarding the direct-to-consumer channel, the matcha green tea marketing strategy was notable; it became a commercial success due to Nestlé's ability to customize its direct offerings to Japanese consumers (*refer to* ◨ Fig. 30.5). When Japanese consumers bought matcha green tea, they had the opportunity to complete a questionnaire that directed them toward a personalized version of the drink. The high adoption rate of this approach suggested that customers clearly identified a greater value, especially in the nutritive benefits they perceived, due to the high customization.

Another direct-to-consumer example that involved embedded technological support concerned the advancement of Nestlé in the Internet of Things (IoT) and artificial intelligence (AI) domains. In particular, in October 2017, Nestlé offered Barista I, a coffee machine that could be operated using a smartphone, to Japanese consumers. Nestlé was then in the process of developing next-generation machines that could be used and synched with Sony Mobile Communications. These machines would be able to receive voice commands to make coffee. According to Akiko Kumagai, the manager of Nestlé in Japan (E-Commerce Division, Nestlé Wellness Business Department):

>> Nestlé Japan has created a digital platform service called Nescafe Connect. The platform is designed to address the issues of Japan's rapidly aging society. A smart tablet connected to our coffee machine (Barista I) makes it possible to communicate with family members who live in different areas of Japan. A part of your daily activities, such as making a cup of coffee, can address communication issues with your families in distance without much effort.

---

23 According to an interview with Greg Beard, CEO of Nestlé Health Sciences. *Nikkei Business Online*, 23 February 2015.

30

□ **Fig. 30.5**   Matcha green tea: Personalization brought to customers. (Source: ▶ https://shop. nestle.jp/front/contents/ambassador/wamb/)

Barista I used Bluetooth short-range wireless communication technology. This allowed for establishing communication with the machine or, more importantly, with the machine's owner. For example, families who lived far from their elderly parents could communicate via smartphones. Elderly citizens may not have been familiar with smartphones, but a coffee machine offered a convenient way to communicate that was enhanced by the Xperia Agent, a personal assistant terminal from Sony Mobile Communications. When a family purchased a Barista I, they registered on the friend list of the application, which enabled all family members to exchange information. According to Kumagai:

» The platform service is designed based on our marketing concept of solving customers' key issues. We would like to further develop the platform to address key issues of our customers – not only communication issues but also more personalized health and nutrition issues.

The partnership between Nestlé and Sony provided a technological link to make the first generation of IoT coffee machines possible. The platform value of the service was expandable. As Akiko explained:

» For example, the platform currently provides our customers with personalized recommendations of daily supplements based on questionnaires regarding customers lifestyles (diet, exercise, etc.), and soon we are going to launch a new service of personalized diet/nutritional recommendations based on an AI [artificial intelligence] analysis of actual photo images of our customers' individual meals.

While Akiko acknowledged that the platform's value creation potential was enormous, she was also discreet regarding the way Nestlé Japan manages personal information on the platform. Akiko stated:

» In fact, we used to consider using more biocentric data of our customers to personalize our service; however, as a food manufacturer, we came to the conclusion that we should not take the risk of handling sensitive, individual biocentric data. If we focus on our marketing mission to address the key issues of our customers in the Japanese market characterized by a rapidly aging society, we do not really need to use the sensitive individual biocentric data to develop our current e-commerce platform service.

30.7.2 Nestlé Products for Hospitals

Regarding medical nutrition, Nestlé acknowledged the potential for the complementarity of its nutritive formula with drugs produced by pharmaceutical companies. Greg Beard, Nestlé Health Sciences CEO, said:

» I think the pharmaceutical industry is our partner. Many of our products are not substitutes for medicines. Rather, they are used as supplements to increase the effectiveness of medicines or to suppress side effects. Indeed, we are working with a pharmaceutical company to collaborate regarding what we can do to provide a better solution for patients.[24]

Nestlé was focused on distributing its own products as well as the products of companies with which it had entered into partnerships. One example of Nestlé's partnerships was that with Ajinomoto, a specialty food and chemical producer with 2014 revenues of $9 billion (*refer to* ◘ Fig. 30.6). This partnership focused on Ajinomoto's diets, which addressed protein-energy malnutrition and provided nutritional care foods (peroral nutrition for medical and nursing care) in Japan. Under the terms of the agreement, Nestlé handled the manufacturing and sales of

| AQUASOLITA® | An oral rehydration solution that effectively and deliciously replenishes water and electrolytes. The refreshing apple flavor is made without excessive sugars and calories. Available in both jelly and powder types. | |
| AMINOCARE® Jelly Leucine 40 | An apple-flavored jelly drink labeled as a food with functional claims. A blend of essential amino acids containing 40% leucine that is reported to support muscle building in people in their 60s and over to maintain muscle mass and walking ability. | |

◘ Fig. 30.6 Example of Ajinomoto nutritional care food sold by Nestlé through the medical channel. (Source: ► www.ajinomoto.com/en/presscenter/press/detail/g2016_02_29.html)

24 Interview with Greg Behar, Nestlé Health Sciences CEO. *Nikkei Business Online*, 23 February 2015.

Ajinomoto's protein-energy malnutrition products. Nestlé also conducted sales and sales promotion activities for nutritional care food through the medical channel pursuant to an exclusive agency agreement, while Ajinomoto focused on product development and clinical research.

Based on the press release that discusses the partnership with Ajinomoto and all the available materials, one can observe that a digital health ecosystem was emerging in Japan. Indeed, the IoT (Internet of Things) theme had become a hot topic, even in the nutrition market, and it was obvious that it was important to constantly monitor the developments in this area among Nestlé's peers, especially the emerging ones.

30.8 Digital Nutrition Platforms: New Entrants

A digital platform enabled data collection, sorted and managed the data, analyzed data with specialized application software, and provided insights and conclusions based on the analysis. A digital platform was similar to the operating system of a smartphone or a computer; it was the ecosystem for the application software, supplying the route for data to reach the correct algorithm.[25]

Several start-up companies had become active in developing digital nutrition platforms. One of the most well-known was Zipongo, which was a relatively new but already well-established player founded in 2010 and based in California. According to the venture capital deals database Crunchbase, as of 2018, the company had conducted eight fundraising rounds, raising in total some \$48 million.[26] In 2018, Zipongo's platform consisted of a number of different apps designed to assist people in changing their nutrition-related behaviors. Depending on the individual's preferences, Zipongo apps provided users with recipes, shopping lists, or restaurant recommendations. The advice was generated algorithmically based on the collected personal data (*refer to* ◘ Fig. 30.7).

Interestingly, Zipongo did not offer its solutions to end users (B2C) directly but rather through their employers (B2B2C), stating that dietary wellness should be part of the corporate culture. For corporate customers, Zipongo developed a two-step process for the data collection of end users. First, employees took a comprehensive nutrition quiz that covered eating habits, allergies, and preferences. This quiz was designed to be retaken at regular intervals to monitor progress. Then, Zipongo worked with biocentric service providers to collect biocentric on-site (i.e., at the corporate customer office), such as blood pressure, cholesterol levels, and body composition. The platform used data to produce recommendations, creating personalized dietary advice for each person. Zipongo worked with specialized health and wellness service providers and had developed solutions that aimed to prevent some chronic diseases, such as diabetes. Zipongo claimed on its website

---

25 "Investors See Payback in Industrial IoT Start-ups." *Bloomberg* "New Energy Finance" letter, January 2018.

26 "Zipongo." *Crunchbase*. www.crunchbase.com/organization/zipongo#section-overview. Accessed 15 October 2018.

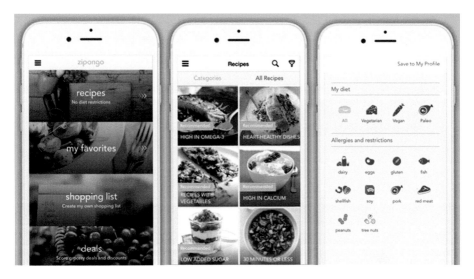

◘ **Fig. 30.7** Example of Zipongo mobile user interface. (Source: ► www.mobihealthnews.com/content/zipongo-raises-18m-move-its-digital-nutrition-platform-wellness-medicine)

that "thanks to our behavioral approach, 75% of our corporate participants report they have developed healthier eating habits." Another example of a nascent digital nutrition platform was provided by Nutrino, a start-up based in Israel. Thus far, it had raised around $ten million via "round A" financing. The company operated a data platform that gathered people's personal biochemistry and then used that information to determine how food affected each user's body. The first public product of the company was released in 2016, and it was called "FoodPrint" (*refer to* ◘ Fig. 30.8). It was a mobile app that allowed people with diabetes to receive an individualized overview of how daily food and lifestyle habits affected their glucose levels. To achieve a broader adoption, Nutrino had established useful partnerships. For example, it collaborated with Abbott so that Abbott digital solutions' (e.g., Abbott LibreLink mobile app) users could synchronize their glucose data with Nutrino's FoodPrint application.

Nutrino was in the early stages of its development, and FoodPrint was the only consumer application it offered. In addition, the company positioned itself as a B2B provider of AI solutions to businesses, which included customized data sets; licenses for its algorithms; integrative solutions for apps, wearables, and devices, and any data related to nutrition.

Zipongo and Nutrino were certainly interesting cases, especially regarding their ability to bring their solutions to the market. However, one could question whether the approaches of the two start-ups were actually useful for Nestlé in the development of its digital nutrition platform, especially as both Zipongo and Nutrino relied on medical data inputs, which raised several issues, including data confidentiality and the cost of gathering and processing data. On the other hand, such data could significantly increase the precision of the personalized advice offered by the platform. This would certainly be one of the dilemmas that Nestlé had to consider in the ongoing evolution of its digital nutrition platform.

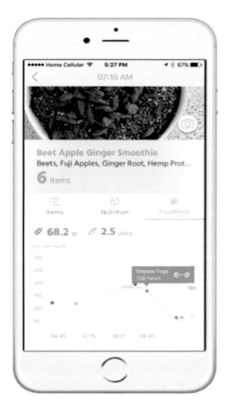

My FoodPrint shows me my blood sugar in relation to my meal, and other relevant events, on a single timeline

◻ **Fig. 30.8**   FoodPrint mobile interface. (Source: ▸ https://nutrino.co/nutrino-helps-make-sense-diabetes/)

For Nannini, several key questions remained unanswered:

- Which part of the emerging digital nutrition ecosystem of Japan does Nestlé believe has the largest potential for a digital nutrition platform?
- Should the Nestlé digital nutrition platform be built for B2C or B2B?
- Depending on the choice between B2C or B2B, which customer segments within B2C or B2B should the Nestlé platform target? Which distribution channels should be activated?
- How should Nestlé access consumer data and address consumer data protection?
- Should the Nestlé digital nutrition platform support only products and services offered by Nestlé and its partners/joint ventures, or should it be agnostic?
- What lessons could Nestlé learn from the successes of start-ups that offer digital nutrition platforms in terms of partnerships and access to consumer data?

Reference

Gupta, R. C. (2016). *Nutraceuticals efficacy, safety and toxicity*. London: Academic Press.

Rabobank: Building Digital Agility at Scale

Contents

Researcher Lisa Duke prepared this case under the supervision of Professor Michael Wade as a basis for class discussion rather than to illustrate either effective or ineffective handling of a business situation. Copyright © 2019 by *IMD—International Institute for Management Development*, Lausanne, Switzerland (▶ www.imd.org). No part of this publication may be reproduced, stored in a retrieval system, or transmitted in any form or by any means without the prior written permission of *IMD*.

© Springer Nature Switzerland AG 2020
T. Jelassi, F. J. Martínez-López, *Strategies for e-Business*, Classroom Companion: Business, https://doi.org/10.1007/978-3-030-48950-2_31

■ Introduction

Utrecht, Fall 2018. For Nieke Martens and Bart Leurs, summer 2018 marked a pivotal point in the digital transformation of Rabobank.

Progress was being made, but Rabobank needed to move faster to match the levels of service and convenience provided by digital native companies like Uber, Netflix, and Amazon that were fast becoming the reference points for the industry.

Leurs, chief digital transformation officer and a member of the executive board, had hired Martens to set up a Digital Hub that was meant to become the cornerstone of the bank's digital implementation plan. The Hub had been successful as a pilot project, but when they had tried to grow the Hub's operations, problems began to surface. For example, they faced challenges attracting and retaining colleagues from the rest of the bank. The bank's main operating units had been happy to support the Hub when it was a small entity located in the head office but seemed less interested when they had to provide people and resources for the Hub's projects. As the number and range of projects increased, their complexity also began to rise. In particular, the shift from DevOps, or projects largely focused on IT development, to BizDevOps, which focused on end-to-end customer journeys, created a number of challenges.

It was necessary to overcome these problems to achieve the scale and speed of transformation required to compete effectively with traditional and emerging rivals. Rabobank's board was looking for answers.

Leurs and Martens were scheduled to make a proposal to Rabobank's management team on how to move forward with the company's digital transformation. They needed to convince the board and the rest of the bank that now was the moment to take the leap forward. How could they address the tensions in the current organization? Would the lessons already learned be enough to face the coming challenges? Were they ready to move from IT DevOps to full BizDevOps? Did they have a choice?

31

31.1 Rabobank: The Cooperative Bank[1]

Rabobank's origins were derived from the nineteenth century German Raiffeisen model, an agricultural credit cooperative, or a credit union. In the twentieth century, although the cooperative structure remained intact, the bank shifted toward becoming a general bank serving businesses and private customers. It also expanded internationally, growing to include operations in 40 countries. In 2002, Rabobank launched its first Internet bank—focused on savings products—in Belgium, followed by Ireland (2005), New Zealand (2006), and Australia (2007). By the 2010s, new postcrisis financial regulations and governance requirements, changing customer needs, and the rise in digitization meant that a review of the existing governance structure was required. On 1 January 2016, 106 local banks merged with

---

1   Rabobank through the years, ► https://www.rabobank.com/en/images/r652-rabodoordetijd-eng-def.pdf

Rabobank Nederland to create a more integrated company, although it still operated on cooperative principles. By 2019, Rabobank's business model included retail banking, wholesale banking, private banking, leasing, and real estate services. It had approximately 8.3 million clients worldwide: 7.3 million in the Netherlands and one million overseas (*refer to* ◼ Fig. 31.1).

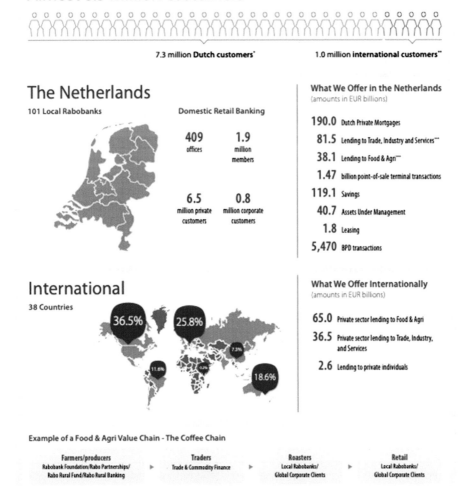

◼ **Fig. 31.1** Rabobank Infographic. (Source: ▶ https://www.rabobank.com/en/images/07-infographic-rabobank-at-a-glance.pdf)

31.2 Digital@Rabobank

Along with many banks, Rabobank had steadily increased its digital offerings, but these remained scattered throughout the organization. In 2016, with customer expectations rising, it decided to centralize many digital initiatives into a "digital bank" sitting in Rabobank's retail domain along with private customer and business customer services. The digital bank brought together expertise on data and analytics, customer experience design, and other digital offerings such as the mobile banking platform. It was able to prioritize digital capabilities not only within its own department but also by working on specific products for both private and business customers. The digital bank also launched its own solutions, such as Rabo eBusiness for business customers. After some time, however, tensions began to emerge between the digital bank and other parts of the organization around the most appropriate portfolio of digital products and services.

Across Europe, fast-moving fintech companies and digital giants like PayPal, Apple, and Google were launching a variety of digital products and services. Faced with increasing competition, most of Europe's traditional banks were embracing digital transformation—moving from high street retail banking to online offerings. In particular, these banks were quickly developing mobile phone apps to offer customers an omni-channel experience.

Of the 50 banks operating in the Netherlands, ING, ABN AMRO, and Rabobank were the largest. ING had already moved aggressively down a digital transformation route and had embraced agile methods to create digital offerings for customers. ABN AMRO was exploring blockchain technology focusing on innovation in fintech, and ING had partnered with many fintech companies to identify disruptive ideas it could apply to its own offerings. ING was seen as a pioneer in digital transformation. Since June 2015, it had integrated agile methodology from its IT DevOps and applied it to Biz DevOps by transforming most of its core head office operations into small multifunctional agile teams with customer focus at their heart. ING's approach[2] was based on chapters (individuals with specific expertise such as data analytics), squads (self-steering, multidisciplinary, autonomous teams of up to nine people), and tribes (a collection of squads, such as mortgage services, typically fewer than 150 people). Rather than transform with its existing workforce, ING placed all employees at its HQ on "mobility"—effectively they were jobless—and made them reapply for a position in the new organization.[3]

In response to this competitive environment, Rabobank leaders decided they needed to move faster to create a stronger digital presence. They wanted to make

2   Perkin, N. (2017). Agile Transformation at ING: A Case Study. Agilebusinessmanifesto, ▶ https://agilebusinessmanifesto.com/agilebusiness/agile-transformation-at-ing/. Accessed May 2019.
3   Jacobs. P, Schlatmann, B., & Mahadevan, D. (2017). ING's agile transformation. McKinsey & Company, ▶ https://www.mckinsey.com/industries/financial-services/our-insights/ings-agile-transformation. Accessed May 2019.

digital the main channel across all customer segments. Bart Leurs, who had joined from ING in 2016 as head of Fintech & Innovation, was appointed chief digital transformation officer in 2017. Underlining the importance of this initiative and the support of senior leaders, he was also appointed a member of Rabobank's Managing Board. The digital transformation would become an integral part of Rabobank's strategic agenda (*refer to* ◙ Fig. 31.2).

Rabobank's digital transformation was driven by four ambitions:

1. Full digital adoption through digital availability—targets were set to increase the availability and use of digital customer journeys.
2. Develop new revenue models to contribute to top-line income growth.
3. Build digital DNA to strengthen Rabobank's digital culture and ways of working, including data-driven decision-making, consumer involvement and customer centricity, and agile methodologies.
4. To be the number one innovation partner for Rabobank's customers—innovating together as per the bank's cooperative culture and traditions.

The acceleration of the bank's digitization would occur across three parallel horizons (*see* ◙ Fig. 31.3). A Digital Hub would focus on Horizons 1 and 2 to change the bank's operating model to deliver customer journeys quickly. The Hub would

◙ **Fig. 31.2** Rabobank's strategic agenda and ten priorities. (Source: Company information)

◙ **Fig. 31.3** The three digital horizons

be central in achieving ambitions 1 and 3, particularly in creating an environment that would be inviting to work in and would attract digital talent. An Inno Hub crossed Horizons 2 and 3, focusing on new business models and open banking. It would have a longer time frame.

Nieke Martens, director of Asset Management, was looking for a new challenge. At her previous employer, she had been head of Digital. She was introduced to Leurs, and after a couple of conversations, it became clear that the role would entail not simply further developing digital but also changing the culture at Rabobank. The key question was how to situate the transformation—as a separate division or integrated? Leurs and Martens visited telecoms companies in the Netherlands and banks in Scandinavia and the United Kingdom to learn how they had approached this challenge. They also considered the cooperative culture of Rabobank and the experience of the separate, digital bank. Martens noted:

» A Digital Hub helps to create momentum because you can support and protect it as it grows, and it can become "digital bacteria" that positively infect other parts of the organization. We decided to house the Hub in our headquarters. We saw in our visits that if it is physically separate from HQ, it creates an integration problem later. We wanted to avoid this. We also didn't want to make it too fancy because then it becomes a kind of museum or a showcase. We want it to be at the core and to make banking more fun, so we chose colors to create a different context for what we were trying to achieve – to start to develop a different culture, to attract everyone at Rabobank. It wasn't so much about changing people but creating an environment in which they can work to be creative and collaborative.

Martens was named head of the Digital Hub in October 2017, and the Hub was launched in January 2018. Leurs and Martens believed that a "public" launch within Rabobank would help drive momentum and put a stake in the ground for Rabobank's accelerated digital transformation. In parallel, as the Digital Hub was launched, other departments across the retail bank decided to start referring to "tribes" rather than "departments." This did not necessarily change the daily working approach to agile methodology, but the language was aligned with agile.

31

31.3 The Digital Hub

Martens deliberately started out with a small team of six people. At that point it was hard to judge just how much work there would be. She inherited two online sales consultants as a result of a request for advice and hired four people herself—one each from IT, business management, data analytics, and compliance. She explained:

» The profiles were specially chosen. We needed the data insights in order to be able to pick the right customer journeys and to make the results very visible in the online management reporting tool – the Daily Digital – that was built by one team member together with colleagues from the Data department. Giving mandates to the squads in the banking environment meant I had to be sure compliance, legal and risk were well covered. The IT experience was needed to complement my knowledge, and business management was crucial as that was the memory of all the work done before I joined.

The two online sales consultants focused on choosing the right customer journeys and then breaking those journeys down into the appropriate stages. They asked various questions, such as "How often is this journey used?" and "What is the data behind the journey?". The IT person looked at developing architecture and reusability rather than reinventing the wheel for each customer journey. Where digital components could be replicated, this was the optimum way forward and would help speed up development. A digital component library was created to house them. The compliance and risk employee oversaw how ideas for customer journeys could be put into practice while meeting compliance requirements. It quickly became clear that someone with seniority in terms of data was needed and was hired as the fifth team member. The sixth member of the team had a business management/organizational design role to track progress and organize staffing for the teams in the Digital Hub. The team borrowed agile coaches from other parts of the organization. Each coach was responsible for three squads. ◗ Figure 31.4 illustrates a week in the life of an agile coach in the Digital Hub. Martens kept her team small but hired trainees and students as necessary.

The Digital Hub started by focusing on three customer journeys, each with its own squad. Each squad comprised ten people drawn from across Rabobank who were 100% dedicated to the customer journey and situated in the Hub. It was agreed with Rabobank's work council that there would be no formal selection process for the squads. The Hub team would have to work with the people available from the businesses at the time, regardless of their suitability. The approach the customer journey teams followed was based on the Spotify[4] version of Agile methodology. Each customer journey would take 12 weeks to complete.

31.3.1 Selecting the Customer Journeys

Rabobank had approximately 400 customer journeys through its digital channels. These journeys had been developed, validated, and implemented over time by various Rabobank teams. The goal of the Digital Hub was to improve and accelerate the use of these digital journeys. Leurs had initially used a global consulting company to help set up the Hub in 2017. Martens was happy with the work done but disagreed on the focus for the customer journeys. The consultants had argued that

---

4   The Spotify version of Agile methodology was based on squads, tribes, and chapters. There were 2 weekly sprints where each squad decided what it was going to work on for those 2 weeks and daily short, focused, stand-up meetings to track progress. Squads had an agile coach who helped improve their way of working and a product owner to define the vision of the product and its features. (Source: ▶ https://medium.com/@media_75624/exploring-key-elements-of-spotifys-agile-scaling-model-471d2a23d7ea).

a

Thursday	
8:00 - 9:00	3-way meeting with HR and another coach on what the skill profile for different roles should look like as we roll out Simplify@Scale.
9:00 - 10:30	Reviews Area Savings. Each of the 8 squads gave a 5–10-minute update on what they achieved and what their next steps are in the next sprint. Representat ives from each squad in the area were present.
10:30 - 12:00	Reviews Area Investments. Same as above; except there are 12 squads.
10:00 - 11:30	Stepped out of the reviews to facilitate a workshop for the board on the agile way of work.
12:00 - 12:15	Daily stand -up coaches; review progress of our own work and our sprint.
13:00 - 14:00	End -of-sprint Investments – PO's of investments do a retro and planning. We mostly focused on retro because we were still working on roadmaps and decided we needed those before we could do a proper planning.
14:00 - 15:00	End-of-sprint savings–same as above –I joined both rituals because I designed the heartbeat and wanted to see how they worked in practice.
15:00 - 15:30	Evaluation of the end-of-sprint.
	The rest of the day: email, looking ahead to next week, admin.
Friday	
	Coach offsite–to make plans and set goals for the next couple of months; as well as getting to know each other better as we are a new team.
Monday	
8:00 - 9:00	Prepping the agile foundation training on Wednesday with a fellow coach.
9:00 -16:30	Participated in the Ideation training for the moonshot campaign. To see if we can use it in our design sprints.
16:30 - 18:00	Catch up with my focus team (my HR line).

31

◻ **Fig. 31.4**   A typical week in the life of an Agile coach at Rabobank. End of sprint/sprint start on Thursdays. Source: Rabobank materials—compiled by an Agile coach

b

Tuesday	
8:00 -9:00	Prep a KPI session for squad AIVO–set approach for the session.
9:00 -9:30	Prep a retro with squad Montecarlo on their expectations of me as a coach.
9:30 -10:00	Daily scrums with 2 of my teams (Montecarlo and AIVO).
10:00 - 11:00	Prepping the agile foundation training (solo).
11:00 - 11:45	Evaluation/improvements of review; session with several participants.
11:45 - 12:15	Stand -up with coaches.
12:30 - 13:00	Briefing on an architecture community session I am going to facilitate.
13:00 - 14:00	Travel to Zeist.
14:00 - 15:30	Train the trainer session on Bowties (incident analysis methodology).
15:30 - 17:00	Email and admin.
Wednesday	
7:30 -9:00	Prepping the agile foundation training.
9:00 -17:00	Giving the foundation training.
Thursday	
8:00 -9:00	Prepping KPI session/email.
9:00 -10:00	KPI session with AIVO team, I facilitated a discussion on what KPIs to use and to define some next steps. The squad was not able to define them themselves and needed someone to guide the discussion.
10:00 - 10:30	Prep a retro with squad AIVO on what their expectations are of me as a coach.
10:30 - 11:45	Time to get some of my other pesky backlog items done.
11:45 - 12:15	Stand -up coaches.
12:15 - 13:00	Define an approach to coach leadership team and chapter coaches within tribe.
13:00 - 15:00	Refining the content of the Scrum master train ing with a fellow coach.
15:00 - 16:00	Coffee/coaching meeting with two coachees in Rabobank (but outside of tribe).

◻ **Fig. 31.4**   (continued)

c

Friday	
9:00 - 11:00	Odds and ends from last week. Set a fellow coach (outside of the tribe) to work on writing part of the training.
	The rest of the day I was off.
Monday	
8:00 - 9:00	Email, planning the week.
9:15 - 10:00	Attend the daily scrums of squads Orientation, AIVO, Montecarlo.
10:00 - 14:00	Refine and prep Scrum master training 23rd.
15:00 - 16:00	Update Head of CI (over from Sydney for the week) on our plans and progress; exchange ideas.
16:00 - 17:00	Planning & sprint start for coaching team.
Tuesday	
8:00 - 9:00	Email, planning the week.
9:15 - 10:00	Attend the daily scrums of squads Orientation, AIVO, Montecarlo.
10:00 - 15:00	Finalise scrum master training with two fellow coaches.
15:00 - 16:00	Follow-up on the KPI discussion with the AIVO team. Review KPIs; feedback on the process and next steps.
16:00 - 16:30	Walk Head of CI through the Squad Health Check tool we used at the digital hub to facilitate the discussion on improvements and next steps.
Wednesday	
7:30 - 10:00	Prep the scrum master training.
10:00 - 17:00	Scrum master training with fellow coach.

31

◘ **Fig. 31.4**   (continued)

Martens's projects were "too simple" and should be "more innovative." Martens commented:

» What we did in the Hub was a deliberate choice not to focus on innovation but instead to solve real issues for customers – dealing with losing your debit cards or opening a joint account – neither was fancy. But if these essential things don't work well, we lose a lot of customers. Small issues have a huge impact on customers. We wanted to be able to measure our impact and used Google Analytics to identify exactly what was happening during these journeys. Where is it easy for customers? Where is it hard? Things that are annoying for customers but also that we could solve in 12 to 13 weeks. If we had chosen journeys that were too innovative, we wouldn't have been able to show that the Hub could deliver. For us, that was really important.

For example, the consultants had suggested a key customer journey such as mortgages. But it would not have been possible to deliver mortgages in the time frame. Martens selected three customer journeys that she believed could realistically be delivered in 12 weeks and would have the highest improvement potential. The first was losing debit cards, which Martens chose on the basis of data from customers. Dutch debit card holders lost their cards more than a million times a year, which was a painful experience. Car insurance was also chosen on the basis of data, which showed online conversion to be very low. The potential upside of improving this conversion was significant. The third journey was the onboarding process for asset management clients based on a frustrating experience that Martens had personally had.

Although Martens selected the first three journeys, after that, a robust decision-making process was developed:

1. An initial selection of digital journeys was made based on:
   (a) The digital journeys with the highest improvement potential based on data (e.g., volume, percentage online, online conversion, customer feedback, call reasons). The criteria were based on the digital key performance indicators (KPIs).
   (b) Suggestions from the organization, supported by data—the majority of these involved creating new digital journeys.
2. Preliminary decisions were made by the management team based on improvement potential/impact on digital KPIs and alignment with the strategic direction.
3. Feasibility determination study by product management and IT with regard to dependency on other initiatives, availability of resources, and timing.
4. Final decision made.

The decision-making process was shared with the management teams of business and retail clients. Martens was aware that the Hub team had to be extremely clear on how customer journeys were chosen, since initially the business units perceived that the Hub alone wanted to decide. A one-page model (*see* ◘ Fig. 31.5) was created and shared across Rabobank. It was strongly communicated that the Hub would only start a customer journey once the business had said yes to it.

A Impact Digital KPI's

- What is the current performance compared to the targets?
- Which customer journeys contribute the most to the targets?

B Strategic Direction

- Does a better customer journey contribute to reducing RKS contact?
- Is the customer journey important from the customer perspective?

C Other Input

- Is the customer journey in the top 10 of customer feedback?
- Which enablers can be included in a squad?
- Which Finalta recommendations can we include?
- Which offline processes are important to digitize?

◘ **Fig. 31.5** Customer journey decision criteria

The process was typically iterative:

Definition

Within the Hub we would analyze all the customer journeys (approximately 400) and for each we had KPIs. We analyzed which journeys have high volumes but really underperform if you look at the targets. We would then go back to the management team in the business, who have the responsibility for all the product groups, to discuss which journey should be picked to resolve, based on our data and advice. The management teams would then decide which to accelerate and digitize. We in the Hub would then form squads around the journeys. The tribe leads remained responsible for the change within the customer journeys, and in the Hub, we change the context for developing them based on multidisciplinary teams and coaches etc. In this way, the squads perform significantly better and faster than they would do if they worked in the traditional way. — Clarien Hoving, Digital Performance Consultant

---

31.3.2 The 12-Week Customer Journeys

To kick-start the journey, each squad went through a 5-day (later 4) launch program "Boostcamp" (*refer to* ◘ Fig. 31.6). The camp supported them to become a fully functioning team. The program started with a "Big Purpose"—a one-liner about what the squad hoped they would achieve. They then refined it during the program to make it their own. Other sessions focused on team dynamics, design thinking, customer experience, and how to conduct customer interviews, data analytics sessions, agile training, and personal development.

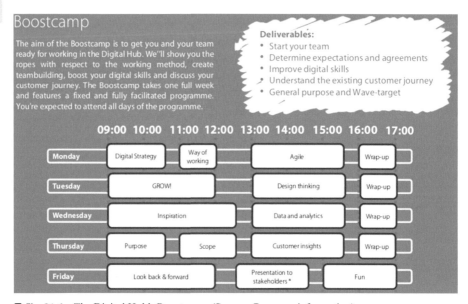

◘ **Fig. 31.6**   The Digital Hub's Boostcamp. (Source: Company information)

There was an agile game to induct team members into what it felt like to work in an agile environment, particularly around multifunctional collaboration. The squad got used to the rituals such as daily stand-ups and planning 2-week sprints. Speakers also presented on how they iterated their customer journeys. This helped shape the squad and develop a common mindset.

After the Boostcamp, each 12-week wave was split into three segments as summarized in ◘ Table 31.1 (*refer to* ◘ Fig. 31.7 *for more details*).

For many squad members, the customer experience part of the process was the most satisfying. Their traditional roles meant they were behind their desks rather than directly interacting with customers. To give their feedback, customers were invited into the user experience center. Some teams also took their prototypes to the nearby Utrecht main station and talked to passersby, many of whom were not Rabobank customers.

Although the target was 12, it was not always possible to keep to it if the solution turned out to be more complex than originally envisaged.

> **Definition**
>
> We try to keep to the 12 weeks, but in reality, we need 3 weeks to make decisions and talk to people outside the squads. We lose a lot of time coordinating between groups before we can start building the solution. It's probably more like 5 weeks than 3. We do manage to implement in around 13 weeks. — Evelien Mooij, Product Owner Joint Account Squad

◘ **Table 31.1** Sprint elements

Design sprint (2 weeks)	The squad starts by understanding the pains and gains in the existing journey by collecting customer feedback and data insights; it continues by drawing up a solution using design screens. The squad brainstorms with solution architects to identify what is possible within Rabobank's IT landscape. The deliverable is a simple paper-based prototype
Realization sprints	The squad then works in 2-week sprints, collaborating with the architects to sharpen the solution. Compliance is involved to ensure the solution is acceptable. The next step is for hub analysts to write up the solution for the development team to start coding
Delivery and monitoring (1 week)	The squad wraps up by going live with everything that has not already gone live. It also finalizes documentation and collaborates with colleagues on implementation and KPI monitoring

After each 12- to 13-week journey, squad members were encouraged to take time out and relax—to go to the beach or somewhere they could simply enjoy themselves. Continuously working in an agile way, with intense focus, could be exhausting. They then returned for a reboost program that included setting individual goals for performance improvement. The coaches helped each individual work on their goals into the next customer journey.

a

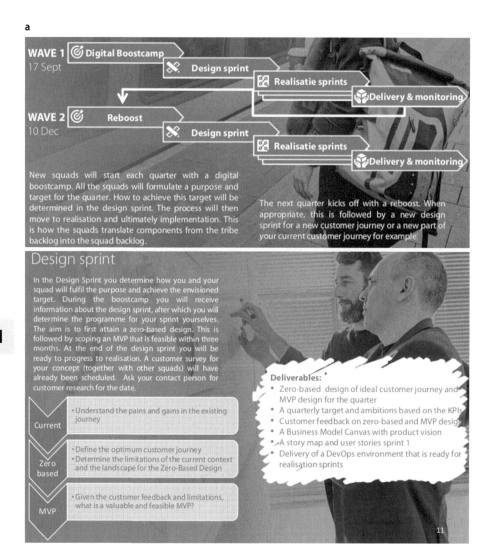

☐ Fig. 31.7   The Sprint roadmap. (Source: Company information)

b

Realisation sprints

During the realisation sprints, you work within the scope of your MVP. You realise everything that is needed to achieve the set target. Adjust your MVP as necessary based on, for example, the customer feedback that you continually gain. It can be gained by testing it with friends and family or through online data insights or interviews with advisers. Another fixed moment for a usability survey of your solution will have already been scheduled in the lab.

Deliverables:
- A measurement plan for accessing KPIs
- Delivery of all required user stories, e.g. DevOps tasks, content creation, implementation of your measurement plan, campaigns and implementation and communications media
- Interim deliveries to production
- Customer feedback from your usability test
- Post MVP vision & roadmap

We work in an agile way within the Digital Hub. This doesn't mean we don't make plans. You have, after all, set a collective aim for the quarter. But it does mean you deliver iterative value and achieve continual self-improvement. You make these iterations daily via the stand-up and for each bi-weekly sprint that includes a review for all stakeholders. This is how you work according to a fixed rhythm towards achieving your aim. Implementing your measurement plan helps to gain insights on customer behavior and adjust upon findings.

Finished the user stories within your area of expertise in the sprint? Support the other areas of expertise in your squad so that you can faster achieve your squad-goal.[12]

Final delivery & monitoring

You wrap up the last week of the Wave (the quarter) and go live with everything that hasn't already gone live in the previous sprints. The right checks for launch will be carried out for this purpose by customers, the Journey Owner, CX, DevOps and possibly the PGC. You inform colleagues for whom this is relevant about the implementation and define improvement points for the next quarter: the quarterly retrospective. You're responsible for the incident management and IT operations of the functionalities you have built. Ensure that you have set up both the incident monitoring and customer behaviour monitoring in such a way that you can optimally learn from it and make adjustments as necessary.

Deliverables:
- (final) Go live of MVP
- Check on Definition of Done – define technical dept
- Document only what is absolutely necessary
- Implemented change activities
- Improvement activities for the next quarter
- Finalise measurement set-up for access to KPI- and incident monitoring

◘ **Fig. 31.7** (continued)

31.3.3 Customer Journey Examples

The journeys all targeted Dutch retail clients. Previously, when a customer lost a debit card, the established wisdom was to focus on replacing the card as soon as possible. Through customer journey interviews, the debit cards squad found that most customers wanted simply to ensure that the lost card could not be used. The squad then focused not only on optimizing the process of reissuing cards but also on allowing customers to block and deblock their cards within 30 seconds of discovering it was missing by using the app.

In terms of car insurance, the customer journey identified that many customers were abandoning the online journey as too many questions were asked. Martens challenged the team not just to halve the number of steps but to radically reduce the process to 5 minutes. The team managed to halve the number of steps required.

The joint account squad looked at how they could make a celebration out of a meaningful event in people's lives. Previously, to open a joint account, one person in the couple had to go into a local branch and then it took over a month for the account to be processed and opened. Understandably, customers were put off by the delay and inconvenience. The squad took a different perspective—this was a lovely time in someone's life. Their solution was that one person simply needed to send an invitation to the other person through the app. It felt personal and gave a sense of togetherness. The impact of adding this simple functionality—with no marketing around it—was that the number of joint accounts quintupled.

31.4 Transformation@Scale

31

After 3 months, it was apparent to Martens that things in the Hub were going very well. She was therefore surprised, after visiting Dutch telecom company KPN, to hear about the many tensions they were experiencing in their digital transformation. She noted:

» That was the moment I realized that our Hub was running too smoothly. That's when I shared with Bart that we had to increase the tension and go faster. So, I decided to scale up from 3 to 10 squads in March, 20 in June and 30 early in July.

Ten squads meant 100 people drawn out of the bank, with a further 100 in June, and 300 in total by July. This approach raised the bar for the bank, and having that number of people out of the regular business and dedicated to fast-paced customer journeys would potentially create shockwaves. The Managing Board were supportive based on the visible success of the original journeys. Refer to ◻ Fig. 31.8 for the Hub development timeline up to August 2018.

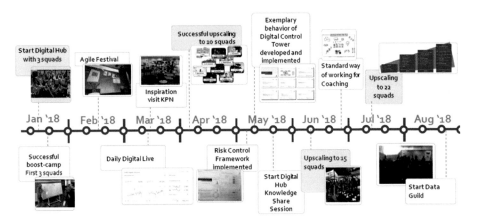

◘ Fig. 31.8 Digital Hub development timeline. (Source: Company information)

31.4.1 **Changing Mindsets and Expectations**

Over time, Martens could see that employees who came into the Hub were changing their mindsets, and customers' expectations of Rabobank's digital services were increasing. Hub participants could see firsthand the significant differences they were making to customers' experiences. Previously, Rabobank employees had typically focused on what competitors were doing; now they were also looking at what digital companies were doing. From Airbnb, for example, they learned that customers do not need an additional device to make a payment, which is what Rabobank required for Internet or mobile payments.

Being able to go to the station quickly and ask passersby for their opinions had been a major revelation. Martens explained:

» It sounds very simple, but it involves a huge cultural mindset change to have someone from, for example, Legal, go to the station and test out the prototype with an actual person – who may or may not be a Rabobank customer. Either way, people could see it had a lot of impact. What we want is not to think on behalf of our customers but instead to just ask them directly – to literally ask them every two weeks if we are going in the right direction.

Instead of focusing on DevOps as before, the digital transformation at Rabobank was making BizDevOps a reality by including data scientists, marketing, commercial, and user experience colleagues as well as a pool of compliance, legal, and risk people.

This transition was not, however, all plain sailing.

31.4.2 Increasing Tensions

With the new squads came increasing challenges and rising tensions, particularly between the Hub and other departments. Before the Hub, the DevOps teams were already working in some form of agile way. Agile was different in the Hub. When DevOps team members joined squads, they had to completely change their way of working, which caused some friction.

31.4.2.1 Aligning Priorities

One example was a customer journey for savings. The default setting was to have functionality roll out on a certain date, for example, July 31. The Hub savings team found that although they were ready, their colleagues outside of the Hub had different timings and backlogs, which resulted in lack of alignment and delays. Everyone was working to different agile rhythms and with different KPIs.

Definition

One of the first teams I coached wanted to give customers more insight into why their payments would fail or not fail. They came up with 20 initiatives to improve this and each of those initiatives had a business case. For example, if we do this, then this is how it's going to benefit the customer and how it's going to benefit our bottom line. We moved forward but then we couldn't get those items on the backlog of other teams who weren't in the Hub, because they had this huge monolithic list of things that they needed to do and finish. Basically, we were not able to implement those improvements. That's where is started to go wrong – our squads couldn't influence the priorities on the other teams' backlogs. — Marc Wagner, Agile Coach

---

31

This was particularly the case with the marketing organization and DevOps capacity from other teams, which had other priorities. Trying to align these in order to deliver within the set time frames was an issue. See ◘ Fig. 31.9 for a typical email illustrating the challenges of managing conflicting priorities between the Hub and other parts of the bank.

Van: Martens, CMM (Nieke)
Verzonden: woensdag 11 april 2018 14:43
Aan: Management Teams Retail Banking
Onderwerp: Prioritize customer journey & scaling-up before summer

".... We have recently noticed that it takes a lot of time to decide on the customer journeys and to allocate the colleagues who will participate in the squads. As you have also noticed, staffing is happening last minute and that is why we want to have a much quicker decision about the squads we choose for the upscaling in June and July. ..."

◘ **Fig. 31.9**   The challenges of aligning priorities at scale

Van: Product Owner
Verzonden: vrijdag 18 mei 2018 13:18
Aan: Martens, CMM (Nieke)
Onderwerp: Prioritize digital IT capacity IT

"… We also have a priority around the capacity of the coming Wave. I'm worried about this. The new wave will start in 1.5 week, and capacity is under pressure.

[…]

In short, if we assume the above situation, we have 2 FTE left for Squad Card Blanche. As far as I'm concerned, not enough so that you can create impact with a squad in 12 weeks.

In my opinion we need at least an extra dedicated Cards person (at least Mon, Tue and Thurs available for the squad) and a journey owner.

If that is not the case, we really have to think about whether we should give it a follow-up…."

■ **Fig. 31.10**   The challenge of attracting and retaining squad members

31.4.2.2 **Attracting and Retaining Squad Members**

The hybrid @scale model caused many other issues. As the number of squads increased, it became harder to fill them properly. Although some were 100% dedicated, others in each squad could devote only 70% or 80% of their time to work in the Hub. Also, squad members were often called back into their departments for regular work. Not only did this affect the length of some customer journeys, but it also created tensions for managers in the main bank. Martens commented:

» There was quite a lot of tension between managers and the people in the Hub about "who is the boss?" and "Hey, these are my people, but I hardly see them" or "I don't have any say in what they're doing." A manager would come back to us and say he wanted his employee back as he had another project in his area that had a greater priority.

■ Figure 31.10 shows an email illustrating this challenge.

Individuals who had worked in the Hub were reluctant to return to business as usual after the customer journey was completed. The energy created through collaboration in the Hub and working with colleagues from different parts of the bank was lost when individuals returned to their usual roles. On other occasions, the businesses had an external demand that they had to meet and had to pull people back from the Hub.

> **Definition**
>
> One of the teams in the Hub was responsible for improving the onboarding process for asset management clients within Rabobank. All the other activities we left to customer services, outside of the Hub. Then we got an urgent request from the Financial Markets Authority to give more clarity on a specific part of the onboarding process. The Hub team were working only on part of that, so we had to get them out of the Hub and back into their line team to work on the FMA request. There was a lot of frustration because people were saying "I have to work on this regulatory thing, and I want to work on the online on-boarding." The other issue was that with the split, people didn't feel responsible for the whole client journey. — Bart Horsten, Wealth Tribe Lead

31.4.3 Professional Jealousy

With only certain parts of a customer journey in the Hub and the rest in the business, professional jealousy arose. Individuals felt that the "fun stuff" went into the Hub and the Hub team got recognition for it, whereas the more mundane part remained in the business unit, and the teams there did not receive any recognition. In IT, for example, the Hub focused on app development and new architecture, whereas the IT division focused on replacing legacy systems. This type of work was less exciting and often harder.

Jealousy also flared when a video of squad members playing games during the launch week was circulated outside the Hub. People in the Hub were accused of just having fun and not doing any real work, while those back in the daily business were working hard.

> **Definition**
>
> We'd hear, "Where's all the serious work? And where's all the acceleration?" That was an interesting challenge because it's a very basic human thing that if you give people another color shirt, they immediately become an outsider. We gave all the squads an orange hoodie and told them they're now part of the Digital Hub, so we sort of accidentally by design created this feeling. It wasn't intentional because we actually wanted it to spread out to the whole of the organization. — Kimberly Schelle, Consultant Digital Hub

The teams were meant to be autonomous, but with different owners coming from the business but not being part of the teams, there were inevitable frictions through lack of regular interaction. Similarly, it was a challenge getting individual squad members' skills up to a certain level when they were not dedicated to a journey or were being pulled across several squads due to lack of available expertise.

31.4.4 Conflicts Around Roles and Responsibilities

A further tension for managers was that they could no longer determine what their reports would focus on. There were conflicts between the focus of product owners in the Hub and the line manager in the business unit who wanted the individual to do something else. This resulted in individuals in the Hub feeling guilty toward their squad because they could not deliver what was required because their line manager was demanding other work to be completed. This was particularly true for the software developers.

❏ Figure 31.11 shows how conflicts and confusion about roles and responsibilities manifested in project discussions as well as more mundane matters such as who to ask for approval to go on vacation.

There was also an issue of interpretation of the role people played in the Hub and their expectations. Outside of the Hub, product ownership was a function with

Van: Schelle, KJ (Kimberly)
Verzonden: woensdag 16 mei 14:43
Aan: ...
Onderwerp: Potential squad optimize customer communication

"...Risk 1: ownership - unclear
- X finds this an important topic and wants it to be picked up in the fall, not necessarily in a dedicated form of squad
- Y is enthusiastic about starting a squad on this subject, but sees ownership at X, audit finding lies with digital channels
- Sales Bedrijven is enthusiastic about squad on this subject, but this topic was not placed on the top list in the MT Business Consultation on squads in September.
..."

Van: Martens, CMM (Nieke)
Verzonden: maandag 29 januari 2018 11:33
Aan: ...
Onderwerp: Vacation

"... For me this is fine but this question belongs to X, he remains responsible for HR matters."

Van: [Product owner]
Verzonden: maandag 29 januari 2018, 8:16
Aan: Martens, CMM (Nieke)
Onderwerp: Vacation

"... I want to ask for approval to go on holiday from 29 April to 11 May. Like to hear if that is OK for you...."

▫ Fig. 31.11 Examples of confusion about roles and responsibilities within the Hub

long-lived tenure. In the Hub, it was a role with a fixed period. There were frictions when an individual was told they would not be appointed to the function after the Hub.

Similarly, there were also issues with performance management. Line management was normally responsible for the performance of individuals, but in the Hub, the line manager had no oversight. Interestingly, the Hub team had no previous knowledge of the performance of people coming into the Hub. Establishing new KPIs to manage responsibility and capability, as well as performance, started to become an issue.

31.5 Building the Digital Organization

The Hub had initially been successful at a small scale, but this was not fast enough to effect meaningful change throughout Rabobank. Increasing the number of squads had led to more tensions and challenges, both within the Hub and across the existing business units. Martens and Leurs discussed their options. Martens summarized:

>> It became clear when we had the new squads in the hybrid model of a Digital Hub and business as usual that this wasn't going to work if we wanted to grow more. In July when we tried to scale up further it became very hard to find people free to work with us. People in the bank started to wake up and think, "Wow this thing is growing, what does it mean for me?" It became clear that we had to build an organization to take digitization forward in a different way.

Martens and Leurs had to present the options for the best way to meet Rabobank's digital goals to the Managing Board. The question was what were the options for moving forward?

Printed by Printforce, the Netherlands